Boston Institute of Finance

Stockbroker Course

Boston Institute of Finance

Stockbroker Course

Series 7 and Series 63 Test Preparation

WILEY

John Wiley & Sons, Inc.

Published by John Wiley & Sons, Inc., Hoboken, New Jersey
Published simultaneously in Canada

Library of Congress Cataloging-in-Publication Data:

Boston Institute of Finance
    Boston Institute of Finance stockbroker course: series 7 and series 63 test preparation / The Boston Institute of Finance.
    p. cm.
    ISBN-10 0-471-71235-3 (paper/cd-rom)
    ISBN-13 978-0-471-71235-0
    1. Stockbrokers—Problems, exercises, etc. I. Title.
    HG4621.B677 2005
    332.63' 076—dc22

                                                        2004027076

Printed in the United States of America

10 9 8 7 6 5 4 3 2 1

CONTENTS

PREFACE

Passing the Series 7 and Series 63 exams is necessary for anyone who wants to sell stocks. But before taking the exams, one must be fully prepared. The *Boston Institute of Finance Stockbroker Course* will provide everything you need to know to pass these exams. More importantly, the material in this book and CD will provide a strong foundation for embarking on your career in the securities industry.

This material has been successfully used for many years to provide classroom training for Series 7 and Series 63 exam preparation. It has been organized and simplified to provide the most efficient learning possible. Indeed, over 80,000 financial professionals have used this material to pass the Series 7 and Series 63 exams. In short, this material is tested and proven.

We've combined the Series 7 and Series 63 content because most securities professionals require both accreditations. Series 7 certification is required by federal law. Series 63 certification is required in 40 states. Generally, once you've mastered the Series 7 material, preparation for Series 63 is comparatively easy. Nonetheless, there are unique aspects to the Series 63 body of knowledge that require independent study to pass the exam. Again, everything you need to know to pass the Series 63 exam is here.

The book contains the core knowledge and information you'll need to master to pass the exams. The attached CD provides a variety of questions and answers to review your retention of the content and to prepare for the exam. For the Series 7 material, the CD contains chapter review questions and answers, six short exams and six longer sets of questions and answers, and a final exam. The Series 63 material contains questions and answers. The combination of the text and the questions and answers will provide you with unparalleled preparation for the exams.

Congratulations on your choice of the *Boston Institute of Finance Stockbroker Course* as your guide to preparing for the Series 7 and Series 63 exams and to prepare for your career as a professional in the securities industry.

Boston Institute of Finance, Inc.

SERIES 7 STUDY GUIDE

INTRODUCTION

Each year, the securities industry becomes more interesting and challenging. New products and investment techniques are constantly appearing, which give industry personnel more choices to service investors.

You will find the *Boston Institute of Finance Stockbroker Course* a very rewarding experience. One main goal of the course is to enable a candidate to pass the Series 7 examination in order to become a registered representative (RR). Another important goal of the course is to help a person become a well-trained RR, in order to better serve his or her clients.

Our course is constantly being improved and updated, and we are convinced that it is the best course available today. *Study is essential.* Remember, your goal is not just to pass the examination, although this is certainly your initial short-term objective. Your long-term objective is to acquire knowledge that will assist you in pursuing your career objectives.

Series 7 Examination

The Series 7 examination is administered to securities industry personnel by the National Association of Securities Dealers (NASD). It is a six-hour, 250-question examination. The Series 7 examination is a computer-based test offered on the PROCTOR® System at certain centers throughout the country. PROCTOR is a computerized testing system in which the candidate answers the questions by touching the bottom of the computer screen or the computer keyboard. At the end of the examination, the candidate is given his score and an analysis of how he did on major sections of the test.

The Series 7 candidate is given scratch paper and is allowed to use a calculator, which must run silently. Programmable-memory calculators, calculators with a print device, or calculators without an independent power source are prohibited from being used by any candidate.

A candidate must pass the Series 7 examination in order to be registered with an NASD or New York Stock Exchange (NYSE) member firm as a general securities representative. An individual who passes the Series 7 examination is allowed to sell all types of equity products except commodities.

The passing grade on the Series 7 examination is 70%. Therefore, candidates must answer 175 questions correctly out of a total of 250. In some cases, a candidate is given 130 questions on each part of the Series 7 examination. In this instance, five questions on each half of the examination are experimental questions and do not count toward the candidate's grade. The five experimental questions on each half are not identified to the candidate.

To take the Series 7 examination, a candidate must obtain a ticket, normally by completing a U-4 Form and sending it to the NASD. The Series 7 ticket obtained from the NASD is valid for a ninety-day period. In order to take the Series 7 examination, a candidate must call a Professional Development Center to take the exam on a PROCTOR computer terminal.

A candidate needs to take one form of personal identification that contains the candidate's signature and a photograph. No reference materials can be taken to the testing area, except for a calculator.

The approximate breakdown of the Series 7 examination is as follows:

Subject area	Approximate number of questions	Percentage of exam
Options	50	20%
Municipal securities	50	20
Investment companies/variable annuities	20	8
Direct participation programs	20	8
Corporate securities	20	8
Securities industry regulations	20	8
Exchange operations	20	8
Economics and securities analysis	15	6
Margins	15	6
US government securities	10	4
Retirement plans and taxation	10	4

How to Study

Studying is not the same as reading a story. Studying requires effort, reflection, thought, and questioning. The purpose of studying is to add to your knowledge and increase the information in your memory. If you think of a mind as a storehouse, material you read often passes through the building and entertains on the way. Some material may remain within the building, but this was not the purpose of reading. When you study, the intent is to add inventory in the storehouse. Hopefully, the effort will be enjoyable, but this is not the purpose of your study effort.

We believe that the coverage in our course is very thorough. It would be difficult for those preparing examination questions to create many that are completely foreign to those you have covered in your practice examinations. Questions on the actual examination may be different, but for the most part, practice questions will have referred to similar facts and calculations.

How to Take the Practice Examinations

On the accompanying CD, a variety of questions and answers are provided, including chapter review questions and sample exams. The purpose of testing a candidate at the end of each section is to identify areas of strength and weakness. A passing grade on the practice questions at the end of each section and the additional practice questions is 80% for our course. A candidate should restudy any questions he or she answered incorrectly.

A candidate might also use a check–double check system. If a question seems difficult—even if you finally know you have selected the correct answer—place one check mark beside it. If the question is one you did not really know how to answer (you guessed), then place two check marks beside it. After completing the exam, study the material relating to questions you have checked, with special emphasis on material relating to those you have double-checked. This is an excellent method of reinforcing your knowledge in those areas where such reinforcement is most needed.

Question-Answering Tips

1. *Read the full question.* This cannot be repeated too often. Study the question to make certain you understand it. For example, when you calculate margin problems, you might be asked how much is the required margin or how much is the required deposit. Both choices might be given as answers, but only one is correct. You must make certain you are answering the question actually asked—not the one you may think is being asked.

2. *Pace yourself.* You will be allowed three hours for each of the two 125-question parts of the actual examination. On practice exams accompanying this course, we recommend trying to answer 125 questions in two hours. This will help you to feel more than comfortable with a three-hour period, but be careful not to waste an inordinate amount of time on any one question. All questions are weighted equally. If you find a question that you have difficulty with, guess at the answer. Place a check mark beside the question on the exam, and after you complete the exam, go back to that question and try again. Note that you should guess at an answer. *Never leave a blank.* A blank will count against you just as much as a wrong answer. At least you have a chance of getting the answer correct if you guess. Furthermore, if you leave a blank, you may, by mistake, place the answer to the next question in that space. This might not be discovered until much later and you would have a time-consuming problem in changing all your answers to their correct location.

3. If you are not certain of the correct answer, you may be quite certain that some answers are incorrect. Eliminate these first. The correct answer then may be quite evident.

4. *Simplify when possible.*

   a. If a question is lengthy, much of the information may be extraneous. Try to eliminate material that is not pertinent. Narrow the question down—it will be easier to answer.

   b. Assume, for example, that you are asked an arithmetic question that appears to be unfamiliar. It may be possible to clarify the approach by using numbers that are easier to work with. For example, in the section on financial analysis, you will be given a formula to find earnings per share. If a company has total earnings of $4,500,000 and there are 15,000,000 shares of common stock outstanding, you would find earnings per share by division.

   $$\frac{\$4,500,000}{15,000,000} = \$0.30$$

   I know that 8 divided by 4 = 2. Now, if I have the 8 and the 2, but the 4 is missing, how would I find it? The answer should be obvious—by dividing the numerator 8 by the answer 2. Obviously, then you would solve your actual problem by dividing the numerator, $4 million by $0.30 and find that the number of shares outstanding is 15 million.

5. *Use your imagination.* The intent of the study course is to provide thorough knowledge. If you have studied properly, you will understand concepts. *It is a mistake to prepare for an examination by simply trying to memorize answers to questions.* The exam is constantly changing. If you have memorized questions and answers, you will be lost when a new question appears. However, if you understand concepts and ideas, you will be able to use your imagination and successfully answer any new question presented.

6. *Be certain to get a good night's sleep before the exam.* The study course has provided you with the necessary information. If you have studied properly, the amount of information gained by late-night study will be more than offset by the incorrect answers you will get if you are tired when you take the exam.

We are convinced that you are now using the best preparation course available to trainees preparing for the Series 7 examination. The pass rate of those using our course is ample proof that we are correct in our conviction.

Study hard, pass the Series 7 examination, and have a successful career in the securities industry.

The Boston Institute of Finance

1 CORPORATE SECURITIES

STOCKS AND BONDS

Individuals seeking to invest their savings are faced with numerous financial products and degrees of risk. Individual investors can invest in a corporation as an equity owner or as a creditor. If they choose to become an equity owner, they will hopefully benefit in the growth of the business. They can purchase common stock or preferred stock in the corporation.

Assume an investor purchases 1,000 shares of ABC Corporation common stock. ABC has 100,000 shares of common stock outstanding. Our investor owns 1% (1,000 divided by 100,000 = 1%) of the outstanding shares. He will receive 1% of any dividends paid by the corporation and would receive 1% of any remaining assets upon dissolution of the corporation, after all creditors have been paid.

Our investor would receive a stock certificate evidencing his ownership of 1,000 shares of common stock of ABC Corporation. He could sell his 1,000 shares, or any lesser amount, at any time. Our investor hopes to be able to sell his shares at a higher price than he paid for them. In other words, he hopes to realize a capital gain on the sale of the shares.

Our investor would also like to receive dividends on his 1,000 shares. Assume ABC pays a quarterly dividend of $0.20 per share. Our investor would receive a quarterly dividend of $200 or an annual dividend of $800. The two main reasons an investor would buy stock in a corporation are

1. To receive any dividends paid by the corporation
2. To hopefully realize a capital gain on the sale of the shares

However, there is risk associated with owning stock in a corporation. If the corporation goes bankrupt, the investor will lose his entire investment, but his personal assets are not at risk. The investor's loss is limited to the amount invested in the corporation. Therefore, an investor in a corporation has limited risk.

An investor can choose to purchase a debt instrument of a corporation instead of becoming an equity owner. Assume an investor purchases a $1,000 par value 6% bond due in 2010 in ABC Corporation. In this case, our investor has become a creditor of ABC Corporation. ABC agrees to pay our investor $60 per year in annual interest. At maturity in the year 2010, ABC agrees to pay our investor the par value of $1,000. If ABC goes bankrupt, our investor would be paid off before preferred or common stockholders. However, our investor would receive only $60 per year in annual interest regardless of how profitable the corporation becomes.

These are the two basic choices facing an investor. He can choose to invest in a corporation as an equity owner or as a creditor. If a corporation becomes very profitable, an investor would benefit as an equity owner. If a corporation experiences financial difficulties, the investor would be in a better position as a creditor. We will examine in more detail an individual's rights as an equity owner and as a creditor or bondholder of a corporation.

MONEY AND CAPITAL MARKETS

There are two general markets for funds: the money market and the capital market. The **money market** refers to transactions in short-term debt instruments, while the **capital market** refers to the market for long-term debt and equity securities.

Commercial banks are the chief source of money market funds. The demand for such funds comes from the United States government, brokers, and commercial borrowers.

Rates charged in the money market are influenced by differences in

- *Maturities.* The longer the maturity of the loan, the higher the interest rate.
- *The borrower's credit rating.* The poorer the credit rating, the higher the interest rate.
- *The demand for funds.* The greater the demand, the higher the interest rate.

The **prime rate** is the interest rate charged on loans made by commercial banks to their best customers (firms with good credit ratings). When interest rates on short-term securities are high enough, individual investors may withdraw their funds from financial institutions and invest directly in the money market. This process is referred to as **disintermediation**.

Money market instruments are any high-grade, liquid debt securities that will mature in one year. Securities having a maturity longer than one year are normally referred to as capital market instruments.

Probably the most widely held short-term debt instruments are US Treasury bills. However, there are a variety of other money market instruments widely used by banks, corporations, and individuals, including federal funds, US government obligations, repurchase agreements, state and municipal obligations, bankers' acceptances, commercial paper, brokers' and dealers' loans, and negotiable certificates of deposit.

The capital market contains long-term debt and equity instruments. The word *market* implies a group of buyers and sellers of capital funds. Those businesses needing long-term funds comprise the demand side of this market. The supply side consists of those individuals who, as investors, seek to invest their savings. The prices at which these funds are purchased or sold are expressed as yields on bonds or notes. The investment banking system is the mechanism through which funds flow from their sources on the supply side to users on the demand side. The market for distributing securities to the public and trading outstanding securities are known as **securities markets**.

COMMON STOCK

Securities that evidence ownership in a corporation are called **equity securities**. They can be divided generally into two types: common stock and preferred stock. Common stock will be discussed first.

Common stock is an equity security because it represents part ownership in a corporation. In general, it presents the greatest opportunity for capital gain to the investor. If the company prospers and grows, the value of the common stockholders' investment will increase. While the possible gain to the common stockholder is unlimited, his loss is limited to the purchase price paid for the shares.

Common stockholders in a corporation normally have the following rights:

- *Limited liability*. The stockholder is not liable for the losses and liabilities of a corporation and cannot lose more than what he paid for his stock. Limited liability is very important to a common stock investor.
- *Proportionate ownership*. The stockholder's ownership of the corporation is in the same proportion as his stock is to all the common stock outstanding. If a company has 100,000 shares of stock outstanding, the owner of 2,000 shares is entitled to 2% of the dividends paid to common stockholders or 2% of the assets left over in the case of liquidation after all other claims have been paid.
- *Transfer rights*. The shareholder has the right to transfer his ownership to another party or give away the shares if he chooses.
- *Dividends*. As an owner, the stockholder may share in the profits of the corporation. Such dividends must be paid out of retained earnings and may not impair capital. Usually, the stockholders cannot force directors to declare dividends even though earnings are sufficient; but, once the directors have legally declared a cash dividend, it becomes a current liability of the corporation and its payment can be enforced by the stockholders. This right, then, is to receive dividends when, as, and if they are declared by the board of directors. Dividends are paid on common and preferred stock and American depositary receipts—*not* on rights or warrants. The amount of dividends paid can significantly affect the market price of a stock. Dividends can be paid out of earnings from prior years even if the corporation realizes a loss in a particular year.
- *Corporate books*. A stockholder has the right to examine the list of stockholders. It does not mean the stockholder can examine detailed financial records of the corporation.
- *Preemptive rights*. When a new issue of common stock is sold, the shareholder frequently has the right to subscribe to that number of new shares permitting him to maintain his proportionate ownership in the corporation. The stockholder can sell his rights if he does not choose to exercise them.
- *Voting*. The shareholder has the right to vote, in proportion to his holdings, at stockholders' meetings or by proxy if he does not attend the meeting.
- *Protection*. The shareholder has the right to take actions to protect the corporation against the wrongful acts of management. These wrongful acts are called **ultra vires** acts.
- *Dissolution*. This refers to the right of the common stockholder to a claim against the assets of the corporation upon dissolution. It is a residual right since the stockholder as an owner is last in priority. All debts and other securities owners must be satisfied first. The common stockholder receives the remainder after all other debts of the corporation and claims of preferred stockholders are paid.

- *Stock certificate.* The stockholder has the right to obtain a stock certificate evidencing his ownership in the corporation. To sell or transfer the shares, the stockholder must sign the certificate exactly as his name appears on the front. The stockholder's signature must be guaranteed by a broker/dealer or bank. The signature and guarantee must be acceptable to the transfer agent, which is normally a commercial bank.

STOCK CERTIFICATES

A stock certificate is negotiable, which means the rights of ownership can be transferred to another party. On the back of the stock certificate there is a form which, when filled out, transfers ownership. Stock can also be assigned to banks or other lenders. A separate assignment form is filled out for this purpose, and the corporation does not change the name of the owner on its books as it does when the certificate itself is transferred. A transfer agent, normally a commercial bank, performs the task of issuing new certificates and recording the transaction in the stock record book. The transfer agent must make certain that the number of new securities issued is the same as the number canceled. Both the old and new certificates are sent to the registrar bank. The registrar's duty is to check the work of the transfer agent and make certain that stock was not improperly issued or fraudulently transferred. The registrar bank functions could be performed by separate divisions of the same bank.

Most stock certificates bear the legend "fully paid and nonassessable," which assures that the stock was not sold at a price less than the par value and no additional assessments against the stockholder can be made. Most states, however, require par value to be fully paid and nonassessable.

A stock certificate may be registered in the investor's name or be held in street name for the investor. Assume a stock certificate is registered in the name of William H. Johnson. In order to sell the stock certificate, it must be signed "William H. Johnson" on the back of the certificate. The broker/dealer or a bank must guarantee the customer's signature. The signature and guarantee must be acceptable to the transfer agent in order to transfer the shares to the new owner. Stock certificates are negotiable instruments when they are property signed by the stockholder.

If a stock certificate is in street name, it means that the securities are held in the name of the broker but owned by the customer. Stock in street name is easier to sell since the customer does not have to sign the certificate to make it negotiable. All securities held in a margin account are in street name. If the stock is owned by the customer but held in street name, the customer is referred to as the beneficial owner of the shares.

TYPES OF STOCK

There are various terms used on a corporation's books to describe the status of its common stock. The usual terms are **authorized, issued, outstanding,** and **treasury**. (See Exhibit 1.1)

Exhibit 1.1: Classification of common stock

Assume ABC Corporation has the following types of common stock in its capital structure:

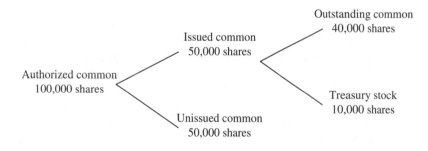

Authorized common	*Issued common*
1. Number of shares the corporation has actually the power to issue (100,000 shares).	1. Amount of stock the corporation has issued (50,000 shares).
2. It is stated in the corporate charter.	2. It is equal to the summation of outstanding stock and treasury stock (50,000 shares).
3. Requires a vote of the stockholders to increase this amount.	3. If the corporation has no treasury stock, issued stock is equal to the outstanding stock and may be referred to as issued and outstanding shares.

Unissued common	*Treasury stock*
1. The number of shares still available to be issued at a later date without a vote of the stockholders.	1. Does not vote.
2. Does not vote.	2. Does not receive dividends.
3. Does not receive dividends.	3. The shares are not used in earnings per share calculations.
4. The shares are not used in earnings per share calculations.	4. The shares are authorized and issued stock but not outstanding stock.
	5. Appears on the balance sheet as a deduction from issued stock.

Authorized common stock is the amount the corporation has the power to issue. This amount is stated in the corporate charter and does not change unless the charter is amended. If a corporation wants to issue more shares than are authorized in the charter, the corporate charter must be amended. Such an amendment normally requires a majority vote of the outstanding shares.

Authorized stock is divided into two groups: issued and unissued. A corporation usually keeps some of its authorized shares unissued for possible use at a later date for the acquisition of other companies, for stock option plans for officers and directors, or for other purposes. Issued stock is divided into outstanding and treasury stock. Outstanding stock is that which has been issued and is in the hands of stockholders, including officers and directors of the corporation.

Occasionally, issued stock is purchased in the market by the issuing corporation. Stock of its own that a corporation reacquires is called treasury stock. It is considered to be issued stock, but not outstanding stock. It cannot vote or share in dividends and is not considered to be an asset of the company. Treasury stock is authorized and issued stock but not outstanding stock. It appears on the balance sheet as a deduction from issued stock to derive outstanding stock. A corporation may acquire treasury stock to use for making future acquisitions, to sell to its employees under stock option plans, because the board of directors feels the price is exceptionally low and decides to buy it back, or to increase earnings per share (since only the number of shares outstanding is used in calculating earnings per share). Therefore, treasury stock (or reacquired stock)

- Does not vote
- Does not receive dividends
- Is issued stock but not outstanding stock
- Is not used in earnings per share calculations

VOTING RIGHTS

Common stock is voting stock and, through this vote, the common stockholder is given the right to vote for the board of directors. The board of directors appoints the management of the corporation. Common stock is the one type of security that *must* be issued by a corporation. Stockholders have the right to vote on such matters as the election of directors, changes in the charter or bylaws, or changes in the purposes for which the corporation was organized.

There are two methods of voting for positions on the board of directors. They are regular (or statutory) and cumulative. To illustrate these systems, assume that a stockholder owns 100 shares of stock and that six persons are to be elected to the board of directors. Under the regular or statutory system of voting, the stockholder could cast 100 votes each for six of the persons running for the office of director. Casting 100 votes each for six persons means that the stockholder casts 600 votes.

If the cumulative voting system is used, it is necessary to first multiply the number of shares times the number of directors to be elected. In this example, 100 shares times six directors would give the stockholder 600 votes. This is the same number he had under the regular or statutory system. The difference is that under the cumulative system, these 600 votes may be cast in any way desired by the stockholder. Six hundred might be cast for the election of one person to the board, or 300 each might be cast for the election of two directors. The 600 total may be voted as a block for one person or divided in any manner desired by the stockholder. The cumulative system gives the minority stockholders a greater opportunity to obtain representation on the board.

Some corporations also give voting rights to preferred stockholders in the event that preferred dividends are passed (not paid). A proxy, giving details of issues to be voted on at the annual meeting, must be sent to all stockholders before the meeting. It must also give the holder an opportunity to instruct his proxy (or representative) on how to vote his shares if he does not attend the meeting.

A method of concentrating control in a company is the establishment of a voting trust. Stockholders deposit their stock with a group of persons acting as trustees, and the title is transferred to the trustees, who then have full power to vote the stock. In exchange, the stockholders receive **voting trust certificates** which entitle the holder to receive the dividends and to have his shares returned when the trust terminates. These certificates, which are actively traded on the New York and other stock exchanges, are also referred to as **certificates of beneficial interest**.

Occasionally, there is more than one class of common stock, with the "other" class (sometimes referred to as **"Class B"** stock) frequently having all the same rights as the **"Class A,"** with the exception of the right to vote.

The common stockholder may have the preemptive right to maintain his equity position in his company. This permits him to subscribe to additional stock in the event that the company decides to raise capital through the sale of additional shares.

A final classification is guaranteed stock, for which another corporation guarantees the dividend, which becomes an unconditional fixed charge of the guarantor. Such a situation normally occurs when one company becomes a subsidiary of another, guaranteeing to pay the dividend on the common stock of the subsidiary.

Common stocks are frequently divided into four quality classes.

1. **Growth stocks** are stocks that have shown better-than-average appreciation over a period of time. Growth in sales and earnings is larger than the average of common stocks. Characteristically, growth stocks are difficult to select in advance; they pay low dividends and give low yields; they sell at high price/earnings ratios; they are highly speculative in their early years, and full growth may require a long holding period. Growth stocks normally have low dividend payout ratios and earn a high rate of return and may fluctuate widely in price.
2. **Blue chip** is the popular term commonly applied to the stock of a strong, well-established corporation that has demonstrated its ability to pay dividends in both good times and bad.
3. **Special situation** is the term applied to the common stock of a company wherein the stock's potential is not related merely to the company's day-to-day business. A special situation may result from such events as hoped-for recovery under new management, discovery of a valuable natural resource on the corporate properties, the introduction of a popular new product, or a possible takeover.
4. **Defensive issues** are those of established companies in industries relatively unaffected by the business cycle, for example, food, public utilities (e.g., natural gas companies), tobacco companies, and clothing stocks. However, steel companies, machine tool companies, aerospace companies, home appliances, and building material stocks are clearly not defensive stocks. Public utility stocks use leverage or borrowed funds extensively to increase their rates of return. They are sensitive to interest rate movements and normally have high dividend payout ratios. When interest rates rise, prices of public utility shares normally fall.

VALUATION OF COMMON STOCK

Valuation of common stock requires understanding of certain terms relating to kinds of value and certain ratios used in security analysis.

Three terms are commonly used in referring to the value of stock.

1. Par value
2. Book value
3. Market value

In the certificate of incorporation, common stock may be assigned a par or fixed value. The par value is printed on the stock certificates. Par value does not represent the book value or the market value of the stock. If the par value of common stock is $5, this is the price at which the stock was originally issued. Par value may also be called face value.

The amount of money, in excess of par value, received by the corporation at the time of the sale of stock is carried on the balance sheet as **capital surplus, paid-in capital,** or **paid-in surplus**. Assume a corporation sells 1,000 shares of stock to the public at $12 per share. The par value of the stock was $5. In this case, $5,000 would be credited to the common stock account and $7,000 (the amount of stock sold above par value) would be credited to capital surplus.

Book value means tangible net asset value, since intangible assets, such as goodwill, are excluded. Total liabilities, preferred stock, and intangible assets are first deducted from total assets. The difference is divided by the number of common shares of stock outstanding. Book value is, then, the net worth of the corporation less intangible assets divided by the number of common shares outstanding. Tangible net assets also may be found by adding the common stock, capital surplus, and retained earnings accounts found in the company's balance sheet and subtracting intangible assets. Book value is equal to tangible net asset value per share.

The formula to compute book value per common share is

$$\frac{\text{Stockholder's equity} - \text{Preferred stock} - \text{Intangible assets}}{\text{Common shares outstanding}}$$

Assume XYZ Corporation has the following financial situation:

Total assets	
(Including goodwill of $1,000,000)	$10,000,000
Total liabilities	$ 4,000,000
Preferred stock	$ 2,000,000
Common shares outstanding	1,000,000

Book value per common share would be

$$
\begin{array}{rl}
\$10,000,000 & \text{Total assets} \\
- \ 4,000,000 & \text{Total liabilities} \\
\hline
\$ 6,000,000 & \text{Stockholder's equity (net worth)}
\end{array}
$$

$$\frac{\$6,000,000 - \$2,000,000 - \$1,000,000}{1,000,000 \text{ common shares outstanding}} = \frac{3,000,000}{1,000,000} = \begin{array}{c}\$3 \text{ book value per} \\ \text{common share}\end{array}$$

The book value per share of a company is affected by such things as

• A stock split
• Writing off tangible assets

If a stock split occurs, the number of shares outstanding increases and book value per share decreases. If a company writes off the value of a tangible asset from its books, book value per share will be lowered because tangible net assets will be a lower figure.

However, the book value per share of a company is not affected by such things as

• Changes in the market price of a company's stock
• Writing off intangible assets

PREFERRED STOCK

Preferred stock is an equity security—evidence of ownership. It merits the word *preferred* since it is entitled to receive dividends before the common stockholders and usually also has a prior claim to corporate assets if the corporation is dissolved. The preferred stockholder, in the event of dissolution, is paid at the par value rate. If there is no par value, the preferred stockholder is paid at a value that is assigned at the discretion of the directors. (See Exhibit 1.2).

Exhibit 1.2: Order of payment in corporate liquidation

1. Taxes
2. Senior lien bonds (such as first mortgage bonds)
3. Bank loans, accounts payable, debentures, and/or unsecured debt
4. Subordinated debentures
5. Preferred stock
6. Common stock

If the preferred stock has a par value, dividends are stated as a percentage of par (e.g., $100 par value, dividends 5% of par). If the stock is no-par, dividends are stated in dollars per share. Dividends are paid only if declared by the board of directors.

When preferred stocks are issued sequentially (first preferred, second preferred) by a corporation, usually the dividend requirements of the first preferred have to be met before those of the second. There are a variety of types of preferred stocks, including prior preferred, cumulative preferred, participating preferred, convertible preferred, and callable preferred.

Prior preferred stock, or preference stock, as it is sometimes called, has claims against dividends and assets that come before other types of preferred stock. An investor would have to check the prospectus of the preferred stock issue to determine if the preferred issue has a prior claim on dividends and assets.

Cumulative preferred stock has an additional feature. If the business does not make a profit, the stockholders—preferred and common—do not normally receive a dividend. The dividends that the cumulative preferred stockholders should have received will accumulate, however. If the corporation eventually makes a profit, before the common stockholders may receive any dividend the cumulative preferred stockholders will be entitled to the current year's dividend and those dividends accumulated from prior years. Such stocks, with dividends in arrears, are a profitable investment if the investor is able to purchase them at a reasonable price shortly before the arrearage is paid.

Participating preferred stocks also have a special feature. They are entitled, as usual, to a specific dividend (e.g., $5 per share) before any dividends may be paid to common stockholders. Participating preferred stockholders are, however, not only entitled to this specified amount per share, but afterward participate with the common stockholders in additional corporate earnings distributed as dividends. Therefore, for participating preferred stock, the dividends are fixed to a minimum amount but not to a maximum amount.

Convertible preferred stocks can be converted into a certain number of common shares, usually within a specific time period, at the option of the owner. For example, a share of $100 par could have the privilege of converting into four shares of common. If the preferred is selling at par, then as long as the common is selling under $25, conversion would make no sense. But once it begins trading over that level, the preferred would trade for at least four times the price of the common. Some convertible preferred stocks never lose their conversion rights (perpetual); others must be converted before a certain date (limited); and still others do not have the right to exercise the privilege for a number of years (delayed).

Convertible preferred stock will likely fluctuate more than other types of preferred when interest rates are stable. The convertible preferred will move with the market price of the common stock.

If the preferred stock is callable preferred, the issuing corporation will have the right to call and retire the stock at a specific price. This is advantageous to the company, especially during periods of falling interest rates, but disadvantageous to the investor, who would lose his stock at precisely the time he wanted to hold on to it. A sinking fund or a regular retirement of the stock each year at a specified price is normally part of present preferred stock issues.

Dividends on preferred stock are paid only if declared by the board of directors. Preferred stockholders have a prior claim on the assets of a corporation ahead of common stockholders. Dividend rates on preferred stock may be fixed or variable.

When preferred stock has certain advantages, it also has certain limitations. It usually does not have the right to vote nor does it have a preemptive right. From the investor's point of view, it must be remembered that dividends depend on earnings. Dividends will usually be less liberal than dividends on common stock in a very profitable firm and they are not as certain a return as bond interest, which must be paid by the corporation regardless of profit. From the corporate point of view, interest on bonds is deductible as an expense before taxes, while dividends paid to stockholders cannot be deducted for tax purposes.

Assume Johnson Manufacturing Company issued new securities that were described as $5.20 cumulative, convertible, voting, preferred stock. This description would indicate to an investor that

- Johnson Manufacturing Company must pay dividends on this new security before any dividends may be paid to existing holders of common stock. This is true of all preferred stock issues.
- If, in any year, the dividend on this preferred issue is not paid, the dividend must be made up in the future before dividends may be paid to common stockholders. An investor would know this because the preferred issue is cumulative.
- The owners of this new security may, at their option, exchange these shares of preferred stock for shares of another security. These preferred shares can be exchanged for shares of common stock in Johnson Manufacturing Company. The preferred stock and common stock in Johnson Manufacturing Company represent separate security issues.
- The description also indicates that the issue has voting rights. However, the description does not state that the issue is callable.

CORPORATE BONDS

Corporate bonds issued by a corporation normally have a par value of $1,000 or $5,000. Assume a corporation issues a $1,000 par value bond with an interest rate of 7% maturing in the year 2000. The investor is a creditor of the corporation and is entitled to be paid $70 annual interest and to receive $1,000 when the bond matures in the year 2000.

The investor can sell the bond prior to maturity if he chooses. Corporate bonds pay interest semiannually. Our investor would receive $35 every six months, or an annual interest payment of $70.

The funded debt of a corporation includes bonds, notes for maturities of five years or longer, and possibly long-term bank loans. The money or property acquired by a corporation under the condition that a definite sum of money must be paid by the corporation at some distant future time represents its **funded indebtedness**.

Bonds are separate and individual obligations of a corporation. They are considered to be part of the company's capital structure and represent a long-term liability. There are two distinct parts of each bond contract.

1. The first part is the bond itself.

   a. The bond is a primary contract between the corporation and the investor.
   b. It represents a definite time with periodic payments of interest.

2. The second part is a supplementary contract known as an **indenture, trust indenture,** or **deed of trust**. This is

   a. A supplementary agreement or contract under which all bonds of a single issue are grouped.
   b. An elaborate instrument that represents the collective security of the bondholders.
   c. A description of the general rights of the individual bondholder.
   d. An instrument that can be changed only with the assent of a majority of the bondholders; often, at least two-thirds of the bondholders must agree.

Legally, the bond itself is the primary instrument. It represents the individual right of action of its owner to sue a defaulting debtor, get a judgment, and levy execution. The indenture is normally administered by the trustee for the benefit of the bondholders.

Corporate bonds are a form of debt and are a promise on the part of the corporation to pay a sum of money (usually $1,000) at a specified future date along with interest payments (usually semiannually) to the holder. Failure on the part of the corporation to make these payments on time is considered to be a default and the holder of the bonds has the right to take legal action to force the company to fulfill its promises. These bonds are originally sold with a maturity, or due date, of five, ten, or even thirty years in the future. Although the great majority of these bonds are in denominations of $1,000, a few are denominated in smaller or larger amounts.

The bonds are either in coupon form, with detachable coupons that the holder must clip off and present for interest payments, and the bond must be presented for payment at maturity date; or in registered form whereby the name of the owner is recorded by the corporation and a check is sent to him for his interest and principal. A third, less common form, is registered as to principal only, with detachable coupons. A bondholder is obviously better protected from loss or theft by holding registered rather than coupon bonds. Transfer of registered bonds is accomplished in the same manner as that of common stock; the certificate is submitted to the transfer agent and a new one is issued in the name of the bondholder.

Since the interest on the bond goes to whoever has possession on a coupon date, it would not be equitable for a person who has held a bond for, say, five months not to get his pro rata share of interest. Therefore, a system has been devised whereby the purchaser of the bond pays to the seller, at the time of the transaction, an amount called **accrued interest**. This payment compensates the seller for the interest to which he is entitled on the bond since the last interest payment. For example, a 6% bond pays $30 in interest twice a year. If the coupon dates were January 1 and July 1, and the seller sold his bond for settlement on May 1, he would receive approximately $20 in accrued interest: $5 per month from January 1 to April 30.

Interest on corporate bonds is subject to all income taxes (federal, state, and local).

There are three types of value referred to in discussing bonds.

1. **Par value** (face value) is the amount stated on the face of the bond.
2. **Market value** is the price at which a bond may currently be purchased.
3. **Redemption value** (maturity value) is the price at which the bond will be redeemed.

Bonds are not usually quoted in dollars but in eighths as a percentage of face value. Thus, a $1,000 bond would be quoted at 100 when sold at par. Corporate bonds are quoted in points. Each point for a $1,000 bond represents $10 or 1% of par value. Bonds that sell for a price greater than par are said to be selling at a premium. Thus, a $1,000 par value bond quoted at 102¾ would sell for $1,027.50—$27.50 or 2¾ more than par.

Bonds that sell for less than par are said to sell at a discount. Thus, a $1,000 par value bond quoted at 92½ would sell for $925—a 7½% discount from par.

Assume a bond is quoted at 97⅞—find its dollar price. A quote of 97⅞ represents 97 full points plus ⅞ of a point, or $978.75.

$$
\begin{array}{lll}
97 \text{ full points x } \$10 & = & \$970.00 \\
⅞ \text{ point x } \$10 & = & \underline{8.75} \\
& & \$978.75
\end{array}
$$

Assume a bond is quoted at 103¾—find its dollar price. A quote of 103¾ represents 103 full points plus ¾ of a point, or $1,037.50.

$$
\begin{array}{lll}
103 \text{ full points x } \$10 & = & \$1,030.00 \\
¾ \text{ point x } \$10 & = & \underline{7.50} \\
& & \$1,037.50
\end{array}
$$

To change a bond quote to a dollar amount, an investor can use the point method, as previously illustrated, or calculate it as a percentage of par value. Both calculations will result in the same amount. For example, assume a bond is quoted at 84½. Find the dollar amount at which the bond is selling.

Point method
$$
\begin{array}{lll}
84 \text{ full points x } \$10 & = & \$840.00 \\
½ \text{ point x } \$10 & = & \underline{5.00} \\
& & \$845.00
\end{array}
$$

Percentage of par method
84½% of $1,000 = 0.845 x $1,000 = $845

MORTGAGE BONDS

Mortgage bonds are secured by mortgages on real estate. These may be first mortgage bonds or junior issues known by such terms as *general, second, consolidated, or refunding,* or they may be closed- or open-end.

If the bonds are closed-end, additional bonds with the same priority of lien (e.g., first) may not be issued and junior issues will be more difficult to sell.

If the bonds are open-end, additional bonds may be issued in the future as part of the same issue under the same indenture. This is desirable if the corporation expands and has to raise more funds, since one large issue will probably be more economical and the senior issue easier to sell. Usually, there are a number of restrictions on the issuance of additional bonds. For example, the number of bonds that may be issued is restricted relative to the value of the property pledged as collateral. An earnings test must be satisfied relating the current and prospective debt service (principal and interest) changes to earnings. A measure of liquidity has to be present, usually a specified amount of net current assets. Finally, there is often a requirement that a certain level of stockholders' equity be maintained. When additional first mortgage bonds are issued, they are usually designated by either a number or letter series.

A compromise is the limited open-end mortgage. With this mortgage, a maximum dollar amount is set for bonds that may be issued with the same priority of lien.

When open-end or limited open-end bonds are issued, an after-acquired clause must be included. This states that any property acquired in the future shall also be pledged for the bonds in question. The investor's safety requires that restrictions be placed on the issuance of more bonds. If such a clause is used with a closed-end mortgage, there is a serious problem if more funds are needed since it is impossible to issue additional mortgage bonds.

First mortgage bonds are the best secured since they have a prior claim on the assets specified in the indenture.

COLLATERAL TRUST BONDS

Collateral trust bonds are secured by assets other than real property—generally, by stocks and bonds and, occasionally, by patents or other intangibles.

The indenture carries the details of the pledge of assets to secure the debt, specifies who is to hold the assets as collateral, and states the conditions under which these assets may be held and released. Ordinarily, the collateralized securities are issued in amounts of 65-75% of the value of the collateral itself.

Pledged securities are generally deposited with the trustee before the collateral trust bonds are issued. The title to the pledged securities may remain in the name of the debtor company issuing the bonds or be transferred to the trustee. If title remains with the debtor, the trustee is given the power to transfer ownership in case of default. The payment of interest and principal on these bonds comes from the interest and dividends on the collateral and not from the earnings of the corporation itself.

The credit position of collateral bonds depends on several factors. These include the credit standing of the issuing company, the collateral pledged, and the terms of the indenture regarding the relationship of the value of the pledged securities to the collateral trust bond issue and the replacement of collateral that declines in value.

EQUIPMENT TRUST CERTIFICATES

These debt obligations are used primarily to finance capital equipment purchases in the transportation industry. When the certificates are issued, title to the equipment (often the rolling stock of a railroad or airplanes) is held by an independent trustee, normally a bank. In other words, equipment trust certificates are secured by liens on equipment.

The certificates mature serially (i.e., a portion each year), but title to the equipment remains with the trustee until the certificates are paid in full.

Under the so-called Philadelphia Plan, the title to the equipment is held by the trustee, which leases it to the corporation. The annual lease payments are used to pay principal and interest, and when all debt charges have been satisfied, title passes to the lessor.

Under the New York Plan, the buyer takes title to the equipment and then executes a chattel mortgage to secure the obligations issued under it.

Purchase money bonds are used to get funds to purchase property. These have many of the characteristics of equipment trust bonds.

DEBENTURE BONDS

Debenture bonds have no specific property pledged as security when the bonds are issued. If the issuer defaults, these bonds have the same claim as any other unsecured debt. These bonds depend on the credit standing of the company, and no specific property can be taken to satisfy the debt. Therefore, debenture bonds are backed by the full faith and credit of the company itself.

The indenture contains the nature of the promise to pay and any restrictions. The presence of protective covenants is of even greater importance to the bondholder than in the case of mortgage bonds. The credit standing of these bonds depends entirely on the strength of the issuer.

SUBORDINATED DEBENTURES

Subordinated debentures have a claim on the assets of the corporation that comes after all debts secured and unsecured.

Regular debentures have a claim on the assets of the corporation on a par with bank loans, accounts payable, and other unsecured debts. A subordinated debenture is the last type of debt to be paid off in a corporate liquidation. However, a subordinated debenture (which is a debt instrument) is paid off before preferred and common stockholders.

Usually, the subordination does not affect the obligation to pay interest or pay the principal at maturity, but only has an effect in the event of the liquidation or reorganization of the corporation.

GUARANTEED BONDS

The purpose of one corporation's guaranteeing the bonds of another is to enable the latter to borrow money at a lower interest rate. The marketplace will grant these bonds almost the same stature as it grants the direct debt of the guarantor. The guarantee sometimes is prompted by a leasing arrangement whereby the lessee guarantees bonds issued by the lessor. Normally, the guarantee is for both interest and principal. Sometimes a group of companies will agree to guarantee the debt of another, under a joint and several agreement, whereby each of the guarantors agrees to guarantee the debt issues in question.

INCOME BONDS

With income bonds, interest payments are not due unless the company's earnings are sufficient. The indenture may say that interest payments are cumulative. Thus, if they are missed in any year or years, they will accumulate and be paid to bondholders when earnings permit. The payment of interest on income bonds must be approved and declared by the board of directors. Such bonds trade "flat" with no accrued interest. The trust indenture will spell out in detail how earnings will be defined.

Since corporations that issue these bonds are often in the hands of a receiver who sometimes succeeds in reaching an adjustment with the creditors, these are sometimes referred to as **adjustment bonds**.

Income bonds should not be recommended to an investor who gives high priority to income and safety of principal. This is because the bondholder will not receive income unless it is earned. Better choices for such an investor would include

- High-quality corporate bonds (first mortgage or equipment trust certificates)
- Municipal general obligation bonds

CONVERTIBLE BONDS

Convertible bonds are convertible into common stock according to the terms stated in the indenture. Convertible bonds in many instances are convertible debentures.

Convertibles may reduce the cost of capital to the corporation since it may be possible to sell bonds more easily and at a lower interest rate if an attractive conversion feature is added. This results in an interest saving to the corporation.

The conversion price is the amount of par value exchangeable for one share of common stock: that is, if the conversion price is $50 and the par value is $1,000, it means the holder of the bond will receive 20 shares if he converts. In this example, the conversion ratio is 20 to 1.

$$\frac{\$1,000 \text{ Par value}}{\$50 \text{ Price convertible at}} = 20 \text{ Shares}$$

The parity price is the price the stock must sell at to be on exact equality with the bond. For example, if the bond above was selling at $1,200, the parity price would be found by dividing the market price by the number of shares into which the bond could be converted.

$$\frac{\$1,200 \text{ Market price}}{\underset{20}{\text{\# of shares received on conversion}}} = \$60 \text{ Parity price}$$

DEBT RETIREMENT

Bonds will eventually reach maturity. This means that the issuer will be faced with the necessity of redeeming them and this redemption will require cash.

The most usual method of retiring bonds is to establish a sinking fund. Money is paid to a trustee who generally uses it to buy back the outstanding bonds. The bonds may be purchased in the open market if it is possible to do so at a reasonable price.

Some bond issues require the corporation to retire a percentage of the issue (often 1 to 3%) by lot each year. The call is announced by publishing the bond numbers in the financial press, usually thirty to sixty days beforehand. The bonds may be called at par or, at times, a few percentage points above par. The company is normally permitted to purchase the bonds in the open market if they are trading under the call price.

Most bond issues are also callable in their entirety at some point, usually five to ten years after issuance, at the option of the issuer. **Call protection** is that period during which such bonds are not callable (e.g., the first five years after issuance). This provision enables a corporation, after this period, at its option, to reduce its borrowing costs by, for example, paying off an older bond issue with a 9% coupon, with the proceeds of a new bond issue bearing an interest rate of 5%. Issuing new bonds for the purpose of using the proceeds to pay off an existing bond issue is known as **refunding**. The company can also rid itself of unfavorable indenture provisions in the same manner, or extend its maturity schedule. A low call price, therefore, is obviously attractive to the issuer. Most often, a premium must be paid to the bondholder to call his bonds away from him, a premium that declines the longer the company waits to refund. These various call features are always spelled out in the indenture. If bonds are called, the creditworthiness of the company improves, as does the debt-to-net-worth ratio. A forced conversion takes place on a convertible bond when the company elects to call its bonds when the market value of the stock is higher than the redemption price of the bond.

Most municipal bonds and some corporate bonds are **serial bonds**. This means that the bonds issued are divided into series. The different series mature at different times. In other words, serial bonds mature in installments on successive dates. Serial bonds are normally noncallable and retired only on their specified maturity dates. They may carry a different coupon for each maturity and are quoted on a yield basis (e.g., 7.5%) rather than a dollar price basis (e.g., 101⅛). Usually, part of the entire issue—a series—will mature annually or semiannually. A typical maturity schedule would have either equal or ascending numbers of bonds maturing from one to ten or fifteen years from the issue date.

When these bonds are purchased, the buyer knows the maturity date, since the maturity date for each series is known and the bonds are not selected by lot. An advantage of such bonds to the corporation is that an established redemption price makes financial planning easier. However, the corporation faces a greater threat to solvency, since serial bonds must be paid when due. The longer-term serial bonds normally carry a lower interest rate. In other words, interest charges are progressively reduced to the corporation with an issue of serial bonds. The longer-term serial bonds are issued at a discount, and the investor receives a higher yield on the longer-term bonds.

Serial bonds are most frequently used with equipment trust certificates. The issuance of serial bonds will permit a corporation to reduce its total interest costs over the life of a bond issue since the yield will vary according to the length of time to each maturity date. Although serial bonds are divided into series, they should not be referred to as series bonds. The term **series bonds** refers to bonds having the same maturity date in a serial bond issue, those having the same priority of lien but issued at different dates, bonds with different priorities of lien, and types such as Series EE or HH US government bonds.

Quite often, a corporation does not rid itself of debt when it pays off a bond issue. Instead, it uses a system commonly used by the federal government known as **refunding**. Refunding means retiring a present bond issue by issuing new securities. New bonds, for example, might be issued and the cash proceeds used to pay off an old bond issue. This might be due to the old bond issue's reaching maturity or because a change in market conditions, such as a lowering of interest rates, means that the company's expenses will be less if it calls in an old bond issue and issues new bonds. If interest rates have dropped sufficiently, it will be less costly to pay the call premium and the cost of a new issue than to continue paying the interest rate specified on the old bond issue.

ZERO COUPON BONDS

In recent years, a new type of bond called a **zero coupon bond** has become a popular investment. Zero coupon bonds could be corporate, US government, or municipal bonds. However, we will describe zero coupon treasury bonds, which seem to be very popular.

A zero coupon bond is purchased by an investor at a deep discount price, and the bond pays all of its interest at maturity. The difference between the discount price paid by the investor and the value received by the investor at maturity represents the interest.

Assume an investor buys a zero coupon treasury bond $1,000 principal value with fifteen years to maturity. This zero coupon bond will cost the investor $189.23. The yield to maturity for the investor is 12%. For an investment of $189.23 the investor will receive $1,000 in fifteen years. However, the Internal Revenue Service states that the owner is receiving an annual return on the bond, but the income is being reinvested at the implied yield instead of being paid out. This results in taxable income to the investor even though no money is received by the investor.

Zero coupon bonds are good investments for tax-sheltered vehicles such as individual retirement accounts or Keogh plans. They are available in various maturities and discount prices. Also available are zero coupon municipal bonds on which imputed interest is free from taxation.

BOND QUALITY

Many factors affect the quality of a bond, including

- Earnings coverage of interest and fixed charges
- The lien protection possessed by the bond issue
- The marketability of the bond
- The issuing firm's past credit history and reputation

These factors and others are combined by several rating agencies whose task it is to summarize the investment quality of the bond with a single, simple rating. Chief among the rating agencies are Standard & Poor's Corporation (S&P) and Moody's Investors Service. While Moody's and S&P are the principal bond-rating services, there are two others: one is Fitch, a subsidiary of S&P; the other is Dun & Bradstreet (D&B),

of which Moody's is a subsidiary. Moody's and S&P issue ratings in order to assess the default risk associated with a bond.

A summary of their ratings is presented below.

Standard & Poor's bond ratings[*]

AAA	Highest grade
AA	High grade
A	Upper medium grade
BBB	Medium grade
BB	Lower medium grade
B	Speculative
CCC	Outright speculation
CC	Outright speculation
C	Reserved for income bonds
DDD	No interest being paid
DD	In default with rating indicating
D	Relative salvage value

[*] *For rating categories AA to BB, a plus sign is added to show high relative standing, a minus sign to show low relative standing.*

Moody's bond ratings[*]

Aaa	Best quality
Aa	High quality
A	Higher medium grade
Baa	Lower medium grade
Ba	Possess speculative elements
B	Generally lack characteristics of desirable investment
Caa	Poor standing, may be in default
Ca	Speculative in a high degree—often in default
C	Lowest grade

[*] *Bonds of the highest quality within a grade a designated by adding a "1" (e.g., A-1 and Baa-1).*

The first four categories of S&P and Moody's ratings represent "investment-grade" issues. Those bonds are suitable for purchase by prudent investors seeking dependable income. Debt issues rated below investment grade have some speculative characteristics.

Higher-quality debt issues of the same face value, maturity, and coupon, when compared to low-quality debt issues, have lower yields and higher market prices. The reason is that investors are willing to purchase high-quality, low-risk bonds for a lower yield than they would require for lower-grade bonds with greater uncertainty. A lower-quality bond will have a lower market price and higher yield than a higher-quality bond.

CALL PROVISIONS

Bonds are frequently issued with a provision that enables the issuer to call in or redeem the bond prior to stated maturity. This feature is included in order to protect the company should better opportunities (such as a lower interest rate) arise.

The inclusion of a call provision, however, reduces the value of the bond as an investment as it introduces uncertainty over the period of time the bond will be outstanding and, thus, changes the yield rate on the bond. Because of this, the issuer must offer the inducement of a call premium and extra payment over and above the par value to the investor should the issuer choose to call the bond before maturity. For example, if the company wishes to call the bond two years after issuing, it might have to agree to redeem the bonds at a price of 106 ($1,060 per $1,000 bond) as opposed to its par price. Call premiums generally decrease over time.

Call protection is the fixed time period after which a bond is issued during which the bondholder is assured that he will be able to keep the investment if he wishes. A low call price is attractive to the issuing corporation since calling their bonds will be less costly. It is not attractive to the investor. When a corporation calls its bonds, the credit standing of the company will improve (it is paying its debt early), and the company's debt-to-net-worth ratio decreases, as previously mentioned.

INTEREST RATE RISK

The usual reason for use of the call provision is the expectation of future variability in interest rates. Bonds frequently must be issued when interest rates are high. When rates subsequently fall, the issuing company may desire to call the bond and issue another one with a lower interest in its place. This illustrates a risk—specifically, the interest rate risk that faces investors and issuing corporations that deal in long-term interest-bearing securities. A change in the market rate of interest not only affects the amount of interest a corporation must pay for new money, it also affects the amount of yield the investor receives and the value of securities already issued. Since the interest paid on a bond is constant, bond prices will vary inversely with interest rates. Bonds with long maturities will have their prices affected more by a change in the general level of interest rates than will bonds with shorter maturities. Long-term bonds will decrease in price more than short-term bonds, when interest rates rise. Long-term bonds will increase in price more than short-term bonds, when interest rates fall.

YIELDS

Since the interest paid on the bond is a fixed legal obligation of the company, and since the interest rates fluctuate, the yield on the bond becomes a crucial point.

There are four types of yield calculations relating to bonds.

1. *Nominal yield.* This is sometimes referred to as the coupon rate. It is the rate printed on the bond or the face rate. If a bond states on its face that it will pay 6% per annum, then the nominal yield is also 6%.

2. *Current yield.* The market value of bonds will fluctuate with changes in interest rates in the economy and the changing attitudes of investors. The face rate of interest—the actual amount of interest paid—will not change. If the bond is a 4% $1,000 par value bond, it will pay $40 per year in interest. If it is a 6% bond, it will pay $60 per year. But if the market value of the bond fluctuates, the current yield will differ from the coupon rate.

$$\text{Current yield} \quad = \quad \frac{\text{Annual interest paid}}{\text{Market price}}$$

   If the bond pays $40 per annum interest and the bond is currently selling for $950, then the current yield is 4.2%, or slightly above the coupon rate of 4%. If the market price was $1,060, the current yield would be 3.77%.

3. *Yield to maturity.* At maturity, a $1,000 par value bond is always worth $1,000 regardless of what the investor originally paid. If the purchased bond is held until maturity, the rate will have to take into consideration the loss of any premium paid or the accumulation of any discount from par value. This yield to maturity is a compound rate of interest which takes the reinvestment of current interest earnings on the bond into consideration. The yield to maturity can be approximated by the formula

$$\frac{\text{Annual interest payment} + \text{Total discount/Number of years to maturity}}{(\text{Current bond price} + \text{Par value})/2}$$

or

$$\frac{\text{Annual interest payment} + \text{Total premium/Number of years to maturity}}{(\text{Current bond price} + \text{Par value})/2}$$

If, for example, the 4% bond had been purchased for $950 with ten years remaining to maturity, the yield to maturity would be

$$\frac{\$40 + 50/10}{(950 + 1,000)/2} = \frac{40 + 5}{975} = \frac{45}{975} = 4.620$$

If the bond had been purchased for $1,060, the yield to maturity would be

$$\frac{\$40 - 10/60}{(1,060 + 1,000)/2} = \frac{40 - 6}{1,030} = \frac{34}{1,030} = 3.3\%$$

4. *Yield to call.* Since the call provision that exists on some bonds creates uncertainty, the yield to maturity would also represent an uncertain value. To compensate for this, a somewhat different yield rate is calculated, which gives the yield to the call date (the earlier date, if there are several call date options),

rather than the yield to maturity. In this calculation, the call price (par value plus the call premium) would be substituted for the par value.

The yield to call can be approximated by the following formula, assuming the call price is $103 and the bond was purchased for $1,000. The bond can be called in five years and has an interest rate of 4%.

$$\frac{\text{Annual interest} + \text{Total premium or discount to call date/Number of years to maturity}}{(\text{Current bond price} + \text{Call price})/2}$$

$$\frac{\$40 + 30/10}{(1{,}000 + 1{,}030)/2} = \frac{40 + 6}{1{,}015} = \frac{46}{1{,}015} = 4.53$$

YIELD BOOK

The actual, precise calculation of yield rates is somewhat involved mathematically. To calculate the yield on every bond would be a laborious and time-consuming task. To simplify the problem, a set of tables involving virtually all possible combinations of price, interest rate, and period to maturity have been compiled into what is known as the **Yield Book (Basis Book)**. With the aid of this volume, the calculation of any bond yield is a simple matter.

Yields are stated in percents and hundredths of a percent, such as 5.86% or 7.51%. Such quotations are referred to as **basis prices**. The hundredths of a percent are known as basis points, with 1% equaling 100 basis points. Basis points are used because they are more flexible than fractions and there is less confusion over relative proportions when discussing changes in interest rates (i.e., a change is expressed as an increase or decrease of so many basis points). Basis prices indicate yield to maturity. If a registered representative tells a customer that a bond is selling at a 6.30 basis, this means that the bond will yield 6.30% if held to maturity. Therefore, if the basis price of a bond is higher than the coupon rate, the bond must be selling below par (at a discount). If both rates are the same, the bond is selling at par. If the basis price is lower, the bond is selling above par (at a premium).

RIGHTS

Rights are commonly used when a corporation wishes to raise funds through the sale of additional common stock. Rights are also called **subscription rights** because the holder has the right to subscribe to a new issue at less than the present market price. Because the holder of common stock frequently has the right, often referred to as the **preemptive right,** to maintain his proportionate position in the equity of a corporation, a corporation will often sell stock to its own stockholders through a privileged subscription or a preemptive rights offering. This offering must first be approved by a vote of the stockholders and then letters must be sent to all stockholders advising them of the terms of the offering. These terms would be the number of shares to which a stockholder is entitled to subscribe, based on the number of shares he presently owns. For example, since one right is issued for each share outstanding before the new issue, if stockholders are permitted to purchase one new share for each 10 held, a stockholder who owns 100 shares would receive 100 rights and be able to purchase 10 new shares. The number of rights needed to purchase one new share is always the ratio of the number of shares previously outstanding to the number of shares in the new issue. Thus, if there were 100,000 shares outstanding and a new issue of 10,000 shares, 10 rights would be needed to acquire 1 new share. These rights would be sent to the stockholder as of a stipulated record date, entitling him to return them within a prescribed period (usually two or three weeks) with his check, to purchase the additional stock. Rights may be traded separately from the stock. Since rights not exercised become worthless, stockholders who do not wish to exercise them should sell them to someone who will exercise them. If someone wishes to acquire some of the new shares, he may purchase the rights. For the rights to have value, they must entitle the holder to purchase securities at less than the current market value.

There are two formulas for calculating the value of rights. First, before the ex-rights date while the stock is selling with rights (cum rights)

$$\text{Value of a right} = \frac{\text{Market price} - \text{Subscription price}}{\text{Number of rights} + 1}$$

R = Value of a right; M = Market price; S = Subscription price; N = Number of rights needed to buy one share.

$$R = \frac{M - S}{N + 1}$$

An example may help to illustrate this problem. Assume the selling price of common stock of Company A is $30 a share and the company is now offering its stockholders the right to purchase one new share at $24.50 for each 10 held. The theoretical value of a right is

$$R = \frac{M - S}{N + 1} = \frac{\$30.00 - \$24.50}{10 + 1} = \frac{\$5.50}{11} = \$0.40 \text{ Value of a right before the ex-rights date}$$

The "1" in the denominator mathematically corrects the fact that the current market value of the stock includes the value of the right that will be acquired when a share is purchased.

On and after the ex-rights date, when the stock is selling without rights, the formula is

$$R = \frac{M - S}{N}$$

Since before the ex-rights date the market price of the stock includes the value of the right that the purchaser of the stock will receive, this market price will decline by the value of the right, since on and after the date the purchase of the stock will no longer receive a right. Referring to the example, the value of a right on or after the ex-rights date would be

$$R = \frac{M - S}{N} = \frac{\$29.50 - \$24.50}{10} = \frac{\$5.00}{10} = \$0.50 \text{ Theoretical value of a right on or after the ex-rights date}$$

The offering terms would also state the date on which the new stock would be issued and give the address of the office to which the subscriptions should be mailed. The stockholder will maintain his proportionate ownership in the corporation only if he exercises his rights. Otherwise, his proportionate ownership in the corporation will decrease.

If the holder of the common does not want to exercise the rights, he can sell his holdings in the market through a broker. The market value of the rights is subject to the same supply-and-demand factors that influence the price of any security and will vary from the theoretical value depending on the demand for the rights and the interest in the new stock issues. If a shareholder wished to establish a gain but not lose any stock, he could sell part of his stock in the open market and replace it with subscription stock. Or, if he felt the stock would go down over the short term, he could sell short the shares to be purchased and then cover his short position with subscription stock.

Key points to remember concerning rights include

- They allow a common stockholder to subscribe to a new issue of common stock before it is offered to the public.
- They normally have a life span of two to four weeks.
- They are freely transferable.
- Holders of rights are allowed to subscribe to the common stock at less than the market price.
- To subscribe to the common stock an investor must send the rights to the corporation or its agent plus the subscription price of the new shares.

WARRANTS

A warrant is a marketable option that gives the holder the long-term right to buy a certain number of common shares, usually unissued shares, at a specified price during a specified time period. They are sometimes issued with bonds as a means of reducing the interest rate a company must pay. They are also frequently used in conjunction with reorganization and mergers and, since they pay no dividends and may eventually expire without value, they are normally of more interest to the speculator than the investor. They are sometimes used to compensate the underwriter of the issue, in place of the normal underwriting fee. The warrant exercise spells out not only the exercise price at which the common stock can be purchased, but also the number of shares and the date on which the warrant expires, although some warrants have a perpetual life. Others are issued with a definite life span. Such warrants cannot be exercised until a specified period of time has transpired. Some warrant terms change over time, with either the price at which the stock can be purchased increased, or the number of shares that can be purchased decreased.

Warrants are freely transferable and may be traded separately from common stock on a national securities exchange. The subscription price of a warrant is related to the market price of the underlying security. Warrants may be used in a new issue of common stock to increase its attractiveness.

AMERICAN DEPOSITARY RECEIPTS

American depositary receipts (ADRs) are negotiable receipts issued by an American depositary stating that a certain number of foreign shares have been deposited with the overseas branch of the depositary or with a custodian. These assist the American investor, since foreign stock is often in bearer form. The purpose of an ADR is to facilitate US trading in foreign securities. Dividends on these bearer shares would be paid in foreign funds to those presenting the certificates at the office of the firm (usually a bank) selected to disburse the dividends. Notices of dividend payments or stockholder meetings could not be mailed to the shareholder since the shares are not registered. Since some trading practices in foreign companies are different from trading practices in the United States, and since foreign currencies and customers are involved, the trading of foreign securities and the settlement of estates partly in foreign securities would be difficult. The ADR, however, is in registered form, and the holder of the ADR is treated exactly the same as the holder of a security in an American corporation. The price of the ADR will fluctuate with the fluctuation of the price of the foreign shares on deposit. Since the holder of an ADR receives dividends, as he would from American companies in which he had invested, the American investor usually considers the ADR to be simply stock in the foreign corporation, although, of course, technically this is not true.

REAL ESTATE INVESTMENT TRUSTS

The purpose of the **real estate investment trust (REIT)** is to enable the smaller investor to invest in real estate. Authorized by congress in 1960 with the passage of the Real Estate Investment Trust Act, real estate investment trusts are, normally, business trusts running twenty years after the death of the last person named in the trust. A trust indenture spells out the functions of the trustees and their powers to act for the benefit of the shareholders. The shares, which are certificates of beneficial interest, are transferable. The indenture also states the maximum number of beneficiaries and the maximum number of holdings the trust may have. There are three major classifications of REIT activities: long-term mortgages, equity in ownership properties, and short-term real estate construction and development loans. Sources of REIT income are: rent from real property; interest on obligations secured by real property; gains from the sale of real property; distributions from and gains on the sales of securities, including other REITs; and abatement or refunds of taxes on real property. REITs thus attempt to make a profit on the spread between what they pay for money and the interest and rent they receive on mortgages and real estate. A typical capital structure could consist of 20% equity, 40% long-term debt, and 40% bank loans and commercial paper.

As long as the REITs meet certain standards, like mutual funds, they escape corporate income taxes if they distribute 90% of net income to shareholders. They must use an external management company, obtain 75% of their income from interest and rents, and invest 75% of their assets in mortgages and real estate. The REIT may also distribute capital gains, which the beneficiary treats as a capital gain, using the holding period of the REIT as his own. The REIT cannot have loss carryover for tax purposes, nor can it pass operating losses through to the shareholder. REITs are traded in the over-the-counter market and many are listed on the New York Stock Exchange.

SPECIAL SITUATIONS

The term *special situations* is frequently applied to the common stock of a company in which the stock's potential is not related merely to the company's day-to-day business. Typically, a special situation may result from such events as hoped-for recovery under new management, discovery of a valuable natural resource on the corporate properties, the introduction of a popular new product, or a potential takeover.

COLLATERALIZED MORTGAGE OBLIGATIONS

Collateralized mortgage obligations (CMOs) are mortgage-backed bonds secured by a pool of mortgage loans. A normal pass-through security, such as a Government National Mortgage Association (GNMA) security, passes through interest and principal payments to investors. However, when mortgage loans are prepaid (homeowner sells or refinances the mortgage), principal is returned to the holder of the security. This may occur when interest rates are low and the holder will reinvest at lower return rates. CMO are a type of derivative security.

CMOs attempt to reduce the repayment risk by dividing their pool of mortgages into classes, called **tranches**. The first tranche will receive all principal repayments before the second tranche receives any prepayments. The second tranche will receive all prepayments before the third tranche receives any prepayments.

An issuer of a CMO distributes cash flow from the mortgages to different classes or tranches of short-, medium- and long-term maturities. Tranches pay different rates of interest and normally mature in two, five, ten, or twenty years. The final tranche of a CMO is referred to as a **Z-bond**. A Z-bond is also referred to as an accrual or accretion bond. Holders of Z-bonds receive no cash flow until earlier tranches are paid in full.

CMOs are normally collateralized by the following:

- GNMA (Ginnie Mae)
- Federal National Mortgage Association (FNMA, Fannie Mae)
- Federal Home Loan Mortgage Corporation (Freddie Mac)
- Federal Housing Administration (FHA) mortgage loans
- Conventional mortgages

Other important points to remember concerning CMOs are

- CMOs are backed by mortgages that are often repaid prior to maturity. CMOs have

  - *Implied call risk*. This is the risk that principal will be returned sooner than expected.
  - *Extension risk*. This is the risk that the life of the security may be longer than anticipated.

- CMOs are traded over the counter (OTC) in the secondary market with markups and markdowns applied.
- Interest payments to investors are subject to both federal and state income taxes. The portion of the payment that represents a return of principal to the investor is not taxable.
- Most CMOs carry a AAA credit rating.
- The primary risks investors in CMOs take include

  - Liquidity
  - Average life sensitivity
  - Price sensitivity

- CMO tranches pay a variable rate of interest which is normally measured against the London Interbank Offered Rate (LIBOR).
- Planned amortization classes (PACs) are CMOs that most resemble bonds because they have a sinking fund structure which means investors will receive payments over a predetermined period with stable cash flow. PACs have a less-than-average exposure to call risk.
- CMOs carry higher coupon rates than US Treasury securities. Investors in CMOs can earn a better return than on US Treasury securities and still own a quality investment. CMOs normally have a higher yield than corporate bonds. CMOs will fluctuate in price in response to changing interest rates.
- CMOs are issued in minimum amounts of $1,000 and may pay interest monthly, quarterly, or semiannually, depending on the terms of the issue and how it is structured.
- The main types of mortgage securities available are pass-throughs and CMOs.
- In certain instances, mortgage securities may be stripped and interest only (IO) and principal only (PO) securities are issued.
- Mortgage securities are purchased by life insurance companies, commercial banks, pension funds, corporations, and charitable organizations.

INTEREST RATE AND BOND CONCEPTS

A clear distinction must be made between the rate of interest on a bond and its yield. The interest rate is stated on the bond and indicates the amount the owner of the bond will receive periodically from the issuer. If the interest rate is 8%, the holder will receive $80 per year. However, the yield to maturity (or call) on this bond is the relation of the total interest that will be received, plus any capital gain (or minus any capital loss) on the investment, to the average amount invested until the bond matures (or is called). Obviously, if the interest rate is 8% but the purchaser pays only $900 for the bond, the yield to maturity (or call at par) will be greater than 8%.

There is an inverse relationship between interest rates and bond prices. The market price of outstanding bonds declines when interest rates rise and increases when interest rates decline. This permits the yield on these outstanding bonds to equal (or at least move in the same direction as) the yield on newly issued bonds with higher or lower interest rates.

Short-term interest rates respond more quickly and fluctuate over a wider range than long-term interest rates. The same can also be said for the fluctuation of yields on short-term issues compared to yields on long-term issues.

The price of long-term bonds is more greatly affected by a change in the level of interest rates than is the price of short-term bonds. The longer a bond has before maturity, the greater the leverage effect of a shift in the level of interest rates on its price. For a specific change in yields, the fluctuation in the market prices of bonds will be greater the longer the period to maturity. If interest rates rise, the price of long-term bonds falls more than the price of short-term bonds. If interest rates fall, the price of long-term bonds increases more than the price of short-term bonds.

To minimize the interest rate risk in a bond portfolio, an investor should purchase bonds with short maturities. Bonds are also subject to the purchasing power risk or the inflationary risk. If an investor purchases an investment-grade bond, the risk of default is not high. However, he will be taking a repurchasing power risk. Assume the investment-grade bond has ten years remaining to maturity. When the investor receives the principal amount in ten years, the purchasing power of the dollars received will be less.

All new issues of US government, federal agency, municipal, and corporate bonds are now being issued in fully registered or book entry form only, as a result of changes in federal tax law. However, many bearer bonds and bonds registered as to principal only are outstanding and will be for many years.

If a bond is described as *safe*, this means that interest and principal will be paid on time. Investment-grade bonds are expected to be "safe" and not default.

Assume a $1,000 par value bond is issued by ABC Corporation, Inc. on January 2, 1993, with a 6% interest rate. The bond has a maturity date of January 2, 2013, and is callable at 103. The current yield on the bond when it is issued is 6%. However, if interest rates rise to 8% by July 2, 1993, the bond's market price will decrease to $750.

$$\frac{\$60 \text{ Annual interest}}{\$750 \text{ Market price}} = 8\%$$

The price of the ABC Corporation bond will decrease in price in order to make the yield competitive with current yields available in July 1993. When the ABC Corporation bond was issued in January 1993, its yield was competitive with current yields at that time. However, when interest rates rise, bond prices must fall and yields increase to be competitive with current yields. If, instead, interest rates fell to 4% on July 2, 1993, the market price of the bond would have risen to $1,500.

$$\frac{\$60 \text{ Annual interest}}{\$1,500 \text{ Market price}} = 4\%$$

SETTLEMENT OF TRANSACTIONS

The securities industry has decided to shorten its standard settlement period to three business days following trade date (T + 3). This change is effective in June 1995.

In the securities industry, a trade is considered settled when a customer pays for a securities purchase. Assume on Monday, June 12, 1995, a customer purchases 100 shares of Disney for a total purchase price of $5,400. Settlement date for the transaction is Thursday, June 15. The customer's funds are required to be at the broker/dealer's office by settlement date to "settle" the money owed on the purchase.

Regulation T of the Federal Reserve requires payment by the fifth business day after trade date. The Federal Reserve's Regulation T gives a two-day grace period past settlement before a broker/dealer must take action. If the customer has not paid by the close of business on the fifth business day after trade date, the broker/dealer must either obtain an extension of time for payment from the appropriate regulatory agency or cancel or liquidate the unsettled portion of the transaction.

Prompt payment in the securities industry is necessary to maintain the financial integrity of the broker/dealers. The customer's payment is due by settlement date, because the 100 shares of Disney will be delivered by the selling broker/dealer on settlement date. Once a customer pays for a security purchase in full, the entire risk on the position is the customer's. If the customer did not pay the broker/dealer for the security purchase, the customer's broker/dealer would still have to pay for the 100 shares of Disney, when it is delivered by the selling broker/dealer.

When a securities transaction takes place, the two important dates are

1. *Trade date*. The date on which the transaction is executed in the marketplace

2. *Settlement date.* The date on which payment is due from the customer on a security purchase or the securities are due from the customer on a sale. The customer must deposit funds on a purchase of securities or deliver securities on a sale in order to settle the transaction.

When a customer purchases a security, he is long the security. Long, in the securities industry, means ownership. A long sale is when a customer sells a security that he owns and the proceeds of the sale are credited to the customer's account on settlement date. A short sale occurs when a customer sells a security he does not own. A short sale requires a customer to deposit margin money to secure his promise to buy the stock back at some future date. A short sale must be done in a margin account and always represents risk to the broker/dealer.

To summarize, effective in June 1995 the securities industry will adopt a three-day settlement period (T + 3) for corporate and municipal securities. Regulation T of the Federal Reserve allows a two-day grace period past the standard settlement date before a broker/dealer must take action. If the customer has not paid for a security purchase by the fifth business day after trade date, the broker/dealer must obtain an extension of time or cancel or liquidate the unsettled portion of the transaction.

If the securities transaction is for $1,000 or less, a broker/dealer would not have to obtain an extension of time and would not have to cancel or liquidate the transaction. US government securities and municipal securities are exempt from the provisions of Regulation T. The standard US securities settlement period is as follows:

- *Corporate securities*—The third business day following trade date (T + 3).
- *Municipal securities*—The third business day following trade date (T + 3).
- *Investment company securities*—The third business day following trade date (T + 3).
- *US government securities*—Next business day following trade date (T + 1).
- *Options*—Next business day following trade date (T + 1).

When a customer purchases a security in a cash account, the account is debited or charged for the amount of the purchase. Assume a customer buys 100 shares of ABC for a total purchase price of $6,500. The funds to pay for the purchase are due in the account by three business days following trade date. When the customer deposits a check into the account, the account is credited for $6,500. The money balance in the account is zero, and the customer is long 100 shares of ABC. Assume two months later the customer sells the 100 shares of ABC for a net amount of $7,800. This is a long sale, and $7,800 would be credited to the customer's account on settlement date. The customer requests a check, and a $7,800 check is sent to the customer, making the money balance in the account zero.

To summarize, the Federal Reserve established a term referred to as the *payment period*. The payment period is defined as the number of days in the standard US securities settlement cycle plus two business days. Also, The Federal Reserve created a new *government securities account*. The government securities account exempts transactions involving government securities for customers from Regulation T.

2 FINANCIAL ANALYSIS

A business uses various financial statements in order to monitor its financial condition. The two main financial statements used by a business are the balance sheet and the income statement. This chapter will analyze the major financial statements used by business and the financial ratios that describe profitability and solvency of a company.

THE BALANCE SHEET

The balance sheet is a statement of the financial condition of a business at a particular moment. The balance sheet is also called a **statement of financial condition**. The purpose of a balance sheet is to present the financial position of the business at a single point in time. It presents the resources of the business: the assets or property, the claims to property, and the property rights that the business possesses. The assets are counterbalanced by the claims other people or businesses have against the property of the business preparing the balance sheet. (See Exhibit 2.1)

Exhibit 2.1: Information in a balance sheet

A corporate balance sheet is the starting point in assessing a company.

Can determine

1. Book value per share of common stock
2. Net worth
3. Financial strength of the corporation
4. Working capital
5. Capitalization ratios
6. Long-term funds contributed by owners and lenders

Cannot determine

1. Operation ratio
2. Expense ratio
3. Accounts receivable turnover
4. Inventory turnover

The claims against the assets of a business are of two types.

1. Claims of creditors against the assets
2. Claims of owners against the assets

The claims of creditors are either short-term claims (current liabilities) or long-term claims (long-term debt). The claims of the creditors must be paid off in a liquidation before the owners of the business receive any money.

The claims of the owners against the assets are reflected in stockholders' equity. Since the claims of the creditors must be paid in full before the owners can be paid, the owners are said to have a residual claim against the assets. Assume ABC Corporation has the following financial statement:

Assets	$100,000
Liabilities	35,000
Stockholder's equity	$ 65,000

ABC Corporation liquidates the assets and receives $100,000. The liabilities of $35,000 must be paid off and the owners or stockholders would receive $65,000.

The balance sheet presents a picture of the assets of a business and the claims against the assets of a business as of one particular date. An equation is often used in relation to a balance sheet. It is referred to as the basic balance sheet equation and is expressed as follows:

$$Total\ assets = Total\ liabilities + Net\ worth$$

Stockholders' equity is also called **net worth**. This equation states that the total assets of a business is equal to the claims against the assets. The total liabilities are the claims of the creditors against the assets. The net worth represents the claims of the owners against the assets.

The balance sheet also presents information concerning the sources of the monies (or funds or capital) that were used to purchase or obtain the assets. The word *capital* has several meanings. In the financial analysis or accounting sense, it is commonly considered to mean long-term or permanently invested money, or money available for long-term or permanent investment. More simply put, the liabilities and owner's equity represent the sources of the funds, and the assets represent the uses of the funds. Because the process of obtaining monies and disbursing monies is a continuous and dynamic one, the balance sheet expresses relationships that will change immediately after a balance sheet has been prepared. When reading a particular balance sheet, it should be understood that the conditions will have already changed and the financial position or condition of the particular business unit may possibly be quite substantially different than it was on the date specified in the statement. Therefore, the older a statement, the less reliable it is as an indicator of the current condition.

The purpose of any set of financial statements is to provide information on which the reader may rely in order to make a decision. Obviously, the best statements would be the most current, since most decisions are made concerning *future* events.

Assets

Assets are defined as property owned by a business. Assets have value to a business. Assets may have value because of their ability to provide future services (machinery) or because they can be sold for cash (inventory). The main assets carried on the balance sheet of a business enterprise are

- Current assets
- Fixed assets
- Intangible assets

Assets on a balance sheet are normally listed in order of their liquidity. Therefore, current assets are listed at the top of the balance sheet. Current assets are assets expected to be turned into cash within one year.

Current assets. As previously defined, current assets are assets expected to be turned into cash within one year. Current assets are normally listed in the order of liquidity, with the most liquid assets listed first. Liquidity refers to the ease in which an asset can be turned into cash. Certain assets are very liquid, such as marketable securities. Other assets such as buildings or machinery are not very liquid since they cannot easily be turned into cash.

The main current assets carried by a corporation are

- Cash and equivalents
- Accounts receivable
- Inventory

Cash and equivalents include balances in checking accounts and cash equivalents such as treasury bills and money market fund balances. Accounts receivable represent money due to the company from customers who have purchased goods or services. Inventory represents merchandise on hand to be sold in order to produce cash flow for the business.

Inventories normally consist of three separate categories.

- Raw materials
- Work in process
- Finished goods

Raw materials represent basic materials with which the company starts production; work in process includes items that are in the manufacturing process; and finished goods are the items that have finished the manufacturing process.

Inventories are normally valued on the balance sheet at the lower of cost or market value. During periods of rising prices, inventory values on the balance sheet will be considerably less than their replacement cost.

Inventory usually will physically move through the business operations on a first-in, first-out (FIFO) basis. That is, the oldest goods on hand will be the first shipped. While this routine is followed physically, it does not have to be followed in the accounting process. Cost (or value) can flow through the records on a FIFO basis; but it can also flow through on a last-in, first-out (LIFO) basis. The rationale behind this seemingly backward way of handling inventory costs is related to inflation. In periods of rising prices, FIFO will result in a higher net income than LIFO. In periods of falling prices, LIFO will show a higher net income than FIFO. (See Exhibit 2.2.)

Exhibit 2.2: Inventory valuation methods

1. **FIFO**—First inventory purchased is the first inventory sold.

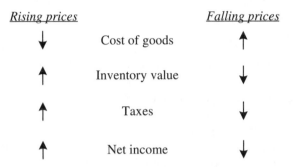

Rising prices		*Falling prices*
↓	Cost of goods	↑
↑	Inventory value	↓
↑	Taxes	↓
↑	Net income	↓

2. **LIFO**—Last inventory purchased is the first inventory sold.

Rising prices		*Falling prices*
↑	Cost of goods	↓
↓	Inventory value	↑
↓	Taxes	↑
↓	Net income	↑

Fixed assets. A fixed asset is an item that has a life in excess of one year. The main fixed assets of a business include

- Land
- Buildings
- Furniture and fixtures
- Equipment

Fixed assets, with the exception of land, can be depreciated. The federal tax code states that unimproved land cannot be depreciated. Fixed assets have finite lives (other than land) due to wear and tear or obsolescence. Depreciation is the method used to allocate the cost of the fixed assets to the operation of the business and to spread this cost over the service life of the asset.

Depreciation. Business assets wear out over time and must be replaced. The tax code provides for reasonable annual deduction from taxable income for the wear and tear for property used in the business. The Economic Recovery Tax Act of 1981 changed the manner in which depreciation was computed. Prior to January 1, 1981, depreciation deductions taken were either straight line or an accelerated method (sum-of-the-years' digits or double-declining balance). The accelerated methods charged more depreciation in early years and less in later years.

Depreciation is an expense item to a business entity and, therefore, reduces taxable income. However, depreciation is a noncash charge. This means that it is an expense that does not result in cash being paid out. Assume a business has net income after taxes of $10 million and a depreciation expense of $2 million. What is the company's cash flow? Cash flow is net income adding back noncash charges such as depreciation.

Net income	$10,000,000
Depreciation	+ 2,000,000
Cash flow	$12,000,000

The main types of depreciation include straight line, double-declining balance, sum-of-the-years' digits and modified accelerated cost recovery system (MACRS). MACRS assigns assets useful life periods such as three, five, or ten years. The basis of an asset for depreciation purposes under MACRS is the cost of the asset.

Depletion. For certain business assets such as oil and gas wells, mines, and other natural deposits, the tax code allows a deduction for depletion. There are two basic methods for computing depletion allowances under the tax code.

1. Cost depletion
2. Percentage depletion

Cost depletion allows the owner of an oil well, for example, to deduct a cost per unit for the oil that is sold. Assume a person buys an oil well for $1 million that is estimated to contain 250,000 barrels of oil. The cost per barrel of the oil is $4. The individual is allowed to deduct $4 per barrel of oil sold from his taxable income. If he sells 20,000 barrels of oil, an $80,000 depletion deduction is allowed.

Percentage depletion generally allows more generous deductions to be taken under the tax code. The percentage depletion deduction is derived by taking a fixed percentage of gross income generated by the property. However, the percentage depletion deduction cannot exceed 50% of the taxable income generated by the property. Taxable income in this case represents gross income minus allowable deductions. Depletion deductions reduce taxable income and are therefore beneficial to an investor. However, depletion deductions are normally subject to recapture under certain circumstances.

Intangible assets. Intangible assets are ownership rights that have no form or substance. Earlier, the value of the asset was defined as the value of the rights that the owner had in that asset. That generally referred to physically existent, tangible items (with the possible exception of accounts receivable). In the case of intangibles (such as goodwill and trademarks), there is no physical existence, only the rights the asset represents.

The main types of intangible assets include

- Goodwill
- Patents
- Copyrights
- Trademarks

Although any business may enjoy a considerable advantage over its competitors because of the goodwill it has developed over a period of time, this asset can only be used or added to the balance sheet in a very specific and limited circumstance. Goodwill derives solely from the acquisition of a subsidiary or from the merger of two or more companies where the purchase price of the acquired company is greater than the value of the assets acquired. In short, goodwill, appearing on a balance sheet, can be acquired only through merger or acquisition—it *cannot* be developed internally.

Since the value of goodwill is established as the excess of the purchase price over the value of the assets obtained, it probably has little relationship to reality. For this reason, the common practice is to write off goodwill as rapidly as possible. A minimum period of sixty months is specified by accounting convention. Goodwill cannot be deducted for tax purposes, however.

A patent gives the owner the exclusive right to a product or process. A registered trademark allows only the owner to use that name or mark. Copyrights similarly give the owner exclusive control over certain written works. All of these assets involve costs of acquisition and costs of protection (i.e., costs incurred to prevent infringement of the right to sole use or possession). These costs become the basis for value of these assets on the balance sheets.

As with goodwill, the value of these intangible but legally enforceable rights is not calculable. How much is the trademark *Coca-Cola* worth? Or the name *IBM*? Can a reasonable value be assigned to them? These assets are almost impossible to value unless the intangible asset is sold to willing buyers.

Because of the lack of basis for valuation, these assets, like goodwill, are generally written off. Unlike goodwill, however, the amortization of these assets can be deducted for tax purposes, except where the asset is acquired by direct purchase. In this latter circumstance, the asset is considered a capital asset (as goodwill is also classified) and, therefore, cannot be depreciated or amortized. Any gains or losses involved will be recognized when the firm disposes of the asset.

Liabilities

Liabilities are the claims of the creditors against the assets of the business. These are legally enforceable rights and payment must eventually be made within a proper time period or on contractually agreed dates. Unlike assets, there is no valuation problem in dealing with liabilities. The amounts are fixed in all categories except one. The only exception is contingent liabilities where the final amount cannot be readily determined until some future event occurs.

As with assets, liabilities are listed in order of liquidity. Current liabilities are listed first, followed by long-term liabilities, also referred to as **long-term debt**.

Current liabilities. Current liabilities are those liabilities expected to be paid off within one year. Current liabilities normally consist of items such as

- Accounts payable
- Salaries payable
- Taxes payable
- Dividends payable
- Short-term notes payable
- Accrued expenses payable
- Current portion of long-term debt payable

Long-term debt. Long-term debt is debt of a business that is not expected to be paid off in one year. The most common types of long-term debt for a business are bonds and bank loans with more than one year to maturity. The bonds may be various types, such as

- First mortgage bonds
- Convertible bonds
- Income bonds
- Debentures
- Subordinated debentures

Stockholders' Equity

Stockholders' equity represents the owners' interest in the business and consists of

- Preferred stock
- Common stock
- Paid-in capital
- Retained earnings

The amount representing preferred stock on the balance sheet of a corporation represents the amount of preferred stock sold at par value. Dividends on preferred stock must be paid before common stockholders can receive a dividend. Preferred stockholders are owners of a corporation along with common stockholders.

The amount representing common stock on the balance sheet is the value of common stock sold at par value. Any amount received by the corporation above par value is credited to paid-in capital or capital surplus.

Retained earnings represents the sum of all earnings retained in the business since its inception. Net income is credited to retained earnings and all dividends are paid out of retained earnings, whether they are cash dividends or stock dividends.

Common stockholders' equity is the summation of common stock, capital surplus, and retained earnings. Common stockholders' equity does not include preferred stock.

Stockholders' equity is increased by

- Net income
- The sale of a new issue of stock
- The sale of treasury stock

Stockholders' equity is decreased by

- The declaration of a cash dividend
- The repurchase of common or preferred stock
- A net loss

However, stockholders' equity is not affected by a stock split or a stock dividend.

Working Capital (Net Working Capital)

Working capital is generally defined as the capital that constantly circulates through the operating cycle of the business in order to provide the necessary resources. Circulating capital is constantly being reinvested. Cash is invested in inventory; inventory is sold and converted into accounts receivable; cash is then collected; and the cycle starts over. Working capital or circulating capital is differentiated from fixed capital, which roughly corresponds to the fixed assets. The fixed assets, while important and necessary from the standpoint of production, do not in themselves participate in the operating cycle. Because of the dependence of the business on this working capital cycle, the importance of working capital cannot be overemphasized. Without constant replenishment in sufficient quantity through the operating cycle, the flow of cash or funds through the business would slowly dry up.

Net working capital (often referred to as working capital) represents the liquid resources of the business and is measured by the difference between the current assets and the current liabilities. The formula for computing working capital is

$$\text{Current assets} - \text{Current liabilities} = \text{Working capital}$$

It is a measure of the liquidity of the firm and indicates how well the firm is handling its current affairs. The larger the net working capital position, the more liquid the firm, since the quantity of current assets is not subject to the immediate claims of creditors.

Since working capital is defined as the difference between current assets and current liabilities, any change in working capital must originate in the noncurrent portions of the balance sheet. It should be obvious, for instance, that any increase in inventory on the one hand and a similar increase in accounts payable on the other will have no effect on working capital, since the increase is the same on both sides. Basically, working capital is increased by the following items:

- Net income
- Cash flow from depreciation and other noncash charges
- Sale of noncurrent assets
- Sale of securities (debt or equity)

Just as funds are increased by activity in noncurrent items, funds are lost or decreased in a similar manner. The principal sources of decreases in working capital are

- Net losses from operations
- Purchases of noncurrent assets
- Elimination or reduction of long-term debt
- Redemption of preferred stock
- Cash dividends on equity securities

INCOME STATEMENT

An income statement for a business enterprise shows the sources of income (sales) and the distribution of the income (expenses). A condensed income statement would appear as follows:

Net sales
Less: Cost of sales
Gross profit margin
Less: Selling expenses
          Administrative expenses
          Depreciation
Operating income
Gain or loss from extraordinary items
Net income before interest and taxes
Less: Income expense
Net income before taxes
Less: Taxes
Net income

Less: Preferred dividends
Net income available to common stockholders

The income statement shows income and expense items, while the balance sheet reflects assets, liabilities, and stockholders' equity. The income statement shows whether a business has realized a net profit or a net loss over the past year. The net income or net loss is transferred to the retained earnings account on the balance sheet.

Operating Income

The difference between net sales and the total of the operating expenses (cost of goods sold plus selling and administrative expenses, including depreciation) yields the **operating income** for the period. This particular figure is important as a measure of the efficiency of the business. It pertains only to the primary mission of the business and does not include extraordinary items which, if included, could easily distort the figure and provide an erroneous impression.

Operating income is the primary measure of the ability of the company to put its goods or services into the market. It can be expressed as a percentage of net sales, and this ratio is called the profit margin ratio.

$$\frac{\text{Operating income}}{\text{Net sales}} = \text{Profit margin ratio}$$

The profit margin ratio shows the percentage of the sales dollar available to pay interest and taxes. After interest and taxes are deducted from operating income, the remainder is net income.

$$
\begin{array}{l}
\quad\text{Operating income} \\
-\ \underline{\text{Interest expense}\qquad\quad} \\
\quad\text{Net income before taxes} \\
-\ \underline{\text{Taxes}\qquad\qquad\quad} \\
\quad\text{Net income}
\end{array}
$$

However, the complement of the profit margin ratio is the operating ratio. The operating ratio is expressed as operating expenses (cost of goods sold, selling and administrative expenses) divided by net sales. If the operating ratio is 65%, the profit margin ratio would be 35%. The two ratios added together would equal 100%.

A manager operating a business would like the profit margin ratio to increase as a percentage of net sales and the operating ratio to decrease. However, interest and taxes are not deducted in computing operating income. If the profit margin for a particular business increases, this does not mean that net income will increase by the same percentage. Interest expense may have increased by a greater percentage than the increase in operating income. Therefore, it is important to remember that operating income is computed before interest and taxes are deducted and net income is derived by deducting all expenses from net sales.

Dividends and Retained Earnings

Since the stockholders are entitled to the residual earnings of the corporation, the retained earnings belong to them. If any distribution of earnings is made to the stockholders, this distribution or dividend must be deducted from retained earnings regardless of the form the dividend may take. Dividends can be declared payable or distributable only by the board of directors of the corporation, and once declared cannot be rescinded except by majority vote of the stockholders. A company is not required to pay dividends to its stockholders, even if earnings exist. The dividend is immediately deducted from retained earnings as soon as it is declared. That portion of earnings not paid as a cash dividend increases retained earnings and stockholders' equity.

If the dividend is to be paid in cash (a promissory note for a future cash payment), a current liability is established that can only be extinguished on payment. The deduction from retained earnings and the establishment of the current liability would be for the full amount of the dividend. When a cash dividend is declared

- Working capital is reduced
- Retained earnings are reduced
- Current assets are not affected
- Capital surplus (paid-in surplus) and par value are not affected

Some stockholders incorrectly believe that retained earnings represents cash. This, of course, is not true. Such stockholders, at times, are able to exert sufficient pressure on the directors to force payment of a dividend when cash may not be available. The stockholders may be satisfied with a stock dividend. This situation is frequently encountered in growth companies. The earnings of such companies may have high annual percentage growth, yet the companies may have only a small cash balance. The payment of a cash dividend in such a case is unlikely.

When the cash dividend is paid by the corporation, cash is reduced, and the current liability, which is dividends payable, is eliminated. On the payment of a cash dividend, current assets are reduced since cash is paid out.

A stock dividend does not change stockholders' proportionate equity in the corporation, but it does reduce retained earnings. Since the payment of a cash dividend is related to the amount of retained earnings, a stock dividend reduces the possible cash dividends that can be paid.

If the stock dividend is relatively small (e.g., less than 20% of the presently outstanding stock), the amount transferred from retained earnings is usually calculated on the basis of market price of fair value of the stock. The entry could be a debit to Retained earnings, a credit to capital stock for the par value (or stated value) of the stock, and a credit to capital surplus for the difference between the par value (or stated value) and market price.

If the stock dividend is relatively large (e.g., more than 20% of the presently outstanding stock), then only the par value (or stated value) of the stock is transferred from the retained earnings account to the capital stock account.

The following examples will illustrate the two methods used to record the effect of a stock dividend:

ABC Corporation has the following stockholders' equity:

Common stock $10 par 10,000 shares outstanding	$100,000
Paid-in capital	50,000
Retained earnings	150,000
Total stockholders' equity	$300,000

The market price of ABC Corporation stock is $20 per share.
Assume that ABC declares a 10% stock dividend; the entry would be

Debit retained earnings	20,000	
Credit common stock		10,000
Credit paid-in capital		10,000

ABC's stockholders' equity would be as follows:

Common stock $10 par 11,000 shares outstanding	$110,000
Paid-in capital	60,000
Retained earnings	130,000
Total stockholders' equity	$300,000

If ABC declared a 100% stock dividend, the following entry would be made:

Debit retained earnings	100,000	
Credit common stock		100,000

ABC's stockholders' equity would be reflected as follows:

Common stock $10 par 20,000 shares outstanding	$200,000
Paid-in capital	50,000
Retained earnings	50,000
Total stockholders' equity	$300,000

Ownership of company assets or claims against company assets do not change with a stock dividend. All that changes is the number of pieces of paper evidencing that ownership.

The effect of a stock split and stock dividend is similar in that, in both cases, the market price of a company's stock will decline and the proportionate ownership of each stockholder will be unchanged. They are handled quite differently on the company's books. In the case of a stock split, par value is reduced and the number of shares proportionately increased. Nothing else is affected. When a stock dividend is paid, par value remains unchanged, while the retained earnings account is decreased and the common stock account increased. In both cases, total stockholders' equity, paid-in capital surplus, cash, and working capital are not affected.

Shareholder approval is required for a company to have a stock split. Approval is not required for a stock dividend, the sale of treasury stock, or a primary distribution of additional shares (assuming the stock is authorized but unissued).

When there is more than one class of stock outstanding, it is necessary to determine the amount of income or earnings related to each class of stock or, more importantly, to the common stock since their portion is residual.

Generally, stock issues are limited to preferred and common. While the latter may be issued in several classes, in most cases only one class will possess dividend rights. *Class* common stock such as class A or class B is created usually in order to divide the rights pertaining to the stock. For instance, class A stock would be granted all of the rights except the right to vote. Class B would have none of the rights except the right to vote. Other divisions are, of course, possible.

If preferred stock is outstanding, the amount of earnings pertaining to the preferred stockholders must be deducted before the earnings available to common stockholders can be calculated. Since the preferred dividend rate is specified in the description of the stock, this is a relatively simple task.

Preferred dividends can be complex in nature depending on the amount of inducement which has been made to get the potential stockholders to purchase the issue. Two features often added to preferred issues are

1. Making the issue **cumulative**
2. Making the issue **participating**

A cumulative issue of preferred means that any dividends *not* declared will accumulate and must be paid before any dividends can be declared on the common stock. As with common stock, dividends can be paid only out of earnings, and no dividends can be paid unless and until it is declared payable by a specific act of the board of directors of the corporation. If the directors do not declare a regular dividend, it is said to be **passed**. But if the dividend in question is on cumulative preferred stock, at some time in the future it must be declared and paid before a dividend can be declared on the common stock.

It is not uncommon to find substantial arrearages in preferred dividends in companies that are experiencing financial difficulties (e.g., no preferred dividends for fifteen or twenty years). Where these arrearages are substantial, a frequent tactic on the part of the corporation is to get the preferred stockholders to compromise by offering an immediate payment in full settlement with the promise of continued dividends in the future. The preferred stockholders will usually accept the compromise since the alternative is a continuance of nothing.

Earnings Per Common Share

An item of importance to the analyst is the amount of earnings that accrue to each share of common stock of the corporation. Basically, this is a simple calculation involving the total of the earnings available to the common stockholders divided by the number of common shares outstanding.

For example, if earnings available to the common stockholders amount to $2 million and there are 500,000 shares of common stock outstanding, then $2 million divided by 500,000 = $4 earnings per share (EPS). The price of common shares in the open market is affected by the current earnings and future earning power of the company. The current EPS has a significant influence on the market price of the stock.

EPS will be affected by the nature of the securities issued by a company. If a company uses a debenture paying 9% interest, the EPS will be higher than if the company uses the same dollar value of preferred stock paying a 9% dividend. The reason, of course, is that interest on the debenture is deducted before taxes, while dividends are deducted after taxes.

In situations involving simple capital structures consisting of only common stock or common stock and nonconvertible senior securities, the calculation of EPS is also simple. Capital structure refers to only the long-term and permanent capital of the corporation. It consists of stockholders' equity plus long-term debt. Capital structure is also referred to as the capitalization of a corporation. However, corporations frequently have complex structures involving senior capitalizations which are convertible into common stock at some specified price or ratio. The existence of these convertible securities clouds the calculation of EPS since there exists the question of what the EPS would be if some or all of the convertible securities were converted.

In order to solve this dilemma, in corporations with convertible securities, two earnings per share figures are calculated: primary EPS and fully diluted EPS.

EPS on a **primary basis** assumes that the denominator includes common stock and **common stock equivalents** if such common stock equivalents would significantly dilute earnings (e.g., 3% or more). Common stock equivalents are those securities currently capable of conversion, exchange, or subscription.

Warrants and stock options are generally considered common stock equivalents, while convertible bonds and stocks are so considered only if their stated interest or dividend rate is less than two-thirds of the prime interest rate. If such an adjustment is made to the denominator of this ratio, the numerator, reflecting earnings available to common stockholders, must be increased to represent the amount that would have been available if interest and/or preferred dividends on these convertibles had not been paid.

Calculating EPS on a **fully diluted basis** is the most conservative method. It assumes that the common stock is fully diluted—that all options, warrants, and convertibles were turned into stock at the beginning of the period. Again, the previously discussed adjustments must be made to both the numerator and denominator of the ratio.

EPS may be affected by many things besides the usual profit- (or loss-) making activities of a firm. They would be increased by such things as a tax loss carryforward, a reduction of corporate income tax rates, or the retirement of bonds. They would also be affected by the acquisition of another corporation through a bond issue, the spinoff of a subsidiary, and changes in the method of inventory valuation.

A security is classified as a common stock equivalent if it meets certain tests.

- *Stock rights.* Stock rights are always considered common stock equivalents and would be converted to common stock at the beginning of the period.
- *Options.* These securities are considered common stock equivalents if the exercise price is less than the average market price for the period. This determination is made at the end of the accounting period.
- *Convertible securities.* These are considered common stock equivalents if, at the time of issue, the cash yield on the security is less than two-thirds of the prime bank lending rate. The rationale behind this rule is that, if the purchaser were willing to accept such a low yield, then the conversion feature must be a significant element in the security's value. This determination is made only at the time of issue. Once made, it is never changed.

The effect of all security conversions is to increase the number of shares outstanding. However, with rights, warrants, and options, a complication exists since the exercise of these securities involves a cash payment to the corporation. To prevent distortion from the effects of this cash payment, the proceeds are considered to be used to purchase treasury stock at market value.

XYZ Corporation

Rights outstanding	10,000 shares at $20 per share
Theoretical proceeds	10,000 x $20 = $200,000
Market price of stock	$50
Theoretical treasury stock purchase	$200,000 ÷ by $50 = 4,000 shares

Common stock equivalent of rights outstanding therefore equals $10,000 - 4,000 = 6,000$ shares.

So, to calculate fully diluted EPS, 6,000 shares would be added as the common stock equivalent for the rights outstanding. The same calculation would be made for warrants and options. However, no adjustment is made, in any case, unless the number of options, warrants, or rights exercisable equals 3% or more of the common stock outstanding.

Convertible bonds and preferreds generally do not require a cash payment at conversion, so the full conversion is added to shares outstanding. But, in the case of bonds, the net income figure must be adjusted to restore interest payments made to the debtholders with suitable allowances made for tax effects. In the case of convertible securities, the net income and the number of shares must be adjusted.

In primary EPS, only actual common stock outstanding plus common stock equivalents are considered. In fully diluted EPS (secondary EPS), all potentially dilutive securities are considered. Thus, the fully diluted EPS is always a lower figure than primary EPS.

Stock Split and Reverse Stock Split

A stock split and reverse stock split also have a negligible effect on the financial condition of the corporation. In the case of a stock split, the number of shares outstanding is multiplied by the ratio specified in the split; the par value is divided in the same manner, but no transfer is made from retained earnings, since dollar values remain unchanged.

The common stock account (and possibly capital surplus) is increased and the retained earnings account is decreased to the extent the stock dividend is relatively large in proportion to shares already outstanding. The stock dividend may tend to keep the stock price lower than otherwise.

Assume a 2-for-1 stock split. Before the split, the illustration might indicate

Common stock $10 par
2,000,000 shares authorized
1,830,000 shares outstanding

After the split, the same illustration might indicate

Common stock $5 par
4,000,000 shares authorized
3,660,000 shares outstanding

In such a situation, a customer owning 100 shares before the split would receive a new certificate for another 100 shares. His proportionate share of ownership would, of course, be unchanged.

The only real impact of the stock split is on the market price of the stock. A 2-for-1 split will cut the price in half (assuming other factors such as general market conditions are constant); a 3-for-1 split will drop the price to one-third of its original value. This move may keep the stock price within a theoretical optimum range.

A reverse stock split has the same effect but in the opposite direction. The number of shares outstanding is reduced and the par value and the market price are increased. The effect is both to consolidate ownership and to increase the market price of the stock. (See Exhibit 2.3.)

Exhibit 2.3: Stock splits and reverse stock splits

A stock split

- Increases number of shares outstanding
- Decreases par value
- Will not affect stockholders' equity
- Will not affect working capital
- Will not affect total assets
- Will not affect retained earnings
- Primary purpose is to decrease market price of stock

A reverse stock split

- Decreases number of shares outstanding
- Increases par value
- Will not affect stockholders' equity
- Will not affect working capital
- Will not affect total assets
- Will not affect retained earnings
- Primary purpose is to increase market price of stock

Dividends—cash and stock

The declaration of a cash dividend

1. Decreases working capital
   (A current liability, dividends payable, is increased.)
2. Decreases retained earnings
   (The amount of the dividend is charged to retained earnings when it is declared.)
3. Decreases stockholders' equity
   (When retained earnings is reduced, stockholders' equity is reduced by the same amount since retained earnings is a component of stockholders' equity.)

The payment of a stock dividend

1. Increases number of shares outstanding.
2. Increases amount in the common stock account.
3. Decreases retained earnings.
4. Will not affect stockholders' equity.
5. Will not affect par value.
6. Will not affect working capital.
7. Will not affect treasury stock.

Assume a company has 4,000,000 shares of common stock outstanding and $5,920,000 income available for common stockholders. There is a 1-for-4 reverse stock split. The new EPS would be

$$\frac{4{,}000{,}000 \text{ common shares outstanding}}{4} = 1{,}000{,}000 \text{ shares outstanding after reverse split}$$

$$\frac{\$5{,}920{,}000 \text{ income available for common}}{1{,}000{,}000 \text{ common shares outstanding}} = \$5.92 \text{ new EPS}$$

Using the income statement shown in Exhibit 2.4 and the balance sheet shown in Exhibit 2.5, we can perform basic financial analysis of a company by using ratios. A ratio is computed by dividing one number by the other so that the numerator is measured in terms of the denominator.

Exhibit 2.4: Income statement

General Disaster Corporation
Income Statement
Year Ended December 31
(000s omitted)

Net sales		$120,000
Less cost of goods sold		75,000
Gross profit		$ 45,000
Less Selling expense	$8,000	
Administrative expense	15,000	
Depreciation	3,000	$26,000
Net income before interest/taxes		19,000
Less interest expense		1,600
Net income before taxes		$17,400
Less taxes		7,500
Net income		$ 9,900
Less preferred dividends		300
Net income available to common		$ 9,600

Exhibit 2.5: Balance sheet

General Disaster Corporation
Balance Sheet
As of December 31

Assets		
Current assets:		
Cash and equivalents		$15,800
Accounts receivable		13,500
Inventory		14,200
Total current assets		43,500
Fixed assets:		
Land and buildings	$40,500	
Equipment	31,000	
Furniture and fixtures	8,000	
Total fixed assets	$69,500	
Less accumulated depreciation	15,200	$54,300
Intangible assets		100
Total assets		$97,900
Liabilities		
Current liabilities:		
Accounts payable	$16,700	
Accrued liabilities	6,400	
Current portion of long-term debt	2,000	
Total current liabilities	25,100	
Long-term debt	26,000	
Total liabilities		76,200

Stockholders' Equity

Preferred stock	$6,000
Common stock	1,830
Paid-in capital	6,700
Retained earnings	7,170
Total stockholders' equity	$21,700
Total liabilities and stockholders' equity	$97,900

Notes

Dividends paid to common stockholders	$1,800,000
Market price of common stock per share	$ 50
1,830,000 common shares outstanding $1 par	1,830,000

Four basic categories of ratios are used in financial analysis.

1. Profitability ratios
2. Liquidity ratios
3. Long-term solvency or leverage ratios
4. Efficiency or turnover ratios

Profitability Ratios

Whether the company is profitable can be determined by inspecting the bottom line of the income statements to see if it is either a net income or a net loss. But *how profitable* is another question. (See Exhibit 2.6 for a summary of financial ratios.)

Exhibit 2.6: Summary of financial ratios

The following ratios provide critical information about the health and performance of a company:

Profitability ratios

a. Rate of return on sales $= \dfrac{\text{Net income}}{\text{Net sales}}$

b. Margin of profit $= \dfrac{\text{Operating income}}{\text{Net sales}}$

c. Operating ratio $= \dfrac{\text{Operating expenses}}{\text{Net sales}}$

d. Return on invested capital $= \dfrac{\text{Net income} + \text{Interest on debt}}{\text{Total capital}}$

e. Dividends per share $= \dfrac{\text{Total dividends paid to common stockholders}}{\text{Common shares outstanding}}$

f. Current yield $= \dfrac{\text{Annual dividends per share}}{\text{Market price per share}}$

g. Return on common equity $= \dfrac{\text{Net income available to common stockholders}}{\text{Total common equity}}$

h. Earnings per share $= \dfrac{\text{Net income available to common stockholders}}{\text{Common shares outstanding}}$

i. Price-earnings ratio $= \dfrac{\text{Market price}}{\text{Earnings per share}}$

j. Dividend payout ratio $= \dfrac{\text{Dividends on common stock}}{\text{Earnings available to common}}$

or

Dividend payout ratio $= \dfrac{\text{Dividends per share}}{\text{Earnings per share}}$

k. Operating income to operating assets $= \dfrac{\text{Operating income}}{\text{Operating assets}}$

l. Return on assets ratio $= \dfrac{\text{Net profit after tax}}{\text{Total tangible assets}}$

Short-term liquidity ratios

a. Current ratio $= \dfrac{\text{Current assets}}{\text{Current liabilities}}$

b. Quick asset ratio $= \dfrac{\text{Current assets} - \text{Inventory}}{\text{Current liabilities}}$

c. Cash asset ratio $= \dfrac{\text{Cash assets}}{\text{Current liabilities}}$ (Cash + Marketable securities)

Long-term solvency ratios

a. Debt to equity ratio $= \dfrac{\text{Total long-term debt}}{\text{Total stockholders' equity}}$

b. Interest coverage ratio $= \dfrac{\text{Earnings before interest and taxes}}{\text{Interest charges}}$

c. Preferred dividend coverage $= \dfrac{\text{Net income after tax}}{\text{Preferred dividends}}$

d. Coverage of fixed charges $= \dfrac{\text{Net income}}{\text{Interest} + \text{Preferred dividends}}$

Leverage ratios

a. $\dfrac{\text{Long-term debt} + \text{Preferred stock}}{\text{Total capital}}$

b. $\dfrac{\text{Common stockholders' equity}}{\text{Total capital}}$

Efficiency ratios

a. Receivables turnover $= \dfrac{\text{Net sales}}{\text{Average receivables}}$

b. Days sales outstanding in receivables $= \dfrac{\text{Receivables} \div \text{Sales}}{360}$

c. Inventory turnover $= \dfrac{\text{Sales}}{\text{Year-end inventory}}$

Other ratios

a. Book value per share $= \dfrac{\text{Stockholders' equity} - \text{Intangible assets} - \text{Preferred stock}}{\text{Common shares outstanding}}$

b. Working capital per share $= \dfrac{\text{Current assets} - \text{Current liabilities}}{\text{Common shares outstanding}}$

c. Cash flow = Net income + Depreciation and other noncash assets

d. Common stock ratio $= \dfrac{\text{Common stock} + \text{Paid-in surplus} + \text{Retained earnings}}{\text{Total capital}}$

e. Return on equity ratio $= \dfrac{\text{Net income}}{\text{Stockholders' equity}}$

Several measures, either singly or as a group, can be used to describe the business profitability in relative terms.

Net income to net sales or rate of return on sales. This ratio measures the company's efficiency in converting sales revenue into profits.

The rate of return on sales for General Disaster Corporation is equal to

$$\frac{\text{Net income}}{\text{Net sales}} = \frac{\$9,900}{\$120,000} = 8.3\%$$

Margin of profit. The margin of profit (profit margin) ratio is found by dividing the income remaining after deducting all of the usual costs of operating the firm from net sales by net sales. The income remaining after deducting these costs is referred to as **operating income** or **operating profit**. It represents the funds available for such purposes as the payment of interest, taxes, and dividends.

$$\text{Margin of profit} = \frac{\text{Operating income}}{\text{Net sales}} = \frac{\$19,000}{\$120,000} = 15.8\%$$

Operating ratio (expense ratio). This is the reciprocal of the margin of profit ratio. It is found by dividing the usual costs of operating the firm by net sales. Together, the margin of profit ratio and the operating ratio must total 100%. The operating or expense ratio does not include interest expense or taxes in the numerator. Interest and taxes are not as easily controlled as the other expenses may be.

$$\text{Operating ratio} = \frac{\text{Cost of sales and operating expenses}}{\text{Net sales}}$$

$$\frac{\$75,000 \text{ cost of sales} + \$26,000 \text{ operating expenses}}{\$120,000 \text{ net sales}} = \frac{\$101,000}{\$120,000} = 84.2\%$$

Return on invested capital. The preceding ratio measured the efficiency of that capital supplied by common stockholders. Total capitalization includes all long-term funds—those funds provided by bondholders as well as both common and preferred stockholders. Since the return to bondholders is in the form of interest, this must be included in the numerator and preferred dividends will, of course, not be deducted.

$$\text{Return on invested capital} = \frac{\text{Net income} + \text{Interest on debt}}{\text{Total capital}}$$

$$\frac{\$9,900 \text{ net income} + \$1,600 \text{ interest}}{\$21,700 \text{ stockholders' equity} + \$26,000 \text{ bond}} = \frac{\$11,500}{\$47,700} = 24.1\%$$

Return on common equity. The ratio of income available to common stockholders divided by total common equity (common stock, paid-in capital and retained earnings) measures the efficiency of the investment made by common stockholders in the business.

$$\text{Return on common stockholders' equity} = \frac{\text{Net income available to common stockholders}}{\text{Common stockholders' equity}}$$

$$\frac{\$9,600 \text{ net income available to common stockholders}}{\$15,700 \text{ total common equity}} = 61.1\%$$

Earnings per share. As discussed under a previous section, the amount of EPS constitutes a vital piece of information for the analyst since stock prices are so closely related, both in the present and the future, to earnings. The methods used in calculating EPS were presented in that discussion and will not be repeated here. For General Disaster Corporation, the EPS (assuming the debentures and preferred stock issues are not common stock equivalents) are

$$\text{Earnings per share} = \frac{\text{Net income available to common stockholders}}{\text{Common shares outstanding}}$$

$$\frac{\$9,600 \text{ net income available to common stockholders}}{1,800 \text{ common shares outstanding}} = \$5.25 \text{ EPS}$$

Dividends per share. The dividends per share ratio is found by dividing the total dividends paid to common stockholders by the number of shares of stock outstanding.

$$\text{Dividends per share} = \frac{\text{Total dividends paid to common stockholders}}{\text{Common shares outstanding}}$$

$$\frac{\$1,800 \text{ dividends on common stock}}{1,830 \text{ common shares outstanding}} = \$0.98$$

Current yield on common stock (dividend yield). A yield refers to the rate of return earned on an investment. The current yield is a ratio which relates the annual dividend on the corporation's stock to its market price. Assume a market price of $50.

$$\text{Current yield} = \frac{\text{Annual dividends per share}}{\text{Market price per share}}$$

$$\frac{\text{Dividends per share}}{\text{Market price}} = \frac{\$0.98}{\$50} = 2.0\%$$

Dividend payout ratio. This is a simple ratio that states the proportion of earnings paid to the stockholder in the form of dividends.

$$\text{Dividend payout ratio} = \frac{\text{Dividends on common stock}}{\text{Earnings available to common}}$$

$$\frac{\$1,800 \text{ dividends on common stock}}{\$9,600 \text{ earnings available to common}} = 18.8\%$$

Price-earnings ratio. Generally, the market value of a commodity or item is, theoretically, a function of its value or service utility to the owner. The value of an income-producing asset is the amount of income it produces in relation to its price. The more income it produces, the greater its price and vice versa. By dividing the market price per share of the company stock by its EPS, one arrives at the price of the stock expressed as a multiple of earnings. By doing this, one can more easily follow how stable the price of the stock is, as the earnings figures fluctuate. Assume a price of $50 for General Disaster common.

$$\text{Price-earnings ratio} = \frac{\text{Market price}}{\text{EPS}}$$

$$\frac{\$50 \text{ market price}}{\$5.25 \text{ EPS}} = 9.5x$$

Present and future earnings and dividends per share are directly related to the market price of a company's stock. For example, assume that a company has a current price-earnings ratio of 15 and earns $1 per share (market price = $15). If earnings are expected to increase at a rate of 20% per year, in five years they will be approximately $2.49 per share. If the stock continues to sell at 15 times earnings, the market price per share would be approximately 37⅜.

Operating income to operating assets. The primary relationship of assets to earnings can be measured relatively easily using two ratios.

1. Operating income to operating assets
2. Return on total assets or return on investment

The first of these two ratios examines only operating data, that is, operating income and operating assets. Operating assets are total assets less intangible assets.

$$\text{Operating income to operating assets ratio} = \frac{\text{Operating income}}{\text{Operating assets}}$$

The measure is a general test of the efficiency of the assets to produce an acceptable return. It suffers primarily from a lack of a uniform definition of what constitutes the operating assets and whether or not interest expense is an operating item. These objections are somewhat muted by the use of the return on total assets ratio.

$$\text{Rate of return on total assets} = \frac{\text{Net income}}{\text{Total assets}}$$

Contrary to earlier profitability ratios, this ratio shows fairly level performance. The ratio is sometimes calculated using net income before taxes.

Short-Term Liquidity

If a business cannot pay its debts as they become due, it is regarded as technically insolvent, even though its assets are in excess of liabilities. Because of this, the company's liquidity or quantity of liquid assets available to pay the obligations is an important analytical consideration. Generally, the liquidity of a business is measured by the relative proportion of liquid assets to current obligations. The three basic measures are

1. Current ratio
2. Quick asset ratio
3. Cash asset ratio

Current ratio. Under the theory that the operating cycle of the business will turn all current assets to cash eventually, a fair measure of the business's ability to pay its current debt is the ratio of current assets to current liabilities.

$$\text{Current ratio} = \frac{\text{Current assets}}{\text{Current liabilities}}$$

Quick asset ratio. The quick asset ratio or acid test ratio is a more stringent measure of corporate liquidity than the current ratio. The discussion of inventory pointed out that there is some problem with inventory values since they cannot be considered firm until the sale actually takes place. Because of this uncertainty, the analyst adjusts the analysis of liquidity by removing inventory from the calculation and comparing the smaller total to the liabilities.

$$\text{Quick asset ratio} = \frac{\text{Current assets less inventory}}{\text{Current liabilities}}$$

Cash asset ratio. This ratio is concerned with the coverage of current liabilities by cash and equivalents. The cash asset ratio for the General Disaster Corporation is

$$\text{Cash asset ratio} = \frac{\text{Cash and equivalents}}{\text{Current liabilities}}$$

$$\frac{\$15,800 \text{ cash and cash equivalents}}{\$25,100 \text{ current liabilities}} = 0.6:1$$

In this case, the cash asset position is insufficient to cover current liabilities.

Long-Term Solvency Ratios

Just as the firm must maintain a stable and sufficient current position to meet current debts, the firm must also maintain itself solvent over the long term as well. It should be clear or at least made clear, that simply maintaining solvency in the current period is not a guarantee of long-term solvency. Long-term stability and solvency is the result of long-term planning, of preparing the company to meet long-range goals, of proper asset acquisition decisions and financing decisions, of maintaining operations to maximize long-term profitability, and a host of other long-term objectives.

Debt-to-equity ratio. This simple calculation expresses the amount of long-term debt as a proportion of equity.

$$\text{Debt to equity} = \frac{\text{Total long-term debt}}{\text{Total stockholders' equity}}$$

$$\frac{\$26,000 \text{ total long-term debt}}{\$21,700 \text{ total stockholders' equity}} = 1.20\%$$

The ratio is expressed either as a percentage or in ratio form.

Interest coverage ratio. Since the majority of the debt is interest bearing, the ability to pay that interest is a decidedly important aspect of both long-term financial solvency and debt-carrying ability. Interest is paid before taxes; therefore, the appropriate measure for the interest would be income before interest and taxes.

$$\text{Interest coverage ratio} \quad = \quad \frac{\text{Earnings before interest and taxes}}{\text{Interest charges}}$$

$$\frac{\$19,000 \text{ net income before interest and taxes}}{\$1,600 \text{ interest charges}} \quad = \quad 11.9x$$

Preferred dividend coverage. Just as debt payments precede distributions to owners, the payments or dividends for preferred stockholders take precedence over payments to common stockholders. Coverage of the preferred dividend is computed in the same fashion as the debt coverage.

$$\text{Preferred dividend coverage} \quad = \quad \frac{\text{Net income after tax}}{\text{Preferred dividends}}$$

$$\frac{\$9,900 \text{ net income}}{300 \text{ preferred dividends}} \quad = \quad 33x$$

On the surface, this ratio would indicate that there is a better coverage for the preferred stockholders than for the debtholders. Given the fact that the debt has precedence over the preferred stockholders, this cannot be the case. The senior securities must be included and, in this case, the calculation would be more of a **times fixed charges** ratio.

$$\text{Coverage of fixed charges} \quad = \quad \frac{\text{Net income}}{\text{Interest + Preferred dividends}}$$

$$\frac{\$9,900}{\$1,600 + \$300} \quad = \quad 5.21$$

If appropriate, the fixed charge coverage ratio should be expanded to cover lease payments if they are significant or material fixed charges and if the leases are noncancelable. The ratio could also, of course, be refined by including debt service with interest and preferred dividends. This would then be divided into income before interest and taxes plus depreciation.

Leverage Ratios

Financial leverage refers to the degree that bonds and preferred stock (fixed return capital) are employed in the financial structure of the company. A conservative capital structure would be one consisting entirely, or primarily, of common stock, while one involving a relatively small percentage of common stock would be trading heavily on its equity and involve considerably greater risk.

Utilities are the traditionally highly leveraged industry. Utilities normally have a large proportion of long-term debt in their capital structure. Historically, their operating profit has been relatively stable and the percentage of long-term debt in their capital structure high. Because of the inverse relationship between bond prices and interest rates, the market price of the common stock of public utilities tends to move downward as interest rates rise.

Leverage is many times referred to as *trading on the equity*. Therefore, it can be said that the utility industry engages in a great deal of trading on the equity.

Also, since leverage magnifies earnings results, companies with potentially variable earnings should avoid leverage since it will only increase the variability.

Total capital may also be referred to as

- Capital
- Total capitalization
- Capital structure

Leverage makes

- Earnings more volatile.
    - Increases the rate of return on common stock in profitable years.
    - Decreases the rate of return on common stock in unprofitable years.

- The market price of the company's common stock more erratic
- The dividends paid by the company less stable if dividends declared are related to annual earnings

The debt-to-equity ratio can also be used to measure financial leverage. It measures the amount of debt a company has as a percentage of its equity.

Efficiency or Turnover Ratios

The manner in which a firm manages its affairs is frequently revealed by the activity rate of turnover of some of the assets. Turnover ratios are calculated by dividing the asset in question into a relevant base.

Receivables turnover and collection ratio. The relative speed by which receivables are collected can be measured two ways.

1. The turnover of receivables during the year, and
2. The number of days sales outstanding in receivables.

$$\text{Receivables turnover} = \frac{\text{Net sales}}{\text{Accounts receivable}}$$

This would indicate that General Disaster is turning over its receivables a little better than eight times a year. Actual collection cannot, of course, be determined since some receivables would be collected almost immediately after sale and some may be collected only after a long delay.

$$\text{Days sales outstanding in receivables} = \frac{\text{Receivables}}{\text{Sales}/360} = \frac{\$1,500}{\$120,000/360} = \frac{13,500}{333.3} = 40.5 \text{ days}$$

Inventory turnover ratio. The speed with which inventory turns over during the period is an indication of the relative salability of the products. This, of course, depends on the industry. As with other ratios, change is important.

Inventory turnover can be computed by dividing sales by year-end inventory.

$$\text{Inventory turnover} = \frac{\text{Sales}}{\text{Year-end inventory}}$$

$$\frac{\$120,000}{\$14,200} = 8.5x$$

Other Ratios

Book value per common share (net tangible assets per share). This ratio indicates the net worth of an individual common share or the amount of assets that theoretically would accrue to the common stockholders, if all assets and liabilities were to be liquidated at book values. It is also used in comparison to market value per share when measuring the value of the stock as an investment. The calculation of book value excludes intangible assets and the value of preferred stock on the books of the company. The formula for book value per common share is

$$\frac{\text{Stockholders' equity} - \text{Intangible assets} - \text{Preferred stock}}{\text{Common shares outstanding}}$$

$$\frac{\$21,700 - \$100 - \$6,000}{1,830} = \frac{\$15,600}{1,830} = \$8.52$$

Working capital per share. A somewhat better measure of the current value of a company is its value of working capital or net current assets per share. The figure has been frequently used as the basis for mergers and acquisitions.

$$\text{Working capital per share} = \frac{\text{Current assets} - \text{Current liabilities}}{\text{Common shares outstanding}}$$

$$\frac{\$18,400}{1,830} = \$10.05$$

3 INVESTMENT BANKING

Investment banking is concerned with the long-term financing of corporations through the sale of equity or debt securities. Most large corporations do not attempt to sell their own securities to the public. Instead, they engage the services of an investment banker to assist them.

An investment banker is a firm that acts as a middleman between the corporation and the public investors. It provides certain services to the issuing corporation. One important service is to advise the corporation on the type security to sell and the price of the issue. The investment banker will assist the corporation in the preparation of the various forms required by the Securities Act of 1933. In certain types of underwriting, the investment banker will purchase the securities from the issuing corporation for resale to the public. In these instances, the investment banker is underwriting the issue and risking its own capital in the distribution of the securities.

SELECTION OF THE INVESTMENT BANKER

There are two basic methods of selecting an investment banker.

1. Negotiated
2. Competitive bidding

The **negotiated method** is most common for industrial corporations. The investment banking firm works with the issuing corporation to determine the actual amount of money needed by the corporation and the type of security best suited to the corporation's capital structure. The performance of such services and the rendering of such advice plays an important role in the competition between investment banking firms and in the ability of firms to retain their corporate customers.

If the securities offered are issued by a municipal corporation, a railroad, or a utility, they must normally be acquired by the **competitive bidding method**. Sealed bids are submitted for the security offered, and the investment banker or syndicate submitting the highest bid gets the issue. This represents the lowest net interest cost to the issuer.

DISPOSAL METHODS

There are also two basic methods that may be used by the investment banker to dispose of securities.

1. Public offering
2. Private placement

As the name indicates, the **public offering** method is used when the securities acquired by the investment banker are distributed to the general public. A public offering of securities must be registered with the Securities and Exchange Commission (SEC) before distribution. Most of this section is concerned with the public offering method of distributing securities.

INVESTIGATION

In the negotiated underwriting, there is a direct relationship between a corporate issuer and an investment banking house acting as an originator. These negotiations may continue for many months before the parties agree as to the amount and type of security that best meets the issuer's needs and is best suited to current market conditions. To have a successful underwriting, it is extremely important from the viewpoint of the investment banker to buy an issue that can be readily and profitably sold.

TYPES OF SECURITIES OFFERINGS

There are two types of securities offerings.

1. Primary distribution
2. Secondary distribution

A **primary distribution** occurs when a corporation is selling previously unissued shares. This does not necessarily mean that it is the first time a corporation is selling its shares to the public. For example, assume

General Motors decides to sell additional shares of stock to the public. If the shares are previously unissued shares, General Motors is engaging in a primary distribution. In a primary distribution, the proceeds of the sale are received directly by the issuing corporation for use in the business.

A **secondary distribution** is the redistribution of shares previously outstanding. For example, an officer of a corporation may decide to sell a large block of securities to the public. This is a secondary distribution since the shares of stock had been previously outstanding in the hands of the officer.

The securities in a secondary distribution may have to be registered before they can be sold. Registration would be necessary if the seller is in a control relationship with the issuer. If the issue must be registered before it can be sold, it is referred to as a **registered secondary**. If an exemption is available under the Securities Act of 1933, the shares do not have to be registered before they can be sold, and the distribution is referred to as a **spot secondary** (**unregistered secondary**). In a secondary distribution, the proceeds of the sale are received by the selling stockholders and not the issuing corporation.

A particular offering of securities could be made up of a primary and secondary distribution. It would be referred to as a **split offering**.

UNDERWRITING AGREEMENT

The underwriting agreement is a contract between the investment banker and the issuing corporation. This agreement is signed the evening before or on the morning of the effective date of the security issue. The underwriting agreement is then filed with the SEC and becomes a part of the registration statement.

The underwriting agreement is signed in either of two ways.

1. Severally but not jointly
2. Severally and jointly

An underwriting agreement that is signed **severally but not jointly** means that each investment banker limits his liability in the underwriting only to that portion of the issue it has agreed to purchase. Assume an investment banker has agreed to underwrite 20% of a new security issue. In this case, the investment banker is obligated to the issuing corporation for only 20% of the issue. The investment banker is not obligated to the corporation for unsold shares of other syndicate members. When an underwriting agreement is signed **severally but not jointly,** it is called a **western account**. A western account is divided as to sales liability. It is sometimes referred to as a divided account or divided syndicate. Underwriting agreements for corporate securities (either corporate stocks or corporate bonds) are normally signed severally but not jointly.

An underwriting agreement that is signed **severally and jointly** means that each underwriter has assumed full financial responsibility to the issuer. This type of agreement is normally used only for municipal bonds. An underwriter in this type of agreement could be held responsible for the inability of other syndicate members to sell the issue. If an underwriting agreement is signed severally and jointly, it is known as an **eastern account**. An eastern account may also be called a united or undivided account.

Types of Underwriting Agreements

The main types of underwriting agreements entered into by an investment banker and a corporation issuing securities are

- Firm-commitment agreement
- Best-efforts agreement
- All-or-none agreement
- Standby agreement
- Mini-maxi agreement

In a **firm-commitment** underwriting, the investment banker actually purchases the securities directly from the issuer and attempts to resell them to the public at the public offering price. In this case, the investment banker underwrites or guarantees to purchase the securities from the issuer. In this type of agreement, the investment banker is referred to as the **underwriter**.

A **best-efforts** agreement is one in which the investment banker does not actually purchase the securities from the issuing corporation. Instead, the investment banker acts as an agent and agrees to use its "best effort" in order to sell the securities to the public. This type of agreement results in less risk to the investment banker than a firm-commitment underwriting.

An **all-or-none agreement** is a type of best-efforts agreement that states that the entire issue is canceled unless it can be completely sold. This type of distribution can take several days or weeks to complete. A corporation might use an all-or-none agreement if it needed a certain amount of funds in order to proceed with a project. Under this type of agreement, no sales are final until all of the issue is sold.

In a **standby** underwriting, the investment banker agrees to purchase and distribute any part of an issue that is not sold. This type of agreement is most often done in connection with a rights offering to stockholders. For example, assume the issuing corporation is attempting to sell 500,000 shares of common stock to its existing stockholders. If the stockholders purchased 300,000 shares, the investment bankers would purchase the remaining 200,000 shares.

A **mini-maxi** agreement is a type of best-efforts agreement under which, if a minimum (mini) percentage is distributed, the issue is not canceled even though the entire issue (maxi) is not sold.

Market-Out Clauses

Underwriting agreements normally contain a provision that relieves the underwriters of their obligation to purchase the securities if certain events occur. The provision in the agreement that releases the underwriter from his obligation to purchase the security is called a **market-out clause**.

Events that could allow the underwriters to take advantage of the market-out clause include

- A substantial change in the financial position of the issuer prior to the effective date
- A substantial change in economic, political, or market conditions (outbreak of war, suspension of trading in securities on the New York Stock Exchange) prior to the public offering

The underwriters may feel that it would be inadvisable to attempt to market the securities as a result of the changes and would invoke the market-out clause.

FORMATION OF UNDERWRITING SYNDICATE

An investment banking firm does not normally choose to underwrite a security issue on its own because of risks involved. It decides, instead, to gather a group of investment bankers together to underwrite the issue. This group of investment bankers gathered to underwrite a security issue is called a **syndicate**. The originating underwriter will normally act as the managing underwriter or syndicate manager for the group.

Syndicate Manager

The syndicate manager has many important functions related to the underwriting process. The responsibilities of the syndicate manager include

- Formation of the underwriting syndicate
- Deciding which firms will be included in the selling group
- Establishing the underwriter's retention
- Stabilizing the issue, if necessary, in the aftermarket
- Allocating shares for group sales
- Allocation of shares, if it is a hot issue

Agreement among Underwriters

The members of the underwriting syndicate sign a document called an **agreement among underwriters**. This agreement describes the rights and liabilities among the underwriters themselves. The agreement among underwriters is also referred to as a **purchase group agreement**. This document is usually signed after the due diligence meeting. The agreement is between the manager of the syndicate and each member, and between each member and every other member. The agreement among underwriters

- Gives the managing underwriter responsibility to act on behalf of the underwriting syndicate (such as stabilizing the issue on behalf of the syndicate)
- Sets the amount of the management fee to be paid to the syndicate manager
- Authorizes the syndicate manager to qualify the issue in various states (blue-skying the issue)
- Describes how the payment and delivery of the securities will be completed

The agreement among underwriters normally contains a penalty syndicate bid clause, the purpose of which is to make certain that the participants do not distribute to traders and speculators intent on only making a quick profit. This clause in the agreement among underwriters states that if a participant's customers sell the security to the managing underwriter in the aftermarket at the stabilizing bid price, then

- The managing underwriter will not allow the member his or her underwriting compensation or selling group compensation on that transaction.
- The managing underwriter will penalize the member a certain amount per share or bond.
- The managing underwriter will reconsider whether that member should participate in the managing underwriter's future offerings.

Syndicate members are required in the agreement among underwriters to offer the security at the established price. If the issue becomes sticky, the managing underwriters may release the syndicate members from their obligation to offer the stock at this price. The syndicate members must receive that authorization from the managing underwriter before they can offer the stock at a price below the public offering price.

SELLING GROUP

The selling group is made up of a group of National Association of Securities Dealers (NASD) member firms, chosen by the managing underwriter, who will assist the underwriting syndicate in selling the shares to the public.

The selling group firms have no financial responsibility to the issuing corporation for unsold shares. The selling group firms receive a selling concession for selling the shares to the public. The selling concession represents a portion of the underwriting spread. Selling group firms do not get involved in negotiations with the issuer concerning the new securities issue. They are involved only in the selling of the shares to the public.

Even though the syndicate manager cannot offer these securities for sale to prospective selling group members before the effective date of the registration, s/he may take preliminary steps, including the sending of a **red herring**. When the registration is effective, a selling group agreement and prospectus will be sent to these prospective selling group members.

DUE DILIGENCE MEETING

Usually, near the end of the twenty-day cooling-off period, the managing underwriter will conduct a due diligence meeting. This meeting is attended by corporation officials and members of the underwriting syndicate and their legal and accounting staff. Attendance by syndicate members is mandatory.

The purposes of the due diligence meetings are

- To make a complete review of the information in the registration statement and to prepare the final prospectus
- To negotiate terms to be included in the formal underwriting contract between the issuer and investment banker

The public offering price of the issue is not determined at this meeting. It is determined the night before or in the early morning hours of the effective date. Underwriters are allowed to withdraw from the underwriting at this meeting without any financial or legal liability to the corporation.

UNDERWRITING SPREAD

The underwriters receive compensation for the risks they incur by receiving a portion of the underwriting spread, depending on their role. The underwriting spread is the difference between the public offering price and the proceeds to the issuer. The amount of the spread varies with

- The size and type of the issue
- Type of business of the issuer
- The business history of the issuer

The average spread on stock issues will normally be larger than the spread on bond issues.

Selling group firms are paid a selling concession out of the underwriting spread for selling shares to the public. The selling concession may also be referred to as the **selling group discount**. Selling group firms may allow a portion of the selling concession to broker/dealers who are not selling group members. The portion of the selling concession allowed to firms that are not members of the selling group is called the **reallowance**.

Assume the XYZ Manufacturing Company is selling a new issue of 300,000 shares to the public. The following information describes the new issue:

	Per share	*Total proceeds*
Public offering price	$28.00	$8,400,000
Underwriting spread	1.60	480,000
Proceeds to the issuer	26.40	7,920,000

Underwriting spread (gross spread)

Management fee	$.16
Selling concession	.96
Underwriter's compensation	.48
Total underwriting spread	1.60

Assume that two NASD member firms will act as underwriters (Member Firm A and Member Firm B). Member Firm A will act as the managing underwriter. The selling group will contain one firm, Member Firm C, in addition to Member Firms A and B, which will receive a 50,000-share allotment. Member Firm A and Member Firm B will each underwrite 150,000 shares. The total amount of the underwriting spread would be distributed as follows:

MEMBER FIRM A: Managing Underwriter, Underwriter

1. Compensation as managing underwriter

    300,000 shares x 0.16 management fee = $48,000

    $48,000 = Total management fee

2. Compensation for shares sold directly to public (acting as underwriter and retailer)

$28.00	Selling price
26.56	Cost
$ 1.44	Per share compensation

    $1.44 x 125,000 shares = $180,000

3. Compensation for shares given up to the selling group

$27.04	Selling price to Firm C
26.56	Cost
$ 0.48	Compensation as underwriter

    $0.48 x 25,000 shares = $12,000

SUMMARY: Compensation to Member Firm A

$ 48,000	Management fee
180,000	Shares sold to public
12,000	Shares given up to selling group
$240,000	Total compensation

MEMBER FIRM B: Underwriter

1. Compensation for shares sold directly to public

$28.00	Selling price
26.56	Cost
$ 1.44	Per share compensation

2. Compensation for shares given to selling group

$27.04	Selling price to Firm C
26.56	Cost
$ 0.48	Compensation as underwriter

    $0.48 x 25,000 shares = $12,000

SUMMARY: Compensation to Member Firm B

$180,000	Shares sold to public
12,000	Shares given up to selling group
$192,000	Total compensation

MEMBER FIRM C: Selling Group Firm

$28.00	Selling price
27.04	Cost
$ 0.96	Selling concession

$0.96 x 50,000 shares = $48,000

$48,000 = Compensation to selling group firm

SUMMARY: Underwriting Spread Compensation

$240,000   Member Firm A
192,000   Member Firm B
<u>48,000</u>   Member Firm C
$480,000   Total compensation to underwriters and selling group

THE SECURITIES ACT OF 1933

The Securities Act of 1933 is sometimes referred to as the **Truth in Securities Act**. Its basic purpose is to make certain that new securities offered to the public are fully and clearly described in the registration statement and prospectus. Under this law, the SEC attempts to make certain that there is a full disclosure of all significant material facts concerning a security to be offered to the public on an interstate basis.

It should be noted that the SEC does not approve securities registered with it, does not pass on the investment merit of any security, and never guarantees the accuracy of statements in the registration statement and prospectus. The SEC merely attempts to make certain that all pertinent information is disclosed in the registration statement and prospectus by requiring that

- The issuer file a registration statement with the SEC before securities may be offered or sold in interstate commerce
- A prospectus that meets the requirements of the Act be provided to prospective buyers
- Penalties (civil, criminal or administrative) be imposed for violations of this Act

Exempted Securities under the 1933 Act

The Securities Act of 1933 makes it unlawful to sell or deliver a security through any instrument of interstate commerce unless a registration statement is in effect. However, certain securities are exempted from the registration requirements of the Act. The following issues qualify as exempted securities:

- Any security issued or guaranteed by the United States or any state or any political subdivision of a state (federal government issues and municipal securities are exempted securities)
- Any note, draft, bill of exchange, or bankers' acceptance that has a maturity at the time of issuance not exceeding nine months (Commercial paper and bankers' acceptances with a maturity of nine months or less are exempted securities.)
- Any security issued by a religious, educational, charitable, or not-for-profit institution (shares by a benevolent association)
- Any securities issued by a savings and loan association, building and loan association, cooperative bank, or similar institution
- Any security issued by a common or contract carrier, the issuance of which is subject to the provisions of the Interstate Commerce Act
- Certificates issued by a receiver or by a trustee in bankruptcy with the approval of a court.
- Any insurance endowment or fixed annuity contract
- Any security exchanged by the issuer with its existing security holders exclusively, where no commission or other remuneration is paid or given directly or indirectly for soliciting such exchange
- Any security offered and sold only to persons resident within a single state or territory, where the issuer of such security is a person resident and doing business within such state or territory (Sale of intrastate securities of locally incorporated firms is exempt.)
- Any security offered to the public when the total amount is $5 million or less (For such issues, the SEC has adopted Regulation A, which exempts the issue from registration requirements if certain specified conditions are met, such as the filing of an offering circular and notification with the SEC.)
- Issues of small-business investment companies. A small-business investment company is a privately owned and privately operated company that has been licensed by the Small Business Administration to provide equity capital and long-term loans to small firms.

Exempted Transactions under the 1933 Act

In addition to exempting certain securities, the Act also exempts certain transactions.

- Transactions by any person other than an issuer, underwriter, or dealer (An isolated individual-to-individual sale is exempt.)
- Transactions by an issuer not involving any public offering (Private placement is exempt.)

- Broker transactions executed on the unsolicited request of customers (Unsolicited orders received from customers are normally exempt.)

Registration of Securities

A security may be registered with the SEC by filing a registration statement in triplicate. The registration statement must be signed by the principal executive officer, the principal financial officer, and by a majority of the board of directors.

All of the signers are subject to criminal and civil penalties for willful omissions and misstatements of material facts.

Red-Herring Prospectus

A red-herring prospectus is a preliminary prospectus. It is given to prospective purchasers during the twenty-day waiting period between the filing date of the registration statement and the effective date. The red-herring prospectus does not contain information such as the public offering price or the underwriter's spread. The term *red herring* was given to the prospectus because the front page contains a statement printed in red ink, which states

A Registration Statement relating to these securities has been filed with the Securities and Exchange Commission but has not yet become effective. Information contained herein is subject to completion or amendment. These securities may not be sold nor may offers to buy be accepted prior to the time the Registration Statement becomes effective. The Prospectus shall not constitute an offer to sell or the solicitation of an offer to buy nor shall there be any sale of these securities in any state in which such offer, solicitation or sale would be unlawful prior to registration or qualification under the securities laws of any such state.

The purpose of issuing a red-herring prospectus is to acquaint potential investors with essential facts concerning the issue. A red-herring prospectus summarizes many of the important details contained in the registration statement. It can never be used to solicit orders, only indications of interest. These indications of interest are not binding commitments. They are not binding on the broker/dealer or the customer. A registered representative is not allowed to mark the red-herring prospectus in any way. S/he cannot write comments or statements on this document.

In recent years, the SEC has requested that the issuer include a maximum range for the public offering price on issues that have not previously been registered under the Securities Act of 1933. The maximum range set in the red-herring prospectus is not always binding. The final public offering price may be set outside of the range with SEC approval.

Unless an exemption applies, it is unlawful for any person to use the mails or any other instrument of interstate commerce to offer a security for sale unless a registration statement has become effective. Therefore, a security can be offered for sale only after a registration statement is effective.

A security can be offered for sale during the period between the filing and effective date, but a written offer is forbidden unless it meets the requirements of a statutory prospectus as defined under Section 10 of the Act. If the firm uses written offers, such as advertisement in newspapers or magazine articles, it would be considered an illegal offer to sell. The written offers would not meet the requirement of statutory prospectus and, therefore, would not be permitted under the Act.

However, the Act does permit the use of tombstone ads between the filing and effective date. The written material that may be used during this period to offer a security for sale is limited to a preliminary prospectus and a tombstone ad. Such a preliminary prospectus or tombstone ad cannot be accompanied by the firm's research report.

SEC Rule 134 specifically defines communications that are not deemed a prospectus. The Rule states that the term *prospectus* shall not include a notice, circular, advertisement, letter, or other communication published or transmitted to any person after a registration statement has been filed if it contains only

- The name of the issuer of the security
- The full title of the security and the amount being offered
- A brief indication of the general type of business of the issuer

A tombstone advertisement meets the requirements of SEC Rule 134 and may be used during the period between the filing of the registration statement and the effective date.

SEC Rule 135 states that a notice given by an issuer that it proposes to make a public offering of securities to be registered under the Act is not deemed to offer any securities for sale if the notice states that the offering will be made only by means of a prospectus and contains only basic information, such as the name of the issuer, the title, amount, and basic terms of the securities proposed to be offered.

SEC Rule 135(a), concerning generic advertising, states that a notice, circular, advertisement, letter, sign or other communication, published or transmitted to any person which does not specifically refer by name to the securities of a particular investment company, to the investment company itself, or to any other investment company not exempt under the Act, is not considered an offer to sell if it is limited to general statements. Such statements might include explanatory information relating to investment company securities generally, the nature of investment companies, and an explanation of investment companies with different objectives.

To summarize, during the period between the filing date and effective date of the registration statement

- No sales of the security may take place.
- Offers of the security may take place, but a written offer may only be made through a preliminary prospectus or a red herring prospectus (tombstone advertising permitted during this period).
- Brokers may answer unsolicited requests for information by sending out a preliminary prospectus and accept unsolicited orders for the security.
- Brokers cannot send out the company's research report or any report projecting the company's future sales and earnings.

Final Prospectus

A registration statement is normally a very long and complex document for an investor to read. The Act requires the preparation of a shorter document called a prospectus. The prospectus summarizes the information contained in the registration statement. It must contain all the material facts in the registration statement, but in shorter form. The prospectus must be given to every person solicited and to every person who purchases or indicates an interest in purchasing securities. The purpose of a prospectus is to provide the investor with adequate information to analyze the investment merits of the security. Even if an investor does not intend to read a prospectus, it still must be given to him. It is unlawful for a company to sell securities prior to the effective date of the registration statement.

The final prospectus must contain a statement that the SEC neither approves nor disapproves of the security. The final prospectus must be dated. A statement concerning possible stabilizing transactions must also be included.

A statement regarding the obligation of dealers to deliver a prospectus for a certain period after the date of the prospectus must be included in a final prospectus. Assume the prospectus is dated December 12, 1989, for a particular security issue of common stock. The statement in the final prospectus would read

Until March 11, 1990 (ninety days after the date of this prospectus), all dealers effecting transactions in the common stock may be required to deliver a prospectus. This delivery requirement is in addition to the obligation of dealers to deliver a prospectus when acting as underwriters with respect to their unsold allotments or subscriptions.

The final prospectus does not contain copies of underwriting contracts or opinions of counsel. This information would be included in the registration statement for the security.

Effective Date of Registration Statement

On the date a registration statement becomes effective, securities may be sold to the public by the investment bankers. The effective date of a registration statement is the twentieth calendar day after filing the registration statement with the SEC, provided it is in proper form. The twenty-calendar-day waiting period before the registration becomes effective is called the **cooling-off period**. The purpose of the cooling-off period is to allow the public time to study the information in the registration statement and prospectus. The SEC may accelerate the effective date of a registration statement if it is in the public interest to do so.

A copy of the final prospectus must be delivered to each purchaser with a confirmation or with the delivery of the security, whichever occurs first. Additional sales literature may be used by the firm as long as the sales literature is preceded or accompanied by a prospectus. Funds may be accepted by the broker/dealer from customers at this time.

A dealer or underwriter acting as principal must deliver a prospectus to a purchaser during the forty-day period after the effective date of the registration statement or the beginning of the public offering of the securities, whichever is the later date. If the issuer is distributing securities for the first time, a prospectus must be delivered by the dealer or underwriter when acting as a principal during the ninety-day period following the offering date.

If the issuer is filing reports with the SEC under Section 13 or 15(d) of the Securities Exchange Act of 1934, the dealer or underwriter does not have to deliver a prospectus during the forty- and ninety-day periods following the effective date when acting as principal. However, whenever an underwriter is offering any portion of the original commitment, a prospectus must be delivered to the purchaser.

Stop Orders

The SEC will issue a stop order when a registration statement is not complete or is inadequate in a material way. If a stop order is issued prior to the effective date, an amendment to the registration statement will be required. When the amendment has been properly filed, the SEC will state this to the issuer. The registration statement will be effective on the effective registration date or the date the amendment has been properly filed, whichever date is later.

The SEC may issue a stop order to suspend the effectiveness of the registration even after the effective registration date. The SEC would take this action if the registration statement included any untrue statement of a material fact. The SEC may subpoena the issuing corporation's records to determine whether a stop order is necessary.

Liabilities under the 1933 Act

The Securities Act of 1933 provides penalties for false and misleading statements contained in the registration statement or prospectus. If misrepresentations were intentionally made, the individuals responsible are subject to criminal prosecution. The civil liabilities allow a purchaser of a security under a registration statement containing a false statement of material fact or omission of a material fact, to sue

- Every person who signed the registration statement
- All directors of the issue
- Attorneys
- Accountants
- Appraisers
- Underwriters

A person would be exempt from liability if he could prove he had reasonable grounds to believe, after investigation, that the statements contained in the registration were accurate.

Stabilization of the Issue (SEC Rule 10b-7)

The agreement among underwriters contains a stabilization clause that allows the syndicate manager to enter into stabilizing activities on behalf of the underwriting syndicate.

Stabilization is necessary to certain distributions in order to have a successful distribution. Persons in the aftermarket may decide to sell their shares a short time after the offering date. If this selling caused the price of the issue to drop in the aftermarket, the distribution in the primary market would be seriously affected, because investors would not want to pay a fixed price for a security that is trading at a lower price in the aftermarket.

An underwriter is stabilizing when he makes bids at or below the public offering price while offers are being made at the public offering price. Under no circumstances can an underwriter bid above the public offering price of the security during stabilization. The managing underwriter is attempting to fix or peg the price of the security in the aftermarket to the public offering price of the new issue in the primary market.

SEC Rule 144

The Securities Act of 1933 was designed to provide full and fair disclosure for securities sold in interstate commerce. SEC Rule 144 (see Exhibit 3.1) was designed to prohibit the creation of public markets in securities of issuers where adequate information is not available to the public. However, where adequate public information concerning an issuer is available, SEC Rule 144 permits the sale of limited amounts of securities owned by affiliates of the issuer and by persons who own restricted securities of the issuer. If the provisions of SEC Rule 144 are not complied with, the seller of the securities and the broker may be subject to both civil and criminal liabilities.

Exhibit 3.1: SEC Rule 144

The important points concerning SEC Rule 144 can be summarized as follows:

1. In order to sell securities under this rule, the shares must have been owned for at least one year, unless the shares are control stock. If the shares are control stock, the one-year holding period does not apply.

2. In computing the one-year holding period, there must be excluded any period during which the person selling the security either

   a. Has a short position in the security, or
   b. Owned a put on the security.

3. Adequate public information concerning the issuer must be available at the time of the sale.
4. The shares can be sold through a broker's transaction or the shares can be sold directly to a market maker.
5. At the time the sell order is placed with the broker/dealer, a Form 144 notice of offering must be filed with the SEC and is effective for ninety days.
6. The amount of securities that may be sold by an affiliate of the issuer is limited to

   a. 1% of the outstanding shares, or
   b. The average weekly volume traded during the preceding four calendar weeks, whichever is greater.

7. The purpose of SEC Rule 144 is to notify the SEC that unregistered securities are being sold to the public.

For the purposes of SEC Rule 144, an **affiliate** of an issuer is a person that directly or indirectly, through one or more intermediaries, controls or is controlled by, or is under common control with such issuer. The term *person,* when used in reference to a person for whose account securities are to be sold in reliance upon this rule, includes, in addition to such person

- Any relative or spouse of such person, or any relative of such spouse, who shares in the same home as such person
- Any trust, corporation, or estate in which such persons collectively own 10% or more of the total beneficial interest

SEC Rule 144 covers both the sale of unregistered (restricted) securities and the sale of securities by an affiliate of the issuer.

An affiliate of the issuer would normally be an officer or director of the issuer or a stockholder owning 10% or more of any class of equity securities. Securities owned by affiliates of an issuer are referred to as **control stock**. In order to sell either unregistered securities or securities on behalf of an affiliate of the issuer, the sales must meet all of the following conditions in order to comply with SEC Rule 144:

1. The shares must have been owned by the investor for at least one year. (This provision does not apply to holders of control stock. There is no holding period for owners of control stock.) The holding period applies to unregistered shares.
2. The shares must have been fully paid for at least one year prior to the sale. In computing the one-year holding period, there shall be excluded

   a. Any period during which the person for whose account the securities are sold had a short position in the security or an option to dispose of the security (put) or any security convertible into the security of the same class.
   b. If the securities sold are nonconvertible debt securities, there shall be excluded any period during which the person has a short position in, or any put or other option to dispose of, the security (put) or any nonconvertible debt security of the same issue.

3. Sales may be made only through a broker's transactions or the stock can be sold in a transaction directly with a market maker. A broker can execute a sell order as agent for the seller and receive no more than the customary commission, but may not solicit buy orders.
4. The amount of securities that may be sold in any three-month period by an affiliate of the issuer is limited to

   a. 1% of the outstanding shares as shown by the most recent report or statement published by the issuer, or
   b. The average weekly reported volume of trading in such security on all securities exchanges and reported through automated quotation systems during the four calendar weeks preceding the filing of the notice of sale, whichever is greater.

   Concurrently with the placing with a broker of an order to execute a sale of any securities under Rule 144, a notice of sale on Form 144 must be filed with the principal office of the SEC in Washington, D.C. A notice of sale does not have to be filed if the amount of securities sold during any 90-day period does not exceed 500 shares and the aggregate sales proceeds do not exceed $10,000.

The person filing the notice must have a bona fide intention to sell the securities within a reasonable time after the filing of such notice.

If the securities are to be sold by a nonaffiliate of the issuer, the unregistered stock may be sold without volume limitation provided that

- For exchange-listed or NASDAQ stocks, the shares have been fully paid for at least three years, or
- For over-the-counter (OTC) stocks, the shares have been fully paid for at least four years.

In both instances, the securities sold must be of an issuer who is currently filing reports with the SEC under Section 13 or 15(d) of the Securities Exchange Act of 1934. Also, in both cases, the person selling the shares must have been a nonaffiliate for the preceding three months before the sale and the seller must comply with all other provisions of SEC Rule 144.

5. Specified current information concerning the issuer must be available.

The one-year holding period associated with SEC Rule 144 applies only to the sale of unregistered securities and not to the sale of control stock (stock owned by a person in a control relationship with the issuer). For example, assume the president of XYZ Corporation received a bonus of 15,000 shares of XYZ stock from the corporation. The one-year holding period would apply to these shares because they were received directly from the corporation and were not previously registered under the Securities Act of 1933.

Assume, instead, the president of ABC bought 1,000 shares of ABC stock through his broker/dealer in an ordinary trade on the New York Stock Exchange. These shares are not subject to the one-year holding period requirement. The shares can be sold immediately provided all the other requirements of Rule 144 are complied with.

SEC Rule 145

SEC Rule 145 states that it will be deemed an offer to sell under the Securities Act of 1933 when there is submitted to security holders a plan or agreement whereby the security holders are required to decide whether or not to accept a new or different security in exchange for their existing security. Such plans or agreements could cover

- Reclassification other than stock splits and changes in par value
- Mergers, consolidations, and similar plans of acquisition except where the sole purpose of such a transaction is to change the issuer's domicile
- Certain transfers of assets where there is a subsequent distribution of such securities to those voting on the transfer of the assets

Unless an exemption can be found, these transactions are subject to the registration requirements of the Securities Act of 1933 and, therefore, full disclosure must be made to shareholders.

SEC Regulation D: Private Placement Exemption

In a major effort aimed at facilitating the capital formation needs of small business, the SEC has adopted Regulation D. Regulation D contains Rules 501 through 506. SEC Rules 501 through 503 set forth definitions, terms and conditions that apply generally throughout Regulation D. SEC Rules 504 through 506 exempt certain transactions from the registration requirements of federal securities laws, provided the offering meets the requirements contained in these rules.

Therefore, if an issuer of securities meets the requirements of Regulation D, the issue can be sold without meeting the full registration requirements that nonexempt issues must meet. Regulation D offerings are subject to antifraud or civil liability provisions of federal securities laws.

SEC Rule 506 provides an exemption for offers and sales to no more than thirty-five purchasers. Accredited investors, however, do not count toward that limit. The thirty-five persons, other than accredited investors, must meet certain sophistication standards. Unsophisticated investors may participate in the offering if a purchase representative (accountant or lawyer) is present representing the unsophisticated investor. SEC Rule 506 prohibits any general solicitation or general advertising. Both SEC Rules 505 and 506 require information to be given to nonaccredited investors. For offerings up to $5 million, the information disclosure requirements to nonaccredited investors under SEC Rules 505 and 506 are identical. For offerings in excess of $5 million, the information disclosure requirements are more comprehensive under SEC Rule 506.

SEC Rule 501 classifies an **accredited investor** for the purposes of Regulation D into eight separate categories. Investors are considered to be accredited under the rule only if the issuer and any person acting on the issuer's behalf has reasonable grounds to believe, and do believe after reasonable inquiry, that the investors come within one of the categories in the definition.

The eight separate categories of accredited investors under Regulation D include

1. Institutional investors (i.e., banks, insurance companies, or investment companies).
2. Private business development companies.
3. Tax-exempt organizations.
4. Directors, executive officers, and general partners of the issuer.
5. $150,000 purchasers provided the total purchase price does not exceed 20% of the investor's net worth at the time of the sale. For natural persons, the joint net worth of the investor and the investor's spouse may be used in measuring the ratio of the purchase to net worth.
6. Individuals with $1,000,000 of net worth or $1,000,000 of net worth for the investor and the investor's spouse.
7. An individual who has an income in excess of $200,000 in each of the last two years and who reasonably expects an income in excess of $200,000 in the current year.
8. Entities made up of accredited investors.

SEC Rule 147: Intrastate Offerings

Section 3(a)(11) of the 1933 Act exempts from the registration requirements of the Act

Any security which is part of an issue offered and sold only to persons resident within a single state or territory, where the issuer of such security is a person, resident and doing business within, such state or territory.

This exemption is available only if the entire issue is offered and sold exclusively to residents of a single state. If any sale takes place to nonresidents, the entire issue loses its exemption. The purpose of this exemption is to allow issuers to raise money on a local basis, provided the business was operating primarily within that state. The following conditions must be met in order to have a distribution qualify as an intrastate offering:

- The securities must be offered or sold exclusively to persons resident in one state, and the persons purchasing the securities must have their principal residence within the state.
- The issuer of the securities must be a resident doing business primarily within the state. In order to be considered a resident, the corporation must meet the following requirements:
  - It must be incorporated in the state.
  - Its principal office must be located in the state.
  - At least 80% of its gross revenues must be from operations located within the same state.
  - At least 80% of its assets must be located within the state.
  - At least 80% of the proceeds of the offering must be used within the state.
- The proceeds of the offering must be used primarily for business purposes within the state. For a period of nine months from the date of the last sale by the issuer of any part of the issue, resale of any part of the issue by any person shall be made only to persons resident within the same state or territory. This will satisfy the requirements that the issue "come to rest" in the state in order to claim the exemption.

For the purpose of determining the residence of purchasers (offerees) of this distribution

- A corporation, partnership, trust, or other form of business organization will be considered a resident of the state if, at the time of the offer and sale, it has its principal office within the state.
- An individual must have his or her principal residence within the state. An individual is not considered a resident if s/he has a vacation home within the state.

Any person acquiring securities from an issuer under this exemption is acquiring unregistered securities that can be resold only if registered under the Act or pursuant to an exemption. Issuers must take required steps to preserve the exemption provided by the rule by

- Placing a legend on the certificate stating that the securities have not been registered under the Act, and setting forth the limitations on resale
- Issuing stop transfer instructions to the issuer's transfer agent
- Obtaining a written representation from each purchaser as to his or her principal residence

Regulation A Offering

The Securities Act of 1933 exempts from the registration requirements an issue of securities offered to the public when the total amount offered is $5 million or less. This is sometimes referred to as the **small-offering exemption**. The purpose of the rule was to allow an issuer who was selling a limited amount of securities to do so without complying with the full registration requirements of the Act. This exemption allows small companies to raise limited amounts of capital without the expense of full registration involved.

The aggregate amount offered by the issuer or affiliates of the issuer cannot exceed $5 million during any twelve-month period. There is no restriction on the number of purchasers in a Regulation A offering, provided only $5 million or less is raised by the corporation.

Within ten business days prior to the initial offering date, a notification on Form 1-A must be filed with the regional office of the SEC for the region in which the issuer's principal business operations are conducted. Securities cannot be sold under this regulation unless an offering circular is furnished to the person to whom the securities are expected to be sold at least forty-eight hours prior to the mailing of the confirmation of sale to such person. However, if the issuer is required to file reports pursuant to Section 13(a) or 15(d) of the Securities Act of 1934, the offering circular may be furnished with or prior to the confirmation of sale.

For a period of ninety days after the date in which the securities were offered to the public, the dealer must furnish a copy of the offering circular to the purchaser prior to or with the purchaser's receipt of the confirmation of the sale. No written offer shall be made under this regulation unless an offering circular containing the information required under the regulation precedes or accompanies the written offer. However, a tombstone advertisement is permitted under this regulation.

The offering circular used in the sale of securities under this regulation must be kept current. If an offering is not completed within nine months from the date of the offering circular, a revised offering circular must be prepared.

The offering circular that will be used by the issuer must be filed with the notification to the SEC. If the offering circular is amended or revised, the amended circular must be filed with the appropriate regional office of the SEC at least ten business days prior to its use. The issuer may distribute a preliminary offering circular during the ten-business-day period prior to the effective date.

The preliminary offering circular would not contain information such as the dealer offering price, underwriter's discount, or selling concession. The SEC, at its discretion, may authorize the commencement of the offering prior to the expiration of the ten-business-day period upon written request for such authorization.

Regulation A offering allows corporations to raise capital with less stringent filing requirements up to $5 million. An offering circular is filed with the SEC instead of a prospectus.

Shelf Distribution

The Securities Act of 1933 contains provisions that allow stockholders the right to sell their shares over a period of time instead of selling them all at once. When a stockholder engages in this type of transaction, it is called a **shelf distribution**.

The selling stockholder may sell his shares at prevailing market prices within nine months following the effective date of the offering. It is the selling stockholder's responsibility to ensure that the prospectus is kept current. Each order ticket must be marked "distribution." The broker/dealer handling the transaction must inform the contra broker that it is shelf distribution stock involved in the trade.

If the transaction is done in the OTC market, a current copy of the prospectus must be given to the buyer before settlement date. If the transaction is executed on a stock exchange, copies of the prospectus must be filed with that stock exchange where they are available for inspection.

THE SECURITIES EXCHANGE ACT OF 1934

The Securities Act of 1933 was passed to make the sale of new issues to the public in interstate commerce subject to federal regulation. The Securities Exchange Act of 1934 extended this federal regulation to all phases of trading in existing securities. Its objective is to prevent unfair and unequitable practices and to bring trading on securities exchanges and OTC markets under federal control.

This Act established the Securities and Exchange Commission. The SEC consists of five persons appointed by the president and administers all federal laws regulating the securities business, except those regulating the extension of credit. This Act also defines many terms, including **broker**, **dealer**, and **exchange**.

The Board of Governors of the Federal Reserve was authorized by the Act to establish regulations governing the use of credit for the purchase or carrying of securities. The Federal Reserve has issued Regulations T, U, and G governing this area. The major areas under the Securities Exchange Act of 1934 will be analyzed.

Registration under the 1934 Act

The Securities and Exchange Act of 1934 requires many different groups and organizations to register with the Securities and Exchange Commission. Among them are

- Corporations having listed securities.
- Brokers and dealers operating in interstate commerce (includes those operating on exchanges and in OTC markets).
- National securities exchanges
- National securities associations (NASD, Municipal Securities Rulemaking Board [MSRB]).

Hypothecation

SEC Rules 8c-1 and 15c-1, adopted by the SEC under the Securities Exchange Act of 1934, specify three general prohibitions that brokers and dealers must observe in regard to the hypothecation of their customers' securities. A broker/dealer may not hypothecate or pledge securities carried for the accounts of his or her customers

- In such a way as to permit the securities of one customer to be commingled with the securities of other customers, unless the broker/dealer first obtains the written consent of each customer
- Under a lien for a loan made to the broker or dealer in such a way as will permit such securities to be commingled with the securities of any person other than a bona fide customer
- In such a way as to permit the liens or claims of pledges thereon to exceed the aggregate indebtedness of all such customers in respect to securities carried for their accounts

Insider Transactions

SEC Rule 10b-5 prohibits persons from trading securities based on inside information. This rule applies to all persons, whether they are insiders in a corporation or members of the general public.

Insiders in a corporation are normally officers, directors, and principal stockholders (persons owning 10% or more of the outstanding shares). However, any person may be considered an insider if

- The person directly or indirectly has access to material inside information, and
- S/he uses this information in the marketplace for his or her own benefit.

Certain persons who are not officers, directors, or principal stockholders could obtain material inside information as a result of their employment. Examples include

- Attorneys
- Accountants
- Reporters for financial publications
- Research analysts for broker/dealers
- Laboratory technicians

These persons who possess the inside information must refrain from using it in the marketplace, refrain from recommending the security, and must not disclose the information to the public. Disclosure to the public, in most cases, should come from the corporation. This would avoid potential liability that could accrue to a person who disclosed information that was later proven to be false.

The SEC and the NASD use certain factors to determine whether an individual acted on inside information in a particular transaction. The first test is that the information must be material. It must be of sufficient importance to have an effect on the stock in the marketplace. If a reasonable man would consider the information important, then it is probably material information. Examples of information that, in most cases, is considered material, are

- Earnings projections
- Dividend increases or decreases
- Merger or acquisition
- Major lawsuit
- Introduction of a new product

• Discovery of a valuable natural resource on company property

The second factor considered is whether the information was nonpublic. It is generally considered to be public information when it is released to the public by the news media. However, the general public should be given time to digest the news, especially when the news is complex. Therefore, officers and directors should not be placing buy or sell orders for their own account immediately after the news is released to the public because the SEC may still consider this acting on nonpublic information.

The third important factor is whether or not the information was a factor in the person's decision to buy or sell the stock. The SEC presumes that the information was an important factor in the purchase or sale decision. It would be up to the individual to prove that the information was not the reason the stock was purchased or sold at that time.

An officer, director, or principal stockholder is prohibited from realizing short-swing profits in the equity securities of their issuer. Any profits realized from purchase and sales activity by an officer, director, or principal stockholder within a six-month period may be recovered by the issuer.

An officer, director, or principal stockholder of an issuer is prohibited from engaging in a short sale or short-against-the-box transaction in any equity security of the issuer.

Officers, directors, and principal stockholders must file a report with the SEC showing the amount of shares they own. Any changes in ownership of the shares must be reported to the SEC.

TOMBSTONE ADVERTISEMENTS

It is important to be able to understand tombstone advertisements. They are used to publicize new issues. Technically, such advertisements do no more than identify the security, state the price, and indicate by whom orders will be executed, and from whom an offering prospectus may be obtained. Actually, however, such information may be extremely important and should be carefully examined by anyone interested in the issue. Details presented in the fine print are quite often extremely significant and should not be overlooked. Several examples of tombstone advertisements will be presented and discussed.

Common Stock

Exhibit 3.2 is a tombstone advertisement for 910,000 shares of class B common stock of Wang Laboratories, Inc. First, note four points that are common to every tombstone. These will not be noted again in the discussion of any tombstone presented in this section.

1. A statement will appear on every tombstone indicating that the offering is made only by a prospectus, which can be obtained by those underwriters who can legally offer the securities in the state of the interested purchaser.
2. The names of the underwriting syndicate members appear on the tombstone, usually at the bottom of the advertisement.
3. The managing underwriter or underwriters appear at the top of the list indicating members of the syndicate.
4. Each tombstone advertisement bears the date of its publication.

Exhibit 3.2: Tombstone advertisement for Wang Laboratories

Because the list of members of the underwriting syndicate may be quite lengthy, some of the names of firms in the syndicate may be eliminated on the example.

Examining this particular tombstone will reveal that the par value of the stock is $0.50 and that the offering price is $9.875 per share.

Preferred Stock

Exhibit 3.3 is a tombstone ad for four million shares of General Telephone & Electronics Corporation no par preferred stock. The offering price is $27.50 per share plus accrued dividends, if any, from the issue date. Note that, since the stock is no-par, the dividend rate of $2.475 per share is stated.

Exhibit 3.3: Tombstone advertisement for General Telephone and Electronics

Notes

Exhibit 3.4 concerns $50 million of notes issued by the Bucyrus-Erie Company. The ad indicates that the notes due on April 1, 1983, will pay 7¾% interest. The *price 100%* means that the notes will sell at their par value plus the indicated accrued interest.

Exhibit 3.4: Tombstone advertisement for Bucyrus-Erie

Debentures

There are two examples of tombstone ads presented concerning debentures. The first of these, Exhibit 3.5, announces the issue of $10 million of 7% debentures due in 1997 by the Limited Stores, Inc. They are to be sold exactly at par plus accrued interest. The reader of this ad who might be interested in these debentures should note three specific points other than those already mentioned.

Exhibit 3.5: Tombstone advertisement for The Limited Stores

1. These are "subordinated" debentures. The holder of a subordinated debenture has a claim on the assets of a corporation, which comes after all other debts.
2. These debentures are redeemable by the corporation. Because redemption will occur when it is to the corporation's advantage—not the investor's—anyone interested in possibly purchasing this issue should carefully examine the prospectus to discover specific details concerning such a redemption. What is the redemption price? Is there **call protection**—any period of time that must elapse before the corporation is permitted to call the debentures?
3. The debentures are convertible into common stock at $22.75 per share. Is this close to the current market price of the company's common stock? If not, what is the possibility, in the opinion of the prospective purchaser, of the market price of the stock reaching this amount?

Exhibit 3.6 is a tombstone for $100 million of City Investing Company debentures due in 1997 along with 800,000 shares of common stock. The offer is actually for 100,000 units, with each unit consisting of one $1,000 debenture and eight shares of common stock with a par value of $1.25 per share. Each unit is offered for a price of $1,000 plus certain accrued interest. Since the $9\frac{1}{8}\%$ debentures are straight debentures—not subordinated—they have a claim on company assets equal to other unsecured debt. Note that these are **sinking-fund debentures,** meaning that the company will set aside a fund at regular intervals to redeem the bonds.

Exhibit 3.6: Tombstone advertisement for City Investing

Mortgage Bonds

Exhibit 3.7 refers to $35 million of First Mortgage Bonds paying 9% interest and due in 2008, issued by the United Telephone Company of Ohio. These bonds are being offered at a discount since the price is indicated as being 99.18% (of par) plus accrued interest. Any calculation of yield to maturity would have to recognize both the annual interest of 9% and the capital gain occurring when the bonds are eventually redeemed at their par value.

Exhibit 3.7: Tombstone advertisement for United Telephone

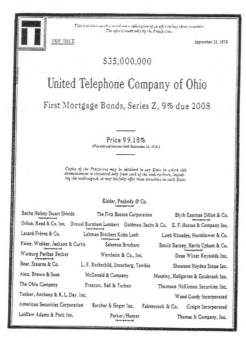

Serial Bonds

Two examples of serial bonds are presented. Both are municipals. One is a general obligation bond. The other is a revenue bond. Exhibit 3.8 is an advertisement of $77,300,000 of bonds issued by the State of Wisconsin. The ad clearly states that these are general obligation bonds—that they are "direct and general obligations of the State of Wisconsin and the full faith, credit and taxing power of the State will be irrevocably pledged to the payment of the principal, interest and redemption price thereof." Other information contained in the ad indicates that these bonds are issued in $5,000 denominations and the bonds from 1989 to 2003 are callable beginning on November 1, 1988, at "varying premiums." This means that if the bonds are called, the holder will receive a premium above par.

Anyone examining this ad should clearly understand the information presented in each column of the table. The first figures indicate that $2,270,000 of the total bond issue will mature in 1979. These bonds will pay the holder annual interest of $237.50 (4¾% x $5,000). This is a stated rate (nominal yield) of 4¾%, but the fourth column indicates that the actual yield to maturity will be 4.40%. This means that these bonds are being sold at a premium since the yield to maturity is less than the stated rate of interest.

Note that the stated interest rate increases as the maturity dates get longer, as does the yield to maturity. Those maturing in 1979 have a stated rate of 4¾% and a yield to maturity of 4.40%, while those maturing in 2003 bear a stated rate of 5.10% and a yield to maturity of 5.60%. Those bonds maturing in 1993 have a "100" beside them in the "yield or price" column. This indicates that these bonds are being sold exactly at par and the yield to maturity will be the same as the stated rate. In this table, those bonds with maturity dates prior to 1993 are being sold at a premium as evidenced by the fact that the yield to maturity is less than the stated rate. Those maturing after 1993 are being sold at a discount, since the yield to maturity is greater than the stated rate. The interest on these bonds is, as stated in the ad, exempt from present federal income taxes.

Exhibit 3.8: Tombstone advertisement for the State of Wisconsin

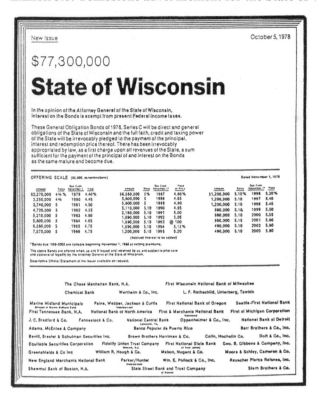

Exhibit 3.9 is a tombstone for $92,900,000 of bonds issued by the Salt River Project Agricultural Improvement and Power District of Arizona. They are electric system revenue bonds and, therefore, are not backed by the full faith and credit of the State of Arizona. The payment of interest is dependent on the earnings of the Salt River Project electric system.

The principal and semiannual interest is due on January 1 and July 1 each year, and the first interest payment will be on July 1, 1979. The information indicates that this interest is exempt from both federal income taxes and the income tax of the State of Arizona. These bonds are also issued in denominations of $5,000 and are available in one of two forms—either registered as to principal only with bearer coupons or fully registered.

These bonds are callable any time after January 1, 1989. "In inverse order of maturities" means that the last maturing bonds must be called first, and "by lot within a maturity" means that those holding bonds within a maturity (e.g., 1998) will have their bonds called by the drawing of a number. When bonds are called, holders will receive 102% of par if their bonds have maturity dates from January 1, 1989, through December 31, 1990, and exactly par, but no more than par value, if their bonds mature after January 1, 1997. Between 1990 and 1997, they might receive more than par but not less. In every case, the holder of a called bond will also receive any accrued interest due to the call date. A sinking fund is to be established and, beginning January 1, 1999, the 2008 and 2018 term bonds must be redeemed out of this sinking fund. The details of this redemption requirement are described in the official statement, which may be obtained from any of the members of the underwriting syndicate. Note that the stated rate on these bonds is the same for all maturities, but the yield to maturity constantly increases for later maturity dates. Since these yields to maturity are lower than the stated rate until 1997, it means that bonds with maturities before that date are being offered at a premium. From 1997 on, they are offered at par. These bonds are rated Aa by Moody's and A+ by Standard & Poor's.

Exhibit 3.9: Tombstone advertisement for Salt River Project

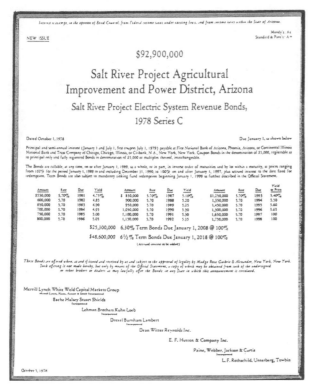

Tender Offer

Exhibit 3.10 is an announcement of a tender offer. It is an offer to purchase 5 million shares of Ashland Oil, Inc. stock at $47 per share. Information presented clearly indicates that this ad is not an offer to purchase. Such an offer may be made only through the "Offer to Purchase" and related "Letter of Transmittal," which has been mailed to all stockholders. If stockholders wish to tender their shares, Ashland will purchase up to 5 million shares tendered by 5 P.M. Eastern Standard Time on October 20, 1978.

The ad also indicates that holders of Ashland's Cumulative Preferred Stock, $5.00 convertible series of 1969, $5.00 convertible series of 1970, and $2.40 convertible series of 1970, and holders of Ashland's 4¾% convertible subordinated debentures for conversion and tender the common shares received. Among other items of information, the ad also indicates that the company will not pay any fees or commissions to anyone for soliciting tenders, is not making any recommendation to any shareholder as to whether to tender stock, and has selected the Chase Manhattan Bank in New York as the depository for the offer.

In order for a person to legally tender shares, he must own the security to be tendered. Under SEC rules, a person is deemed to own a security if

- He or his agent has title to it.
- He has purchased the security, or has entered into an unconditional contract to purchase it but has not yet received it.
- He owns a security convertible into or exchangeable for it and has tendered such security for conversion or exchange.
- He has an option to purchase or acquire it and has exercised such options.
- He has rights or warrants to subscribe to it and has exercised such rights or warrants.

A person is considered to own or be long a security only to the extent that he has a net long position in the security. For example, if a person is long 500 shares of ABC in one account and short 500 shares of ABC in another account, he does not have a net long position in the security. Any sales he enters into will be considered short sales.

However, a customer who is long 500 shares of a security and short 500 shares of the same security, could take advantage of a tender offer in the security by covering the 500-share short position. In other words, if the customer repurchased the 500-share short position, he would then be left with a 500-share long position. The customer would then be able to tender the 500-share position to the company making the tender offer.

The following three types of tender offers would be legal:

1. A custodian tendering shares from an account he is managing under the Uniform Gifts to Minors Act/Uniform Transfer to Minors Act
2. A trustee tendering shares from a trust account
3. A person tendering his own shares either fully paid or from a margin account, even if the margin account is restricted

By tendering shares from a margin account, a person is reducing the risk associated with the account by turning shares into cash. However, a person cannot tender shares that he borrowed through a short margin account. In this case, the person does not own these shares and, therefore, cannot tender them.

The tombstone ads presented are only illustrations. The purpose of presenting them is to call attention to the amount and types of information that may be obtained from a careful examination of such advertisement. Every registered representative should be able to interpret such information.

Principal stockholders are persons who own 10% or more of an equity security of a publicly traded corporation. Principal stockholders are insiders in a corporation and are prohibited from selling their company's stock short or even short against the box. Principal stockholders (insiders) must report any changes in beneficial ownership in their company's stock to the SEC. Also, principal stockholders (insiders) are prohibited from engaging in short-term swings in their company's stock. A short-term swing occurs when an insider buys and sells at a profit within a six-month period. If an insider engages in a short-term swing, the profit is recoverable by the company. Assume John James is the president of ABC Corporation. He wants to sell shares he has held only four months at a profit. The registered representative should tell Mr. James that he will have to forfeit the profit on the sale, because he will have engaged in a short-term swing.

Exhibit 3.10: Tombstone advertisement for Ashland Oil

4 MUNICIPAL SECURITIES

INTRODUCTION

State and municipal securities are either general obligations of the issuer (a state, city, or town) or revenue bonds payable only from a specific source of revenue (such as tolls or water or sewer charges). The bonds are readily marketable, for the most part, with the better-known and higher-quality bonds enjoying the most liquid markets. There is a tremendous diversity of issuers, with different maturities and coupons for each issuer. Probably the single most important characteristic of these bonds is the fact that the interest paid is free from all federal income taxes. If a resident of a state owns obligations of his own state or cities, towns, or authorities within his state, the interest on these bonds is normally free from his own state income tax as well. He must pay state income taxes (if his state has an income tax) on municipal bonds issued outside his state. Interest received on bonds issued by United States territories or possessions, such as Commonwealth of Puerto Rico bonds, is free from all income taxes—federal, state or local. The federal tax-exempt status of municipal bonds originated from the doctrine of mutual tax reciprocity developed by the United States Supreme Court. The doctrine holds that interest received from US government securities is exempt from state and local income taxes. If this tax exemption on municipal bonds were eliminated, the result would probably be an increase in the yield of newly issued municipals.

Federal tax exemption is obviously advantageous to the investor. The higher the investor's tax bracket, the greater the advantage. The equivalent yield an investor would have to earn on a fully taxable security to provide the same after-tax income as a municipal security can be calculated by subtracting the investor's tax bracket from 100% and dividing the yield on the municipal security by the answer. For example, assume an investor in the 28% tax bracket purchases a municipal bond yielding 9%. To get the same after-tax yield on a corporate bond, that security would have to yield 12.5% (100% − 0.28 = 0.72, therefore, 0.09 divided by 0.72 = 0.125 or 12.5% equivalent yield).

Since the interest on municipal bonds is exempt from federal income taxes, a client buying municipal bonds on margin is not allowed to use the interest charged on his debit balance as a tax deduction. Such a deduction would be illogical because a tax expense would then be deductible, while the interest received would not be taxable.

Historically municipal securities have been purchased by commercial banks, insurance companies, and individuals in order to obtain the benefit of tax-exempt interest. However, charitable organizations and pension funds generally have not been major purchasers of municipal securities since they are tax-exempt organizations themselves and do not need the benefit of tax-exempt income from municipal securities.

When municipal bonds are purchased by an investor in a primary distribution at a discount, the difference between that price and par is treated as tax-free interest. Consequently, where such bonds, originally issued at a discount, are sold by the original or subsequent holders before redemption, each holder of the bond to the date of maturity is entitled to apportion the amount of discount at which the obligation was issued according to the period of his holding. Any other capital gain that results from either the sale or maturity of municipal bonds is treated as a capital gain and taxed accordingly.

Examples

1. Municipal bond issued at $800 in a primary distribution and held by the original purchaser until it matures at $1,000. The $200 gain is exempt from federal income tax.
2. Municipal bond issued at $800. Matures in 20 years at $1,000. Original purchaser holds bond 4 years and sells the bond for $890. Federal income tax must be paid on a capital gain of $50 computed as follows:

$$\frac{\$200 \text{ discount}}{20 \text{ years to maturity}} = \$10 \text{ amortized per year}$$

$800	Cost of bond
+ 40	Amortization for 4 years
$840	Cost basis for bond
$890	Sales proceeds
−840	Cost basis for bond
$ 50	Capital gain for tax purposes

3. Municipal bond issued at its par value of $1,000, purchased by an investor at $800 in the secondary markets and sold by the investor at par. Federal income tax must be paid on a capital gain of $200.
4. Municipal bond purchased at $1,000 by an investor and later sold by the investor at $1,100. Federal income tax must be paid on a capital gain of $100.
5. If an investor purchases a municipal bond at a premium and holds it until maturity, the amount of the premium cannot be deducted as a capital loss. Assume an investor purchases a municipal bond for $1,200, which will mature in five years. If the investor holds the bond until maturity, the $200 loss cannot be deducted as a capital loss. The investor must amortize the amount over the remaining life of the bond. Therefore

$$\frac{\$200 \text{ (amount of premium)}}{5 \text{ (number of years to maturity)}} = \$40 \text{ amortized each year}$$

This amortization reduces the cost basis of the bond from $1,200 to $1,000.

$1,200	Original purchase price
− 200	Amount amortized over 5 years
$1,000	Cost basis of bond for tax purposes

Therefore, no capital gain or loss is incurred for federal tax purposes.

$1,000	Proceeds at maturity
−1,000	Adjusted cost basis of the bond
$ 0	Gain or loss for federal tax purposes

Assume that the investor sold this particular bond for $1,100 at the end of two years rather than holding it until maturity. In this case, the capital gain or loss computation would be as follows:

$1,200	Cost of bond
− 80	Amortized over 2 years ($40 per year)
$1,120	Cost basis of bond
$1,120	Cost basis
−1,100	Proceeds from sale
$ 20	Capital loss for tax purposes

In other words, if an investor purchased a municipal original issue discount bond and held it to maturity, he would **not** have a taxable gain. If he purchased any other municipal at a discount and held it to maturity, he **would** have a taxable capital gain. If he purchased a municipal bond at a premium and held it to maturity, he would **not** have a tax-deductible capital loss.

TYPES OF MUNICIPAL BONDS

The main types of municipal bonds are

- General obligation bonds
- Revenue bonds
- Special tax bonds
- New housing authority bonds
- Moral obligation bonds

General Obligation Bonds

General obligation bonds (GOs) are unconditionally guaranteed by a political unit that has the power to levy taxes. They are often referred to as "full faith and credit" bonds, and their holders receive an unconditional guarantee that the interest and principal will be paid on time.

GOs issued by a state would most frequently be supported by one or a combination of the following types of taxes:

- Income tax
- Sales tax
- Gasoline tax

GOs issued by a city or town (local government) are normally supported by a real property tax—an ad valorem tax on the assessed value of real property.

There are two types of GOs.

1. Unlimited-tax GOs
2. Limited-tax GOs

Unlimited-tax GOs carry the backing of the full taxing power of the issuer. However, limited-tax GOs are not secured by all of the taxing power of the state or local government. Limited-tax GOs are supported by the pledge of a tax that is limited as to its rate or amount. For example, such bonds may be secured by a maximum property tax. It is important for any prospective investor to know if the limited taxing power behind these bonds has already been fully or partially used. If all of the limited taxing power has been used, no margin of safety exists for the protection of the bondholder. This is why limited-tax GOs generally sell at a lower price (higher yield) than unlimited-tax GOs having the same quality and maturity.

A municipality could obtain money to pay off its general obligation debt from all of the following sources:

- Fines
- License fees
- The collection of delinquent taxes
- Property taxes

GOs may be subject to limitations on their issuance. The authority for issuing municipal bonds comes from either the constitution of the state or from statutory authority. Voters' approval may be required, in some instances, before a GO may be issued.

A law requiring voters' approval will state whether a simple majority or a two-thirds approval is required. If voters' approval is not required, the power to issue municipal bonds is in the hands of the administrative officials.

A state or municipality may be subject to a limit on the amount of debt it can legally incur. This debt limit refers to the legal maximum debt-incurring power of the issuer. A level debt service bond issue is one for which the combined annual payments of principal and interest are approximately equal.

A bond attorney, before rendering his legal opinion, will research the statutes of a state to make certain that the bond issue conforms. After the bond attorney is satisfied that there is a statutory authority for the issue, he will make certain that there is constitutional authority. The state constitution will be closely examined by him to make certain that the statutes enacted by the state legislature do not violate the constitution.

Revenue Bonds

Revenue bonds are financed by "user charges." This means that the principal and interest are payable from income received from users of the system. These are revenues derived from the operation of a particular municipal enterprise, such as a toll bridge or turnpike. Interest and principal are both dependent on the earnings of this municipal enterprise.

Revenue bonds are intended to be self-liquidating. **Self-liquidating revenue bonds** are those in which the financed project generates funds to retire the bonds. The concept related to revenue bonds is that the users of the facility should pay for the facility.

These bonds are not subject to the ordinary debt limitations of the issuer, and may be issued by states, political subdivisions, and intrastate and interstate authorities. There is a wide variety of projects constructed from the proceeds of revenue bond issues whose revenues are pledged to service their bonds: toll roads and bridges, water and sewer plants, electric generating facilities, and so forth. A feasibility study by independent experts is essential to a revenue bond issue. Such a study is necessary to determine the need for or estimated use of the facility and the ability of the facility to produce the service at a price consumers are willing to pay.

Revenue bonds normally carry a higher coupon rate than GOs of the same issuer. They do not require a citizen referendum as GOs may, and, since interest is paid out of the earnings of a municipal enterprise, the interest payments do not deplete the general revenue of the state or municipality.

However, revenue bonds are not generally as safe as GOs. Banks are prohibited from underwriting and from dealing with customers on a principal basis, in most municipal revenue issues, by the Glass-Steagall Act of 1933. However, banks can deal on a principal basis and act as an underwriter in GOs. Banks acting as agent for customers (not as principal) may accept customer orders for all of the following types of securities:

- Corporate stock
- Corporate bonds
- Municipal GOs
- Municipal revenue bonds

In certain instances, when a revenue bond is sold, sufficient funds are obtained in order to cover interest expenses during the construction period of the project. In other words, the interest is said to be **capitalized**.

This capitalized interest, which is derived from the bond proceeds, is invested to earn income prior to its use. It is then used to meet interest payments during the construction period of the particular project.

The revenue bond indenture, which is the basic instrument for the security of revenue bonds, describes the manner in which the trustees must apply revenue to the costs of operation. The order of application is often referred to as the **flow of funds**. Although the application differs from one bond issue to the next, a typical bond issue would have the following funds or accounts through which the revenue would pass:

- *Operation and maintenance (O&M) fund.* The first repository is the O&M fund, which is used for the regular operating income and expenses of the project.
- *Bond serial account.* Funds are deposited here until the semiannual interest payment, the principal of any maturing serial bonds, and the sinking fund requirement for the term bond issue payments have been accumulated.
- *Debt service reserve fund.* Ordinarily, funds are accumulated here in an amount equal to one year's principal and interest requirements on the serial bonds and either one or two years' interest on the term bonds. If earnings are insufficient to make principal and interest payments, this reserve can be used.
- *Reserve maintenance fund.* An amount is set aside here for maintenance, usually an amount recommended by a consulting engineer.
- *Renewal and replacement fund.* Money to replace equipment or to provide for repairs that are necessary at irregular intervals is set aside in the renewal and replacement fund.
- *Surplus fund.* Here, all the remaining funds are deposited and are used for such purposes as redeeming bonds (via the optional sinking fund); payment to the local municipality in lieu of taxes, or for any other improvements or extensions to the project. If funds are required to be set aside to retire term municipal revenue bonds, for example, they would normally be deposited in the sinking fund.

It is sometimes helpful to visualize these various funds as water buckets; as soon as one is filled, the excess spills over to the next, and so on down the line.

The indenture usually contains various protective covenants as follows:

- A rate covenant that requires the issuer to charge rates sufficient to cover all debt service requirements, plus a margin of safety of 10% or higher. The term **coverage** as it relates to a revenue bond issue means the number of times which earnings for a period exceed the debt service payable in that period. The rate covenant requires that the rates and fees charged customers will be fixed so that net revenues always cover debt service by some predetermined ratio. The rate covenant for a highway bond, for example, would provide for toll rates to be maintained which are sufficient to meet all financial requirements, including reserves. A municipal bond's rate covenant would require that rates be maintained sufficient to cover payments into the following funds:
  - Operating and maintenance fund
  - Debt service fund
  - Debt service reserve fund

However, the rate covenant does not require that rates be sufficient to cover payments into the sinking fund.

- Other covenants require that adequate insurance be maintained at all times; that the plant and equipment be kept in good working order; that no discrimination be practiced in hiring policies or in services provided; that a consulting engineer of good reputation be retained; and that records be published and a report, audited by an outside auditing firm, be made. Most municipal bonds have a catastrophe call covenant and a financial reporting covenant. The catastrophe call covenant would apply if a project financed by a municipal revenue bond were destroyed by a fire or other catastrophe during the construction period. The financial reporting covenant requires that periodic financial reports be issued concerning the facility.
- Another covenant relating to a municipal issue is the restriction on the sale of additional bonds. A closed-end indenture prohibits the sale of additional bonds payable from the revenues of the project, except as necessary to complete the project. An open-end indenture permits the sale of additional bonds but, ordinarily, an earnings test has to be met. For example, the indenture might state that additional bonds could be sold if net revenues available for debt service for the past year were equal to 150% of debt service requirements for the present and proposed bonds. Usually, junior lien bonds (those payable from revenues left over after all first lien debt service charges have been satisfied) can be sold without an earnings test, as long as all other funds are current.

Certain municipal bonds have a defeasance covenant in the bond's indenture. Assume a municipal issuer has $1 million in debt outstanding. Additional money is borrowed by the issuer and invested in US government securities with the same maturity date as the previous issue. Since funds are available to retire the previous debt, the debt and any restrictive covenants attached are removed as a liability by the issuer or **defeased**.

The US government securities are deposited with the trustee when the municipal bond is prerefunded. The bondholders no longer have a claim against the pledged revenues of the previous issue. This procedure is allowed provided the bond's trust indenture contains a defeasance covenant.

If a revenue bond is additionally secured by the taxing power of the issuer, it would be classified as a GO. A bond whose principal and interest is payable from project revenues and also by the taxing power of the issuer is often referred to as a **double-barreled security**. A double-barreled municipal bond has its debt service secured by two separate sources. It is general obligation-backed and revenue-backed. If the net revenue is insufficient to service the debt for a double-barreled municipal bond as previously mentioned, the municipality may use any of the following sources to satisfy the obligation:

- Fines
- Ad valorem tax collection
- Assessments of additional taxes
- Collected back taxes

A municipality could create a municipal authority to sell bonds in order to finance construction of a public school. Assume the municipal government makes periodic payments to the authority to provide for the issue's debt service. The payments are made from direct taxes collected by the municipality. This type of issue would be classified as a GO.

To summarize, the indenture is a document that describes the rights of bondholders and the duties of the trustees who act to protect the interests of the bondholders. The indenture contains information concerning

- Redemption features
- Flow and application of funds
- Pledges to maintain rates

However, a bond's indenture does not contain information concerning reoffering yields or selling concessions.

Special Tax Bonds

Special tax bonds are payable only from the proceeds of a special tax, such as a liquor or cigarette tax. Another example would be highway bonds payable only from the proceeds of a gasoline tax. Special tax bonds are often classified as revenue bonds because they are payable only from the proceeds of a special fund. Some special tax bonds are payable primarily from a special tax, but also are secured by the full faith and credit of the state or municipality. In this case, the bonds are classified as GOs.

Special assessment bonds are another type of special tax bond. They are primarily secured by charges on directly benefited property. Such charges are in the form of an assessment against those who benefit from the construction of the facilities for which the bonds were issued. An example would be special assessment bonds issued to finance the improvement of streets and sidewalks. In recent years, most special assessment bonds have also been secured by the full faith and credit of the issuer and, therefore, would be classified as GOs.

New Housing Authority Bonds

These bonds are issued by local public housing authorities. Known as PHAs, they are secured by the annual net revenues of the local public housing authority, low-income housing projects and, far more important, from annual contributions of the Public Housing Authority of the United States. They are backed by the full faith and credit of the US government for the payment of interest and principal if the issuer's funds are not sufficient to meet obligations. Therefore, PHAs are considered to be of very high quality.

Other Types of Municipal Bonds

Industrial revenue bonds are municipal bonds wherein the proceeds of the issue are used to finance the construction of facilities or to purchase equipment which is leased to a corporation. The amount of the lease payments is set high enough to meet all of the costs associated with the bonds, including principal and interest. State and local governments use industrial revenue bonds in order to attract industry into an area. Industrial revenue bonds may also be referred to as industrial development bonds. The interest on these bonds is still tax-exempt if the proceeds are used for certain public purposes (even though the facilities may be operated by a private company), such as construction of

- Harbors
- Airports
- Mass transit systems
- Water, sewer and electric systems

Pollution control bonds have been issued frequently in recent years in an attempt to improve the environment. The proceeds of the bond issue are used to construct pollution control facilities, which are then leased to a private corporation. Interest received on a municipal industrial development bond is not tax-exempt to the holder if he is a substantial user of the system.

A lease rental bond, another type of municipal bond, is a bond secured by lease payments made by the party leasing the facility.

A moral obligation bond is a municipal bond that is secured by revenues from a financed project and additionally by a nonbinding undertaking that any deficiency in pledged revenues will be reported to the state legislature, which may make up any shortfall. The state legislature has the authority to allocate funds to support debt service payments, but it is not legally required to do so. If the issuer of a moral obligation bond defaults, legislative appropriation would be required for payment.

UNDERWRITING MUNICIPAL BONDS

New issues of municipal bonds are sold in the primary market. General obligation municipal bonds are sold on a competitive bidding basis. Revenue municipal bonds may be sold on a competitive basis or a negotiated basis. In either case, one firm will act as the managing underwriter. The managing underwriter forms an underwriting syndicate and a selling group. The managing underwriter is best described as the dealer that directs all of the underwriting group's activities.

The underwriting syndicate can be formed as an eastern account or western account. An eastern account is also called an undivided or united account. The eastern account is undivided as to sales and undivided as to liability. Syndicate members participate in the liability for unsold portions in proportion to their original participation in the account. Even if a syndicate member underwriting 20% of the issue in an eastern account sells all of the bonds allotted to it, the syndicate member must still take 20% of any unsold bonds of the entire syndicate.

A western account is also called a divided account. In a western account if a syndicate member underwriting 20% of an issue sells all of the bonds allotted to it, then it has no further liability for unsold bonds of the entire syndicate.

New issues of municipal bonds may be issued as serial bonds or term bonds. Serial bonds mature in installments on successive dates. Serial municipal bonds are normally quoted on a yield-to-maturity basis. The first step an underwriter must take before bidding for a serial issue is to determine a scale. The scale on a new issue of municipal bonds contains the various offering yields to maturity.

Term municipal bonds mature on a single date. Term municipal bonds are normally quoted at dollar prices and have mandatory sinking fund provisions attached.

After the underwriting syndicate is formed, the manager sends out a syndicate account letter identifying

- The duration of the account
- Each member's participation in the account
- The manager who is acting as agent for the syndicate

The syndicate letter describes the priority schedule employed to determine the allocation of the new issue of municipals. If a syndicate manager allocates bonds in a manner different from the priority established in the agreement among underwriters, the syndicate manager must be able to justify his allocation under MSRB rules.

A syndicate manager usually allocates municipal bonds according to the following priorities:

- **Presale orders.** These are orders the syndicate received before it actually offered the bonds.
- **Group net orders** (net orders sold for the benefit of the account). These are orders received once the offering has begun at a net price.
- **Group orders.** These are purchases by dealers who are not concession members of the syndicate. The dealers will receive the concession.

- **Designated orders.** Orders received from investors in which the concession and, in some cases, the takedown will be received by two or more members of the syndicate.
- **Member orders.** These are purchases by members of the syndicate at the takedown for their own account or for sales to investors or other dealers. If the bonds are sold to an investor the syndicate member keeps the entire amount of the takedown. If the sale is made to a dealer, the dealer will receive the amount of the concession.

Municipal syndicate orders are filled in sequence. Assume a municipal syndicate is reoffering $500,000 of GOs. The orders received by the manager as of the date the bonds can be confirmed for delivery are

- $250,000 designated orders
- $250,000 group orders
- $250,000 member orders

In this case, assuming normal priority provisions are followed, designated and group orders will be filled. Member orders will not be filled at all.

Assume a municipal bond is being offered to the public at $1,000 with a $5 spread. A municipal syndicate account member can buy the bonds at the takedown $995 and sell them for $1,000 to a public customer. Assume the concession is $2.50 per bond. A syndicate member can sell to a municipal dealer who is not in the syndicate at $997.50. The dealer will earn a concession of $2.50 per bond when selling the bonds to the public. Assume a municipal syndicate is composed of ten members and it is preparing to enter a bid on a municipal issue. At the final price meeting, two members dissent. In this case, either

- All syndicate members can reach a consensus agreement on the price and proceed with the bid, or
- The syndicate members who agree on the bid can go ahead with it. The other members would then drop out of the syndicate.

Equivalent Yield

Yields on a municipal bond are frequently on a taxable equivalent basis (i.e., at a rate that makes them equivalent to a taxable bond, for a given personal tax rate, before taxes). The **equivalent yield** for a municipal bond may be calculated by subtracting the holder's tax bracket rate from 100% and dividing the yield on the municipal bond by the answer. For example, assume an investor is in the 28% tax bracket and that he owns a municipal bond yield 5%. Equivalent yield would be found by subtracting 28% from 100% and then dividing the 5% yield.

$$\frac{0.05}{0.72} = 6.9\%$$

This means that this person would have to make an investment yielding 6.9% before taxes to receive the 5% after-tax yield he receives on the municipal bond. If, for any reason, this tax-exempt privilege should be removed, the yield on municipal bonds would very probably have to be increased to make their yields competitive with other securities. This would, of course, increase the cost of borrowing by state and local governments.

CHARACTERISTICS OF MUNICIPAL BONDS

Municipal bonds are available in the following forms:

- Bonds fully registered as to principal and interest
- Coupon bonds registered as to principal only
- Coupon bonds (bearer bonds)
- Book entry

A fully registered bond has the owner's name on the bond certificate, and interest is mailed by check to the bondholder by the paying agent, generally on a semiannual basis. A major advantage of a registered bond is that, if it is lost, the bondholder has some protection. In order for a registered bond to be transferred, the bond certificate must be made negotiable by an endorsement (signature of the owner or all co-owners). All new issues of municipal bonds are required to be fully registered under federal tax law.

Coupon bonds are generally **bearer** bonds. They do not have the owner's name on the certificate, and the bond may be transferred by delivery. Coupons are attached to the bond. A bearer bond has the advantage of being more marketable, since no endorsement is required for sale. However, the bondholder must bear the risk of losing the bond. Some bonds may be interchangeable between registered and coupon form. In some cases, such a change is at the expense of the bondholder.

A coupon bond may be registered as to principal only. This means that the bond certificate is issued in the name of the owner, but with bearer coupons. The coupons must be detached as each interest payment is due and cashed by the bondholders. However, at the maturity date, the owner of a bond registered as to principal only is the only one who can be paid the principal amount.

The interest that will be paid on a municipal bond will be indicated on the bond certificate, if it is a registered bond. Interest is usually paid semiannually. On a coupon bond, the interest rate will be shown on the coupons attached to the bond. Accrued interest is calculated on a 30/360 basis—30-day months and a 360-day year. In calculating the contract price, when municipal bonds are purchased the regular way, accrued interest is computed from (and including) the last interest payment date up to (but not including) the settlement date. On trades between dealers, settlement would be in clearinghouse funds and not in federal funds.

Accrued interest on a bond is

- Always less than the full coupon payment
- Always added to the purchase price of the bond

If interest payments are in default, the bonds are traded without accrued interest. The past unpaid coupons are attached and the bond is said to be **traded flat**. On a new issue, accrued interest is normally calculated from the **dated date** appearing on the tombstone ad. Assume the dated date is June 1 for a particular municipal bond issue. If an investor purchases the bond for settlement on June 1, no accrued interest will be paid. However, if the settlement of the transaction was June 10, the customer will pay nine days of accrued interest. Accrued interest for a municipal bond is always computed up to, but not including, settlement date.

The dated date for a municipal bond is the date from which interest accrues. Municipal bonds normally pay interest semiannually. For example, if the dated date for a bond is June 1, the municipal bond will normally pay interest on December 1 and June 1. However, a municipal issuer may want to issue a bond June 1, 1986. Therefore, the dated date will be June 1, 1986. The municipal issuer wants the interest payment dates to be July 1 and January 1. In order to get the bond on a January–July cycle for interest payment purposes, the first coupon must cover a seven-month period. This would be called a long coupon. If it covered less than a six-month period, it would be called a short coupon. Therefore, the first coupon on this bond would be for seven months (June 1, 1986–January 1, 1987). The second coupon and all remaining coupons will cover a six-month period.

Municipal bonds are usually issued in either $1,000 or $5,000 denominations. Most of the recent issues (especially the larger issues) have been in $5,000 denominations. Purchasers of large amounts of municipal bonds may request larger denominations if they prefer them. The $5,000 denomination is preferred by underwriters and institutions because of the reduced number of bonds that must be handled and stored. Therefore, the minimum denomination municipal bonds are issued in is $1,000. However, they are more frequently issued with minimum denominations of $5,000.

Municipal bonds are generally of three types with respect to maturity schedules.

1. Term bonds
2. Serial bonds
3. Serial bonds with a balloon maturity

A term bond is an issue that has a single maturity date. For example, a twenty-year $10 million bond issued January 1, 1978, and maturing January 1, 1998. Mandatory sinking fund provisions are usually associated with a term municipal bond. Such a mandatory sinking fund provision is required to make certain that sufficient funds will be available to retire the bonds on the maturity date.

A serial bond is a single issue that has varying maturity dates. For example, a twenty-year $20 million issue could mature at the rate of $1 million each year. In this case, one-twentieth of the entire issue would mature each year.

A serial bond with a balloon maturity is one which is serial for part of the issue with a final balloon term amount due at maturity. For example, a $50 million bond issue could be composed of $20 million in serial bonds maturing at various times and $30 million in term bonds maturing at one time.

Some municipal bonds are callable by the issuer. This means that the bonds may be redeemed at the option of the issuer before maturity. Under such an optional call provision, the bonds may be callable at par but, in most cases, they are callable at a predetermined premium over par. For example, the premium may be 103% of par until a certain date (e.g., January 1, 1983), and at a declining redemption price thereafter. If a bond is callable at 103%, this would be $1,030 for a $1,000 bond and $5,150 for a $5,000 bond. Some municipal bonds have mandatory call provisions, and the issuer must repurchase a certain amount of bonds as stated in this indenture. The call provision is advantageous to the issuer because, if interest rates decline, the issuer might call a high coupon bond and issue a bond with a lower coupon rate, thereby saving interest costs. This is disadvantageous to the bondholder because it places a ceiling on appreciation possibilities. A purchaser is unwilling to pay too high a price for the bond, if the bond may be called away from him or her for some specified amount.

The following statements can be made concerning municipal bonds with call provisions:

- If the municipal bond is called in after interest rates decline, investors will be forced to reinvest at lower rates.
- The premium, if any, received by investors does not generally compensate for the loss of investment return if the bonds are called.
- The bonds will generally be called when the issuer can refund the issue at lower interest rates.
- Premium bonds with a call feature will not appreciate as fast as comparable bonds without a call feature in a declining interest rate market.

In almost all cases, revenue bonds are callable prior to maturity either from surplus funds or the use of a mandatory sinking fund. If they are serial bonds, the call may be by maturity or inverse numerical order. Term bonds are usually called by lot. To check whether a particular bond has been called, Standard & Poor's Called Bond Record can be checked.

If a municipal bond is called prior to maturity, it is said to be prerefunded. When there is an advance refunding on municipal bond issues, refunded securities are most often secured by the escrow of US Treasury obligations. Municipal bonds may be prerefunded in order to

- Reduce interest costs
- Restructure the debt
- Liberalize provisions in the indenture

When a long-term speculative-grade municipal bond is prerefunded, the quality of the bond generally improves.

SECONDARY MARKET AND TRADING PRACTICES

The secondary market for municipal bonds refers to trading in outstanding issues. Municipal bonds are traded in the over-the-counter (OTC) market. All types of municipal bonds are traded in the OTC or secondary market. Some examples include

- Special tax bonds
- Dollar bonds
- Defaulted securities
- Tax anticipation notes
- Bonds registered as to principal
- Bearer bonds
- Bonds offered regular way
- Bonds listed in the Blue List
- Bonds issued after a syndicate breakup

Functions that occur in the secondary market for municipal bonds include

- The purchase and sale of bonds dealer to dealer
- Maintaining markets for dollar bonds (bonds quoted at dollar prices such as 88⅝ instead of a yield basis)
- Maintaining markets for bonds that are in default

However, a purchase of a new issue of municipal bonds does not occur in the secondary market. It occurs in the primary market. Therefore, when a new issue of municipal bonds is sold in the OTC market, it is said to be distributed in the primary market.

Once the new issue is sold, it is traded in the OTC market and is said to be traded in the secondary market.

In the secondary market, the following factors affect the marketability of municipal bonds:

- Whether the bonds are registered or bearer
- Block size, rating, and maturity
- Call feature, whether it is a local or national issue

- Coupon and dollar price

A quotation given by a municipal securities dealer in the secondary market is

- Subject to prior purchase or sale
- Subject to a subsequent price change
- May be nominal (for information only and not firm)

However, when a municipal securities dealer gives a quote, it does not necessarily mean that it represents the best bid or offer in the entire municipal market. It does represent the best bid or offer from one municipal securities dealer, but not necessarily the best in the marketplace.

In the municipal securities marketplace, a practice known as *taking bonds firm* for a certain time period has developed. When one municipal dealer takes bonds firm from another dealer at a certain price, an understanding exists between the two dealers. A municipal dealer can take a certain amount of bonds firm with or without a recall period.

Assume Trader Y has $50,000 of Commonwealth of Massachusetts 7% 2010 general obligation bonds in its inventory. Trader X calls Trader Y and asks to take the bonds *firm for one hour without recall* at 80. Trader Y agrees. This means

- Trader X controls the bonds for one hour.
- Trader Y cannot change or alter the price for one hour.
- Trader X and Trader Y have agreed on the purchase price.
- Trader X has protected himself from the sale of the bonds by Trader Y except by prior agreement.

The following are *NOT* true concerning the understanding between Trader X and Trader Y:

- That Trader X will automatically own the bonds after one hour. This is not true because at the end of the hour, Trader X will either buy the bonds from Trader Y or the firm price commitment will end and Trader Y is free to sell the bonds to anyone.
- That Trader Y can sell the bonds to anyone during the hour but only at a better price. This is not true because, during the hour Trader Y cannot sell the bonds except by prior agreement with Trader X, even if he receives a higher bid.

Assume that Trader X takes a block of bonds firm from Trader Y at 85 firm for one hour with a five-minute recall. This means that Trader Y is permitted to recall his bonds at any time but he must give Trader X an option to buy the bonds for five minutes. Trader Y may show the bonds to other prospective purchasers indicating that these bonds are out firm and subject to recall. Trader X has first call on Trader Y's bonds for one hour. However, if Trader Y exercises his recall provision, Trader X has five minutes to buy the bonds or the firm price commitment ends.

It is attractive to a buying municipal securities dealer to take bonds firm because

- The firm does not have to buy the bonds before it sells them.
- The firm can control the bonds for a specific time period.

Municipal bond traders are responsible for maintaining positions in municipal securities. They purchase and sell municipal securities for the account of the municipal securities dealer. They also provide bid quotations and appraisals relating to municipal securities.

BROKER'S BROKER

In the municipal securities business, certain firms specialize in handling orders for other municipal securities dealers. These firms are referred to as **broker's brokers**. Most of the broker's brokers are located in New York City. A municipal securities dealer may receive an order to sell a large amount of a particular issue. The municipal securities dealer may turn the order over to a broker's broker, who will work the order for them.

The broker's broker will obtain better exposure for the order. A broker's broker acts as agent and charges a commission to the municipal securities dealer or institution using its services. A broker's broker does not normally maintain an inventory or act as principal. A broker's broker does not normally trade for its own account or bid on new issues of municipals. However, a broker's broker does execute trades for dealer banks, institutions, and other municipal securities dealers. A broker's broker gives out information about the municipal market to other dealers and institutions. One additional reason an institution might use the services of a broker's broker is to maintain anonymity in the sale of a large block of municipal bonds.

JOINT ACCOUNTS

In certain instances, municipal securities dealers will form a joint trading account. A joint account is an account formed by two or more municipal dealers to purchase or distribute a block of municipal securities. When participating in a joint account, a municipal trader could

- Purchase bonds for an accumulation account
- Effect transactions from its own or a related portfolio
- Sell bonds in excess of his liability in the account

However, when participating in a joint account, a municipal securities dealer cannot provide quotes indicating that there is more than one market for the security.

LEGAL OPINION

Before municipal bonds are issued, the state or local government will employ a law firm specializing in municipal borrowing to give a legal opinion concerning the bonds. An investor should make certain, when purchasing municipal bonds, either in a primary distribution or in secondary trading, that the bonds are accompanied by a legal opinion. If an investor does not have a legal opinion with his bonds, the bonds may not be salable or may only be salable with a substantial discount. Most municipal bonds in recent years (but not all of them) have the legal opinion printed on the bond certificate. If the legal opinion is not printed on the bond, the investor must obtain a copy with delivery and carefully safeguard the opinion, as well as the bond certificate. The legal opinion is provided by an independent law firm.

The legal opinion (the statement made by the independent bond attorney) contains the following six points:

1. An opinion that the interest on these bonds is free from existing federal income taxes.
2. A reference to the laws that permit this bond issuance.
3. A statement that the issue is in compliance with all applicable legislative acts, court rulings, and state constitution.
4. Specifications of the terms of the offering, including information about maturities and call features.
5. Identification of any tax limitations on the issue (applies only to GOs) and a statement that the bond issue has been reviewed.
6. An identification of sources of payment and any prior pledges of these funds and assurance that the proceeds of the issue are to be used for the stated purpose.

The legal opinion does not imply market acceptance, does not state that the bond is a suitable investment, does not guarantee the safety of the bond, does not guarantee the accuracy of information in the offering circular, nor act as an evaluation of the creditworthiness of the bond. The legal opinion will not state that the revenues will be adequate on any project to service the debt or that the payments of interest and principal will be made on time. The legal opinion indicates that the bonds have been legally issued. In other words, it covers the validity of issuance. However, a municipal bond attorney can never guarantee that principal and interest will be paid on time for a particular issue.

The legal opinion on a municipal revenue bond would be concerned with the following factors:

- Its exemption from federal taxation
- Authorization to issue the securities
- A limitation on the pledge of revenues, if a limitation exists

However, the legal opinion on a municipal revenue bond would not be concerned with the suitability of the bond for investment purposes.

The bond attorney's duties include

- Determining that the bonds have been legally issued (in accordance with applicable statutes)
- Determining that the issuer is qualified for tax exemption
- Examining or preparing original drafts of proceedings before adoption

However, the bond attorney does not examine all the bonds to see that they are correctly printed and that all coupons are attached. This would be done by the issuer or the underwriter. The primary function of a municipal bond attorney is to render an opinion as to the tax exemption and legality of the issue.

A municipal bond attorney may issue an *unqualified legal opinion* on the securities to be issued. An unqualified legal opinion is also called a *clean legal opinion*. No irregularities are noted in the bond issue.

A municipal bond attorney could issue a qualified legal opinion stating that the municipal issue is subject to certain limitations such as a limitation on the rate of taxation that might be levied for the payment of the bonds.

If factors are present that might bring into question any aspect of the opinion, such as a lawsuit relating to the issuance of the bonds, the bond attorney makes reference to this factor and may express an opinion that such factor is without merit (a no-merit opinion). If the bond attorney feels that there is a basis for the lawsuit, he will issue a qualified legal opinion, not expressing an opinion concerning the outcome of the lawsuit.

SHORT-TERM TAX-EXEMPT SECURITIES

It is common practice for state and municipal governments to issue short-term securities in order to obtain additional working capital until funds are received from taxes or other sources. Municipalities issue short-term notes for interim financing and not permanent financing. The principal types of short-term tax-exempt securities issued by state and local governments are

- Project notes
- Tax anticipation notes
- Revenue anticipation notes
- Bond anticipation notes
- Grant anticipation notes

Project notes (PNs) are short-term notes issued by local governments. The proceeds are used for urban renewal and housing assistance programs. These notes are primarily obligations of the public housing authorities (local housing authorities), if the funds are used for housing assistance. If the notes were issued by a local urban renewal agency (local public agency) they are primarily obligations of the urban renewal agency. However, these project notes are secured by the full faith and credit of the US government. The US government must pay any deficiency in funds when the notes are due for payment of either principal or interest.

PNs are considered to be the highest-quality municipal obligations. They would be most appropriate for consideration by an investor whose primary concerns are preservation of capital and minimal market risk. However, they are not sources of permanent financing.

Tax anticipation notes (TANs) are issued by municipalities in order to finance current operations in anticipation of future tax receipts. **Revenue anticipation notes (RANs)** are issued by municipalities to finance current operations in anticipation of the receipt of revenues other than general tax receipts. **Bond anticipation notes (BANs)** are issued to obtain funds for projects that will be financed by the sale of bonds. They might be used for short-term borrowing for capital projects by state and local governments. The BANs are then paid from the proceeds of the bond issue. **Grant anticipation notes (GANs)** are issued on the expectation of receiving grant money from the federal government. Tax, revenue, bond and grant anticipation notes are all usually GOs.

Moody's Investors Services rates tax, revenue, bond, and grant anticipation notes using a MIG 1 through MIG 4 rating system. MIG 1 is the best-quality notes, and the quality decreases through MIG 4 (adequate quality). MIG ratings do not apply to PNs, but only to tax, revenue, and bond anticipation notes.

PRICING

Municipal bonds that mature serially are quoted, in most cases, on a yield basis plus accrued interest. The words **yield basis** mean that the price stated is the investment return that will be obtained if the bond is held until maturity. For example, a quote on a yield basis for a 7% municipal bond maturing on March 1, 2008, might be 7.50% bid and 7.40% offered. This means that, if the investor purchased this municipal bond at the ask price, he would obtain a yield to maturity of 7.4%. When serial bonds are issued, they are priced at their yield to maturity.

To find the actual dollar amount the investor would pay to purchase this bond, reference should be made to a basis book. A basis book may also be referred to as a yield book or bond value book. A basis book will show the dollar price an investor will pay for a bond, provided the yield is known. Assume the 7% municipal bond maturing on March 1, 2008, was purchased at a basis of 7.4% for settlement on March 1, 1979. An excerpt from a sample page in a basis book is shown in Exhibit 4.1.

Exhibit 4.1 A typical basis book page

YEARS AND MONTHS

7%

Yield	26-6	27-0	27-6	28-0	28-6	29-0	29-6	30-0
6.50	106.28	106.32	106.37	106.41	106.45	106.49	106.53	106.56
6.60	104.98	104.98	105.04	105.08	105.11	105.14	105.17	105.20
6.70	103.70	103.72	103.75	103.77	103.79	103.82	103.84	103.86
6.80	102.44	102.46	102.47	102.49	102.50	102.52	102.53	102.55
6.90	101.21	101.22	101.22	101.23	101.24	101.25	101.25	101.26
7.00	100.00	100.00	100.00	100.00	100.00	100.00	100.00	100.00
7.10	98.81	98.81	98.80	98.79	98.78	98.78	98.77	98.77
7.20	97.65	97.63	97.62	97.61	97.59	97.58	97.57	97.55
7.30	96.51	96.48	96.46	96.44	96.42	96.40	96.39	96.37
7.40	95.38	95.35	95.33	95.30	95.28	95.25	95.23	95.21
7.50	94.28	94.25	94.21	94.18	94.15	94.12	94.09	94.07
7.60	93.20	93.16	93.12	93.08	93.05	93.01	92.98	92.95
7.70	92.14	92.09	92.05	92.01	91.96	91.93	91.89	91.85
7.80	91.09	91.04	90.99	90.95	90.90	90.86	90.82	90.78
7.90	90.07	90.01	89.96	89.91	89.86	89.81	89.77	89.72
8.00	89.06	89.00	88.95	88.89	88.84	88.79	88.74	88.69
8.10	88.08	88.01	87.95	87.89	87.83	87.78	87.72	87.67
8.20	87.11	87.04	86.87	86.91	86.85	86.79	86.73	86.68
8.30	86.15	86.08	86.01	85.94	85.88	85.82	85.76	85.70
8.40	85.22	85.14	85.07	85.00	85.93	85.87	85.80	85.75

The basis book is organized by coupon rates. The page referred to in Exhibit 4.1 has a coupon rate of 7%. The basis book shows the years and months to maturity in columns across the top of the page. The different yield values are designated in a column to the left side of the page, usually in 0.10% increments. The yield table itself contains dollar prices. Therefore, each yield value, when traded to the specific number of years remaining on the bond, shows the corresponding dollar price. In the example, the yield of 7.4% on a bond, with 29 years remaining, shows a dollar price of 95.25, which equals $952.50.

In order to find the dollar price of a bond in a bond table, it is necessary to know the following three items:

1. Yield
2. Maturity date
3. Settlement date

The same analysis can be done in reverse by stating that a 7% bond purchased at 95.25 (95¼) with 29 years remaining until maturity would have a yield to maturity of 7.4%.

A dollar price or yield between those provided by such a table can be calculated by using the available information and interpolating. The idea of interpolation is to calculate the percentage difference between the information provided (basis percentages or dollar prices) and to apply that information to the "other side" to calculate the number in question.

Assume that in considering the 30-year 7% bond, available information indicates that the dollar price is 106.56 at a 6.50% basis and 105.20 at a 6.60% basis. You are now asked what the yield would be given a dollar price of 105.88.

The difference between the two prices provided is 1.36 (106.56 – 105.20). The difference between 105.20 and the price questioned, 105.88, is 0.68; 0.68 is 50% of 1.36. You would then take 50% of the total difference between the two basis values (6.60 – 6.50 = 0.10) and add this amount (0.05) to the lower basis provided (6.50 + 0.05) and find that a dollar price of 105.88 would produce a yield of 6.55%. Again, either the higher or lower number can be used if the difference is exactly 50%, but, in any instance when the number in question is not exactly halfway between the two provided, it would be necessary to base the calculations on either the lower or the higher.

Some municipal bonds are called **dollar bonds** because the price is stated as a dollar amount. In most cases, dollar bonds are term bonds (bonds which mature all at one time).

The average dealer's market spread on a $1,000 bond is usually one-half to one point, which is $5 to $10 per $1,000 bond. However, smaller inactively traded issues with longer maturities may have a spread of two points ($20 per $1,000) or more.

Spreads are wider for small trades and it is not advantageous to be trading in and out of municipal securities in small amounts. An investor is better off purchasing at least $25,000 worth of municipal securities, if possible, if he plans on reselling and not holding them to maturity. By purchasing a larger amount, the marketability of the securities is improved. An investor would expect a higher unit price when selling larger blocks of municipal securities (i.e., $100,000 worth) than when selling $5,000 worth. The terms *all or none* and *multiples of* are frequently used in agency transactions in this market and refer to seller's offering terms.

Marketability is also affected by the reputation of the issuer. Therefore, an investor will find that a municipal bond issued by a well-regarded state or local government is more readily marketable than a small issue of an obscure locality that is a great distance from the investor's home. In the case of the small issue, the investor may have difficulty finding a buyer for the securities.

Another factor to consider concerning the marketability of municipal bonds is whether the bonds are registered or in bearer form. Bearer bonds (coupon bonds) trade at slightly higher prices and are somewhat easier to market than registered bonds.

Municipal securities are greatly affected by interest rate changes. They tend to fluctuate to a greater degree than comparable US government or corporate securities when interest rates rise or fall. This is caused, many times, by commercial banks that buy municipal securities in large quantities when money is readily available and sell them when money tightens. However, many purchasers of municipal securities, both individual and institutional purchasers, are not affected by these fluctuations because they hold the municipal securities until maturity.

If interest rates are expected to rise, a municipality would borrow long term; if they are expected to fall, it would borrow short term. Municipalities would attempt to retire debt when interest rates are high. During periods of high interest rates when bond prices are low, a municipality wishing to retire debt would bid to attract tenders. In other words, they would bid in an attempt to have investors sell their bonds. During periods of low interest rates when bond prices are high, a municipality would not bid to attract tenders.

There are certain significant relationships between interest rates and yields. When the general level of interest rates rises or falls, short-term rates change more sharply than long-term. During periods of **easy money,** debt issues of the same quality will generally have both long- and short-term yields below normal, and short-term yields will be lower than long-term. The reverse would generally be true when money is tight. In periods of easy credit conditions, the yield curve will normally slope upward from the shortest maturity to the longest (short-term rates will be lower than long-term). This relationship even held true (contrary to taxable issues) during the tight money period of 1973. In periods of **tight money,** the yield curve is inverted or negatively sloped. The demand for short-term credit is high and interest rate level on short-term credit is high. Short-term US government debt, such as Treasury bills, would have a rate of return higher than long-term US debt, such as Treasury notes or bonds.

In secondary markets, short-term discount bonds appreciate more rapidly when interest rates decline than either short-term premium bonds or long-term bonds. Steadily declining interest rates would cause the reverse, in that short-term discount bonds would depreciate less rapidly.

Declining interest rates naturally encourage refunding. Issuers then find it attractive to call in outstanding high-interest-rate securities, paying them out of proceeds of the sale of new securities bearing a lower rate of interest.

SOURCES OF INFORMATION ON MUNICIPAL BONDS

There are four important sources of information available concerning municipal bonds.

1. White's Tax Exempt Bond Market Ratings
2. The Blue List
3. Munifacts Wire Service
4. The Bond Buyer

White's Municipal Bond Ratings rank where the yields for 20-year bonds would fall in relationship to each other. A very secure municipal bond is assigned the number 100. If a particular municipal bond assigned 100 yields 5.80%, a bond with a rating of 95 should have a yield of approximately 6.1%. White's ratings for municipal bonds reflect the marketability risk associated with the bond.

The Blue List is a publication that is distributed nationally each morning by Standard & Poor's. The Blue List shows municipal bonds owned by dealers, which are being offered for resale. The Blue List is a daily publication that lists approximately 50 to 75% of the dollar volume of all the outstanding secondary issues for sale in the United States. The Blue List is an indicator of the size of the secondary market for municipal securities. The Blue List contains the following information:

- Number of bonds available for sale
- Name of the bond (the issuing authority)
- Coupon rate
- Maturity date of the bond
- Yield or price
- Name of the dealer offering the bond
- Purpose of the bond

The Blue List does not contain the bond's quality rating.

The Munifacts Wire Service carries offerings of securities along with their yields and concessions. It is the principal news wire service that serves the municipal industry.

The Bond Buyer is the name of an organization located in New York City that publishes *The Daily Bond Buyer* and *The Weekly Bond Buyer*. *The Daily Bond Buyer* is published Monday through Friday. It is the industry's national trade paper. *The Weekly Bond Buyer* is published once a week on Monday and it contains all of the same information as appeared in *The Daily Bond Buyer* for the previous week.

Any significant new issue of a municipal bond will be advertised in *The Daily Bond Buyer* through a notice of sale. *The Daily Bond Buyer* normally contains information such as the following concerning the proposed new issues:

- Date, time, and place of sale
- Size of the issue
- Maturity schedule
- Call features
- Type of bond
- Interest payment dates

However, *The Daily Bond Buyer* does not contain the bond's rating. *The Daily Bond Buyer* is used by municipal dealers when placing a bid for competitive municipal issues. The dealers use the Bond Buyer worksheets to prepare their bid and submit it on the bid form.

The Daily Bond Buyer also publishes two measures that are closely followed in the municipal industry.

1. The Placement Ratio
2. The Thirty-Day Visible Supply

The Placement Ratio is the proportion of all competitive and negotiated bond issues over $1 million that were sold during the week. The Placement Ratio is a very good indicator of the demand for municipal securities by investors. It is compiled weekly as of the close of business on Thursday.

An 80% placement ratio means that municipal dealers sold 80% of the total municipal securities underwritten that week. This means that 20% of the total issues that were brought to market were still in the municipal dealers' inventories.

The Thirty-Day Visible Supply is a measure of all municipal offerings that are scheduled to come into the marketplace in the next thirty calendar days. The Thirty-Day Visible Supply volume is a good indicator of the expected supply in the new issue market for municipals. The volume is broken down into two separate numbers.

1. Issues of GO and revenue bonds to be sold on a competitive basis
2. Issues of GO and revenue bonds to be sold on a negotiated basis

Issues of municipal notes are not included in these numbers.

The Bond Buyer also publishes *The Bond Buyer Index*, which is the weekly average yield of a group of twenty general obligation municipal bonds with twenty-year maturities on a given day. *The Bond Buyer Index* is compiled once a week as of Thursday. It is a weekly composite of twenty-year municipal bond yields. *The Index* is composed of dealers' estimates of the yield that a hypothetical twenty-year bond would have to carry if that issue came to market during the week. These estimates are gathered weekly by The Bond Buyer. It is a good indicator to buyers of the yield they would receive if they purchased a similar bond.

The Bond Buyer's Revenue Bond Index is the average weekly yield of twenty-five specific revenue bonds with thirty-year maturities.

NEW ISSUES

In most states, new issues of municipal bonds must be sold by a competitive bidding method rather than by negotiated methods of underwriting. An **official notice of sale** is published in the local newspapers and other publications by the municipality inviting bids to be made by investment bankers. The notice of sale is normally available from the issuer, underwriter, or approving attorney.

The municipality will award the issue to the investment bankers whose bid results in the lowest net interest cost to the issuer. If more than one investment banker bids the same rate, the one bidding the highest premium will get the issue. Each bidder must submit a good-faith deposit check normally in an amount from 2% to 3% of the par value of the bonds being sold.

It should be noted that the good-faith deposit placed with an issuer by an underwriter will

- Be returned to unsuccessful bidders
- Be forfeited if the underwriter fails to perform under the terms of the bid
- Be applied in payment for the new issue at the time of settlement

Under the Tax and Fiscal Responsibility Act of 1982, which became law on September 3, 1982, most debt obligations issued after December 31, 1982, are required to be registered, including those issued by the United States and state and local governments. The primary exceptions to the Act include

- Obligations not offered to the public
- Obligations maturing in one year or less from date of issue
- Obligations sold outside the United States to non-US citizens

These registration requirements for state and municipal obligations became effective on July 1, 1983, at which time the interest income on otherwise tax-exempt obligations was no longer exempt if the registration requirements were not met. Issuers of debt obligations will not be allowed an interest deduction on obligations not meeting the registration requirements, may not reduce earnings and profits for such interest, and are liable for an excise tax equal to 1% of the principal amount for each year from date of issue to maturity. A holder of a bond not in compliance with the registration requirements may not, on disposition thereof, deduct any losses or receive capital gain treatment.

To summarize, a notice of sale for a municipal issue normally contains certain information, such as

- The requirement concerning a good-faith deposit
- The time and date of the sale
- The name of the approving attorney
- Call features associated with the bond, if any
- Registration provisions
- What expenses the bidder must pay
- Bid limitations as to coupon rates
- A statement that the issuer can waive any irregularity in the bid

However, a notice of sale for municipal securities *does not* contain

- The bond's rating
- A statement guaranteeing the ability to service the debt
- A statement describing the security set aside collateralizing the issue
- Offering yields

The notice of sale is a document provided by the issuing municipality, which announces the pending sale of a municipal issue. The notice of sale contains the specific criteria for awarding a bond issue.

In most cases, a syndicate is involved in handling the issue of securities in the primary market. The manager of the syndicate is the dealer who directs all of the underwriting groups' activities. In forming a syndicate account, a municipal syndicate account letter is used. This letter must include such things as the designation of the manager as agent for the account, the duration of the account, each member's participation, and the priority schedule used to determine allocation of the bonds.

Every syndicate must provide for an order period during which orders are accumulated prior to allocation. Customer orders must be given priority over orders submitted by syndicate members or other municipal securities dealers, and priority rules adopted by the syndicate must be disclosed to the public on request. The order of importance, from highest to lowest, relative to priorities that the syndicate manager usually applies in allotting municipal bonds, was mentioned previously.

The most detailed financial information about a new issue of municipal bonds is generally contained in the official statement. The municipal securities dealer underwriting the issue must

- Send each purchaser a preliminary form of official statement, if available.
- Send a final form of the official statement, when available, to each purchaser.
- Furnish a copy of the official statement to other municipal securities dealers, if requested.

OFFICIAL STATEMENT

The **official statement** is the disclosure document for municipal securities and

- Is prepared voluntarily by the issuer with assistance from the investment banker. The Municipal Securities Rulemaking Board (MSRB) cannot require an issuer to prepare an official statement.
- Contains the most detailed financial information concerning a new issue and its issuer, complete information about the bond sale, and facts about the economic and social life of the community.
- On many large national issues, an **offering circular** is prepared by the investment bankers to be mailed to prospective purchasers. It is a summary of many of the important points contained in an official statement.
- Each customer must be furnished with a copy of the official statement by the municipal securities dealer underwriting the issue; if not available in final form, a preliminary form must be sent.
- A copy of the official statement must be given to other municipal dealers by the underwriter, if requested.

The official statement is a document voluntarily provided by an issuing municipality, which discloses material information about a new issue of municipal securities such as

- The purpose of the issue
- The use of the proceeds of the issue
- How the proceeds will be repaid

The official statement contains the most detailed financial information available concerning the new municipal issue. The official statement on a new issue of municipal securities is normally requested by underwriters from issuers for disclosure purposes and is given to retail purchasers. Details of call provisions relating to a municipal security are contained in the official statement. Investors use information in the official statement to assess the credit quality of the securities. The official statement does not have to be filed with the Securities and Exchange Commission (SEC) since municipal securities are exempt from the registration requirements of the 1933 Act. They are also exempt from the issuer reporting requirements of the Securities Exchange Act of 1934. However, municipal securities and all other securities are subject to the antifraud provisions of the Securities and Exchange Act of 1934.

There are, of course, rules applying to specific problems that might be encountered in distributing a new issue. For example, a syndicate concerned with such a new issue may be oversubscribed on the long end. In other words, there is an oversupply of buyers interested in acquiring those bonds with the longest maturities. In such case, certain maturities will only be confirmed during the order period for orders entered as group net. This means that each member of the syndicate will share in these sales in direct proportion to his or her underwriting commitment.

Investment bankers who receive the securities from the issuer offer them for sale in the primary market. A firm that is a member of the underwriting syndicate buys the bonds at the offering price less a **takedown**. A quote of 5.8% less ½ would mean 5.8% yield to maturity less $5 per $1,000. Assume, for example, that the takedown is ¼ of a point. The syndicate members could buy a $1,000 bond for 99¾ and reoffer it at $1,000 par. They would earn ¼ of a point on subsequent sales at par. On a new issue, the spread is the difference between the syndicate cost and the average offering price.

The term **total takedown** in a municipal underwriting is best described as the total of the selling concession and the additional takedown. For example, a municipal underwriting may offer the following compensation:

$$\text{Selling concession} + \text{Additional takedown} = \text{Total takedown}$$
$$\tfrac{1}{4} + \tfrac{1}{8} = \tfrac{3}{8}$$

A member of the underwriting syndicate, when selling the bonds to a customer, would earn ⅜ (total takedown). A member of the selling group would earn ¼ (selling concession) when selling the bonds to a customer. The selling concession is also referred to as the reallowance. A point in reference to the takedown or selling concession is 1% of par value or $10 per $1,000 bond and $50 per $5,000 bond.

The term **concession** may refer to

- The amount of syndicate profit a dealer may be allowed if he sells bonds for another account
- The amount of takedown allowed to a dealer not an account member
- The discount from list one dealer may offer another in the secondary market

The first step in determining a **bid** for a new municipal bond issue is to determine the **scale**. The scale contains offering yields to maturity. Normally, shorter maturities have lower coupons than longer ones. If the reverse is true, the scale is said to be **negative** or **inverted**.

In a municipal securities underwriting, members of the syndicate sign an agreement among underwriters. This document is not signed by the bond counsel, the trustee, or the issuer.

REGULATION

Rules for the municipal securities business are established by the MSRB. Its rules apply to

- Municipal brokers and dealers
- Bank municipal dealer departments
- Organizations acting as financial consultants to municipalities, as well as underwriters of municipal securities

If a municipal securities dealer is registered with the SEC, this indicates that the SEC has received certain background information concerning the organization, such as financial statements, lists of officers, and directors. However, the SEC does not

- Approve the business conduct of the firm
- Approve the financial standing of the broker/dealer
- Guarantee that everyone associated with the firm is duly qualified

MUNICIPAL SECURITIES RULEMAKING BOARD

Before the passage of the Securities Acts Amendments of 1975, the activities of municipal securities broker/dealers and bank municipal dealers were relatively unregulated. However, as a result of the Securities Acts Amendments of 1975, municipal securities broker/dealers and bank dealers must now be registered with the SEC. Under the legislation, banks are allowed to register a separately identifiable department as a municipal securities dealer. The separate department is considered to be the municipal securities dealer and not the bank itself.

The 1975 Act created the MSRB to establish rules for the municipal securities industry. The SEC and National Association of Securities Dealers (NASD) were given the responsibility of enforcing MSRB rules as they apply to broker/dealers. The Board of Governors of the Federal Reserve System, Comptroller of the Currency, and Federal Deposit Insurance Corporation have the responsibility of enforcing MSRB rules as they apply to bank municipal dealers. In the area of fraud, the SEC has exclusive jurisdiction over both municipal securities firms and bank municipal dealers.

MSRB Rules

The MSRB has established rules covering all aspects of the municipal securities business. MSRB rules covering the following areas will be examined:

- Professional qualifications
- Recordkeeping, discretionary accounts, and customer complaints
- Uniform practices
- Customer confirmations
- Quotations and sales reports
- Sales during the underwriting period
- Execution of transactions
- Suitability of recommendations and transactions
- Gifts and gratuities
- Professional advertising
- Disclosure of control relationship

- Financial advisory activities
- Information obtained in fiduciary capacity
- Improper use of assets
- Supervision
- Transactions with employees of other professionals
- Availability of Board rules
- Prices and commissions
- Reciprocal dealings with municipal securities investment companies
- Disclosures in connection with new issues
- Arbitration

As previously mentioned, prior to the Securities Acts Amendments of 1975, broker/dealers engaged exclusively in municipal securities transactions were not required to be registered with the SEC. The Securities Acts Amendments of 1975 required municipal securities broker/dealers to register with the SEC. This piece of legislation created a new self-regulatory organization, the MSRB, to formulate rules to regulate all firms transacting business in municipal securities including bank municipal dealer departments.

The MSRB has the primary rule-making authority for municipal securities broker/dealers subject to oversight by the SEC. However, the MSRB does not have examiners for inspections of municipal broker/dealers. Therefore, MSRB rules must be enforced by other organizations on behalf of the MSRB. For broker/dealers, MSRB rules are enforced by

- The SEC
- The NASD

For bank municipal dealer departments, MSRB rules are enforced by

- The Board of Governors of the Federal Reserve System
- The Comptroller of the Currency
- The Federal Deposit Insurance Corporation (FDIC)

The SEC has regulatory authority over both broker/dealers and bank municipal dealer departments in the area of fraud. MSRB rules, in addition to regulating municipal broker/dealers and bank municipal dealer departments, also regulate organizations acting as consultants to municipalities and underwriters of municipal securities. However, the MSRB has no rule-making authority over the issuers of municipal securities (cities, towns, states). MSRB rules are enforced by the NASD on the New York Stock Exchange and NASD member firms.

Commissions charged on municipal securities transactions are fully negotiable under the MSRB and SEC rules. The MSRB cannot set minimum commission rates to be charged on municipal transactions. However, the MSRB has established rules and regulations in areas such as

- Qualification examinations
- Uniform settlement procedures
- Quotations
- Gifts and gratuities
- Professional advertising
- Execution of transactions

When a municipal securities broker/dealer registers with the SEC, the SEC requests certain background organization information. However, as previously mentioned, registration with the SEC does not imply that the

- SEC has approved the financial standing of the registrant
- SEC has approved the business conduct of the registrant
- SEC has determined that all persons associated with the registrant are duly qualified under all securities laws

Professional qualifications. A municipal securities broker/dealer is not allowed to engage in the business of effecting transactions in municipal securities unless the firm and every natural person associated with the firm is registered in accordance with the rules of the Board.

Every municipal securities firm must register at least two municipal securities principals and one financial and operations principal with the following exceptions:

- If the municipal securities broker/dealer is a member of the NASD and conducts a general securities business, or if the municipal securities firm has fewer than eleven persons associated with it in whatever capacity, it must qualify only one municipal securities principal.
- Bank municipal dealers do not have to qualify a financial and operations principal. NASD member firms that have a person qualified as a financial and operations principal under NASD rules are deemed to have satisfied the MSRB requirement of having a financial and operations principal.

Municipal securities principals are persons engaged directly in the management or supervision of the firm's municipal securities business. Financial and operations principals are persons responsible for

- Approval of financial reports required by the SEC or any self-regulatory organization, approving all transactions
- Overall supervision of individuals who assist in the preparation of such reports and the maintenance of the firm's books and records

In order to be registered as a municipal securities principal or a financial and operations principal, a person must pass a comprehensive examination, unless he or she qualifies for exemption. Persons who perform only clerical or ministerial functions and who do not solicit orders or communicate with customers do not have to be registered.

The term **municipal securities representative** refers to a person associated with a municipal securities broker or dealer, other than in a supervisory or clerical capacity, who engages in one or more of the following activities:

- Underwriting, trading, or sales of municipal securities
- Financial advisory or consulting services for issuers in connection with the issuance of municipal securities
- Research or the rendering of advice with respect to municipal securities
- Any activities other than those specifically enumerated above that involve communications directly or indirectly with public investors in municipal securities

A municipal securities representative who has not been previously qualified as a municipal securities representative cannot transact business with the public or be compensated on a commission basis for transactions in municipal securities for a period of at least ninety days following commencement of the person's association with the firm. During this ninety-day period, the trainee must be compensated on a straight salary and may discuss the purchase and sale of municipal securities with other securities dealers. However, the trainee cannot do such things as

- Discuss with individual customers the sale of municipal securities
- Advise individual customers or institutions, such as insurance companies or banks, to purchase municipal securities
- Purchase municipal securities for the investment portfolio of a bank or insurance company

A trainee must qualify as a municipal securities representative within 180 days following the commencement of the trainee's association with the firm or he or she must cease performing any of the functions of a municipal securities representative. A municipal securities representative, once s/he is qualified, can sell all types of municipal securities and US government and agency issues, including

- General obligation municipal bonds
- Revenue bonds
- Special tax bonds
- New Housing Authority bonds (PHA bonds)
- Industrial revenue bonds
- Short-term tax exempts (PNs)
- US Treasury bills, notes, and bonds
- Federal agency issues

However, a person who qualifies **solely** as a municipal securities representative cannot engage in sales of

- Corporate stocks or bonds
- Investment company shares, including tax-exempt unit investment trusts and municipal bond funds
- Direct participation programs

Recordkeeping. MSRB rules concerning recordkeeping require certain books and records to be maintained by a municipal dealer and kept current. These include

- Records of original entry—**blotters**
- Account records showing all activity in customer accounts
- Securities records showing all positions for each municipal security
- Subsidiary records reflecting municipal securities in transfer and securities borrowed or loaned
- Put options and repurchase agreements (on municipal securities)
- Records for agency transactions and principal transactions
- Records of syndicate transactions
- Copies of confirmations and certain other notices to customers
- Financial records, customer account information, and customer complaints

Administration of discretionary and other accounts. Except for institutional accounts, municipal securities broker/dealers must maintain a record for each customer containing the following information as far as it is applicable:

- Customer's name and residence or principal business address
- Whether the customer is of legal age (the date of birth does not have to be obtained)
- Tax identification or Social Security number
- Occupation
- Name and address of employer
- Name and address of beneficial owner or owners of such account if other than the customer and if transactions are to be confirmed to such owner or owners
- Signature of the municipal securities representative or general securities representative introducing the account and the signature of a municipal or general securities principal indicating acceptance of the account
- With respect to discretionary accounts, the customer's written authorization to exercise discretionary power or authority with respect to the account, written approval of the municipal securities principal who supervises the account, and written approval of a municipal securities principal with respect to each transaction in the account, indicating the time and date of approval
- Whether the customer is employed by another broker, dealer, or municipal securities dealer
- In connection with the hypothecation of the customer's securities, the written authorization of the customer

Each broker/dealer must obtain this information at or before the completion of a transaction in municipal securities, with or for the account of a customer. All of this information, with the exception of the tax identification or Social Security number, must be obtained prior to the settlement of a transaction. Transactions in discretionary accounts must not be effected except to the extent clearly permitted by the prior written authorization of the customer and accepted in writing by the principal. A municipal securities principal must approve the discretionary account in writing before it can be accepted by the firm. A municipal securities principal must promptly review and approve in writing each transaction in municipal securities effected with or for a discretionary account. The principal must, at regular and frequent intervals, review all customer accounts in which transactions in municipal securities are effected, to detect and prevent irregularities and abuses. The MSRB principal reviewing transactions in a discretionary account for a customer would be concerned with such things as

- Whether the transaction was effected in accordance with discretionary account authorization
- Whether the price is fair and equitable for the security

A customer, under MSRB rules in a discretionary account, does not have to authorize each transaction in writing for the account. Once the discretionary authorization papers are signed by the customer, then discretionary powers are given to another person. The person who has the discretionary power can decide what securities to buy or sell without prior approval of each transaction by the customer.

The term **discretionary account** means the account of a customer with respect to which a broker/dealer is authorized to determine what municipal securities will be purchased, sold, or exchanged by or for the account. Transactions in such an account may only be effected if the broker/dealer first determines that it is suitable for the customer, or unless it is specifically authorized by the customer.

Under MSRB rules, a firm handling a discretionary account for a customer

- May not effect transactions that are excessive in size or frequency in view of the resources of the customer
- Must approve each discretionary order in writing on the day the order is entered; it does not have to be approved prior to its entry

Assume an employee of a municipal securities dealer wants to open a discretionary account and have a registered representative in the same office handle the account. Does the employee have to give the registered representative written authorization before trades can be executed on a discretionary basis? The answer is "yes." Every discretionary account requires prior written authorization even if the person owning the account is an associated person with the municipal dealer.

Customer complaints. Every municipal securities broker/dealer must make and keep current a record of all written complaints of customers and those persons acting on behalf of customers, and what action, if any, has been taken in connection with each complaint. **Complaint** means any written statement alleging a grievance involving activities of the broker or dealer with respect to anything concerning the customer's account.

The rules require municipal securities brokers and dealers to establish, maintain, and enforce written supervisory procedures to assure compliance with MSRB rules. One of the required procedures is the designation of at least one qualified municipal securities principal as responsible for supervising the activities in municipal securities of the broker/dealer and at least one such individual for each branch office. Another requirement is the prompt review and written approval by the designated municipal securities principal (or by a general securities principal specifically authorized by rules of the Board) of the handling of all written customer complaints pertaining to transactions in municipal securities. Such review and written approval is required for

- The opening of each customer account introduced and carried by a municipal securities broker or dealer in which transactions in municipal securities may be effected
- Each transaction in municipal securities
- The handling of all written customer complaints pertaining to transactions in municipal securities
- All correspondence pertaining to the solicitation or execution of transactions in municipal securities

Uniform Practice Rules

The MSRB has also established uniform practice rules. These rules concern definitions and rules of trading concerning settlement date definitions, information that must be contained in confirmations, and delivery of securities.

The **settlement date** is the day used in price and interest computations and the day delivery is due unless otherwise agreed by the parties. A **business day** is one recognized by the NASD as a day on which securities transactions may be settled. Settlement dates are

- For *cash* transactions, trade date and settlement date are the same day.
- For *regular way* transactions, the third business day following the trade date. The statement or term *T + 3* for a municipal trade indicates the municipal security settles regular way in three business days.
- For *when, as, and if issued* transactions, settlement date is a date agreed upon by both parties which shall not be before the normal settlement date.

MSRB rules are similar to NASD rules concerning confirmations and delivery of securities. However, it is important to point to certain MSRB rules in these areas.

- The minimum denomination municipal bonds are available in is $1,000. However, municipal bonds are more frequently issued with $5,000 denominations. This is true whether the bonds are in bearer or registered form. Municipal bonds are also issued in book entry form.
- A *good delivery* of a security is accomplished when the seller delivers a properly endorsed certificate with all legal items attached to the buyer.
- When municipal securities are delivered by one municipal securities dealer to another, it is assumed that (unless otherwise agreed), the following will be true for a good delivery:
  - Trade will settle three business days from the trade date.
  - Bond is in bearer form.
  - Bond is noncallable.
  - Legal opinion will accompany the bond (unless the bond is sold ex-legal).
  - Bonds are in denominations of $1,000 or $5,000.
  - Seller delivers to the buyer in the buyer's office on settlement date.

- Bond number, coupon rate, and maturity date can be identified on the certificate.
- Delivery of a municipal securities certificate can be rejected for
  - A missing legal opinion.
  - No assignment with a registered bond.
  - A mutilated coupon.
  - Incorrect delivery instructions.
  - The bonds being sold as bearer and delivered in registered form.

However, under MSRB rules, a delivery of a municipal security cannot be rejected for a missing CUSIP number on the certificate. In order for a municipal securities dealer to make a good delivery to the purchaser of municipal bonds that are in default, only unpaid coupons should be attached.

- The following is a summary of the information that must be contained on a confirmation under MSRB rules:
  - Trade and settlement dates
  - Capacity in which the transaction was effected
    - A principal for its own account
    - An agent for the customer
    - An agent for a person other than the customer
    - An agent for both the customer and another person
  - Name, address and telephone number of the dealer
  - The total dollar amount of the transaction
  - The name of the issuer
  - A description of the security
  - A designation whether the securities were purchased or sold
  - The total dollar amount of any commission
  - Whether the bonds are callable

However, MSRB rules *do not* require a confirmation to contain information such as

- Debt service coverage for a revenue bond
- The quality rating for a municipal bond
- The commission per bond (only the total commission must be shown)
- The taxable equivalent yield or full details of the call feature
- The name of the paying agent

Quotations. Quotations for municipal securities must be bona fide. Quotations must not be distributed or published unless they represent a bona fide bid for, of offer of, municipal securities by the broker or dealer making the quotation. All quotations, unless otherwise indicated at the time made, shall be subject to prior purchase or sale and to subsequent change in price. This in no way prohibits requests for bids or offers or nominal quotations if such quotations are clearly stated as such when made. A **nominal quotation** or **subject quotation** means an indication of price given solely for informational purposes. MSRB rules concerning quotations relating to municipal securities cover

- The distribution of bids
- The distribution of offers
- Requests for bids
- Requests for offers

Prices stated in a quotation must be based on the best judgment of the broker/dealer of the fair market value of the municipal securities that are the subject of the quotation. A quotation is considered **bona fide** if the broker/dealer making it is prepared to purchase or sell the security at the price stated in the quotation and under the conditions, if any, specified when the quotation is made. No broker/dealer must knowingly misrepresent a quotation relating to municipal securities made by another broker/dealer.

No municipal securities broker/dealer participating in a joint account shall, together with other participants in the account, distribute or publish quotations relating to the securities which are the subject of the account, if the quotations indicate more than one market for the same securities.

MSRB rules prohibit a municipal securities dealer from giving a quotation relating to municipal securities unless the quotation represents a bona fide bid for, or offer of, securities. A municipal dealer can publish a quotation stating bid wanted (BW) or offer wanted (OW). These are considered nominal quotations.

Under MSRB Rule G-13, the price stated in a quotation for municipal securities must be based on the best judgment of the person making the quotation as to the fair market value of the securities at the time the quotation is made.

MSRB rules do not require that the price stated in a quotation represent only the fair market value of the securities for which the quotation is made, but rather that the price stated has a reasonable relationship to the fair market value of the securities, taking into account all relevant circumstances, such as a firm's inventory position overall and in respect of a particular security, and a firm's anticipation of the direction of the movement of the market for the securities. The following are three examples of how this provision would apply:

1. Assume that a dealer submits a bid for bonds, knowing that they have been called by the issuer. The bonds are not general market bonds and the fact that they have been called is not widely known. While called bonds ordinarily trade at a premium, the dealer's bid is based on the value of the bonds as though they had not been called, and is accepted by the dealer on the other side of the trade who is unaware of the called status of the bonds. In these circumstances, the bid clearly would not have been based on the best judgment of the dealer making it as to the fair market value of the bonds.

2. The provision would also apply to the situation in which a dealer submits a bid for bonds based on valuations obtained from independent sources, which in turn are based on mistaken assumptions concerning the nature of the securities in question. The circumstances indicate that the dealer submitting the bid knows that the securities have a substantially greater market value than the price bid, but the fact that independent valuations were obtained, albeit based on mistaken facts, clouds the dealer's culpability. The best judgment standard of this rule would apply in this situation.

3. The provision would also apply in the situation in which a dealer makes a bid or offer of a security without any knowledge as to the value of the security or the value of comparable securities. While the Board does not intend that the best judgment of a dealer as to the fair market value of a security would be second-guessed for purposes of the rule, the Board does intend that the dealer be required to act responsibly and to exercise some judgment in submitting a quotation. In other words, a quotation that has been *pulled out of the air* is not based on the best judgment of the dealer and, in the interests of promoting free and open markets in municipal securities, should not be encouraged.

Reports of sales or purchases. No municipal broker/dealer or associated person can distribute or publish any report of a purchase or sale of municipal securities unless they have no reason to believe that the reported transaction is fictitious or to further any fraudulent, deceptive, or manipulative purposes.

Under MSRB rules, a municipal securities dealer that distributes or publishes a report of a sale or purchase of municipal securities is required to know or have reason to believe that the transaction is not fictitious or in furtherance of any fraudulent, misleading, or deceptive purpose. MSRB rules do not require the reporting of sales or purchases of municipal securities, but establishes requirements for any such report. A report of a short sale is not prohibited under MSRB rules. Short sales of municipal securities are allowed but not commonly entered into by a municipal securities dealer.

Sales during the underwriting period. Specific rules apply to orders placed during the underwriting period of a new issue of municipal securities. The rules require that certain information be made available to members of the syndicate concerning orders for securities held in the syndicate. Providing members of a syndicate with access to information concerning any orders is appropriate since all members of the syndicate have a proprietary interest in the securities owned by the syndicate and are, therefore, entitled to information concerning the sale of such securities.

Execution of transactions. Broker/dealers, when executing a municipal securities transaction for a customer, must make a reasonable effort to obtain a price for the customer that is fair and reasonable in relation to prevailing market conditions. A broker/dealer acting as a **broker's broker** shall be under the same obligation. (A broker's broker is one who effects transactions for other broker/dealers.)

Suitability of recommendations and transactions. A broker/dealer must not recommend a transaction to a customer unless the broker/dealer, after reasonable inquiry

- Has reasonable grounds to believe that the recommendation is suitable for such customer on the basis of information furnished by the customer concerning the customer's financial background, tax status,

investment objectives, and any other similar information concerning the customer known by the broker/dealer
- Has no reasonable grounds to believe that the recommendation is unsuitable if all such information concerning the customer is not furnished or known

Therefore, under MSRB rules, when a municipal securities dealer is attempting to determine suitability, it is reasonable to question a customer concerning

- Investment objectives
- Tax bracket or tax status
- Financial background
- State of residence
- Structure of the customer's existing portfolio

It is not necessary under MSRB rules to question a customer concerning his or her investment experience. However, many municipal firms do inquire about a customer's investment experience.

If a broker/dealer informs a customer that a transaction is unsuitable, the broker/dealer may afterward provide advice concerning the securities, if so requested by the customer, and execute transactions in the securities if the customer so directs the representative.

Churning is prohibited. Transactions must not be recommended or effected for a discretionary account that are excessive in size or frequency in view of information known to the broker or dealer concerning the customer's financial background, tax status, and investment objectives.

Gifts and gratuities. In the conduct of their business, brokers and dealers in municipal securities must deal fairly with all persons and cannot engage in any deceptive, dishonest, or unfair practice. No municipal securities broker or dealer shall, directly or indirectly, give or permit to be given, any service or gift with value in excess of $100 per year to a person other than an employee or partner of the broker or dealer if the payments or services relate to the municipal securities activities of the employer of the recipient of the payment or service. The term *employer* includes a principal for whom the recipient is acting as agent or representative. This rule against giving anything of value in excess of $100 per year to a person will not

- Be deemed to prohibit occasional gifts of meals or tickets to theatrical, sporting, and other entertainment events; the sponsoring of Internal Revenue Service (IRS)-recognized legitimate business functions; or gifts or reminder advertising, provided that such gifts are not so frequent or so expensive as to raise a suggestion of conduct inconsistent with high standards of professional ethics
- Apply to contracts of employment with or compensation for services rendered by another person provided there exists prior to the employment or rendering of service, a written agreement between the broker/dealer and the person performing such services, which includes the nature of the services, the amount of the proposed compensation, and the written consent of the person's employer

Under MSRB rules, the following gifts and gratuities would be permitted:

- Reminder advertising valued at $50
- Tickets to a sporting event valued at $100
- A restaurant bill valued at $130 for a customer and a dealer
- Accommodations at an economic conference for a customer valued at $180
- A cash gift of $100
- A dinner and a hockey game for a customer

Under MSRB rules, a municipal securities representative cannot make a gift in excess of $100 per year to

- A customer of the municipal securities representative
- A treasurer of an issuer of municipal securities
- An employee of another municipal dealer who executes transactions for the representative's firm

The following gifts made by a municipal securities representative to a customer would be in violation of the MSRB rules and therefore prohibited:

- A two-week expense-paid trip to Hawaii
- A cash gift of $500
- A television that costs $350
- A weekly gift of $25
- Vintage wine valued at $140

- A washing machine valued at $325
- A Cadillac valued at $22,600
- A yacht valued at $45,000
- A condominium valued at $169,900

Professional advertising. Advertising or similar communications must not contain information concerning the facilities, services, or skills of the broker or dealer that is materially false or misleading. Furthermore, such communications must be approved in writing by a municipal securities principal or general securities principal prior to first use. Written approval of a principal is not required before each use of the ad, only the first use. Records of all such communications must be made and kept current in a separate file. Advertising relating to municipal securities would include offering circulars, market letters, and summaries of official statements. However, an official statement issued by a municipality is not considered advertising under MSRB rules.

In an advertisement, a municipal dealer could state that the firm guarantees timely execution of orders. However, a municipal dealer could not guarantee

- That they will repurchase a customer's bonds at cost
- That the customer will always collect interest on the bonds
- That the customer will realize capital gains on the sale of the bonds

Disclosure of control relationship. A **control relationship** is deemed to exist if a broker, dealer, or municipal securities dealer controls, is controlled by, or is under common control with the issuer of the security or a person other than the issuer who is obligated with respect to debt service on the security. For example, a control position would exist between a municipal dealer and an issuer when an officer or director of the underwriter is in a position of authority over the issuer of the municipal bonds. No broker or dealer can effect a transaction in a municipal security for the discretionary account of a customer if that broker or dealer has a control relationship unless, before entering into a contract with the customer, the broker or dealer discloses the nature of the control relationship to the customer. The disclosure must either be in writing or else supplemented by the sending of a written disclosure on the confirmation at or before the completion of the transaction.

Financial advisory activities. The purpose of MSRB rules is to establish ethical standards and disclosure requirements for brokers or dealers who act as financial advisors to issuers of municipal securities. A financial advisory relationship exists when a broker or dealer renders or enters into an agreement to render financial advisory or consultant services for an issuer with respect to new issues of municipal securities for compensation. This includes advice concerning the structure, timing, and terms relating to an issue. Such a relationship does not exist, however, when such advice is rendered by a broker or dealer in the course of acting as an underwriter.

A financial advisory relationship must be evidenced in writing prior to, upon, or promptly after, the beginning of the relationship (or promptly after the selection of the issuer if the issuer has not been determined at the time the relationship commences). The writing must set forth the basis of compensation forces to be rendered, including provisions relating to the deposit of funds with or use of fiduciary or agency services offered by the broker or dealer, or any person in a control relationship with the broker or dealer.

No broker, dealer, or municipal securities dealer having a financial advisory relationship with respect to a new issue of municipal securities can acquire as principal (alone or with others) any portion of such issue or arrange for such acquisition by a control person unless

- If the issue is to be sold by the issuer on a negotiated basis

  - The financial advisory relationship has been terminated in writing, and at or after termination, the issuer has expressly consented in writing to such acquisition or participation.
  - The broker or dealer has expressly disclosed in writing to the issuer at or before such termination that there may be a conflict in changing from the capacity of financial advisor to purchaser and the issuer has acknowledged receipt of such disclosure in writing, and
  - The broker or dealer has expressly disclosed in writing to the issuer at or before such termination the source and anticipated amount of all remuneration and the issuer has expressly acknowledged in writing the receipt of such disclosure, or

- If the issue is to be sold by the issuer at competitive bid, the issuer has expressly consented in writing prior to the bid to such acquisition or participation.

This rule does not prohibit a broker or dealer having such a financial advisory relationship with respect to a new issue from purchasing such securities from an underwriter for its own trading account or for the account of customers so long as the action is not intended to contravene the intent of the rule. Brokers or dealers subject to this rule must maintain a copy of the written disclosures, acknowledgments, and consents required in a separate file.

Such a financial advisory relationship must be disclosed in writing to each customer who purchases such securities from the broker or dealer at or before the completion of the transaction with the customer.

Information obtained in a fiduciary capacity. No broker or dealer having access to confidential, non-public information concerning the ownership of municipal securities that was obtained in the course of acting in a fiduciary or agency capacity for an issuer or for another broker or dealer shall use such information to solicit purchases, sales or exchanges of municipal securities except with the consent of such issuer or broker or dealer, or person on whose behalf the information was given.

Improper use of assets. No broker or dealer shall make improper use of municipal securities or funds held on behalf of another person. Furthermore, no broker or dealer shall guarantee a customer against loss in or share in the profits or losses of

- An account carried or introduced by the broker or dealer
- A transaction in municipal securities with or for a customer

Bona fide put options and repurchase agreements ordinarily issued in the course of business are not guarantees against loss and may be used.

These rules do not prohibit an associated person of a broker or dealer from participating as an individual in an investment partnership or joint account providing that the participation is solely in direct proportion to the financial contribution made by the person to the partnership or account.

Supervision. Each broker or dealer is obligated to supervise the activities of its associated persons with respect to municipal securities and the conduct of its municipal securities business. One or more municipal securities principals and financial and operations principals must be designated as responsible for supervising activities and business and enforcing supervisory procedures.

Brokers and dealers must establish, maintain, and enforce written supervisory procedures to assure compliance with the rules of the MSRB and other rules and regulations. At a minimum, such procedures must provide for

- The designation of at least one duly qualified municipal securities principal as responsible for supervision of the associated persons of the broker or dealer with respect to municipal securities. In addition, at least one duly qualified municipal securities principal should be designated for supervising such activities in municipal securities for each branch office or other location in which an associated person engages in such activities.
- The prompt review and written approval of all municipal transactions by the designated municipal securities principal (or general securities principal).

Under MSRB rules, all municipal securities transactions must be approved in writing by a municipal securities principal. This is normally done at the end of the trading day when the order tickets or purchase and sales journal are reviewed and initialed by the municipal securities principal. All orders must be approved in writing by a municipal securities principal including orders entered by

- Individuals
- Trust departments
- Insurance companies
- Commercial banks

Transactions with employees of other professionals. A broker or dealer is prohibited from opening or maintaining an account in which municipal securities transactions may be effected for a customer who is employed by, or the partner of, another municipal securities broker or dealer, or for the spouse or minor child of such person, unless the firm first gives written notice to the broker or dealer by whom the person is employed or with whom the person is a partner.

In such accounts, transactions in municipal securities may not be effected unless the broker or dealer

- Simultaneously sends the employer a duplicate copy of each confirmation sent to the customer
- Acts in accordance with any written instructions the employer may have provided with respect to transactions effected

If the employing dealer does not issue any special instructions to the firm carrying the account, then monthly statements do not have to be sent by the carrying firm to the employing firm. However, duplicate copies of confirmations must still be sent by the carrying firm to the employing firm.

Assume First Ohio, a municipal securities dealer, has been asked to open an account for Mrs. Jones. Mrs. Jones's husband is employed by California Securities Corporation, which is also a municipal securities dealer. Under MSRB rules, First Ohio may open an account for Mrs. Jones, but it must give written notice to California Securities Corporation.

Under MSRB rules, if an employee of Municipal Securities A wants to open an account with Municipal Securities B, Municipal Securities Dealer B must

- Before establishing the account, send written notification to Dealer A.
- Accept orders only in full compliance with written instructions provided by Municipal Securities Dealer A.
- Submit duplicate copies of transaction confirmations to Dealer A.

Availability of Board Rules

Municipal securities brokers and dealers must keep a copy of the MSRB rules in each office in which any activities covered by the rules may occur. These rules must be available for examination by customers promptly on request.

Prices and Commissions

No municipal securities broker or dealer shall purchase such securities for its own account from a customer, or sell from its own account to a customer, except at an aggregate price (including markdowns or markups) that is fair and reasonable, taking into consideration all relevant factors, including

- The best judgment of the broker or dealer as to the fair market value of the securities at the time of the transaction, and of any securities exchanged or traded in connection with the transaction
- The expense involved in effecting the transaction
- The fact that the broker or dealer is entitled to a profit
- The total dollar amount of the transaction
- The price or yield of the security
- The maturity of the security

No municipal securities broker or dealer shall purchase or sell municipal securities as agent for a customer for a commission or service charge in excess of a fair and reasonable amount, taking into consideration all relevant factors, including

- The availability of the securities involved in the transaction
- The expense of executing or filing the customer's order
- The value of the service rendered by the broker or dealer
- The amount of any other compensation received in connection with the transactions

However, certain factors should not be considered by a municipal securities dealer in determining the amount of compensation to be charged on a particular transaction. Factors that should not be considered include

- The customer's financial status
- The value of the dealer's inventory

The MSRB does not have a 5% markup policy. To determine whether a markup on a particular municipal transaction is fair, the previously mentioned factors must be considered.

Commissions charged on a municipal securities transaction under MSRB rules are fully negotiable between dealers and customers. The MSRB cannot set minimum rates since this would be illegal under federal law. A municipal dealer also cannot recover depreciation in its inventory through higher markups. For example, assume a municipal dealer bought a particular municipal bond for $1,000. The bond, after two weeks, is selling at $900 as a result of an increase in interest rates. The municipal dealer cannot take into consideration the market decline of $200 in determining the markup. The markup must be computed from the market price and not the cost.

MSRB rules require that if a transaction in callable securities is effected on a yield basis, dollar prices must be calculated to the lower of the price to call or the price to maturity.

RECIPROCAL DEALINGS WITH MUNICIPAL SECURITIES INVESTMENT COMPANIES

Municipal securities firms are not permitted to solicit transactions in municipal securities from an investment company as compensation for shares sold of the investment company.

DISCLOSURES IN CONNECTION WITH NEW ISSUES

When a new issue is being sold, the broker or dealer must, at or prior to the time of sending a final written confirmation of the transaction, send the customer

- A copy of the official statement in final form, voluntarily furnished by or on behalf of the issuer (or an abstract or other summary of such statement prepared by the municipal securities broker or dealer).
- In connection with a negotiated sale of a new issue, the following information concerning the underwriting arrangements:
  - Underwriting spread.
  - Amount of any fee received by the broker or dealer as agent for the issuer in the distribution of the securities, and
  - Initial offering price for each maturity in the issue to be offered by the underwriters.

Therefore, under MSRB rules, a customer purchasing a new issue of municipal securities must be given

- An official statement, assuming one is available, on the issue
- A confirmation stating the purchase price of the security

If the official statement in final form is not available when the final confirmation is sent, an official statement in preliminary form, if any, shall be sent. However, the official statement in final form (or abstract or summary thereof) must be sent to the customer promptly after it becomes available to the broker or dealer. The documents referred to in these rules must also be sent, on request, to any broker or dealer to which new issue municipal securities are sold.

ARBITRATION

Every municipal securities broker or dealer is subject to an arbitration code thoroughly described in the rules. The rules cover the appointment of committees and procedures. Matters subject to arbitration include every claim, dispute or controversy arising out of, or in connection with, the municipal securities activities of a municipal securities broker or dealer. Any claim, dispute, or controversy shall be submitted to the arbitration pursuant to the arbitration code at the instance of

- A municipal securities broker or dealer against another such broker or dealer
- A person other than a municipal securities broker or dealer against such a broker or dealer
- A municipal securities broker or dealer against a person other than a municipal securities broker or dealer provided that the submission to arbitration is pursuant to a specified agreement to arbitrate

SEC ANTIFRAUD RULES

The 1934 Securities and Exchange Act antifraud provisions prohibit actions, such as

- Indicating to customers that an all-or-none municipal underwriting is a firm commitment
- Omitting material information about a municipal issue from a dealer's offering circular
- Using a manipulative technique to affect the price of a municipal security

However, selling a municipal security short is allowed under SEC and MSRB rules. Municipal securities are not normally sold short by traders because the trading market for many municipal securities is limited which makes covering the short position a difficult task.

MUNICIPAL BOND SWAPPING

A municipal bond swap is a transaction in which municipal bonds in one portfolio are sold and the proceeds are used to purchase other municipals of comparable value. One main purpose of swapping municipal bonds is to establish a capital loss. A capital loss results if the municipal bond is sold at a price less than the investor's cost. The proceeds of the sale can be used to buy another municipal bond with a different coupon, maturity, or issuer.

Municipal bond swaps can be used in order to

- Consolidate holdings into more manageable (and marketable) lots

- Gain an increased amount of current income
- Gain an increased yield to maturity
- Establish a loss to offset capital gains or income
- Improve cash flow
- Upgrade the quality of his holdings

INSURANCE

The following agencies insure municipal bonds:

- Municipal Bond Insurance Association (MBIA)
- American Municipal Bond Assurance Corporation (AMBAC)
- Financial Guaranty Insurance Company (FGIC)
- Bond Investors Guaranty (BIG)

When a municipal issue is insured, the payment of interest and principal is guaranteed by the insurance company in the event of the issuer's default. Insured municipal bonds normally carry a AAA rating. The primary reason a municipality would insure a new issue of municipal bonds would be to lower the coupon rate on the issue.

RATING SERVICES

As with corporate securities, state and municipal securities are also rated by various agencies, the chief examples of which are Standard & Poor's Corporation (S&P), Moody's Investor's Service, and Fitch's Investor's Service. Moody's does not rate bonds of issuers having less than $600,000 in debt financing. Therefore, a municipal bond may be nonrated because the issuer's debt is relatively small.

Because of local interest in local securities, there are a number of smaller rating services that specialize in rating local securities, especially those too small for the large national organizations to investigate.

The state and municipal ratings are similar to the corporate ratings described earlier, except that "C" is the lowest-rated bond and is awarded to those municipal securities that have extremely poor prospects of ever achieving a recognized investment standing. It must be remembered that the rating services emphasize default risk, not market risk, yield, or marketability.

Because it is quite difficult to investigate all of the relevant facts surrounding municipal issues (such as the legality of the issue, the economic condition and prospects of the issuing unit, the present and past financial condition), the rating services provide a distinct and valuable service to the investment community. Because of these very extensive and detailed investigations, the bond rating directly affects the interest rate that the municipality will be forced to pay on a proposed issue.

It is a usual practice to rate the issue **before** it is marketed by rating the municipality in general. For example, all of the Macon County, Georgia, GOs carry the same rating. In other situations, separate issues may be rated individually. For example, Cook County, Illinois, GOs are rated together, but Cook County School District and High School bonds are individually rated.

As the bond ratings are reviewed periodically, especially in connection with a new issue, the rating may change. It is not uncommon for a rating change from Aa to A to mean an additional fifty basis points (½ of 1%) on the interest rate. A change from a Baa would be even worse.

S&P and Moody's ratings of municipal bonds emphasize the default risk associated with the bonds. Some municipal bonds are not rated because the issuer's total debt is relatively small, as previously mentioned. (See Exhibit 4.2.)

Exhibit 4.2: Bond Rating Service Categories

STANDARD AND POOR'S BOND RATINGS*

AAA	Highest grade
AA	High grade
A	Upper medium grade
BBB	Medium grade
BB	Lower medium grade
B	Speculative
CCC	Outright speculation
CC	Outright speculation
C	Reserved for income bonds
DDD	No interest being paid

DD	In default
D	Relative salvage value

* For Standard & Poor's categories AA to BB, a plus sign is added to show high relative standing, a minus sign to show low relative standing.

MOODY'S BOND RATINGS**

Aaa	Best quality
Aa	High quality
A	High medium grade
Baa	Lower medium grade
Ba	Possess speculative elements
B	Generally lack characteristics of desirable investment
Caa	Poor standing, may be in default
Ca	Speculative in a high degree, often in default
C	Lowest grade

** For Moody's rating categories, bonds of the highest quality within a grade are designated by adding a "1" (e.g., A-1 and Baa-1).

The first four rating categories for Standard & Poor's and Moody's represent municipal bonds that are considered "investment grade": If a municipal bond is considered investment grade, it means that the bond has a high probability of paying interest and principal. Banking law in certain states requires that securities in a bank's portfolio be both marketable and investment grade.

Therefore, for Standard & Poor's, the following ratings are considered investment grade:

1. AAA
2. AA
3. A
4. BBB

For Moody's, the following ratings are considered investment grade:

1. Aaa
2. Aa
3. A
4. Baa

Therefore, bonds with speculative characteristics for Standard & Poor's begins with ratings of BB and for Moody's Ba. The Rating Services must be given current financial information by the municipal issuer.

Assume a customer purchases a municipal bond rated Aaa by Moody's. The customer is primarily interested in increasing his return but still maintaining investment grade quality.

A municipal bond rated A by Moody's can be described as an investment grade municipal bond with high or medium quality.

DEBT SERVICE

The term **debt service** refers to the total payment needed for interest on and repayment of the principal amount of the debt. For example, the debt service on a mortgage would be the total interest and principal charge required on a monthly basis.

Serial municipal bonds mature in installments on successive dates. Serial issues may have a level debt service. The term **level debt service** means that the annual combined payments of principal and interest are equal each year and the bonds will be retired by the final maturity date.

If a new municipal serial bond issue has a level debt service, then principal payments will increase and interest payments will decrease as the bond approaches maturity. This is because in the early years, a greater portion of the payment is applied on the interest and less on the principal. As the bond approaches maturity, a greater portion of the payment is applied on the principal.

TAX RATE

Tax rates for municipalities on real property are expressed in mils. A mil is 1/10 of a cent. It can also be stated at $1 per $1,000 of assessed valuation. Therefore, a 7 mil would produce $7 in tax revenues for each

$1,000 of assessed valuation. A mil, when stated in decimal form, is 0.001 (1/10 of one cent). Therefore, 5 mils could be stated as 0.005 or 7 mils at .007.

The mil rate is used to determine the dollar amount of tax revenue generated on real property. For example, assume a municipality has a 7-mil tax rate on $1 million of assessed valuation. What amount of tax revenues will be generated by this tax rate?

The computation can be done in either of two ways.

1. Amount of assessed valuation x Mil rate expressed as a decimal

$$\text{Assessed valuation} \quad x \quad \text{Mil rate as decimal} \quad = \text{Tax revenues generated}$$
$$\$1,000,000 \quad x \quad .007 \quad = \$7,000$$

2. Determining the number of thousand dollars of assessed valuation x $1 per mil.

$$\frac{\$1,000,000 \text{ assessed valuation}}{\$1,000} = 1,000 \text{ thousands of dollars of assessed valuation}$$

$$1,000 \text{ x } 7 \text{ mil rate} = \$7,000 \text{ tax revenues generated}$$

Assume instead that a city has a tax rate of 5 mils. Full valuation of the city is $400 million and property is assessed on a 50% basis. How much will the tax levy produce in dollars?

The dollar amount can be computed in either of two ways.

1. $400,000,000 full valuation x 50% = $200,000,000 assessed valuation
    $200,000,000 x .005 (mil as a decimal) = $1,000,000 tax revenue generated.

2. $400,000,000 x 50% = $200,000,000 assessed valuation

$$\frac{\$200,000,000}{1,000} = 200,000 \text{ thousands of dollars of assessed valuation}$$

$$200,000 \text{ x } 5 \text{ mils per } \$1,000 = \$1,000,000 \text{ tax revenue generated.}$$

MUNICIPAL DEBT STATEMENT

To satisfy the requirements of bylaws and local regulations, the municipality involved generally must publish annually a debt statement that gives all particulars concerning all debt issues outstanding. Included in this statement, which is also made available to investors, are certain ratio calculations, principal among which are the net overall debt to assessed valuation and net overall debt to estimated real valuation. These ratios, as mentioned earlier, establish whether the net overall debt is within both reasonable limits and any statutory limits that may exist.

Net overall debt for a municipality may be determined as follows:

Total bonded debt of municipality
– Self-supporting debt
– Sinking funds
Net bonded debt
+ Floating debt
Net direct debt
+ Net overlapping debt
Net overall debt

The total bonded debt of the municipality is reduced by the amount of self-supporting debt and sinking funds (for other than the self-supporting debt), reflecting the net bonded debt of the municipality. Any floating debt the municipality has is added to net bonded debt to determine net direct debt. The floating debt is debt that will normally be paid off in the current year. It is usually borrowing in anticipation of future revenues (tax anticipation borrowing). Net overlapping debt is added to net direct debt to determine the net overall debt of the municipality. Overlapping debt is that part of the debt of other taxing units for which residents of a particular municipality are responsible.

Overlapping debt refers to debt of governmental units sharing the same tax base. It refers to debt of other public bodies that must be taken into consideration when determining the debt of a particular issuer. A city or town could have overlapping debt from

- The county
- A road district
- A school district

However, a city or town would not normally be responsible for overlapping debt from the state in which the city or town is located. Analysts examining a municipal GO would be interested in certain ratios and indicators, including

- Ratio of net overall debt to assessed valuation
- Ratio of net overall debt to estimated real valuation
- Per capita debt of the municipality
- Tax collection record
- Amount of overlapping debt
- Property valuation trends
- Direct and overlapping debt to population
- Assessed valuation to estimated valuation
- Stability of management

The analyst examining a municipal general obligation bond would be looking for warning signals of a declining credit situation, including

- Rapid increase in debt outstanding
- Current operating deficits
- Increasing levels of unfunded pension liabilities
- Increasing tax delinquencies
- Decline in property values

REVENUE BONDS

Revenue bonds are issued to construct certain specified facilities. These could include toll bridges; toll roads; skating rinks; golf courses; water, sewer, and electric systems; and hospitals and nursing homes. The revenue generated from the facility is pledged to pay both principal and interest on the bonds as well as the operating expenses of the facility. Interest is payable only if earnings exist, or out of the debt service reserve fund. Principal is due at maturity, regardless of earnings.

In general, there must be a close correlation between the total costs of debt service and operation of the facility, as well as an economic justification for the facility. Equally important to the success of the entire venture is a lack of competing or potentially competing facilities. Unfortunately, the foresight and planning of many municipal projects is incomplete in this regard, and we find state toll highways constructed parallel to federally built free expressways; toll bridges connected to major through routes served by toll-free bridges; and many other instances in which the revenue was never produced and the bonds proved worthless.

The basic criteria for the success of a revenue bond must be the revenue-generating ability of the facility. Not only must the revenue pay for the interest and principal payments on the bond, the revenue must also cover both normal upkeep and maintenance plus remodeling and improvement costs as well. It is generally the practice to require a margin of safety of at least a 10%, and preferably larger, excess of revenue over projected costs. The **coverage test** is the number of times earnings for a period exceed the debt service payable in that period.

The legal requirements associated with revenue bonds are usually far less stringent than those associated with GOs. Their issuance is not affected by legal limits on debt issued by the community. They do not create an increase in debt service from the general tax revenue. The issuance of revenue bonds usually does not require the approval of the citizens. In short, the question of legality of the issue is greatly simplified.

Since legality is not a major problem, the principal protection offered to the investor, besides the revenue-generating ability of the facility, is the protective covenants that are associated with the bond issue. The principal covenant here would be the pledge of the revenues generated to service the debt. A further protection is the provision of an auditing or review authority to make sure the provisions regarding the application of revenues (especially the disposition of excess revenues) is being properly adhered to. The specific security will vary to some degree due to the nature of the issue. Hospital revenue bonds, for example, are secured by net project revenues plus pledged endowment income.

Analysts examining a municipal revenue bond issue would be interested in certain ratios and factors, including

- Facility's management and financial history
- Provisions of the indenture, including protective covenants
- Likelihood of attaining adequate revenues

- Estimated future debt service coverage ratio
- Reserve
- Provisions fund requirements
- Flow of funds for the issuance of additional bonds
- Rate covenant

An analyst doing a feasibility study relating to a municipal revenue bond would be concerned with factors such as

- The need for the facility
- Similar projects in the area that might compete with the facility
- The population in the project area
- Coverage ratios
- The quality of the management operating the facility

An analyst reviewing an airport revenue bond would consider the following factors relevant:

- The amount of tourism in the area
- Energy costs in the area
- Passenger traffic trends

MARKETABILITY

Regardless of the type of municipal security (e.g., general obligation or revenue), an investor must consider marketability. Marketability is affected by such factors as

- Block size
- Bond rating
- Maturity date
- Coupon
- Dollar price
- Call feature
- The name of the issue
- Whether the bond is traded only locally or nationally
- Whether the bond is registered or bearer

MUNICIPAL BOND UNIT INVESTMENT TRUSTS

Municipal bond unit investment trusts issue shares that represent units in a particular municipal bond portfolio. A unit investment trust is a type of investment company that

- Passes tax-exempt income to investors
- Is organized under a trust indenture
- Sells units normally in multiples of $1,000
- Does not have a board of directors but has a board of trustees
- Issues redeemable shares (the certificates may be tendered to the trustee at any time for redemption)

Each unit investment trust is a separate entity created by an indenture. As the bonds in the portfolio mature or are called, the size of the fund is reduced. The life of these unit investment trusts is usually limited to the life of the bonds in the portfolio. An investor will pay a sales charge of approximately 3½% to 5% to purchase a unit investment trust.

An investor would purchase a tax-exempt unit investment trust for

- Diversification of issuers
- Geographic diversification
- Ease in the collection of interest

The Tax Reform Act of 1976 allowed the formation of investment companies to manage municipal bond portfolios and to pass through tax-exempt income to investors. Open-end investment companies that invest in municipal bonds can buy and sell the bonds in the portfolio in an attempt to generate a higher return. If interest rates rise, the bonds in the portfolio will fall in value. If interest rates fall, the bonds in the portfolio will rise in value. These managed investment companies may be load or no-load funds. The load funds levy a sales charge up to 8½%, while no-load funds do not levy a sales charge.

ADDITIONAL CONCEPTS: MUNICIPAL BONDS

Other important concepts relating to municipal bonds include

- A municipal dealer who is asking for a workable indication is seeking a likely bid from another municipal dealer.
- If a customer purchases a municipal bond in the secondary market at 90 and sells it seven years later at 98, his gain is $80.
- Presale orders are normally filled first relating to a new issue of municipal bonds and member orders are filled last. The priority sequence for filling orders for a new municipal issue would be

  - Presale
  - Group net
  - Designated
  - Member

- The price at which a municipal bond would be tendered to an issuer is determined by the issuer.
- Amortization of a municipal bond is accomplished by reducing the premium over the remaining life of the bond.
- The legal opinion on a municipal bond attests to the tax exemption and legality of the issuer. The legal opinion on a new issue of municipal bonds is written by the bond attorney (bond counsel) working for an independent law firm.
- If the bond counsel or bond attorney gives an "unqualified legal opinion" on a municipal bond, it means that the bond counsel is rendering an opinion that is not subject to any limitations.
- Municipal bond trades settle in clearinghouse funds, which are available on the next business day, as opposed to federal funds, which are available immediately.
- A broker's broker executes orders for other municipal dealers and institutions. A broker's broker

  - Does not deal directly with the public
  - Does not trade for its own account
  - Does not bid on new issues

  A broker's broker gives out information about the municipal market to other municipal dealers and customers. Municipal dealers use a broker's broker to get better exposure on an order and to maintain privacy relating to the transaction.

- A *put bond* allows the holder to redeem the issue at specified intervals before maturity and receive full face value. In return for this privilege, the purchaser of a put bond receives a lower yield.
- A *control relationship* exists between a municipal securities dealer and a municipal issuer when an officer of the underwriting firm is in a position of authority over the issuer of municipal bonds. A control relationship must be disclosed to the customer in all types of municipal transactions, whether executed as agent or principal.
- A *joint account* is an account formed by two or more municipal securities dealers for the purpose of purchasing and distributing a block of municipal securities. While participating in a joint account, a municipal securities dealer cannot provide quotes indicating more than one market for the securities, which are the subject of the account.
- An investor wanting market information on municipal securities would normally consult the Blue List. The Blue List is an indicator of the size of the secondary market for municipal bonds.
- The amount by which the par value of a municipal bond exceeds the market price is described as the discount. The amount by which the market price of a municipal bond exceeds the par value is described as the premium.
- Municipal bonds that are callable may be redeemed prior to maturity by the issuer. The issuer, when calling term bonds with a sinking fund, normally make the selection randomly.
- A municipal revenue bond may be called because

  - The municipal facility is destroyed by a fire or catastrophe.
  - Interest rates in the economy are declining.
  - Funds are available in the surplus account to call the bonds.

  However, municipal revenue bonds normally do not have a statutory debt limit. Statutory debit limits apply to general obligation municipal bonds.

- In the analysis of a municipal revenue bond, the following factors would be examined:
  - Protective covenants
  - Feasibility study
  - Comparison with similar projects

  However, budgetary practices of the issuer would be more important to GOs than to municipal revenue bonds.
- When analyzing the creditworthiness of a municipal issuer, the net overall debt is the sum of the direct debt and the overlapping debt of the issuer.
- The creditworthiness of a general obligation municipal bond could be determined by using the ratio of direct and overlapping debt to market valuation.
- New municipal securities trainees are subject to a ninety-day apprenticeship period. During this ninety-day period, the municipal trainee *may not*
  - Discuss the purchase or sale of municipal securities with individual or institutional customers
  - Be compensated on a commission basis
- The municipal trainee may discuss the purchase or sale of municipal securities with other municipal security dealers, provided the trainee is compensated on a straight salary basis.
- Municipal bonds are normally issued in serial maturities, and two separate calculations can be used to determine the lowest interest cost to the issuer. The calculations are used to determine the
  - Net interest cost
  - True interest cost
- The **net interest cost (NIC)** is derived by adding the total volume of interest payments for the entire offering and dividing by the amount of bonds outstanding times the years they are outstanding. If the bonds were issued at a discount, the amount of the discount is added to the interest payments as if it were an outlay by the issuer. If the bonds were issued at a premium, the amount would be subtracted from the interest payments. The **true interest cost (TIC)** takes into consideration the time value of money, while the net interest cost calculation does not.
- Municipal bond confirmations would include certain information such as whether the transaction was a purchase or sale, the identity of the dealer, and the capacity in which the dealer acted. However, full details of the call feature would be described in the official statement and not on the confirmation. The fact that a municipal bond is callable and the call dates would be stated on the municipal bond. Also, the name of the paying agent would not be stated on the municipal bond confirmation.

5 US GOVERNMENT SECURITIES

INTRODUCTION

The debt of the federal government may be divided into two broad categories—marketable and nonmarketable. Marketable government securities consist of securities such as US Treasury bills, notes, and bonds. Nonmarketable securities are securities such as Series EE and Series HH Bonds. These securities are unconditionally guaranteed by the US government and are considered to be the highest quality. The major portion of the federal debt is marketable—the securities can be transferred directly from one owner to another. Most of the nonmarketable debt is in the form of savings bonds, which are registered and must be purchased from and sold through banks. Interest on US government securities is exempt from state income taxes but subject to federal income taxes. Marketable US government debt includes Treasury bills, Treasury notes, Treasury bonds, flower bonds, and cash management bills.

TREASURY BILLS

Treasury bills are short-term direct obligations of the federal government. They offer an investor an extremely liquid investment of the highest quality. Treasury bills bear no interest, and the holder does not receive an interest check. They are sold at auction at a discount from par. They are marketable but not redeemable until maturity. The interest received is the difference between the discounted price paid and par, and is taxed as ordinary income. The lower the price of the bills, the higher the yield to maturity.

Treasury bills come in minimum denominations of $1,000. Treasury bills normally have maturities of three, six, and twelve months. Three-month Treasury bills may also be referred to as 91-day bills, or 13-week bills, while 6-month bills are referred to as 182-day bills or 26-week bills.

In the new-issue market, where Treasury bills are offered by the US Treasury, which uses the Federal Reserve banks as agents, bills having maturities of three months and six months are sold at a weekly auction. Issues with a one-year maturity are usually sold monthly. Treasury bills may be purchased in the secondary market with maturities as short as one day. Treasury bills represent the largest dollar volume of the various money market (short-term) instruments. They are used by the US Treasury to finance deficits in the federal budget. Treasury bills are traded only in the over-the-counter market, and there is a narrow spread between bid and ask prices quoted by primary dealers. Because of their high quality and short maturity, bills normally have the lowest yields of any taxable securities. A long-term policy of investing in Treasury bills would result in a stable principal and a fluctuating rate of return. The return earned on US Treasury bills is exempt from state income tax, but subject to federal income taxes. Treasury bills are not callable by the US government prior to maturity.

Small investors normally place noncompetitive tenders with the Federal Reserve for Treasury bills. The noncompetitive tenders are filled at the average price of competitive tenders submitted by institutions and the small investor is guaranteed to have his or her order filled.

The discount—the difference between the purchase price of the securities and the amount of the check submitted in payment—will be mailed to the purchaser after the issue date. The Treasury will report ownership and income information to the Internal Revenue Service (IRS) using Social Security numbers and employer identification numbers as the method of identification.

Treasury bills are the only US government securities that are quoted on a yield basis. Their bid and ask price, therefore, will differ from those quoted for other government issues. A Treasury bill might be quoted as

Bid	Ask
5.95	5.80

The bid is higher than the ask since these numbers indicate the price as a discount from face value. The larger number, representing the largest discount, is therefore really a lower dollar price. The ask price indicates that if the bill is purchased at the ask price and held to maturity, the yield on the investment, calculated at an annual rate, is 5.80%.

A basis point for a US Treasury bill is equal to 1/100 of 1% par value (0.01%). Therefore, for a one-year $10,000 US Treasury bill, one basis point would be equal to

$$\$10,000 \times .0001 = \$1.00$$

For a one-year $1 million Treasury bill, a basis point would be equal to

$$\$1,000,000 \times 0.0001 = \$100 \text{ annual amount}$$

For a $1 million US Treasury bill with a 182-day maturity (a half year), a basis point would be equal to one-half of the annual amount.

$$\$1,000,000 \times 0.0001 = \$100$$

$$\frac{\$100}{2} = \quad \$50 \text{ basis point for six-month maturity}$$

For a $1 million US Treasury bill with a 91-day maturity (one-quarter of one year), a basis point would be equal to one-quarter of the annual amount.

$$\$1,000,000 \times 0.0001 = \$100$$

$$\frac{\$100}{4} = \quad \$25 \text{ basis point for 91-day bill}$$

CASH MANAGEMENT BILLS

Treasury bills known as cash management bills are normally issued several times a year to raise cash for very short periods of time (ten to twenty days). Cash management bills are issued in minimum denominations of $1 million and are normally purchased by institutions.

TREASURY NOTES

Treasury notes are interest-bearing obligations of the US government and come in various denominations from $1,000 to $1 million. They are issued in book entry form, pay interest every six months, are not callable prior to maturity, and have maturities of two to ten years. They mature at face value. Treasury notes are quoted at a percentage of their face value in 1/32nds of 1%, as are Treasury bonds. Thus, a bid of 98.4 would be converted into a dollar price of $981.25 as follows:

$$
\begin{array}{ll}
98 = & \$980.00 \\
4/32 \text{ of } 1\% \text{ of par} & 1.25 \\
& \$981.25
\end{array}
$$

TREASURY BONDS

Treasury bonds are similar to Treasury notes except that maturities are over ten years and some issues are callable at par, five years prior to maturity. If callable or redeemable prior to maturity, they are known as **term** bonds. This call feature is expressed as June 15, 1989/94, with the earlier date, June 15, 1989, the callable date, and the latter, June 15, 1994, the maturity date. Although the Treasury rarely exercises its privilege to call these bonds at face value at a time between these two dates, yields to maturity are calculated only to the call date. There is a statutory limit which is changed from time to time by Congress, which limits the rate of interest the Treasury can pay on long-term debt. Outstanding issues of Treasury notes and bonds are available in registered or bearer form. New issues of Treasury notes and bonds are available in book entry form and can be purchased from the Federal Reserve banks without paying a commission.

Treasury notes and bonds trade in 32nds and settle on a next day basis in federal funds. Treasury bills and Treasury notes are not callable, but Treasury bonds may be called prior to maturity. Treasury bills have a $10,000 minimum denomination, while Treasury notes and bonds have a $1,000 minimum denomination.

US Treasury securities are issued regularly with a wide range of maturities. There is a larger dollar amount outstanding in Treasury securities than any other security. US Treasury securities have virtually no credit risk but do have a market risk relating to interest rates.

FLOWER BONDS

Certain issues of US Treasury bonds are referred to as **flower bonds**. These flower bonds are redeemable at face value in the payment of federal estate taxes. In other words, if the decedent had an estate tax bill of $10,000 and had in his possession at the time of his death $10,000 par value of US Treasury bonds at $4\frac{1}{2}\%$, due May 15, 1994, (assuming it is a flower bond issue), then these bonds could be used to satisfy the entire tax requirement. This is true even though the market value of these bonds was substantially less than $10,000. Flower bonds are direct obligations of the US government.

Since most of these flower bonds were issued with very low coupon rates, they sell at deep discounts from par value. A revision of the federal tax code eliminated the concept of flower bonds for Treasury bond issues after April 1971. However, earlier issues have maturity dates extending to 1998.

MARKETABILITY: US TREASURY SECURITIES

Treasury issues are normally more marketable than any other type of security. At almost all times, primary dealers are ready to buy and sell quantities of these securities with very narrow spreads. The market stability of these issues varies inversely with income return. Extremely short-term bills are relatively unaffected by price variations but generally have the lowest return.

Marketable government securities are extremely liquid and extremely safe. They are, however, affected by two primary investment risks: the interest rate risk and the purchasing power risk. There is an inverse relationship between interest rates and bond prices. If interest rates rise, bond prices tend to fall. Since interest and principal are payable in dollars, a decline in the purchasing power of the dollar will affect the holder of either marketable or nonmarketable securities. A decline in the purchasing power of the dollar always affects those holding fixed income investments severely; this is precisely because the return, in terms of numbers of dollars, is fixed. For this reason, those who hold investments having a fixed long-term maturity value are severely affected by a decline in the purchasing power of the dollar.

SERIES EE BONDS

The Treasury also issues nonmarketable bonds, which are mainly Series EE bonds and Series HH bonds. Series EE bonds are nonmarketable and nontransferrable and cannot be used as collateral for a loan. They can be purchased at most banks and post offices and can be redeemed wherever they are sold. They can be registered in the name of one person, in the names of two co-owners, or in the name of one person and a beneficiary who will automatically become the owner if the registered owner dies. They are purchased at discount from par, with denominations ranging from $50 to $10,000. No one individual may purchase more than $15,000 par value in a calendar year. Bonds registered in co-ownership form may be applied to the holdings of either co-owner or apportioned between them, up to a maximum of $30,000 face amount. They may be redeemed for cash before maturity according to their schedule after a six-month holding period. The longer the bond is held, the higher the percentage return.

SERIES HH BONDS

Series HH bonds are similar to Series EE bonds except that they are sold at face value and interest is paid semiannually by check. They are redeemable at par any time after the first six months, but, like Series EE bonds, the actual yield increases the longer they are held. The most important characteristics of both Series EE and HH bonds are their safety and their ready conversion to cash at a fixed rate. Both Series EE and HH bonds are registered in the owner's name and neither may be used as collateral for a loan.

FEDERAL AGENCY BONDS

The bonds sold by the various government agencies and government-sponsored enterprises (GSEs) are distinguished by the fact that such bonds are considered to be of high quality. They carry interest coupons and enjoy active and liquid markets. Federal agency issues are considered to be nonrisk assets for banks by bank regulatory authorities. Federal agency bonds are also referred to as **government agency bonds**. Federal agency issues have various interest accrual periods, which could be monthly, semiannually, nine months, twelve months, or to maturity.

Federal agency issues are normally considered low-risk investments. New issues are book entry, while outstanding issues are available in registered form or in bearer form with interest coupons attached. Federal agency issues are exempt from registration requirements of the Securities Act of 1933 and the reporting requirements of the Securities Exchange Act of 1934.

Federal agency issues trade in 32nds and regular way settlement is normally the next business day in federal funds. Accrued interest on federal agency issues is computed on a 30/360 basis, while Treasury bills, notes, and bonds are computed on the actual number of days in a year.

The main government agencies or government-sponsored enterprises are

- Federal farm credit banks

- Federal home loan banks
- Federal National Mortgage Association (Fannie Mae)
- Government National Association (Ginnie Mae)
- Federal Home Loan Mortgage Corporation (Freddie Mac)
- Student Loan Marketing Association (Sallie Mae)

Federal Farm Credit Banks

The Farm Credit System provides loans to farmers and farm-related businesses. The Federal Farm Credit banks issue the federal farm credit banks consolidated systemwide bond. These bonds are issued in book-entry form only. The interest earned on these bonds is subject to federal income tax but exempt from state income tax. The bonds are considered to be of very high quality. Federal farm credit bonds are backed by federal land banks, federal intermediate credit banks and banks for cooperatives, which are part of the Farm Credit System.

Federal Home Loan Banks

This agency consists of twelve regional banks owned entirely by their members (savings and loan associations, savings banks, homestead associations, and insurance companies), which make loans to these members to finance home building by granting mortgage loans. The funds for these loans are generated by bond offerings. The bonds are backed by loans for residential mortgages. Federal home loan banks issue both notes and bonds. The notes have maturities of less than one year with interest payable at maturity. Federal home loan bank bonds are issued with minimum denominations of $10,000. These bonds pay interest semiannually, which is subject to federal income tax, but exempt from state and local tax.

Federal National Mortgage Association (FNMA) (Fannie Mae)

Fannie Mae provides a degree of liquidity for government-insured mortgages in the secondary market, by buying and selling residential mortgages. Fannie Mae issues mortgage-backed securities by pooling conventional mortgages. Interest and principal repayments are passed through to the holders of the mortgage-backed securities. Fannie Mae securities are not backed by the US government, but Fannie Mae can borrow a specific amount of money from the US Treasury.

Fannie Mae debentures are issued in book-entry form with minimum denominations of $10,000. Interest on these debentures is payable semiannually. The interest received on Fannie Mae securities is subject to both federal income tax and state and local taxes. Securities issued by Fannie Mae are considered exempt securities under the Securities Exchange Act of 1934. Fannie Mae debentures and common stock are highly marketable, unlike the short-term notes, which are not marketable. Fannie Mae's common stock is listed and traded on the New York Stock Exchange (NYSE).

Government National Mortgage Association (GNMA) (Ginnie Mae)

Ginnie Mae is a wholly owned agency of the US government. Ginnie Mae's primary purpose is to guarantee securities, which represent to investors an undivided interest in pools of mortgage-backed securities, thereby increasing the availability of home mortgage money.

Ginnie Mae fully modified pass-through securities are backed by the full faith and credit of the US government and therefore the timely payment of interest and principal is guaranteed. The Ginnie Mae pass-throughs come in minimum denominations of $25,000 and they represent a share in a pool of Federal Housing Authority (FHA) or Veterans Affairs (VA) single or multifamily mortgages. Ginnie Mae pass-throughs pay interest and principal to investors monthly. The term **pass through** is derived from the fact that the principal and interest payments, less mortgage servicing, are literally passed through to the investor on a monthly basis. Ginnie Mae pass-throughs are issued in registered form. These securities are highly marketable. A portion of the principal on paydown is a return of capital and not taxable to the investor. Interest received on securities issued by Ginnie Mae is subject to both federal income tax and state and local taxes.

Federal Home Loan Mortgage Corporation (Freddie Mac)

Freddie Mac is a publicly traded corporation listed on the NYSE. Freddie Mac also issues mortgage-backed securities. Freddie Mac, along with Fannie Mae, links together mortgage lenders with investors. Freddie Mac pools conventional mortgages and issues mortgage-backed securities to investors.

Freddie Mac securities are *not* guaranteed by the US government. Interest received on Freddie Mac mortgage-backed securities is fully taxable at the federal, state, and local levels.

Student Loan Marketing Association (Sallie Mae)

Sallie Mae provides liquidity for student loans by buying them from lending institutions and reselling them to investors as securities. Sallie Mae is a publicly traded corporation (GSE) listed on the NYSE. Sallie Mae securities are *not* backed by the US government. Interest received on Sallie Mae debt obligations is subject to federal income taxes, but exempt from state and local income taxes.

To summarize, Ginnie Mae obligations are backed by the US government. Obligations of Fannie Mae, Freddie Mac, and Sallie Mae are *not* directly backed by the US government and are referred to as GSEs. Interest received from debt obligations of Ginnie Mae, Fannie Mae, and Freddie Mac is subject to federal, state, and local income taxes. Interest received on Sallie Mae obligations is subject to federal income tax, but exempt from state and local taxes.

TREASURY DIRECT SYSTEM

In 1987, the US Treasury created its Treasury Direct program, which mandated that all newly issued Treasury bills, notes, and bonds be maintained in book-entry form. The Treasury Direct System opens a single master account for each owner in which Treasury bills, notes, and bonds are held. The information maintained in the account includes the customer's name, address, telephone number, taxpayer identification number, and bank account information.

The owner or owners of the account can purchase additional Treasury securities or transfer securities to another account. The owner will receive a statement of account from the Treasury, which is a record of purchases, sales, deposits, and withdrawals to the account.

When a Treasury Direct account is opened, the US Treasury notifies the designated bank of the customer that it will be receiving electronic payment of funds. These funds will be credited to the checking or savings account designated by the customer. The Treasury has a similar program in effect concerning the direct deposit of Social Security checks. The direct deposit system means that there will be no lost checks in the mail and the owner of the account has immediate access to his funds.

The Treasury Direct program allows accounts to be opened in the name of individuals, partners, corporations, trustees, executors, and guardians. To open a Treasury Direct account, a new account request form must be submitted. If the account will be maintained in joint names, both owners must sign the request form.

When securities are held in book-entry form, no definitive certificate is available to the purchaser. The purchaser receives a confirmation and statement listing his or her ownership of the security. Since the Treasury has a list of the owners of its securities, book-entry securities are considered to be registered. Book-entry securities are transferred by journal entry.

FEDERAL FUNDS

Federal funds are reserves of member banks held by the Federal Reserve that are in excess of requirements. Banks that have these reserves may loan them (usually overnight) on an unsecured basis to banks that have reserve deficiencies.

The main points to remember concerning federal funds are

- Federal funds are excess reserves of Federal Reserve member banks that are loaned to other banks, usually overnight, at the federal fund rates.
- The federal funds rate is a leading indicator of short-term rates and is normally the most volatile rate in the money market. It is a very sensitive indicator of monetary conditions.
- It is normally higher than the rate charged at the Federal Reserve's discount window.
- If the federal funds rate is rising, it indicates that banks are borrowing heavily to meet reserve requirements and that excess reserves of member banks are shrinking.
- The federal funds effective rate is the daily average rate of interest costs of federal funds throughout the country.
- Smaller regional banks are normally a source of federal funds.
- The supply of federal funds is affected by changes in member bank reserve requirements.

REPURCHASE AGREEMENTS

US government securities are sold in the over-the-counter (OTC) market. Dealers buy and sell from their own inventories at their own risk. This increases the liquidity of government securities and permits the maintenance of the broad, active market so important to the US Treasury. During the period when the Treasury is selling a new issue of securities, these dealers take large amounts of the new issue intending to sell them to investors. It would be difficult for the market to absorb such new issues without dealer participation and prices would be temporarily severely depressed.

Government securities dealers are also used by the Federal Reserve System when it attempts to influence money and credit. It is through these dealers that the Fed conducts open market purchases and sales. It is these dealers who first feel the effect of Federal Reserve operations, which then spread to the entire financial markets.

Dealers finance the major portion of their positions with borrowed funds. Such short-term loans to large government securities dealers are of obvious importance in the functioning of the money market. These loans are of two types. One is a **demand loan,** similar to a broker's call loan. The dealer retains title to the securities but transfers the securities to a lender as collateral for a loan.

The other type involves a **contractual arrangement** under which the securities are actually sold to the lender, but the borrowing dealer agrees to repurchase them at the sale price plus interest. Banks and other money market lenders also use such loans and repurchase agreements to make short-term adjustments in their positions.

Using such a **repurchase agreement,** temporary funds may be borrowed overnight for a specified period of days or occasionally longer (up to eighteen months) at a fixed rate of interest without any risk of loss due to market fluctuations. Under the **buy-back** arrangement, the dealer agrees to sell and later repurchase and, simultaneously, the lender agrees to purchase and later resell, specified securities. (See Exhibit 5.1.)

Exhibit 5.1: Repurchase agreement

Dollar National Bank
Quincy, Vermont

February 2, 1970

Mr. Roger W. Brown
Rockwell Lumber Company
Rockwell, Vermont 02295

Dear Mr. Brown:

In accordance with your instruction we confirm having sold you <u>100,000 US Treasury</u> <u>Notes 5% due November 15. 1970,</u> owned by this bank at par flat for delivery and payment on <u>February 2, 1970.</u>

The securities will be held by us in safekeeping for your account. We enclose our Safekeeping Receipt No. <u>986555.</u>

We also confirm the purchase from you of the above securities for delivery and payment on <u>February 17. 1970.</u> At that time we will remove the securities from safekeeping and credit your account for the above amount plus interest or forward our cashier's check at your request.

The effect of this transaction will be earnings of <u>$328.77</u> for the period <u>February 2 to February 17</u> which represents <u>8%</u> per annum on the amount invested for <u>15</u> days.

We appreciate the opportunity to be of service.

Very truly yours,
(Signed) Alexander W. McDonald

Vice President

Summary

1. Agreement between the buyer and seller to reverse a trade at a specified time and specified yield (repo rate).
2. US government securities dealers use repurchase agreements to finance their inventories.
3. Interest rates are determined by negotiation between buyer and seller.

Under repurchase agreements, an institution seeking to borrow funds for a few days will sell short-term US government securities to another investor. At the same time, it agrees to repurchase the same securities at a time and price which provides a predetermined yield (repo rate) calculated on the actual number of days using a 360-day year. The sale price and yield may be determined using an actual day calculation basis without a fixed maturity. The agreed-upon yield is closely related to other money market instrument yields.

BANKERS' ACCEPTANCES

These short-term instruments are used primarily to finance imports and exports. A buyer of goods draws an order on his bank, instructing the bank to pay a specified amount at a specified time to the seller. The bank that accepts this draft is, in effect, guaranteeing it. The seller of the goods can present this draft at his own bank and receive payment in full, minus a discount reflecting current short-term interest rates. Acceptances, then, trade in the secondary market, at a discount, and are purchased by investors who receive payment in full from the accepting bank at maturity date. The accepting bank charges a fee for this guarantee, but runs only a small risk, since the seller's bank has already forwarded draft and shipping documents to the acceptor. (See Exhibit 5.2.)

Exhibit 5.2: Bankers' acceptance

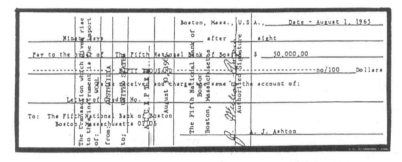

Summary

1. Drafts or bills of exchange that become money market instruments when payment is guaranteed by a bank or other financial institution.
2. They are designed primarily to enable businessmen to finance foreign trade.
3. They are issued on a discount basis.
4. They normally mature in nine months or less.
5. They are collateralized loans guaranteed by a financial institution that are sold to investors at a discount.
6. They are not callable.

COMMERCIAL PAPER

These securities are unsecured corporate promissory notes issued with maturities from 30 to 270 days. Notes are issued in multiples of $1,000 from $5,000 to $5 million or more. Other corporations, commercial banks, insurance companies, and mutual funds are major purchasers. This paper is frequently issued by finance companies, and major finance companies sometimes place the paper directly with the purchaser instead of selling it in the marketplace. These securities are issued both directly by the borrowers to the lenders and indirectly through dealers who underwrite the paper and, in turn, sell it to ultimate lenders. The paper is issued in bearer form at the prevailing discount rate on the basis of a 360-day year. Commercial paper is normally issued at a discount from par. (See Exhibit 5.3.)

Exhibit 5.3: Commercial paper

Summary

1. Represents unsecured promissory notes of corporations.
2. Normally has a maximum maturity of nine months (270 days). If it is issued for more than nine months, it must be registered with the Securities and Exchange Commission (SEC).

3. It is normally issued in bearer form at a discount from par. Some commercial paper may be issued "plus interest."
4. May be sold directly by the issuer to investors such as money market funds, pension funds and industrial firms.
5. Commercial paper is not callable but is freely negotiable.
6. Commercial paper is not guaranteed by the Federal Deposit Insurance Corporation (FDIC).

BROKERS' AND DEALERS' LOANS

Not really money market instruments, brokers' loans are those made to brokers to finance margin purchases by the brokers' customers. Thus, the funds borrowed by an individual from a broker to buy stock are, in fact, provided by commercial banks. The loans are secured by stocks left in street name with the broker and are evidenced by either demand notes (call loans), which must be paid on the demand of the lender, or time notes, which can run up to six months. The call rate can fluctuate from day to day and is closely tied to the rates of money market instruments. Dealers' loans are loans made to those dealers who take positions (make markets) in securities. The loans help finance these inventories and are backed with securities (usually US government bonds and bills). The interest rate paid also closely follows the rate in the short-term market.

NEGOTIABLE CERTIFICATES OF DEPOSIT

These are negotiable certificates issued by banks in return for time deposits. They have been issued in amounts ranging from $100,000 to $1 million. The minimum amount must be $100,000 on orders to be traded in the money market. The maturity is normally negotiated directly between the purchase of the CD (actually the depositor or lender) and the bank. If the holder of the CD needs his funds before maturity date, he can sell this instrument in the open market since it is negotiable. Prices are quoted on a yield basis, calculated on an actual day basis and a 360-day year. (See Exhibit 5.4.)

Exhibit 5.4: Negotiable certificate of deposit

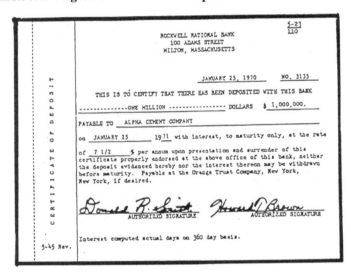

Summary

1. To be negotiable, a CD must have a face value of $100,000.
2. They are guaranteed by the issuing bank.
3. Negotiable CDs are not callable.
4. The issuing bank will redeem the CD at maturity at its face value plus the stated interest.
5. Maturities of one year or less are common, but some CDs have maturities of three to five years.
6. They are not callable.

TREASURY RECEIPTS

Treasury receipts are stripped coupon Treasury bonds. They trade at deep discounts and are very volatile. All of the interest accrued is paid in one payment at maturity.

The underlying bonds are held by a custodian bank for the beneficial owner, and payment is made by the custodian bank to the holder at maturity. Purchasers are able to lock in a rate of return for a predetermined period.

Other important points concerning Treasury receipts include

- Treasury receipts are traded by many brokerage firms.
- Interest and principal payments on the stripped bonds are guaranteed by the US Treasury and, therefore, Treasury receipts carry the highest credit ratings.
- Interest on Treasury receipts is taxable on accrual even though the investor receives only one payment at maturity.
- Individuals normally purchase Treasury receipts for retirement plans such as individual retirement accounts (IRAs) and Keoghs that have no current tax liability.
- Treasury receipts are created by brokerage firms. For example, a twenty-year US Treasury bond is transformed into forty-one separate units representing the forty semiannual interest payments and the final principal payment. Therefore, forty-one separate zero coupon Treasury receipts are created.

EURODOLLAR BONDS

Eurodollar bonds are bonds issued by American or European corporations outside of the United States. Interest and principal on these bonds is paid in eurodollars, not in any foreign currency. Eurodollars are American dollars held on deposit in banks in European countries.

Eurodollar bonds are not registered with the Securities and Exchange Commission (SEC) and, therefore, cannot be initially offered for sale in the United States. Eurodollar bonds are normally sold at lower than US interest rates. Eurodollar bonds could be issued by American corporations, foreign corporations, domestic and international banks, and foreign governments.

INTERBANK MARKET FOR FOREIGN CURRENCIES

Major banks throughout the world trade American dollars and foreign currencies on a daily basis. The interbank market for foreign currencies is a decentralized market. The market is essentially free from government regulation. Trading in the interbank market for foreign currencies is normally conducted in large amounts ($1 million to $5 million).

It is common for central banks of leading industrial nations to take actions that affect their own currencies and other currencies. For example, if the American dollar is falling in relation to the euro and Japanese yen, central banks might buy American dollars. The Bank of Japan might sell billions of yen in exchange for American dollars. The US Federal Reserve, the central bank of Germany and Britain, might also sell yen or euros in exchange for American dollars.

Assume the American dollar declines from 158.6 yen to 121.2 yen and from 1.95 Swiss francs to 1.57 Swiss francs. The top officials of the US Treasury and the Federal Reserve Board decide to intervene and stop the falling dollar. The New York Federal Reserve Bank will buy dollars in exchange for yen or Swiss francs by placing orders with large banks or foreign currency traders in the US or overseas. If the Federal Reserve is short of yen or Swiss francs to carry out the deal, it will borrow them from the Japanese or Swiss central banks and repay them at a later date. The Federal Reserve, by placing the order to purchase dollars, raises the demand for dollars and raises the supply of yen or Swiss francs. This action tends to boost the price of American dollars in relation to the Japanese yen and the Swiss francs. (See Exhibit 5.5.)

Exhibit 5.5: Strong dollar vs. weak dollar

Certain factors that tend to cause a strong dollar or a weak dollar can be summarized as follows:

Strong dollar	*Weak dollar*
1. Rising interest rates	1. Falling interest rates
2. Federal budget surplus	2. Federal budget deficit
3. Central banks buying dollars	3. Central banks selling dollars
4. Balance of payments surplus	4. Balance of payments deficit
5. Foreign investors buying Treasury securities	5. Foreign investors selling Treasury securities
6. Foreigners buying stock in US companies	6. US investors buying stock in foreign companies
7. Federal reserve tightening money supply	7. Federal reserve easing the money supply
8. Balance of trade surplus	8. Balance of trade deficit
9. Deflation	9. Inflation
10. Optimism about US economic policy	10. Pessimism about US economic policy

The Federal Reserve must be careful since interest rates tend to increase when the central banks purchase dollars and take money out of circulation. Central bank intervention will not turn the dollar upward for long if economic and political events have convinced banks, businesses, investors, and speculators that the currency will lose buying power in the future.

ADDITIONAL CONCEPTS

Treasury bills are normally auctioned on a Monday and settle the following Thursday. Treasury bills may be purchased by investors from Federal Reserve banks, which act as agents for the US Treasury.

Treasury notes and Treasury bonds are sold at or near par value, and interest is paid on a semiannual basis. Treasury notes, Treasury bonds, and Treasury strips are capital market instruments. Treasury bills are money market instruments.

US Treasury bills, notes, bonds, and strips and federal agency issues are exempt from the registration requirements of the Securities Act of 1933. They are referred to as exempt securities. Corporate equity and debt issues are nonexempt securities and must be registered under the Securities Act of 1933.

Treasury bills and Treasury strips do not have a stated interest rate and, therefore, no nominal yield. Treasury notes and Treasury bonds have an interest rate stated such as $4\frac{1}{4}\%$ or $5\frac{7}{8}\%$.

Money market instruments are short-term debt obligations such as Treasury bills, commercial paper, bankers' acceptances, repurchase agreements, federal funds, and negotiable certificates of deposit of a year or less. Money market instruments, since they are debt obligations, do not pay dividends. Money market instruments are normally exempt from the registration requirements of the Securities Act of 1933. Treasury bills have the most active secondary market of the various money market instruments. Capital market instruments include equities (common stock); preferred stock; corporate bonds; US government notes, bonds, and Treasury strips; American depository receipts (ADRs); mortgages; and warrants.

Government agency or government-sponsored corporation debt obligations have a higher yield than Treasury bills, notes, or bonds. The higher yield reflects a slightly higher risk than direct obligations of the US government. However, government agency debt is considered to be of very high quality in the marketplace.

The financial news often contains stories concerning **derivative securities**. Derivatives are securities that derive their value from other securities. Derivative investments can be straightforward, such as equity, stock index, foreign currency, and interest rate options. Collateralized mortgage obligations are a type of derivative security. Other more complicated derivative investments include interest rate swaps, inverse floaters, and equity-linked bank deposits. Derivatives can be used by institutional investors to reduce risk on their stock and bond portfolios. Institutional investors can hedge their portfolios using derivatives such as stock index, foreign currency, and interest rate options. However, more risky derivatives can be used as very speculative investments generating large profits or losses. Investors using derivatives should be clearly aware of the types of risk they are assuming.

6 OVER-THE-COUNTER MARKETS

INTRODUCTION

Most securities trading in the United States takes place on stock exchanges or in the over-the-counter (OTC) market. Stock exchanges are located in a central place. The OTC market is a network of thousands of market makers and traders connected by telephones and computers. Prices in the OTC market are determined by negotiations between broker/dealers (market makers and traders). The OTC market is a negotiation market. Buyers and sellers do not meet and execute trades by negotiation through telephones and computers. On stock exchanges, buyers and sellers meet on a trading floor and trading is done on an auction basis.

The OTC market is primarily regulated by the National Association of Securities Dealers (NASD). The OTC market and stock exchange trading make up secondary market trading in securities in the United States. The primary securities market is also referred to as the **new issue market**. In the primary securities market, underwriters purchase securities from issuing corporations and resell the securities to the public. The secondary market consists of trading on national securities exchanges and in the OTC market. Participants in the secondary market include

- Order-entry firms
- Market makers
- Traders
- Public customers

The OTC market is basically composed of two types of equity securities: (1) NASDAQ securities and (2) non-NASDAQ securities. NASDAQ is also referred to as the **NASDAQ Stock Market**. NASDAQ is the NASDs automated quotation system. It is a computerized trading system, which provides subscribers bid and ask prices of securities traded on the system, and for the New York Stock Exchange (NYSE) issues. Securities traded on NASDAQ are separated into two classes.

1. NASDAQ national market securities
2. NASDAQ small-cap securities

NASDAQ national market securities are the higher-quality, more actively traded NASDAQ securities. Securities such as Microsoft and Intel are NASDAQ national market securities. NASDAQ market makers are required to make a continuous, firm, two-sided market of at least 100 shares, but possibly more than 100 shares depending on the trading volume in the security.

NASDAQ small-cap securities are securities that do not meet the listing requirements to be included as a national market security. Since NASDAQ small-cap securities are less actively traded, NASDAQ market makers have lower required quotation sizes. The more actively a security is traded, the narrower the spread. The less actively traded security has a wider spread and more risk associated with trading it.

Non-NASDAQ OTC securities consist of OTC bulletin board securities and pink sheet securities. Non-NASDAQ OTC securities are made up of mostly speculative securities. These securities are suitable only for customers who can assume a great deal of risk and are capable of evaluating the risk.

MAKING A MARKET IN A SECURITY

What is meant when a firm is said to be "making a market in a security"? Assume that a firm is making a market in the shares of XYZ Corporation. This means that the firm stands ready to buy and sell shares of XYZ Corporation at quoted prices. The quoted prices are the bid price and the ask price. A firm who makes a market in a security on an exchange is called a **specialist** and in the OTC market is called a **market maker**.

For example, a market maker may quote the stock of XYZ as follows:

XYZ Corporation

Bid	*Ask*
25	25.50

The **bid price** is the price at which the market maker will buy the stock; the **ask price** is the price at which the market maker will sell the stock. The difference between the bid and ask price is the **spread**. The spread, in this case, is $0.50. An actively traded stock has a narrow spread, and a less actively traded stock would have a wider spread.

If a retail firm wants to buy stock from the market maker, it will have to pay the ask price. If a retail firm wants to sell the stock to the market maker, it can do so at the bid price. A market maker may have a long or short position in a security in which it makes a market. If the firm has a **short position,** it means that the market maker has *sold more securities than it has purchased.* The market maker has sold securities that it does not own, and must borrow in order to make delivery of the shares to the buyer. Obviously, it is advantageous to have a long position when the market is rising and a short position when the market is falling.

FIRM AND SUBJECT MARKETS

In non-NASDAQ securities, a market maker may quote two types of securities in which it trades. The first type of market that can be quoted is a **firm market**. Firm market prices represent prices at which a security can actually be bought or sold. A firm market is good for at least one trading unit. A trading unit is normally 100 shares of stock or 10 bonds. Therefore, if a market maker quotes a firm market, it will buy at least 100 shares at the bid price, or sell at least 100 shares at the ask price of a non-NASDAQ security. Backing away from a firm quote is a violation of NASD rules.

To quote a firm market, the market maker would state any of the following:

- "The market is 15–15.50."
- "It is 15–15.50."
- "We can trade it 15–15.50."
- "15–15.50"

The second type of market that can be quoted by a market maker is a **subject market**. A subject market represents prices that are subject to confirmation. In other words, they are not firm prices.

To quote a subject market, the market maker would state any of the following:

- "It is quoted 15–15.50."
- "It is 15–15.50 subject."
- "It is 15–15.50 small"

A **workout market** is a subject market. It is defined as a range between which a dealer feels he can obtain the security within a reasonable period of time.

Bid	*Ask*	
32	32.25	300 by 700

The market maker will buy up to 300 shares on his bid of 32, and sell up to 700 at his ask price of 32.25. This is referred to as a quote and size. The quote and size can also be reflected in a shortened form as follows:

$$32–.25 \quad 3 \text{ by } 7$$

To be a market maker in a particular security, a broker/dealer must have on file certain information about the company, such as its latest annual report and prospectus, and have a reason to believe that the company's filings with the Securities and Exchange Commission (SEC) are current. To be a market maker in a particular security, the broker/dealer does not need SEC, NASD, or the company's approval.

When executing an OTC agency transaction for a customer, an NASD member may interject a third party between itself and the best available market only if the total cost or proceeds of the transaction are better than the prevailing interdealer market for the security. If an NASD member firm interjects a third party between itself and the best available market causing the customer to pay a higher price, this is called **interpositioning**. Interpositioning is prohibited under NASD rules, since the customer would receive a less favorable price.

BID OR OFFERING WANTED

In certain instances, a market maker wants to buy or sell a security but does not receive any bids or offers. In this case, it will publish a quotation stating **bid wanted** or **offer wanted**. The term bid wanted (BW) means that the market maker wants to sell the stock and is asking for bids. The term offer wanted (OW) means that the market maker wants to purchase stock and is asking for offers from prospective sellers. BW and OW are always subject quotes.

EXECUTION CAPACITIES

A firm will normally act in one of two capacities in its dealings with customers. It may act as a broker and purchase or sell stock on the instruction of its customers. When a firm acts as a broker, it purchases stock as agent for its customers and charges a commission. For example, a firm purchases 100 shares of XYZ at a $25.50 ask price and charges the customer a commission of $50. When a firm acts as a broker, it must disclose the amount of the commission charged to the customer on the confirmation.

The second capacity in which a firm may act is as a dealer. When a firm acts as a dealer, it charges its customers a markup, but does not charge a commission. For example, a dealer may purchase 100 shares of XYZ at $25.50 (ask price from a market maker as principal). The dealer then marks up the stock a certain percentage. Assume the stock is marked up and sold to the customer at $26. The price of $26 is called a **net price**. A net price to the customer includes a dealer markup. In this example, the markup was $0.50.

NASDAQ LEVELS OF SERVICE

NASDAQ was introduced by the NASD on February 8, 1971. It provides a subscriber to the service instantaneous bid and ask quotations in any security quoted on NASDAQ and last sale information.

There are three levels of NASDAQ service which are available to subscribers.

1. *Level I.* Used mainly by brokers; consists of a computer terminal which gives a registered representative the inside market in the security. The inside market is the highest bid and the lowest ask price in the security. For example, assume the following market exists for XYZ on NASDAQ:

Bid	*Ask*	*Spread*
30.00	30.50	0.50
30.12	30.75	0.63
30.25	31.00	0.75

The inside market is 30.25–30.50. The price of 30.25 is the highest bid, while 30.50 is the lowest offer in the security.

2. *Level II.* Used mainly by traders; it consists of a computer terminal which displays the current firm quotations of all market makers in a particular stock.

3. *Level III.* Used by market makers, it provides the current firm quotations of all market makers, but also allows the market maker to input quotations in the securities in which they make a market.

NASDAQ market makers are required to report daily volume transacted in each issue to the NASD at the end of the day. The NASD also requires NASDAQ market makers to report data on securities quoted in the system on a monthly basis as determined by the Board of Governors. The NASD reviews market makers' performance on a monthly basis.

NASDAQ market maker must be open for business at 9:30 A.M. Eastern time, and close no sooner than 4:00 P.M. Eastern time. Firms may close their hours of trading only on the hour or on the half-hour. A market maker can still enter quotes outside these hours provided the system is in operation and appropriate notification to the operator of the NASDAQ system of its desire to enter quotes.

Some of the main points to remember concerning NASDAQ are

- NASDAQ market makers must report daily volume in each authorized issue and file monthly reports with the NASD.
- NASDAQ market makers must be open for business from 9:30 A.M. to 4:00 P.M. Eastern time.
- There is no waiting period for security to be quoted on NASDAQ. Once a registration statement is effective, the security can be quoted on NASDAQ.
- For initial inclusion in NASDAQ, an issue must have two registered and active market makers. For continued inclusion, the issue must have one registered and active market maker.
- It establishes qualifications for registered market makers and others who subscribe to the system's service.
- The system permits firm quotations to be entered into it and instantly changed by market makers.
- NASDAQ will normally suspend trading in a security when
  - The company requests that it be suspended.
  - Material facts will be disclosed shortly about the company.
  - The net worth of the company becomes negative.
  - The company files for bankruptcy.

- NASDAQ market makers must report transactions in NASDAQ/NMS securities through the Transaction Reporting System within ninety seconds after execution. Transactions not reported within ninety seconds after execution must be designated as late. In transactions between two registered market makers, the transaction must be reported by the seller.
- Companies listed on NASDAQ can issue nonvoting stock.
- To be quoted on NASDAQ, a security must

  - Have at least two market makers
  - Have a minimum number of stockholders
  - Have a minimum number of shares outstanding

- NASDAQ quotations released to the news media

  - Reflect interdealer quotations
  - Reflect the inside market (highest bid and lowest offer)
  - Represent subject quotes
  - Represent quotes at a specific time of day (normally 4 P.M. Eastern time)

MARKUPS AND MARKDOWNS

NASD rules state that markups and markdowns must be fair, taking into consideration all relevant circumstances. Markups and markdowns should not generally exceed 5%. However, 5% is a guide, not a rule. If a broker/dealer charges a markup in excess of 5%, s/he will have to be able to justify it based on all relevant circumstances concerning the transaction.

When broker/dealers charge a markup or markdown on a securities transaction, they are acting as principals (dealers). If broker/dealers act as agents, they charges a commission. A broker/dealer cannot charge a markup and a commission or a markdown and a commission on the same transaction.

TYPES OF SECURITIES TRADED

There are many different types of securities traded in the OTC market. The following is a partial list:

- US government securities, municipal bonds, and bank securities
- Insurance company securities, closed-end funds, and most corporate bonds
- New issues of securities after the distribution is completed
- Railroad equipment trust certificates and securities of foreign corporations
- Corporate stock, preferred stock, warrants, and rights

THIRD AND FOURTH MARKETS

When securities that are listed on the NYSE or another national securities exchange are traded over the counter, they are said to be traded in the third market. Large blocks of listed securities can be traded in this market without affecting the auction price on the floor of the NYSE. A **block** is defined as a trade of 10,000 shares or more. A fourth-market trade takes place between two institutions without a broker/dealer. For example, a mutual fund buys securities directly from a life insurance company or bank's portfolio.

TYPES OF ORDERS

In the OTC market, round-lot and odd-lot orders are not separated. For example, an OTC trade involving 365 shares would be entered on one order ticket. The main types of orders that are used in the OTC market are summarized as follows.

Market Order

A market order is an order to buy or sell a security at the best price available in the market. The trader handling the order will try to obtain the best price available for his or her customer.

Limit Order

A limit order is an order to buy or sell a security at a specific price or better. A limit order to buy is entered below the current market price of a security. For example, assume XYZ is selling at $50 per share. A person could enter a limit order to buy 100 shares of XYZ at $40 per share. This limit order to buy could be executed only at $40 per share or less. The limit price of $40 is the price above which the customer does not want to pay. Of course, s/he would be willing to pay less than $40 per share. The brokerage firm could not execute the order for the customer at a price above $40 per share.

A limit order to sell is placed above the current market price of a security. For example, assume ABC stock is selling at $30 per share. A customer could place a limit order to sell 100 ABC at $35 a share. A limit order to sell is normally placed by a customer who has a long position in the security. The customer in this case wants to sell the security, but only if s/he receives $35 a share or higher. The brokerage firm could not execute the order for the customer at a price below $35 per share.

All-or-None Order

An all-or-none order requires that the entire amount of the order be executed—a lesser amount will not be accepted by the customer. For example, if a customer wants to purchase 700 shares of ABC Company, the broker/dealer must find a market maker willing to sell 700 shares at once. If the market maker wants to sell only 300 shares, no transaction can take place. An all-or-none order does not have to be executed immediately.

Alternative Order

This is an order to do either of two alternatives. For example, a customer places an order to sell 500 shares of ABC at 55 or buy 500 shares of ABC at 50. The execution of one side of the alternative order will automatically cancel the other side.

Assume that the buy order for 500 shares at 50 is executed; the 500-share sell order at 55 is automatically canceled. If a partial execution takes place, an identical number of shares is automatically canceled for the other order. For example, if 300 shares of ABC are bought at 50, the remaining order would be either sell 200 shares of ABC at 55 or buy 200 shares of ABC at 50.

Fill-or-Kill Order

A fill-or-kill order must be executed at once in its entirety or not at all. A complete execution is necessary for a fill-or-kill order. However, the complete execution does not necessarily have to be at one price. In a fill-or-kill order, the customer requests a specific price. For example, the customer might enter an order to buy 3,000 shares of XYZ at 22 FOK (fill or kill). The customer does not want to pay more than $22 a share. However, s/he would be willing to accept an execution of 2,000 shares at $21.80 and 1,000 shares at $22, since it is an even better execution than buying 3,000 shares at $22.

Good-Till-Canceled Order

A good-till-canceled (GTC) order is also referred to as an **open order**. It remains open until it is canceled or executed.

Day Order

A day order is an order that expires at the end of the day unless executed. Limit orders entered by customers will be entered as either day orders or GTC orders (open orders).

ARBITRAGE

Arbitrage may be defined as the purchase or sale of a security in one market together with an offsetting sale or purchase of the same (or equivalent security) in another market. This technique may be used for either OTC securities or those traded on exchanges.

Arbitrage transactions may be divided into two types.

1. Riskless arbitrage
2. Risk arbitrage

Riskless arbitrage can be done when a difference in price exists between two markets in the same security. For example, assume ABC stock is trading at $72 per share on the Chicago stock exchange and $71.90 per share on the NYSE. A trader could sell short 100 shares at 72 on the Chicago stock exchange, and buy 100 shares on the NYSE at $71.90 for a $0.10 profit. Assuming these transactions can be executed at these prices, it is a riskless transaction.

Another riskless arbitrage situation could exist between a convertible bond and common stock. For example, assume a convertible bond is selling at $1,000 and is convertible into 20 shares of common stock. The common stock is selling at $55 per share. Therefore, a riskless arbitrage situation exists. The common stock that can be obtained on a conversion would be worth $1,100. To arbitrage, the trader should buy the convertible bond and sell short the common stock. If the common stock and the convertible bond are selling at parity, then no arbitrage situation exists.

A risk arbitrage situation might develop as a result of a tender offer. For example, consider the following situation:

XYZ Company announces a plan to acquire the *Los Angeles Times* Newspaper Company. The terms are one XYZ share for four *Los Angeles Times* shares. XYZ shares are trading at $45 a share, and the *Los Angeles Times* shares are trading at $17 per share. XYZ's board of directors meet to discuss the proposal. There is concern about the merger's being legal under antitrust laws. The trader at the brokerage firm of Dale & Williams purchased XYZ shares and sold *Los Angeles Times* shares short. The trader has engaged in a risk arbitrage transaction.

SMALL ORDER EXECUTION SYSTEM

The Small Order Execution System (SOES) is the NASD's automatic trade execution system for certain size customer agency orders in NASDAQ/National Market System (NMS) and NASDAQ small-cap securities. This system also automatically reports the trade to NASDAQ and sends details to the clearing corporation to be issued for comparison and settlement.

Automatic execution systems, such as SOES

- Provide instantaneous executions of certain size market and marketable limit orders
- Report completed trades immediately

However, a customer order is not guaranteed a better execution or a better price on every transaction entered into the system.

SEC RULE 15c2-6 (Penny Stock Cold Calling Rule)

The SEC has adopted Rule 15c2-6 to help protect investors from high-pressure sales tactics often used to sell highly speculative securities (penny stocks).

This rule applies to certain non-NASDAQ OTC securities selling at less than $5 per share. Under this rule, before a registered representative can sell a non-NASDAQ OTC security selling less than $5 per share to a customer, the registered representative must determine in writing that the security is a suitable investment. The customer's written agreement must be obtained before the transaction can take place. This rule is often referred to as the **penny stock cold calling rule,** even though it covers non-NASDAQ securities selling at less than $5 per share.

SEC Rule 15c2-6 requires the following:

- Before a registered representative can sell most penny stocks to a customer, the broker/dealer must obtain the customer's investment objectives, current financial situation, and investment experience.
- Before selling the customer a penny stock, the broker/dealer must put the customer's financial information in a suitability statement and explain to the customer why high-risk penny stocks are an appropriate investment for him.
- The broker/dealer must obtain the customer's signature on its suitability statement to show that the customer verified the accuracy of the financial information.
- The broker/dealer cannot sell a security covered by this rule to a customer if the registered representative does not obtain financial information from the customer.
- The customer must be sent a copy of the suitability statement.
- The registered representative must tell the customer, in writing, the identity and quantity of the security being offered to him or her.
- The broker/dealer must obtain the customer's signed purchase approval. The customer's written approval is required until s/he has purchased the securities of three companies covered by this rule. Thereafter, the broker/dealer is not obligated to obtain the customer's written approval.
- Before the sale is complete, the broker/dealer must receive the written agreement from the customer. The customer is not obligated to buy the security if s/he does not send the signed agreement to the broker/dealer.

SEC Rule 15c2-6 *does not* apply to the following:

- Securities listed on a national securities exchange, securities quoted on NASDAQ, or securities issued by a registered investment company.
- Put or call options issued by Options Clearing Corporation.
- Securities selling at $5 per share or above.

- Sales made to established customers who have made a security transaction or deposited funds or securities in their brokerage account more than one year prior to the proposed penny stock transaction. Also, an established customer is a person who has purchased the securities of three companies covered by the rule from the same broker/dealer.
- Transactions not recommended by the broker/dealer.
- Transactions in which the broker/dealer is not a market maker in the security being sold, and its sales-related revenue from transactions subject to this rule does not exceed 5% of total sales revenue.

The SEC has stated its intention to enforce this rule vigorously. The purpose of the rule is to give the customer time to decide whether to invest in highly speculative securities.

MISCELLANEOUS CONCEPTS: OTC MARKET

The following miscellaneous concepts relate to the OTC market:

- Assume a security listed on the NYSE, such as IBM, is traded in the OTC market. If IBM is traded over the counter, it is said to be traded in the third market. Market makers who trade listed securities in the OTC market are called third-market makers.
- The Federal Reserve System is the agency that decides which OTC securities can be purchased on margin by public customers. Listed securities, which are securities listed on stock exchanges, can automatically be bought on margin.
- Pink sheets show published wholesale stock prices at which dealers are willing to trade and are inter-dealer quotations. Yellow sheets show published corporate bond prices at which dealers are willing to trade. The Blue List is a standard source of daily price quotations for municipal bonds.
- If a broker/dealer buys a large block of stock from an institution, this is referred to as **block positioning**. A block is defined as a trade involving 10,000 shares or more.
- NASDAQ Level I computer terminals are normally used by registered representatives, which gives the inside market or inside quote on a security. However, on Level I the market makers are not listed. Therefore, orders cannot be executed by registered representatives on Level I terminals. The orders are sent to the traders who execute the transactions on Level II NASDAQ terminals.
- Customers are at risk on a security purchase beginning with the trade date. The trade date is the date on which the security is purchased. The settlement date is the date on which the transaction is due for payment.
- Customer orders have priority over firm (broker/dealer) orders in the OTC market and on stock exchanges.
- Customer confirmations of securities transactions must be sent out by the next business day following trade date (T + 1). If a firm is a market maker in the security sold to the customer, this fact must be stated on the confirmation.
- A firm may act as agent for both the buyer and the seller in a securities transaction and charge both a commission. It must be disclosed on the confirmation that the firm acted as agent for the customer and agent for another person (the customer on the other side of the transaction). This situation may occur in a cross transaction. For example, a customer may place an order to buy 100 ABC at 23, and another customer may place an order to sell 100 ABC at 23. In this case, the firm will execute the transaction as a cross. This means that the buy order and sell order are matched together and each customer is charged a commission. Each customer confirmation must note the commission charged to the customer and that the firm acted as agent for another person.

7 NATIONAL ASSOCIATION OF SECURITIES DEALERS REGULATIONS

The passage of the Securities Exchange Act of 1934 by the Congress of the United States extended federal regulation to all areas of trading in listed securities. However, there was no effective federal regulation covering trading in the over-the-counter (OTC) securities market. Congress felt that federal regulation should extend to the OTC market. Basically, it had two choices.

1. Expand the Securities and Exchange Commission (SEC) staff to monitor the OTC market, or
2. Permit a self-regulatory organization to monitor the OTC market.

Congress chose the second alternative. In 1938, it passed the Maloney Act, permitting national associations of broker/dealers, which became Section 15(A) of the Securities Exchange Act of 1934. The NASD is a national association of broker/dealers operating under the Maloney Act. Trading practices in the OTC market for corporate securities is subject to regulation by the NASD and the SEC. The NASD is still subject to review by the SEC. All disciplinary actions of the NASD are reviewed by the SEC.

CERTIFICATE OF INCORPORATION

In its certificate of incorporation, the purposes of the NASD are stated as follows:

1. To promote just and equitable principles of trade
2. To provide a medium through which the membership may consult and cooperate with governmental and other agencies in the solution of the problems affecting the industry
3. To administer and enforce rules of fair practice and to prevent fraudulent and manipulative acts and practices
4. To promote self-discipline among members; to adjudicate differences between members and between members and the public

BYLAWS OF THE NASD

The bylaws of the NASD contain a number of articles dealing with membership requirements, qualification of registered personnel, administration of the NASD, and other areas. Some of the more important sections of the bylaws concern membership rules, branch offices, qualification of associated persons, and NASD committees.

Who is eligible for membership in the NASD? Any broker/dealer who, in the normal course of business, transacts any branch of the investment banking or securities business in the United States is eligible to join the NASD. A broker would be defined as an individual, partnership, corporation, or other legal entity effecting transactions in securities for the account of others, but not including banks. Bank-owned subsidiary corporations may become NASD members.

A dealer would be defined as an individual, partnership, corporation, or other legal entity engaged in the business of buying and selling securities for its own account. The definition would not include banks or any other person or institution that buys or sells securities for its own account, but does not normally engage in this activity as part of their normal business operation.

Membership in the NASD is important to a broker/dealer if it wants to operate in the OTC market, because NASD regulations prohibit NASD members from granting discounts or concessions to non-NASD members. NASD members are prohibited from joining with nonmembers in the distribution of new issues of securities. Most firms decide that to operate successfully in the OTC market, it will be necessary to join the NASD.

If a broker/dealer wants to join the NASD, it must

- Register its firm with the SEC
- Meet the minimum capital requirements imposed by the association
- Qualify two individuals as principals and one as a financial principal by having them pass supervisory examinations
- Qualify registered representatives by having them pass a securities examination

NASD membership or registration is not available to applicants except by an order of the SEC in the following situations:

- Where the broker/dealer has been suspended or expelled from a national securities exchange for violating just and equitable principles of trade
- Where the SEC or a stock exchange has an order revoking or denying the registration of the broker/dealer
- Where the individuals have been convicted in the last ten years of a felony or misdemeanor involving crimes such as embezzlement or misappropriation of funds
- Where the individuals do not meet the training and experience standards or other standards that the NASD Board of Governors may feel are necessary

The NASD requires that members notify them concerning the opening and closing of branch offices. A branch office is defined as an office (including a corporate subsidiary) that is

- Owned or controlled by the member
- Located in the United States
- Engaged in the investment banking or securities business

A branch office may also be an office of supervisory jurisdiction. An office of supervisory jurisdiction must have a registered principal supervising the activities of registered representatives in that office. Each office of supervisory jurisdiction must have an NASD principal designated to carry out supervisory procedures. The supervisory procedures must be in writing. Each firm must designate to the NASD its branch offices and its offices of supervisory jurisdiction.

The NASD requires that certain personnel in member organizations be registered with it and pass qualifying examinations. The four main classes of registration are

1. General securities principal
2. Financial and operations principal
3. General securities registered representative
4. Registered options principal, senior registered options principal, and compliance registered options principal

The NASD requires that all corporations and partnerships have at least two persons registered as principals. The following individuals must be registered as principals:

- Persons engaged in management or supervision of the firm's investment banking or securities business
- Persons involved in the training of principals associated with the member. Therefore, the following would normally have to be registered as principals:

  - Sole proprietors
  - Partners
  - Officers
  - Managers of offices of supervisory jurisdiction
  - Directors
  - Managers of investment banking activities

Since September 1, 1972, every broker/dealer must designate a financial principal, who will be responsible for the preparation and approval of financial statements and net capital computations. To qualify as a financial principal, a person must pass a comprehensive examination, unless specifically exempted by the NASD.

A registered representative is defined by the NASD as every partner, officer, or employee of a member engaged in any of the following activities:

- Solicitation or handling of listed or unlisted securities business
- Sale of listed or unlisted securities on an agency or principal basis
- Solicitation of subscriptions to services provided on a fee basis, such as investment management or advisory services

A branch office of a member is not permitted to transact options business with the public unless the principal supervisor of the branch accepting options transactions has been qualified as a registered options principal. This requirement does not apply to a branch office that has no more than three registered representatives so long as the options activities of such a branch are appropriately supervised by a registered options principal.

The NASD requires that every member shall provide for the diligent supervision of all customer accounts and orders related to options by a general partner (if a partnership) or officer (if a corporation) of the member who is a registered options principal and who has been specifically identified as the member's senior registered options principal. Such individual may delegate to qualified employees responsibility and authority for supervision and control of each branch office handling transactions in options provided that the senior registered options principal has overall authority and responsibility for establishing appropriate procedures of supervision and control over such employees.

Every member must also designate and specifically identify a compliance registered options principal. This individual may be the senior registered options principal. He shall have no sales functions. His responsibility is to review and propose appropriate action to ensure the member organization's compliance with securities laws and regulations and exchange rules relating to the firm's option business. The compliance registered options principal must furnish regular reports to the compliance officer (if he is not the compliance officer) and to other senior management of the member organization. The prohibition against this individual's having any sales functions shall not apply to a member organization that has received less than $1 million in gross commissions in one of the preceding two fiscal years or that currently has ten or fewer registered representatives handling option accounts.

The NASD also has certain limited categories of registration for persons who intend to sell only certain investment products or engage in specific areas of activity. The limited categories of registration include

- Investment company and variable products representative
- Direct participation programs representative

The NASD is divided into thirteen separate districts. Each district has a district committee consisting of individuals elected for three-year terms. Each district must also have a district business conduct committee. However, in actual practice, the district committee functions as the direct business conduct committee.

The NASD district business conduct committee has original jurisdiction for hearing trade practice complaints against an NASD member. A decision of the NASD district business conduct committee may be appealed to the Board of Governors of the NASD. If an NASD member wants to appeal a decision of the Board of Governors of the NASD, he or she can appeal it to the SEC.

The Board of Governors of the NASD manages the affairs of the Association. The Board of Governors elects the officers of the NASD. For a rule violation, the NASD may impose the following penalties on a member firm or a person associated with a member:

- Fine
- Censure
- Suspension
- Expulsion

ADVERTISING RULES

A separate file of all advertisements, sales literature, and market letters, including the name(s) of the person(s) who prepared them and/or approved their use, must be maintained for a period of three years from the date of each use, the first two years in a place readily accessible to examination or spot checks. All advertising to be used by member firms must be submitted for review within five business days after initial use, unless the advertising has been approved by a stock exchange. Advertising material would generally include

- Material for use in a newspaper or magazine
- Radio or television advertising

Advertising literature does not include

- Tombstone ads
- In-house material
- Personal recommendations designed for one client

A tombstone ad is an ad that identifies only the member, security to be offered, and price of the security. No sales literature is contained in a tombstone ad.

It is a violation of the rules of fair practice to

- Publish any advertisement that contains untrue or misleading statements
- Make statements in any advertisement which are exaggerated
- Make promises of specific results in any advertisement
- In any advertisement, give opinions which have no reasonable basis founded on inquiry by the member

Statements in sales literature or in conversation with customers stating or implying a specific gain expected in the price of a security, a higher price after a split, or promises of a specific number of shares of a new issue if a client places an order for existing securities are examples of those violating securities industry regulations.

In making recommendations, the member must have a reasonable basis for the recommendation and disclose

- Price at the time the original recommendation is made
- That the member usually makes a market in the issue, if this is true
- If applicable, that the member intends to buy or sell the securities recommended for the firm's own account, unless the ownership is merely nominal
- The ownership, if any, of options, rights, or warrants to purchase the security recommended, unless ownership is nominal.

Sales literature used to solicit purchases of common stock under NASD rules must state

- The name of the member firm
- The date the material was originally published
- The price at the time the material was distributed

Sales literature, under NASD rules, does not have to disclose the member firm's inventory or investment position. The member must also provide or offer to furnish, on request, available investment information supporting the recommendations.

Material referring to past recommendations may be used if it sets forth all recommendations as to the same type, kind, grade, or classification of securities made by a member within the last year. Such references cannot imply that these recommendations would have been profitable to any person nor that they indicate the general quality of a member's recommendations. Longer periods of years may be covered if they are consecutive, include the most recent year, and contain the required information.

Testimonial material must make clear that such experience does not indicate future performance or results obtained by others. It must state whether any compensation was paid to the maker and, if it implies an experienced opinion, the qualifications of the maker.

RECOMMENDATIONS MADE TO CUSTOMERS

It is the member's responsibility to see that all recommendations made to customers are suitable as far as the member knows the facts. Statements concerning a company's financial status and future can be made only if they have a reasonable basis founded on inquiry by the salesman. The member has the responsibility to obtain the facts on both the customer and the company recommended and to sell at a price related to the market.

Certain practices have been interpreted by the NASD to be violations of the NASD rules of fair practice. The following is a partial list:

- Recommending speculative low-priced securities to customers, without knowledge of the customer's financial situation
- Churning or excessive trading in a customer's account
- Short-term trading in mutual fund shares
- Establishment of fictitious accounts to hide certain transactions
- Transactions in discretionary accounts without prior written permission of the customer
- Unauthorized use of a customer's funds or securities
- Private transactions by a registered representative without the employer's knowledge
- Recommending a purchase beyond a customer's financial ability to meet the commitment

PRIVATE SECURITIES TRANSACTIONS

NASD rules prohibit an associated person, such as a registered representative, from participating in a private securities transaction unless prior written notice is given to the broker/dealer. A private securities transaction is a securities transaction outside the regular course or scope of an associated person's employment with the member firm.

Assume a registered representative has been asked by a real estate agent to help sell condominium units that are not registered with the SEC. This is an example of a private securities transaction because it would be outside of the registered representative's regular scope of employment.

Under NASD rules, the registered representative must give the member firm prior written notice before engaging in a private securities transaction. The written notice must

- Describe in detail the proposed transaction and the person's proposed role
- State whether the person has received or will receive selling compensation in connection with the transaction.

If the registered representative will receive selling compensation, the member firm which has received written notice must advise the associated person or registered representative in writing stating whether the member

- Approves the associated person's participation in the proposed transaction
- Disapproves the person's participation in the proposed transaction

If the member firm approves the associated person's participation in the private securities transaction, then the transaction must be recorded on the books and records of the member firm. The member firm must supervise the associated person's participation in the private securities transaction as if the transaction were executed on behalf of the member. If the member firm disapproves the associated person's participation, then the associated person must not participate in the private securities transaction in any manner, directly or indirectly.

In the case of a private securities transaction in which an associated person will not receive any compensation, the member firm must promptly provide the associated person with written acknowledgment of the notice. The member firm may, at its discretion, require the associated person to adhere to specified conditions in connection with his participation in the transaction.

EXECUTION OF RETAIL TRANSACTIONS

It is the member's responsibility to obtain the best possible price for a customer under the prevailing market conditions. The member cannot interject a third party between the member and the best available market, unless the member can show that the customer obtained a better price. A member cannot give his orders to other broker/dealers to be executed for customers, unless the member can demonstrate that the customers are receiving the best possible prices.

PROMPT RECEIPT AND DELIVERY OF SECURITIES

A member may not accept a purchase order from a customer unless the member has determined that the customer placing the order, or his agent, agrees to receive securities against payment in an amount equal to any execution, even if the execution is only part of a larger order.

No member may mark a sell order received from a customer as a long sale unless one of the following conditions is present:

- The member has the security in its possession.
- The customer is long the security in his account with the member.
- Assurance is received from the customer that the security will be delivered in good deliverable form within three business days
- The security is on deposit with another broker/dealer, bank, or depository, and instruction has been given to deliver the securities against payment.

PROXY MATERIAL

A member must forward to each beneficial owner of securities all proxy material, annual reports, and other material furnished to it by the issuer of the securities. This would be necessary when customer securities are in street name. If the securities are registered in the name of a customer, the proxy material would be sent directly to the customer. The person soliciting the proxies will reimburse the member for expenses. However, a member does not have to send proxy material to persons residing outside of the United States. Proxy costs are payable by the issuer of the securities.

NASD HOT ISSUE RULES

An NASD member participating in the distribution of a new issue of securities to the public is required to make a bona fide public offering at the public offering price. Failure to make such a bona fide public offering at the public offering price is known as **free riding and withholding**.

This is especially important when a member is distributing a **hot issue**. A hot issue is an issue that, on the first day of trading, sells at a premium over the public offering price. For example, the issue may have been offered to the public at $10 a share and, on the first day of trading, rises in price to $11 a share.

Instances when underwriters or selling group members are free riding or withholding include

- Selling blocks to the accounts of partners or officers
- Maintaining positions by selling to members or their families
- Selling the securities to brokers and dealers outside the selling group who position the securities to sell later at a higher price

Can a member withhold any securities of a hot issue for its own account or the account of officers, directors, partners, or employees? The answer is "no." A member may not withhold shares of a hot issue for its own account or sell shares of a hot issue to officers, directors, partners, employees, or members of their immediate families.

Under NASD rules, a member could *not* sell any shares of a hot issue to

- An officer of the member
- A director of the member
- A partner of the member
- An employee of the member whether registered or unregistered with the NASD
- Employees of other broker/dealers

An NASD member *may* sell shares to the following customers provided that it is in accordance with their normal investment practice with the member, and the aggregate of the securities so sold is insubstantial and not disproportionate in amount as compared to sales to members of the public, and that the amount sold to any one of such persons is insubstantial:

- Senior officer of a bank, such as a bank president
- Senior officer of an insurance company
- Senior officer of an investment company
- A member of the immediate family of an officer of the distributing broker/dealer provided that the officer does not contribute directly or indirectly to the support of such member of the immediate family
- A finder of the issuer (an individual who brings together the issuer and the investment banking firm)
- Another NASD member for the account of a customer

The term *immediate family* under NASD rules means parents, mother-in-law or father-in-law, husband or wife, brother or sister, brother-in-law or sister-in-law, children, or any other relative to whose support the member or person associated with the member contributes directly or indirectly. It does not include

- Aunts or uncles
- Grandmothers or grandfathers
- Nieces or nephews

Hot issues are issues that trade at an immediate premium from their offering price. A hot issue could be an equity security in a primary or secondary distribution, or could even be a debt issue.

CHARGES FOR SERVICES

Any charges for services performed by the member, including services such as safekeeping of securities or transferring securities, shall be reasonable and not unfairly discriminatory between customers.

NASD MARKUP POLICY

The NASD rules of fair practice state that a broker/dealer must charge a fair price. If the member does a trade on a principal basis, the markup charged must be fair. If the member does a trade on an agency basis, the commission charged must be fair. A broker/dealer cannot charge a markup and a commission on the same transaction even if it is disclosed to the customer.

The NASD defines a **markup** as the difference between bought and sold prices or between price and price plus commission. The NASD has developed a markup policy that covers this area. The NASD markup policy is known as the 5% policy since the NASD has determined that markups generally should not exceed 5%.

Three important points should be remembered concerning markups.

- The 5% policy is a guide or guideline, not a rule.
- A markup of 5% or less may be considered unreasonable.
- The determination of the fairness of markups must be based on consideration of all relevant factors, of which percentage markup is only one factor.

The relevant factors that the NASD will take into consideration in determining the fairness of a markup include

- *Type of security.* The markup on stocks will generally be higher than the markup on bonds.
- *Availability of the security in the market.* Inactive securities will normally have a higher percentage markup than active securities.
- *Price of the securities.* It is expected that lower-priced securities will normally have a higher percentage markup than the higher-priced securities.
- *Amount of money in the transaction.* Small transactions will normally have a higher percentage markup than large transactions.
- *Disclosure.* This is considered to be a factor, but not a justification by itself. In other words, if an NASD member warns a customer in advance that the markup on a particular transaction is going to be high, such disclosure will be looked upon with favor, but will not by itself justify the high markup.
- *Patterns of markups.* Each markup by itself must be fair, but the NASD will give attention to the general pattern of markups charged by the firm.
- *Nature of member's business.* It is expected that firms offering more services may charge a slightly higher markup.

One point that should be remembered is that excessive expenses are not a justification for a higher markup. If a firm has expensive office furniture and fixtures, it could not pass on these costs in the form of higher markups to customers.

What specific types of transactions does the NASD markup policy apply to? It applies to the following types of transactions:

- *Riskless or simultaneous transactions.* These are situations in which a member buys a security from a market maker to fill an order in the same security previously received from a customer.
- *Sales to customers from inventory.*
- *Purchase of a security from a customer.* In this case, the markdown must be reasonable.
- *Agency transactions.* In this case, the commission charged must be fair.
- *Proceeds transactions.* This is a transaction in which a customer sells a security and uses the proceeds of that sale to purchase another security at or about the same time. The profit or commission on the securities sold must be considered in computing the markup on the securities purchased by the customer. (The markup policy applies to the combined profits on both sides.)

What types of transactions would *not* be covered by the NASD markup policy? It would not apply to

- Listed securities traded on an exchange; in this case, the stock exchange would have justification.
- The sale of securities wherein a prospectus or offering circular is required to be delivered and the securities are sold at a specific public offering price. This means that the sale of new issues and registered secondaries, and the sale of open-end investment company shares, are not covered by the markup policy since such shares are always sold with a prospectus and at a specific public offering price.
- US government securities or municipal securities.

To summarize

- The NASD markup policy is a guideline, not a rule.
- A markup of 5 % or less could be considered excessive.
- The NASD markup policy applies to secondary market trading in OTC equity securities.
- The markup is based on the inside market price (highest bid and lowest ask).

- A riskless or simultaneous transaction must conform to the NASD markup policy. A riskless or simultaneous transaction occurs when a broker/dealer purchases a security from a market maker, marks it up, and immediately sells it to a customer to fill an order. For example, a customer places an order to buy 100 shares of ABC with a broker/dealer. The broker/dealer purchases 100 shares at $35 from a market maker and immediately sells it to the customer at $35.75. The amount of the markup is ¾ of a point or $0.75. The percentage markup on the trade is

$$\frac{\text{Amount of the markup}}{\text{Broker/dealer's contemporaneous cost}} = \frac{\$0.75}{\$35} = 2.1\% \text{ markup}$$

The percentage markup of 2.1% is well within the guideline of 5%. Percentage markup is one factor used under NASD rules to determine the fairness of a markup. Other relevant factors, such as the size of the transaction, the availability of the security, and any disclosures made to the customer are also considered. A broker/dealer's contemporaneous cost can be used to determine percentage markup. However, assume a broker/dealer purchased 100 shares of XYZ on Monday at $25 per share. The broker/dealer placed the security into its inventory account. On Thursday, the market price of XYZ is $20 per share. A customer places an order for 100 shares of XYZ at the market. The broker/dealer must mark up the security from its present market price of $20 per share and cannot mark it up from $25 per share since it is not a contemporaneous cost. The broker/dealer might sell the stock to the customer at $21.50 net. The word *net* means that the price paid by the customer includes a markup or markdown. This transaction includes a markup of ½ of a point or $0.50.

- The NASD markup policy does not apply to new issues (primary distributions), the sale of open-end investment company shares, registered secondary distributions, the purchase of a listed security, a municipal bond transaction, or a US government transaction.

CONFIRMATIONS

A member must send a customer a written confirmation on or before the first business day following the trade date. A confirmation gives a customer the complete details concerning his or her trade. It contains information such as

- Name of the security purchased or sold
- Price at which the trade was executed
- Number of shares or units purchased or sold
- Capacity in which the broker/dealer acted
- Amount of commission charged if the broker/dealer acted as agent

When a firm acts as broker, it must furnish or be prepared to furnish, information as to the date and time of the transaction, the source and amount of the commission received by the member from all sources, and the identity of the purchaser or seller.

If a member acts as a broker for a customer in transactions in listed securities in the third market, at a price that is in line with the current price on the exchange plus or minus a differential, with the retail firm absorbing the differential, a legend should be used on the confirmation to the customer that explains these facts in order to ensure adequate disclosure to the customer.

All customers of a broker/dealer must be sent a confirmation concerning the details of a particular trade. Instances in which the obligation to furnish a confirmation exists include

- If a bank purchases securities for its investment portfolio, a confirmation must be sent to the bank since it is a customer of the broker/dealer.
- If an insurance company purchases stock for its own account, the insurance company must be furnished with a confirmation.
- If an individual who resides in a foreign country purchases securities, that individual must be furnished with a confirmation.

DISCRETIONARY ACCOUNTS

A discretionary account is an account in which the customer gives to the broker/dealer the right to purchase and sell securities for his or her account without securing prior customer consent for each transaction. No member or registered representative is allowed to exercise any discretionary power in a customer's account unless such customer has given prior written authorization and the account has been accepted in writing by the member. A registered representative cannot accept an order from one spouse (e.g., the husband) to execute a trade in the other spouse's account unless written instructions have been received from the other spouse (e.g., the wife) authorizing such orders.

All discretionary orders must be approved promptly and in writing. They must be approved on the same day they are placed, but not prior to execution. All discretionary accounts must be reviewed at frequent intervals to detect and prevent transactions that are excessive in size or frequency.

What if a customer tells a registered representative to buy 100 shares of XYZ but to enter the order only when he believes the price is right? Would this be considered a discretionary order? The answer is "no." If a customer instructs a registered representative to purchase or sell a definite amount of a specified security, but gives discretion as to the price and time, this is not considered to be a discretionary transaction. However, if a client gives her registered representative a sum of money and instructs him to buy whatever security he thinks best, the order is discretionary and the registered representative would need prior written authorization before executing it.

If a registered representative handles a discretionary account, he must

- Obtain prior written authorization from the customer
- Designate each such order as discretionary
- Not make transactions that are excessive in size or frequency (churning)

DEALING WITH NONMEMBERS

A member cannot grant any nonmember broker/dealer any selling concession, discount, or allowance not allowed to members of the general public. A member cannot join with a nonmember broker/dealer in any distribution of an issue of securities to the public. The term *nonmember* includes suspended or expelled dealers or anyone not admitted to membership in the NASD. Eligibility in the NASD is limited to broker/dealers transacting any branch of the investment or securities business. Banks are not eligible to become NASD members.

OTHER PROVISIONS OF THE NASD RULES OF FAIR PRACTICE

Other provisions include

- No member or person associated with a member shall give directly or indirectly, anything of material value in excess of $100 per person per year to any person, principal, proprietor, employee, agent, or representative of another person, without the prior knowledge and consent of the employer.
- No member may give anything of value to any person for the purpose of influencing or rewarding such person in connection with publishing or circulating information intended to influence the market price of a security.
- A member must disclose to a customer a situation wherein the member is controlled by, controlling, or under common control with the issuer of a security the customer intends to purchase. If the disclosure is not made in writing, it must be supplemented by the giving or sending of written disclosure at or before the completion of a transaction. Firms normally make the disclosure with a notation on the confirmation.
- A member acting as a broker for a customer or for both a customer and another person, or a member acting as a dealer and receiving a promise of a fee from a customer for advising a customer with respect to securities shall, at or before the completion of any transaction with or for the customer, in any security in the primary or secondary distribution of which the member is participating or in any way financially interested, give the customer written notice of the existence of such participation or interest.
- A member in any way financially interested in the primary or secondary distribution of a security not admitted to trading on a national securities exchange shall not represent that such security is being offered to a customer *at the market* or at a price related to the market price unless the member has reasonable grounds to believe that a market for the security exists besides a market over which the member has control.
- If a member holds customers' securities that are fully paid for, these securities must be segregated and clearly identified as belonging to the customer. Also, excess margin securities must be segregated for the account of a customer. Excess margin securities are securities owned by the customer in excess of 140% of a customer's debit balance.
- No member shall guarantee a customer against loss in any securities account or securities transaction. Assume a new stock issue is sold to the public at $20 per share. One month after the offering, the stock is quoted $14\frac{3}{8}$ bid–15 ask. A customer who purchased the new issue at $20 per share is unhappy that the price decreased. He wants his registered representative to buy back the shares at $20 per share. The

registered representative is not allowed to do this under any circumstances since it is prohibited, under NASD rules and rules of other self-regulatory organizations, to guarantee a customer against loss.

- No member or person associated with a member shall share directly or indirectly in the profits or losses in any account of a customer, unless such member or person obtains prior written authorization from the member carrying the account. In addition, the member or person may share only in direct proportion to that amount invested in the account.
- A member must obtain certain information from customers when opening an account, such as name, address, whether the customer is of legal age, signature of the registered representative, and signature of the partner, officer, or manager. Discretionary accounts require the customer's occupation as well as the signature of each person authorized to exercise discretion.
- Members must keep a separate file of all written complaints received from customers. The separate file of written complaints must be kept for six years, the first two years in a readily accessible place.
- A member must make available to any bona fide customer, upon request, a copy of the firm's most recent balance sheet or statement of financial condition. The balance sheet or statement of financial condition must be made available to the customer immediately.
- The **reciprocal brokerage rule** states that sales of investment company shares shall not be a qualifying or disqualifying factor in the selection of a broker/dealer to execute portfolio transactions.
- The **antireciprocal rule** states that it is inconsistent with just and equitable principles of trade and a violation of the rules of fair practice for any member to engage in any of the following activities:

  - To provide sales personnel any incentive or additional compensation for the sale of shares of specific investment companies based on the amount of brokerage commissions expected from any source.
  - To recommend specific investment companies to sales personnel if such companies are recommended or selected on the basis of brokerage commissions received or expected from any source.
  - To grant sales personnel any participation in brokerage commissions received by the member from portfolio transactions of any investment company whose shares are sold by such member, or from any covered account if such commissions are directed by, or identified with, such investment company or covered account.
  - To use sales of shares of any investment company as a factor in negotiating the price of, or amount of brokerage commissions to be paid on, a portfolio transaction of an investment company or of any covered account.
  - These rules do not prevent a member from compensating its sales personnel based on total shares of investment company shares provided such compensation is not designed to favor or disfavor sales of shares of particular investment companies on a basis prohibited by the NASD.

The sale of variable contracts of an insurance company by an NASD member is subject to the rules of fair practice. A member may not participate in the offering of variable contracts unless the sales load is fair, taking into consideration all relevant circumstances. No member who is a principal underwriter as defined in the Investment Company Act of 1940 may sell variable contracts through another broker/dealer unless (1) such broker/dealer is a member, and (2) there is a sales agreement in effect between the parties.

NASD CODE OF PROCEDURE

The Code of Procedure of the NASD was established for the purpose of handling trade practice complaints relating to violations of the rules of fair practice. The NASD district business conduct committee has original jurisdiction for hearing complaints against NASD members.

In certain complaints against NASD members, the facts are not in dispute and the respondent does not wish to have a hearing. In this case, a respondent may waive a hearing and accept a summary complaint procedure. A summary complaint procedure may be accepted by a member in a situation in which the facts are not in dispute and the member waives a hearing and accepts the summary complaint procedure.

If a member accepts a summary complaint procedure, the maximum penalty that a district business conduct committee can impose on a member is censure and/or a fine of $2,500.

As mentioned earlier, a member may appeal any decision of the district business conduct committee to the Board of Governors. If a member feels that the Board of Governors has not acted properly, it may appeal the decision to the SEC. A decision of the SEC may be appealed to the Circuit Court of Appeals in the federal court system.

UNIFORM PRACTICE CODE

All OTC transactions in securities (except for transactions cleared through a registered clearing agency and exempt securities) are subject to the provisions of the Code. In trades between members, failure to deliver the securities sold or failure to pay for securities as delivered on or after the settlement date, does not effect a cancellation of the contract. The remedy of the buyer or seller is provided for according to the buy-in or sellout provisions of the Code unless the parties mutually consent to cancel the trade.

Trade Date

Trade date is the date on which a securities transaction occurs between two parties. Dealer A buys 100 shares of XYZ from Dealer B on Monday, December 10. Monday, December 10 is referred to as the trade date for this transaction.

Settlement Date

The Uniform Practice Code defines the term *delivery date* with regard to securities transactions. **Delivery date** is used interchangeably with **settlement date** and means the date designated for the delivery of securities. Delivery dates vary for different types of securities transactions.

For a transaction that is done regular way, delivery shall be made at the office of the purchaser on, but not before, the third business day following the date of the transaction. Therefore, if a transaction is executed on March 5, a Thursday, the regular-way settlement date is Sunday, March 8. The trade date in this transaction is March 5, the date on which the securities transaction took place. If there were a holiday between the trade date and the settlement date, it would not be counted in arriving at the settlement date. For example, if March 8, a Sunday, was a holiday, regular-way settlement in our transaction would be Wednesday, March 11. (See Exhibit 7.1)

Exhibit 7.1: Trade and settlement dates

			MARCH 20XX			
SUN.	MON.	TUES.	WED.	THURS.	FRI.	SAT.
	Trade		Settlement			
1	2	3	4	5	6	7
8	9	10	11	12	13	14
15	16	17	18	19	20	21
22	23	24	25	26	27	28
29	30	31				

If the trade date is Monday, March 2, the settlement date or regular-way settlement date or regular way settlement would be three full business days later for listed and unlisted stocks and bonds. For US government securities, the settlement date would be the next business day after the trade date (Tuesday, March 3). For a cash transaction, the settlement date would be Monday, March 2, the same as the trade date.

Assume that Thursday, March 5, is a holiday and the securities markets are closed. If the trade date is still Monday, March 2, the settlement date would be Friday, March 6.

For corporate stocks, corporate bonds and municipal bonds, regular-way settlement is the third business day after the trade date. For US government securities, regular-way settlement is the following business day after the trade date. If a transaction is done for cash (a cash transaction), delivery shall be made at the office of the purchaser on the date of the transaction. This type of transaction is normally done at the end of the year to recognize a gain in that taxable year or in a situation wherein the customer needs the money immediately and does not want to wait until the regular-way settlement date.

A customer selling stock in a cash transaction will have to accept less than a person selling the same stock in a regular-way transaction at the same time. This is because the buyer in a cash transaction must have the funds available for payment on the same day as the trade, while the buyer in a regular-way transaction has three business days after the trade date to pay for the transaction.

Seller's Option Contract

A seller's option contract requires delivery to be made at the office of the purchaser on the date on which the option expires, usually not more than sixty calendar days after the trade date. The Uniform Practice Code of the NASD does not set a maximum number of days that can be used in a seller's option contract. However, NYSE rules provide for a maximum time period on a seller's option contract of sixty calendar days after the trade date. Most NASD members have accepted this limit when entering into seller's option contracts. A seller's option contract can be settled with a delivery of borrowed securities. In a seller's option contract, the seller is allowed to deliver the stock before the expiration of the option, provided one business day's written notice is given to the purchaser.

A customer might use a seller's option contract if he wanted to sell a security while traveling overseas. Assume he enters into a seller's option thirty-day contract since he expects to be overseas approximately one month. Instead, he returns home in two weeks. He then signs the certificate, and his broker gives the purchasing broker one business day's notice. The selling broker can then deliver the security to the buying broker on the next business day, and the buying broker must pay for the transaction and accept delivery.

When-Issued Contract

A when-issued or when-distributed contract differs from other contracts in that the securities called for have not yet been issued or distributed, and the issue or distribution date may not have been determined. A date for the settlement of such contracts must be determined after the date of issue or distribution of the securities becomes known. If the securities which are eventually issued or distributed differ substantially from those contemplated in the contract, the contract could not be settled and must be canceled.

For example, assume the stock of ABC Company is trading at $50 per share. The board of directors of ABC announces a 2-for-1 split. ABC stock will trade at $50 and the when-issued stock will start trading at $25 per share. This is because the stockholders must still approve the stock split and if they do not, the when-issued contracts are canceled. This is why the contracts are properly called **when, as, and if issued,** and **when, as, and if distributed,** even though in the industry they are most often referred to as **when-issued** and **when-distributed** contracts.

Ex-Dividend Or Ex-Rights Date

An investor must purchase a stock before this date in order to be entitled to the distribution. This date for transactions in stocks, except for cash transactions, is normally the second business day before the record date, provided the record date falls on a business day. If it does not fall on a business day, the ex-dividend date would be the third business day before the record date.

- **Cash** transactions shall be ex-dividend or ex-rights on the business day following the record date.
- SEC Rule l0b-17 requires corporate directors to make **timely announcements** of distributions concerning publicly traded securities. This is to permit the NASD's uniform practice committee to take appropriate action. *Timely* means that the committee must be notified by the corporation at least ten business days before the record date.
- The ex-dividend date on open-end investment company shares is the date designated by the fund or principal underwriter.

Record Date

The record date is a date fixed sometime in advance by a corporation that is going to pay a dividend. The corporation pays the dividend to persons whose names are on the books of the company on this date. Use the calendar shown in Exhibit 7.2 to calculate some examples.

Exhibit 7.2: Record and ex-dividend dates

			APRIL 20XX			
SUN.	MON.	TUES.	WED.	THURS.	FRI.	SAT.
1	2	3	4	5	6	7
					Ex-dividend	
8	9	10	11	12	13	14
		Record				
15	16	17	18	19	20	21
22	23	24	25	26	27	28
29	30					

If a company announces that it will pay a dividend to stockholders of record on April 17, the ex-dividend date would be two full business days before the record date. If the record date is not a business day (Saturday, Sunday, or holiday), the ex-dividend date would be three business days before the record date.

The last day that a customer can purchase the security in a regular-way transaction and still receive the dividend is Thursday, April 12. The ex-dividend date is Friday, April 13. If the customer purchases the stock on Thursday, April 12, the trade will settle on the record date and the customer is entitled to the dividend. Starting on Friday, April 13, the stock trades ex-dividend (without the dividend).

Due Bill

A due bill is a promise to pay a distribution of cash, rights, or securities. If a security is sold before it trades ex-dividend or ex-rights and delivered too late for transfer on or before the record date, it must be accompanied by a due bill for the distribution to be made. In this instance, the seller in the transaction would receive from the issuing corporation a dividend distribution to which he is not legally entitled. Therefore, when the seller delivers the certificate to the buyer in this instance, a due bill must accompany delivery.

A due bill for a cash dividend is a postdated check, which is also called a **due-bill check**.

Reclamation and Rejection

The term **reclamation** as used in the Uniform Practice Code means a claim for the right to return or to demand the return of a security previously accepted. A properly executed uniform reclamation form must accompany securities on reclamation or return.

For example, assume Broker/Dealer A delivered the wrong security to another broker/dealer in error. Broker/Dealer A would fill out a uniform reclamation form and send it to the other broker/dealer reclaiming the security delivered in error.

Buy-In

A contract that has not been completed by the seller according to the terms specified may be closed out by the buyer not sooner than the third business day following the date delivery was due. On the day after settlement or any subsequent day, the purchasing broker/dealer who has not received the security may deliver a written notice of buy-in to the seller's office not later than noon his time, two business days preceding the execution of the proposed buy-in. If the seller fails to effect delivery in accordance with the buy-in, the buyer may close the contract by purchasing the security in the best available market for the account and liability of the party in default. Immediate notice must be given to the seller by telegram, hand delivery, or other comparable written media, as to the price and quantity purchased.

Sellout

If a purchasing firm fails to accept delivery of securities according to the terms of the contract (other than for valid NASD reasons), the seller may sell out the security without notice in the best available market for the account and liability of the party in default. The party executing the sellout must inform the broker/dealer as promptly as possible by telegram, hand delivery, or other comparable written media of the quantity of securities sold and the price received.

Confirmations or Comparisons

Each party to a transaction, other than a cash transaction, must send a uniform comparison or confirmation on or before the first business day following the date of the transaction. Comparisons or confirmations of cash transactions must be exchanged the day of the trade. Comparisons or confirmations must be compared on receipt to determine whether any discrepancies exist.

If any discrepancies do exist, a corrected uniform comparison or confirmation must be sent by the party in error. These rules do not apply to transactions that clear through the National Securities Clearing Corporation or any other clearing organizations registered under the Securities Exchange Act of 1934.

If a broker/dealer receives a confirmation or comparison relating to a transaction which it does not have on its records, a DK notice should be sent to the contra-broker. This Official NASD DK notice is used for unmatched trades and is always sent to the contra-broker (the other side of the trade). The DK notice is never sent to the customer or self-regulatory organizations such as the NASD or the NYSE.

GOOD DELIVERY OF SECURITIES

The term *good delivery* as it is used in the securities business means that a stock certificate is delivered by the selling broker to the buying broker in a form permitting ownership to be readily transferred. The requirements for a good delivery of securities under NASD rules are summarized as follows:

- On the back of a registered stock certificate, a legal document called an **assignment and power of substitution** is printed, which allows for transferring ownership of the certificate. In order to make a registered certificate negotiable, the person owning the certificate must sign it exactly as his or her name appears on the front of the certificate. Therefore, if a certificate is registered in the name of "Paul Michael Jones," the certificate must be signed "Paul Michael Jones" on the back of the certificate or on a stock power. Signatures such as "P.M. Jones" or "P. Michael Jones" are not acceptable. Once the stock certificate is properly signed or a stock power is properly signed, the certificate is fully negotiable and transfer of ownership can take place. A stock power is a separate piece of paper that is almost identical to the back of a stock certificate. The signed stock power, when attached to the certificate, makes it negotiable. If a signature to a certificate is erased, corrected, or altered, the certificate must be accompanied by an explanation on the original certificate signed by the person executing it in order to be acceptable for transfer. If a stock certificate is owned by joint tenants, all joint tenants must sign the certificate in order to be a good delivery.

- For a good delivery of stock certificates, the following rules apply concerning the denominations the certificates may be in:

  - If the transaction is for 100 shares, good delivery would be one certificate for 100 shares or certificates totaling 100 shares. Therefore, a transaction for 100 shares would be a good delivery in each of the following examples:

    - 1 certificate for 100 shares
    - 5 certificates each for 20 shares
    - 2 certificates each for 50 shares
    - 100 certificates each for 1 share
    - Any other combination of certificates totaling 100 shares would be considered good delivery.

  - If the transaction is greater than 100 shares and a multiple of 100 shares, good delivery would be one certificate for the exact amount of the contract, or in multiples of 100 shares or in amounts in which units of 100 shares can be made or a combination thereof equaling the amount of the contract. The following examples might be helpful:

Transaction	*Denomination of certificates*	*Good delivery*
400 shares	One certificate for 400 shares	Yes
	Four 100-share certificates	Yes
	Eight 50-share certificates	Yes
	Five 80-share certificates	No
600 shares	Twelve certificates, 50 shares each	Yes
	Twenty-four certificates, 25 shares each	Yes
	Six certificates for 80 + six for 20 shares	Yes
	Five certificates for 60 + six for 50 shares	No

- If the transaction is for more than 100 shares but not in a multiple of 100 shares, good delivery would be multiples of 100 shares or amounts from which units of 100 shares can be made or combination thereof, plus either the exact amount for the odd lot or smaller amounts equaling the odd lot. The following examples illustrate this example:

Transaction	Denomination of certificates	Good delivery
525 shares	One 500-share + one 25-share certificate	Yes
	One 400-share + one 100-share + one 25-share	Yes
	One 500-share + twenty-five 1-share certificates	Yes
	Ten 50-share + one 120-share + one 5-share certificates	Yes
	One 525-share certificate	No

- If the transaction is for less than 100 shares (an odd lot), good delivery would be a certificate for the exact amount of the contract. Therefore, a transaction for 49 shares would be a good delivery with 1 certificate for 49 shares or any combination totaling 49 shares.

Other important points concerning a delivery of securities include

- A mutilated security is not a good delivery unless properly authenticated by the trustee, registrar, transfer agent, or issuer. The delivery of a bond that bears a coupon which has been mutilated as to the bond number or signature must bear an appropriate endorsement authorized by the paying agent in order to be a good delivery.
- Delivery of certificates called for redemption is not a good delivery unless the entire issue is called.
- Each assignment and power of substitution form allows a person to appoint an individual as attorney for him, to transfer the shares (power of substitution portion). The person sending a signed certificate or a signed stock power through the mail could insert the broker/dealer's name in the appropriate space. If this is done, only the broker/dealer can make the certificate negotiable again by his signature. This is added protection for the person signing the certificate in case it is lost in the mail.
- A certificate is not a good delivery with an assignment or power of substitution executed by a person since deceased or an infant.

The following schedule summarizes the requirements that must be met to effect a transfer of securities for certain types of registration:

Certificate in the name of	Signature and documents required
An individual	Signature of individual
Joint tenants	Signature of all joint tenants
Corporation	Signature of officer authorized to sign plus a corporate resolution that the officer has the authority to act for the corporation
Partnership	Signature of a general partner plus a certification from the partnership that the person is a general partner with authority to sign

INVESTMENT COMPANIES AND THE NASD RULES OF FAIR PRACTICE

Section 26 of the rules of fair practice cover the sale of investment company shares. The following statements cover the important points contained in Section 26 of the rules of fair practice:

- The lowest price at which an underwriter may sell shares of an open-end investment company to a member is the net asset value per share.
- An NASD member may purchase shares of an open-end investment company from the underwriter only

  - For his own investment.
  - To cover purchase orders already received (not to make a market in the security).

- A broker/dealer may purchase shares of an open-end investment company from an NASD member underwriter at a price other than the public offering price only if

  - The buying broker or dealer is also a member, and
  - A written sales agreement is in effect between the parties at the time of the sale.

- An NASD member may not use an upcoming dividend or distribution to induce the purchase of investment company shares (called selling dividends).

- NASD members must promptly pay underwriters for sales of investment company shares. If the payment is not received within ten business days after the transaction date, the NASD must be notified.
- It is contrary to just and equitable principles of trade to sell just below the breakpoint. The breakpoint is the point at which the sales charge is reduced.
- In any transaction between dealers and customers, the public offering price must be maintained.

REGISTERED REPRESENTATIVES—NASD RULES

The NASD regulates member firms (brokerage firms) and associated persons (officers, directors, partners, and registered representatives). Clerical personnel are not considered associated persons. Registered representatives must always act in the best interest of their customers. They can be disciplined for violating

- Federal securities laws
- State securities laws (blue-sky laws)
- Rules and regulations of the self-regulatory organizations (SROs), such as the NYSE, NASD, Municipal Securities Rulemaking Board (MSRB), and regional stock exchanges

When an individual seeks registration with the NASD, a U-4 form must be filed along with a copy of the person's fingerprints. The U-4 form asks questions about a person's background. If an individual who is registered is disciplined by any regulatory agency, this fact must be promptly reported to the NASD. For example, if a person has an insurance or real estate license suspended, the NASD must promptly be notified by an amendment to the U-4 form.

If a registered representative is terminated by a member firm, a U-5 form must be filed with the NASD and a copy must be sent to the registered representative.

8 EXCHANGE MARKETS

The New York Stock Exchange (NYSE) is the largest national securities exchange in the United States. It is located in New York City in lower Manhattan. Securities of most major US corporations are traded on the NYSE.

The NYSE is a self-regulatory organization (SRO) that regulates its own members. The National Association of Securities Dealers (NASD) and the Municipal Securities Rulemaking Board (MSRB) are also self-regulatory organizations. The NYSE and other self-regulatory organizations

- Conduct member firm examinations
- Enforce fair standards of trading
- Provide arbitration facilities to resolve disputes
- Require member firms to keep a high level of solvency (liquid assets)
- Enforce rules of fair practice
- Require members to be qualified

EXCHANGE MEMBERSHIP

The NYSE is a not-for-profit corporation with 1,366 individual members who own seats (memberships). Only individuals may own a seat on the Exchange. When one or more of the individuals owning a seat is associated with a firm, the entity is referred to as a **member firm**. Since more than one individual member may be associated with the same member organization, the number of member organizations is much less than the number of individual members.

The price of a **seat** is determined by supply and demand. The purchaser must not only be able to pay the agreed upon price to the seller, but also must be approved by the board of directors and pay the fees required by the exchange.

The membership of the exchange elects a board of directors to govern its affairs. The board of directors is composed of members of the exchange and representatives of the general public.

Members of the exchange may conduct their business either as sole proprietors, partnerships, or corporations. Any member who is general partner, officer, or employee may qualify a firm or corporation as a member organization.

ALLIED MEMBERS

An allied member of the NYSE is any natural person who is a general partner, a principal executive officer, or any employee who controls a member organization. An allied member must agree in writing to abide by the constitution of the exchange. An allied membership is not transferable and terminates if an allied member dies or is expelled.

TYPES OF EXCHANGE MEMBERS

Due to its size, most of the attention of this section must be focused on the NYSE. The NYSE has different types of members transacting business on the exchange. The main classification of exchange members is as follows:

- **Commission house broker.** This is an exchange member who executes orders for customers of his member organization.
- **Two-dollar broker.** He transacts orders for other exchange members and receives a fee for his services. The fee varies with the size of the transaction.
- **Specialist.** Exchange member who is given the responsibility to maintain a fair and orderly market in any security in which he is the registered specialist on the exchange floor.
- **Registered competitive market maker.** An individual whose dealings in a security on the exchange floor for his own account must contribute to the maintenance of price continuity and to minimizing the effects of a temporary disparity between supply and demand. At the request of a floor official, a regis-

tered competitive market maker must make a bid or offer for his own account in any stock traded on the floor in order to contribute to maintenance of a fair and orderly market in such stock.

- **Competitive trader** (formerly called registered trader). An individual member who executes trades on the floor for his own account and hopes to profit from short-term market fluctuations.
- **Bond broker.** He performs a function similar to a commission broker. He executes orders for customers of the firm he represents.

Another important securities exchange in the United States is the American Stock Exchange, which is also located in New York City. The American Stock Exchange is also organized as a not-for-profit corporation. The operations of the American Stock Exchange are governed by a board of directors elected by the membership, which is composed of exchange members and representatives of the general public.

Besides the NYSE and the American Stock Exchange, there are several regional stock exchanges considered to be **national exchanges**. These regional stock exchanges are located in the following cities:

Chicago Stock Exchange	Chicago, Illinois
Pacific Stock Exchange	Los Angeles, California
Philadelphia Stock Exchange	Philadelphia, Pennsylvania
Boston Stock Exchange	Boston, Massachusetts
National Stock Exchange	All-Electronic Trading

FUNCTIONS

All American exchanges perform certain basic functions.

- They provide a marketplace where securities may be bought and sold quickly, with little variation from the current market price in normal markets.
- They permit fair price determination. A fair price is defined as whatever price buyers and sellers in a free market can agree upon as reasonable.
- They perform other functions, such as reporting sales and quotations, performing regulatory functions relating to their members and releasing information on listed companies.

DOUBLE-AUCTION SYSTEM

On the New York and American exchanges, and to some degree on the regional exchanges, trading is done in the manner of a two-sided auction. In the more familiar auction, there is one auctioneer-seller, and (hopefully) many buyers. On the exchanges, there are many sellers and many buyers. This is called the **double-auction system**.

As an example, consider the NYSE. On the floor, there are a number of trading posts. At each post, certain specific listed securities are traded. Buyers wanting to purchase AT&T stock will go to the post where AT&T is traded. Prospective sellers will do the same. Meeting at that post as a crowd, they will shout prices at which they are willing to buy or sell. As a result, there is a free market, and prices are determined by buyers and sellers.

Securities listed on stock exchanges are referred to as **listed securities**. Listed securities are

- Automatically marginable
- Can be sold short only on an uptick or zero-plus tick
- May be delisted if they fail to meet listing requirements

To determine if an issue will be listed, the following factors are analyzed by the NYSE.

- The earnings history for the company
- The company's dividend payout ratio
- The current market price of the company's shares

RULES OF TRADING

There are, naturally, rules governing trading on exchanges, but these rules exist primarily to prevent any one person or group from obtaining an unfair advantage. In other words, these rules exist to protect the double-auction system. Bidding and offering rules on the NYSE are based on priority (first bid or offer), precedence (greatest number of shares), and parity (equal bids and offers), and include

- The highest bid and lowest offer have the floor.

- The first bid or first offer at a price has priority over other bids or offers at that price.
- Any trade or series of trades which removes all of the offers (or bids) at a given price ends the auction and a new auction begins.
- Secret transactions on the floor are not permitted, and all bids and offers must be made orally in an audible voice.

The stock exchanges do not buy, sell, or own stock. They do not take any part in the determination of price. A stock exchange provides a location where buyers and sellers may meet to transact business, establish rules to protect customers and members, and provide certain services. The exchange does not do any business in securities itself and does not set market values of securities.

Under NYSE rules, only members can trade securities on the floor of the exchange. Therefore, the following can trade securities on the NYSE trading floor:

- Specialist
- Floor brokers (two-dollar brokers)
- Competitive traders

TYPES OF ORDERS

There are many different types of orders a customer can give to a member organization. A customer will decide what type of order is most beneficial to him at a particular time. The main types of orders, which a customer can give his or her broker, are as follows:

- *Market order*. A market order is an order to buy or sell at the best price available, when the order reaches the floor of the stock exchange. For example, a customer tells a registered representative to "Buy 100 shares of Telephone at the market for my account." This order will be transmitted to the floor and executed at the best available price. The customer will have established a long position in Telephone. The term *long* in the securities business means *ownership*. The customer is long 100 shares of Telephone.
- *Limit order*. A limit order is an order to buy or sell at a specific price, or better, and may be either a day or good-till-canceled (GTC)order. For example, suppose that a particular stock is selling now at $50 per share and that you would like to sell your shares if the price should rise to $60. You would then place a limit order to sell at $60. If you would like to buy more shares if the price dropped to $40, you would place a limit order to buy at $40.

  Note that a limit order to sell always specifies a price *above* the present market price, while a limit order to buy always specifies a price *below* the present market price. Such an order is only executed at the specified limit price or better. Thus, in the example, stock would be bought only at $40 or below and sold only at $60 or above. There is, of course, the possibility of missing the market. The specified price may never be reached or there may be other orders placed earlier—stock ahead—and the price may move away from the limit before the specific order is exercised. The order, however, never becomes a market order even after the stock sells at the limit. Besides being day orders and GTC orders, limit orders may be immediate or cancel, or fill-or-kill orders.
- *Stop order*. Stop orders are orders to buy or sell when a given price is reached or passed. They may be either day or GTC orders. They are really memorandum orders that become market orders when a given price is reached or passed. For example, assume a customer bought 100 shares of XYZ at $20 per share. XYZ increases in price to $50 per share. The customer places a stop order to sell at $47 per share. If the stock decreases to $47 per share or lower, the stop order is activated. The stop order to sell becomes a market order to sell and the customer sells the stock at the best available price. The purpose of a stop order to sell is to protect an existing profit on the security. A stop order to sell is always placed below the market price of the security. A stop order to buy always specifies a price above the present market price. The purpose here is either to protect an existing profit on a short sale or reduce the possible loss on a short sale. A stop order to sell, however, always specifies a price below the present market price and is used to either protect an existing profit on a long purchase or reduce the loss on a long purchase. A stop order cannot be executed until the given price is reached or passed, it becomes a market order—unlike the limit order—and will be executed regardless of the price.

  There are certain dangers related to stop orders. One is that a temporary reversal of the market may cause an order to be executed. Another is that the order may be executed at several points away from the stop price.

- *Stop limit orders*. Order to buy or sell at a specific price; the order becomes a limit order when the stop price is reached. For example, sell 100 GM at $68 stop $67 limit. When GM trades at $68, the stop is activated and the order becomes a limit order, which must be executed at $67 or higher. American Stock Exchange rules require round-lot stop orders to be entered as stop limit orders. The stop and limit prices must be the same price.
- *Day order*. Order to buy or sell at a specific price or better; the order expires at the end of the day unless executed. All orders are automatically entered as day orders, unless the registered representative receives instructions to enter it as a GTC.
- *Good-till-canceled (GTC) order*. Order to buy or sell at a specific price or better; the order remains open until executed or canceled. GTC orders must be confirmed semiannually. The dates on which the confirmation periods end shall be prescribed by the exchange. Orders properly confirmed retain the same order of precedence on the specialist's book. A GTC order is also called an **open order**.
- *Not-held order*. This type of order gives discretion to the floor broker as to time and price. The floor broker uses his best judgment concerning the proper time to bid for stock (buy) or offer stock (sell) during the auction process. A specialist can never accept a not-held order.
- *Participate but do not initiate (PNI)*. The customer usually gives this type of order to the broker when she has a large order to buy or sell. The floor broker is instructed to participate in the trading, but not to become aggressive, in order to avoid causing a wide price movement in the stock.
- *All-or-none order (AON)*. This is an order in which the customer wants to execute the entire buy or sell order. The floor broker must monitor the trading and buy or sell only when the proper quantity is offered or bid for at the price desired by the customer. The order does not have to be executed immediately.
- *Fill-or-kill order (FOK)*. This type of order must be executed immediately in its entirety or it is canceled. This order requires a complete execution although it does not have to be at one price. Therefore, an FOK order must be executed in its entirety or not at all.
- *Immediate or cancel (IOC)*. This is an order that must be executed immediately, but a partial execution is acceptable. Any part of the order not executed is canceled.

SPECIALIST

A specialist is an exchange member who is responsible for maintaining a fair and orderly market in any security in which he is the registered specialist. Specialists normally work in units, either in partnerships or joint arrangements. During trading hours, a specialist remains at a specific trading post. A specialist may act as a broker or a dealer in a particular transaction, but cannot act as both a broker and a dealer in the same transaction. When acting as a broker, the specialist accepts orders away from the market from floor brokers and enters them in his book. When these orders are executed, the specialist earns a commission, which is called **floor brokerage**. A specialist is a broker's broker and does not accept orders directly from customers.

When acting as a dealer, the specialist buys and sells stocks in which he is registered for his own account. The specialist must be willing to sell stock when there is no other seller, or buy stock when there are no other buyers. Therefore, he risks his own capital in order to maintain fair and orderly markets. The specialist is expected to maintain an orderly succession of trades as close as possible to the last sale. Remember, a specialist does not set prices and does not keep a stock from rising or falling. He is required only to maintain a fair and orderly market in any security in which he is the registered specialist.

The specialist records all limit orders he receives in his specialist's book. Buy orders are usually entered on the left side of the page, while sell orders are usually entered on the right side of the page. Each page will reflect one whole number.

Assume that the specialist's book in XYZ is as follows:

Buy (bids)	*XYZ*	*Sell (Offers)*
	55	
	.13	
300 Merrill Lynch	.25	
	.38	
	.50	
	.63	200 PaineWebber
		400 A.G. Edwards
	.75	500 Dean Witter

When a specialist is asked for a current quote and size in XYZ, he will reflect the highest bid and the lowest offer and the number of shares. The current quotation in XYZ is $55.25–$55.63 300 by 600. The specialist never reflects any bid or offer except the highest bid and the lowest offer in his book.

A specialist may not compete with any order on his book. He must purchase stock at a higher price than anyone else is willing to pay, or sell at a lower price than anyone else is willing to take. In other words, the lowest price the specialist may bid for stock in this case is $55.26. The highest price the specialist can offer stock at is $55.62. He must bid at least $0.01 higher than the highest bid on his book and offer stock $0.01 lower than the lowest offering on his book.

A specialist must attempt to open a stock for trading as close as possible to the closing price of the previous business day. Market orders, before the opening, are given to the specialist. He must open the stock for trading at a price that will allow all market orders to buy or sell to be executed. Assume a specialist has buy orders for 15,000 shares and sell orders for 11,000. The specialist must find sell orders for an additional 4,000 shares in order to open the stock. A delayed opening would occur when there is a large imbalance of buy and sell orders.

REDUCING ORDERS ON EX-DIVIDEND DATE

On the date a security trades ex-dividend, the specialist will reduce

- Open limit orders to buy in that security
- Open stop orders to sell in that security including stop (unit orders to sell)

These orders will be automatically reduced unless the customer has entered a **do not reduce (DNR)** order. Open limit orders to buy, open stop orders to sell, and open stop limit orders to sell are all orders entered below the market price of the security and are reduced by the specialist.

Price of buy limit or sell stop orders	Dividend amount	Order reduced to
45	$0.12	44.88
47	$0.25	46.75
49	$1.00	48.00

The reason that open limit orders to buy are reduced is that it would be unreasonable to expect the customer to pay the same price for the company's stock after the dividend. Assume a customer places a limit order to buy XYZ at $51 per share. The customer feels that the stock is worth that price and does not want to pay any more than $51. This is the reason a limit order was entered by the customer. The company announces that it will pay a $0.50 per share dividend. On the ex-dividend date, the customer's order must be reduced to a buy order at $50.50 to be in the same position as he was before the dividend was announced. The customer, of course, did not receive the dividend because he did not own the security. The company paid out a portion of its assets ($0.50 per share) and, therefore, is worth less to the potential buyer of its shares.

A sell order is also reduced for a different reason. In this case, the customer did receive the dividend, and when the order is reduced, he would be in the same position after the reduction in price, if the order is subsequently executed. For example, assume the customer had a stop order to sell 100 XYZ at $50 per share. The company announced intentions to pay a dividend of $1. On the ex-dividend date, the stop order to sell is reduced to $49 and, subsequently, activated and executed at $49 per share. The customer would receive $100 in dividends and $4,900 from the sale of the security (excluding commissions). The total of $5,000 is exactly the same amount he would have received if the 100 shares were sold at $50 without a dividend being declared.

The specialist does not reduce open limit orders to sell or open stop orders to buy. Open limit orders to sell are not reduced because the customer wants a certain amount from the sale of stock even though he received the dividend. Open stop orders to buy are not reduced because, in this case, the customer did not receive the dividend. A reduction of the order might cause it to be activated as a result of a dividend, and not as the result of market forces of demand and supply.

A stop limit order to sell would be reduced by the specialist at the opening on the ex-dividend date. Assume a customer has placed an order with the specialist to sell 100 ABC at $50 stop $48 limit. ABC declares a $0.60 dividend. At the opening on the ex-dividend date, the order will appear on the specialist's book as an order to sell 100 ABC at $49.40 stop $47.40 limit.

A stop limit order to sell is essentially the same type of order as a stop order to sell, except that the customer must receive the limit price after the stop is activated. Assume a customer places an order to sell 100 shares of ABC at $52 stop $51 limit. Assume ABC trades at $52 a share. A trade at $52 a share activates the stop and the order becomes a limit order. The order will be executed provided it can be done at $51 or higher. However, if the next trade after the stop is activated takes place at $50.75 and continues to decline in price, the order will not be executed. This is the danger associated with a stop limit order. A stop limit order can be activated, but the order may or may not be executed. The closer the limit price is placed to the stop price, the greater the chance the order may not be executed.

SHORT SALES ON EXCHANGES

The Securities and Exchange Commission (SEC) has established certain rules governing short sales on stock exchanges. Short sales can be made only on a plus tick or a zero-plus tick. This means that a short sale can only be made at a higher price than the last sale price on the consolidated tape. However, if the last sale price is the same as the previous sale, the last change in price must be a plus tick in order to effect a short sale. A plus tick may also be called an uptick. Consider the following example:

Assume a stock trades at prices in this sequence.

$45, $44.88, $44.88, $45, $45

The change in price from $45 to $44.88 is a minus tick. The next sale takes place at $44.88 and is a zero-minus tick. The fourth transaction takes place at $45 and is a plus tick. Stock could have been sold short in this transaction because it was a plus tick. The next transaction takes place at $45 and is a zero-plus tick. Stock could have been sold short at this price also. A short seller does not have to wait until a plus tick or zero-plus tick occurs. The short seller may be the seller in the transaction that establishes the plus tick or zero-plus tick.

Let us combine the concepts associated with short sales and the reducing of orders on the ex-dividend date by the specialist. Assume ABC stock will open ex-dividend after closing at $40 per share on an uptick. The dividend on the security is $0.60. What is the lowest price at which the stock can be offered for a short sale?

Since the stock closed at $40 on an uptick, the short sale rule has been met. The stock will be reduced to $39.40. Therefore, 39.40 is the lowest price at which the stock can be offered for a short sale.

STOPPING STOCK

A specialist is allowed to guarantee a broker an execution at a certain price while the broker tries to obtain the stock at a more favorable price. The procedure is known as **stopping stock**. A specialist can only stop stock (guarantee execution at a certain price) for public customers of member firms.

For example, if a stock is quoted $50–$50.25, the specialist may grant a stop to PaineWebber at $50.25 for 200 shares. This means that PaineWebber is guaranteed to pay no more than $50.25 to purchase the 200 shares. PaineWebber will now try to buy the stock in the crowd at less than $50.25. If this cannot be done, and a seller offers 200 shares at $50.25, PaineWebber will be stopped out. PaineWebber will buy the 200 shares at $50.25. There must be at least a $0.02 spread in the stock before a specialist can grant a stop.

To summarize, stopping stock is a procedure where the specialist guarantees the purchase or sale of a security at a specific price, while the broker attempts to obtain a better price. The actual price at which the order will be executed is not determined. However, the specialist guarantees that the customer will not pay more or receive less than a specific price. The specialist may stop stock only for the account of public customers. No floor governor's permission is required to stop stock. The request to stop stock must come from the floor broker because the specialist is prohibited from granting stops unless specifically asked to do so by a floor broker.

Exchange rules prohibit the specialist from doing the following when trading for his own account:

- Bid or offer stock at the same price as any customer's limit order on his book. If the specialist wants to bid for stock for his own account, he must bid at least $0.01 higher than the highest bid on his book. If the specialist wants to offer stock from his own account, he must offer the stock at least $0.01 lower than the lowest offer on his book.
- Activating any customer's stop order on his book except by an execution.
- Stopping stock for any member's personal account. A specialist is allowed to stop stock only for a public customer of an NYSE member firm.
- Compete with any customer's market order. This means the specialist cannot buy as principal until all customer market orders to buy have been executed, and the specialist is not allowed to sell stock as principal until all customer market orders to sell have been executed.

Some of the important points concerning a specialist are summarized below.

- An exchange member responsible for maintaining a fair and orderly market for all stocks in which he is the registered specialist.

- Records all limit orders, stop orders, and stop limit orders received on his specialist's book.
- May act as a broker or dealer in a transaction, but not both in the same transaction.
- When acting as broker, executes limit orders left with him and earns floor brokerage.
- When acting as dealer, buys and sells for his own account and risk.
- Does not deal directly with the public, only with other members (floor brokers, traders).
- Does not set prices and does not try to prevent a rise or fall in the price of the stock.
- May not participate in a proxy contest nor can he be an officer or director of a company in which he is a specialist.
- When asked for a quote, reflects the highest bid and lowest offer on his book.
- When a stock is quoted ex-dividend or ex-rights, the specialist reduces open buy limit orders, stop orders to sell, and stop limit orders to sell.
- The specialist does not reduce

  - Open stop orders to buy, including open stop limits to buy
  - Open sell limit orders
  - Orders marked do not reduce (DNR)

- A specialist may stop stock for the account of public customers of member firms, not for his own account or the account of any member.
- He must open the stock as near to the previous day's close as possible and still execute all buy and sell market orders received before the opening.
- A specialist can accept a market order to buy or sell from a customer and act as principal in the trade. He can also place the following types of orders on his book:

  - Limit order
  - Stop order
  - Stop limit order

  Limit orders and stop orders entered with the specialist must be entered as either day orders or OTC (open) orders. Assume a customer wants to place a buy limit order that is "good through the month" in an NYSE-listed stock. The NYSE member firm can accept this order and place it with the specialist as a GTC order. However, responsibility for cancellation of the order at month-end (assuming it is not executed prior to month-end) rests with the member firm.

- If a customer changes the terms of an order on the specialist's book, the order will lose its priority on the specialist book and will be placed last for all orders at the same price.

TAPE DISPLAYS

All round-lot transactions that take place on the floor of any national securities exchange are reported on the consolidated tape. The consolidated tape is composed of two separate tapes.

1. *Network A.* Reports sales of NYSE-listed issues regardless of where the transaction is executed (exchange or OTC).
2. *Network B.* Reports sales of American Stock Exchange–listed issues regardless of where the trade is executed (exchange or OTC), also sales in regional issues (stocks listed solely on regional exchanges) are reported on this tape.

The consolidated tape reports transactions in listed common stocks, warrants, rights, and preferred stocks. Third- and fourth-market transactions in listed securities are reported on the consolidated tape. Options, commodities, and odd-lot transactions are not reported on the consolidated tape. Transactions in foreign securities and transactions in primary markets are not reported on the consolidated tape.

All round-lot transactions in NYSE-listed issues executed on a national securities exchange or OTC are reported on Network A with the following components:

- Stock symbol
- Price
- Volume
- Qualifications

For example, if 100 shares of General Motors trades on the NYSE at $74, the transactions would be reported on Tape A as follows:

GM Indicates that 100 shares of General Motors traded at $74
74

The reported transaction reflects the symbol and the price. For 100 share trades, the number of shares is not shown. If a transaction takes place and the volume is greater than 100 shares and less than 1,000 shares (200–900), the number of shares would be reported as follows:

2s	=	200 shares	6s	=	600 shares
3s	=	300 shares	7s	=	700 shares
4s	=	400 shares	8s	=	800 shares
Ss	=	500 shares	9s	=	900 shares

In other words, the "s" refers to round lots. Therefore, 5s to a trade in five round lots equal 500 shares. A normal round-lot trade represents 100 shares.

GM   F   C   IBM
2s 74   3s 52 9s 31 4s 70

The tape is reporting that 200 shares of General Motors traded at $74, 300 shares of Ford traded at $52, 900 shares of Chrysler traded at $31, and that 400 shares of IBM traded at $70.

If a transaction is effected for 1,000 shares through 9,900 shares, the transactions are reported as follows:

ABC   XYZ   TBS
10s 52   25s 61   48s 74

The tape is reporting that 1,000 shares of ABC traded at $52, 2,500 shares of XYZ traded at $61, and 4,800 shares of TBS traded at $74.

If a transaction is effected for 10,000 shares or more, the exact volume is printed.

HTN   CNN   HBO
10000s 35   14000s 55   18000s 44

The tape is reporting that 10,000 shares of HTN traded at $35, 14,000 shares of CNN traded at $55, and 18,000 shares of HBO traded at$ 44.

Certain inactive securities (mostly preferred issues) on the NYSE have round lots equal to 10 shares instead of 100 shares. These transactions are reported on the tape with the letters "s" printed between the volume and price.

MNR Indicates that 60 shares of Mighty Northern Railroad traded at $58 a share
6s 58
s

Transactions in preferred stocks are indicated by the symbol "Pr."

RCA Pr
4s 65

The tape is reporting that 400 shares of RCA preferred stock traded at $65 on the NYSE.

If a transaction is reported on a delayed basis, it would be shown as follows:

CBS.SLD
41.25

This transaction indicates that 100 shares of CBS traded at $41.25 was reported out of sequence. In other words, there was a delay in reporting this transaction relating to CBS.

If trading on the NYSE in particular securities is halted for regulatory reasons, trade reports from other markets will not be displayed as they occur. Instead, they will be stored and displayed as a group after the market closes. Actually, all other markets normally halt trading in a security when the NYSE declares a regulatory halt.

ODD-LOT TRANSACTIONS

Odd lots are defined as any number of shares that is less than the normal unit of trading. The normal unit of trading in most stocks on the NYSE is 100 shares. Therefore, an odd-lot order, in most securities, would be less than 100 shares. In certain inactively traded securities on the NYSE, the normal trading unit is 10 shares. An odd lot for these securities would be an order for less than 10 shares.

CONSOLIDATED QUOTATIONS

Electronic quotation machines provide traders and registered representatives with up-to-the-minute prices and quotations. The quotations are designated by symbols relating to each exchange and are summarized as follows:

Exchange	*Symbol*
Boston	B
Instinet	O
Chicago	M
New York	N
NASDAQ	T
Philadelphia	X
Pacific	P

INTERMARKET TRADING SYSTEM

The Intermarket Trading System (ITS) is a communications network that links together the New York, American, Chicago, Pacific, Philadelphia, and Boston Stock Exchange trading floors. The ITS communications network keeps floor brokers and specialists constantly aware of competing market bid and ask prices.

Terminals are available on each of the exchange floors showing bid and ask quotations and size for each eligible security in the system. The ITS enables buyers and sellers to obtain the best prices in the stocks included in the linkage, and also enables specialists and floor brokers in one market to buy and sell for their own accounts (or as agent for the account of another) in competing markets.

NYSE BOND TRADING

The greatest majority of bond trading takes place in the OTC market. The reason is that many bond trades are so large that the auction process does not appear to be as efficient as the dealer process.

The NYSE requires that all orders for the purchase or sale of listed bonds must be sent to the floor for execution, except in the following instances:

- When the order is for the purchase or sale of ten bonds or more
- When a better price may be obtained off the floor
- When customer requests that the order be executed off the floor

Therefore, under NYSE rules, all orders for nine listed bonds or less must be sent to the floor for execution. The only exception to the rule is when the customer directs that the order be executed off the floor. The trading unit for listed bonds is normally $1,000.

SUPER DOT

The Super Dot System operating on the floor of the NYSE is an electronic order-entry system linking NYSE member firms directly to the trading floor. The system routes market and limit orders directly to the post where each stock is traded, or to the member firm's booth on the trading floor, and promptly reports executions back to the firms.

Member firms can enter market orders and limit orders in round or odd lots directly from their order rooms. The system automatically executes orders from their order rooms. The system automatically executes orders when a $0.01 spread exists in a stock and reports them back within five seconds. The automatic execution is based on the best quote in the Intermarket Trading System. Customer orders placed through the Super Dot System receive competitive executions. However, customer orders placed through the system are not guaranteed better executions than could be obtained outside the system.

PROGRAM TRADING

In recent years, a great deal of discussion has arisen concerning a trading strategy referred to as **program trading**. Program trading is a generic term given to a number of strategies that take advantage of computers to buy and sell large blocks of stock simultaneously. Certain types of computer-generated trading is widely accepted. However, a program trading strategy called *index arbitrage* has caused much debate.

Index arbitrage is used by a handful of sophisticated traders to cash in on disparities between stock and futures prices. Traders buy or sell baskets of stocks while at the same time executing offsetting trades in stock index futures or options. Traders profit by trying to capture price discrepancies between stocks and index futures or options. If stocks are temporarily cheaper than futures, an arbitrager will buy stocks and sell futures. Program trading can make market swings more steep.

ADDITIONAL CONCEPTS

The following information on exchange operations is important to understanding how transactions are executed.

- A specialist can act as agent or as principal in a securities transaction. A specialist, when acting as agent

  - Maintains the specialist book
  - Establishes the opening price in each security in which he is the assigned specialist

- A specialist, when acting as dealer or as principal

  - Maintains an orderly market in his assigned securities
  - Handles odd-lot orders

- Transactions reported on the consolidated tape do not include commissions. Assume a customer purchases 100 shares of XYZ at $58 a share with a $0.50 commission. The transaction would be reported on the consolidated tape at $58 a share.
- A secondary distribution is a large block of securities traded normally at the close of business of the NYSE. Assume an officer of an NYSE-listed security wants to sell 500,000 shares. This is a secondary distribution, which will be executed in the OTC market and the seller will pay the transaction costs.
- Assume a customer buys 100 shares of ABC at $30 per share. ABC increases in price to $80 per share. The customer has an unrealized gain on ABC of $50 per share ($5,000). To attempt to protect the gain, the customer could place a stop order to sell 100 shares of ABC at $75 per share. If the stock trades at $75 per share or lower, the stop order is activated. The customer would sell the stock at the best available price.
- The NYSE has a circuit breaker rule, which stops trading for one hour (Level 1 halt), if the Dow Jones Industrial Average (DJIA) declines by 10% from its previous day's close before 2:00 P.M. (ET). A Level 2 halt is a decline of 20% and a Level 3 halt is a decline of 30%. A Level 3 halt would suspend trading for the remainder of the trading day. Program trading curbs go into effect if the DJIA moves up or down by 2%.
- Registered persons must sit for the regulatory element of continuing education on the second anniversary of their first registration date and every three years thereafter.

9 EXCHANGE REGULATIONS

This chapter will explore New York Stock Exchange (NYSE) rules and regulations. NYSE rules relating to associated persons, including registered representatives, will be covered. NYSE rules relating to communications with the public, handling customer accounts, settlement of transactions, and other areas will also be examined.

REGISTERED REPRESENTATIVES

A registered representative (RR) is an associated person of a member firm and must be registered with the NYSE and National Association of Securities Dealers (NASD) before performing the functions of an RR. To become registered, an individual must be employed by a member firm and complete a U-4 form and submit fingerprints. The individual must pass the Series 7 examination demonstrating knowledge in various areas of the securities industry.

The normal training requirement for NYSE registered representatives is four months. The training requirement and/or examination requirement for an individual candidate may be waived at the discretion of the exchange for good cause.

RRs and officers of a member organization must sign a statement indicating that they will not

- Guarantee the payment of the debit balance in a customer's account without the prior written consent of the exchange.
- Guarantee a customer against loss in his or her account.
- Share, directly or indirectly, in the profits or losses of any customer's account.
- Engage in outside business activities without prior written notice to their employer.
- Engage in private securities transactions without prior written notice to their employer.
- Open a securities account with another broker/dealer without prior written notice to their employer.
- Rebate any part of the compensation they receive as RRs.
- Commingle customer funds with their own funds. All customer funds received by RRs must be promptly given to the member firm.

RRs must agree in writing that they will do the following:

- Notify the NYSE promptly if they become involved in any litigation, criminal action, or bankruptcy proceeding or their securities license is suspended or revoked.
- Appear before any NYSE committee upon their request to give evidence or produce records relating to any investigation.
- Agree to arbitration to resolve any controversy between them and their member firm or any other member firm arising out of their employment or termination. Arbitration may be requested by either party in a dispute and the contra-party must submit to the arbitration proceeding.
- Agree to appear and testify in any dispute for a ninety-day period following their termination.

Besides signing agreements concerning their activities, certain other rules relating to RRs are important. For example, RRs may not

- Be employed in a nominal position because of commissions which their own account brings to the firm
- Take a leave of absence without their firm's approval

However, with the prior permission of the exchange, RRs may

- Operate from their residence.
- Advertise their home address in any normal manner.
- In such case, their residence address is considered as constituting an office of their employer.

Concerning speaking and teaching activities, the prior approval of the exchange is not required for single talks, courses, or lecture series on investment subjects or outside speaking activities before community groups and institutions if

- They have the consent of a general partner, allied member, or competent authorized delegate.

- The member organization assumes responsibility for the general content and the speaker's educational approach.
- In talks and lectures sponsored by public or private groups, personnel should not recommend specific securities or methods of investing.

Therefore, under NYSE rules, RRs must receive permission from their employer before giving seminars, lectures or speeches relating to the securities industry. Prior permission from the NYSE is not required.

NYSE rules require a member organization to maintain a log of all talks and lectures given by its employees reflecting the following information for a specific talk or lecture:

- The name of the person giving the talk
- The name of the group sponsoring the talk
- The subject matter discussed

The retention period required for logs of all talks and lectures given by the personnel of a member organization is three years.

IF RRs want to give a talk sponsored by a public or private group concerning securities

- They must obtain prior approval from a member, allied member or competent authorized delegate.
- They cannot recommend specific securities or methods of investing.
- The broker/dealer must maintain a record of the speech for three years.

A leave of absence may be granted to an RR by a member organization without the prior approval of the exchange, provided

- The member organization retains a written record of the leave.
- The RR is not physically present at any office of the employer and does not act as a registered representative.
- The RR does not leave to engage in any other business or be employed by another corporation, firm, or individual or serve as a partner, officer, or director of any other partnership or corporation.

Other important points concerning registered representatives are

- Any advice given to a client must be based on good faith and informed judgment of investment facts, not rumor.
- A client's interest shall always be the first consideration of an RR.
- The wholesale recommendation of a single security to all clients, without attention to each individual's investment situation, is unsuitable.
- RRs' responsibility is greatest when they recommend the purchase of highly volatile securities in little-known companies.
- RRs must never allow their personal investment actions to influence the advice they give to their clients.
- If an RR is suspended by the NASD for a violation of NASD rules, s/he must promptly notify the exchange.
- An RR, member, member organization, or employee may not give a gratuity of more than $50 per person per year to any employee of the exchange, other member, nonmember broker or dealer, or news or financial media, without the prior written consent of the recipient's employer.
- An RR may be a director of up to three corporations not in the securities business without the prior approval of the exchange.
- An RR could be censured, fined, suspended, or expelled for violating rules and regulations. Member firms can be held responsible for failing to properly supervise RRs who violate industry rules.

COMMUNICATIONS WITH THE PUBLIC

Member firm communications with the public must be truthful and in good taste. Member organizations must conform to the following guidelines concerning written communications:

- Recommendations must be reasonable and supporting information must be provided.
- When a specific security is recommended, the member organization must disclose if
  - The firm usually makes a market in the security recommended.
  - The member organization or its partners or officers hold options on the security recommended.
  - The member organization was the manager or co-manager of a public offering of the security within the last three years.

- Any material concerned with past recommendations made in connection with purchases or sales is acceptable if it covers and includes all of the following:

  - At least a one-year period.
  - A list of all the issues in a specific universe or clearly definable area, which can be fully isolated and circumscribed, recommended during the period.

- The date and price of each recommendation on the recommendation date and at the end of the period shown or when the sale was suggested, whichever date is earlier.
- The number of issues recommended, the number that advanced, and the number that declined. In the event that a list of past recommendations is offered but not included in the material, it must be made clear that

  - The period was one of a generally rising market, if such is the case.
  - There is no implication in the material of any future performance or that the customer cannot lose by following the firm's recommendation.
  - If the record is averaged, such results would have been obtained only if each issue had been purchased when recommended and sold at the end of the period covered or when the sale was recommended. The impact of commissions must also be addressed.

The rules of the exchange also require that each market letter, research report, and all sales literature prepared and issued by a member or member organization for general distribution be approved in advance by a member, allied member, or competent authorized delegate.

Also, it is important to know that research reports must be prepared or approved by a supervisory analyst acceptable to the exchange. If the firm does not have a person so qualified with the exchange to approve such material, it must be approved by a qualified supervisory analyst in another member organization.

Therefore, under NYSE rules, research reports prepared by a member firm of the NYSE for public distribution must

- Be approved in advance by a partner, officer, or a person the member firm so designates
- Be approved in advance by a supervisory analyst acceptable to the exchange
- Be approved by a qualified supervisory analyst employed by another member firm if two member firms have so arranged
- Be retained at least three years by the member firm that prepared the material

All market letters, sales literature, and research reports referring to the market or to specific companies or securities must be kept for three years, and copies retained must

- Contain the name or names of the preparers
- Contain the name or names of persons approving issuance
- Be readily available for inspection

Member organizations which desire to broadcast NYSE quotes on radio or television programs must obtain exchange approval by submitting an outline of the material to be covered in the program.

CONDUCT OF ACCOUNTS

Member firms must, through a general partner or principal executive officer, learn the essential facts concerning every customer, every cash and margin account, every order, and every individual holding a power of attorney over a customer's account. All accounts must be supervised by the member firm in a diligent manner. A branch-office manager may approve the opening of a customer's account, but that account must be approved within a reasonable time by a general partner, principal executive officer, or a person specifically authorized to approve the opening of accounts.

If an employee of an NYSE member firm wants to open a securities account with another member firm, prior written consent must be obtained from the employing member firm. Also, duplicate copies of confirmations and statements must be sent by the carrying firm to the employing firm if the account is approved. NYSE employees need prior written permission from the NYSE to open a securities account, but duplicate confirmations are not required. Officers of banks do not need written permission of their employer to open a securities account.

A member organization cannot carry an account on its books in the name of someone other than the customer who owns the account. However, an account may be designated by a symbol or number if the member organization has obtained a written statement from the customer attesting to the ownership of the account.

A member, allied member, or employee of a member organization cannot exercise any discretionary power in a customer's account without obtaining

- Prior written authorization of the customer
- Prior approval of a general partner or principal executive officer responsible for giving such approval

Member organizations must send customer statements at least quarterly to any customer who had a money position, security position, or an entry in the account during the preceding quarter.

Assume a customer asks her RR to send her confirmations to her investment advisor. This can be done under NYSE rules provided a written request is obtained from the customer.

Every member organization must make available to any customer, partner, stockholder, or subordinated lender of such organization, at their request, a statement of its financial condition. Therefore, if a customer opens an account with an NYSE member firm and requests a copy of the firm's statement of its financial condition, the firm must make the statement available to the customer. The member firm does not have to give customers a copy of its income statement and does not have to disclose its inventory or investment positions to customers.

A member organization is required to maintain a record of every order transmitted to the floor for a period of three years. Each order must include the type of order, time of entry, and time of execution. Also, the designation of the customer's account and terms of the order must be included on the firm's record. NYSE rules require that sell orders must be marked "long" or "short" on the order ticket. In a long sale, the customer agrees to deliver the security by settlement date.

A change in the account name or designation on an order cannot be made unless it has been approved by a member, allied member, or a person authorized to approve this type of transaction. The person who authorizes the change must be personally informed of the reasons for the change and indicate their approval in writing on the order ticket or other record of the firm.

What if an order is executed at a certain price ($55) but reported to the customer at a different price ($54)? Which price shall be binding on the customer? In this example, the customer would be required to pay the price at which the order was actually executed ($55). The fact that an order was reported in error to the customer does not relieve the customer from paying the correct contract price.

DEALINGS AND SETTLEMENTS

In this section, some of the important points contained in the NYSE Constitution relating to dealings and settlement of security contracts will be discussed. All contracts executed on the floor of the exchange are settled in one of the following ways:

- *Regular-way contract (T + 3).* Delivery of the stock by the seller is due on the third business day following the trade date—this is the usual way listed stocks are settled. For US government notes or bonds, regular-way settlement is the first business day following the trade date.
- *Cash transaction.* Delivery of the stock by the seller is due on the same day as the transaction. Transactions made at or before 2:00 P.M. are due before 2:30 P.M.; those made after 2:00 P.M. are due within thirty minutes after the transaction.
- *Seller's option contract.* Due on the date of expiration of the contract.
- *When issued and when distributed.* Due on a date determined by the exchange.

Transactions in stocks (except cash transactions) will trade ex-dividend (without the dividend) on the second business day before the record date. The record date is a date fixed in advance by the corporation paying the dividend. The dividend is paid to persons whose names are on the books of the corporation on the record date.

If an individual purchases stock before the ex-dividend date, he is entitled to the dividend. However, if the transaction takes place before the ex-dividend or ex-rights' date, and the delivery is made too late to have the shares transferred into the buyer's name by the record date, the seller must give the buyer a due bill for the amount of the dividend.

A due bill is a written promise to pay a distribution of cash, rights, or securities. In the case of a cash dividend, a due bill is in the form of a due-bill check, which is payable on the date the dividend is paid by the company.

ACCRUED INTEREST ON BONDS

The next subject to be discussed is the manner in which bonds are handled with regard to the settlement of contracts. Unless otherwise stated by the exchange, all contracts in bonds shall be traded "and interest". In other words, the purchaser, when he buys a bond, pays the contract price plus the accrued interest from the last payment date up to, but not including, settlement date. Interest is computed on a 360-day year on corporate and municipal bonds. Each calendar month is considered a 30-day month. Interest begins to accrue on the last interest payment date.

Consider the following example:

Assume the payable dates for XYZ bonds, for interest payments, are January 15 and July 15. The bond is purchased for settlement on April 19. How many days accrued interest will be paid by the purchaser? Since the settlement date is April 19, accrued interest will include through April 18.

January 15–January 30	16 days
February	30 days
March	30 days
April	18 days
Total	94 days

Remember, every month is considered to have thirty days, and interest is computed from the last payment date up to, but not including, settlement date.

Assume the customer purchased the bond for $1,000 (par) and the interest rate on the bond was 6%. The amount of accrued interest the customer would pay is calculated as follows:

$$\$1,000 \quad \text{x} \quad \frac{6}{100} \quad \text{x} \quad \frac{94}{360} = \$15.67$$

Therefore, the total contract price to be paid by the customer is $1,015.67.

For US government bonds, interest is computed on the actual number of days in a month. If a month has 31 days, the interest is computed on the 31 days. For example, assume a regular-way trade is done on June 3 in $1,000 US Treasury 5% 1996. Assume that the last interest payment was March 15. The amount of accrued interest that the customer will pay is computed as follows:

March 15–31	17 days
April	30 days
May	31 days
June	3 days
Total	81 days

$$\$1,000 \quad \text{x} \quad \frac{5}{100} \quad \text{x} \quad \frac{81}{365} = \$11.10$$

The total contract price that the customer will pay is $1,011.10.

The accrued interest is added to the contracts of both the buyer and seller. The buyer pays the accrued interest and the seller receives the accrued interest.

ARBITRATION

Any controversy that arises between parties who are members, allied members, member firms, or member corporations, must be settled by arbitration proceedings at the request of any such party.

However, if the controversy is between a member and a nonmember, the dispute can only be brought to arbitration at the request of a nonmember. A nonmember can force a member to arbitrate a dispute, but a member cannot normally force a nonmember to arbitrate. The decision of a majority of the arbitrators shall be final and cannot be appealed to the board of directors. Arbitration is less costly and more efficient than litigation.

LISTING AND DELISTING OF SECURITIES

Prior to the company's stock's being listed on a stock exchange, the following factors are considered by the stock exchange's listing committee:

- The earnings record for the company
- The number and location of the company's stockholders
- The assets of the company
- The voting rights policy of the company

The exchange requires certain minimums with regard to earnings, assets, market value shares outstanding, and number of shareholders to initially list a company's securities. The exchange would also consider delisting a security when the market value, shares outstanding, and number of shareholders fall below certain levels.

The listing agreement between the company and the exchange is designated to provide timely disclosure to the public of earnings statements, dividend notices, and other information that may affect security values or influence investment decisions. The exchange requires actively operating companies to agree to solicit proxies for all meetings of stockholders.

VOTING RIGHTS

As a matter of general policy, the exchange has for many years refused to list nonvoting common stocks, but that policy has changed.

What if a company that still meets listing requirements wants to delist its stock? The NYSE will not allow a company to delist unless the delisting proposal is approved with a substantial majority of the outstanding shares voting to delist. The exchange defines a substantial majority to be 66⅔% of the outstanding shares voting in favor of delisting the security, together with a failure of 10% of the individual holders to object.

OFF-BOARD TRANSACTIONS

The NYSE market responsibility rule states that members, member organizations, and affiliated persons may not, in NYSE listed securities

- Cross agency orders in their offices
- Effect principal trades in their offices
- Effect off-board principal trades

The rule also states that agency transactions off-board with third-market makers and nonmember block positioners may be effected only if public limit orders on the specialist's book are satisfied. Such specialist's orders may be satisfied immediately before the over-the-counter (OTC) transaction. If the OTC transaction is effected first, such specialist's orders existing on the specialist's book at the time of the OTC transaction must be satisfied. NYSE rules also state that, with certain specified exceptions, members may not effect transactions in the OTC market in a subscription right admitted to dealings on the exchange.

Members are free to execute, as agents, customer orders to buy or sell listed securities in the OTC market with other persons so long as they do not also act as agents for the other persons. Members are, however, not normally permitted to act as principals in any exchange-listed security in the OTC market or act as agents for both buyer and seller in any OTC trade of a listed security.

THE TELEPHONE CONSUMER PROTECTION ACT

The purpose of the 1991 Telephone Consumer Protection Act (TCPA) is to protect residential telephone customers from receiving unwanted live telephone solicitations. Under the TCPA, telephone solicitations may be placed only from 8:00 A.M. to 9:00 P.M. local time of the called party. Also, the caller must provide the called party with the identity of the caller and a telephone number or address at which the caller may be contacted.

If the called party indicates that s/he does not want to be called in the future, the company making the call must place that person's telephone number on a **do-not-call list**. The do-not-call list must be kept permanently by the broker/dealer or company.

The Act does not apply to any caller who has an established business relationship with the called party. An established business relationship exists with a telemarketer (calling party) if the called party (customer) has made an inquiry or transaction regarding products or services offered by the calling party or employing entity. However, if the customer states that s/he does not want to receive any further solicitations from the caller or their employing entity, the business relationship ends. That person's name must be placed on the do-not-call list.

SUITABILITY

The term *suitability*, in the securities industry, means that a customer's securities investments fit their investment objectives, financial situation, and needs. An RR obtains information from a customer concerning estimated annual income, estimated net worth, liquid assets, employment status, age, marital status, dependents, and investment knowledge.

A customer's investment objectives may be long-term growth, aggressive (speculative) growth, or current income with protection of principal. The allocation of a customer's assets between equities, bonds, and money market instruments must be determined. In other words, the principles of asset allocation are applied to a customer's overall financial situation.

Normally, young investors will have a high percentage of their assets in common stocks or equity funds. As they move into middle age, their portfolio will normally include some debt obligations. Older persons who have retired will generally have a high percentage of their assets in debt obligations and a small percentage in equity investments.

MISCELLANEOUS NYSE RULES

Under NYSE rules, a member firm, upon written instructions from a customer, may hold a customer's mail for up to two months if the customer is traveling in the United States. The mail can be held, upon written instructions from the customer, for up to three months if the customer is traveling abroad. At the end of the two- or three-month period, the mail must be sent back to the customer and cannot be sent to any other person.

Member organizations are required, under NYSE rules, to make complete checks into the background of all their personnel, including

- Clerical personnel
- RRs
- Employees who will be bonded

Employment applications must be kept for three years after the person leaves the employ of the member firm.

10 CUSTOMER ACCOUNTS

This section will analyze the various types of customer accounts and the procedures that should be used in opening these accounts. Each type of securities account requires certain documents before a customer can transact any business.

A registered representative (RR) should have a thorough knowledge of the various accounts. Certain procedures should be strictly followed by the RR in order to avoid confusion and possible litigation. If a customer's account is handled improperly by an RR, the firm may be liable for any losses sustained by the customer.

The two main types of accounts normally opened by a customer are

1. Cash accounts
2 Margin accounts

CASH AND MARGIN ACCOUNTS

A **cash account** is one in which customer transactions are conducted with the understanding that settlement will be prompt. A customer should pay for a security purchase at least by the settlement date (three business days after the trade date). However, Regulation T of the Federal Reserve Board states that if a customer does not pay in full for a purchase of securities by the close of business on the fifth business day after the trade date, the broker must cancel or liquidate the transaction unless

- The amount of money due does not exceed $1,000, in which case the broker/dealer does not have to sell the customer out.
- The security is unissued, in which case the customer must pay within five business days from the date the security is made available.
- The shipment of securities is incidental to the consummation of the transaction, in which case the five-business-day period is extended by the number of days required for such shipment, but no more than five additional business days.
- The understanding between the broker/dealer and the customer is that payment is to be made on delivery. This is referred to as a COD (cash on delivery) or a DVP (delivery vs. payment). The settlement date is thirty-five calendar days after trade date.

Regulation T states that, if a transaction is canceled or liquidated because a customer failed to make prompt payment, the account must be frozen for ninety calendar days. The customer would not be able to make any purchases (except for an exempt security) unless sufficient funds are already held in the account before the order is processed.

Therefore, if a customer purchases 100 shares of ABC on Tuesday, June 8, payment must be received from the customer by the close of business on Tuesday, June 15. If payment is not received by the broker by this date, the transaction or unsettled portion must be canceled or liquidated, if no extension of time is obtained.

It is important to remember that a customer should pay for a security purchase at least by the settlement date. Regulation T describes the time frame in which a broker/dealer must act (close of business on the fifth business day after trade date), if the payment is not received.

A broker/dealer may request an extension of time for payment by a customer from the appropriate regulatory agency (stock exchange, National Association of Securities Dealers [NASD] or Federal Reserve bank), if unusual circumstances are present. For example, the customer may be in the hospital or out of town and unable to pay promptly. The extension of time for payment must be obtained by the close of business on the fifth business day after trade date. If an extension is not obtained and a security purchase is not canceled or liquidated, then the broker would be in violation of Regulation T.

A **margin account** is different from a cash account because, in a margin account, the customer does not pay in full for a security purchase. The customer deposits a specific percentage of the purchase cost and borrows the remainder from the broker. Transactions in margin accounts represent more risk to a customer than a cash account transaction.

Regulation T requires that a purchase in a margin account be paid for by at least the fifth business day after trade date. This is the same requirement as for a cash account. In a margin account transaction, the customer should deposit the specific percentage of the purchase cost by the settlement date. However, the broker/dealer has a two-day grace period before canceling or liquidating the transaction or its unsettled portion as required under Regulation T. In a margin account transaction, the broker/dealer can request an extension of time for payment from the appropriate regulatory authority, if unusual circumstances are present.

A customer is also required under Regulation T to promptly deposit any securities sold in a cash account into the account. Regulation T does not define the time frame in which a customer must deposit securities that s/he sold in a cash account. However, SEC Rule 15c33 requires a broker/dealer to buy in a customer if the customer does not deliver a security that s/he sold within ten business days after settlement date. An extension of time may also be obtained concerning requirement to buy in the customer if unusual circumstances exist.

CUSTOMER ACCOUNT DOCUMENTATION

Before a customer is allowed to transact business in a securities account, the following information is normally obtained from the customer on a new account form:

- Customer's name, address, and telephone numbers (work and home)
- Social Security number or taxpayer identification number
- Whether the customer is a citizen
- Age
- Occupation
- Bank and broker references
- How the account was acquired

The customer's full name must be obtained including any titles (e.g., Dr. John Smith). A customer's account can be designated by a symbol or number (numbered account) provided the customer signs a written statement attesting to the ownership of the account. A customer may desire to open a numbered account for privacy reasons.

The broker/dealer must maintain the customer's current mailing address and home and business telephone numbers. Internal Revenue Service (IRS) regulations require the customer to give the broker/dealer his Social Security or taxpayer identification number. If a customer does not provide his Social Security or taxpayer identification number to the brokerage firm, s/he will be subject to backup withholding. In other words, the broker/dealer will withhold a certain percentage of the proceeds of the customer's sales.

Customers must be of legal age to open a securities account with a broker/dealer. The legal age may be eighteen or twenty-one, depending on the state or specific policy of the broker/dealer. Therefore, if a sixteen-year-old wants to open a securities account in his name, this is prohibited.

SERVICING CUSTOMERS

Some customers will not seek the advice of RRs concerning purchases and sales of securities. These customers are only looking for good service from the RR (execution of orders and receiving their securities properly registered). However, it would still be proper for an RR to advise a client against the purchase of a highly speculative security if s/he felt it was in the customer's best interest not to purchase the security. The customer may still want to purchase the security, and the RR should clearly mark the order as unsolicited. Many broker/dealers require all of their orders to be designated as solicited or unsolicited.

An RR is never allowed to guarantee a specific rise or fall in the price of a security under any circumstances. For example, an RR can never say to a customer, "Buy this stock at $20; it is going to $80, I guarantee it." This type of statement is strictly prohibited. However, an RR could say, "The stock looks attractive at $30; from a technical point of view there is support at $25 and resistance at $35." An RR could also make a statement such as, "I recommend you buy the stock at $40, it has been showing steady growth. I'll put a copy of our research report in the mail to you."

Many customers, however, will rely on the investment advice of their RR. The degree to which they rely on the RR's advice will vary from complete dependence to casual inquiries.

Before RRs can give proper advice to a customer, they must be sure of the customer's investment objectives. If the customer wants an RR to recommend specific securities to fit into the customer's personal financial plan, other important information would have to be obtained, including, but not limited to

- The customer's available liquid assets
- Other assets owned by the customer, such as real estate and insurance

- Other marketable securities owned by the customer
- Financial obligations of the customer (needs of dependents)
- The customer's temperament

Any investment advice given by an RR should be based on informed judgment of current investment information concerning the company. If a customer inquires about XYZ and the RR is unfamiliar with the company, s/he should say "This is a company I have not followed closely. Let me look into the company and get back to you."

RRs' responsibility is greatest when they recommend the purchase of a highly speculative security or the purchase of a little-known, inactively traded company. The advice given by an RR should never be influenced by the representative's personal investment decisions.

All RRs should keep two important records in order to service their customers properly.

1. Portfolio record of their customers' securities holdings
2. Cross-referenced record of securities held by customers

The **portfolio record** lists each customer and his or her securities holdings, along with other information such as: full name; home address and telephone number; business address and telephone number; investment objectives; power of attorney, if any; special instructions; and any other related information.

The cross-referenced record can assist RRs in keeping customers informed of important developments concerning their companies. Each page of the record contains a particular security. Under the name of the security is listed each customer's holding. RRs would be able to write to each customer or call the customer to discuss the company, if they felt it was necessary to do so.

DISCRETIONARY ACCOUNTS

An RR may not accept any orders to execute transactions from a person other than the customer, without prior written authorization from the customer. However, a customer may decide to give trading authorization to another person (i.e., investment advisor). The customer may give a third party either limited trading authorization or full trading authorization.

Limited trading authorization may be given by the customer to another person by signing a **limited trading authorization form**. This form gives a third party the right to purchase or sell only for the account of the customer. No money or securities may be withdrawn from the account except by the customer. Therefore, an RR with limited trading authorization may purchase or sell all types of securities for a customer (stocks, bonds, warrants). However, no money or securities may be withdrawn by the RR.

A customer may give full trading authorization to a third party by signing a **full trading authorization form**. This authorization gives a third party the right to purchase or sell for the customer and withdraw money and/or securities.

If full discretionary powers are given to an RR, officer, or partner of the broker/dealer, the account is considered a **discretionary account**. Prior written authorization must be received from the customer before any discretionary transaction may be executed.

In any account in which the customer gives trading authority to another person, the account should be reviewed frequently to detect transactions that are excessive in size or frequency. This review should be conducted to detect any possible *churning* of a customer's account.

A broker/dealer who is carrying an account of a client of an investment advisor must obtain the following information:

- The client's name and address
- Acceptable evidence of the investment advisor's authority
- Written instructions from the client as to the address to send the confirmations

Trading authorization may be given to third parties by individuals, joint tenants, partnerships, or corporations. However, fiduciaries cannot usually grant trading authorization to third parties.

A limited or full trading authorization is also referred to as a limited or full power of attorney. A power of attorney is created when an individual allows another person to act on his behalf. The broker/dealer must have on file the limited or full trading authorization (power of attorney) before any orders are accepted from the third party (investment advisor).

When an RR is given trading authorization over a customer's account, the account, as mentioned previously, is referred to as a discretionary account. The RR must designate each order ticket as *discretionary* at the time the order is entered. In a discretionary account, excessive transactions in the account to generate commissions are prohibited. Excessive transactions in a discretionary account is referred to as **churning** the account and is prohibited under securities laws.

A discretionary order is one in which the RR decides what stock to buy or sell for the customer. For example, the customer sends in $40,000 and says to the RR, "Buy whatever stocks you think are best for my account." This is a discretionary order and cannot be executed by the RR without prior written authorization from the customer.

However, a customer can give an RR discretion concerning time and price without prior written authorization. Assume a customer says to an RR "Buy 100 shares of General Motors for my account and enter the order when you think the price is right." This is not a discretionary order since the customer decided what security to purchase and the number of shares. In other words, the customer decided the security and quantity. This order can be accepted as given and does not have to be executed as soon as possible. The RR can watch the market for a short time in an attempt to obtain a better price for the customer.

The main points to remember concerning a discretionary account are

- Prior written authorization must be obtained from a customer before a discretionary order is entered in his account.
- Frequent supervisory reviews of discretionary accounts must be made by the broker/dealer.
- Churning the account is prohibited. Churning refers to excessive trading in a discretionary account in order to generate commissions.
- Discretionary orders must be reviewed on a timely basis by a supervisory person. A timely basis means that the orders must be initialed on the day entered. They do not have to be approved before they are entered.
- The discretionary account must be approved by the broker/dealer before any orders can be accepted. NASD rules require an NASD principal to approve the account. New York Stock Exchange (NYSE) rules require that a discretionary account be approved by an officer, partner, or allied member of the firm.
- If the owner of a discretionary account dies, the trading authorization given to the third party terminates immediately.
- If the owner of a discretionary account wants all customer statements and confirmations for the account to be sent to the agent (investment advisor) only, this is allowed. However, the owner must waive his or her right to receive the confirmations and monthly statements in writing.
- If a customer guarantees a broker/dealer that a power of attorney is in the mail, the firm cannot accept an order for the account on a discretionary basis. The broker/dealer must have the signed power of attorney in its possession and the account must be approved before any orders can be accepted.
- Even though a discretionary account has been approved and all proper papers are on file, unlimited trading privileges do not exist in the account. The RR must still act in the best interest of the customer.
- Confirmations and statements cannot be sent to the RR on the customer's behalf. This is allowed in the case of a third party (investment advisor) if the customer waives his right to receive them in writing. However, this is not allowed with an RR. Statements must be sent to the customer.
- Checks or securities in a discretionary account cannot be issued in the name of an RR. All checks and securities must be drawn to the owner of the account.
- The discretionary authorization given by a customer to the broker/dealer and/or RR is good until revoked. Annual or periodic renewal in writing is not required.

PAYMENT AND DELIVERY INSTRUCTIONS

The broker/dealer should obtain information from the customer concerning the payment and delivery of securities when opening the account. The most common instructions a customer would give to the broker concerning the handling of money and securities are

- Transfer and ship to the customer.
- Hold in street name. **Street name** means the securities are held in the broker/dealer's name or its nominee name but owned by the customer. All margin securities are held in street name by the broker/dealer.
- Transfer and hold in safekeeping for the customer.
- Send the check to the customer on settlement date relating to a sale.

APPROVAL OF ACCOUNTS

Under NYSE rules, every new account must be approved by a general partner, principal executive officer, or a specifically authorized person. The approval must be in writing on the account form or a document that is part of the permanent records of the firm. NASD rules require that a customer's account be approved by a member, partner, officer, or manager, on the account card. If a customer requests, regulations require that s/he be furnished the broker/dealer's most recent balance sheet immediately. The broker/dealer does not have to give a customer an income statement or a copy of its investment or inventory accounts.

SUPPLEMENTARY DOCUMENTATION REQUIRED—MARGIN ACCOUNT

Certain other documents must be completed by the customer when opening a margin account. These documents are necessary to protect the firm and the customer and to avoid possible litigation. They describe the terms and conditions under which business is to be transacted in the margin account.

The main supplementary documents that must be completed by a customer for a margin account include

- *Hypothecation agreement.* This document describes the terms and conditions under which a margin account for a customer will be operated. This agreement allows the firm to pledge a customer's securities as collateral for a loan to the firm. The broker/dealer is also given the right to liquidate the securities if it feels it is necessary for the firm's protection. A hypothecation agreement is also known as a **customer's agreement** or a **margin agreement**. This document must be signed by a customer before any business may be transacted in a margin account.
- *Loan consent agreement.* This document authorizes the broker/dealer to lend a customer's securities to itself or to others. It is important in facilitating short sale transactions for customers. Even though it is not essential that a customer sign this document to open a margin account, most brokerage firms require that it be signed as a matter of policy for every margin account.
- *Credit agreement.* Broker/dealers are required under federal law to disclose to their customers information concerning how credit will be extended in a margin account. Firms normally have customers sign this form to evidence their understanding of the credit agreement.

CUSTOMER ACCOUNTS AND DOCUMENTS

A cash account opened for a customer requires a new account report form (new account form) to be completed. A margin account for an individual customer requires, in addition to a new account form

- Hypothecation agreement (margin agreement)
- Loan consent agreement
- Credit agreement

A **joint account** requires that a joint account agreement be signed by both customers, which binds them both to the terms of the agreement. A corporation opening a cash account requires, in addition to a new account form

- Copy of corporate charter or bylaws
- Resolution from the board of directors authorizing a specific person or persons to enter orders on behalf of the corporation

Assume a husband and wife have a joint account and the husband dies. The wife would normally be required to present the following documents to have the securities registered in her name:

- Copy of death certificate
- Affidavit of domicile
- Inheritance tax waiver

Assume that a customer, Mr. Jones, is legally declared incompetent and his daughter is appointed as conservator for the customer. Only the daughter is allowed to enter orders for the account. Mr. Jones could not enter orders for the account since he was legally declared incompetent by a court.

A **trust agreement** requires, in addition to a new account form, a certified copy of the trust agreement. A guardian account requires, in addition to a new account form, a copy of the guardian appointment certificate issued by a court.

Under Securities and Exchange Commission (SEC) rules, customers must be sent a statement of account if they have an open security position or money balance at least quarterly. Even if the security position or money balance is eliminated during the quarter, a customer must receive a statement for that particular quarter.

SEC rules also require a broker/dealer to send *semiannual statements* of their financial condition to customers, which must include

- An unconsolidated balance sheet
- A statement of net capital
- Subordinated loan information

FIDUCIARIES

Fiduciaries are persons vested with legal rights and powers to be exercised for the benefit of another person. The term **fiduciary** covers a wide variety of activities and individuals, such as directors of corporations, attorneys acting for their clients, trustees managing trusts, and others serving in responsible positions. A fiduciary is always acting for the benefit of another person. In a fiduciary relationship, one party is placing confidence in another party to act in good faith and for his or her benefit.

For example, a custodian managing the account of a minor under the Uniform Gifts to Minors Act is a fiduciary. The custodian must always act in the best interest of the minor and always as a prudent man.

Every state has a statute or well-established judicial rule directing and limiting the conduct of a fiduciary. These laws are generally divided into two main types.

1. Prudent man rule
2. Legal list rule

The **prudent man rule** states that, in acquiring, investing, and managing property for the benefit of another, a fiduciary shall exercise the judgment that men of prudence, discretion, and intelligence exercise in the management of their own affairs. A prudent man will, in most cases, seek diversification of investments and reasonable income with safety of principal. Under the prudent man rule, fiduciaries are allowed to invest in equity securities.

Legal list states allow fiduciaries to invest in securities that are on a list of approved securities. This list of approved securities for investments by fiduciaries is usually published annually by the state's banking department.

Fiduciaries cannot normally enter into highly speculative transactions. Therefore, if a fiduciary wants to open a margin account, the fiduciary must present documentation stating that margin trading is permitted. In this case, it would be wise to have the broker/dealer's legal counsel review the documentation before any margin trading begins. Also, a power of attorney should not be accepted by a broker/dealer from a fiduciary. This is because a fiduciary (such as custodian or executor) may not normally delegate trading authorization to a third party.

Examples of fiduciaries include

- Executors
- Administrators
- Guardians
- Trustees
- Custodians
- Receivers in bankruptcy
- Conservators of incompetents

An **executor (executrix)** is a person named in a will to settle the estate of a deceased person. An **administrator** is a person appointed by a court to settle the estate of a person who died without a will. A **guardian** is a person appointed by a court to handle the property of another living person. A **trustee** is a person who manages a trust pursuant to a trust agreement. A **receiver in bankruptcy** is a court-appointed person who handles the affairs of a bankrupt company or a company that is reorganizing under court supervision. A **conservator** of an incompetent is a person appointed by the court to handle the affairs of a person who is no longer capable of handling his or her own affairs.

UNIFORM GIFTS TO MINORS ACT / UNIFORM TRANSFER TO MINORS ACT

This type of account will be discussed separately because it should be thoroughly understood by an RR. The Uniform Gifts to Minors Act has been amended in many states and is referred to as the Uniform Transfer to Minors Act. We will refer to the two statutes as **UGMA/UTMA.** Because a minor cannot be bound by the terms of a contract, broker/dealers will not open accounts for them. Minors have a legal right to void contracts at their option, and this could result in losses to the broker/dealer. Therefore, broker/dealers prohibit minors from opening securities accounts in their own names unless they open it pursuant to UGMA/UTMA statutes with a custodian.

States have adopted either UGMA or UTMA, which permits a donor to make a gift of securities to a minor by registering the securities in the name of the adult as custodian for the minor. The custodian of the account manages the account for the benefit of the minor. The custodian should manage the account in a prudent manner seeking reasonable income and protection of principal. The custodian should not be investing in a very speculative security because of the risks involved. The custodian must not engage in speculative transactions such as

- Uncovered option writing
- Selling securities short
- Commodity futures trading

However, covered call writing would be allowed since it is a conservative option strategy used to generate income.

It is important to remember that the donor gives up all rights to any property transferred to a minor under this statute. Any gift made under the UGMA/UTMA is irrevocable and the donor may not take the gift back at a future date. Once the securities are registered in the name of the custodian for the minor's benefit, the gift is complete and the minor becomes the sole owner of the securities. When the minor reaches the age of majority, any cash and securities in the account are transferred by the custodian to the person who has just reached the age of majority.

The **donor** must be an adult, since a minor cannot make a gift under the Act. The donor appoints the custodian and can appoint himself custodian if s/he chooses. Securities, mutual fund shares, money, annuities, and life insurance of any amount may be given to a minor. Only fully paid securities may be given, since margin accounts are prohibited. The gift must be made during the donor's lifetime and not through a will.

The donor must fully understand that the gift is an irrevocable donation. The securities and funds in the account must be turned over to the minor when the minor reaches the age of majority. The gift is considered completed when the securities are registered by the custodian for the minor. Taxes on dividends, interest, or capital gains realized in the UGMA/UTMA account are the tax responsibility of the minor. Normally, any tax returns are submitted by the custodian and taxes due are paid from funds in the account.

The **custodian** is a fiduciary and must manage the account in the best interests of the minor, not for his personal benefit. Joint custodians are not permitted. Only one custodian and one minor are allowed per account. The custodian can manage the account as s/he deems advisable. S/he can invest funds, sell securities or other assets, and reinvest the proceeds. For example, in a rights offering, the custodian could sell stock and exercise the rights. S/he could donate funds and exercise the rights. The custodian could sell the rights and invest in another security or hold the funds for future investment.

The custodian retains management control over the account until the minor reaches majority, at which time any securities or funds that have not been expended must be turned over to the minor. If the custodian resigns, is removed by court order, or dies before the minor reaches the age of majority, a successor custodian will be appointed.

Only the custodian has management control over the assets in the account. Parents of the minor have no management authority over the assets unless one of the parents is the custodian. For example, if an uncle set up an UGMA/UTMA account for his nephew, only the uncle would have management authority over the account.

The custodian, at his discretion, may use custodial property for the support, maintenance, education, general use, and benefit of the minor. The assets in the account cannot be used to benefit the custodian. The custodian should apply the prudent man rule to managing the assets in the account. Detailed records should be kept by the custodian concerning transactions in the account.

Stock certificates in a UGMA/UTMA account must be registered in the name of the custodian for the minor, for example, John Smith as Custodian for John Smith Jr. under the Uniform Transfer to Minors Act of Massachusetts. The registration of the securities completes the gift.

Income and capital gains realized by the account are taxable to the minor only, not to the donor or the custodian. The minor's Social Security number must be obtained for the account, since the minor is the legal owner of the securities. If the minor dies, the custodial property becomes part of the minor's estate. When the minor reaches majority, control of the account is transferred from the custodian to the minor: Any checks paid out of a UGMA/UTMA account must be paid according to the name of the account (John Smith as Custodian for John Smith Jr.). Checks must never be paid to the custodian's name.

ACCOUNTS OF DECEASED PERSONS

If a customer of a broker/dealer dies, the firm should immediately cancel all outstanding orders (limit orders, stop orders). The account should be frozen until the necessary instructions and documents are received from the executor or administrator of the estate.

If the deceased person was a joint tenant in the account, the surviving person normally must present a death certificate, affidavit of domicile, and an inheritance tax waiver before the assets in the account are released. If the deceased person was a tenant-in-common with another person, the account must be frozen until instructions are received from the executor or administrator with necessary papers. Under no circumstances should the securities be given to the surviving person in a tenancy-in-common account.

If the deceased person was a partner in a partnership account maintained by the broker/dealer, it is necessary to obtain authorization from the surviving partners before executing any orders in the partnership. This is because a partnership is normally dissolved upon the death of a partner. The account is usually frozen until the necessary authorization is obtained.

JOINT OWNERSHIP OF SECURITIES

Securities purchased jointly by customers are generally registered in one of two ways.

1. Joint tenancy with rights of survivorship
2. Tenancy-in-common

Any joint tenant owns an undivided interest in the securities. However, the handling of the interest in the securities in the event of death of a co-owner differs greatly. Under joint tenancy with rights of survivorship, if one of the joint tenants dies, the entire interest passes to the remaining joint owner without going through probate.

In a joint tenant with rights of survivorship account

- Orders may be placed by either party.
- Correspondence relating to the account may be mailed to either party.
- Checks may be mailed to either party; however, any checks paid out must be drawn to the owner of the account. All checks paid out of any account must be drawn payable to the owner of the account.

In a tenancy-in-common, if one of the tenants dies, his interest will pass to his estate and not to the other joint owner. There is no right of survivorship in a tenancy-in-common. For example, assume two brothers, William and James Johnson, open an account as tenants-in-common. William Johnson owns 60% interest, and James owns 40% interest in the account. If William dies, his 60% interest will pass to the estate of William Johnson, which will become the owner along with James Johnson.

TRANSACTIONS IN CUSTOMER ACCOUNTS

When an order is executed for the account of a customer, an order ticket is written up by the RR. An order ticket normally contains the name of the customer, security, trade date, price, quantity purchased or sold, type of account, and market of execution. Order tickets must be marked long or short under security industry regulations.

If any errors have occurred in the execution of an order, the RR should immediately notify an officer or partner of the firm. The RR should not attempt to correct the error with subsequent executions without proper approval.

The order ticket is normally used by a brokerage firm to prepare a written confirmation of the transaction, which will be sent to the customer. A confirmation must be sent to the customer disclosing the details of the trade. The confirmation must be sent out to the customer on the business day following the trade date. An order ticket and confirmation should be compared to ensure accuracy and to avoid possible back-office problems. A typical confirmation will contain the following information:

- Name of the customer
- Trade and settlement date
- Description of security
- Quantity purchased or sold
- Price of execution
- Contract amount
- Interest, commissions, taxes, or any other charges (if applicable)
- Net amount due to broker or customer

Customer confirmations must disclose the capacity in which the broker/dealer acted for the customer. The broker/dealer may have acted as

- Customer's agent
- Principal
- Bona fide market maker
- Agent for another person (in a cross the broker/dealer would act as agent for both parties)

Confirmations must be sent out promptly to customers. **Promptly**, in this instance, is defined as the next business day following trade date. All customers must be sent confirmations whether they are individual customers or institutional customers, such as banks or insurance companies.

BROKERAGE BACK-OFFICE DEPARTMENTS

An RR should have a basic understanding of the functions performed by the back-office departments of a typical stockbrokerage firm. The following is a summary of the back-office departments and their functions:

- *Order Department.* Orders to purchase or sell securities for customers are transmitted to this department by registered representatives. The orders are then sent to the exchange floor (listed security) or to the over-the-counter (OTC) market-maker firm (unlisted security) for execution.
- *Purchase and Sales (P&S) Department.* The principal functions of the P&S Department are to verify the accuracy of executed orders and to send confirmations of transactions to customers.
- *Margin Department.* This department is responsible for controlling all aspects of credit extension to customers. It will compute required margin in customers' accounts and issue Regulation T margin calls, maintenance calls, or house calls to its margin customers.
- *Cashier's Department.* This department maintains custody of securities in the firm's possession. It handles receipts and deliveries of securities transactions, customer transfers, and bank loans. This department does not get involved with the execution of orders.
- *Dividend Department.* This department accounts for all dividends receivable and payable by the firm. It issues dividend claims to other brokers and to customers, as necessary.
- *Proxy Department* This department is responsible for obtaining proxy material to be distributed to customers concerning securities held in street name for customers.
- *Stock Record Department.* This department maintains the firm's stock record. A stock record shows, for each security, the owner and location of the security.
- *Reorganization Department.* This department handles the exchange of one security for another in a brokerage firm, such as converting convertible bonds.

Follow the typical route an order would take through the various back-office departments. If a customer gives an order to an RR, the order is transmitted to the Order Department (sometimes called the Wire Room). The Order Department transmits the order to the appropriate market and receives an execution report. The order ticket is then sent to the P&S Department, which prepares the customer confirmation and sends a copy to the Margin Department. The Margin Department checks to see that all of the provisions of Regulation T have been complied with. The P&S Department also sends a report of the transaction to the Cashier's Department. The Cashier's Department will receive or deliver the security and also receive or make a money payment. If securities have been received by a firm, the Cashier's Department is responsible for the transfer and delivery of securities to the customer or the placing of securities in safekeeping for the customer.

To summarize, the transaction is processed as follows:

Order Department → P&S Department → Margin Department → Cashier's Department

CENTRAL ASSET ACCOUNTS

Many brokerage firms are presently combining various financial transactions into one account for the convenience of customers. These accounts are referred to as central asset accounts. The individual brokerage firms have particular names for their own central asset accounts. These accounts allow customers to combine in one account securities purchases, check writing, and credit card transactions. Other financial transactions are also available in a central asset account. Although these accounts vary from firm to firm, the following summarizes the main features of most central asset accounts:

- A brokerage account allowing margin transactions to be executed
- A checking account allowing unlimited check writing
- Credit card privileges, normally American Express, VISA, and MasterCard

- Excess funds swept automatically into a money market fund
- One monthly statement summarizing all financial transactions processed through the account

Most central asset accounts require a minimum initial investment ranging from $1,000 to $20,000, depending on the particular brokerage firm. Some brokerage firms offer securities research, check-cashing privileges, discount brokerage, and pay-by-phone privileges in a central asset account. The industry is changing in this area, and more financial services will be available to customers using central asset accounts in the near future.

MISCELLANEOUS CONCEPTS CONCERNING CUSTOMER ACCOUNTS

Registered representatives should be guided by the following rules and practices in regard to customer accounts:

- An RR must always attempt to provide customers with good service, sound advice, and ethical practices. Assume a customer wants to purchase a security that the RR feels is not a good investment. In this case, the representative should inform the customer that s/he does not feel this particular security is a proper investment, considering the customer's investment objectives, financial situation, and needs. If the customer still wants to purchase the security, the RR should enter the order and mark the order ticket **unsolicited**. An unsolicited order is an order in which the customer has totally decided on his own which security to buy or sell. A solicited order is one in which the broker calls the customer and requests the customer to purchase or sell a particular security.
- Assume an account has been assigned to an RR and the information states: "The customer is fifty-five years old and earns approximately $70,000."
  The RR should first validate the account information. After validating it, the RR can then talk to the customer concerning his investment objectives and possible investment strategies.
- An RR can execute orders for his spouse's individual account provided the spouse's prior consent is obtained for each transaction. The spouse's account is treated as any other customer's account would be treated. If the RR obtained a power of attorney from his spouse, it would then be a discretionary account. The RR, in a discretionary account, could enter buy and sell orders without the prior approval of his spouse. However, the spouse could revoke the discretionary agreement at any time.
- Under security regulations, a broker/dealer is prohibited from carrying an account in the name of a minor only. An account opened under the UGMA/UTMA is allowed. However, an account in the name of a minor only is prohibited. An account in the name of a person other than the customer is not allowed under security industry regulations. Other prohibited accounts include accounts for legal incompetents and accounts for residents of states in which the broker/dealer or RR is not authorized to do business.
- In determining a customer's financial profile, the RR should take into consideration the customer's temperament, marital status, educational needs of dependents, and equity in his home.
- Assume a customer tells an RR that s/he is leaving the country for a month and s/he wants the RR to exercise discretion on his portfolio while s/he is away. The RR must obtain prior written authorization to exercise discretion. Without prior written authorization, the RR cannot enter orders in the customer's account on a discretionary basis.
- If an RR makes a mistake executing an order, s/he must immediately notify his or her supervisor for instructions on how to correct the error.
- If a customer wants to open an account designated by a number only (numbered account), this is permitted provided the customer signs a written statement attesting to ownership of the account.
- If a material change has occurred in a customer's financial status, the client's information file must be promptly updated.
- Over the long term, common stocks have been the most profitable investment for investors followed by long-term bonds and money market instruments.
- A customer retiring at age seventy would probably have an investment objective of current income and preservation of capital.

11 MARGIN ACCOUNTS

PART I

INTRODUCTION

Many customers of broker/dealers who purchase securities choose to pay for the purchase in full. If a customer pays in full for a security purchase, the transaction is executed in a *cash account*. In a cash account transaction, there is no risk to the broker/dealer once the securities have been paid for by the customer. The entire market risk of the security position is borne by the customer.

However, certain customers prefer to purchase securities on a margin basis to possibly benefit from the use of leverage. Regulation T issued by the Board of Governors of the Federal Reserve System regulates the extension of credit by broker/dealers. All broker/dealers must handle margin transactions in accordance with Regulation T. Regulation T does not cover commodity transactions.

Regulation T permits different types of accounts to process customer securities. However, most customers open cash and/or margin accounts. These two accounts will be analyzed in depth.

To open a cash account a customer must complete a new account report form. A customer's signature is not required in most cases to open a cash account. In this type of account, a customer agrees to pay for a security purchase promptly, but at least by the fifth business day after trade date. Settlement date for a regular-way transaction in equity securities is the third business day after trade date. The broker/dealer wants a customer to pay by settlement date. However, if a customer still has not paid by the close of business on the fifth business day after trade date, the broker/dealer must either

- Obtain an extension of time from the appropriate regulatory agencies (normally the National Association of Securities Dealers [NASD], stock exchange, or Federal Reserve bank), or
- Cancel or liquidate the unsettled portion of the transaction.

Under Regulation T, a broker/dealer may, at its option, disregard any sum due from the customer not exceeding $1,000. Therefore, if a customer purchases $400 in securities and does not pay by the fifth business day after trade date, the broker/dealer does not have to cancel or liquidate the transaction. This exemption eliminates the need to request extensions of time relating to small transactions.

However, if a customer purchases $10,000 worth of securities in a cash account, the entire $10,000 must be obtained from the customer. The $1,000 rule does not allow the customer to deposit $9,700 and owe the broker/dealer $300. In order to qualify for the exemption, the purchase itself must be for $1,000 or less. If a customer purchased $10,000 and deposited $9,700, the remaining $300 worth of securities would have to be sold out by the broker/dealer if no extension was obtained.

The broker/dealer must state the reason it is seeking the extension of time for payment and it must be requested in good faith. If the customer has not paid by the end of the extension, the transaction will probably have to be canceled or liquidated. A second extension of time for a trade is difficult to obtain from a regulatory agency without a very good reason.

If a check has not been received by a broker/dealer for a customer purchase by the fifth business day after trade date, an extension of time will be requested routinely in most cases. This is because many times the check has been mailed by the customer but has not been received by the broker/dealer. The brokerage firm does not want to sell out a customer purchase unless absolutely necessary. If a customer is sold out in a cash account by a broker/dealer because a customer did not make prompt payment (payment by the fifth business day after trade date), the account must be frozen for ninety calendar days. If a customer wants to purchase securities during this ninety-day period, sufficient funds to pay for the purchase must be in the account before the order is accepted and processed. The ninety-day freeze rule does not apply to an exempt security.

To summarize concerning transactions in a cash account

- The entire risk of the transaction rests with the customer once the securities have been paid for.
- A customer must pay for any securities purchased by the fifth business day after trade date. An extension of time must be obtained if the customer cannot pay by the fifth business day after trade date. If an extension of time is denied, the transaction must be canceled or liquidated.

- In order to request an extension of time, the broker/dealer must determine that the customer is acting in good faith. The regulatory agency will grant an extension of time provided they feel that the broker/dealer is acting in good faith.

The second type of account that a customer can open is a *margin account*. A margin account is used for financing transactions in

- Equity securities listed on a national securities exchange (namely, common stock, preferred stock, warrants, and rights)
- Over-the-counter (OTC) margin securities (list of OTC stocks or bonds designated by the Federal Reserve Board that are considered eligible to be purchased on a margin basis)
- Convertible bonds, corporate bonds, US government bonds, and municipal bonds

All transactions not specifically authorized for inclusion in another account must be recorded in a margin account.

REQUIRED DOCUMENTS—MARGIN ACCOUNT

A customer who wants to open a margin account must complete a new account report form, customer's agreement, loan consent agreement, and credit agreement. The customer's agreement is also referred to as the margin agreement or hypothecation agreement.

The customer's agreement must be signed by the customer before any transactions can be done in a margin account. The customer's agreement describes the conditions under which a margin account will be handled. The customer's agreement gives the broker/dealer extending credit certain rights, including the right to

- Sell the securities in the account, if necessary, in the event the customer does not meet a margin call.
- Charge the customer interest on the debit balance.
- Rehypothecate the securities at a bank.

The loan consent agreement authorizes the broker/dealer to lend the customer's securities to itself or others. Although it is not essential that a customer sign this agreement in order to maintain a margin account, many brokerage firms require it to facilitate the handling of short-sale transactions. Short-sale transactions will be discussed later in this section.

Securities and Exchange Commission (SEC) Rule 10b-16 requires a broker/dealer extending credit in a margin account to disclose to the customer the terms and conditions relating to the financing. Many brokerage firms require customers to sign the credit agreement. By signing the agreement, the customer is agreeing to the terms.

The credit agreement discloses to a customer

- That interest is charged on the debit balance
- The manner in which annual interest is computed
- That the interest rate can be changed without notice
- The nature of any lien retained by the broker/dealer in the security as collateral and the conditions under which additional collateral can be required

The interest charged on the debit balance is based on the broker's call loan rate, which is the interest rate the broker/dealer pays on the money it borrows from the bank collateralized by customer securities.

A debtor–creditor relationship is created between the customer and the broker in a margin account. The broker is the creditor because he is lending money to the customer (debtor). The securities are held by the broker in street name as collateral for the loan. Securities held in street name are owned by the customer but held in the name of the broker and are fully negotiable. The broker can sell the securities, if necessary, to satisfy the loan (debit balance).

LONG MARGIN ACCOUNT

In order to begin margin analysis, it is important to learn the terms that will be used throughout the section. The first three terms that must be thoroughly understood for a long margin account are

- Market value long
- Debit balance
- Equity

The term **market value long** refers to the total value of the securities held long in the account. The word *long* means ownership and refers to the securities the customer owns.

The term **debit balance** is defined as the amount of money the customer owes to the broker and is sometimes called the **ledger balance**.

Equity refers to the customer's interest in the account or the customer's net worth in the account. It is the market value long of all securities in the account minus the debit balance.

The amount that is initially deposited by a client in a margin account and the equity that must be maintained in such accounts are determined by selecting the greater of the following:

- Regulation T requirements
- Exchange margin requirements
- House margin requirements

REGULATION T REQUIREMENTS

Regulation T is a federal regulation that covers the extension of credit by broker/dealers and exchange members on security transactions. The Federal Reserve Board of Governors was given the authority to govern credit extension in the securities industry by the Securities Exchange Act of 1934. Regulation T sets forth the amount of cash and/or securities that must be deposited with the broker by a customer when a security is purchased on margin. (See Exhibit 11.1)

Exhibit 11.1: Regulation T summary

Regulation T, a regulation of the Board of Governors of the Federal Reserve System, is concerned with the extension of credit by broker/dealers.

Regulation T allows the following securities to be purchased on margin:

- *Registered security.* Any security listed on a national securities exchange. A registered security may be purchased on margin.
- *OTC margin securities.* List of OTC companies that may be purchased on margin under Regulation T. This list is published by the Board of Governors of the Federal Reserve System and includes OTC stocks and bonds.
- *Exempt securities.* US government securities and municipal securities are exempt from the provisions of Regulation T. The margin requirements for these securities are determined by the appropriate regulatory bodies (i.e., the NYSE and the NASD).

All other securities not covered in categories 1, 2, or 3 are considered unregistered securities. Unregistered securities may not be purchased on margin. They must be purchased in a cash account.

Consider the following example:

Customer A purchases 500 shares of ABC Corporation at $20 per share. Assume the Federal Reserve Board margin requirement is 50%. This means that the customer must deposit 50% of the cost of the securities in cash. The word *margin* refers to the amount of money and/or securities a customer puts up when he purchases a security in a margin account. The Federal Reserve margin requirements may also be referred to as the Regulation T margin requirement, the initial margin requirement, or simply the margin requirement. All of these terms refer to initial margin requirements. After Customer A purchases the stock, the account appears as follows:

Market value long	$10,000
Debit balance	10,000
Equity	$ 0

A Regulation T call will be issued by the broker to the customer because of the purchase. The customer must deposit $5,000 in cash or marginable securities with a loan value of $5,000 within seven business days after the trade date. Regulation T calls are issued as a result of a purchase by a customer, not because of a decline in the market value of the securities in the account. In this example, it is assumed that the customer will pay for his security purchase with a deposit of cash. Therefore, after the money is deposited, the account will appear as follows:

Market value long	$10,000
Debit balance	−5,000
Equity	$ 5,000

In a long margin account, the following formula is very important:

$$\text{Market value long} - \text{Debit balance} = \text{Equity}$$

In other words, the total amount of securities owned by the customer minus what is owed to the broker equals the customer's interest or net worth in the account.

The $5,000 that the customer deposited reduced the debit balance from $10,000 to $5,000.

The customer has equity in the account of $5,000. At the present time, the account is properly margined. This means that the equity is equal to the Regulation T requirement.

The Regulation T requirement refers to the amount of equity required in the account under the provisions of Regulation T. If the Regulation T requirement is greater than the equity in the account, the account is restricted and no money or securities may be withdrawn by the customer. The equity does not have to be maintained at the Regulation T requirement level. Regulation T is concerned with initial requirements and not maintenance requirements.

The formula to determine the Regulation T requirement for a long position is

Market value long x Federal reserve margin requirement = Regulation T requirement

The example account is properly margined, but because there is no Regulation T excess, the broker may not pay any money or securities to the customer out of the account.

The term **Regulation T excess** refers to the amount of money that may be withdrawn from the account by the customer. To compute Regulation T excess, assume that the Federal Reserve margin requirement is 50%.

The formula for computing Regulation T excess under the margin required method is

Equity – Regulation T requirement = Regulation T excess

Return to the original example account.

Market value long	$10,000
Debit balance	– 5,000
Equity	$ 5,000

It has already been stated that this account has no Regulation T excess. This can be proved by using the two formulas previously presented. First, determine what the Regulation T requirement is for the account; then, compare the equity to the Regulation T requirement. If the equity is greater than the Regulation T requirement, there is Regulation T excess that may be withdrawn by the customer or used for new purchase commitments.

FORMULA: Regulation T requirement

Market value long	x	Margin requirement	=	Regulation T requirement
$10,000	x	50%	=	$5,000

FORMULA: Regulation T excess

Equity	–	Regulation T requirement	=	Regulation T excess
$5,000	–	$5,000	=	$0

However, assume the 500 shares of ABC Corporation increase in price to $40 a share. The account would appear as follows:

Market value long	$20,000
Debit balance	– 5,000
Equity	$ 15,000

After the increase in the market value of the securities in the account, Regulation T excess is computed as follows:

FORMULA: Regulation T requirement

Market value long	x	Margin requirement	=	Regulation T requirement
$20,000	x	50%	=	$10,000

FORMULA: Regulation T excess

Equity	–	Regulation T requirement	=	Regulation T excess
$15,000	–	$10,000	=	$5,000

The $5,000 of Regulation T excess is also called **excess equity**. The entire $5,000 is available for withdrawal by the customer or may be used for new purchase commitments.

From the original position, assume that the 500 shares of ABC Corporation declined in price to $15 a share instead of rising in price. The account would appear as follows:

Market value long	$7,500
Debit balance	– 5,000
Equity	$ 2,500

Market value long	x	Margin requirement	=	Regulation T requirement
$7,500	x	50%	=	$3,750

Equity	–	Regulation T requirement	=	Regulation T excess (or restriction)
$2,500	–	$3,750	=	($1,250)

In this case, the Regulation T requirement is greater than the equity and the account is a restricted account. No money or securities may be paid out of the account to the customer, assuming there is no balance in the customer's special memorandum account. The special memorandum account will be discussed later in the section.

If the Regulation T requirement is greater than the equity, the account is restricted by the difference. Therefore, the account is restricted in the amount of $1,250. The formulas can be stated as follows:

Equity > Regulation T requirement = Excess equity

Regulation T requirement > Equity = Restricted amount

By computing the Regulation T requirement in a margin account and comparing it to the equity, we can determine that the account either

- Has excess equity which can be withdrawn by the customer or used toward new purchase commitments, or
- Is a restricted account, which means no cash or securities can be withdrawn, or
- Is properly margined and, therefore, has no excess equity and the account is not restricted

The equity in the account does not have to be maintained at the Regulation T requirement level. The Regulation T requirement is used to determine whether or not money can be taken out of the account. It is not concerned with maintenance requirements, which will be discussed later in this section. (For a summary of Regulation T see Exhibit 11.1.)

NYSE MAINTENANCE REQUIREMENTS

The next subject area that will be discussed is the maintenance margin requirement of the NYSE. The NYSE requires a customer to maintain at least 25% of the market value of the securities long in the account as equity. In other words, the equity in the account can never fall below 25% of the market value long. If the equity does fall below 25% of the market value long, the customer will receive a maintenance call from the broker for the difference between the amount of equity and 25% of the market value long. A maintenance call is due promptly.

Assume the following example:

Market value long	$10,000
Debit balance	– 3,500
Equity	$ 6,500

What is the maintenance requirement? The maintenance requirement is 25% of the market value long.

$10,000 x 25% = $2,500 Maintenance requirement

What is the maintenance excess?

Equity	–	Maintenance requirement	=	Maintenance excess
$6,500	–	$2,500	=	$4,000

Assume that the 500 shares of ABC decline in price to $8 per share. The account would appear as follows:

Market value long	$4,000
Debit balance	– 3,500
Equity	$ 500

The maintenance requirement is $4,000 x 25% = $1,000.

Equity	–	Maintenance requirement	=	Maintenance excess (or Call)
$500	–	$1,000	=	($500)

In this case, since the equity is less than the maintenance requirement, a maintenance call for $500 would be issued to the customer and due promptly.

Firms that are not members of the NYSE are governed by the margin requirement rules of the exchange of which they are members or the NASD. The rules of the other exchanges and the NASD are similar to the NYSE rules.

Computing a few margin problems will ensure an understanding of

- Regulation T requirements
- NYSE maintenance requirements
- Loan value
- Excess equity or restricted account

In each of the following examples, assume a 50% Federal Reserve margin requirement.

Customer C has the following account:

$25,000	Market value long	Regulation T requirement	$12,500 ($25,000 x 50%)
–15,000	Debit balance	Loan value	$12,500 ($25,000 x 50%)
$10,000	Equity	NYSE maintenance	$ 6,250 ($25,000 x 25%)

Customer D has the following account:

$23,000	Market value long	Regulation T requirement	$11,500 ($23,000 x 50%)
–13,000	Debit balance	Loan value	$11,500 ($23,000 x 50%)
$10,000	Equity	NYSE requirement	$ 5,750 ($23,000 x 25%)

It is also possible to calculate when an NYSE maintenance call will be issued as a result of a decline in the market value.

Customer E has the following account:

$22,500	Market value long	Regulation T requirement	$11,250
−15,600	Debit balance	Loan value	$11,250
$ 6,900	Equity		

The formula to determine the market value below which the first NYSE maintenance call would go out is

$$\frac{\text{Debit balance}}{1 - \text{Maintenance requirement}} = \frac{\$15,600}{1 - 25\%} = \frac{\$15,600}{0.75} = \$20,800$$

The first NYSE maintenance call would go out when the market value declined below $20,800.

HOUSE MAINTENANCE REQUIREMENTS

Many brokerage firms establish minimum house maintenance requirements of 30% instead of the 25% maintenance requirements on long positions imposed by the NYSE. Therefore, if the customer's equity fell below 30% of the market value long, a house maintenance call would be issued to the customer. The customer would be required to bring the equity up to the 30% level promptly.

A broker/dealer may use house rules to increase the requirements of Regulation T, NYSE requirements, or NASD margin requirements. A broker/dealer can never set house rules lower than the requirements of Regulation T, the NYSE or the NASD. For example, assume the Federal Reserve margin requirement is 50%. ABC is a very volatile security. A broker/dealer could set a margin requirement of 70% on an initial purchase. The broker/dealer could even refuse to loan money on the security by requiring the full cash payment on each purchase. In certain instances, a regulatory body, such as the NYSE, may set higher margin requirements on a particular security because of its price volatility.

The formula used to determine the market value below which a house maintenance call would go out is (assume a house maintenance of 30%)

$$\frac{\text{Debit balance}}{1 - \text{Maintenance requirement}} = \frac{\$15,600}{1 - 30\%} = \frac{\$15,600}{0.70} = \$22,286$$

The first house maintenance call would go out when the market value declined below $22,286.

Certain concepts must be clearly understood concerning margin accounts. The following chart will be helpful.

Margin Transaction Table 1

Transaction	*Market value long*	*Debit balance*	*Equity*
Increase market value	Increase	No effect	Increase
Decrease market value	Decrease	No effect	Decrease
Purchase of security	Increase	Increase	No effect
Sale of a security	Decrease	Decrease	No effect
Cash deposit	No effect	Decrease	Increase
Cash withdrawal	No effect	Increase	Decrease
Deposit of securities	Increase	No effect	Increase
Withdrawal of securities	Decrease	No effect	Decrease

Up to this point, it has been assumed that all margin purchases will be paid for with a deposit of cash. Assume that a customer wants to pay for a security purchase by depositing fully paid securities instead of cash. The following example will illustrate this situation.

Assume a customer buys $10,000 worth of securities on margin. The customer wants to pay for the purchase by depositing fully paid securities. What must be the market value of the fully paid securities deposited to satisfy the Regulation T requirement? Assume a Regulation T requirement of 50%.

To find the amount of fully paid securities that must be deposited, the following formula can be used:

$$\frac{\text{Required cash deposit under Regulation T}}{\text{Loan value}}$$

$$\$10,000 \times 50\% = \$5,000 \text{ Regulation T cash deposit required}$$

Since the Regulation T requirement is 50%, the loan value is 50%.

$$\frac{\text{Required cash deposit under Regulation T}}{\text{Loan value}} = \frac{\$5,000}{0.50} = \$10,000$$

$10,000 in fully paid securities must be deposited to meet the Regulation T requirement.

The answer can be proved by analyzing the account

```
$10,000   Securities purchased
+10.000   Securities deposited
$20,000   Market value long
```

```
$20,000   Market value long    Regulation T requirement ($20,000 x 50%)   =   $10,000
–10,000   Debit balance        Excess equity                                          0
$10,000   Equity
```

The account is properly margined as a result of the deposit of $10,000 worth of fully paid securities. Note that the debit balance was not affected by the deposit of securities; it remained at $10,000. The $10,000 debit balance was created by the purchase of securities of that amount.

DEBIT BALANCE

The debit balance in a margin account is increased by

- The cost of additional securities purchased
- A withdrawal of cash
- Interest charged on the debit balance

The debit balance in a margin account is decreased by

- Net proceeds from securities sales
- Deposits of cash
- Cash dividends and interest received

The debit balance in a margin account would not be affected by a stock dividend. Assume the following account:

Long	*Market price*	*Market value long*	*Debit balance*
200 shares ABC	$55	$11,000	$3,000

Assume ABC pays a 10% stock dividend. On the ex-date, the customer would be long 220 shares of ABC and the market price would decline proportionately. At that time, the account would appear as follows:

Long	*Market price*	*Market value long*	*Debit balance*
220 shares ABC	$50	$11,000	$3,000

Therefore, the stock dividend increased the number of shares long in the account and decreased the market price. The total market value long and the debit balance in the account were not affected.

Assume a customer's account appears as follows:

```
$20,000   Market value long
– 8,000   Debit balance
$12,000   Equity
```

The account is charged $450 in interest and credited $275 in dividends. What is the new debit balance in the account?

Interest charged on the debit balance increases the debit balance, while dividends credited reduce the debit balance.

```
$8,000   Debit balance
+ 450   Interest charged
$8,450
– 275   Dividends
$8,175   New debit balance
```

The interest rate charged to customers on the debit balance in a margin account is based on the call loan rate, also called the broker's loan rate. This is the rate at which the broker/dealer borrows money from the bank collateralized by customer securities. For example, if the broker/dealer is paying a call loan rate of 8%, customers might be charged 9% interest on the debit balance.

PART II

MINIMUM EQUITY REQUIREMENTS

Part I discussed the methods used in computing equity, Regulation T requirements, excess equity, and NYSE maintenance requirements. This section will expand on these concepts.

Remember that the Federal Reserve Board margin requirements are initial requirements. The examples have used 50%, 60% and 65% as the margin requirement. The requirement is changed by the Federal Reserve

Board of Governors when they feel it necessary to do so, raising the margin requirement to dampen credit and lower the margin requirement to encourage the use of credit.

The NYSE (Rule 431) requires a minimum equity of $2,000 for all initial margin transactions in a margin account, except that no deposit is required in excess of the cost of any security purchase. This is an initial requirement. If a customer wishes to open a margin account, he must deposit at least $2,000 in cash and/or securities having a market value equal to $2,000.

Some examples will help to illustrate these concepts. Assume a 50% margin requirement in the examples.

Customer A buys 100 shares of XYZ at $14 per share in an initial transaction in a margin account. How much cash must the customer deposit?

$$100 \text{ shares} \times \$14 = \$1,400 \text{ Total cost}$$

The customer must deposit $1,400 to satisfy the NYSE initial margin requirement. The customer does not have to deposit more than the cost of the securities. When the customer pays in full for the security purchase, there is no risk to the broker/dealer as a result of the transaction. The security is fully paid for and owned by the customer. If the security became worthless, the entire loss of $1,400 would be the customer's.

Assume Customer A buys 100 shares of ABC at $24 per share in an initial transaction in a margin account. How much cash must the customer deposit?

$$\$2,400 \times 50\% = \$1,200 \text{ Regulation T requirement}$$

In this case, the customer must deposit the NYSE initial requirement of $2,000.

If the customer purchased a security while the equity in the account was below $2,000, the customer would be required to deposit either the amount necessary to bring the equity to the $2,000 level or 100% of the cost of the security purchase, whichever is less.

Assume the equity in a customer's account is $700. The customer purchases $1,000 worth of securities. How much cash must be deposited by the customer, assuming a 50% margin requirement?

To bring the account to the $2,000 equity level would require a deposit of $1,300. If the customer paid for the transaction in full, he would have to put up $1,000. Therefore, the customer would be required to deposit the lesser amount of $1,000.

The customer does not have to maintain the equity at the $2,000 level. However, the customer would not be allowed to make a withdrawal to cause the equity to drop below the $2,000 level. The equity may go below the $2,000 level because of a decrease in the market value of the securities; however, the customer would receive a call for more funds only if the equity in the account decreased below the NYSE maintenance or house maintenance requirements.

The following analysis can be used for meeting an NYSE maintenance call. Assume the following account. The market value of the securities has decreased to the point that the equity in the account is $1,000 below the NYSE maintenance requirement. The margin requirement is 50%.

$20,000	Market value long	NYSE maintenance requirement $5,000
−16,000	Debit balance	
$ 4,000	Equity	

The customer is issued an NYSE maintenance call for $1,000 and does not meet the call. NYSE calls are due immediately. This is defined to mean that the customer must take immediate steps to bring the account up to the required equity (deposit a check in the mail on the same day or the next day at the latest). Since the customer did not meet the NYSE maintenance call, the broker/dealer must liquidate securities to meet the NYSE maintenance call. To determine the amount of securities the broker/dealer must sell, the following formula may be used:

$$\frac{\text{Amount of NYSE maintenance call}}{\text{NYSE Maintenance requirement}} = \frac{\$1,000}{.25} = \$4,000$$

$4,000 in securities must be liquidated to meet the NYSE call. In order to meet an NYSE maintenance call, the broker/dealer must liquidate securities equal to four times the amount of the call.

Assume the $4,000 in securities is sold to meet the NYSE maintenance call. The account would appear as

$16,000	Market value long	NYSE maintenance requirement	$4,000
− 12,000	Debit balance	Equity	$4,000
$ 4,000	Equity	NYSE maintenance call	0

Assume the same account is subject to a house maintenance requirement of 30%.

$20,000	Market value long	House maintenance requirement	$6,000
− 16,000	Debit balance	Equity	$4,000
$ 4,000	Equity		

The customer is issued a house maintenance call for $2,000. In this case, the following formula can be used to determine what amount of securities must be sold to meet the house call:

$$\frac{\text{House maintenance call}}{\text{House maintenance requirement}} = \frac{\$2,000}{0.30} = \$6,666.66$$

$6,666.66 in securities must be sold to meet the house call, which is 3• times the amount of the house call. When this is done, the account would appear as

$13,334	Market value long	House maintenance requirement	$4,000
−9,334	Debit balance		
$ 4,000	Equity		

The next subject to be discussed is the issuance of Regulation T calls to customers. Remember, Regulation T calls apply to new positions and not to maintenance.

Assume the following margin account of Customer Smith. The margin requirement is 50%.

$20,000	Market value long	Regulation T requirement	$10,000
−4,000	Debit balance	Maintenance requirement	$ 5,000
$16,000	Equity	Excess equity	$ 6,000

Customer Smith now purchases 400 shares of EFG at $40. How much money must the customer deposit to meet a Regulation T call?

$16,000 x 50% = $8,000 margin required on purchase

Margin requirement − Excess equity = Regulation T call to customer
$8,000 $6,000 $2,000

The customer must deposit $2,000 within five business days after the trade date in order to meet the Regulation T call. If the customer does not deposit the $2,000 by the fifth business day after trade date, the broker must liquidate enough securities to meet the call or apply for an extension of time if unusual circumstances exist.

However, if a customer purchases stock and, as a result of the transaction a margin call of $500 or less is generated, the firm does not have to issue a call to the customer (the $500 rule). If a trade results in a margin call in excess of $500, the entire amount of the call must be obtained.

In the preceding example, the customer purchased $16,000 worth of securities. He had to deposit $2,000 to meet Regulation T call, which was generated as a result of the purchase. A question frequently asked is "How much stock could the customer have purchased on margin without putting up additional money?" This concept is known as the **buying power** in the account. The buying power in the account refers to the amount of stock a customer can purchase without depositing additional funds in the account.

The formula for determining buying power can be stated as follows:

$$\text{Buying power} = \frac{\text{Excess equity}}{\text{Federal reserve margin requirement}}$$

For our problem, the buying power in the account before the purchase was

$$\frac{\text{Excess equity}}{\text{Federal reserve margin requirement}} = \frac{\$6,000}{0.50} = \$12,000$$

Therefore, the customer could have purchased $12,000 worth of securities without putting up additional cash or securities. However, the customer chose to purchase $16,000 worth of securities and, therefore, was required to deposit $2,000 to meet the Regulation T call.

RESTRICTED MARGIN ACCOUNTS

It is important to examine restricted accounts for some further analysis. Assume the following margin account. Regulation T requirement is 50%.

$20,000	Market value long	Regulation T requirement	$10,000
−13,000	Debit balance	Maintenance requirement	$ 5,000
$ 7,000	Equity		

$ 7,000	Equity
10,000	Regulation T requirement
($3,000)	Restricted

The account is restricted in the amount of $3,000. Because the account is restricted, no money or securities may be withdrawn by the customer, assuming there is no money in the special memorandum account. The special memorandum account will be analyzed later in this section.

Regulation T allows the withdrawal of a security from a restricted margin account provided

- A cash deposit equal to 50% of the market value of the security is placed in the account, or
- Margin securities having a loan value equal to 50% of the market value of the security being withdrawn are deposited into the account, regardless of other Regulation T or NYSE requirements.

Therefore, if a customer wants to withdraw $5,000 worth of securities from the restricted account where Regulation T is 50%, he would have to deposit either

- $5,000 x 50% = $2,500 in cash, or

- $\dfrac{\$2,500}{.50 \text{ loan value}}$ = $5,000 in securities

The $5,000 in securities have a loan value of $2,500, which is 50% of the $5,000 market value of the security withdrawn.

Should a customer sell stock in a restricted account, some of the money may be withdrawn. This introduces a new concept—the **retention requirement,** which refers to the amount of money that must be retained in a restricted margin account as a result of a long sale by a customer or a withdrawal of securities.

The current Regulation T retention requirement is 50%. Therefore, 50% of the proceeds of a long sale by a customer must be retained in a restricted account. The other 50% of the proceeds of the sale may be released to the customer.

Return to the original account. Margin requirement is 50%.

$20,000	Market value long	Regulation T requirement	$10,000
−13,000	Debit balance	Restricted amount	$ 3,000
$ 7,000	Equity		

The customer sells $2,000 worth of securities. How much money may be released to the customer? After the sale, the account can be recalculated as follows:

$18,000	Market value long	Regulation T requirement	$9,000
−11,000	Debit balance	Restricted amount	$2,000
$ 7,000	Equity		

The account is still restricted after the sale; however, the customer is entitled to 50% of the proceeds of the sale.

$2,000 x 50% = $1,000 may be released to the customer

If the sale had generated any excess equity in the account, the customer would be entitled to withdraw the excess equity.

Assume now that a customer has a restricted margin account and decides to purchase more securities. Does he have to deposit enough cash to take the account off restriction? The answer is "No." The customer has to meet the margin requirement on the new purchase commitment. Consider the following account. Regulation T requirement is 50%.

$18,000	Market value long	Regulation T requirement	$9,000
−10,000	Debit balance	Restricted amount	$1,000
$ 8,000	Equity		

If the customer purchases $1,200 worth of securities, he will receive a Regulation T or federal call for $600.

$1,200 amount of purchase x 50% = $600 Regulation T call

Assuming the customer deposits the $600 within seven business days, the account would appear as follows:

Original account		*Purchase*	*Adjusted account*	
$18,000	Market value long	$1,200	Market value long	$19,200
−10,000	Debit balance	1,200	Debit balance	−11,200
$ 8,000	Equity	0	Equity	$ 8,000

The customer deposits the $600 required margin.

Deposit

$19,200	Market value long		Market value long	$19,200
−11,200	Debit balance	(600)	Debit balance	−10,600
$ 8,000	Equity	$600	Equity	$ 8,600
$19,200	Market value long		Regulation T requirement	$ 9,600
−10,600	Debit balance		Restricted amount	$ 1,000
$ 8,600	Equity			

In this case, when the customer meets the federal or Regulation T call, the account is still restricted by $1,000.

Assume that the customer does not make the required deposit within five business days after the trade date and no extension of time for payment is obtained from the appropriate regulatory authority (NASD, stock exchange, or Federal Reserve bank). In this case, the broker/dealer must liquidate securities to cover the amount of the Regulation T call. Consider the following example. Margin requirement is 50%.

$$\begin{array}{ll} \$40,000 & \text{Market value long} \\ \underline{-24,000} & \text{Debit balance} \\ \$16,000 & \text{Equity} \end{array}$$

The customer purchases $6,000 worth of securities and receives a federal or Regulation T call for $3,000 ($6,000 x 50%). The customer does not pay within five business days after the trade date and no extension of time is obtained. What amount of securities must the broker/dealer liquidate in order to meet the federal or Regulation T call?

The broker/dealer, in order to meet a federal or Regulation T margin call by a liquidation of securities, must sell securities equal to

- The amount of the call divided by 0.50, or
- The amount needed to make the account properly margined after the sale, whichever is less.

In this example, the amount that must be sold can be determined as follows:

$$\frac{\$3,000 \text{ amount of call}}{0.50 \text{ amount released}} = \$6,000 \text{ in securities that must be sold}$$

The amount of the call is divided by 0.50 because the retention requirements of 50% will release only 50% of the proceeds of a sale. Therefore, a Regulation T call must be divided by .50 in order to determine the full dollar amount of securities that must be sold to yield a releasable amount equal to the call. In the example, the amount of the call, $3,000, represented 50% of the securities sold, which was $6,000.

The amount needed to make the account properly margined is computed next. The amount that must be sold under this alternative in an account with a 50% Federal Reserve margin requirement is determined by the following formula:

$$\frac{\text{Amount of restriction after purchase}}{0.50} = \text{Amount of securities that must be sold to make account properly margined}$$

After the purchase of $6,000 worth of securities, the account would appear as follows:

$$\begin{array}{ll} \$46,000 & \text{Market value long} \\ \underline{-30,000} & \text{Debit balance} \\ \$16,000 & \text{Equity} \end{array}$$

$46,000 x 50% = $23,000 Regulation T requirement

$$\begin{array}{ll} \$23,000 & \text{Regulation T requirement} \\ \underline{-16,000} & \text{Equity} \\ \$\,7,000 & \text{Restricted amount} \end{array}$$

$$\frac{\$7,000 \text{ amount of restriction}}{0.50} = \$14,000$$

Therefore, the broker/dealer would have to sell $6,000 in securities if the customer did not meet the Regulation T call of $3,000, the lesser requirement.

Assume the following margin account for a customer (50% margin requirement):

$$\begin{array}{ll} \$20,000 & \text{Market value long} \\ \underline{-10,000} & \text{Debit balance} \\ \$10,000 & \text{Equity} \end{array}$$

The customer purchases $8,000 worth of securities and does not meet the margin call of $4,000 ($8,000 x 50%). The broker/dealer is forced to liquidate securities in order to meet the call. What amount of securities must be liquidated?

The broker/dealer would have to liquidate the lesser of the following two requirements:

1. The amount of the call divided by 0.50
2. The amount needed to make the account properly margined after the sale (amount of restriction after the purchase divided by 0.50)

In the example, this would be

1. $\dfrac{\$4,000 \text{ call}}{.50} = \$8,000$

   or

2. Amount of the restriction after the purchase divided by 0.50

After the purchase, the account appears as follows:

$$\begin{array}{ll} \$28,000 & \text{Market value long} \\ \underline{-18,000} & \text{Debit balance} \\ \$10,000 & \text{Equity} \end{array}$$

$28,000 x 50% = $14,000 Regulation T requirement

$14,000   Regulation T requirement
−10,000   Equity
$ 4,000   Amount of restriction

$$\frac{\$4,000 \text{ amount of restriction}}{0.50} = \$8,000$$

Therefore, the broker/dealer must sell $8,000 worth of securities in order to meet the Regulation T call, since both computations require the same amount of securities to be sold.

SAME-DAY SUBSTITUTION

The next area to be explored concerning restricted accounts is the **same-day substitution privilege**. The same day substitution privilege refers to selling a security in a margin account and purchasing another security at the same time. The substitution purchase must be made on the same trade date as the sale.

Therefore, in every margin substitution, there is a commitment (purchase of a security or a short sale), and a liquidation (long sale or purchase to cover a short position). A commitment transaction requires additional margin (purchase of a security or a short sale). A liquidation transaction reduces margin requirements by reducing the long or short positions in the account (long sale or a purchase to cover a short position).

For example, a customer in a restricted margin account could sell 100 shares of XYZ at $50 and purchase 200 shares of ABC at $25 on the same trade date, without depositing additional funds. This is referred to as an **equal substitution**. The status of the customer's account is exactly the same after the equal substitution.

The equal substitution could also have been the short sale of 100 shares of XYZ at $50 and the purchase to cover 200 shares of ABC at $25 on the same day in a short account. Short accounts will be explored in detail later in the section.

However, the substitution would not have been the purchase of a security and a short sale since both of these transactions would be commitments and additional margin would be required on each. If a customer executed both a long sale and a short cover (assuming he had a mixed account), this would be two liquidating transactions and not a margin substitution. Therefore, to have a margin substitution, a customer must execute a commitment transaction and a liquidating transaction.

Consider the following restricted account. The margin requirement is 50%.

$10,000   Market value long   Regulation T requirement $5,000
− 7,000   Debit balance   Restricted amount $2,000
$ 3,000   Equity

The customer buys $5,500 of stock and sells $4,000 worth of another security on the same trade date. This is referred to as an unequal substitution. In this case, the purchase cost exceeds the sales proceeds by $1,500. The customer must meet the margin requirement on the net purchase of $1,500.

$5,500   Cost of purchase
−4,000   Proceeds of sale
$1,500   Excess of purchase cost over sales proceeds

$1,500 x 50% = $750 required margin deposit

$750 must be deposited into the account within five business days to satisfy the Regulation T requirement.

The next example examines an unequal substitution in a restricted account where the sales proceeds exceed the purchase cost. Assume the following margin account. The margin requirement is 50%.

$20,000   Market value long   Regulation T requirement $10,000
− 14,000   Debit balance   Restricted amount $ 4,000
$ 6,000   Equity

The customer sells $10,000 worth of securities and purchases $7,000 worth of different securities on the same day. In this case, the customer is allowed to withdraw 50% of the net sales proceeds calculated as follows:

$10,000   Sales proceeds
− 7,000   Cost of purchase
$ 3,000   Net sales proceeds

$3,000 net sales proceeds x 50% = $1,500

$1,500 may be withdrawn by the customer

RULES CONCERNING SAME-DAY SUBSTITUTION IN A RESTRICTED ACCOUNT

Equal substitutions (where the cost of the security purchased equals the sale proceeds) do not require any deposit of funds. If the cost of the purchase exceeds the sales proceeds, the margin requirement must be met on the net purchase. If the sales proceeds exceed the purchase commitment, 50% of the net sales proceeds may be released to the customer (normally it will be credited to the special memorandum account (SMA) and available for withdrawal by the customer). SMAs will be discussed in Part IV of this chapter.

In a nonrestricted account, if the cost of the purchase is greater than the sales proceeds, the margin requirement must also be met on the net purchase. The amount of excess equity in the account may be applied against the net purchase.

Consider the following account. Margin requirement is 50%.

$40,000	Market value long	Regulation T requirement	$20,000
– 10,000	Debit balance	Excess equity	$10,000
$30,000	Equity		

The customer buys $20,000 worth of ABC and sells $4,000 of XYZ on the same day.

$20,000	Purchase
– 4,000	Sales proceeds
$16,000	Net purchase

$16,000 x 50% = $8,000 margin required on purchase

However, since the account has excess equity of $10,000, $8,000 of the $10,000 in excess equity can be used to meet the Regulation T call. If the amount of the excess equity were not sufficient to meet the margin required on the net purchase, the customer would have been issued a Regulation T call for the additional amount.

In a nonrestricted account, the account must be recalculated to determine the additional excess equity generated, if the sales proceeds on the same-day transactions exceed the purchase commitment.

REHYPOTHECATION

When a customer purchases securities on margin, the customer puts up a certain amount of money (margin requirement) and borrows the difference from the broker/dealer.

Assume the Federal Reserve margin requirement is 50%. If a customer purchases $10,000 worth of securities, he must deposit $5,000 into the account by the fifth business day after the trade date. Therefore, the account would appear as follows:

Market value of securities long	$10,000
Debit balance	–5,000
Equity	$ 5,000

In this example, the debit balance represents the amount of money the customer owes to the broker/dealer. The broker/dealer is allowed to pledge a certain amount of a customer's securities at a bank in order to obtain funds to help finance the transaction. This procedure is called **rehypothecation** and it is regulated under SEC rules.

For rehypothecation purposes, a broker/dealer can pledge 140% of a customer's debit balance in securities at a bank to obtain funds to help finance the transaction. Therefore, in this case, the broker/dealer could pledge $7,000 worth of the customer's securities at the bank and obtain a loan of $5,000 from the bank.

A broker/dealer is not allowed to pledge or loan the customer's securities to obtain an amount in excess of the customer's indebtedness, which is $5,000 in the example. If a broker/dealer wants to lend the customer's securities to other broker/dealers, the same rules apply. In other words, a broker/dealer cannot lend the customer's securities in excess of 140% of the customer's debit balances to another broker/dealer and could not obtain funds in excess of the customer's indebtedness.

WHEN-ISSUED SECURITIES

The next topic that will be discussed briefly concerns a purchase by a customer of a security on a **when-issued** basis. A purchase of a security on a when-issued basis is subject to NYSE requirements, which require a customer to deposit either

- $2,000, or
- 25% of the total cost, whichever of the two is greater

This margin requirement applies to a customer purchase in either a cash or margin account. Assume a customer purchases 400 shares of ABC at $30 a share in a margin account. How much must the customer deposit to meet the NYSE requirement?

The customer must deposit either $2,000, or $12,000 total cost x 25% = $3,000.

Therefore, the customer must deposit $3,000 to meet the NYSE requirement. After the stock goes regular way, the customer would be required to bring the margin up to 50%. If the purchase was made in a cash account, the additional 75% must be deposited by the customer no later than five business days after the securities go regular way.

NEW ISSUES

The Securities Exchange Act of 1934 prohibits a broker/dealer from extending credit to a customer to purchase a security that is part of a primary distribution. Under this Act, a broker/dealer cannot extend credit to a customer in order to purchase shares of an open-end investment company. Closed-end investment company shares may be purchased on margin if they are listed on an exchange or are on the OTC margin securities list. However, open-end investment company shares can be deposited into a margin account and credit extended on the shares after thirty days.

PART III

SHORT MARGIN ACCOUNTS

This section will focus on short margin accounts. A short sale is the sale of a security that the seller does not own. If an individual thinks the price of the security will decline, and he hopes to repurchase it at a lower price later, he may choose to sell the stock short.

When a customer sells a stock short, the broker borrows the stock for the customer and makes delivery to the buyer. A short sale is a margin transaction and subject to Regulation T requirements. The broker must deposit the cash value of the shares with the party from whom he borrowed the stock. If the price of these shares goes up, the broker will be subjected to a mark to the market. This means that he will have to deposit more money with the lender of the stock.

The party lending the stock may call for its return at any time or the borrower may return the stock at any time to the lender. The security sold short may be borrowed by the short seller's broker from one of the following sources:

- The short seller's own brokerage firm
- Another stock brokerage firm
- A large financial institution

If the security is borrowed from another broker or institution, a cash deposit equal to 100% of the current market value of the securities must be deposited with the lender.

All short sales of equity securities must take place in a margin account. Short sales are subject to the same federal margin requirements as long purchases in a margin account. Any type of security may be sold short, although in most cases only listed common stock and OTC margin stocks are sold short.

For a short account, it is necessary to understand three important terms.

- Credit balance (total credit balance)
- Market value short
- Equity

The **credit balance** is the amount of the proceeds generated by the short sale plus the required margin deposit from the customer. The credit balance may not be withdrawn by the customer. However, it is considered an asset of the customer.

The **market value short** is the total market value of the securities sold short by the customer and is a liability of the customer because he must repurchase these securities at a later date. The customer may purchase these securities at a higher or lower price than he sold them short at, depending on the market conditions for that security after the short sale.

The **equity** in a short account is the difference between the amount of money in the account (total credit balance) and the market value of the securities sold short (market value short). The formula for computing equity in a short account is

Credit balance – Market value short = Equity

The formula for computing the Regulation T requirement in a short account, assuming a margin requirement of 50%, is

Market value short x 50% = Regulation T requirement

The formula for computing the NYSE maintenance requirement (see Exhibit 11.2) in a short account for stocks selling at $5 and above per share is

Market value short x 30% or $5 per share, whichever is greater

For stocks selling below $5 per share, the NYSE maintenance requirement is

Market value short x 100% or $2.50 per share, whichever is greater

Exhibit 11.2: NYSE maintenance requirements summary

Long account	=	25% of the market value long
Short account	=	30% of the market value short or $5 per share, whichever is greater, for stocks selling at $5 per share or above; or 100% of the market value or $2.50 per share, whichever is greater, for stocks selling below $5 per share

Regulation T requires that in all margin accounts, the long and short positions must be calculated as one account. The computation for excess equity must be done on the combined long and short positions. Some margin problems will illustrate this point. Assume a 50% margin requirement. Assume Customer Williams opens an account by selling 200 shares of a listed security short at $50 per share. The calculation for the total credit balance in the account after the trade is as follows:

200 shares sold short at $50 = $10,000 (proceeds of sale)

$10,000 x 50% = $5,000 (margin required on the short sale)

$10,000 proceeds of sale + $5,000 margin required = $15,000 credit balance

The formula for computing equity in a short account is

Credit balance – Market value short = Equity
$15,000 – $10,000 = $5,000

In a short margin account, a fluctuation in the market value short does not affect the credit balance in the account. If the market value short in the account increases, equity in the account decreases. If the market value short decreases, equity in the account increases.

If a customer deposits money into a short margin account, the credit balance increases and equity increases. If a customer withdraws a portion of the credit balance, the credit balance decreases and equity in the account decreases.

Assume a customer makes an initial short sale in his margin account of 1,000 shares of XYZ at $10 per share. In this case, the customer must deposit either 30% of the market value short or $5 per share, whichever is greater, to meet the NYSE maintenance requirement.

$10,000 market value short x 30% = $3,000
or
1,000 shares x $5 per share = $5,000

The customer must deposit the greater of the two requirements, which is $5,000.

If the maintenance requirement on a customer's transaction is greater than the initial requirement, then the customer must meet the maintenance requirement on the trade.

Assume a customer sells 1,000 shares short at $2 per share. What would be the NYSE minimum margin requirement on this transaction?

Since the stock is selling for less than $5 per share, the NYSE minimum margin requirement would be the greater of the following two requirements:

1. 100% of the market value in cash, which in this case would be $2,000, or
2. $2.50 per share which would be $2.50 x 1,000 = $2,500

Therefore, the NYSE minimum margin requirement on this transaction would be $2,500.

Assume a customer opens both a long account and a short account with a broker/dealer. When a customer has both a long and short account with a broker/dealer, it is referred to as a mixed account. Assume the following mixed margin account (Federal Reserve margin requirement is 50%):

Long account	*Price*	*Market value*	*Debit balance*
300 CBS	$30	$ 9,000	$10,000
500 NBC	20	10,000	
200 ABC	25	5,000	

Short account	*Price*	*Market value*	*Credit balance*
200 HTN	$35	$7,000	$18,000
100 ITN	40	4,000	

The total equity in the mixed margin account can be computed as follows:

Long account		*Short account*	
Market value long	$24,000	Credit balance	$18,000
Debit balance	−10,000	Market value short	−11,000
Equity	$14,000	Equity	$ 7,000

The total equity in the mixed margin account is $21,000 consisting of $14,000 in the long account and $7,000 in the short account. A formula can be used to compute the total equity in a mixed margin account. The formula is total equity (TE) is equal to market value long (MVL) plus credit balance minus market value short (MVS) minus debit balance.

In the example, the formula can be proved as follows:

MVL	+	Credit balance	−	MVS	−	Debit balance	=	TE
$24,000		$18,000		$11,000		$10,000		$21,000

To compute whether the account has excess equity or is restricted, the Regulation T requirements for both the long and the short accounts must be combined and compared to the equity.

Market value long x Margin requirement = Regulation T requirement (long account)
$24,000   50% $12,000

Market value short x Margin requirement = Regulation T requirement (short account)
$11,000   50% $5,500

Regulation T requirement (long account)	$12,000
Regulation T requirement (short account)	5,500
Total Regulation T requirement	$17,500

Total equity	$21,000
Total Regulation T requirement	−17,500
Excess equity	$ 3,500

The mixed margin account has excess equity of $3,500 which can be withdrawn by the customer or used to make new commitments. Therefore, the long account has buying power of $7,000.

$$\frac{\text{Excess equity}}{\text{Federal Reserve margin requirement}} = \frac{\$3,000}{0.50} = \$7,000 \text{ buying power in the long account}$$

Instead of using the buying power in the long account, it could be used in the short account. We can compute the short selling power in the short account by using the following formula:

$$\frac{\text{Excess equity}}{\text{Federal Reserve margin requirement}} = \frac{\$3,500}{0.50} = \$7,000 \text{ short selling power in the short account}$$

Therefore, a customer with a mixed margin account containing $3,500 of excess equity could either

- Purchase $7,000 of securities in the long account, or
- Sell short $7,000 of securities in the short account.

Assume the customer purchased $7,000 of securities in the long account. The mixed margin account would appear as follows:

Long account		*Short account*	
Market value long	$31,000	Credit balance	$18,000
Debit balance	−17,000	Market value short	−11,000
Equity	$14,000	Equity	$ 7,000

The total equity in the mixed margin account remains at $21,000. The new Regulation T requirements would be

Market value long x Federal Reserve margin requirement = Regulation T requirement
$31,000   50% $15,500

Market value short x Federal Reserve margin requirement = Regulation T requirement
$11,000   50% $5,500

Total equity	$21,000
Total Regulation T requirement	−21,000
Excess equity	$ 0

Therefore, the account is properly margined after the $7,000 purchase in the long account. If, instead, the customer sold short $7,000 worth of securities in the short account (100 shares at $70 a share), the mixed margin account would appear as follows:

Long account		*Short account*	
Market value long	$24,000	Credit balance	$25,000
Debit balance	−10,000	Market value short	−18,000
Equity	$14,000	Equity	$ 7,000

The total equity in the mixed margin account remains at $21,000. The new Regulation T requirements would be

Market value long x Federal Reserve margin requirement = Regulation T requirement
$24,000   50% $12,000

Market value short x Federal Reserve margin requirement = Regulation T requirement
$18,000   50% $9,000

Total equity	$21,000
Total Regulation T requirement	−21,000
Excess equity	$ 0

Therefore, the account is properly margined after the $7,000 short sale in the short account.

Any study of short sales would not be complete without an explanation of the procedure known as **selling short-against-the-box**. Selling short-against-the-box refers to a situation in which a customer sells a security short even though he has a long position in the same security. In this case, the customer may not want to sell out his long position because he would be subject to a capital gains tax in that year. He would prefer to sell short-against-the-box and effectively freeze or hold his position at the prices existing when he went short-against-the-box.

Selling short-against-the-box is not considered a sale for tax purposes by the Internal Revenue Service (IRS). This is because the broker treats the transaction similar to a normal short sale in which a customer has no position in the stock. The broker must borrow the securities sold short-against-the-box. The customer's stock is held by the broker and not delivered out of the account. Consider the following situation:

Customer A is long 500 shares of EFG at $10 a share and decides to sell it short-against-the-box. The accounts would appear as follows:

	Short account
$5,000	Credit balance
− 5,000	Market value short
$ 0	Equity

	Long account
$5,000	Equity
− 500	NYSE maintenance requirement
$4,500	Excess equity

If the customer decides to withdraw this excess equity, the accounts would appear as follows:

	Short account		*Long account*
$5,000	Credit balance	$5,000	Market value long
− 5,000	Market value short	− 4,500	Debit balance
$ 0	Equity	$ 500	Equity

If the market value of the short position increases to $5,200, the account would appear as follows:

	Short account		*Long account*
$5,000	Credit balance	$5,200	Market value long
− 5,200	Market value short	− 4,500	Debit balance
$ (200)	Equity	$700	Equity

The NYSE maintenance requirement for a short-against-the-box position is 10% of the long position with the short position marked to the market.

NYSE maintenance requirement = $5,200 x 10%	=	$520	Long
Short mark to market	=	200	Short
Total NYSE maintenance requirement	=	$720	

Total equity for the accounts = $700 + ($200) = $500 equity

$500	Equity
−720	NYSE maintenance requirement
$220	NYSE maintenance call

The customer is now required to deposit an additional $220 to meet the NYSE maintenance requirement following the market value increase.

Earlier in this section a formula was used that calculated the market value below which an NYSE or house maintenance call would be issued. For a short margin account, a formula can also be used to calculate the market value above which an NYSE maintenance call would be issued. The formula to determine the market value above which an NYSE maintenance call would be issued for a short margin account is

$$\frac{\text{Credit balance}}{1 + \text{NYSE maintenance requirement}}$$

or

$$\frac{\text{Credit balance}}{1.30}$$

Assume the following short margin account:

$26,000	Credit balance
−10,000	Market value short (100 shares X @ $100 each)
$16,000	Equity

To what market value could the account increase before an NYSE maintenance call would be issued?

$$\frac{\$26,000 \text{ credit balance}}{1.30}$$

Assume the market value short increased to $20,000. The account would appear as follows:

$26,000	Credit balance
−20,000	Market value short
$ 6,000	Equity

$20,000 market value short x 30% = $6,000 NYSE maintenance requirement

$6,000	Equity
− 6,000	NYSE maintenance requirement
$ 0	NYSE maintenance excess

If the market value short increased above $20,000, the account would receive an NYSE maintenance call. The account's equity at the present time is exactly equal to the NYSE maintenance requirement. In other words, the account has no NYSE maintenance excess and is not subject to an NYSE maintenance call.

The following chart will be helpful in understanding the basic concepts of a short account:

Margin Transaction Table 2

Transaction	Credit balance	Market value short	Equity
Increase market value short	No effect	Increase	Decrease
Decrease market value short	No effect	Decrease	Increase
Sale of a security short	Increase	Increase	No effect
Covering purchase	Decrease	Decrease	No effect
Cash deposit	Increase	No effect	Increase
Cash withdrawal	Decrease	No effect	Decrease

Since a short sale constitutes a margin transaction, Regulation T requirements and NYSE maintenance requirements must be met. However, the NYSE initial equity requirement of $2,000 also applies. Consider the following example:

Assume a customer opens a margin account and his initial transaction is to sell 100 X short at $15. How much cash must be deposited by the customer? Assume a Regulation T requirement of 50%.

100 shares x $15 = $1,500 proceeds of short sale

$1,500 x 50% = $750 Regulation T requirement

However, the customer must deposit $2,000 to meet the NYSE initial equity requirement. When the $2,000 is deposited, the account will appear as follows:

$3,500	Credit balance
− 1,500	Market value short
$2,000	Equity

The customer would not be allowed to make any withdrawals from the account that would reduce the equity below the $2,000 level. The equity may decrease below $2,000 as a result of market fluctuations. The customer is not required to maintain the equity at the $2,000 level.

A short sale by a customer is always considered to be a margin transaction because there is always risk to the broker. Therefore, the $2,000 minimum equity rule of the NYSE must always be met.

Assume the market value of X increases, equity in the account decreases. The equity in the account protects the broker/dealer in case the customer does not meet a margin call. Assume the market value of the stock immediately increased to $40 per share in the marketplace as the result of a tender offer bid by another company. This is an extreme example; however, it does illustrate an important point. If the market value of X increased to $40 per share, the account would appear as follows:

$3,500	Credit balance
− 4,000	Market value short
$(500)	Deficit

In this case, the credit balance in the account is not sufficient to repurchase the security sold short. Therefore, the broker/dealer is in an unsecured position. The customer would receive an NYSE maintenance call for $1,700 ($4,000 x 30% + $500 deficit). When the $1,700 is deposited in the account, it would appear as follows:

$5,200	Credit balance
− 4,000	Market value short
$1,200	Equity

After the deposit of $1,700, the account has sufficient equity to meet the NYSE maintenance requirement. The equity in the account is $1,200, and the NYSE maintenance requirement for the account is $1,200 ($4,000 market value short x 30%).

The purpose of this example was to illustrate that a short sale by a customer always represents a risk to the broker/dealer. The greater the customer's equity in the account, the lower the risk to the broker/dealer.

PART IV

SPECIAL MEMORANDUM ACCOUNT

This section will explore an account frequently misunderstood—the special memorandum account (SMA). The SMA is used in conjunction with a margin account.

Because the value of securities held in a margin account fluctuates, any excess equity in the account can disappear quickly. For this reason, the SMA was created. A broker will automatically transfer the excess equity from the margin account to the SMA when a computation reflecting excess equity exists. When the transfer is made, the amount that is transferred into the SMA will not decrease as a result of the decrease in value of securities in the margin account.

The following example should be helpful in illustrating the concept of an SMA. Assume the margin requirement is 50%.

$16,000	Market value long	Regulation T requirement	$8,000
− 8,000	Debit balance	Excess equity	$ 0
$ 8,000	Equity		

The account has no excess equity, and the SMA balance is zero; however, if the market value in the account increases to $24,000, the account would appear as follows:

$24,000	Market value long	Regulation T requirement	$12,000
− 8,000	Debit balance	Excess equity	$ 4,000
$16,000	Equity		

Assume that the broker is using the memorandum method of maintaining the SMA. Under this method, excess equity is posted to a memorandum account for future use by the customer. Therefore, $4,000 of excess equity would be posted to the SMA, and the balance would be $4,000 credit. The customer would have the $4,000 of funds available for withdrawal or to use for new purchase commitments. The balance in the SMA cannot be used to meet a house or NYSE maintenance call.

The SMA is a permanent record of the firm. The SMA can never have a debit balance. The account either has a credit balance representing funds available to the customer or it has a zero balance.

The SMA will normally reflect the following information:

- Customer's name
- Date of any entries
- Amount of any entries
- Balance in account (always either a credit balance or zero)
- Explanation of any entries

Assume that the market value of securities in the example account increased to $30,000. The account would appear as follows. Regulation T is 50%.

$30,000	Market value long	Regulation T requirement	$15,000
− 8,000	Debit balance	Excess equity	$ 7,000
$22,000	Equity	SMA balance	$ 7,000

In this case, an additional $3,000 of excess equity was generated by the increase in the value of the securities from $24,000 to $30,000. Therefore, an entry will be made in the SMA to increase the balance to $7,000. The customer now has $7,000 worth of funds available.

Assume now that the previous account's market value long decreases to $22,000. The account would appear as follows:

| Market value long | Debit balance | SMA |
| $22,000 | $8,000 | $7,000 |

How much cash can the customer withdraw from the account? The customer has equity in the account of $14,000 (Market value long $22,000 − Debit balance $8,000). The SMA has a $7,000 credit balance. The customer may withdraw the amount in the SMA of $7,000. When the customer withdraws the $7,000, the account would appear as follows:

| Market value long | Debit balance | SMA |
| $22,000 | $15,000 | $0 |

The customer was allowed to withdraw the amount in the SMA even though the account is restricted after the withdrawal. This is because the amount in the SMA was properly placed there when the account had excess equity, for the purpose of protecting it from being wiped out by market depreciation. However, the customer may not withdraw an amount from the SMA that would cause the equity in the account to be less than the house (if applicable) or NYSE maintenance requirements. This is a very important point to remember. An example of this point will be helpful.

Assume the following customer's account, 50% margin requirement and 30% house maintenance requirement.

| Market value long | Debit balance | SMA |
| $20,000 | $14,000 | $2,000 |

How much cash can the customer withdraw from the account? In this example, the customer cannot withdraw any cash from the account because any withdrawal would cause the account to fall below house maintenance requirements.

| Market value long | − | Debit balance | − | Equity |
| $20,000 | | $14,000 | | $6,000 |

| Market value long | x | House requirement | = | House maintenance requirement |
| $20, 000 | | 30 % | | $ 6, 000 |

| Equity | − | House maintenance requirement | = | House excess |
| $6,000 | | $6,000 | | $0 |

Since there is no house maintenance excess, any withdrawal will cause the customer to receive a house maintenance call, and this is not permitted. Therefore, it must be remembered that the amount in the SMA may be withdrawn as long as it does not cause a house or NYSE maintenance call. Another way of stating this is to say that the customer may withdraw either the

- SMA balance, or
- House maintenance excess (if applicable) or the NYSE maintenance excess, if the amount is *less* than the SMA balance

Consider the following example. Margin requirement is 50%, house maintenance requirement is 30%.

| Market value long | Debit balance | SMA |
| $20,000 | $12,000 | $4,000 |

How much cash can the customer withdraw from the account? In this case, the customer has equity of $8,000. Remember, never add the SMA balance to the equity in the account. The SMA balance represents funds available for withdrawal by the customer with certain exceptions. Equity in the account is equal to the market value long minus the debit balance.

| Market value long | x | House requirement | = | House maintenance requirement |
| $20,000 | | 30% | | $6,000 |

| Equity | − | House maintenance requirement | = | House maintenance excess |
| $8,000 | | $6,000 | | $2,000 |

In this case, the house maintenance excess is less than the SMA balance; the customer can withdraw only $2,000 from the SMA.

Another restriction concerning the withdrawal of the SMA balance is the $2,000 initial equity rule. A withdrawal from the SMA would not be allowed to cause the equity to go below the $2,000 level.

Consider an example of a sale in a nonrestricted account and the effect on the SMA. Assume a 50% margin requirement in the account.

Market value long	Debit balance	SMA
$40,000	$15,000	$5,000

Assume the customer sells $5,000 worth of securities. What will be the new SMA balance after the sale? The account can be computed as follows:

	Original account	*Sale*		*Adjusted account*
$40,000	Market value long	$(5,000)	$35,000	Market value long
− 15,000	Debit balance	$(5,000)	− 10,000	Debit balance
$25,000	Equity		$25,000	Equity

$35,000 Market value long x 50% = $17,500 Regulation T requirement

$25,000	Equity
− 17,500	Regulation T requirement
$ 7,500	Excess equity

An additional $2,500 may be credited to the SMA.

$7,500	Excess equity after sale
− 5,000	SMA balance after sale
$2,500	Additional amount to be credited to SMA

It is important to note that only the excess equity generated above the present SMA balance is credited to the SMA account. The additional excess equity generated in this example is $2,500 and is added to the SMA. The balance in the SMA will then be $7,500.

The formula for computing buying power can be revised with the introduction of an SMA. The formula for buying power in a long margin account becomes

$$\text{Buying power} = \frac{\text{SMA}}{\text{Federal Reserve margin requirement}}$$

In a restricted margin account, 50% of the proceeds of a long sale are released to the SMA. Assume the following account with a margin requirement of 50%:

$20,000	Market value long	Regulation T requirement	$10,000
− 12,000	Debit balance	Restricted amount	$ 2,000
$ 8,000	Equity		

If the customer sells $1,000 worth of securities, how much money can be released to the customer?

A sale of securities in a margin account will increase the SMA balance. The SMA balance will be increased by the amount of excess equity generated as a result of the sale. If no excess equity is generated, 50% of the proceeds of the sale are released to the SMA.

Original	*After sale*			
$20,000	$19,000	Market value long		
− 12,000	− 11,000	Debit balance	Regulation T requirement	$ 9,500
$ 8,000	$ 8,000	Equity	Restricted amount	$ 1,500

Since no excess equity was generated as a result of the sale, 50% of the proceeds of the sale may be released to the SMA. After this is done, the two accounts appear as follows:

	Margin account	*Special memorandum account*
$19,000	Market value long	$500 Credit
− 11,000	Debit balance	
$ 8,000	Equity	

The formula for computing short selling power can also be revised with the introduction of an SMA. The formula becomes

$$\text{Short selling power} = \frac{\text{SMA balance}}{\text{Federal Reserve margin requirement}}$$

When a customer engages in a long sale in a margin account, at least 50% of the sales proceeds are credited to the SMA, even if the account is restricted. Also, when a customer covers an existing short position in a restricted account by purchasing the security, there is a 50% release to the SMA.

The main points to remember concerning an SMA are

- It is used in conjunction with a margin account.

- The SMA balance represents funds available to the customer with certain restrictions.
- The SMA either has a credit balance or a zero balance. It can never have a debit balance.
- Once an amount of funds has been transferred to an SMA, these funds cannot be decreased by a decline in the market value of securities in the margin account. Excess equity is automatically transferred to the SMA.
- At least 50% of the proceeds of a long sale in a restricted margin account will be released to the SMA. Also, when a short position is covered by a purchase, the release to the SMA is 50%.
- If the account is not restricted, an increase in the market value of securities long in the account will permit an increase in the SMA balance.
- No withdrawal from an SMA would be permitted if the effect of the withdrawal would be to place the account in violation of the house maintenance requirement, the NYSE maintenance requirement, or the $2,000 minimum equity rule.
- The SMA balance can be used to meet Regulation T or federal margin calls on new purchase commitments, but not to meet a house or NYSE maintenance call.
- Any deposit of cash into the margin account is automatically credited to the SMA (assuming the amount is not deposited to meet a Regulation T call).
- The loan value of any deposit of securities is automatically credited to the SMA (assuming the securities are not deposited to meet a Regulation T call).
- If a customer has a mixed margin account, only one SMA would be used with the mixed account. Excess equity generated in both the long and short account would be credited to one SMA.

Miscellaneous Examples

Assume a customer has the following three accounts with a broker/dealer. Regulation T is 50%:

	Current market value	*Ledger balance*	*SMA*
Cash	$36,000	$14,000 CR	
Long margin	$62,000	$31,000 DR	$3,000
Short margin	$26,000	$38,000 CR	

What is the customer's total equity on deposit with the broker/dealer?

The total equity on deposit is computed by adding the equity in the three separate accounts. The equity in the cash account is $50,000, which is the market value of the securities plus the credit balance in the account. The $36,000 of securities must be fully paid for since they are in a cash account.

The equity in the long margin account is $31,000, which is the market value long minus the debit balance. The equity in the short margin account is $12,000, which is the credit balance minus the market value short. Therefore, the total equity in the three accounts is $93,000.

Total equity	
Cash	$50,000
Long margin	31,000
Short margin	12,000
Total equity	$93,000

What amount of cash may be withdrawn by the customer without adding equity?

The customer can withdraw cash in the amount of $17,000. This represents the cash balance in the cash account plus the amount in the SMA.

$14,000	Cash balance in cash account
+ 3,000	Balance in SMA
$17,000	Total cash customer could withdraw without adding equity

Assume an investor has the following margin account. Regulation T is 50%. House maintenance requirement is 30%.

Market value	*Debit balance*	*SMA*
$85,000	$69,000	$4,000

What is the customer's equity in the account?

The customer's equity is $16,000, which is the market value long minus the debit balance.

How much cash can the customer withdraw from the account?

The customer in this case cannot withdraw any money from the account. The reason is that the house maintenance requirement for the account is $25,500, which is greater than the equity. The customer will receive a house maintenance call in the amount of $9,500.

$25,500 House maintenance requirement
$-16,000$ Equity
$ 9,500 House maintenance call

Assume a customer has the following margin account. Regulation T is 50%.

$12,000 Market value long
$-6,000$ Debit balance
$ 6,000 Equity

The account is charged $750 in interest and credited $900 in dividends. What is the new debit balance in the account?

Interest charged on the debit balance in a margin account increases the debit balance while dividends reduce the debit balance.

$6,000 Present debit balance
$+750$ Interest charged
$6,750
-900 Dividends credited
$5,850 New debit balance

Assume a customer has the following margin account. Regulation T is 50%. The debit balance in the account is $45,500.

Market value long
500 ABC at 80
400 XYZ at 62½

What is the customer's percentage of equity in the account?
The market value long in the account is

500 ABC @ 80 $40,000
400 XYZ @ 62½ 25,000
Total market value long $65,000

$65,000 Market value long
$-45,500$ Debit balance
$19,500 Equity

$$\frac{\$19,500 \text{ equity}}{\$65,000 \text{ market value long}} = 30\%$$

Assume in a separate example we are told that the equity in a customer's account is $20,000 and this represents 40% of the long market value of the securities in the account. What is the customer's debit balance?

To determine the customer's debit balance, the market value of securities in the account can be determined by dividing the equity by 40%.

$$\frac{\$20,000 \text{ equity}}{0.40} = \$50,000 \text{ market value long}$$

$50,000 Market value long
? Debit balance
$20,000 Equity

Therefore, the debit balance in the customer's account must be $30,000.

12 OPTIONS

PART I

INTRODUCTION

Options were used about 300 years ago in Holland by tulip growers to hedge their inventory of tulip bulbs. Investors can use options to seek capital gains, hedge against stock positions, or increase their rate of return. The buyer of an option contract has a maximum loss equal to the premium paid. The buyer of an option pays the premium to the writer of the option. The maximum gain to the writer of an option is the premium received.

The buyer of an option has paid the premium to the writer for the right to exercise the option. However, the buyer has the right to exercise the option but not the obligation to exercise it. The buyer of the option has the right to exercise it, sell it, or allow it to expire.

The writer of an option has been paid the premium to perform on the contract, if it is exercised. The writer must sell the underlying security at the exercise price for a call option. The writer of a put option must buy the underlying security at the exercise price. The writer of a call or put option can enter into a closing purchase transaction and close out the position. However, once an option contract has been assigned to a writer, he must perform on the contract. The writer cannot close out his position once he has been assigned.

The two basic standardized option contracts available to investors through the Options Clearing Corporation (OCC) are a call and a put. They are described as follows:

- A call is a negotiable bearer contract giving the buyer the right to buy 100 shares of the underlying stock at a stated price (the strike price) on or before a stipulated date.
- A put is a negotiable bearer contract giving the buyer the right to sell 100 shares of the underlying stock at a stated price (the strike price) on or before a stipulated date.

A person may decide to be either a buyer or a writer of call options, or a buyer or writer of put options. His decision will be based on his own financial objectives and on his analysis of market prospects. If he believes the market price of a security will increase, he would buy a call or sell a put. If he believes the market price will decrease, he would buy a put or sell a call.

A put has the highest value to the buyer when the underlying stock is falling in market value. A person would buy a put in anticipation of the market value of the underlying stock going down. If, for example, a put was purchased with a strike price of $50 and the market price declined to $40, the owner of the option could purchase 100 shares of stock at $40 per share and "put" them to the seller of the option at $50.

Conversely, a call has the highest value to the buyer when the underlying stock is rising in market value. If, for example, a call was purchased with a strike price of $50 and the market price of the underlying stock increased to $60, the owner of the option would "call" the 100 shares from the seller of the option at $50 per share and sell them for $60 per share. The purchaser of a call option will lose if the market price of the underlying stock is below the exercise price on the expiration date.

An investor might buy calls or puts for capital gains purposes. Investors may write calls or puts to generate premium income. Investors can buy puts to protect long positions or buy calls to protect short positions. Calls may be purchased by investors to control additional shares of a corporation. Also, an investor with a diversified portfolio could write call options to increase his rate of return on the portfolio. Options can be used in various ways by investors for either speculation or hedging or to generate additional income.

PREMIUM

The price at which options are bought and sold is the **premium**. The buyer pays the premium and the writer receives it. The money received is kept by the writer, whether the option is exercised or not. The buyer of the option does not receive his premium back. The buyer hopes to recover more than he paid by either exercising the option or selling it at a profit.

The amount of the premium is determined competitively on the option exchange floor by supply and demand. If prices in the stock market are rising, the premium for calls will rise. At such a time, there will be less interest in puts and the premium for puts will decline. The reverse will happen when prices in the market are declining. Three factors that will affect the amount of the premium at a given point in time include

1. *Intrinsic value.* The intrinsic value of an option is the in-the-money amount. An option contract will sell for at least its intrinsic value. Assume an investor buys 1 ABC July 40 call, and the market price of ABC is $43 per share. The intrinsic value of the ABC option is $3 per share or a total premium of $300. If the market price of the underlying security is above the strike price for a call option, the option is in-the-money by that amount. For a put option, the amount by which the market price is below the strike or exercise price is the in-the-money amount.

2. *Time value.* The remaining time an option has until expiration will also be reflected in the premium. The longer the time period remaining until the option expires, the higher the premium. The reason is that the underlying stock will have a longer period in which it might move in the desired direction— higher in the case of a call, lower in the case of a put.

   Assume that a customer purchased 1 XYZ October 30 call for $7 when XYZ stock was selling at $33 a share. The customer paid a total premium of $700. This option has an intrinsic value of $300. This is the amount by which the market price of XYZ exceeds the exercise price of the option. The additional $400 of the premium was paid for the remaining time left until expiration.

   Assume another customer purchases 1 ABC April 50 call for $3 when ABC is selling at $49 per share. In this case, the option has no intrinsic value because the market price of ABC is less than the exercise price. Therefore, the total premium of $300 paid by the customer is for the time value of the option.

3. *Volatility.* The volatility of the underlying stock also affects the premium of an option. The greater the volatility of the underlying security, the higher the premium of the option. This is because the purchaser of an option on a volatile security has a greater chance of making a profit. There is greater likelihood that the market price will rise if a call is purchased or fall if a put is purchased.

CALL OPTION

Listed put and call options (options traded on a national exchange) will be analyzed thoroughly in this section. First, a listed call option contract will be examined. Assume a customer purchased 1 ABC July 40 call for $4. This option can be analyzed as follows:

1	*ABC*	*July*	*40*
Number of options contracts each covering 100 shares of the underlying security	Underlying security	Expiration month	Strike or exercise price
Call type	For a premium of $4 per share the total premium is $400 ($4 x 100 shares)		

The customer in this case has paid a total premium of $400 to the writer of the call. He has purchased the right to buy or call 100 shares of ABC from the writer at a fixed price of $40, and has paid a total of $400 for this right. The most the customer who purchased this option can lose is the total premium he has paid of $400. Assume the price of ABC stock increases to $50 and the customer exercises the option and sells the stock. What is the customer's profit or loss on the transaction?

If the customer exercises the option, he must purchase 100 shares of ABC at $40 per share for a total purchase price of $4,000. The customer then sells the stock and receives the total market value of $5,000.

$$\begin{array}{ll} \$5,000 & \text{Sales proceeds} \\ -\underline{4,000} & \text{Exercise price} \\ \$1,000 & \text{Profit on exercise} \end{array}$$

However, in order to determine the total profit or loss on the transaction, the total premium paid by the customer must be deducted from the profit realized on the exercise.

$$\begin{array}{ll} \$1,000 & \text{Profit on exercise} \\ -\underline{\ \ 400} & \text{Total premium} \\ \$\ \ 600 & \text{Profit on transaction} \end{array}$$

When the customer purchased this call option contract (1 ABC July 40 call), one of the following three possible results would occur:

1. This call option could expire unexercised. In this case, the customer would lose $400, which is the amount of the premium. The $400 loss would be a capital loss to the customer. The most the purchaser of an option can lose is the amount of the premium. The purchaser of a call option has a limited loss potential.
2. The option contract could be exercised by the customer. In the previous example, it was assumed the option was exercised when the market price of ABC was $50 per share. This resulted in a $600 profit for the customer. The customer in this example would exercise the option only if the market price of the underlying security was above the exercise price of the option. The writer has nothing to say about the exercise of the option contract.
3. The customer could enter into a closing sale transaction. A closing sale transaction refers to a transaction by which a customer closes out an existing long option position by selling that option in the marketplace. Assume the customer sold his 1 ABC July 40 call for $9. This customer would have realized a $500 capital gain. If the customer, instead, sold the option for $1, he would have realized a $300 capital loss.

This same option can be analyzed from the point of view of the writer of the option. The writer in the example has received a total premium of $400. The writer received the premium of $400 for agreeing to sell 100 shares of ABC at $40 per share if the option is exercised against him. The writer can enter into a closing purchase transaction in order to terminate his position as a writer at any time, provided he has not yet received an exercise notice. If he receives an exercise notice, he must perform on the contract. In other words, he must sell the security at the exercise price to the person who exercised the option.

When the writer sells 1 ABC July 40 call in an opening transaction and receives the premium of $400, one of three results will occur.

1. The option contract could expire unexercised. If this occurs, the writer will realize a capital gain of $400.
2. The option could be exercised against the writer. In this case, the writer would have to sell 100 shares of ABC at $40 per share to the person exercising the option against him.
3. The writer could enter into a closing purchase transaction. In other words, he would terminate his position as a writer. If the writer purchased the option at $2, he would realize a capital gain of $200. If, instead, the writer purchased the option at $7, he would have a $300 capital loss.

The buyer of a call option feels that the price of the underlying security will increase above the exercise price. In other words, he is bullish on the stock. If the underlying security does increase in price, the buyer of the call can exercise it or sell it in the marketplace. Assume a customer purchases 1 XYZ Jan 30 call for $3. In other words, the customer has paid a total premium of $300 for the call option ($3 per share x 100 shares covered by the option contract). In order for the customer to break even, the underlying security must be selling at $33 per share. At a market price of $33, the customer is in a breakeven position because, if he exercised the option, he could call the stock away from the writer at $30 per share and sell it in the marketplace at $33. The $300 profit on exercise would exactly offset the $300 total premium paid by the customer. If the price of the security increased above $33 a share, the customer would have an unrealized profit. The term **unrealized profit** means that the transaction is presently profitable but has not been closed out by the customer.

The writer of a call option does not feel that the price of the underlying security will increase in price above the exercise price. In other words, the writer of a call option is bearish on the underlying security. Assume a customer writes 1 ABC October 20 call for a premium of $4. In order for the writer of this call to be in a breakeven position, the market price of the underlying security must be $24 a share. If the option were exercised, the writer would have to sell the security at $20 per share, which is selling in the market at $24 a share. The writer would lose $400 on the exercise which would exactly offset the $400 total premium received by the writer. If the market price of the underlying security increased above $24 a share, the writer would have an unrealized loss on the transaction. The writer of an uncovered call has unlimited loss potential.

PUT OPTION

Next, a listed put option will be examined. Assume a customer purchased 1 XYZ January 50 put for $6. This option contract can be analyzed as follows:

1	*XYZ*	*January*	*50*
Number of options contracts each covering 100 shares of the underlying security	Underlying security	Expiration month	Strike or exercise price
Put type		For a premium of per share premium, therefore the total premium is $600 ($6 per share x 100 shares)	

The customer in our example has paid a total premium of $600 for the right to sell, or put to the writer, 100 shares of XYZ at $50 per share, if he chooses. The customer who purchased this put option feels that the underlying security will decrease in price. Assume the market price of XYZ decreased to $30 per share. The owner of the option can purchase the security in the marketplace at a cost of $3,000 (100 shares x $30 per share). He can then exercise the option and put stock to the writer at $50 per share. The customer would realize a $2,000 profit on the exercise of the option. The premium of $600 is subtracted from the profit on exercise and results in a $1,400 net profit.

When the customer purchases this put option, 1 XYZ January 50 put, one of three possible results will occur.

1. The put option could expire unexercised and the customer would lose $600, which is the amount of the premium. The loss would be a capital loss to the purchaser.
2. The put option contract could be exercised by the customer. In the previous example, it was assumed that the option was exercised when the market price of XYZ was $30 a share. The exercise resulted in a $1,400 profit to the customer. The customer in this example would exercise the option only if the market price of the underlying stock was below the exercise price of the option.
3. The customer could enter into a closing sale transaction. Assume the customer sold the put option for $8, the customer could realize a $200 capital gain. If, instead, the customer sold the put option for $3, he would have realized a $300 capital loss.

This same put option can be analyzed from the point of view of the writer. The writer of the put option received the premium of $600. The writer was paid the premium of $600 because he agreed to buy 100 shares of XYZ at $50 per share if the option is exercised against him. The writer of the put option does not feel that the underlying security will decrease in price. If the underlying security decreases below $50 per share, the writer of the put option will lose money on the exercise. This is because he will be forced to pay $50 a share for the security that would be selling below $50 per share.

When the writer sells 1 XYZ January 50 for a premium of $6, one of three possible events will occur.

1. The option contract could expire unexercised and the writer will realize a capital gain of $600.
2. The option contract could be exercised against the writer. The writer would have to buy 100 shares of XYZ at $50 per share.
3. The writer could enter into a closing purchase transaction. The writer would realize a $200 capital gain. If, instead, the writer purchased the option for $9, he would realize a $300 capital loss.

The buyer of a put option feels that the price of the underlying security will decrease in price below the exercise price. In other words, he is bearish on the stock. If the underlying security does decrease in price, the buyer of the put can exercise it or sell it in the marketplace. Assume a customer purchases 1 XYZ April 40 put for $5. In other words, the customer has paid a total premium of $500 for the put option ($5 per share x 100 shares covered by the option contract). In order for the customer to break even, the underlying security must be selling at $35 per share. At a market price of $35, the customer is in a breakeven position because, if he exercised the option, he could buy the stock in the market for $35 per share and put it to the writer at $40 per share. The $500 profit on exercise would exactly offset the $500 total premium paid by the customer. If the price of the security declined below $35 per share, the customer would have an unrealized profit.

The writer of a put option does not feel that the price of the underlying security will decrease in price below the exercise price. In other words, the writer of a put option is bullish on the underlying security. Assume a customer writes 1 ABC April 30 put for a premium of $3. In order for the writer of this put to be in a breakeven position, the market price of the underlying security must be $27 per share. If the option is exercised, the writer would have to purchase at $30 per share a security that he could only sell at $27 per share. The $300 loss on the exercise would be exactly offset by the $300 total premium he received and the writer would break even.

The buyer of an option may also be referred to as the holder or purchaser. The buyer of the option has gone "long" the option. The term *long* means ownership in the securities industry. The buyer has the right, but not the obligation, to exercise it, sell it in a closing sale transaction, or allow it to expire.

The writer of an option is the person who sold the option, the seller or the person went short the option. The term *short* means that the investor sold the option in an opening sale transaction. The writer who went short the option created an opening short position in the option.

The exercise price of an option contract is also referred to as the *strike price* of the option. Assume a customer buys 1 XYZ April 50 call option at $4. If the market price of XYZ is above $50 per share, the option is in-the-money by that amount. Assume XYZ stock is selling at $57 per share. The option contract is in-the-money $7 per share or a total dollar amount of $700. The premium is never figured into the in-the-money or out-of-the-money amount.

Call option writers may be either uncovered call writers or covered call writers. **Uncovered call** writers do not own the underlying security and have unlimited loss potential. In any example, if a customer sells a call or sells a put, it is assumed to be uncovered unless it is specifically stated that it is covered. A **covered call** position is when the customer is long the stock and short a call on the same security. A covered call can be executed in a cash account, while an uncovered call must be executed in a margin account.

PART II

TYPES OF SPREADS

Option customers have various choices when they deal in options. Customers can buy calls or puts and write calls or puts. They can engage in spread transactions, straddles, or combinations. Each option strategy has a different risk–reward potential (see Exhibit 12.1). The buyer of a call has a maximum risk of the premium paid. The maximum gain to the buyer of a call is unlimited. The buyer of a put has a maximum loss equal to the premium paid and a maximum gain equal to the aggregate exercise price minus the premium.

Exhibit 12.1: Risk–reward chart—Calls and puts

Position	*Maximum gain*	*Maximum loss*
Call buyer	Unlimited	Premium paid
Call writer	Premium received	Unlimited
Put buyer	Exercise price minus premium paid	Premium paid
Put writer	Premium received	Exercise price minus premium received
Covered call writer	Premium received	The market value of security minus the premium received

Customers seeking limited profits with limited risks might engage in spread option transactions. With spreads, a customer has limited profit potential but also has limited loss potential. Customers who want to take greater risks in search of greater potential profits might choose straddles or combinations.

A **spread** is defined as the simultaneous purchase and sale of an option covering the same underlying security with different expiration dates, strike prices, or both. Spreading options is a hedging strategy that is used by investors to reduce, but not eliminate, risk. The option spreader engages in a transaction with well-defined risks and potential for better-than-average gains on the money he risks. The spread is the dollar difference between the customer's buy and sell premiums. In a **debit spread,** the cost of the option purchased is greater than the proceeds of the option sold. A debit spread must widen for a customer to realize a profit. In a **credit spread,** the sales proceeds are greater than the cost. A credit spread must narrow for a customer to realize a profit. To determine whether a spread is a debit or credit spread, look at the net premium paid or received.

The main types of option spreads are

- Calendar spread
- Price spread
- Diagonal spread

A **calendar spread** is also called a **time** or **horizontal spread**. A calendar spread is the simultaneous purchase and sale of an option contract covering the same underlying security with the same strike price but with different expiration dates.

Buy 1 ABC July 40 call

and

Sell 1 ABC October 40 call

This is a calendar spread because the expiration months are different.

A **price spread** is also called a **vertical** or **money spread**. In a price spread, a customer simultaneously purchases and sells an option contract covering the same underlying security with the same expiration month but with different strike prices. The main types of price spreads are

- Bullish spreads
- Bearish spreads

In a **bullish spread,** an investor is bullish on the price of the underlying security, believing that it will rise in value. In a bullish spread, the investor buys the lower strike price and sells the option with the higher strike price. For example, assume a customer engages in the following transactions when ABC stock is selling at $45.

Buys 1 ABC July 40 call at $6

and

Sells 1 ABC July 50 call at $1

This is a **bullish call spread,** and the customer will realize a profit if the underlying stock increases in value. Assume ABC stock increases in value to $52 per share.

The ABC July 40 call is sold for $13 and the ABC July 50 call is purchased at $3. The customer has realized a profit of $500. A $700 profit was realized on the July 40 call and a $200 loss was realized on the July 50 call, resulting in a net profit of $500.

The customer realized a profit on the bullish call spread because the price of the underlying security increased. If the price of ABC stock had decreased to $32 and both options had expired unexercised, the customer's loss would have been $500. The $500 is the net debit premium.

Assume a customer engages in the following transaction with the market price of ABC stock at $45:

Buys 1 ABC July 50 call at $1

and

Sells 1 ABC July 40 call at $6

This is a **bearish call spread**. In a bearish call spread, the investor buys the higher strike price and sells the lower strike price. The customer will profit if the price of the underlying security decreases. Assume the price of ABC decreases to $34 and both call options expire unexercised. The customer realizes a $500 profit. The $500 is the net credit premium. If the price of ABC increased to $60, the customer's loss would be $500. The customer would lose $1,000 on exercise minus the $500 net credit premium received.

In a **bullish put spread,** a customer buys a put with a lower strike price and sells a put with a higher strike price. The customer expects the price of the underlying security to increase. Assume a customer engages in the following transaction with the market price of ABC at $40:

Buys 1 ABC July 40 put at $2

and

Sells 1 ABC July 50 put at $12

This is a bullish put spread. If the price of ABC increases to $60, both puts will expire and the customer will realize a $1,000 profit, which is the net credit premium. In a bearish put spread, the customer feels that the underlying security will decrease in price. Assume the customer engages in the following transaction with the market price of ABC at $45:

Buy 1 ABC July 50 put at $7

and

Sell 1 ABC July 40 put at $2

Assume the market price of ABC decreases to $30 per share. The customer sells the July 50 put for 22, and the July 40 put is purchased for $12. The customer's profit is $500.

A **diagonal spread** is the purchase and sale of option contracts on the same underlying security with different expiration dates and strike prices. For example, assume a customer engages in the following transactions:

Buys 1 ABC July 40 call

and

Sells 1 ABC October 50 call

This is a diagonal spread. This type of spread requires consideration of factors existing in both calendar and price spreads. In a calendar or price spread, only one element varied (the expiration month or exercise price). In a diagonal spread, both expiration month and exercise price are different.

Let us now look at the maximum profit and maximum loss calculation for a spread. Assume a customer has the following spread option position:

Sell 1 ABC July 60 call at $1
Buy 1 ABC July 50 call at $7

This is a price or vertical spread because the strike prices are different. It is also a debit spread since the net premium due to the broker/dealer is $600. The spread can also be described as a bullish spread, since the customer purchased the option with the lower strike price and sold the option with the higher strike price.

Since this is a bullish call spread, the customer will make money if the price of the underlying security increases in value. Assume the market price of ABC increases substantially. In this case, both call options will be exercised and the customer will realize a profit of $400. A $1,000 profit was realized on the exercises less the net premium of $600, resulting in a net profit of $400.

If, instead, the price of the underlying security decreases in value, both call options will expire worthless. The customer will have a $600 capital loss equal to the net premium paid. Therefore, for this call option spread, the following can be summarized:

Sell 1 ABC July 60 call at $1
Buy 1 ABC July 50 call at $7

To summarize

Price or vertical spread	Strike prices different
Debit spread	Cost exceeds sales proceeds
Bullish spread	Buy low strike price, sell high strike price
Maximum profit	$400
Maximum loss	$600

Assume in this example that the customer has the following spread option position:

Short 1 XYZ Jan 70 call at $6
Long 1 XYZ Jan 80 call at $1

This is also a price or vertical spread. However, this is a credit spread because the net premium of $500 is credited to the customer's account. The spread can also be described as a bearish spread since the customer will make a profit if the underlying security decreases in value. It is a bearish spread, by definition, because the customer bought the option with the higher strike price and sold the option with the lower strike price.

Since this is a bearish spread, the customer will make money if the price of the underlying security decreases in value. Assume the price of the underlying security decreases substantially and both call options expire worthless; the customer will have a profit of $500 equal to the net premium received.

If, instead, the price of the underlying security increases substantially, both call options will be exercised and the customer will realize a loss of $500. He will realize a $1,000 loss on exercise minus the $500 net premium received, resulting in a $500 loss.

Therefore, for this call spread, the following can be summarized:

Short 1 XYZ Jan 70 call at $6
Buy 1 XYZ Jan 80 call at $1

To summarize

Price or vertical spread	Strike prices different
Credit spread	Sales proceeds greater than the cost
Bearish spread	Buy higher strike, sell lower strike
Maximum profit	$500
Maximum loss	$500

Investors would engage in spread transactions to limit risks. However, spreads offer only limited profit potential. To determine if a spread is a debit or credit spread, compute the net premium. If the cost of the option purchased is greater than the proceeds of the option sold, it is a debit spread. To profit on a debit spread, the spread between the two options must widen. In other words, the premium for the option purchased increases in value more than the premium for the option sold.

In a credit spread, the proceeds of the option sold are greater than the cost of the option purchased. For a customer to profit on a credit spread, the spread between the options must narrow. In other words, the premium for the option sold decreases more than the premium for the option purchased.

STRADDLES AND COMBINATIONS

A **straddle** is defined as a put and a call on the same underlying security with the same strike price and same expiration date. An investor can buy a straddle or write a straddle. Assume an investor or customer buys 1 ABC July 40 put at $4 and buys 1 ABC July 40 call at $4.

> Long 1 ABC July 40 put at $4
> Long 1 ABC July 40 call at $4

This is a **long straddle,** because it is a put and a call on the same underlying security with the same strike price and expiration month. It is a long straddle because the customer is buying both options. If the customer sold both option positions, it would be a **short straddle**.

In the example of the long straddle, the customer must pay the option in full with a deposit of $800. The maximum loss to the customer is $800, which is the amount of the total premium paid. The maximum profit to the customer is unlimited as a result of the long call position.

A customer would purchase a straddle to take advantage of a major move in the price of a security, regardless of the direction of the move. If the underlying security increases in value, the call option can be exercised, and if the underlying security decreases in value, the put can be exercised.

Assume a customer enters into a short straddle as follows:

> Sells 1 XYZ April 60 put at $3
> Sells 1 XYZ April 60 call at $3

This is a short straddle and the writer receives a total premium of $600. The maximum profit to the writer of this straddle is $600, the amount of the total premium received by the writer. The maximum loss to the writer of this straddle is unlimited, because the customer is short an uncovered call. A customer would write a short straddle because he does not expect much fluctuation in the price of XYZ during the life of the straddle.

To summarize, a customer who enters into a long straddle has a maximum loss potential equal to the total of the premiums paid on the put and call. The maximum gain potential to the purchaser of a straddle is unlimited since he is long a call. The writer of a straddle (short straddle) has a maximum gain potential equal to the sum of the two premiums received. The maximum loss to the writer of a straddle is unlimited because of the short uncovered call position.

A **combination** is a put and call position with different strike prices, expiration months, or both. A combination is combining a put and a call in any way other than a straddle. A straddle is a put and a call with the same strike price and expiration month. A combination has a different strike price or expiration date on the put and call position. Assume a customer sets up the following option position:

> Long 1 ABC July 40 call at $4
> Long 1 ABC Oct 50 put at $3

This position is a long combination, because it is a put and a call on the same underlying security with different strike prices and expiration dates. The maximum gain to the customer is unlimited on the combination, while the maximum loss is $700, representing the total premium paid. If, instead, the customer wrote the July 40 call and the Oct 50 put, it still would be a short combination. The maximum gain to the writer is $700 and the maximum loss is unlimited.

LONG-TERM EQUITY ANTICIPATION SECURITIES

Long-term equity anticipation securities (LEAPS™) are long-term options on blue chip securities, which gives the owner or holder of the option the right to purchase or sell shares of stock at the exercise price, on or before the expiration date for up to two years in the future. LEAPS are available in both calls and puts on blue-chip securities. LEAPS expire on the Saturday following the third Friday of the expiration month.

Investors who want to take a longer-term view of the stock market can purchase LEAPS instead of buying the underlying security directly. Assume an investor considers XYZ to be a solid long-term buy, he can buy XYZ LEAPS calls. If an investor wants to hedge against a market decline over the long term, he can buy XYZ LEAPS puts on the securities in his portfolio.

By purchasing LEAPS calls, investors can profit from the appreciation of certain quality securities, using much less capital than required to purchase the securities themselves. The purchase of a LEAPS call or put offers the buyer limited risk equal to the premium paid. An investor buying LEAPS calls or puts has a leveraged profit potential with a limited risk.

LEAPS are also available on the S&P 100 Index™ and the S&P 500 Index.™ LEAPS index options settle in cash based on the difference between the closing value of the index on the last trading day and the strike price of the options. The S&P 100 LEAPS (OEX LEAPS) have an American-style exercise, which means they can be exercised at any time prior to expiration. The S&P 500 LEAPS (SPX LEAPS) have a European-style exercise, which means they can only be exercised by the holder just prior to expiration (normally on the last trading day). Index LEAPS have a cash settlement.

LEAPS calls and puts (Equity LEAPS) have expirations of two years from the issue date. LEAPS index options have expirations up to thirty-nine months from the time they are issued. LEAPS are similar to equity options in that a premium of 1 equals $100. A premium of 3½ for a LEAPS call or put equals $350.

LEAPS can be viewed as alternatives to stock ownership without the short-term risk associated with normal equity options. LEAPS can be used to take advantage of a risking market or to protect against a decline in the price of a particular security. LEAPS are issued and guaranteed by OCC and the options disclosure document delivery requirements apply to the buyers and writers of LEAPS.

MAXIMUM RISK AND MAXIMUM PROFIT

The maximum risk to the buyer of a call option is the amount of the premium. Assume a customer buys 1 ABC July 70 call at $6. The most the buyer of this call can lose is $600. The buyer of a call has limited risk.

The maximum gain to the buyer of this call option is unlimited. There is no limit on the upside of the market price of the underlying security. Therefore, the buyer of a call option has limited risk but an unlimited profit opportunity.

The writer of a covered call has a maximum profit opportunity equal to the premium received on the sale of the option. During the life of the call, the writer gives up the appreciation potential in return for the premium. However, if the call option expires, the investor would then be long the stock and at this time would benefit from a price increase. The maximum loss to the writer of a covered call is the market value of the security position minus the premium received. Assume a customer buys 100 shares of ABC at $30 per share and writes 1 ABC October 30 call for $3. The customer's maximum loss potential is $2,700. If the stock goes to zero, the loss is $3,000 minus the $300 premium for a net loss of $2,700.

The writer of an uncovered call has a maximum profit potential equal to the amount of the premium received from the sale of the call. If the option expires, he will keep the premium and profit by that amount. However, the writer of an uncovered call has unlimited dollar risk. Assume an investor sells 1 XYZ October 40 call at $4. The writer has received the premium of $400. The writer of this call must sell 100 shares of XYZ at $40 per share, if the option is exercised against him.

Assume the price of XYZ increases rapidly to $90 per share and the call option is exercised against him. The loss is $4,600. The writer realizes a $5,000 loss on exercise minus the $400 premium received, resulting in a $4,600 net loss.

Therefore, the writer of an uncovered call has unlimited risk. In our example, XYZ could have increased to $110 per share or any other price. The writer of an uncovered call has a limited profit opportunity, but unlimited loss potential.

The maximum loss to the buyer of a put option is limited to the amount of the premium. The maximum profit to the buyer of a put option is the exercise price of the put minus the premium paid for the option. Assume a customer buys 1 ABC July 50 put for $6. The maximum loss the customer can realize is $600. The maximum profit the customer can realize is $4,400. If the stock goes to zero (into bankruptcy), the customer could purchase the stock for zero and put it to the writer at $50 per share. The profit on exercise would be $4,400, which is the $5,000 profit on exercise minus the $600 premium paid.

The maximum profit to the writer of a put option is limited to the amount of the premium. The maximum loss is limited to the exercise price minus the premium received. Assume a customer sells 1 XYZ October 60 put for $7. The maximum profit potential to the customer is $700, which is the amount of the premium. The maximum loss potential is $5,300. If the stock goes to zero, the customer, on exercise, would have to pay $60 per share. The loss would be $6,000 minus the premium of $700, resulting in a $5,300 net loss on the transaction.

The maximum risk and maximum profit potential for option buyers and writers can be summarized as follows:

Position	Maximum risk	Maximum profit
Call buyer	Premium paid	Unlimited
Covered call writer	Market value of security minus premium	Premium received
Uncovered call writer	Unlimited	Premium received
Put buyer	Premium paid	Exercise price minus premium paid
Uncovered put writer	Exercise price minus premium received	Premium received
Debit spread	Net debit paid	Profit on exercise minus net debit
Credit spread	Loss on exercise minus net credit	Net credit received
Long straddle	Total premium paid	Unlimited
Short straddle	Unlimited	Total premium paid
Long combination	Total premium paid	Unlimited
Short combination	Unlimited	Total premiums received

TAXES ON OPTIONS

Options are considered capital assets, and gains and losses are capital gains and losses under federal tax laws. If a call option or put option expires, a capital loss for the amount of the premium is realized by the buyer. The writer of a call option or put option realizes a capital gain at the time of the expiration of the option.

On a closing sale transaction or a closing purchase transaction, a capital gain is realized if sales proceeds exceeded the purchase price. For example, a customer buys a call option for a premium of $4 and sells the call option at a later date for $7. The customer realizes a $300 capital gain. If a customer writes a call option for $8 and purchases the call option at a later date for $9, the writer would realize a $100 capital loss.

On the exercise of a call option, the premium is added to the exercise price for the exercising holder and added to the sales proceeds for the writer. Assume a customer buys 1 ABC July 60 call for $4 and exercises the call. For tax purposes, $6,400 is the cost basis to the holder and is also the sale proceeds to the writer.

$6,000   Exercise price $6,000   Exercise price
+ 400   Premium paid   + 400   Premium received
$6,400   Cost basis—holder $6,400   Sales proceeds—writer

On the exercise of a put option, the premium is subtracted from the exercise price to determine the sales proceeds to the holder and the cost basis to the writer.

Assume a customer buys 1 XYZ October 80 put for $7 and exercises the put. For tax purposes, $7,300 is the sales proceeds to the holder and is also the cost basis to the writer.

$8,000   Exercise price $8,000   Exercise price
− 700   Premium paid   − 700   Premium received
$7,300   Sales proceeds—holder $7,300   Cost basis—writer

Therefore, on the exercise of call options, the premium is added to the exercise price to determine the cost basis to the holder and added to the exercise price to determine the sales proceeds to the writer. The buyer of the call option paid the premium, which increases his cost basis. The writer of the call option received the premium which increases the sales proceeds for tax purposes.

On the exercise of put options, the premium is subtracted from the sales proceeds for the holder because the premium was paid by the holder. The writer of the put option received the premium which is treated as a reduction of his cost basis.

Normally, the purchase of a put on a particular security will destroy the holding period of the stock, if it has been held one year or less at the time of the purchase. Assume 100 shares of ABC is purchased at $50 a share and on the same day 1 ABC July 50 put is bought at $4 by a customer. The customer identifies the put as a hedge, and a notation is made on the firm's records. This is referred to as a **married put**. The holding period of the stock will determine whether the gain or loss is short term. If the put expires, the put premium is added to the purchase price of the stock and is not a capital loss.

$5,000   Cost of stock
+ 400   Expiration of married put
$5,400   Cost basis for stock

Assume the stock is sold two years later for $6,500. A long-term gain of $1,100 is realized by the customer.

BASIC OPTION CONCEPTS

Options offer an investor a great deal of leverage. For a $500 investment, the customer has an opportunity for an unlimited gain. The purchaser of a put does not have an opportunity for unlimited gains, but still has leverage on his investment.

A call option can also be used by an investor to protect a short position. In other words, options can be positioned against securities. Assume a customer has the following position:

Long 1 ABC July 50 call and short 100 shares of ABC

The long call position will protect the customer if ABC increases in value. The customer could exercise the call and receive 100 shares of ABC. The 100 shares of ABC could be delivered in settlement of the short position. Since the customer could call the stock away at $50, any rise above $50 would not affect the customer.

An investor can obtain certain advantages by purchasing call options in a number of different companies, including

- If the underlying stocks decline, the investor's loss would be limited to the amount of the premiums.
- If the underlying stocks moved upward, the investor could participate in the upward movement.
- Added diversification would be provided to the investor only until the calls expire.

The writer of a call option receives the premium and must perform on the option if it is exercised against him. Being short an uncovered call is the most speculative option transaction. For example, a customer writes 1 XYZ October 60 call. Exciting news is released about XYZ, and the stock rapidly increases to $95. The call is exercised against the writer.

The writer of the option would have to buy the stock at $95 and have it called away from him at $60, resulting in a $3,500 loss on exercise.

$6,000   Sell
− 9,500 Buy
$3,500   Loss to writer

The writer of an uncovered call has an unlimited loss potential. The most the writer of an uncovered call can make is the amount of the premium. Therefore, an uncovered call writer can only make a limited profit and has an unlimited loss potential.

The writing of covered calls is a conservative strategy in order to generate income. For example, a person with a portfolio of blue-chip stocks would write call options to generate income. If the calls expire, a short-term capital gain is generated to the writer. If the calls are exercised, the writer sells the stock at the strike price, receives the proceeds of the sale, and keeps the premium.

The buyer of a put limits his risk to the amount of the premium. However, the buyer of a put has a limited opportunity for gain. The maximum profit potential to the buyer of a put is the aggregate exercise price less the premium paid. Assume a customer buys 1 ABC July 70 put for $8. The maximum profit the customer could realize is $6,200. If the stock goes to zero (company goes out of business), the customer could buy the stock for zero and put the stock to the writer at $70. The customer would realize a profit of $7,000 on exercise, less the $800 premium paid. The final net profit for the customer is $6,200, which is the maximum profit the customer could have realized.

If a customer has a limited amount of money and the market is declining, he should buy puts. A customer also might buy a put to protect a long stock position.

Assume a customer owns 100 shares of ABC at $80 per share. The customer is concerned that ABC stock may decrease in price in the near future. The customer does not want to sell the 100 shares of ABC, but he still wants to obtain protection against a decline in the price of ABC. In this case, the customer should buy 1 ABC put. Assume that it is now May and the customer buys 1 ABC October 80 put for $6. While the customer owns the ABC put, he has complete downside protection after paying the premium. If ABC stock goes to zero, the customer can exercise the put and sell the stock at $80 per share.

However, it is important to know how long the customer has owned the 100 shares of ABC when the put is purchased. If the 100 shares of ABC were owned more than the long-term requirement when the put was purchased, then there is no effect on the holding period of the stock. Any gain or loss on the sale of the 100 shares of ABC is considered long-term.

If, instead, the 100 shares of ABC were not held for more than the long-term requirement, the purchase of the put would destroy the holding period of the stock. The holding period on the long stock will start over when the put is liquidated or expires.

Buying a put is considered by many investors to be more advantageous than selling short equity securities because

- It requires a smaller capital commitment.
- It has a lower loss potential.
- An investor does not have to wait for an uptick in the stock.

The writer of a put receives the premium and if the put is exercised, the writer must buy the underlying security at the strike price. The writer of a put is bullish on the underlying security. The maximum profit the writer of a put could realize is the amount of the premium. Assume a customer writes 1 XYZ October 70 put at $7. The maximum profit to the writer in this example is $700, which would be a short-term capital gain if the put expired. The maximum loss to the writer of the put is $6,300. If the underlying security goes to zero and the put is exercised against the writer, the maximum loss is $6,300.

$ 0	Market value of XYZ
7,000	Exercise price to the writer
$7,000	Loss on exercise
$7,000	Loss on exercise
– 700	Premium received by the writer
$6,300	Maximum loss to the writer

LISTED OPTION CONTRACTS

The Chicago Board of Options Exchange (CBOE) commenced operations on April 26, 1973. Later, options trading began on the American Stock Exchange; Inc., Philadelphia Stock Exchange, Inc.; New York Stock Exchange, Inc.; and the Pacific Stock Exchange, Inc. All of the options exchanges except the CBOE use a specialist system to trade options just as in the trading of stocks and bonds. Persons authorized by the CBOE to engage in transactions on the CBOE floor include

- Order book official
- Floor broker
- Competing market makers

ORDER BOOK OFFICIAL

The order book official is an exchange employee who is assigned a post to execute transactions in specific classes of options. The order book official maintains a book for all public orders that are left with him relating to a particular class. He is responsible to record and execute all public orders left with him. Public orders have priority over all other orders on the CBOE floor. Put and call options covering the same underlying security are traded at the same post on the floor. Trading takes place in front of the order book official at a particular post.

The order book official maintains a separate book for public orders for puts and calls. Only market orders or limit orders from public customers are placed in the book. Stop orders, spread orders, and straddles are *not* accepted for the book. Orders in the book automatically take priority over all other orders at a particular price. Therefore, all orders on the book at a particular price must be executed before any orders from the floor can be executed at the same price or better.

THE FLOOR BROKER

Normally, floor brokers execute public orders acting only as agent. The floor brokers charge a fee for executing the order (brokerage fee). Floor brokers receive orders from the brokerage houses and execute them on the floor. They place limit orders on the order book official's book. A floor broker always must use due diligence in executing orders according to the instructions he receives.

MARKET MAKERS

Market makers on the CBOE floor act as dealers for their own account. Every market maker on the floor is assigned to a particular class of options and competes with other market makers assigned to the same class. The more active the option, the more market makers the exchange assigns to it. The competing market makers improve liquidity and execution of public orders.

The market maker's principal function is to maintain a fair and orderly market. He must buy and sell for his own account if the prices are not continuous or if there is a temporary difference between supply and demand.

TRADING ROTATIONS

The order book official opens and closes trading in options each day. He does this through means of **trading rotations**. These are described as very brief time periods during which bids, offers and transactions in only a single, specified option contract can be made. The order book official commences an opening trading rotation promptly following the opening of the underlying security on the principal exchange where it is traded. The order book official first calls for the bids, offers, and transactions in a single option series having the nearest expiration date. He then does this in order with each series having the nearest expiration date. The procedure is then repeated for these series following successive expiration dates until he has gone through all existing expiration dates.

TRADING HALTED

In order to maintain a fair and orderly market, trading may be halted by the CBOE in a class of options if two floor officials agree. If the conditions causing trading to be halted are determined by the directors to no longer be present, or if they determine that the resumption of trading best serves the maintenance of a fair and orderly market, trading will be resumed. When, in the judgment of any two floor officials, because of an influx of orders or other unusual circumstances, the interest of maintaining a fair and orderly market so requires, the officials may declare the market in one or more classes of option contracts to be **fast**. The officials then may assign the options traded at the post to other posts, authorize order book officials to execute transactions, and/or direct that one or more trading rotations be employed. Trading rotations may also be used to open the market in an option after a trading halt.

If trading is halted in ABC stock that is listed on the New York Stock Exchange (NYSE), trading in listed options on ABC stock will be halted at the same time by the CBOE.

SPECIALISTS AND REGISTERED TRADERS

Exchanges other than the CBOE use the specialist system. On the American Stock Exchange, registered option traders who elect to engage in exchange options transactions are designated as specialists on the exchange with respect to options transactions effected on the floor.

In a manner prescribed by the exchange, each specialist and registered options trader engaging in options trading shall file with the exchange and keep current a list identifying all accounts for stock, option, and related securities trading in which they may engage in trading activities or over which they may exercise investment discretion. They may not engage in any trading of such securities in any account not reported.

OPTIONS CLEARING CORPORATION (OCC)

OCC plays a distinctly important role in listed option transactions. Details of its operations are given in its prospectus. A general description of its function is that once it has determined that there are matching orders from a buyer and seller and that the premium has been paid, the direct link between these two parties is severed. As far as the option buyer is concerned, OCC is the seller, and as far as the option writers is concerned, OCC is the buyer. This permits these two parties to act independently of each other. OCC is the issuer and guarantor of all listed option transactions including equity, stock index, foreign currency, and interest rate options.

Most listed options are offset by a closing purchase or sale transaction before the expiration date. Offsetting occurs when a buyer sells an option he previously purchased or a seller buys back an option he previously sold. There are, normally, no certificates indicating ownership of an option. Ownership is evidenced by the confirmations and statements customers receive from their brokers. If a customer wants a document as evidence of ownership, OCC will issue, on request, a non-negotiable certificate to the clearing member. This certificate indicates that the clearing member holds an option, and it provides a space for the clearing member to certify that the option is held for the customer. Such certificates must be surrendered in the case of a closing sale or exercise or else OCC will not permit these transactions to occur.

COMPARISON—LISTED AND OVER-THE-COUNTER OPTIONS

There are more differences than there are similarities between exchange and over-the-counter (OTC) traded options. The basic similarities are

- On both OTC and exchange-listed options, the strike price (exercise price) is fixed when the option is purchased.
- On both, in the event of stock dividends, stock splits, reverse splits, or other equivalent actions, the option becomes an option for the equivalent in new securities when they are duly listed for trading and the total exercise price is changed accordingly.

For example, in the case of stock dividends, the exercise price and number of shares are adjusted as follows:

$$\text{Adjusted exercise price} = \frac{\text{Old exercise price}}{1 + \text{Decimalized dividend } \%}$$

$$\text{Adjusted number of shares} = \text{Old number of shares} \times (1 + \text{Dividend percentage})$$

If Mr. Jones owns a call option for 100 shares and ABC declares a 5% stock dividend, then on or after the ex-date, the new exercise price and adjusted number of shares would be

$$\text{Adjusted exercise price} = \frac{\$50}{1 + 0.05} = 47\tfrac{5}{8} \text{ (round to nearest } \tfrac{1}{8}\text{)}$$

$$\text{Adjusted number of shares} = 100 \times (1 + 0.05) = 100 \times 1.05 = 105 \text{ shares}$$

If, however, a stock dividend or split is such that one or more whole shares of underlying stock is issued for each outstanding share, the number of shares is not adjusted. In such case, the number of options is proportionately increased and the exercise price proportionately decreased.

As an example, assume one option on 100 shares of stock at an exercise price of $90. Compare what would happen if there were a 3-for-2 stock distribution with the result of a 2-for-1 distribution. In the 3-for-2 distribution, the existing option would be adjusted and cover 150 shares at an exercise price of $60. In the latter case, with a 2-for-1 distribution, the result would be two options, each for 100 shares at an exercise price of $45.

If, after an adjustment, an option covers more than 100 shares, the aggregate premium is determined by multiplying the premium per share by the number of shares covered by the option. For example, in the 3-for-2 distribution just described, if the premium on the option before adjustment was $4 per share, then the aggregate premium after adjustment would be $600 (150 shares x $4).

For other distributions (not cash dividends), such as recapitalization or reorganization of the issuer of the underlying security, or where the previously described adjustments do not seem appropriate to OCC, other adjustments may be made to the exercise price, unit of trading, or number of options that OCC believes to be fair to holders and writers.

Any adjustment in the exercise price is rounded to the nearest one-eighth and any adjustment in the number of shares is rounded to the nearest whole share.

In the case of rights, warrants, or spin-offs, the market price of the underlying stock is reduced by their value. The value is determined by the initial transaction in the right, warrant, or spun-off securities on or after the ex-dividend date. All open positions will include the additional rights, warrants, and spun-off securities unless the expiration date of the rights or warrants is prior to that of the option contract. If they do not expire first, then the exercise of all open positions affected is reduced in value. The value to be used in these adjustments is determined by the exchange.

The difference between exchange-listed and OTC options are

- On listed options, the contract price is not changed by the value of any cash dividend, while on OTC options, the contract price is reduced by the value of the cash dividend on the day the underlying stock goes ex-dividend.

- On exchanges, the strike price is an even dollar amount and a multiple of at least 5 (5-point intervals for securities trading below 50, 10 points between 50 and 200, and 20 points above 200), while the OTC striking price is an exact fractional amount based on the specific current market price of the underlying stock.
- Exchanges have standard expiration dates, while the OTC expiration date can be as short as thirty-five days and as long as one year. The expiration months of certain classes of options are January, April, July, and October. For other classes, they are February, May, August, and November; and for other classes they are March, June, September, and December. Thus, exchange-traded options are standardized into four expiration dates each year. If it wishes to, an exchange may list options expiring in any month. Trading in options of a particular month generally begins about nine months earlier. This means that, at any given time, options in each class, having three different expiration months, are usually open for trading. The longest time a listed equity option contract will generally be open for trading is nine months.
- Exchange-traded options are guaranteed by OCC, while OTC options are guaranteed by an NYSE member firm.
- Listed options are traded on an exchange (not in the third market), while OTC options are traded in the OTC market.

OPENING AND CLOSING TRANSACTIONS

When a customer purchases a call or put option, it is an **opening purchase**. The customer has opened a position by purchasing an option. If the customer later sells the call or put option, it is a closing sale. The customer has closed out an option position by selling.

When a customer writes a call or put option, it is an **opening sale**. The customer has opened a position by selling an option contract. If the customer later buys the option contract back in the marketplace, it is a **closing purchase transaction**. Therefore, an opening purchase transaction creates a long option position. A closing sale transaction closes out or eliminates a long option position. An **opening sale transaction** creates a short option position in either a put or call. A **closing purchase transaction** closes out or eliminates a short option position.

EXERCISING OPTIONS

OCC is the issuer and guarantor of every option contract. Exercise can occur only through OCC. An exercise notice must be submitted to OCC by 8:59 P.M. Pacific time, 10:59 P.M. Central time, 11:59 P.M. Eastern time, on the Saturday immediately following the third Friday of the expiration month. To permit this notice to be submitted to OCC before the expiration time, the exchanges have fixed 2:30 P.M. Pacific time, 4:30 P.M. Central time, 5:30 P.M. Eastern time on the business day immediately preceding the expiration date as the exercise cutoff time.

To exercise an option, an exercise notice in proper form must be tendered to OCC by the clearing member maintaining the account in which the option is held. Therefore, the holder of an option may exercise it only through the broker handling the account in which the option is held.

A tender of an exercise notice to OCC is irrevocable. The exercising holder is contractually obligated to pay the aggregate exercise price for the underlying security on the **exercise settlement date**. This is required even if the underlying security declines in value after the exercise notice is tendered.

An exercise notice properly tendered on any business day will be assigned by OCC on the following business day. Under unusual circumstances, assignments may be delayed and OCC will fix the assignment and exercise settlement date as soon as it deems fair and reasonable. Writers should determine from their brokers the latest time the broker may notify the writer of exercise notices assigned to the broker, since notification may not be until one or two days following the assignment date.

An exercise notice is assigned to a clearing member, randomly selected, having an account with OCC showing the writing of an option of the same series as the one exercised. The clearing member is required to allocate the exercise notice to a customer maintaining a position as a writer in the account either

- On a random selection basis, or
- On a first-in, first-out (FIFO) basis.

There are no price restrictions as to exercise. Options may be exercised regardless of the price at which the underlying stock is trading.

Options are exercisable at any time after they are issued, until the exercise cutoff time, with certain exceptions. The exceptions are

- The exchanges limit the aggregate number of options in each class which may be exercised by a holder or group of holders acting in concert within any three consecutive business days. The specific limits are the same as the position limits covered later in this section. The limits apply whether the options were purchased on one exchange or different exchanges. Exchanges may make exceptions to these limits under unusual circumstances. Puts and calls, even though they cover the same underlying security, are separate classes of options and are not added together for purposes of this rule.

- An exchange may restrict the exercise of particular options within a class of options traded on that exchange if it believes this is in the interest of maintaining a fair and orderly market, is otherwise believed to be in the public interest, or is believed to protect investors. The holder of such an option will not be able to exercise it if his position is with a member of the exchange imposing the restriction. This restriction, however, will not remain in effect for the period commencing ten business days prior to the option's expiration.

- OCC may restrict the exercise of particular options during the ten business days prior to the option's expiration. Under such a restriction, the holder of such an option will not be able to exercise it irrespective of where his position is maintained. If the restriction is imposed on the writers of calls, OCC shall fix a fair settlement value, if any, for such options.

  Instead of delivery and receipt of the underlying security upon exercise, the parties may pay and accept the settlement value fixed for the day the exercise notice is assigned. If the restriction is imposed on the holders of puts based on the suspension of trading in the underlying security, the restriction may be terminated by OCC when the trading suspension has been lifted or when OCC determines that the underlying security has no value. If trading of the underlying stock is halted on the principal exchange on which it is traded, trading in listed options on this stock will be halted at the same time by the CBOE.

- Each exchange may also restrict the exercise of particular options if it determines that the holder, or a group of holders acting in concert, is in violation of the position limits established by that exchange.

The exercise cutoff time for expiring listed option contracts requires customers wishing to exercise an option to instruct their broker prior to 2:30 P.M. Pacific time, 4:30 P.M. Central time, 5:30 P.M. Eastern time, on the business day immediately preceding the expiration.

TYPES OF OPTION EXERCISES

Put and call options can be classified, relating to exercise terms, as either American-style options or European-style options.

The terms *American* and *European* refer to when the options are exercisable and have nothing to do with geographic location of the option markets.

Most options issued and guaranteed by OCC are **American-style** options, which may be exercised by the holder at any time after it is purchased, up to expiration. **European-style** options may be exercised only during a specified period. The specified period in which the European-style option can be exercised may be as short as one business day, just before the option expires. Investors should be aware of the type of option they have purchased or sold in order to be aware of the applicable exercise periods.

Holders of European-style options must be aware that, because of the limited period in which the option can be exercised, the only means of recovering its market value is by selling it in the marketplace. During the period that the European-style option cannot be exercised, it has no intrinsic value. The market price of the European-style option depends on the likelihood that the option will eventually be sold at a profit. Writers of European-style options are subject to assignment of an exercise only during the exercise period.

POSITION LIMITS

The exchanges have established option rules that place limitations on the maximum number of options in each class which may be held or written by a single investor or a group of investors acting in concert. An exchange may order the liquidation of positions found to be in violation of these limits and impose other sanctions.

Options Position Limits are changed at certain times by the CBOE. The rule in effect at the time of this writing was 75,000, 60,000, 31,500, or 22,500 option contracts on either side of the market, depending on the volume in the underlying security. Assume an option on an underlying security ABC qualifies for a 75,000 position limit rule. The customer could have the following positions:

Long 40,000 ABC calls	Long 55,000 ABC puts
Short 35,000 ABC puts	Short 20,000 ABC calls
75,000	75,000

The maximum number of contracts on either side of the market is 75,000 contracts. Remember, position limit rules can change and current limits can be obtained from the CBOE's Web site at cboe.com.

These limits are applicable to the following positions covering the same underlying security:

- Puts and calls separately
- The aggregate of long put positions and short call positions
- The aggregate of short put positions and long call positions

The position limit rule applies to any person acting in concert. **Acting in concert** as it relates to the position limit rule means

- An individual trading options for himself and for a trust or corporation over which he exercises control
- Two or more customers with an agreement or understanding between them to coordinate or bunch their option activities
- A registered representative (RR) or investment advisor with discretionary authority over several customer accounts

The minimum long or short position in any single class of option contracts carried for any single customer that represents a position reportable to the exchange is 200 contracts.

DELIVERY AND PAYMENT

Except for cash-on-delivery (COD) transactions, after a customer exercises a call option contract but before he receives the called stock, the member organization must obtain from the customer either

- Full cash payment of the aggregate exercise price, or
- The required margin deposit if the transaction is effected in a margin account

Once an exercise notice has been assigned to the writer of a call option, he may no longer effect a closing purchase transaction. The writer must deliver the underlying security or, in the case of a put, make the required payment. The exercise settlement date is the third business day following the date the exercise notice is properly tendered to OCC.

As an example, assume Mr. Crombie tenders an exercise notice for a call to OCC on Wednesday, June 4. OCC assigns a firm the notice on June 5. The firm assigns one of its customers the notice on June 6. The settlement date for the called stock would be Monday, June 9.

If an assignment is made to the writer of a call option, the writer must deliver the underlying security. He could not, for example, deliver an escrow receipt to satisfy the assignment. He must deliver the underlying security. The following would satisfy an assignment to the writer of a call option:

- Buying the underlying security in the open market and delivering it.
- Delivering the underlying security the writer currently owns.
- Going short the underlying security, in which case the broker/dealer will deliver the security to the holder of the call option resulting in a short position for the writer. The writer could have to maintain margin on the short position.

If a customer exercises a long put position, he must deposit the underlying stock. This may be in the form of

- The fully paid stock
- A security convertible or exchangeable for the fully paid stock
- The required margin (if any is required) to carry the short position in the stock that would result from delivery

The put writer could pay the put holder on exercise by depositing

- The cash required for full payment
- The cash margin (if any is required) to carry the resulting long position
- Marginable securities to carry the resulting long position

If an exercise notice for a call is properly tendered to OCC prior to the ex-dividend date, the exercising holder is entitled to any cash dividend even though the notice of assignment may not be received by the writer until on or after the ex-dividend date. An uncovered writer may then be required to deliver not only the underlying security, but also the distributed amount even though he is only able to acquire the security on an ex-dividend basis.

OCC's obligations are ended when the underlying security is physically delivered to the exercising clearing member. If securities are not delivered on the exercise settlement date, the exercising clearing member may issue a **buy-in** notice and buy the undelivered securities in the best available market. OCC must pay the exercising clearing member, on the business day following the buy-in, the difference between the price paid when buying-in the securities and the price that would have been payable by the exercising clearing member to the assigned clearing member.

When the holder of a put files an effective exercise notice with OCC prior to the ex-dividend date for a cash dividend, but delivers the underlying stock to the writer to whom the notice is assigned after the ex-dividend date, he must also deliver the cash dividend to the writer.

OPTION PREMIUMS AND COMMISSIONS

The premium for an option is determined in the marketplace on the CBOE floor. The basis for computing nonmember commission charges on options transactions is the total premium involved in the orders. The number of shares covered by an option contract is usually 100; therefore, a premium of $4 per share would be a total dollar premium of $400. In some instances, however, such as an adjustment due to a stock dividend, the contract might be for more than 100 shares. Therefore, a premium of $3, if the unit of trading is 106 shares, is a total dollar premium of $318.

OCC standardizes option contracts with regard to contract size, strike price, and expiration date. Premiums for option contracts are determined by supply and demand on the CBOE floor. As the price of the underlying security increases, call premiums on the security increase and put premiums decrease.

MISCELLANEOUS OPTION CONCEPTS

- Assume option contracts trade on ABC Corporation stock as follows:

Calls	*Puts*
ABC April 60	ABC April 60
ABC April 70	ABC April 70
ABC April 80	ABC April 80

- There are two classes of options in this example. This is a class of ABC calls and a class of ABC puts. Calls and puts on an individual security are never in the same class. The term *series* refers to each separate option contract within a class. There are three separate call series and three separate put series. The three-call series collectively makes a class of calls, and the three-put series makes a class of puts.
- Call option writers may be uncovered writers or covered writers. An uncovered call writer does not own the underlying security and has unlimited risk. Uncovered call options must be written in margin accounts, and margin money must be deposited by the customer. An uncovered writer is also referred to as a *naked* writer. A covered call writer is long the underlying security in the account or has an escrow receipt or depository receipt for the security. If an option is exercised against a covered call writer, the long stock can be delivered to the exercising holder. The broker/dealer does not have risk on a customer's covered call position. However, if a customer defaulted on an uncovered call position, the broker/dealer would have to purchase the stock and deliver it to settle the contract.
- Assume a customer buys 1 XYZ July 70 call at $7. The customer decides to exercise the option. The customer informs his broker to exercise and the broker/dealer notifies OCC. OCC randomly assigns the exercise to a broker/dealer who has a short option position in an XYZ July 70 call. The broker/dealer reassigns the option exercise to a customer, on either a FIFO basis or a random basis. The customer who has been assigned must sell the 100 shares of XYZ to the exercising holder at $70 per share.

PART III

CUSTOMER ACCOUNTS

The foremost objective of exchange rules is customer protection. When considering approval of an option customer's account, a member organization must attempt to obtain a detailed outline of the customer's financial needs, financial situation, and investment objectives.

Such information should be used by the member organization both to initially approve a customer's account for option trading and to determine whether or not a recommendation to purchase or sell an option contract is suitable for the customer.

Before recommending the purchase or sale of an option to a customer, due diligence must be used to obtain information concerning

- Changes in investment objectives since the initial approval of the account
- Changes in the customer's financial situation since initial approval of the account
- The customer's present and future financial needs

RRs should make only suitable recommendations to customers. As a rule of thumb, to comply with suitability criteria, for someone seeking advice on options, an RR normally should not recommend committing more than 15% to 20% of that person's investment assets to options.

Recommendations to customers to write an uncovered option contract (either put or call) are subject to higher suitability standards. They are considered unsuitable unless, upon information furnished by the customer, the person making the recommendation has a reasonable basis for believing that the customer has such knowledge and experience in financial matters that he may reasonably be expected to be capable of evaluating the risks of such a transaction and be financially capable of carrying such an uncovered position.

The customer's account must be approved for option transactions no later than the time an initial order is accepted. At or prior to the time the customer's account is initially approved for options transactions, a member organization must provide the customer with a current options disclosure document.

Furthermore, under exchange rules, a copy of each amendment to an options disclosure document must be provided to each previously approved customer not later than the time the next confirmation of a transaction is provided.

Within fifteen days after a customer's account has been approved for options transactions, a member organization must obtain from the customer a written agreement that the account will be handled according to the rules of the CBOE (on which the options are traded) and the rules of OCC.

A customer trading unlisted options is not automatically approved to buy, sell, or trade listed options. Customer accounts that were initially approved solely for covered call writing must be reapproved for put buying, put writing (covered or uncovered), or put spreading.

An existing options agreement that refers only to call options is insufficient for a customer dealing in put options. A new options agreement covering both puts and calls must be obtained from the customer before the initial put transaction.

Customer accounts must be properly supervised. If a registered options principal delegates responsibility for supervision of customer accounts to an employee, he must establish appropriate written procedures of supervision and control over such employee. While a branch-office manager may initially approve a customer's account for options trading, the approval must be confirmed within a reasonable time by a registered options principal.

Under option exchange rules, order tickets must contain information such as

- Designation of the customer's account
- Type of option and number of contracts traded
- The name of the underlying security
- The time of the order's receipt on the floor and time of report of execution

Written confirmations of transactions in option contracts must be furnished promptly to customers. Such confirmations must show the

- Underlying security, expiration month, and exercise price
- Number of option contracts, premium, and commission
- Trade date and settlement date
- Whether the transaction is a purchase or sale

- Whether it is a principal or agency transaction
- Whether the transactions are exchange or other transactions

Statements of account, except with exchange permission, must be sent by member organizations to customers showing security money positions and entries. They must be sent at least quarterly to all accounts having a position during the preceding quarter and at least monthly to all accounts having an entry during the preceding month. Customers who are day-trading options must be provided statements of account at least monthly.

A member organization is permitted to send communications to a customer in the care of another person

- If the customer has given the member organization written instructions, and
- Duplicate copies are sent to the customer at another address designated in writing by him.

If the customer of a member organization wishes to initiate arbitration proceedings, the customer must file a written statement requesting arbitration with a designated official of the exchange.

DISCRETIONARY OPTION ACCOUNTS

In order for a broker/dealer to exercise discretionary authority in an option account for a customer:

- Prior written authorization must be obtained from the customer.
- The customer's account must be accepted in writing by a registered options principal.
- Each order must be identified as discretionary at the time it is entered.
- There must be frequent supervisory review of the account by a compliance registered options principal to prevent transactions that are excessive in size or frequency.
- Each discretionary order must be approved and initialed on the day entered by the branch-office manager (BOM) who would normally be a registered options principal (ROP). If the BOM is not ROP qualified, his approval must be confirmed within a reasonable time by an ROP.
- A record must be made of every discretionary order that includes the customer's name, whether it is a purchase or sale, the number of contracts, premiums, and the date and time of the transaction.

Under CBOE rules, a discretionary authorization does not have to be renewed annually in writing. The authorization is good until revoked by the customer.

OPTION COMPLAINTS

Member organizations must maintain and keep current a separate central log, index, or other file for all options-related complaints. The term **options-related complaint** means any written statement by a customer alleging a grievance arising out of or in connection with listed options. This central file must be located at the principal place of business of the member organization or such other principal office designated by the member organization. The central file must describe the nature of the complaint and record the action the broker/dealer took to resolve the complaint.

Each option-related complaint received by a branch office must be forwarded to the office in which the central file is located not later than thirty days after receipt, and a copy must be maintained at the branch office that is the subject of the complaint. A record of written options complaints must be maintained by a broker/dealer for a period of six years, the first two in a readily accessible place.

OPTION ACCOUNT RECORDS

Under CBOE rules, the customer account records must contain certain information concerning the customer's background and financial information including the basis for any estimates made by the firm. The date an options disclosure document was sent to the customer as well as the RR's name and the name of the approving ROP must be stated. The types of transactions the account is approved for must be reflected on the firm's records. If it is a discretionary account, this fact must be stated.

Refusal of a customer to provide any of the information must be noted on the customer's records. The member organization must then use the information provided together with other information available in determining whether and to what extent to approve the account for options transactions.

Under CBOE rules, the following points are correct concerning customer background and financial information:

- Financial information that the customer supplies must be verified by the broker/dealer within fifteen days after the account has been approved for options transactions.

- If the firm becomes aware of material changes concerning existing customers, a copy of background and financial information on file must be sent to the customer within fifteen days after the firm becomes aware of the change.
- This information must be sent to the customer by the firm for verification within fifteen days after the account is approved for options transactions unless it is contained in the customer's account agreement.

Assume Mr. Smith is opening an option account with your firm and he is asked to verify and, if necessary, correct the background and financial information that he has supplied the firm. Mr. Smith never responds to the request. Under CBOE rules, the broker/dealer may consider the information to be verified.

Assume Mr. Johnson wants to open an account to trade options but he refuses to provide the firm with specific information because he feels it is personal information and not of their concern. Under CBOE rules, the broker/dealer must make a note of the customer's refusal on its records and in deciding the extent to which the account may be approved, may use other available information.

SUMMARY—OPTION CUSTOMER ACCOUNTS

The following is a summary of other important points relating to option customer accounts:

- If the customer's account has previously been approved for other securities transactions, including OTC options, it must be reevaluated and specifically approved for listed options transactions prior to accepting an option order from the customer.
- A customer's account may be approved only for certain types of options transactions and not for others. For example, a customer's account may be approved for call transactions only or for other limited activity.
- A written record must be maintained noting the date the account was approved and bearing the signature of the ROP who is responsible for approving the account.
- Within fifteen days after the account has been approved for options, the firm must have obtained a written account agreement signed by the customer.
- Information considered in approving an account for options transactions must be reflected in the written records of the account.
- With respect to accounts in which options trading authorizations have been granted to a third person who is not an employee of the firm, including a person acting on behalf of an investment partnership or an investment club, each firm should satisfy itself of the agent's authority to act and that such authority relates to options trading. Similarly, before approving accounts of trusts, pension funds, profit-sharing plans, or other fiduciaries, for options trading, firms should satisfy themselves that the instruments under which the fiduciary is acting permit options trading.
- For natural person customers (not institutions), the firm must request investment objectives, employment status, estimated annual income, net worth, and liquid assets, as well as marital status, dependents, age, and investment experience and knowledge.
- Every member firm that conducts a public options business is required to designate one senior registered options principal (SROP). The SROP has overall authority and responsibility for supervision of all nonmember customer option transactions. The SROP may delegate the duty to review option activities within the firm to employees (generally ROP qualified) under his direct control. Such delegation does not relieve the SROP of his responsibility for overall supervision and control over the firm's option activities.
- Every member firm that conducts a public options business must designate one compliance registered options principal (CROP). The CROP may not have a sales function unless the firm either

  - Has received gross commissions on its option business of less than $1 million in either of the two preceding years, or
  - Has ten or fewer RRs handling option accounts.

- Background and financial information of customers who have been approved for options transactions must be maintained at both the branch office servicing the customer's account and the principal supervisory office having jurisdiction over that branch for the most recent six-month period.

OTHER TYPES OF OPTION ACCOUNTS

Assume ABC Broker/Dealer has a policy of allowing trustees to maintain an option account in which put and call options are purchased. Under option exchange rules, ABC Broker/Dealer should obtain the following information from a trustee opening an option account:

- New account report form
- Option agreement
- Proof that an options disclosure document (ODD) has been given to the trustee
- Copy of the trust agreement

A letter of consent from the individual granting or creating the trust is not required. A copy of the trust agreement must be examined to ensure that the trustee has the power to engage in transactions in option contracts.

Under CBOE rules, if one option account is to be used to guarantee another account, certain requirements must be met. Assume a husband and wife open separate accounts. The husband agrees to guarantee his wife's account for margin purposes and have the accounts consolidated for the determination of the required margin. Under CBOE rules, if one account is guaranteed by another account, the accounts may be consolidated for the determination of the required margin if a written guarantee is executed and the guaranteeing account is not owned by the member organization or affiliated persons of the member organization.

RULES CONCERNING OPTION COMMUNICATIONS

Put and call options issued by OCC (the only options listed on any of the exchanges) are registered under the Securities Act of 1933 and, therefore, the full disclosure requirements of the 1933 Act are fully applicable to the offer and sale to customers of these options. Moreover, under SRO (self-regulatory organization) rules, disclosure requirements apply to all options customers—both buyers and writers. Under these rules, customers must be furnished with a current ODD either before or at the time their account is approved for options transactions.

Many firms hold option seminars in their communities to generate interest in options. It is appropriate under SRO rules to deliver to each participant a current ODD at the time such a seminar is held. An ODD is required to be delivered if written materials are distributed at the seminar.

All advertisements issued by a member firm pertaining to options must be approved in advance by the CROP or his designee. Advertisements must be submitted for approval to an exchange at least ten days prior to publication or broadcast. Copies must be retained for three years by the firm using such material, and the material must contain the names of persons who prepared and approved the material. Advertising includes any sales material utilized by a member firm that reaches a mass audience through public media such as newspapers, periodicals, magazines, television, radio, telephone recording, motion pictures, audio or video device, billboards, signs, or any mail solicitation that is not required to be accompanied or preceded by a current ODD. Recommendations, specific or otherwise, of option strategies are not permitted in any advertisement. The use of past or projected performance figures, including annualized rates of return, is not permitted in any advertisement pertaining to listed options.

Sales literature includes any written communication (not defined as an advertisement) distributed or made available to customers or the public that contains any analysis, performance report, projection, or recommendation, with respect to options. Sales literature also includes any seminar texts, lectures or similar events and any exchange-produced materials. Sales literature must be preceded or accompanied by a current ODD. The most common types of option sales literature include market letters, research reports, option worksheets proposing option strategies, exchange-produced materials, and seminar texts.

Other important points relating to option sales literature include

- Sales literature requires prior approval by the CROP or his designee, but it does not have to be filed with the exchange.
- Copies must be retained for three years by the firm using such material.
- A current ODD must precede or accompany the distribution of any sales literature relating to options.
- All communications (oral and written) concerning options must not contain promises of specific results or omit material facts.

Other miscellaneous CBOE rules with which a registered representative should be familiar include

- A member organization may make an off-the-floor trade for a customer only if

- It is an opening or closing transaction for a premium of $1 or less, or
- A better price can be obtained off the floor.

- An oral recommendation by an RR to a customer must be followed by a statement relating to the risks.
- A member organization may not restrict the size or frequency of a customer's option transactions unless such limitation has been practiced historically in that firm's customer relationships.
- If an RR violates exchange rules, the exchange may fine, censure, suspend, or bar the RR and could also discipline the broker/dealer for failing to properly supervise the RR.
- An RR can never sell a call option contract for the corporation that issued the underlying security. In other words, a corporation cannot write call options against its own security.

OPTIONS DISCLOSURE DOCUMENTS (ODD)

In an attempt to provide options customers with written material that would be easier to read than OCC prospectus, the ODD was prepared by the regulatory authorities. The document is entitled *Characteristics and Risks of Standardized Options.*

Under CBOE rules, every member organization must deliver a current ODD to each customer at or prior to the time the customer's account is approved for options transactions. At or prior to the time a customer's account is approved for options, the customer must be furnished the ODD pertaining to that category of options.

A copy of each amendment to an ODD must be furnished to each option customer not later than the time the next confirmation of a transaction is sent to a customer. If a customer requests a copy of the current prospectus of OCC, the member organization must furnish it to the customer. However, most customers will probably be satisfied reading the ODD, which provides a more plain-language explanation of the risk–reward relationship of options trading.

STOCK INDEX OPTIONS

In recent years, stock index options have become very popular with investors. Stock index options are based on the same principles as options on equities. Stock index options allow investors to profit from and protect against price movements in the stock market in general rather than in individual securities.

In our examples, the Standard & Poor's (S&P) 100 stock index option will be used. However, the same principles would apply to the other stock index options. The S&P 100 option has become the most actively traded of all listed options. The S&P 100 market index is made up of 100 blue-chip stocks on which the CBOE currently trades equity options and it also trades on the CBOE.

The main difference between the S&P index option and equity options is that the S&P index option has a cash settlement. In equity options, the exercise requires delivery of the underlying securities. However, when an index option is exercised, only cash changes hands; the assigned writer must pay the exercising holder cash equal to the difference between the closing value of the index on the exercise date and the exercise price of the option multiplied by the specific index multiplier. The index multiplier for the S&P Index option is $100. The symbol for the S&P 100 index option on the ticker tape is OEX. Stock index options can be used to profit from a market swing or to hedge a diversified portfolio.

Assume a customer buys one June OEX call option at $4 when the S&P 100 Index closed at 150.00. One month later, the S&P index closed at 168.00. The customer decides to close out his position by exercising the option. What is the customer's profit or loss?

168.00 x $100	=	$16,800	Sell
150.00 x $100	=	15,000	Buy
		1,800	Profit on exercise
		400	Premium
		$ 1,400	Net profit

If instead the index decreased in value and the option expired, the customer's maximum loss was limited to the amount of the premium paid ($400).

Assume that a customer expects a market decline in the near future and he purchases 1 S&P 160 put for $4\frac{3}{8}$ when the S&P index closed at 162.00. Three weeks later, the S&P index closes at 151.50. The customer exercises the put. What is the customer's profit or loss?

160.00 x $100	=	$16,000	
151.50 x $100	=	15,150	
		$ 850	Profit on exercise

$850.00	Profit on exercise
437.50	Premium paid
$412.50	Net profit

A customer could use stock index options to hedge a diversified portfolio of securities. Assume the customer feels that a steep, temporary market decline is about to begin. The customer could either sell call options on the S&P 100 stock index or buy puts on the index. The investor could hedge market risk to the extent of the call premiums received. If he bought puts on the index, the decrease in the market value of the portfolio would be at least partly offset by an increase in the value of the puts.

Investors who own securities face three main risks.

1. Market risk
2. Industry risk
3. Firm-specific risk

Market risk influences every security to some extent. Market risk is affected by changes in investors, attitudes, inflation, expectations, interest rates, and fiscal policies. The S&P stock index option contract allows investors to hedge the market risk related to a stock portfolio. Market risk may be referred to as systematic risk.

Industry risk is affected by factors relating to a specific industry. Components of industry risk include foreign competition, labor problems, shortages of raw material, outdated products, and changes in the regulatory environment. The general stock market may be increasing while a particular industry is not participating in the increase.

Firm-specific risk is the risk associated with the individual security. The company's earnings may fall short of expectations, or a major lawsuit may be brought against it by another corporation.

Portfolio diversification can reduce industry and firm-specific risk. However, market risk cannot be greatly reduced by diversification. Market factors cause changes in the value of a diversified portfolio of securities.

To summarize some of the main points relating to the S&P 100 index option contract

- The underlying index is the S&P 100 index. The S&P 100 index is a broad-based, value-weighted index that gives greater weight to stocks with larger capitalization (more shares outstanding). The S&P 100 index is composed of 100 blue-chip stocks such as IBM, General Motors, Exxon, and General Electric. The S&P 100 index measures the market performance of the 100 blue-chip stocks that comprise it. To compute the index, the market price of each of the stocks is multiplied by its outstanding shares. The total of the market values are added together to obtain the aggregate market value of the stocks in the index. In order to determine the current value of the index, the aggregate market value is divided by the base value and multiplied by 100. Base values are adjusted over time to reflect changes in capitalization relating to mergers, acquisitions, stock splits, or substitution of companies.
- The S&P 100 index options have a cash settlement. If a customer exercises a put or call, she is entitled to the in-the-money amount of the option. This is the difference between the exercise price and the closing value of the index on the exercise date multiplied by 100 (index multiplier). Therefore, on the exercise of a stock index option, only cash changes hands. The exercising holder of the option receives the amount by which the option is in-the-money.
- The dollar value of the index is determined by multiplying the index value by $100. If the index is at 142.40, the dollar value of the index is $14,240 (142.40 x $100). If the index is at 162.20, the dollar value of the index is $16,220 (162.20 x $100). The index multiplier for the S&P 100 Index is $100.
- S&P 100 Index options expire on a monthly basis. The expiration date is the Saturday following the third Friday of the expiration month.
- Option premiums are expressed in points. Each point is equal to $100. As with equity options, for premiums of 3 or above, minimum fluctuations are $\frac{1}{8}$. For premiums below 3, minimum fluctuations are 1/16. Therefore, a quote of $8\frac{5}{8}$ for S&P 100 index options equals $182.50. A quote of 2 3/16 equals $218.75.
- Exercise prices are normally set at five-point intervals to bracket the current value of the index. New exercise prices are introduced when the current value of the index approaches the upper or lower limits of existing strike prices.
- The aggregate exercise price of an S&P index option is the exercise price multiplied by the index multiplier. For example, the aggregate exercise price of an S&P 160 index option is $16,000 (160 x $100).

- The CBOE has the discretion to open trading in index options each day even though trading may not have opened in a substantial number of stocks in the underlying index. The present level of the index is continually updated during the trading day.
- Stock index options appeal to investors because of their versatility. Investors who anticipate a rising stock market could buy call options on the S&P 100 index. Investors who anticipate a falling stock market could buy puts on the S&P 100 index. Investors, in this way, could profit from stock market moves without investing in a diversified portfolio of stocks. Investors can use stock index options to hedge an existing portfolio. An investor could sell calls and buy puts on the S&P to hedge against market declines. Investors could also hedge specific stock positions against market risk by using stock index options. He could buy a put on the S&P index to protect against an individual security declining in price. If the market decreases, the profit on the put could offset the decrease in the price of the individual security. Also, index options can be used by investors who want to preserve capital. Assume an investor's primary objective is preservation of capital but he would like to participate in potential increases in the market. The investor could place most of his funds in safe short-term securities such as Treasury bills and use the balance to buy some call options on the S&P 100 index. If the market increases, he will make a profit on the calls. If the market does not increase, the most he can lose is the amount of the premiums. The remainder of his portfolio would be generating income with minimal risk.

The CBOE also trades S&P 500 index options (SPX). The American Stock Exchange trades the Major Market Index (XMI) and the Philadelphia Stock Exchange trades the Gold/Silver Index Option (XAU). Various other index options are traded by regional stock exchanges and the NYSE on their options trading floors.

Nonequity options, including broad-based stock index options, are subject to special tax treatment. Broad-based stock index options cover securities from different industries. The normal short- and long-term capital gains rules do not apply to broad-based stock index options. Instead, at the end of the year, these contracts are marked to the market and are deemed to have been sold at their present market value. Also, regardless of the holding period of the stock index option, any gain or loss on the option is considered 60% long-term and 40% short-term. Other equity options (options on individual securities) and narrow-based stock index options are subject to regular capital gains treatment. Narrow-based stock index options are options based on specialized industries such as the Oil and Gas Index, NYSE Telephone Index, Computer Technology Index, Oil Index, Airline Index, Gold/Silver Index, and PSE Technology.

Assume a customer purchases 1 S&P 150 call at 4. At the end of the year the premium of the option has increased to 16. The customer has held the option for two months. What is the tax treatment for federal tax purposes?

$$\begin{array}{ll} \$1,600 & \text{Assumed sale at market value} \\ \underline{400} & \text{Cost} \\ \$1,200 & \text{Gain} \end{array}$$

$$\begin{array}{lcll} \$1,200 \times 60\% & = & 720 & \text{Long-term gain} \\ \$1,200 \times 40\% & = & \underline{480} & \text{Short-term gain} \\ & & \$1,200 & \text{Total gain} \end{array}$$

The customer reports a long-term gain of $720 and a short-term gain of $480 on his federal tax return. Even though the stock index option was not sold by the customer, under the special tax treatment, it is considered to have been sold at its present market value. The option was held only two months prior to year-end. However, under the special tax treatment, it is considered to have been sold at its present market value, with 60% of the gain considered long-term gain and 40% short-term. This special tax treatment applies to interest rate options and foreign currency options.

OPTIONS ON FOREIGN CURRENCIES

To understand the risks associated with foreign currency options, an investor must be familiar with some basic concepts relating to foreign currencies. Each sovereign country has its own currency that it uses within its own borders. However, when transactions take place between countries or citizens of these countries, it is necessary to price these transactions in one of the nation's currencies. The relative value of one country's currency compared to another country is expressed in terms of **exchange rates**. The exchange rate is expressed in US dollars. A foreign exchange rate represents the price of one currency in relation to another currency at a particular moment in time.

Foreign exchange rates are either set by governments or are allowed to float freely. Most Western countries allow their exchange rate to fluctuate in value in relation to the US dollar. However, governments intervene in the marketplace, using their central bank to affect exchange rates. Governments buy the weaker currency and sell the stronger currency.

Foreign currency trading exists in large financial centers throughout the world, and primary trading takes place by the world's international banks. Trading in foreign currencies is normally done in units of $1 million to $5 million. Individuals can purchase foreign currency for travel or other purposes in the retail foreign currency market. However, prices in the retail market may vary from prices in the wholesale interbank market.

Currency	*Units underlying each contract*	*Symbol*
Euro	62,500	EU
Swiss francs	62,500	SF
Canadian dollars	50,000	CD
British pounds	31,250	BP
Japanese yen	6,250,000	JY
Australian dollar	50,000	AD

A call option on a foreign currency allows the holder to purchase units of the underlying currency at the option exercise price, which is stated in US dollars. An investor would buy call options to profit from a strengthening foreign currency in relation to the US dollar. Therefore, assume an investor feels that the Swiss franc will increase in price relative to the US dollar. He should buy call options on the Swiss franc. If he feels that the Swiss franc will decrease in price, he should buy put options on the Swiss franc.

Premiums for foreign currency options are quoted in US cents per unit of the underlying currency for euros, Swiss francs, Canadian dollars, and British pounds. Premiums are in hundredths of a cent per unit for Japanese yen.

A premium of 2.00 for a SF option represents $0.02 per SF. Since each option represents 62,500 SF, the total option premium would be $1,250 ($0.02 x 62,500).

A premium of 8.2 for an option on British pounds would represent a total option premium of $2,562.50. A premium of 4.00 for an option on Swiss francs would represent a total option premium of $2,500 ($0.04 x 62,500). A premium of 6.00 for an option on Canadian dollars would represent a total premium of $3,000 ($0.06 x 50,000). A premium of 2.6 for an option on Japanese yen would represent a total premium of $1,625 ($0.00026 x 6,250,000).

Assume a customer purchases one SF June 40 call and pays $850 for the option. The SF spot or cash price has risen to 44 ($0.44). The customer exercises the option. What is the customer's profit or loss?

Spot price SF	44	Sell
SF June	40	Buy
	$0.04	Profit

$0.04 Profit x 62,500 = $2,500 profit on exercise

$2,500	Profit on exercise
850	Premium paid
$1,650	Net profit

To summarize the main points relating to foreign currency options

- If the value of a foreign currency increases in relation to the US dollar, call premiums on foreign currency will increase and put premiums on foreign currency will decrease.
- If the value of a foreign currency decreases in relation to the US dollar, put premiums on foreign currency will increase and call premiums on foreign currency will decrease.
- The Philadelphia Exchange trades options on foreign currencies with American-style and European-style exercises and options with end-of-the-month expirations.
- Foreign currency transactions in the interbank market involve very large amounts. Investors are at a disadvantage because prices are not as favorable in the retail market as compared to the wholesale interbank market.
- There is no systematic reporting of last sale information relating to foreign currencies. It is difficult for investors to obtain timely information about the foreign currency market. Also, the interbank market in foreign currencies operates twenty-four hours a day. The hours for trading foreign currency options do not conform to the hours in which the foreign currencies are traded.
- Presently, foreign currency options are traded on the Philadelphia Stock Exchange and the CBOE.

- Exercises on foreign currency options are settled through the facilities of OCC. The delivery of foreign currency to satisfy an option exercise must take place in the country of origin of that foreign currency. OCC has set up banking arrangements that allow it to receive or deliver each underlying foreign currency in the country of origin to satisfy option exercises.
- Options are traded on the European currency unit (ECU). The ECU is made up of specialized amounts of different currencies. The ECU is recognized as the official medium of exchanges of the European Economic Community's monetary system. The ECU is mainly intended for use in international commerce. The European Economic Community's monetary authorities may change the currencies comprising the ECU for their particular weightings from time to time.
- If an investor is obligated to receive foreign currency in settlement of a business contract, he could hedge against a decline in the value of that currency by purchasing puts.

YIELD-BASED OPTIONS

Fluctuations in interest rates affect all types of investment products. Interest rate options provide investors with the opportunity to profit from interest rate movements. Interest rate options are traded on the CBOE and are available on the thirteen-week Treasury bill yield, the five-year Treasury note yield, the ten-year Treasury note yield, and the thirty-year Treasury bond yield.

Interest rate option contracts are available in puts and calls. A call buyer of an interest rate option anticipates rising interest rates, while a put buyer of an interest rate option anticipates falling interest rates. Since interest rate options are options on the yield of US Treasury bills, notes, and bonds, they are referred to as **yield-based options**. Yield-based call options will increase in value as interest rates rise. Yield-based put options will increase in value as interest rates fall.

For interest rate options, underlying values for the option contracts are ten times the underlying Treasury yields. If the annualized discount rate on the newly auctioned thirteen-week Treasury bill is 4.5%, the underlying value for the option on the short-term interest rate (Treasury bill yield) would be at 45.00. If the yield to maturity is 7.25% on the thirty-year Treasury bond (option on the thirty-year rate), the underlying value on the thirty-year Treasury bond yield-based option will be at 72.50.

If the yield to maturity on the thirty-year Treasury bond increased from 7.25% to 8.25%, the Treasury bond yield-based call would increase from 72.50 to 82.50.

Interest rate options differ from options on individual securities because the underlying value of interest rate options is based on interest rates. Interest rate options rise and fall in value based on changes in interest rates. Individual equity options values rise or fall based on changes in the market value of the underlying equity security.

Interest rate options have a cash settlement. Assume an investor is holding an expiring thirty-year Treasury bond yield April 75 call option. The call option has a settlement value of 79 at the April expiration time. The investor would exercise the interest rate option and $400 would be credited to her account and $400 would be debited to the writer's account.

$$
\begin{array}{ll}
79.00 & \text{Settlement value} \\
\underline{75.00} & \text{Strike price} \\
4.00 & \text{x \$100 multiplier} = \$400 \text{ cash settlement}
\end{array}
$$

Interest rate options have the same multiplier of $100 as equity options and stock index options. Also, interest rate options have a European-style exercise, which means that the option can be exercised only during a specified period immediately prior to the expiration.

The symbols for the yield-based options are as follows:

- Thirteen-week Treasury bill yield (IRX)
- Five-year Treasury note yield (FVX)
- Ten-year Treasury note yield (TNX)
- Thirty-year Treasury bond yield (TYX)

The premiums on interest rate options are affected by volatility, time remaining to expiration, and the price of the underlying security (Treasury bills, notes, or bonds). Interest rate options purchased by investors will settle at a future date. Therefore, investors must form opinions on what the rates will be at the expiration date. The yields that the marketplace or investors expect on the most recent issue to be present at expiration are referred to as **forward yields** or **forward rates**.

Assume the marketplace projects forward rates that are above the current spot rate. In this case, call options will increase in value and put options will decrease in value. If the marketplace projects forward rates that are below the current spot rate, call options will decrease in value and put options will increase in value.

The following interest rate strategies can be used by investors in interest rate options:

Expectation	*Strategy*
Rising five-year interest rates	Buy five-year yield-based calls
Falling thirty-year interest rates	Buy thirty-year yield-based puts
Rising ten-year interest rates	Buy ten-year yield-based calls
Falling thirteen-week interest rates	Buy thirteen-week yield-based puts

Assume that thirty-year interest rates are at 7.25% and the value of the thirty-year Treasury bond yield-based call is at 72.50 (10 times the underlying Treasury yield). The investor buys one Treasury bond yield-based call at 2½ ($250). Assume thirty-year Treasury bond yields rise and the settlement value for the thirty-year Treasury bond yield-based call is 78.50 (interest rates 7.85%). The investor has a profit of $350.

$$
\begin{array}{ll}
78.50 & \text{Settlement value} \\
\underline{72.50} & \text{Strike price} \\
6.00 \text{ x } \$100 \text{ multiplier} & = \$600 \text{ cash settlement} \\
\\
\$600 & \text{Profit on exercise} \\
\underline{-250} & \text{Premium paid} \\
\$350 & \text{Profit}
\end{array}
$$

To summarize, interest rate options are options based on the yield of US Treasury bills, notes, and bonds. In other words, options are available on short-term, medium-term and long-term rates. Yield-based call options will increase in value as the underlying interest rate rises above the strike price. Yield-based put options will increase in value as underlying interest rates decline below the strike price.

Underlying values for interest rate option contracts are ten times the underlying Treasury yields. An annualized discount rate of 5.5% on a newly auctioned thirteen-week Treasury bill would set the underlying value for the thirteen-week Treasury bill yield-based option at 55.00. A yield to maturity of 8.25% on a thirty-year Treasury bond would place the underlying value of the thirty-year Treasury bond yield-based option at 82.50.

Interest rate options have a cash settlement, and the multiplier is $100. They have a European-style exercise, which restricts exercise to a specified period immediately prior to expiration (normally, the last trading day before expiration). When interest rate options are exercised, the exercising holder receives the amount by which the option is in-the-money as a cash settlement.

CAPPED INDEX OPTIONS

Capped index options (CAPS) give investors the right to participate in upward or downward movements on the S&P 100 index (OEX) and the S&P 500 index to a predetermined level.

CAPS are initially listed with a strike price that is at-the-money and a capped price that is 30 points higher for call CAPS and 30 points lower for put CAPS.

Assume that the OEX is 359.55. Call CAPS would be introduced with a strike price of 360 and a capped price of 390. The 360 strike price plus a 30-point capped interval equals a capped price of 390. Put CAPS would be introduced with a strike price of 360 minus a 30-point capped interval equals a capped price of 330.

CAPS call buyers would profit if the index moved from the strike price up to the capped price. CAPS put buyers would benefit if the index moved from the strike price down to the capped price.

OEX CAPS and SPX CAPS (CAPS on the S&P 500) have a European-style exercise. A European-style exercise means that the option can only be exercised by the holder at or just prior to expiration. However, CAPS have a unique automatic exercise feature. If the underlying index on any day closes at or above the capped price for calls, or at or below the capped price for puts, the option will be automatically exercised. The CAPS buyers would receive the in-the-money 30-point difference between the strike price and the capped price. The CAPS buyer would realize a 30-point profit minus the premium paid. CAPS sellers on exercise would lose 30 points, less the premium received when the CAPS were sold.

Buyers and sellers of CAPS can always liquidate their positions. However, CAPS, unless they are automatically exercised, can be exercised only at expiration (European-style exercise).

OEX CAPS add new series every two months with four-month expirations. SPX CAPS add new series every three months with six-month expirations. Price quotations for both OEX CAPS and SPX CAPS will reflect bids and offers for a minimum of ten contracts.

Assume an investor buys 10 OEX 350 four-month call CAPS at 14. The total cost of the position is $1,400 ($14 x $100 multiplier). The CAPS call buyer would profit if the OEX closed on any given day during the life of the contract at or above 380. In this case, the option contract would be automatically exercised and the CAPS call buyer would realize a profit of

$380 Capped price
350 Strike price
$ 30 Profit on exercise
– 14 Premium
$ 16 Net profit per share

$16 net profit per share x $100 multiplier = $1,600 net profit per contract

$1,600 net profit per contract x 10 contracts = $16,000 net profit on 10 contracts

Other important points concerning CAPS include

- CAPS place a limit on profit potential but have a lower cost than traditional options with the same strike price and expiration date.
- CAPS buyers or sellers can close out their position at any time before the expiration date by selling the option in the marketplace.
- A CAPS buyer's risk is limited to the premium paid. The maximum profit to the CAPS buyer is limited to the 30-point capped interval minus the premium paid. The maximum loss to the CAPS writer is limited to the 30-point capped interval minus the premium received for selling the option.
- Call CAPS and put CAPS are similar to vertical spreads. However, the advantage of CAPS is that they are created with a single trade, instead of the two trades needed to create a vertical spread. Similar to vertical spreads, CAPS have limited risk for both buyers and sellers. Spreads must be executed in a margin account, while CAPS can be executed in a customer's cash account.
- The maximum loss to the CAPS buyer is the amount of the premium paid.
- OEX and SPX CAPS are attractive to investors because their benefits include

  - Lower cost than traditional put and call options with the same strike price and expiration date
  - Limited risk to both buyers and writers because of the capped interval
  - Automatic exercise feature, which gives the buyer a 30-point profit minus the premium paid

- An investor bullish on the stock market over the next several months would purchase OEX call CAPS. An investor bearish on the stock market over the next several months would purchase OEX put CAPS.
- Assume a capped index option has a strike price of 360 and a capped price of 390. The value of the index reaches a high of 392 during a particular trading day, but closes at 389. The automatic exercise feature of the option is not triggered. The index must close at or above 390. Assume on another trading day the index closes (exercise settlement value) at 395. The call option will be automatically exercised and the cash settlement amount would be $3,000 (the amount of the capped interval) and not $3,500.

MARGIN REQUIREMENTS

When a customer writes an uncovered put or call on an equity security, the initial and maintenance margin requirement is equal to 20% of the current market value of the underlying security, plus 100% of the current option premium, with an adjustment for an out-of-the-money option. The minimum margin required on an uncovered put or call on an equity security is 10% of the current market value of the underlying security plus the current option premium.

Assume a customer writes 1 ABC July 60 call for 12 when the market price of ABC stock is $70 per share. What is the margin requirement on this position?

$7,000 x 20% = $1,400

$1,400 + $1,200 (option premium) = $2,600 margin requirement

Assume a customer writes 1 XYZ January 50 call for 1 when the market price of XYZ is 45. What is the margin requirement on this uncovered call?

$4,500 x 20% = $900

$900 + $100 premium = $1,000

$1,000 – $500 out-of-the-money amount = $500 margin requirement

However, since the option is out-of-the-money, we must calculate the minimum margin requirement. If the minimum margin requirement is greater than the initial requirement, the customer must deposit the minimum requirement. The minimum margin requirement is 10% of the market value of the underlying security plus the premium.

$$\$4,500 \times 10\% = \$450$$

$$\$450 + \$100 \text{ premium} = \$550 \text{ minimum margin requirement}$$

Since the minimum requirement is greater than the initial requirement, the customer must deposit the minimum requirement of $550.

The margin requirement of 20% of the market value of the underlying security plus the current premium applies to equity options and narrow-based stock index options. The margin requirement on broad-based stock index options is 15% of the market value of the underlying security plus the current premium with a minimum margin of 10% of the market value of the underlying security plus the premium.

Regulation T of the Federal Reserve Board governs the amount of credit that may be initially extended by a broker/dealer to a customer at the time the customer enters into a securities transaction. The status of the account as a whole must always be tested against the Regulation T requirements when any transaction occurs in a margin account. Exchange requirements are additions to Regulation T—not substitutions—and individual firms may impose even stricter limits than Regulation T or exchange requirements.

Under Regulation T, options purchased by a customer have no loan value in a margin account—they are not considered marginable securities. Whether an option is purchased in a cash or a margin account, a deposit is required equal to 100% of the total cost. In other words, the premium must be paid in full.

Assume, for example, that a customer in a margin account buys 1 WLL August 60 put for 5 and buys 1 WLL August 60 call for 5 when the price of WLL is $60. If the customer has no other cash or securities positions, he would have to deposit $1,000 in his margin account ($500 + $500). In this example, the customer would break even if the market price declined to 50 (buy stock at $50 and put it to the writer at $60 = $10 profit – the total premium cost), or, if the stock increases to 70 (call the stock at $60 and sell it at $70).

The rules of OCC require the clearing member for a buyer to pay the premium to OCC prior to 9 A.M. Central time, 10 A.M. Eastern time, on the first business day following the day on which OCC receives the report of the matched trade.

Only covered writing transactions may be executed in a cash account and are

- In the case of a call

  - The underlying security is held in the account prior to the sale, or
  - An escrow receipt is deposited promptly following the sale (the proceeds are not released until the deposit is made), or
  - A depositary trust certificate is deposited promptly following the sale (the proceeds are not released until the deposit is made).

- In the case of a put

  - The aggregate exercise price is deposited prior to the sale, or
  - A bank guarantee letter is deposited promptly following the sale (the proceeds are not released until the deposit is made).

The **escrow receipt** of a bank custodian must be on a form approved by OCC. It guarantees that the underlying security is held in the customer's account and will be delivered if the option is exercised. The depositary trust certificate does the same. An escrow receipt can be used in either a cash account or a margin account. It is issued for a specific number of shares and a specific option series.

A **Bank guarantee letter** must be on a form approved by the regulatory agencies and certifies that the bank holds funds on deposit equal to the full amount of the aggregate exercise price of the short put and that these funds will be paid if the put is exercised.

An option may be purchased in a cash account and a call may be exercised in a cash account if full cash payment for the underlying security is deposited in the account promptly and before there is any release of proceeds for any resale of such security.

The margin deposit does not have to be provided when any of the following are held in the account:

- The underlying security in the case of a call, or a short position in the underlying security in the case of a put (assuming the margin has been provided on the short stock position).

- Securities immediately convertible into or exchangeable for the underlying security without restriction or the payment of money in the case of a call, provided that the right to convert or exchange does not expire on or before the expiration date of the option.
- An agreement under which a bank that is holding the underlying securities or the required cash is obligated to deliver, in the case of a call, or accept, in the case of a put, the underlying securities against payment of the exercise price upon the exercise of the option.
- A long position in a call on the same number of shares of the same underlying security, which does not expire before the expiration date of the call issued, provided that any amount by which the exercise price of the long call exceeds the exercise price of the short call is deposited into the account.
- A long position in a put on the same number of shares of the same underlying security, which does not expire before the expiration date of the put issued, provided that any amount by which the exercise price of the put issued exceeds the exercise price of such long position is deposited to the account
- A warrant to purchase the underlying security, in the case of a call, which does not expire on or before the expiration date of the call provided that any amount by which the exercise price of the warrant exceeds the exercise price of the call issued is deposited to the account. A warrant used in this manner shall have no loan value in the account.

The following summarizes important points relating to option transactions in cash or margin accounts:

- If a customer purchases a put or call in a cash or margin account, the option must be paid for in full. The customer is required to deposit 100% of the premium. Long options in a margin account have no loan value under Regulation T.
- A spread transaction (buying a call and selling a call or buying a put and selling a put on the same underlying security) must be executed in a margin account. A spread transaction cannot be executed in a cash account.
- In a cash account, if a customer writes a put or call, the option must be covered. A call option written by a customer is covered in a cash account if the customer is

  - Long the underlying security in the account, or
  - Has a bank guarantee letter equal to the aggregate exercise price on deposit.

- In a margin account, a customer could engage in any type of option transaction. However, in a cash account, only transactions that represent no risk to the broker/dealer can be executed. Therefore, in a cash account, a customer could buy puts or calls or write covered puts or covered calls. These transactions represent no risk to the broker/dealer. When a customer buys a put or call, the transactions must be paid in full. On expiration, the entire loss is the customer's. When a customer writes a covered put or call, the funds or stock necessary to perform on exercise is readily available. In a margin account, the customer can engage in risk transactions and is required to deposit margin money. Therefore, in a margin account, a customer could

  - Write uncovered puts and calls
  - Spread options
  - Sell calls against convertible bonds

SUMMARY—IMPORTANT CONCEPTS

An RR should clearly understand the risks and potential profits relating to option contracts. To briefly review, the purchaser of a call option has unlimited gain potential and a limited loss equal to the premium paid. An uncovered call writer has a gain potential equal to the premium received and an unlimited loss potential. A covered call writer has a gain potential equal to the premium received and a loss potential equal to the market value of the underlying security less the premium received.

A put buyer has a gain potential equal to the exercise price of the put minus the premium paid and a loss potential equal to the premium paid. A put writer has a gain potential equal to the premium received and a loss potential equal to the exercise price of the put minus the premium received.

Customers who engage in spreading options have a limited gain potential and a limited loss potential. However, straddles and combinations have unlimited gain potential to the buyers and unlimited loss potential to the writers.

Option position	*Gain/loss potential*
Spread	Limited gain–limited loss
Long straddle	Unlimited gain–limited loss
Short straddle	Limited gain–unlimited loss
Long combination	Unlimited gain–limited loss
Short combination	Limited gain–unlimited loss

SPECIFIC OPTION EXAMPLES

Covered Call

Assume a customer buys 100 shares of ABC at $80 per share and writes 1 ABC July 80 call at $4. This is a **covered call** position. The breakeven price of the stock is now $76 per share. However, if the market price of the stock increases substantially, the call option will be exercised against the customer and he will sell the ABC stock for $80 per share. Therefore, for a covered call position, the maximum profit to the writer is $400. The maximum loss potential is $7,600. If the stock goes to zero (bankrupt), the customer will lose $8,000 on the 100 shares of ABC minus the $400 premium received.

Long Stock–Long Put

Assume a customer buys 100 shares of XYZ at $80 per share and buys 1 XYZ July 80 put at $4. The customer is long the stock and long a put. The maximum loss to the customer on this position is $400. If the price of XYZ decreases, the customer can exercise the put and sell the 100 shares of ABC to the writer at $80 per share. If the stock increases in value, the put will eventually expire, but the customer will still be long the stock. Therefore, the customer's gain potential is unlimited. With a long stock–long put position, the customer's gain potential is unlimited, while his loss potential is limited to the amount of the premium paid. The breakeven price for the customer's position is $84 per share.

Short Stock–Short Put

Assume a customer sells short 100 shares of ABC at $60 per share and writes 1 ABC October 60 put at $6. The customer is short the stock and short a put. If ABC increases substantially in price, the put will expire worthless, but the customer will still be short the stock. Therefore, with a short stock–short put position, the customer's loss potential is unlimited. The customer's gain potential is limited to the premium received of $600.

Bullish Call Spread

Assume a customer buys 1 XYZ July 60 call at $7 and sells 1 XYZ July 70 call at $3. This is a bullish call spread, since the customer is buying the lower strike price and selling the higher strike price. It is also a debit spread with a net debit of 4 ($400). The customer must deposit $400 by the next business day following trade date. The customer's maximum loss potential is $400, the amount of the net debit. The customer's maximum gain potential is $600. If XYZ increases, the customer would realize a $1,000 profit on exercise minus the $400 net debit paid. Therefore, the maximum profit potential is $600 on this bullish call spread.

Straddle

Assume a customer buys 1 ABC July 70 call at $3 and buys 1 ABC July 70 put at $3. This is a long straddle. The customer's maximum loss potential is $600, which is the sum of both premiums paid. The maximum gain potential is unlimited as a result of the long call position. The breakeven price for the call is $76 and the breakeven price of the put is $64. A person who buys this long straddle expects fluctuation in ABC stock.

The writer of this straddle has a maximum gain potential of $600 and an unlimited loss potential. The writer of the straddle does not expect any significant fluctuation in the price of ABC stock prior to the expiration of the options.

In-The-Money and Out-Of-The-Money

Assume a customer buys 1 XYZ May 30 call at $4. The market price of XYZ's stock is $33 per share. This call option contract is in-the-money $3 per share, reflecting a total in-the-money amount of $300. The total premium of $400 represents $300 of intrinsic value and $100 of time value. The premium paid for an option is not figured into the in-the-money or out-of-the-money computation. If the market price of XYZ's stock was $29 a share, the option contract would be out-of-the-money $1 per share, or a total dollar amount of $100.

Assume a customer buys 1 ABC October 60 put at $7, when the market price of ABC stock is $55 per share. This put option is in-the-money $5 per share or a total dollar amount of $500. The total premium of

$700, represents $500 of intrinsic value and $200 of time value.

Assume a customer buys 1 XYZ May 50 call at 1¾, when ABC's market price is $49 per share. The total premium paid for the option is $175. If the market price of XYZ increases above the strike price of $50, the option premium will move dollar for dollar. This means that if the market value of XYZ increases to $54, the call option will be selling for at least $4 ($400).

If the market price of the underlying security is at the same price as the strike or exercise price of the option, the option is selling "at-the-money." Assume a customer buys 1 EFG May 60 call at $2, when the market price of EFG stock is $60 per share. The call option contract is trading at-the-money. The market price of the underlying security and the strike price are the same.

OPTION TERMS

Aggregate exercise price—The exercise price of an option contract multiplied by the number of units of the underlying security covered by the option contract.

Class of options—All option contracts of the same type (e.g., puts or calls) covering the same underlying security.

Closing purchase transaction—A transaction in which an investor who is obligated as a writer of an option intends to terminate his obligation—what an RR should mark on an order ticket being filled out for a customer's order to eliminate a short position.

Closing sale transaction—A transaction that reduces or eliminates a long position in an option contract.

Issuer—In listed option contracts, OCC is the issuer.

Opening purchase transaction—A transaction that creates or adds to a long position in an option contract.

Opening sale transaction—A transaction in which an investor intends to become the writer of an option.

Outstanding long position—Option contract issued by OCC that has not been the subject of a closing purchase transaction and has not reached its expiration date.

Premium—The aggregate price of an option agreed upon between the buyer and writer or their agents in a transaction on the floor of the exchange.

Series of options—Contracts of the same class having the same exercise price and expiration date and unit of trading.

DATES AND TIMES FOR PUT AND CALL OPTIONS

Cash dividend. To be entitled to receive an ordinary cash dividend declared by the issuer of the underlying stock, the holder of a call option must tender an effective exercise notice with OCC no later than noon, Pacific time, 3:00 P.M. Central time, 4:00 P.M. Eastern time on the business day prior to the ex-dividend date. The holder of a put who files an effective exercise notice with OCC prior to an ex-dividend date must deliver the dividend to the writer.

Cease trading. Options cease trading at noon Pacific time, 3:00 P.M. Central time, 4:00 P.M. Eastern time on the business day immediately prior to the day on which that option expires.

Earliest exercise. An option may be exercised on the same day it is purchased.

Exercise cut-off time. Customers wishing to exercise an option must instruct their brokers prior to 2:30 P.M. Pacific time, 4:30 P.M. Central time and 5:30 P.M. Eastern time on the business day immediately preceding the expiration date.

Exercise settlement date. Exercise must be settled on or before 10 A.M. Pacific time, noon Central time, 1 P.M. Eastern time on the settlement date which is three business days following the date the exercise notice is properly tendered to OCC.

Expiration months. Option contracts expire quarterly on either the January, April, July, and October cycle; February, May, August, and November cycle; or March, June, September, and December cycle.

Expiration time. Outstanding options may be exercised by the receipt of an exercise notice in proper form at OCC prior to 8:59 P.M. Pacific time, 10:59 P.M. Central time, 11:59 P.M. Eastern time on the Saturday following the third Friday of the expiration month.

Issue date. Except for options purchased or matched on the last trading day prior to the expiration time, options will be issued at 10:00 A.M. Pacific time, 12 noon Central time, 1:00 P.M. Eastern time on the business day after OCC receives from an exchange a report of a matched trade.

Settlement date for purchase and sale options. Clearing member for a buyer is required to pay that premium to OCC prior to 7:00 A.M. Pacific time, 9:00 A.M. Central time, 10:00 A.M. Eastern time on the first business day following the day on which OCC receives the report of the matched trade.

13 ECONOMIC, MONETARY, AND INDUSTRIAL FACTORS

ECONOMICS

Students studying the economy often ask for a definition of economics. **Economics** is the study of how society uses resources (land, labor, capital goods, and management ability) to produce goods and services and to distribute them to consumers. Under the heading of economics, we analyze topics such as business cycles, economic indicators, inflation and deflation, and the federal reserve system.

The stock market has tended to be a leading indicator throughout history. It normally rises prior to an increase in economic activity and falls prior to a decrease in economic activity. Also, certain economic conditions such as inflation, rising interest rates, and high unemployment tend to have a downward effect on stock prices. Any investment decision must consider all the relevant information that might affect a security's price. This chapter will identify much of the information that is generally accepted as having a material effect on the price of a security.

BUSINESS CYCLES

The economic environment in which firms operate is constantly undergoing periods of relative change with respect to output, production, employment, and rates of interest. These relative changes, over time, reflect a pattern called the **business cycle**. The business cycle is divided into segments or phases called **expansion, peak, recession,** and **trough**. The expansion or recovery phase is characterized by an upturn in business activity wherein output is increasing, investment is increasing, and unemployment is decreasing. The expansion phase ultimately reaches a peak, where it is usually choked off by the unavailability of additional funds for further investment due to the high levels of interest rates. The interest rate increases because the demand for these funds usually exceeds the supply. The peak of the expansion phase may also be characterized by overproduction and buildup of excessive amounts of inventory beyond the present levels of demand. The peak is followed by a downturn, which is called the recession phase. This is characterized by a reduction in output and investment, and an increase in unemployment as firms lay off workers in an attempt to reduce their inventories. The downturn in activity lasts until a bottom or trough is reached and the production activity levels off. How far the activity level of the economy drops determines whether the downturn is classified as a recession or a depression. A recession is a mild decline, while a depression is a steep, long-lasting decline. A recession is often defined as a mild six-month decline in stock prices, business activity, and unemployment. A normal business cycle has a peak–recession–trough–expansion or recovery sequence.

Changes in the business cycle affect firms differently. For example, firms that sell durable goods, such as large appliances and automobiles, tend to experience a downturn in their sales when the overall economy is on the downswing. This occurs because consumers have less income during a recessionary phase and they can postpone their purchases of these durable goods by making the current goods last a little longer. However, the housing industry historically expended its activity in times of recession and limited its activity in times of general economic expansion. This phenomenon occurs because the housing industry is very dependent on the cost of borrowing money. In times of expansion, there is a high demand for funds to continue to finance the needed assets to keep up with expanding sales. The demand for funds near the peak of the expansion phase usually exceeds the supply, which pushes up the interest rate and chokes off housing activity. In periods of recession, interest rates have historically tended to be low, which has induced the housing industry to increase its activity.

ECONOMIC INDICATORS

A leading indicator is one that reaches a high point or low point ahead of the peaks and troughs in the business cycle. Examples of this are new business investments in inventory, new orders for durable goods, new building permits, Standard & Poor's (S&P) stock index, M2 (see the Federal Reserve System section in this chapter), the average workweek of production workers, and "help wanted" advertising.

Coincident indicators reach their high or low points at about the same time the business cycle reaches its high and low points. Examples include manufacturing and trade sales, gross national product (GNP), personal income, and the Index of Industrial Production. (See Exhibit 13.1.)

Exhibit 13.1: US balance of payments deficit

The deficit increases (gets worse) when

- There is an increase in US investment abroad.
- American tourists increase spending abroad.
- US loans to underdeveloped countries increase.
- There is an increase in interest and dividend payments on US securities owned by foreigners.

The deficit decreases (improves) when

- Commodity exports increase.
- Foreign investments in the United States increase.
- Foreign tourists increase spending in the United States.
- There is an increase in the interest and dividends earned by Americans on foreign investments.

Lagging indicators reach their high and low points after the business cycle. Examples include the unemployment rate, the average prime rate, commercial and industrial loans outstanding, and the ratio of consumer installment credit to personal income.

The indicators can help by suggesting the direction in which economic activity is changing, but they will not be of much use in predicting the magnitude or the duration of the indicated change. Several indicators may also be combined to form what is termed a **diffusion index**. The diffusion index is used to overcome the problem that not all indicators of a particular type will move in the same direction with the same magnitude. The diffusion index, therefore, generalizes what is happening in a particular class of indicators.

INFLATION AND DEFLATION

Until recently, downturns in the business cycle, that is, recessions and depressions, were usually characterized by a decrease in the general price level, which is normally called a *deflationary period*. During such a deflationary period, money increases in value. Because the price level is falling, individuals with fixed incomes are better off than those who have incomes that tend to follow changes in the business cycle. During this period, debtors find it difficult to repay borrowed money because their earnings are decreasing. Creditors find it to their advantage because they will be repaid with higher-valued dollars. When the rate of inflation is decreasing rapidly, interest rates in the economy fall. Falling interest rates cause the market value of debt instruments to rise. Expansion phases have been accompanied by inflation, which is a general increase in the price level of goods and services. Individuals on fixed incomes are hurt as their dollars become worth less. Debtors find this situation favorable because they are repaying their debts with cheaper money, while creditors are hurt because they will be receiving those cheaper dollars.

CONSUMER PRICE INDEX

The Consumer Price Index measures the average change in prices for selected goods and services bought by wage earners in selected US cities. The Consumer Price Index is often referred to as the **Cost of Living Index**. The Index is published monthly by the United States Department of Labor's Bureau of Labor Statistics. Prices of approximately 400 goods and services are gathered in 56 cities. The prices are weighted and averaged. The Index is figured on a base period of 100. If the Index is presently at 140, then the cost of living has risen 40% since the base period.

FEDERAL RESERVE SYSTEM

The US government attempts to control and influence the economy by means of fiscal and monetary policy. Fiscal policy relates to the government's influence on the economy through federal taxing and spending programs and is controlled by Congress. Monetary policy refers to the government's attempt to control the money supply and is handled by the Federal Reserve.

Current definitions of the money supply include

M1—currency plus demand deposits, traveler's checks, and other checkable deposits (NOW accounts, credit union share drafts)

M2—M1 + Money market fund balances + Overnight repurchase agreements at commercial banks + Overnight eurodollars + Time deposits of less than $100,000 at commercial banks and thrift institutions

M3—M2 + Time deposits of $100,000 or more at commercial banks and thrift institutions + Term repurchase agreements + Institution-only money market fund balances

The Federal Reserve System attempts to influence the level of interest rates to help meet the goals of the government. These goals vary over time, but the dominant ones are to promote full employment as outlined by the Employment Act of 1946, to promote growth, and to maintain price stability. At any point in time, one of these goals may be dominant.

Often, the Fed's role is to lean against the wind in order to promote stability. In this capacity, the Fed chokes off inflation and overexpansion by contracting the money supply, thereby causing the interest rates to increase. This, in turn, restricts borrowing and slows down the expansion.

If the economy is in recession, then the Fed makes credit more available by increasing the money supply. This decreases interest rates and thereby makes it easier for firms to borrow and invest in projects which will put people back to work producing more goods and services. Increases in the money supply lead to lower interest rates and higher domestic inflation. If GNP and the Consumer Price Index started to decrease, the Federal Reserve would normally increase the money supply.

The tightening of money and credit by the Fed is usually followed by a decrease in securities prices because fewer funds will be available for investment, and economic activity will be slowing down. An expansion of credit by the Fed usually results in increases in securities prices because more funds will be available for investment and it is anticipated that economic activity will pick up.

As previously outlined, the Fed can effect changes in the economy by increasing or decreasing the supply of money. It has a number of tools it can use to do this. First, the Federal Reserve can regulate the flow of money and credit in the economy by

- Lowering the reserve requirement to stimulate the economy
- Raising the reserve requirement to slow down the economy

The second way the Federal Reserve can affect money and credit is by changing the discount rate. The discount rate is the rate charged to member banks that borrow from the Federal Reserve. The Federal Reserve would

- Lower the discount rate to stimulate the economy
- Raise the discount rate to slow down the economy

By decreasing the discount rate, the banks are encouraged to borrow the money and increase their reserve base and thereby create new money. By increasing the discount rate, the banks are discouraged from borrowing and the money supply will not expand. An increase in the Federal Reserve's discount rate would most likely lead to an increase in the

- Prime rate
- Broker's loan rate
- Discount on Treasury bills

An increase in the discount rate would normally make bank loans less available.

A third method of affecting money and credit in the economy is through open market operations. Open market operations refers to the Federal Reserve's purchase or sale of government securities, normally US Treasury bills, but could also be securities such as US Treasury notes or bonds and federal agency issues.

Open market operations are the Federal Reserve's most frequently used method to control money and credit in the economy. Using this method, the Federal Reserve buys government securities to stimulate the economy or sells government securities to slow down the economy.

Federal Reserve open market operations influence

- Interest rate
- M1 (Demand deposits + Currency in circulation)
- Currency exchange rates
- Velocity of money
- Bank reserves

The fourth method the Federal Reserve uses to control money and credit in the economy is by establishing and adjusting margin requirements. The Securities Exchange Act of 1934 gave the Federal Reserve the power to set margin requirements. The Federal Reserve created Regulation T, which establishes rules for the extension of credit to purchasers of securities by broker/dealers. Regulation T covers both cash and margin accounts and requires prompt payment by securities buyers.

The Federal Reserve also created Regulation U, which regulates credit extension by banks when the loan is for the purpose of buying securities on margin. In addition, the Federal Reserve established Regulation G, which covers lending by finance companies and individual lenders when the proceeds of the loan are used to buy securities on margin.

The fifth instrument to be discussed as a control device of the Fed is its ability to exert its influence on member banks and other financial institutions. The Fed can make its feeling known through the public media or through the examiners it sends to member banks. Its efforts to control the money supply by these means are limited by the extent to which it can obtain cooperation from these institutions. This is called **moral suasion**.

The Federal Reserve, through its monetary policy, regulates bank credit and the overall money supply. It is also considered to be the lender of last resort. The Federal Reserve, by its actions, directly controls bank reserve requirements and discount rate levels. However, the Federal Reserve does not control US government spending, taxation, or the budget deficit. Also, the Federal Reserve does not directly set the prime rate. The prime rate is the interest rate charged by commercial banks to their best credit-rated customers. Each commercial bank sets its own prime rate. If the Federal Reserve tightened money and credit in the economy, the first rate to change would probably be the federal funds rate, which is the interest charged by a bank that loans excess reserves to another bank, usually on an overnight basis. A high and rising federal funds rate generally means that banks are having a problem meeting reserve requirements. A low and falling federal funds rate indicates that banks are meeting reserve requirements without much difficulty.

As previously mentioned, an increase or decrease in the money supply is not the ultimate objective of the Fed. The objectives of the Fed are supposedly those that are of highest priority in the eyes of the public. The three goals mentioned as dominating the scene are full employment, maximum growth, and price stability. The government can also attempt to reach these objectives by use of fiscal policy.

To summarize, the following are functions of the Federal Reserve:

- Lending to commercial banks
- Auditing member banks
- Regulating bank credit
- Regulating the overall money supply
- Acting as agent for the US Treasury
- Being the lender of last resort

FISCAL POLICY

Fiscal policy refers to the spending and taxing policies of the federal government. The fiscal policy of the US government is set by Congress. US government fiscal policy is concerned with changes in government spending and income tax rates. If the US government wanted to stimulate the economy by using fiscal policy, it would increase government spending and lower income tax rates. If it wanted to slow down the economy by using fiscal policy, it would decrease government spending and raise income tax rates.

The theory of active manipulation of government taxation and spending to control the business cycle is the Keynesian Theory, named after English economist John Maynard Keynes.

To summarize, fiscal policy refers to the spending and taxing policies of the US government. Fiscal policy is controlled by Congress. To stimulate the economy, Congress would vote to increase government spending and lower income tax rates. To slow down the economy, Congress would decrease government spending and raise income tax rates.

ADDITIONAL ECONOMIC CONCEPTS

The following are key terms commonly used in economic analyses and discussions:

- The US gross national product (GNP) is the total value of all goods and services produced in the country on an annual basis. In order for an analyst to properly compare GNP figures from one year to the next, they must be in constant dollars (adjusted for inflation). The value of net exports (exports minus imports) is included in GNP.
- The **Consumer Price Index** measures the average change in prices for selected goods and services bought by wage earners in selected US cities.
- A **recession** is most often defined as a mild six-month decline in stock prices, business activity, and employment.

- The **prime rate** is the interest rate charged by commercial banks on loans to their best-rated customers, such as AAA-rated corporations.
- The term **disintermediation** refers to the flow of money out of depository institutions such as savings banks into competing money market investments to obtain a higher yield.
- The **business cycle** has periodic upswings and downswings in the economy. The business cycle normally has four stages: peak–recession–trough–recovery (expansion).
- The term **real interest rate** in the economy refers to the current interest rate minus the inflation rate. Therefore, if the current interest rate is 8% and the inflation rate is 5%, the real interest rate is 3%.

FUNDAMENTAL ANALYSIS

The term **fundamental analysis** connotes an examination of the basic factors affecting the issuer of securities and the markets in which the securities are traded. A concern for the fundamentals affecting an issuer is important for both business and nonbusiness security issuers. Fundamental analysis is concerned with such factors as earnings, company outlook, company annual report, and management. Fundamental analysis can be subdivided into quantitative and qualitative analysis. Quantitative analysis concerns the past operations of the issuer of a security, its prospectus within its industry, and the possible future of the industry.

Qualitative analysis concerns information about the goals and objectives of a company, its success in meeting its goals, whether management is aggressive or extremely conservative, the extent of the company's research effort, and new legislation and political action that will affect the company or its industry. Such information is found in financial magazines, newspapers, private surveys, and similar sources.

TECHNICAL ANALYSIS

Analysts are concerned with studying all the information available that might improve the selection of securities. One group of analysts believes that the values of securities are primarily the result of supply-and-demand forces in the market and not of earnings and/or dividends. The supply-and-demand characteristics are based on both rational and irrational occurrences made up of this information and opinions and feelings about what the future holds. This group of analysts believes that the result of these forces is a movement in price that will tend to be followed for a considerable period of time. The shifts in supply and demand are indicated by the changes in the trend.

The analysts who believe in these trends are called **technical analysts** or **chartists**. The technical analyst attempts to recognize a trend and determine when the direction is changing by plotting individual items of information or using moving averages calculated for selected periods of days or weeks. From the chartists' point of view, once a trend line has been established, the stock tends to move in the same line. Their main tools are charts that compare price and volume relationships. Among the most popular of the tools are the Dow Jones Average, the S&P 500, and the New York Stock Exchange Index (NYSE).

Fundamental analysis	*Technical analysis*
Factors considered include	Factors considered include
• Management of a company	• Support and resistance level
• Earnings of a company	• Trading volume
• A company's outlook	• Moving averages
• A company's annual report	• Odd-lot purchases and sales
• Price earnings ratio	• Timing of purchases and sales
	• Advances and declines
	• Charting

Fundamental analysis attempts to predict future stock prices by analyzing a company's earnings, management, product competition, and economic factors. Technical analysis tries to predict future stock price movements based on present and prior trends illustrated on a stock's chart. A stock's chart of its prices may reflect support and resistance levels or other chart patterns.

STOCK MARKET AVERAGES

The main stock market averages or indices followed by investors are

- Dow Jones Industrial Average (DJIA)
- S&P 500
- NYSE Composite Index

- Value Line Index
- Wilshire 5000 Equity Index

The Dow Jones Average is the most popular stock market average because it is among the oldest, best known, and most publicized. It is used by many investors as an indicator of market direction. The Dow Jones Average is really four averages.

1. An industrial average of 30 common stocks; in other words, the DJIA is the market price of 30 selected common stocks divided by a constant.
2. A transportation average of 20 common stocks.
3. A utility average of 15 common stocks
4. A composite average of these 65 common stocks from the industrial, transportation, and utilities industries.

The S&P 500 is an index that consists of 500 stocks made up of 400 industrials, 60 transportation and utility companies, and 40 financial issues. It is further broken down into industry segments. It has an advantage over the Dow Jones Average because it includes a greater number of securities and, therefore, has a broader base. This is a base-weighted aggregate index and shows the relative changes in the stock prices it includes compared to a base year.

The NYSE Composite Index includes all common stocks (not preferred) listed on the NYSE. Every half hour the change in the average price of NYSE shares, expressed in dollars; is printed. It reflects trends in stock prices on a daily, hourly, and even minute-by-minute basis.

Regardless of the average used or the method followed, it is quite evident that predicting a change in the market is far from being an exact science. Hindsight is wonderful but, historically, there is considerable evidence to indicate that the most successful investors have been the ones who have not attempted to determine that particular point in time when the market and/or a particular stock will be high or low, but follow a consistent pattern of investment.

TECHNICAL MARKET THEORIES

Much of technical analysis originates in what is termed the *Dow Theory* developed by Charles H. Dow at the turn of the century. The theory holds that the securities market has three movements, all occurring at the same time. Therefore, according to the theory, the stock market can be forecast accurately by analyzing these trends. The trends studied are called the primary, secondary and minor trends. The primary trend is long term in nature, while the secondary trend is short term. Secondary trends can last from a couple of weeks to several months. The daily fluctuations are termed *minor trends*, and they cannot be of much use due to their short duration. The Dow Theory makes use of the industrial and transportation averages to estimate market position. If both of these averages are going in the same direction, it is supposed to be an excellent indicator of a bull or bear market that will continue for some time.

Assume, for example, that the primary trend is upward. There will be many secondary downward reactions. Each of these downward reactions will be followed by a price recovery that will reach a point exceeding the previous high. If, after this, there is a downward reaction that goes below the low point of the last reaction, there is, then, an indication that the market has gone into a primary downward.

The Dow theorist does not consider the signal of a change to a primary downtrend to be valid unless the same pattern occurs in both the industrial and transportation averages. The entire pattern described would have to repeat itself in reverse to indicate that a primary downtrend has changed to a primary uptrend. One problem with the Dow Theory is that confirmation (movement of both the industrial and transportation averages in the same direction) does not occur until after an already substantial rise or fall.

Breadth-of-the-market analysis is used to study the turning points of the market. It is a good measure of the strength of a bull or bear market. The easiest method of measuring the breadth of the market is to cumulate daily the net number of advancing or declining issues on the NYSE. Each day, the declines would be subtracted from the advances, and the result would be a net positive or negative figure.

This cumulation is continued forever. Naturally, if different analysts begin their cumulations on different dates, their figures will be different; but breadth analysis is primarily interested in *change* rather than in the level. The change during any time period would be the same, regardless of the date cumulation begins. This measurement of breadth is then compared with a market average such as the DJIA. If the breadth index declines to successive new lows, while the DJIA continues to rise, it indicates that a major turndown in stock prices is likely. During a bear market, if the breadth index declines severely for several weeks while the DJIA is falling and trading volume is higher than in previous weeks, it indicates that the bottom of the market has probably been reached.

The total volume of traded stocks is another tool of the technician. This figure is studied because it is believed that volume changes are usually necessary for a price change to occur since volume is an indicator of the supply and demand for stock. The basic beliefs are that, in a bull market, the volume will increase and decline in unison with the price. Therefore, trading volume is a bullish indicator when it is heavy on advances and light on declines. In a bear market, the opposite holds; that is, volume increases with price declines and volume decreases with price increases. Trading volume is a bearish indicator when it is heavy on declines and light on advances. Also, volume usually decreases ahead of major declines and volume increases during market troughs. Sometimes, a sharp drop in stock prices is accompanied by increasing volume after a lengthy period of market decline and is described as a *selling climax*.

The Odd-Lot Theory is used by technical analysts as an indicator of market direction. Technical analysts study the behavior of the small investor who buys in lots of less than 100 shares. The theory is that when the odd lotter increases his buying relative to his selling, the sophisticated investor should sell, and vice versa. The belief is that small investors sell most heavily at the bottom (when they should be buying) and buy most heavily at the top (when they should be selling).

The Short Interest Theory is another technical tool. This theory is based on the short selling that goes on in the market. Short selling is the sale of a stock by an individual who does not actually own it, but who borrowed it from someone else. The short seller makes this move because he believes the price of the stock will fall and he can buy it back later at a lower price than he sold it. Then, he returns this newly purchased stock to the individual from whom he borrowed it. The theory recognizes that these short sales must eventually be covered and that all this buying activity will stimulate demand for the stock.

The short interest ratio is followed more closely than the number of shares sold short. The ratio is found by dividing the latest short interest position by some current column figure, such as the daily average of the preceding month. A low ratio is considered to be bearish and a high ratio bullish. The greater the short interest (short position), the greater the cushion or brake affecting a decline in prices. Therefore, large short interest makes for a technically strong market and small short interest makes for a technically weak market.

CONFIDENCE INDICATORS

Baryon's Confidence Index

Baryon's Confidence Index is calculated by dividing the high-quality bond yields by the higher yields on low-quality bonds. An increase in this index means that the spread between the two types of bonds is decreasing, and this is indicative of expansionary times and an increasing stock market. A decreasing index would indicate a recession in both the economy and the stock market.

S&P Confidence Index

The S&P Confidence Index compares low-priced stocks to high-quality stocks. The low-priced stocks are assumed to be speculative in nature. This index is similar to the Baryon's index described previously. It is assumed that, when the economy is expanding and the market is increasing, individuals will be more apt to assume more risk by buying speculative stocks. During recessions, the investor is more apt to want the security that comes with a high-quality stock. The index number usually decreases before a peak in the market because investor confidence is beginning to decrease and security is sought in quality stocks. If the index begins to increase, it signals the beginning of an increase in the market from a bottom position.

CHARTING

Charts are frequently used by technical analysts to forecast price movements of securities. They are usually used for short-term technical analysis. From the chartist's point of view, once a trend line has been established, the stock tends to move along the same trend line. Brief movements away from this trend line mean an opportunity for profit.

The inverted head and shoulders formation is the exact opposite of the head and shoulders top formation. When the right side of the right shoulder of the inverted head and shoulders formation rises to a point where it penetrates the neckline, the breakout would supposedly indicate the reversal of a downward trend. In other words, it is a bullish sign and indicates an upward movement in prices. It is indicating a reversal of a downward trend. (See Exhibit 13.2.)

Exhibit 13.2: Chart patterns

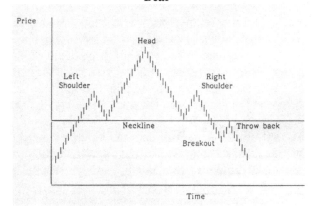

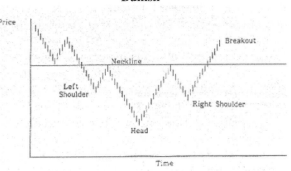

Support and resistance levels are also used by technical analysts. As far as the technical analyst is concerned, **support** and **resistance** levels are important indicators of possible price movement. Exhibit 13.3 illustrates support and resistance. The bottom horizontal line at the left of the chart is a support level. Support is a barrier to price decline. Once this level has been reached, the price is attractive to buyers, and demand will be likely to prevent the price from declining below this level. The resistance level, however, acts as a barrier to price increase. This is the upper horizontal line at the left of the chart. Once price reaches this point, selling tends to occur, which will prevent price from increasing any further.

Exhibit 13.3: Support and resistance levels

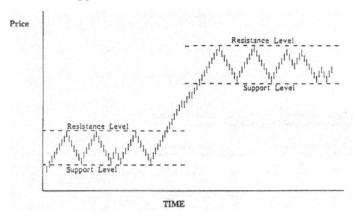

A barrier is, of course, not impenetrable. Quite often, there is a considerable period of time when the support and resistance levels effectively act as barriers. This is considered to be a **congestion area**—a period of time when prices fluctuate sideways only between these two levels. Eventually, however, a point may be reached where price is able to break through one of these barriers and new support and resistance levels are formed. In Exhibit 13.3, price levels finally materialized at higher prices than before.

The technical approach is simply one of the methods used to anticipate future price movements. The purpose is prompt recognition of trends of formations, which will then be interpreted by the chartist. The danger, of course, lies in the interpretation of price movements. Charts do, at times, present signals that can be disastrous to the investor—especially the investor who is not sophisticated in this area.

INDUSTRY ANALYSIS

The preceding sections dealt with the analysis of the economy as a whole to help determine by charting what the course of an individual stock may be over time. Attention will now be focused on analyzing the particular industry or stock undergoing analysis.

Industries, like products and individual firms, have life cycles that are composed of a pioneering stage, expansion stage, stabilization stage, and a decline and death stage.

The pioneering stage is characterized by a rapid increase in the demand for the product of the industry because of its unique new qualities and features. The demand will not only be increasing during this stage, but it will be increasing at an increasing rate. The opportunity for profits attracts more capital into the industry. Weaker firms do not survive this stage as the stronger ones capture a large segment of the market.

The expansion phase is made up of firms that survive the pioneering stage. These remaining firms tend to become stronger with respect to financial resources and market share. Increased competition usually results in improved products and lower product prices. The industry is still growing, but the rate of growth is decreasing. Most of the companies from the expansion stage enter the stabilization stage, which is characterized by a lack of growth or a very slow rate of growth. This stagnated stage may continue indefinitely or an expansion may result due to new technology, or the industry may enter a stage of decline, at which time many of the firms must leave the scene due to declining sales. In an extreme situation, the industry may cease to exist.

Industries can be classified according to how they react to the general trends in the economy. The major classifications in this area are defensive, growth, and cyclical industries.

Defensive industries are hurt the least by recessions and depressions. An example is the food-processing industry. The stock of firms in this category may be held for income purposes, and the total earnings may even increase in times of recession.

Growth industries include firms that are believed to have very large increases in earnings compared to the average, without regard to the economic cycle. The large increase in earnings is often the result of some dramatic change in technology.

Cyclical industries tend to follow the general business cycle. That is, they do well in the expansion phase and poorly in the recession phase. This industry usually has a product whose purchase can be put off until economic conditions recover. An example is the automobile industry, wherein an individual may make his old car last a little longer until the economy recovers from a recession.

EFFICIENT MARKET THEORY

There have been a number of new approaches to security and portfolio valuation in recent years. One of these is sometimes referred to as the **Efficient Market Theory**. According to this theory, the price of an individual security and of the entire market is, at any one moment, the composite view of investors. This view is balanced to reflect differences in opinions, preferences, and views. Each security and the market as a whole is considered to be priced fairly in relation to the ownership risk associated. Security prices are considered to be basically in equilibrium. Under this equilibrium assumption, individual rational investors should structure their portfolios by adjusting the risk element of their investments. Increasing risk should produce higher returns, and vice versa.

Since it is impossible to calculate the universe of risky investments at any one moment, it is more practical to use some average such as the S&P 500 stock price index. In this theory, the market (the index) is considered to be the ultimate in efficient diversification, which could not then be reduced by any additional diversification. Market risk reflects the effect of overall market movements on price changes in each security and every portfolio.

RANDOM WALK THEORY

The **Random Walk Theory** holds that successive changes in stock prices are independent, are evenly distributed, and tend to be repetitive over a period of time. It assumes that the securities market is an efficient marketplace. It also assumes that successive price changes are independent and that these changes follow some probability distribution.

According to this theory, the price of any stock will fully reflect the information that the public receives and the price of a stock will change immediately upon receipt of the new information. The theory does not relate to the level of price or return but to the changes that occur between successive prices.

Those who adhere to this theory believe that it is impossible to forecast a price change based on historical data. This means that this theory is in direct conflict with technical analysis based on the use of past performance to predict future performance. It is also obvious that, according to this theory, a fundamental analyst could be successful in predicting the movements in the price of a stock only if he possesses better information than the rest of the public (inside information or better insight with respect to the future course of the firm).

Numerous studies have been unable to disprove the basic implication of the Random Walk Theory, which is that no mechanical trading rule will produce profits significantly greater than random selection. Statistical evidence also indicates that professional investors have not done better than randomly selected portfolios, adjusted for risk, over a long period.

However, the theory does not deny the possibility of predicting future stock price changes. It accepts the idea that if investment research techniques can accurately forecast future company earnings, these techniques should result in more accurate price forecasts.

It is also reasonable to believe that different sets of critical factors affect every industry and company. These factors must be identified and consistently followed in any sound, analytical approach. Any change in these factors affects the outlook for profit and investment expectations.

BETA ANALYSIS

Risk on a security position may be divided into two components—market risk and specific stock risk. The **market risk** is the risk related to the movement of the entire stock market and is nondiversified to a great extent. The **specific stock risk** is the risk associated with a particular security and its financial condition.

The beta coefficient measures the market risk or systematic risk. If a security has a beta of 1.2, it is expected to fluctuate greater than the general market. If the general market increased 10%, this security would be expected to increase 12%. Therefore, a portfolio manager would want a portfolio of securities with a beta in excess of 1.0, if she expected a rising market. A portfolio manager expecting a falling market would want her portfolio to consist of securities with a low beta (less than 1.0). Securities with a beta of less than 1.0 would be expected to decline less than the general market.

The alpha coefficient measures the expected return on a security regardless of stock market performance. If a security has an alpha of 1.3, it is expected to increase in price by 30% based on factors such as earnings per share. To summarize, beta measures volatility; alpha measures the return expected regardless of the movement of the general market.

FINANCIAL INFORMATION

It is obvious that it is difficult, if not impossible, to predict the future movement of securities prices on a consistent basis. It has also been found that the investor who consistently invests without attempting to forecast future movements in price will have a better chance of success than one who reacts to every little change in the market. It follows, therefore, that it is better to set realistic objectives with respect to investing in securities. For example, knowing that consistent income production is desired, it is possible to select an investment plan that will have a high probability of success. With the objective established, whatever it may be, the first step would be to determine the outlook for the total economic environment to see if it appears consistent with the set objectives. For example, relying on a consistent income from moderately speculative stocks with a predicted recession about to occur may not be advisable when high-quality bonds are available. The amount of risk that the investor is willing to assume becomes an important consideration in choosing securities that may be able to fulfill the objectives. The more conservative investor looking for a consistent income may find more peace of mind in bonds than in stocks. If the investor has the financial ability to diversify his holdings, then the entire portfolio must reflect the investor's attitude toward risk. Consideration must be given to the fact that certain industries might be more capable of fulfilling the needs of the investor; for example, in a recession, a conservative investor may be more inclined to invest in securities in the food industry rather than in the durable goods industry, which will likely follow the economic downturn. After the portfolio is selected, it must be constantly reviewed because changes will occur in the variables originally used in the initial selection.

Perhaps the best available source of new, fresh, and current financial data comes from the various financial newspapers and magazines, both daily and weekly. Chief among them are

- *The Wall Street Journal*
- *The Commercial and Financial Chronicle*
- *Barron's* (weekly)
- *Business Week* (weekly)
- *The New York Times* (financial section)
- *Forbes* magazine (biweekly)
- *The Wall Street Transcript* (weekly)
- *The Money Manager* (weekly)
- *The Financial World* (weekly)
- *The Magazine of Wall Street* (biweekly)
- *The Financial Analyst's Journal* (bimonthly)
- *The Institutional Investor* (monthly)

FINANCIAL EXHIBITS

Certain financial exhibits appear in *The Wall Street Journal* and other financial publications on a daily basis. An informed investor should be able to read and interpret these exhibits. The following exhibits and examples should be helpful by providing experience in interpreting financial data.

Exhibit 13.4: New York Stock Exchange composite transactions

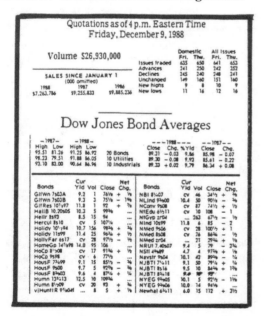

Exhibit 13.4 shows the closing price of NYSE-listed companies. The last price is the closing price of the securities on Monday, December 3, 2001, at 4:00 P.M. Eastern time. Look at Abbott Labs, the sixth security listed in the exhibit. Abbott Labs closed at $55.46, which is up $0.46 from the previous close. Abbott Labs was up 14.5% year to date, its high for the year was $56.25, and its low was $42. The symbol for Abbott Labs is ABT, and its annual dividend is $0.84. Abbott Labs has a yield of 1.5% and a price earnings ratio of 51. The trading volume in Abbott Labs was 4,997,800 shares.

Exhibit 13.5: New York Stock Exchange bonds

Exhibit 13.5 reflects closing prices for NYSE bonds as of the close of business on Friday, December 9, 1988. The letters "zr" after the names of a bond indicates that it is a zero coupon bond. The letters "cv" indicates a convertible bond. The "%j" indicates that the company is in bankruptcy or receivership or being reorganized under the Bankruptcy Act. For NL Industries, the bond has a coupon rate of 9⅜% and matures in the year 2000. The bond pays annual interest of

$$\$1,000 \times .09375 = \$93.75$$

The current yield on the bond is 10.4%.

$$\frac{\$93.75 \text{ annual interest}}{\$901.25 \text{ market price}} = 10.4\%$$

The trading volume in NL Industries was 50 bonds, and the closing price was 90⅛ ($901.25). The bond closed down ⅜ of a point from the previous day. This represents a decrease of $3.75 (⅜ of $10).

Exhibit 13.6: Listed options quotations

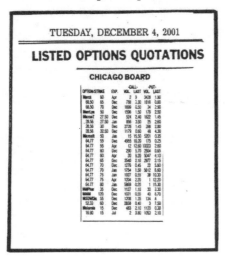

Exhibit 13.6 shows the name of the option and its closing price under it. For example, Merck closed at $68.50, and Microsoft closed at $64.77. The option strike price and expiration month are the next two columns. The volume and last sale for the calls and puts are the final columns. Look at Merck with a strike price of $60 with an April expiration. The last sale of the call was 9 and the last sale of the put was $1.90. The call option contract is in the money $8.50. The call option has an intrinsic value of $8.50 and a time value of $0.50 for a total premium of $9 per share. The put option has no intrinsic value, but has a time value of $1.90 per share.

Exhibit 13.7: Treasury bonds, notes, and bills

Exhibit 13.7 shows prices and yields for US Treasury bills, notes, and bonds. The US Treasury Bill maturing on March 9, 1989, has an annual return of 8.12%. The bid quotation of 7.90% is the annualized percentage return the buyer would like to obtain. The asked quotation of 7.86% is the annualized percentage return the seller wants the buyer to accept.

US Treasury notes and bonds are quoted in thirty seconds of a point. Therefore, an investor who purchased the 11⅞% October 1989 Treasury note at the asked price of 102-12 would pay a dollar price of $1,023.75.

$$102\text{-}12 = \begin{array}{c} 102\ 12/32 \\ 12/32 \text{ of } \$10 \end{array} = 102 = \begin{array}{r} \$1,020.00 \\ \underline{3.75} \\ \$1,023.75 \end{array}$$

The 12¾% November 1989 Treasury note decreased 0.05 from the previous day. This represents a decrease of $1.56 from the previous day's close.

$$5/32 \text{ of } \$10 = \$1.56$$

14 RISKS AND POLICIES

INTRODUCTION

The risks facing the investor are numerous: financial, market, inflation, economic, and social, to name a few. Banks fail, the dollar fluctuates, large cities face insolvency.

The weighing of these risks is a critical factor in the investment advice rendered to clients. Their needs must be balanced in the light of their objectives, financial condition, and the risk of loss of capital.

The registered representative (RR) does not have a crystal ball on his desk. The advice he offers is pragmatic, based on his knowledge of the securities, companies, and the risks associated with both. The purposes of this chapter are to acquaint the reader with the range of risks facing the investor and to apply the knowledge of the risk factor to investment counseling.

Risk conditions will lead to investment strategies. The successful RR must be able to recommend a logical strategy in the face of risk, consistent needs, and the financial condition of the client.

The main types of investment risk associated with investing in securities are

- Credit risk
- Purchasing power risk or inflationary risk
- Interest rate risk
- Market or systematic risk

CREDIT RISK

Credit risk is the risk that an issuer of securities will not make interest or principal payments when they are due. The credit risk is also referred to as *default risk*, *business risk*, or *financial risk*. An investor can minimize credit risk by investing in high-quality securities such as

- US Treasury bills, notes, or bonds
- Most federal agency issues
- AAA- or AA-rated municipal bonds
- AAA- or AA-rated corporate bonds

An investor would be taking considerable risk investing in

- New issues of unseasoned companies
- Highly speculative growth stocks
- Low-rated corporate or municipal bonds

PURCHASING POWER RISK

Purchasing power risk is the risk that money will lose its purchasing power over time. Fixed-income securities are most susceptible to purchasing power risk, which is also referred to as *inflationary risk*. (See Exhibit 14.1.)

Exhibit 14.1: Purchasing power risk (inflationary risk)

Investments most susceptible include

- Savings accounts
- Life insurance
- Series EE and MI bonds
- Face-amount certificates
- Fixed annuities
- US government, municipal, and corporate bonds
- Certificates of deposit

Investments less susceptible include

- Common stocks (especially growth stocks)

- Variable annuities
- Growth mutual funds

Assume an investor purchases a AAA corporate bond in ABC Corporation. The ABC corporate bond has a $1,000 par value with a 7% interest rate and has a maturity of ten years. The investor purchases the bond at par value. Each year the bond will pay $70 in annual interest. At maturity, the investor will receive his $1,000, which is a return on his principal.

Since the bond is rated AAA, the investor is not taking a credit risk. However, the investor is taking a significant purchasing power risk. When the investor receives his $1,000 in ten years, it will certainly buy less in goods and services. The fixed interest payments are also susceptible to inflation. Assume the inflation rate in the economy is 4%. The real interest rate is the current interest rate minus the inflation rate. The bond has a current interest rate of 7% minus the inflation rate of 4%. This gives the investor a real interest rate or real return of 3% on the bond.

Any investments with a fixed rate of return are vulnerable to inflation. Savings accounts; certificates of deposit; and US government, municipal, and corporate bonds are examples of investments that are affected by the purchasing power risk.

Common stock is an investment that is least susceptible to the purchasing power risk. Assume an investor purchases 100 shares of XYZ Corporation at $65 per share. XYZ is a high-quality security. The XYZ common stock pays an annual dividend of $3.20. The current yield of XYZ's common stock is

$$\frac{\$3.20 \text{ annual dividend}}{\$65 \text{ market price}} = 4.9\%$$

Assume at the end of ten years XYZ common stock has a market price of $150 and pays an annual dividend of $7.50. The investor has received excellent returns from his investment in XYZ. The dividend has grown from $3.20 per share to $7.50 per share over ten years. The market value of 100 shares has grown from $6,500 to $15,000 over the ten years. This investor has more than offset the effects of inflation with his investment. However, common stocks are subject to investment risks such as the market risk, capital risk, selection risk, or timing risk.

INTEREST RATE RISK

The **interest rate risk** is the risk that rising interest rates will cause the market price of debt obligations to decline. The interest rate risk affects debt obligations such as US government bonds, corporate bonds, and municipal bonds. The interest rate risk has a greater impact on long-term bonds than on short-term bonds. If interest rates in the economy rise, long-term bonds fall more in price than short-term. If interest rates in the economy fall, long-term bonds rise more in price than short-term bonds.

In order to minimize the interest rate risk, an investor can purchase short-term securities. Assume an investor buys $10,000 of US Treasury bills maturing in three months. The interest rate risk associated with this investment is very small. The investor purchases the Treasury bills at a discount from par value and receives full face value at maturity.

The interest rate risk is minimized if an investor purchases a debt obligation with a variable interest rate. For example, an investor might purchase a municipal bond with a variable interest rate. The interest rate on the municipal bond might be a percentage of the rate paid on selected issues of US Treasury securities on specified dates. The variable interest rate will reduce the interest rate risk on a particular debt issue. When interest rates in the economy increase, the interest rate on the particular bond will also increase. Since the interest rate on the bond increased, the market price of the bond will not decrease in the same manner as a fixed interest rate bond.

MARKET OR SYSTEMATIC RISK

The **market** or **systematic risk** an investor faces is the risk of a decline in the price of securities because of a general falling market. Investors have certain choices to make when building an investment portfolio. How many different securities should be purchased and how many shares of each security? Diversification can lessen risk in a portfolio. However, diversification cannot completely reduce risk. Certain investment periods have been very difficult for investors. During these periods, the general stock market has declined and investors have experienced losses. Market or systematic risk refers to the risk of loss because of a general declining stock market. Market or systematic risk was evident during the following periods:

- October 1929 through 1932 (stock market crash)
- July 1956 through December 1957

- December 1961 through June 1962
- December 1968 through May 1970
- January 1973 through December 1974
- October 19, 1987 (The modern stock market crash)

Carefully selected common stocks can be an excellent investment vehicle over the long term. A solid common stock investment may provide rising earnings, rising dividends, and a rising market price. However, market or systematic risk is always present in the stock market.

OTHER TYPES OF INVESTMENT RISK

Investors face other risks investing in securities in addition to the credit risk, purchasing risk, interest rate risk, and market or systematic risk. Other investment risks purchasers of securities face include

- Political risk
- Social risk
- Capital risk
- Selection risk
- Timing risk
- Liquidity risk
- Call risk
- Exchange risk

Political risks are risks that an investor must assume relating to possible adverse government action. For example, the Tax Reform Act of 1986 impacted unfavorably on tax shelter investments. A company's assets could be nationalized by an unfriendly government. Taxes could be raised on capital gains realized from securities transactions. Any unfavorable government action that impacts on individual securities or the stock market in general is classified under political risk.

Social risks refer to the uncertainties caused by changing social factors. Worries about pollution can favor certain industries and adversely affect others. A Food and Drug Administration (FDA) report on cranberries as a possible cancer-causing food almost wrecked that industry. Noxious automobile emissions and the public outcry for automobile safety meant new products such as catalytic converters, seat belts, and air bags. Such events change consumer demand, which creates new industries and products and eliminates others.

Capital risk is the risk that invested capital will decline in value. It is the risk that an investor may not fully recover the amount of his investment. Capital risk is significant on the purchase of a speculative new issue. Capital risk is almost nonexistent on the purchase of Treasury bills, notes, or bonds that are held to maturity.

Selection risk is the risk that an investor may choose a security that performs poorly even though it is a suitable security. A customer may purchase 100 shares of ABC Corporation at $80 per share. ABC is a high-quality security. ABC earnings for the quarter are down slightly. ABC stock decreases significantly in price.

Very closely related to the selection risk is the **timing risk**. The time risk is the risk of purchasing or selling securities at a disadvantageous time and sustaining losses or lowering gains. Short-term traders are very concerned with timing. ABC may be an excellent company with well-defined long-term potential. However, a trader may be purchasing ABC with the intent of making a five-point gain over a short period of time. The long-term potential of the company is of no great concern to the short-term trader. He is concerned with selling at a profit over the short term and timing is of great importance.

The **liquidity risk** is the risk of adverse changes in the quality of securities originally purchased that permit their convertibility into cash without significant loss of value. For example, a limited partnership investment is very difficult to sell in the secondary market. It is not normally a liquid investment, and investors bear a liquidity risk related to the security.

The **call risk** is the risk associated with the redemption of debt securities prior to maturity. The call risk is not associated with common stock because common stock is not normally callable. An investor who is concerned with the call risk should not purchase a premium bond with a high interest rate, callable at par. This type of bond is likely to be called by the issuer if interest rates fall. Short-term securities such as US Treasury bills, commercial paper, bankers' acceptances, and negotiable certificates of deposit are not callable. US Treasury notes are also not callable prior to maturity, but US Treasury bonds are callable.

The **exchange risk** is the risk of loss on foreign currency exchanges. Foreign securities are susceptible to the exchange risk. Both foreign and domestic debt securities are subject to risks such as purchasing power, interest rate, and political. Assume an investor purchases a Japanese security and sells it at a profit using Japanese yen. She converts the yen to dollars at a time when yen is declining in relation to the dollar. The investor would suffer a loss relating to the exchange risk.

INVESTMENT PORTFOLIO

Basically, there are two broad types of investors: conservative and aggressive. **Aggressive investors** have as their goal the realization of long-term capital gains that are significantly higher than the growth rate of the economy. Aggressive investors follow a portfolio policy that concentrates on the issues of a small number of firms whose prospects seem most favorable. In any given economic period, some industries are characterized as growth, while others decline. The aggressive portfolio policy concentrates investments in a relatively small number of issues that exhibit considerable fluctuation in market price and yield.

Possible investments include common stocks, low-grade bonds, special-situation securities, performance mutual funds, warrants, rights, and low-grade convertibles.

The **conservative investor** will employ a defensive policy to minimize the credit risk. His goals are

- To have the total portfolio grow at a rate similar to the economy and stock market averages
- To attempt to obtain reasonable income with protection of principal

Defensive strategy implies greater diversification when more speculative securities are held in the portfolio. Defensive issues include high-grade securities such as bonds, convertibles, and preferred stock, where the principal and interest (or dividends) are relatively secure. Complete diversification would require dispersing selections by industry, by geographic location, by type of security, and by maturity. To diversify, two methods are generally employed.

1. **Random**—diversifying by selecting issues completely by chance. The firms could be in one or several industries.
2. **Selective**—diversifying by investing in unrelated industries and/or investing in firms in many industries.

Two additional factors must be considered by both aggressive and conservative investors in protecting against credit or financial risk. The first is the ability to hold on to securities during periods of volatile market and price fluctuations. This is especially relevant when the number of issues held is small. The second factor is the quality of investment management available to the client investor. Again, this is of prime importance when the number of securities in the portfolio is small and when the portfolio consists of more speculative issues.

As discussed before, the interest rate risk is that if interest rates rise, the price of debt securities will fall. An associated risk, with callable securities, is that the investor runs the risk of having the debt issue called during periods of low interest rates.

The maturity dates of the securities held in the portfolio represent the hedges against the interest rate risk. The length of the dates to maturity will have different effects, however, on the stability of income and principal of the debt securities. Generally, bonds with long maturity dates exhibit stability of income but fluctuations of principal. Continuous investment in securities with shorter periods to maturity generally result in a stable principal and a fluctuating income.

A defensive strategy against these fluctuations is a diversified portfolio that includes bonds with varying maturity dates. This will average the yields in the portfolio. The client must again exhibit patience and be able to hold on during periods of fluctuations in principal and income. His major consideration will be the choice of the appropriate maturity schedule.

The loss of the dollar's purchasing power is one of the greatest risks facing the investor and must be reconciled with the investment objective, whether it is aggressive or defensive. The aggressive strategy against the purchasing power risk avoids long-term debt issues.

Defensive portfolio structure against the purchasing power risk indicates a balanced portfolio of high-grade bonds and preferred and common stock. The hedge against inflation may be provided by the equity issues, while the preferred stock and the bonds offer downside protection. There is no guarantee that such a portfolio will protect the investor from the purchasing power risk but, historically, such diversification should provide him with greater probability to do so.

Marketability risks can generally be avoided by careful selection of securities. This risk must be viewed in relation to the liquidity needs of the client. Real estate, as an example, may be illiquid. Portfolios with a high proportion of real estate should be balanced with other investment vehicles with a greater degree of liquidity.

INVESTMENT STRATEGIES

The aggressive investor seeks to obtain the maximum return on his investment. Purchases and sales will be made primarily on the basis of changes in the market prices of the issues. Specifically, the investor may employ one or more of the following as part of an aggressive policy:

- He may time purchases and sales to coincide with anticipated market movements of a major scale. This would involve attempting to forecast bull and bear markets by forecasting changes in the general trend of business.
- He may engage in purchases and sales of special-situation stocks.
- He may move from investments in one industry to another.
- He may apply the **Dow Theory,** which attempts to identify primary trends once they are established.
- He may use technical analysis and criteria, such as market volume, year-end tax selling, short selling activity, and market breadth.
- The investor may vary the structure of the portfolio in line with expected market movements. This may include switching from stocks to bonds, from aggressive stocks to more conservative issues.
- He may purchase securities on margin.

The defensive investor will buy and sell securities without regard to changes in the market price. He may employ techniques that are based on timing, maturity cycles, quality maintenance, and yield differentials. These timing techniques include

- **Random walk.** The theory behind random selection is that the present stock movements are totally independent of all past moves and events. This implies that examining past price and volume in an attempt to predict the future is a waste of time. Supporters of this theory hold that at any time the price of a security is a correct valuation due to the extremely efficient securities markets in the United States. According to this theory, since stock prices are **random**, attempts at prediction based on history are valueless.
- **Dollar-cost averaging.** This method involves investing a fixed sum of money ($100) in the same security (ABC Corporation) at regular intervals (monthly) over a relatively long period of time, without regard to the price level of that security. If the prices of the security rise and fall, the average cost of the security must be mathematically lower than the average price. Assume the following stock prices and a monthly investment of $100:

Month	*Investment*	*Price of stock*	*# Shares purchased*
1	$100	$ 8	12.500
2	100	10	10.000
3	100	8	12.500
4	100	5	20.000
5	100	10	10.000
6	100	6	16.666
Total	$600		81.666

The average cost of the shares equals $600 divided by the number purchased (81.666) or $7.35. The average price of $47 (sum of all prices) divided by 6 (number of integers) of $7.83, which is higher than the average cost. Some caveats must be mentioned in conjunction with dollar-cost averaging. First, it must be called just that, *not* "dollar-averaging" or "averaging the dollar." Second, the method simply cannot work if the price of the security always falls. Third, the investor is investing in securities whose prices fluctuate and the method demands consistent investment. The investor can lose money if he sells when the price is low. Dollar-cost averaging does not guarantee a profit.

- **Constant ratio plans.** This is one of the simplest portfolio formula plans. The investment portfolio is divided into two parts: an aggressive portion containing common stocks and a defensive or conservative portion containing high-grade securities. The aim is to keep both sides in balance.
- **Variable ratio plan.** Using this method, the rise and fall of the market will change the percentage of stocks and bonds in the portfolio. If the market rises, a lower proportion of stocks relative to bonds will be maintained. If the market falls, the stocks held will represent a larger proportion.

This is similar to the constant ratio plan except that the aggressive–defensive ratio is adjusted as conditions change in the securities market. When common stock prices rise, one would reduce the percentage invested in common stocks and increase the percentage in bonds and cash. When common stock prices fall, one would increase the percentage invested in common stocks and decrease the percentage in bonds and cash.

- **Constant dollar plan.** This method keeps constant the number of dollars in the portfolio without regard to the mix between stocks and bonds. If the value declines, additional investment is made to reach the desired dollar level. If the value of the portfolio rises, securities are sold.

  The constant dollar plan requires dividing the portfolio into two parts—equity investments and fixed income investments, such as bonds. The equity portion is always kept at a fixed dollar amount by either selling stocks when prices are high or buying when prices are low. The initial task is to make an arbitrary decision determining the dollar amount assigned to the equity and fixed income portions of the portfolio.
- Other defensive policies

  - **Recycling funds with bond maturities.** Under this plan, the investor makes the initial capital investment and uses the proceeds from maturing bonds to purchase new debt obligations.
  - **Quality maintenance.** The purpose of this method is to upgrade the investor's portfolio. The investor would purchase or sell securities in order to maintain the desired quality of issues in the portfolio.
  - **Market yield differentials.** There are various techniques designed to take advantage of yield differentials in the market. One that was already discussed was arbitrage. Others include hedging and techniques similar to those used in commodities trading.

It is fortunate that if an existing portfolio is not satisfactory, it may be changed. Careful portfolio planning is a necessity. As Jeremy Taylor once said, "If thou hast a bundle of thorns in thy lot, there is no need to sit down on it."

SUMMARY —INVESTMENT RISKS

To summarize, the main types of investment risk assumed by customers investing in securities are

- **Inflationary risk**—the risk that money will lose its purchasing power over time (purchasing power risk). Fixed income obligations (bonds) are most susceptible and common stocks are least susceptible.
- **Capital risk**—the risk that a customer may lose principal on an investment.
- **Selection risk**—the risk that the customer may choose a security that performs poorly even though it is a suitable security.
- **Timing risk**—the risk of purchasing or selling securities at a disadvantageous time and sustaining losses or lowering gains.
- **Interest rate risk**—the risk that interest rates may rise and the price of fixed income securities and, often, equity securities will fall. Long-term bonds are most susceptible to this risk.
- **Market or systematic risk**—the risk of a decline in the price of securities because of a general falling market.
- **Credit risk**—the risk that the issuer of a security will be unable to pay interest or principal on the security when it is due. The credit risk is a measure of the creditworthiness of the issuer and is also referred to as the **default risk**.
- **Liquidity risk**—the risk of adverse changes in the quality of securities originally purchased that permit their convertibility into cash without significant loss of value.
- **Risk of legislative change**—the risk that new legislation or changes in federal, state, or local laws may affect potential financial benefits from securities purchased (political risk).
- **Call risk**—the risk associated with the redemption of debt securities prior to maturity.

ADDITIONAL CONCEPTS

Although risk can be reduced, it can never be eliminated.

- Individuals who have investment objectives of current income and preservation of capital would normally purchase high quality-short-term debt obligations such as Treasury bills, negotiable certificates of deposit, bankers' acceptances, or money market funds.
- Assume an individual purchases a AAA corporate bond due in twenty years, a US Treasury bond due in twenty years, and a general obligation municipal bond with AAA rating due in twenty years. The individual owning these three bonds has very little default risk. However, the individual has two risks associated with these bonds.

- Interest rate risk
- Purchasing power risk (risk of inflation)

- Assume an individual owns a corporate bond with a market value of $1,200 callable at 102. The individual in this example has a call risk. If the bond is called at 102 ($1,020), the individual would receive $1,020 for a bond selling at $1,200.
- Assume an investor buys 100 shares of common stock of the following companies:

  - Coca-Cola
  - Johnson & Johnson
  - AT&T

  The default risk is low because these companies carry A+ ratings. However, the investor is assuming a market (systematic) risk and a capital risk. An investor who will need the invested funds in two or three years for college costs should not invest in equity securities. Investors in equity securities do not normally assume an interest rate risk or a purchasing power risk. Investors in equity securities may be subject to a capital risk, selection risk, timing risk, market risk (systematic risk), and possibly a liquidity risk for thinly trading issues.

- An important concept related to the risk of a bond portfolio is the concept called *duration*. Duration is defined as the percentage change in the price of a bond given a 1% (100 basis point) change in yield. A duration of 10 means that the price of a bond will change approximately 10% given a 1% change in the bond's yield. A duration of 5 means that the bond will change approximately 5% given a 1% change in the bond's yield. The greater a bond's duration, the greater the bond's volatility. The longer the term of a bond, the greater its duration. The less frequent the coupon payments, the greater the bond's duration. Duration can be used to measure the risk of a bond portfolio. A pension plan might use duration to measure how sensitive its bond portfolio is to interest rate changes.

15 SECURITIES TAXATION

On March 1, 1913, the Sixteenth Amendment to the Constitution, which gave Congress the "power to levy and collect taxes" on income, became effective. This amendment created the income tax law in the United States that is still in effect today, with many revisions.

The amendment also overturned a Supreme Court decision that had blocked an income tax for almost two decades. Income taxes, at that time, were already in effect in countries such as Great Britain, Australia, Japan, and New Zealand, as well as the state of Wisconsin.

The tax system that was set up included an individual income tax that would apply to individuals and trusts, as well as a corporate income tax. Unincorporated business enterprises are not separately taxed as entities since their proprietors or partners pay taxes on their share of the profits, whether or not the profits are withdrawn from the business. Corporations are taxed, in most cases, as separate entities, and dividends received by shareholders are taxed at their individual income tax rates.

BASIC TAX CONCEPTS

Basic tax concepts relating to investments in the federal tax code include

- All net capital gains will be taxed at the same rate as ordinary income, except that long-term capital gains are taxed at a maximum of 20%.
- Dividends and interest received by individuals is fully taxable as ordinary income.
- Capital losses must be netted against capital gains. Any remaining capital losses can be written off against ordinary income up to a maximum of $3,000 in a year. The excess capital loss carryforward is treated as a short-term capital loss in the following year.
- Losses from passive activities to the extent that they exceed income from passive activities generally cannot be deducted against other income of the taxpayer. Losses that are not deductible in one year may be carried forward and deducted from passive income in following years. When the taxpayer sells his interest in the passive activity, any remaining losses not previously taken may be deducted in full. Passive activities are business activities in which the taxpayer does not materially participate, such as an investment in a limited partnership. Real estate limited partnerships purchased by investors would be considered passive activities. For rental real estate activities in which an individual actively participates, up to $25,000 of losses may be taken each year against nonpassive income of the taxpayer.

CAPITAL GAINS AND LOSSES

Capital gains and losses result from the sale or exchange of capital assets. Land, buildings, stocks and bonds, and certain other types of property are normally considered capital assets. A capital gain is recognized when the amount realized from the sale or exchange of a capital asset is greater than its adjusted cost basis. The basis for securities is normally the cost (purchase price) including commissions. Real estate property costs, in most cases, must be adjusted because of depreciation and improvements. Therefore, when the amount of proceeds realized from a sale exceeds the adjusted cost basis, a capital gain is incurred. A long-term capital gain is a gain on a capital asset held more than twelve months. A short-term capital gain is a gain on a capital asset held twelve months or less. Short-term gains are taxed as ordinary income at the person's tax bracket rate. However, long-term capital gains are taxed at a maximum tax bracket rate of 20%.

Assume a customer in the 20% tax bracket has the following gains and losses:

$8,000 long-term gain
$2,000 long-term loss
$4,000 short-term gain
$6,000 short-term loss

Capital gains and losses must be subtracted to obtain a net capital gain or loss.

$8,000	Long-term gain	$6,000	Short-term loss
-2,000	Long-term loss	-4,000	Short-term gain
$6,000	Net long-term gain	$2,000	Net short-term loss

$6,000	Net long-term gain
-2,000	Net short-term loss
$4,000	Net capital gain

$4,000 net capital gain x 20% = $800 tax liability

The Tax Equity and Fiscal Responsibility Act of 1982 requires brokers to report the gross sales proceeds realized by their customers as well as any other information the Internal Revenue Service (IRS) may request. Brokers must furnish customers with statements of the information supplied to the IRS by January 31 of the year following the year to which the return applies.

If an individual sells a capital asset and the proceeds realized are less than the adjusted cost basis, he has incurred a capital loss. Capital losses must be used first to offset capital gains. If the capital gain is greater than the capital loss, the investor has a net capital gain. For example, if an investor had a capital gain of $10,000 and a capital loss of $3,000, the investor would have a net capital gain of $7,000. If the capital losses exceed the capital gains, a capital loss deduction may be taken on the individual's income tax return not exceeding $3,000. A net capital loss above $3,000 may be carried forward by an investor.

Assume an investor purchases $50,000 worth of XYZ Corporation over a long period of time. He decides to sell $20,000 worth of XYZ. Under federal tax laws, the investor is allowed to specify which shares are being sold to minimize his capital gain. If the investor is unable to specify which shares are being sold, the IRS requires that the first-in, first-out (FIFO) method be used to specify which shares are being sold.

Capital Gains

A short-term capital gain realized on the sale of a security receives no favored income tax treatment. It is taxed as ordinary income and is subject to tax at the person's income tax bracket rate. Therefore, a short-term capital gain is taxed at the rates that apply to other income.

Assume an investor in the 28% tax bracket purchased 100 shares of ABC for $40 a share on January 15. He sold the shares on April 1 in the same year at $60 a share. What amount of tax will he pay? In this case, the investor has realized a capital gain of $2,000. The investor will pay a tax of $560.

$2,000 short-term capital gain x 28 % = $560 tax liability

Capital Losses

A capital loss is incurred when an individual sells a capital asset and the sales proceeds are less than his adjusted basis in the capital asset. If an individual has only capital losses in a year, or his capital losses exceed his capital gains, a capital loss deduction may be taken on an individual's tax return. The maximum amount of capital loss that may be deducted from ordinary income is $3,000. Assume an investor realizes a $12,000 capital loss in a tax year. The investor has no capital gains. The investor could write off $3,000 against ordinary income and carry forward $9,000 to the next tax year.

Capital losses may be written off against ordinary income on a dollar-for-dollar basis. Therefore, assume an individual had only one trade and it resulted in a $1,500 capital loss. The individual has no other capital gains or losses. In this case, he could write off the entire $1,500 against ordinary income.

GAINS AND LOSSES FROM SHORT SALES

A **short sale** is defined in the Securities Exchange Act of 1934 as

> *any sale of a security which the seller does not own or any sale which is consummated by the delivery of a security borrowed by, or for the account of, the seller. A person shall be deemed to own a security if (1) he or his agent has title to it; or (2) he has purchased, or has entered into an unconditional contract binding on both parties thereto, to purchase it but has not received it; or (3) he owns a security convertible into or exchangeable for it and has tendered such security for conversion or exchange; or (4) he has an option to purchase or acquire it and has exercised such option; or (5) he has rights or warrants to subscribe to it and has exercised such rights or warrants; provided, however, that a person shall be deemed to own securities only to the extent that he has a net long position in such securities.*

For income tax purposes, no gain or loss is realized on a short sale until the short sale is covered. If an investor does not own the security he has sold short, any gain or loss realized on the closing of the short sale is a capital gain or loss. Therefore, a short sale (other than short-against-the-box) will result in a capital gain or loss, regardless of the time period between the date of the short sale and the closing date of the short sale.

Assume an investor (who has no position in the stock) sold short 100 shares of ABC at $40 a share on January 10 and closed out the transaction by purchasing 100 shares of ABC at $30 a share on May 15 in the same year. The investor incurred a capital gain of $1,000. If the investor had covered his short at $50 a share (instead of $30) on May 15, the loss of $1,000 would have been a capital loss.

WASH SALES

Wash sales occur when substantially identical securities are purchased within thirty days before or after the sale of the substantially identical securities. Any losses resulting from wash sales are not deductible. The disallowed loss is added to the basis of the new stock or security. Wash sale rules do not apply when a profit is generated on a securities transaction.

Substantially identical securities usually refers to securities of the same corporation. Securities of one corporation are not considered substantially identical with securities of another, nor are preferred stocks or bonds of a corporation identical with common stock of the same corporation. Differences in issue dates, interest payment dates, maturity dates, interest rates, or callable features are reasons for bonds issued to be considered not substantially identical. Preferred stock or bonds, which are convertible into common stock of the same corporation that have relatively the same values and price fluctuations, may be determined to be substantially identical.

Therefore, under wash sale rules, a loss on the sale of a security cannot be deducted on a person's tax return if, within a period beginning thirty days before the sale and ending thirty days after the sale, the person buys a call on the same security.

YEAR-END RULES

As a result of the Tax Reform Act of 1986, capital gains and losses will be recognized as of trade date. Therefore, if trade date is in late December and settlement date for a transaction is in January, the gain or loss is taxable in the prior year. The trade date of the transaction is used in determining the year in which the gain or loss is recognized for tax purposes.

STATE TAXATION

Some states do choose to tax interest received by an investor on other state and municipal obligations. However, the states cannot tax interest received on US government obligations.

Assume a customer lives in Massachusetts. He owns $10,000 in US Treasury bonds with a 5% coupon. His federal tax bracket rate is 28% and his state tax bracket rate is 10%. What is his total tax liability on the interest received?

Massachusetts and every state with an income tax cannot tax the return earned on US Treasury bills, notes, or bonds. However, the federal government taxes the return earned on its securities. Therefore, the total tax liability on the interest received is computed as follows:

$10,000 Treasury bonds x 5% = $500 interest received

$500 interest x 28% = $140 total tax liability

The general rule is that states cannot tax the return earned on US government securities such as bills, notes, or bonds. However, the federal government taxes the return earned on all three. Also, the federal government does not tax the return earned on municipal securities. Therefore, if an investor received $300 in interest on a Commonwealth of Massachusetts bond, the $300 would not be taxable by the federal government.

Assume a customer purchases a $10,000 Treasury bill for $9,500. At maturity, the customer will receive the face amount of $10,000. The customer has a $500 capital gain, which is taxed as ordinary income. If the customer is in the 28% tax brackets, he will pay a federal tax of $140.

STOCK DIVIDENDS

Assume an investor purchased 100 shares of XYZ at $50 per share on January 17. The investor received a 10% stock dividend on May 12 of the same year. All of the shares are sold on June 21 of the same year for $70 per share. What is the capital gain or loss for tax purposes?

As a result of the 10% stock dividend, the investor owned 110 shares at a cost of $5,000. The customer sold the 110 shares on June 21 at $70 per share. The capital gain or loss is computed as follows:

$7,700   Proceeds of sale
− 5,000   Cost of shares
$2,700   Capital gain

If, instead of selling all 110 shares on June 21, the investor sold only 50 shares, the capital gain or loss would be computed as follows:

$$\frac{\$5,000 \text{ cost}}{110 \text{ shares}} \quad = \quad \$45.45 \text{ average cost per share}$$

$70.00   Selling price per share
− 45.45   Average cost per share
$24.55   Profit per share

$24.55 profit per share x 50 shares = $1,227.50 capital gain on 50 shares

AMORTIZATION OF BOND PREMIUMS AND DISCOUNTS

If an investor purchases a taxable bond (i.e., corporate bond) at a premium, the investor may, at his option, amortize the premium over the life of the bond. The cost basis of the taxable bond is reduced by the amount amortized each year. The amount amortized each year is a deduction from adjusted gross income for the investor and reduces taxable income. Therefore, the investor will not have a loss at maturity since the amount of the premium will have been totally written off.

Assume a taxpayer purchases a $1,000 corporate bond maturing in ten years for $1,250. Each year $25 ($250 divided by ten years) could be deducted from the taxpayer's adjusted gross income, and the cost basis of the bond is reduced.

An investor is not required to amortize the premium of a taxable bond. If he does not amortize it, then the amount of the premium will represent a capital loss at maturity. Similar alternatives are available if a corporate bond is purchased at a discount.

Assume a $1,000 7% corporate bond maturing in ten years is purchased for $840. The taxpayer could choose to consider the $160 discount as a capital gain at maturity or could amortize the discount over the life of the bond. Using the straight-line method of accreting the bond discount, the calculation would be

$$\frac{\text{Amount of discount}}{\text{Years of maturity}} \quad \frac{\$160}{10} \quad = \quad \$16 \text{ amount accreted per year}$$

The cost basis of the bond is increased $16 per year. At maturity the calculation is

$1,000   Proceeds at maturity
− 1,000   Adjusted cost basis
$ 0   Capital gain or loss at maturity

The amount of the accretion (accumulation) of $16 represents ordinary income to the investor each year.

Assume that the investor sold the bond at the end of five years for $960. The capital gain or loss would be computed as follows:

$840   Cost of bond
+ 80   Amount accreted over five years
$920   Adjusted cost basis

$960   Proceeds on sale of bond
− 920   Adjusted cost basis
$ 40   Capital gain

The straight-line method of amortizing a bond's discount is also referred to as the straight-line method of accretion. The term **accretion** refers to the increase in the cost basis of the bond each year. The amount of the accreted discount each year represents ordinary income to the holder of a taxable bond.

However, when a corporation issues bonds (having a maturity of more than one year) at a discount from the maturity value, the Tax Equity and Fiscal Responsibility Act of 1982 does not permit the original issue discount to be allocated in equal monthly amounts over the life of the bond. Since the true interest cost, if the bond had not been issued at a discount and the corporation borrowed each year to meet its interest payments, is lower in the early years of a bond's life than in the later years, a formula must be used. Under this formula, the amount of the original issue discount allocable to each year will grow. It will be less in the early years and more in the later years.

If a tax-exempt bond is purchased at a premium, the premium must be amortized. The amortization reduces the basis of the bond, but the amortization is not deductible as it is with a taxable bond.

For example, an investor purchases one Town of Needham 8% bond, due June 30, 1992. The bond was purchased for settlement on June 30, 1987, for $1,300. The premium paid on the bond is $300.

$$\frac{\$300 \text{ premium}}{5 \text{ years}} = \$60 \text{ amortized per year}$$

At maturity, the investor will have no capital gain or loss on the bond.

$$\begin{array}{rl}
\$1,000 & \text{Proceeds at maturity} \\
-\ 1,000 & \text{Adjusted cost basis} \\
\hline
\$\quad 0 & \text{Capital gain or loss at maturity}
\end{array}$$

If a tax-exempt bond is purchased at a discount, the amount of the discount cannot be amortized. Assume an investor purchases a $1,000 face value tax-exempt bond for $800 and holds it until maturity. The investor incurs a $200 taxable capital gain.

CORPORATIONS

Under federal tax law, corporations pay taxes on their net income based on a graduated scale, which Congress changes from time to time. Corporations pay taxes on their net income, and shareholders pay taxes on dividends received from the corporation. This is referred to as the *double taxation of corporation profits*.

If a corporation owns either common stock or preferred stock in a domestic corporation, only 20% of the dividends received by the owning corporation are subject to income tax (with some exceptions). Therefore, 80% of the dividends received by the corporation are normally tax-exempt.

This tax exemption for dividends on stock exists to partially eliminate the triple taxation of corporate earnings. If Corporation A has earnings, it must pay a corporate tax on these earnings. If it distributes any portion of these earnings to stockholders, the stockholders must pay a tax on the earnings. This is double taxation. If, however, the stockholder happens to be another corporation, and the Internal Revenue Code had not provided any exemption, the corporation would have to pay a corporate income tax on these earnings (the second time they would have been taxed) and its stockholders would also have to pay a tax on any of the income derived from these dividends distributed to them. This exemption is the reason why the yields on many high-grade preferred stocks are lower than the yield on bonds. They are not only an attractive corporate investment, but also provide an attractive after-tax yield.

TAX SYSTEMS

Taxes may be either progressive, regressive, or proportionate. The system generally held in highest esteem in the United States is the progressive tax system. When a tax is progressive, individuals with high income pay a higher percentage tax than those with low income. Income taxes and estate taxes are examples of progressive taxes.

When a tax is regressive, individuals with low income pay a higher percentage tax than those with higher income. Any tax that levies a fixed dollar amount on each individual is regressive, since that fixed dollar amount will be a smaller percentage of a high income than it is of a lower income. While this system is generally agreed to be unsatisfactory, there are many examples of it, including property taxes, highway tolls, and most sales taxes.

The third possibility is proportionate taxation. Under this system, every taxpayer pays the same percentage tax regardless of income. There are few examples of proportionate taxation, with the exception of certain state income taxes (e.g., Massachusetts) that are at least somewhat proportionate.

GIFT TAX

The Internal Revenue Code provides for a tax to be levied on the donor of a gift exceeding certain limits. The purpose of the tax is to prevent a person from giving away all of his property before his death, thereby avoiding the estate tax. However, if a person gave away all of his property just before his death, the resulting gift tax would be approximately the same as the estate tax that would have been paid if the property was not given away. This is because gifts and estates are now subject to the same rate of taxation.

However, it is possible to avoid any taxation on certain gifts under the law. A person is allowed to give $10,000 a year away tax-free to as many individuals as he chooses. For example, a person could give four individuals $10,000 each, every year, completely tax-free. It is therefore advantageous for the donor to spread gifts over a period of years to take advantage of the $10,000 annual exclusion to any one person in a year. A husband and wife jointly could give away $20,000 to as many persons as they choose, tax-free.

As a result of the Economic Recovery Tax Act of 1981, an unlimited estate and gift tax marital deduction is allowed. Therefore, transfers of property between a husband and wife will pass free of gift and estate taxes. Congress, in passing this provision, felt that a husband and wife should be considered one economic unit for estate and gift taxes as they are for federal income tax purposes. This Act also states that each spouse will be treated as one-half owner of jointly held property regardless of whether the husband or wife paid for the property.

MARKET DISCOUNT BONDS

For bonds issued after July 18, 1984, the amount of market discount, with certain exceptions, is treated as ordinary income and not a capital gain upon distribution. Assume an investor buys a $1,000 par value corporate bond in 1985 for $920. In this case, $80 represents the amount of market discount. Assume the bond is sold for $1,250 after eight months. The total profit is $330. However, $80 is considered ordinary income and $250 is a capital gain. Prior to this change in the tax code, the entire $330 would have been taxed as a capital gain.

Certain bonds are exempt from this ordinary income rule.

- Tax-exempt obligations such as municipal bonds
- Obligations maturing within one year of issuance
- US savings bonds
- Installment obligations

Therefore, corporate bonds are subject to market discount rules, but municipal bonds are exempt. Also, all short-term obligations, municipal and corporate, are exempt from market discount rules.

SUMMARY—TAX CONCEPTS

To summarize important tax concepts relating to investors

- Net short-term gains are taxed as ordinary income.
- Dividend and interest income received by an investor is fully taxable without any exclusion amount.
- The unearned income in excess of $1,300 of a minor child under fourteen years of age will be taxed to the child at the parent's highest marginal tax bracket rate.

ADDITIONAL CONCEPTS

Taxes need to be considered in all investment decisions.

- Under the federal tax code, wages and salaries are considered to be earned income.
- Dividends, interest, and capital gains are considered to be unearned income. In certain instances, dividends, interest, and capital gains are referred to as *portfolio income*, since they are generated from a portfolio.
- If personal tax rates increase, there would be a greater demand for municipal securities and a lesser demand if personal tax rates decrease.
- A progressive tax requires those with higher incomes to pay taxes at higher rates. In other words, the greater the taxable amount, the greater the tax. Income, estate and gift taxes are progressive taxes.
- A regressive tax places a greater burden on those least able to pay. Sales, excise, and gasoline taxes are regressive taxes.
- The cost basis for stock purchased by an investor is the market value of the securities when acquired plus commissions paid to acquire them.
- Accrued interest paid on the purchase of a bond is not part of an investor's cost basis. However, any commissions paid to purchase bonds are part of the cost basis.
- Assume an investor acquires $40,000 of XYZ over fifteen years. Under federal tax laws, the investor can specify which shares are being sold to minimize the capital gain. If an investor cannot specify which shares are being sold, the investor must use FIFO.
- Wash sale rules apply to both long-sale transactions and short-sale transactions.
- Interest and dividends received on corporate securities and foreign securities are fully taxable at the federal, state, and local levels.

- A foreign tax credit is allowed to US investors against their federal income taxes, for the taxes paid on income earned outside of the United States.
- Assume Mrs. Jones buys 100 shares of ABC at $60 per share. She gives the stock to her son when the market value is $72 per share. The son sells the stock two years later at $75 per share. The gain for tax purposes is $1,500. The son picks up the donor's basis of $6,000.

16 INVESTMENT COMPANIES

INTRODUCTION

Among the unique investments offered by the securities business are investment companies. This chapter will provide an in-depth analysis of this popular investment vehicle. The wide variety of funds offered attests to their acceptability to the investing public. This variety warrants considerable study on the part of the informed registered representative.

The two main types of investment companies are open-end funds and closed-end funds. Open-end investment companies (open-end funds) are also referred to as *mutual funds*. They continuously offer new shares to the public and redeem customer shares on demand. Closed-end investment company shares trade on stock exchanges and in the over-the-counter (OTC) market. Closed-end investment companies (closed-end funds) will be discussed later in this chapter.

An open-end investment company is defined by the Investment Company Act of 1940 as "either a corporation or a trust through which investors pool their funds in an investment portfolio to obtain diversification and supervision of their investments."

The term **mutual fund** is the most popular name for open-end investment companies. Open-end investment companies continuously offer new shares for sale to investors. Moreover, the companies provide a continuous market for the redemption of shares from investors. Thus, the investor buys the mutual fund from the issuing company and sells the shares back to the issuer, either directly or through broker/dealers. Shares of open-end investment companies are not traded on organized exchanges as are corporate shares.

Mutual funds may be purchased either in specific dollar amounts or in a specific number of shares. Sales charges, in the case of **load** funds (no-load funds levy no sales charges), are deducted from the investment and the net investment results in full and fractional shares in the fund. Purchases of investment company shares are carried to three places after the decimal.

Assume a customer invests $1,000 in the XYZ Fund. The ask price of the XYZ Fund is $12. How many shares will the customer purchase?

$$\frac{\$1,000 \text{ amount invested}}{\$12 \text{ ask price per share}} = 83.333 \text{ shares}$$

Assume instead that the ask price of the XYZ Fund was $14 per share. How many shares would the customer purchase?

$$\frac{\$1,000 \text{ amount invested}}{\$14 \text{ ask price per share}} = 71.426 \text{ shares}$$

The shares purchased represent the investor's undivided interest in the mutual fund's portfolio and give the investor the right to vote on certain basic issues similar to the voting right accorded to common stockholders.

The very nature of mutual funds is that risks are pooled into a common portfolio to minimize the risks associated with the smaller portfolio of the individual investor. There are various ways in which the open-end investment company can disperse risks. The objective and type of fund may indicate the dispersion of the risk.

The fund is managed by full-time professionals, and it is likely that their expertise will be greater than that of the individual investor. Moreover, since they are full-time, it is also likely that they will have more time to devote to the management of the fund than the individual investor. It is the primary responsibility of the fund's full-time management to meet the objective of the open-end investment company, as described in the prospectus.

One of the functions of fund management is to obtain the appropriate diversification of the securities in the fund's portfolio while at all times attempting to meet the fund objectives. Another of their responsibilities is to decide on the proper timing of the investment decision. It is management who must decide whether to buy, sell, or hold securities. In addition, the fund's management identifies the tax status of the fund's distributions. A mutual fund generally makes two types of distributions: income distributions and capital gains distributions.

Thus, in theory, the fund management should be more competent and skilled than the individual investor. It is forbidden, however, under Securities and Exchange Commission (SEC) rules to allege or imply that the fund's management or its diversification will guarantee the investor against loss of his investment. Neither can any statement be made that the fund's management or diversification will assure a capital gain. In fact, the SEC forbids any extravagant or misleading claims as to the management ability of the open-end investment company.

DISTRIBUTIONS BY FUNDS

Mutual funds, as previously mentioned, make two types of distributions: income distributions, and capital gains distributions. Income distributions are also referred to as *dividend distributions*. Income distributions are paid from a fund's net investment income. Net investment income is derived from gross investment income less operating expenses. The three principal sources of gross investment income are: (1) dividend income the fund receives from its holdings of common and preferred stock; (2) interest income from the debt obligations in its portfolio, and (3) short-term capital gains realized on the portfolio.

The fund subtracts its operating expenses, such as the management fee, custodial fee, auditor's fee, and costs of printing and publishing reports from gross investment income. Costs associated with advertising may be deducted from gross investment income if a written plan has been approved by its shareholders (12b-1 funds).

The net investment income distributed by an open-end investment company will vary for the following reasons:

- The dividends on the fund's portfolio will vary.
- New bond investments may pay higher or lower interest than previous investments.
- The fund's operating expenses can change.

There is no restriction on how often dividends can be paid out by an investment company. Dividends are paid as often as they are declared by the board of directors, which could be daily. Certain money market funds declare dividends daily and pay them to shareholders monthly.

Capital gains distributions are paid from long-term capital gains realized on the sale of securities in the fund's portfolio. Capital losses are used to offset capital gains. The net long-term gain is distributed to shareholders according to their proportionate holding of shares. Capital gains distributions can normally be paid out only once a year by an investment company.

When the fund makes distributions, the assets of the fund are decreased. If, however, the fund shareholder reinvests these dividend and capital gains distributions, the number of shares owned will increase and will have a compounding effect on his investment. Even though a mutual fund shareholder reinvests capital gain distributions and dividend distributions, he is still taxed on the amount of the distributions.

Capital gains distributions are based on realized gains or losses. The price of fund shares is also affected by unrealized profits or losses on stocks and bonds that have not been sold. The holder of mutual fund shares is not taxed on unrealized profits.

Advertising statements regarding fund distributions are carefully monitored by the SEC. There cannot be any implication that mutual funds will increase the investor's capital or preserve her original capital. Nor can any statement imply that mutual funds can assure a particular return. Even if a mutual fund has increased in value 30% in each of the past three years, the fund's prospectus or a fund salesman cannot state that the fund will increase 30% in the present year.

Mutual funds offer shareholders certain conveniences, including the following:

- Investment decisions are made by full-time fund managers.
- The fund offers safekeeping of security certificates.
- The investor can invest in full or fractional shares.
- The investor can liquidate a portion of his invested capital without reducing the degree of diversification.
- The fund shares may be used as collateral for a bank loan.
- Automatic reinvestment of income dividend and capital gains distributions is available.
- Some funds offer a conversion privilege. This allows the investor to change from one fund to another, within the same family, as his investment objective changes. For example, an investor may change from a growth fund to an income fund without incurring any additional sales charges but would be subject to tax on any capital gain.

TYPES OF FUNDS

The main types of mutual funds offered to investors include

- Diversified common stock fund
- Income fund
- Specialized or sector fund
- Balanced fund
- Bond fund
- Municipal bond fund
- US government securities fund
- Hedge funds
- Dual-purpose funds
- Money market funds
- International funds

Diversified common stock funds invest primarily in common stocks. They may concentrate on **blue-chip** companies or on **growth** companies. The stocks in the portfolio of such a growth fund are normally spread over many different companies and industries. Some common stock funds are classified as aggressive growth funds since they invest in speculative securities to attempt to obtain maximum capital gains.

Some diversified common-stock funds have the dual objectives of growth and income and are referred to as growth and income funds. These funds invest in stocks with potential appreciation as well as in stocks that pay relatively high dividends.

In the case of income funds, the investments are generally concentrated in common stocks of a single industry (such as petroleum), a group of related industries (such as aluminum and steel), or a single geographic area (such as Japan). The objective of specialized funds may be growth, income, or safety of principal. Specialized funds are commonly referred to as **sector funds**.

Balanced funds, as the name implies, provide balance in the portfolio and normally contain bonds, preferred stock, and common stock. Balanced funds usually have a more conservative investment policy than a common-stock fund and offer greater stability. In a rising market, balanced funds have a smaller gain, but, in a falling market, they normally decline less. Such funds appeal to investors who are seeking relative safety of principal.

Bond funds offer the investor safety of principal since the investments are in senior securities. Such investments, however, offer fixed incomes, and the investor must accept the inflationary or purchasing power risk.

Municipal bond funds invest in municipal bonds whose interest is exempt from federal income taxes. Normally, the minimum investment in such funds is one **unit** or $1,000. Income received by an investor from a municipal bond is exempt from federal income taxes.

US government securities funds invest in securities of the US government. In such funds, there is great safety of principal due to the equality of the investment. The investor does face the risk of decreased purchasing power in this type of fund.

Hedge funds attempt to hedge against market declines by engaging in aggressive trading techniques such as short selling. They also customarily allow for borrowing money and place few restrictions on the types of securities they may hold. The term may be applied to any aggressively managed high-risk mutual fund.

Dual-purpose funds have two classes of shares. The intention is to provide investors with either dividends or capital gains. Income shares receive all of the fund's net investment income but none of its capital gains, and capital shares receive all of the fund's capital gains but none of its investment income. This type of fund is theoretically in a position to provide income to investors seeking income, and capital gains to investors seeking capital appreciation.

International funds invest primarily in common stocks of foreign corporations. International funds must also be concerned with the value of the dollar against foreign currencies. When the dollar declines against foreign currencies on foreign exchange markets, foreign stocks and bonds become worth more in terms of dollars, and the net asset values of the funds rise. When the dollar increases against foreign currencies, the value of international fund shares decline.

Money market funds first appeared in the early 1970s when rates in the money market rose above rates on time deposits. These funds offered investors high return and high liquidity. Their funds are invested in high-yield, short-term debt securities.

Money market funds are no-load funds with no redemption fee. They do not issue certificates but send out statements at regular intervals showing deposits, withdrawals, and interest credited to the account. The investor can withdraw funds from such a fund on demand at any time without penalty. Many funds, in fact, provide checks that the investor may make out and cash or use to pay bills, just as he can with bank checks.

Most money market funds have a minimum original investment requirement, and many require checks drawn against the fund to be for some minimum amount. The funds hold portfolios of high, liquid short-term investments. Funds for redemption are available either from new deposits into the funds by investors, from maturing securities, or from the sale of portfolio assets. Since these funds offer the investor safety of principal as well as liquidity and high return, the typical fund prospectus restricts investments to short-term securities (e.g., stocks, bonds, or buying on margin). The more conservative funds invest their assets only in government and agency securities, while those that are more aggressive invest in a wider range of money market securities.

The minimum investment in a money market fund is normally $1,000. The minimum amount an investor can draw checks on for most money market funds is $500. Money market funds normally declare dividends daily and pay them out to shareholders monthly. Most money market funds value their shares by the amortized cost valuation method. Under this method, the cost of the securities is written up to maturity over its remaining life. However, if interest rates rose and share redemptions exceeded sales, the money market fund would be forced to sell shares at prices below those valued by the fund.

MUTUAL FUND COMPARISONS

A customer's representative will often find himself in competition for a client's investments. If the competition is another mutual fund, the investor will be making a comparison based on

- Investment objectives
- Investment policies
- Quality of management
- Nonstatistical factors
- Yield

The objective of the fund must be clearly stated in the fund's prospectus. The investor will then be able to select that fund that most closely resembles her personal investment objective. A fund can change its investment objectives only if it is authorized to do so by more than 50% of the voting securities and by the fund's directors. A retired individual may be interested in investing in a bond fund, money market fund, income fund, or even a growth and income fund. However, she would not be interested in investing in a computer technology fund or a special-situation fund. Even though two funds have the same objectives, they may employ different techniques in attaining them. For example, two growth funds may be identical in objective; but one may invest in blue-chip companies, while the other selects stocks of new companies that seem to offer growth potential.

Quality of management can be measured by actual operating results of the fund. Performance may be compared statistically and nonstatistically. Certain problems arise in statistical comparisons. This year's "darling" may be next year's "dog." The time period selected can be misleading.

The success of the management of a mutual fund is measured by the degree to which it has achieved its stated objectives. Management success is judged not only by how well the portfolio does in accordance with the fund's objective, but also by management's ability to control expenses. Expense management may be analyzed by the use of an expense ratio. The expense ratio is found by dividing operating expenses by the fund's average net assets.

$$\frac{\text{Operating expenses}}{\text{Fund's average net assets}}$$

ADVERTISING BY FUNDS

The SEC has, in recent years, taken a very close look at mutual fund advertising. As a result of analysis, stock and bond mutual funds are required to use current standardized performance figures in their advertising. The funds must include the average annual total return, after expenses, for the most recent one-, five- and ten-year periods. These figures must be printed on the prospectus in typeface that is no smaller than other performance figures.

In addition to requiring uniform calculation of total return, the SEC requires that income funds use a uniformly calculated thirty-day figure in any ads advertising their yield. Also, the SEC requires fund fee tables to illustrate every expense or fee, as well as how much these reduce a hypothetical $1,000 investment for one, three, five and ten years. The fee table must appear in the beginning of all fund prospectuses. The purpose of these fee tables is to make it easier to compare the charges imposed by individual funds. The rules apply to front- and back-end loads and funds that levy 12b-1 fees.

Funds that levy 12b-1 fees are referred to as 12b-1 funds. These fees are named after the SEC regulation that governs them. Both load and no-load 12b-1 funds are allowed to use a portion of the shareholders' assets to pay marketing and advertising costs.

In recent years some funds began charging low loads instead of the normal load of approximately 8½% to 9%. Mutual funds are available today with different loads or sales charges.

- **Load fund**—normally charges an 8½ to 9% sales charge
- **Low-load fund**—sales charge normally 2 to 3%
- **No-load fund**—no sales charge levied on a customer purchase

PUBLIC DISTRIBUTION OF FUND SHARES

Four entities may be involved in the distribution of a mutual fund to the investor.

1. *The fund.* Usually a corporation that owns the investment portfolio—the fund's shares are owned by the investing public. If organized as a corporation, it will have directors and officers carrying out the functions and activities of those in the usual business corporation. If organized as a common-law trust, it does not have directors, officers, or an advisory board—management will be handled by a trustee under the terms of the trust agreement.
2. *The underwriter.* Most funds use the services of a principal underwriter—a firm that has the exclusive contractual right to purchase new shares from the fund at the net asset value per share.
3. *The dealer.* The underwriter makes a contractual arrangement with securities dealers permitting these dealers to continuously offer the fund's shares to the public. The underwriter retains a small portion of the selling commission; the dealer receives the major portion out of which sales representatives are compensated.
4. *The plan company.* Sometimes the underwriter distributes the fund shares to a plan company and this company sells them to investors. **Plan companies** are most often used when the contractual plan method of distribution is selected.

The method of distribution used must always be described in the fund's prospectus. In summary, the public may purchase fund shares by one of the following methods:

- Fund → underwriter → dealer → investor
- Fund → underwriter → investor
- Fund → investor
- Fund → underwriter → "plan company" → investor

PRICES OF MUTUAL FUND SHARES

The **ask price** of open-end investment company shares is the price at which they are sold to the public—the price the investor must pay when he purchases shares. The ask price is also called the **public offering price**. The **bid price** is the price at which the investment company will buy back its own shares—the price the investor will receive when he sells his shares (minus any redemption fee).

The bid price is the net asset value per share (NAVPS) of the fund. This is determined in two steps.

1. Fund assets – Liabilities = Total net assets.

2. $\dfrac{\text{Total net assets}}{\text{Number of shares outstanding}} = \text{NAVPS}$

NAVPS must be determined at least once each business day, as of the close of business of the New York Stock Exchange (NYSE). It should be noted that the fund's assets consist mainly of the portfolio in which the fund has invested. If the market value of the fund has exceeded its cost, the excess is called the fund's *appreciation*. If the cost exceeds market value, this difference is known as the fund's *depreciation*.

The NAVPS varies with the assets and liabilities of the fund. NAVPS increases if the fund's assets rise (i.e., if the securities appreciate) or if the fund's liabilities decrease. NAVPS falls if the securities in the portfolio fall or if liabilities increase.

Open-end companies are prohibited from ever selling their shares for less than the NAVPS. If an investor decides to purchase shares in an open-end investment company, the price paid will be based on the NAVPS next computed after receipt of the order by the dealer. If the fund is a no-load fund, the bid and ask prices will be the same. If the fund has a load (a selling charge), there will be a difference between the bid and ask prices caused by this sales charge.

SALES CHARGES

A sales charge (load) is normally charged only when the fund is sold to the customer. It includes not only the commission to be retained by the dealer and the salesman, but also the underwriter's concession. It does not include the management fee—an operating expense of the fund. The sales charge is based on the ask price. For example, if the NAVPS of a fund is $14.49 (the bid price) and the fund has a sales charge of 8%, the ask price (the offering price) would be found by dividing the $14.49 by 0.92. The divisor is found by subtracting the percentage load from 100%. Note that the ask price could not be found by multiplying the bid price by 8% and adding the answer to the bid price. In the example used, the ask price would be

$$\text{Ask price} \quad = \quad \frac{\$14.49}{0.92} \quad = \quad \$15.75$$

Note the relationship between these amounts.

$15.75   Ask price
– 14.49   Bid price   The $1.26 sales charge is 8% of the ask price of $15.75.
$ 1.26   Load

The bid price is that at which the fund will buy back its own shares. Some funds, however, charge a redemption fee. This fee is usually based on the NAVPS of the shares being redeemed and is generally 1% or less. If, for example, a fund has a bid price of $20, an ask price of $21.50, and a redemption fee of ¾ of 1%, an investor redeeming 1,000 shares would receive $19,850.

$20 x 1,000 shares	=	$20,000
$20,000 x 0.0075	=	– 150
Proceeds to investor		$19,850

The method of calculating the public offering price must be described in the fund's registration statement and prospectus. Information concerning sales charge, redemption fee, or management fee can always be found in the prospectus. Prices quoted in the daily newspaper are bid and ask prices based on that day's close. A person deciding to invest the next day would not pay an amount related to either of these newspaper amounts since his price will be based on the net asset value next computed after the dealer receives his order on that day. The sales charge paid by an investor would be the same, whether the fund shares are purchased through a broker/dealer or wholesaler or from the fund itself. Wholesalers and broker/dealers, in order to sell fund shares, must be registered with the National Association of Securities Dealers (NASD).

Mutual fund companies normally allow investors to swap funds for a nominal charge and avoid another sales charge. A mutual fund company may have a family of funds, such as growth, aggressive growth, growth and income, and income and money market. An investor may sell an income fund and buy a growth fund. Even though the investor is avoiding a second sales charge, the transaction may have tax consequences. The IRS considers the swap a sale of one security and a purchase of another security. If the customer realizes a capital gain on the sale of the income fund, she is subject to federal income tax on the gain. The customer, by immediately reinvesting in the growth fund, does not postpone the tax liability on the realized capital gain.

BREAKPOINTS

A **breakpoint** is the dollar amount required to qualify for a reduced sales charge on purchases of mutual fund shares. A breakpoint schedule might appear as follows:

Amount of purchase	Sales charge
$100–$9,999	8%
$10,000–$24,999	6%
$25,000–$99,999	4%
$100,000 and over	2%

The prospectus must include a table showing a sales charge for different breakpoints. The Investment Company Act of 1940 permits such reduced sales charges by any person making appropriate quantity purchases either in one lump sum, by accumulating the required sum with securities previously purchased, or through a letter of intent (LOI). Two terms require further elaboration. The Investment Company Act of 1940 defines any *person* as

- An individual.
- An individual, his spouse, and their children under the age of twenty-one, purchasing securities for his or their account.
- A trustee or fiduciary purchasing securities for a single trust estate or single fiduciary account (including a pension or similar employee benefit trust under Section 401 of the Internal Revenue Code).

Groups of individuals, such as an investment club, are not a *person* and, therefore, are never eligible for a reduced sales charge due to a quantity purchase.

A **letter of intent** is defined as a letter stating the investor's intention to purchase the required dollar amount over a period not to exceed thirteen months. The letter is binding only on the fund, not on the investor. If the sales charges are reduced during the period, the investor receives the benefit. If they are raised, he can be charged no more than the schedule in effect at the date of the letter. His redemption privileges continue during this LOI time period.

The LOI may, additionally, be backdated as much as ninety days to enable the investor to take advantage of a recent large purchase. The total time covered by the letter, however, must not exceed thirteen months.

Some of the shares purchased by the investors under an LOI may be held in escrow by the fund. If the investor does not meet the obligations of contributing the required dollar amounts within the thirteen-month period, enough shares are redeemed to pay the fund the additional sales charges as they are owed.

Assume a customer signs an LOI to invest $20,000 in a mutual fund. His original investment of $11,000 has increased to $15,000. What amount must the customer invest to maintain his original agreement and obtain the discounted sales charge? The customer must still invest $9,000 to obtain the reduced sales charge. Capital appreciation is not considered in an LOI. The customer is obligated to invest a specific dollar amount in order to obtain the discounted sales charge.

Rights of accumulation permit reduced sales charges on future purchases after the investor has reached a new breakpoint. For example, John Wellington invests $1,000 a month in the ABC Fund. ABC's sales charges are 8% on the first $10,000 and 6% from $10,000 to $25,000. For the first ten months, the sales charges will be $80 each month (8% x $1,000); but on the eleventh month, as the 6% breakpoint is reached, the charge will be reduced and will stay at 6% until the next breakpoint is attained. This is different from the LOI that applies the lower charges to the entire amount invested.

In rights of accumulation, capital appreciation is taken into consideration. Assume a customer invests $13,000 in a mutual fund. The investment appreciates in value to $17,500. The customer will now invest an additional $1,000. What will be the sales charge based on the following information?

Amount invested	Sales charge
$1–$9,999	$8\frac{1}{2}\%$
$10,000–$14,999	$8\frac{1}{4}\%$
$15,000–$19,999	8%
$20,000–$49,999	$7\frac{3}{4}\%$

The sales charge on the additional $1,000 investment by the customer would be 8%. Appreciation is taken into consideration when determining the sales charge in a rights of accumulation purchase. However, a capital appreciation is not taken into consideration in an LOI purchase.

DOLLAR COST AVERAGING

Dollar cost averaging is the investment of a specific sum in the same security or group of securities over a long period of time, without regard to the price level of that security. It may be referred to as **dollar cost averaging** or **cost averaging,** not "dollar averaging" or "averaging the dollar." The key to dollar cost averaging is the mathematical certainty that if the price of a security continually rises and falls, the average cost of the security will be less than its average price. The reason is that when the price is low, the investor will purchase more shares than when the price is high. An example will demonstrate this.

Month	*Amount of purchase*	*Security price*	*Shares purchased*
1	$100	$ 6	16.667
2	$100	5	20.000
3	$100	3	33.333
4	$100	4	25.000
5	$100	8	12.500
6	$100	10	10.000
Totals	$600	$36	117.500

The average price is $6 ($36 divided by 6), but the average cost is $5.11 ($600 divided by 117.500).

A warning must be given in conjunction with this investment method. First, the investor may lose if the security is sold when the price is lower than his average cost. Second, the method requires continuous investment. Third, it requires patience and persistence by the investor, especially during periods of market decline. The investor will not achieve any appreciation on his investment if the price of the security continually falls.

REDEMPTION OF MUTUAL FUND SHARES

Mutual funds must redeem their shares upon request by a shareholder. The shares may be held by the fund's transfer agent or by the investor himself. If the shares are held by the transfer agent, the investor addresses a letter to the fund in care of the transfer agent (usually a custodian bank) stating that he is the registered owner of the fund shares held in an account with a certain account number.

The investor directs that the shares be liquidated and the proceeds be remitted. Enclosed with the letter is a signed stock power with the investor's signature guaranteed by a member firm of the NYSE or a national bank.

If the shares are held by the investor, he requests redemption in writing to the fund (as described above), or orally or in writing to the dealer. The investor presents his certificate or an accompanying stock power with the signature guaranteed in the same manner as above.

The price received by the investor is the NAVPS or bid price next computed after the fund or its agent receives the properly completed redemption request. Therefore, upon redemption, an investor would not immediately know the total dollar value of the redemption. Redemption fees, if any, are deducted from the bid price, and the net amount must be remitted to the investor within seven days. The fund's transfer agent will then cancel the redeemed shares.

The Investment Company Act of 1940 requires that the fund redeem such shares within seven days after they are properly tendered. However, the fund may postpone payment under the following conditions:

- When trading on the NYSE is restricted or when the exchange is closed for other than a holiday or weekend
- When the SEC permits the fund to suspend the redemption right to protect shareholders
- When an emergency makes the disposal of the fund's portfolio or the valuation of its net assets impractical

STRUCTURE OF OPEN-END INVESTMENT COMPANIES

Open-end investment companies must be registered under the Investment Company Act of 1940, which also affects the structure of the fund company. Important provisions include

- The open-end investment company must have net worth of at least $100,000 before its shares may be offered to the public.
- Open-end investment companies may only issue common stock. They may not issue senior securities such as bonds or preferred stock.
- The fund may engage in temporary bank borrowing if the fund maintains a 300% asset coverage on the amount of money borrowed.
- No more than 60% of the fund's directors may be officers or employees of the fund or affiliated with the fund's investment banker, underwriter, or investment advisor.

Therefore, at least 40% must be "outsiders"—persons who are not officers of the fund or affiliated with the fund's investment banker, underwriter, or investment advisor.

Functions performed by the fund's board of directors include (1) the general responsibility for investment policy decisions of the fund, (2) ensuring that the fund management adheres to the stated objectives of the fund, (3) appointing the officers of the fund. In actuality, the board or the fund officers may appoint a committee to manage the investments, or, in most cases, such investment management is delegated to a management company under contract to the fund.

MUTUAL FUND MANAGEMENT COMPANY

An interlocking directorate usually exists between the fund and the contracted management company. An investment advisory agreement must be approved by a majority of the fund's board of directors who are not parties to the contract, and such agreement must also be approved by a majority vote of the fund's shareholders.

A typical investment advisory contract has the investment advisory firm pay the salaries of the fund's officers and employees, and other corporate costs. In return, the fund pays the investment advisor a fee for these services. This fee is typically about ½ of 1% of the fund's average annual net assets. This rate sometimes decreases as the fund's assets increase. This fee cannot be based on the realized or unrealized appreciation of the fund's portfolio, although it may fluctuate with performance.

The Investment Company Amendments Act of 1970 permits a performance fee, if the variation in the fee is based on the investment performance of the fund, averaged over a specified period, and measured against an appropriate securities price index (or other measure) as specified by the SEC. Naturally, all performance, management, and investment advisory fees must be clearly specified in the prospectus. The prospectus must also clearly state that there are contractual limits to these fees.

The Investment Company Act of 1940 also prohibits the fund's purchasing securities on margin (credit) and selling short, unless special permission is received from the SEC. Hedge funds apply for and receive permission from the SEC.

RIGHTS OF FUND SHAREHOLDERS

Mutual fund shareholders have rights similar to common shareholders of other corporations. Complete financial statements must be sent to them at least semiannually. They have the right to vote on certain matters, such as

- Selection of the fund's directors
- Any proposed change in the fund's investment practices, policies, or objectives.
- Approval of the fund's investment advisor
- Any proposed change in the method of calculating the public offering price, management (or other) fees, and redemption price

The shareholders have the final authority since the preceding may be changed only if approved by a vote of more than 50% of the outstanding shares and by the fund directors. Fund shareholders must be sent proxies that allow them to vote without attending the annual shareholders' meeting. Such proxies must be accompanied by the details of the company's contract with its investment advisor and any relationships that may exist between the officers of the fund and its advisor.

FUNCTIONS OF THE UNDERWRITER

The underwriter of a mutual fund is also known as its distributor or sponsor. The functions the underwriter performs are

- Wholesale marketing of the fund shares to the securities dealers, plan companies, or investors. The underwriter has the exclusive right to purchase new shares from the fund at the NAVPS.
- Direct sales to the public through a captive sales organization, if any. If sales are made through advertising alone, there is often a reduced charge or no sales charge at all (as in the case of "no-load" funds).
- Preparation of sales literature. All sales literature must be prepared in conformity with SEC regulations.

When sales charges are made, the underwriter retains a small portion of the total sales charge. This portion is called the **underwriter's concession**. The major portion, received by the dealer, is referred to as the **dealer's concession**. These concessions are not additions to the sales charge when calculating the public offering price, since they are already included in the sales charge.

CUSTODIAN

The Investment Company Act of 1940 requires an open-end investment company to have its assets in the hands of a custodian, usually a national bank, trust company, or other qualified institution. The custodian may perform any essential clerical-type service for the fund and its shareholders. The custodial functions include

- Safeguarding the fund's physical assets
- Disbursing funds for securities purchases
- Receiving funds from securities sales

If the custodian also acts as transfer agent and registrar, its functions also include

- Issuing new fund shares
- Canceling redeemed shares
- Disbursing dividend and capital gains distributions
- Performing clerical functions (i.e., periodic reports, proxy forms, or bookkeeping)

Such services are performed pursuant to a contract between the custodian and the fund. There are certain functions that custodians cannot perform, including

- Any management, supervisory, or investment function
- Taking any part in selling or distributing fund shares
- Offering any protection against the fund's assets depreciating (declining) in value

OWNERSHIP OF MUTUAL FUND SHARES

Investors who purchase fund shares must decide on the form of ownership. The different ways in which mutual fund accounts may be registered are

- *Joint tenants with rights of survivorship.* If one owner dies, the other acquires full ownership. For example, if a husband dies, the wife becomes the sole owner of the fund shares.
- *Tenants in common.* Each owner owns a specified percentage or fractional interest in the fund shares. In the event of the death of one of the owners, the heirs of the deceased inherit his share.
- *UGMA/UTMA custodial account.* Mutual funds may be placed in a custodial account under the Uniform Gifts to Minors Act/Uniform Transfers to Minors Act (UGMA/UTMA). Under this Act, the gift is irrevocable, complete transfer of one person's interest to another person. The shares are registered in the custodian's name for the benefit of the minor and are turned over to him or her upon the attainment of majority.
- *Trust accounts.* Mutual funds may be placed in trust accounts, provided that the trust is properly established.

An attorney should be consulted in such matters of ownership. The registered representative (RR) selling fund shares must realize that she is prohibited from recommending a particular form of ownership since this constitutes the unauthorized practice of law.

TAXATION OF MUTUAL FUNDS

Investors must contend with a system of double taxation in the United States. The corporations in which they invest pay taxes, and the interest or dividends distributed to the investors are further taxed to the investors. If the mutual fund investing in various corporations had to pay taxes as well, triple taxation would exist. To avoid this undesirable situation, the Internal Revenue Code allows a mutual fund to avoid taxation on any income it distributes to its shareholders, if it qualifies as a regulated investment company under Subchapter M of the Internal Revenue Code. In effect, the fund becomes a conduit, or pipeline, through which corporate dividend and interest distributions flow directly to the fund shareholder as if he directly owned the investments. The requirements that the fund must meet to qualify for this special tax treatment under Subchapter M of the Internal Revenue Code are

- It must be a domestic corporation.
- It must be registered with the SEC under the Investment Company Act of 1940 for the entire taxable year, either as a management company or a unit investment trust.
- It must derive at least 90% of its gross income from dividends and interest and capital gains from the sale of securities.
- It must distribute at least 90% of its net investment income as taxable dividends to shareholders (the fund pays taxes on the undistributed investment income at its regular corporate tax rate).
- Less than 30% of its gross income must be derived from the sales of securities held less than three months.

Regulation under Subchapter M and registration with the SEC does not imply in any way that the government regulates or supervises the fund's management or its portfolio.

It is the mutual fund shareholder's responsibility to report all dividend and capital gains distributions to the IRS and state tax agency. Such information is sent to the shareholder by the fund (or its agent) on IRS Form 1099. Income distributions paid to investors by a regulated investment company are taxed as ordinary income.

CLOSED-END INVESTMENT COMPANIES

Some investment companies are closed-end, and a contrast between them and mutual funds (open-end companies) is appropriate. The following table will help to distinguish the two:

Open-end	*Closed-end*
1. No fixed number of shares outstanding. Shares are continuously offered to the public.	1. A fixed capitalization. A fixed number of shares outstanding, like any other company. They do not continuously offer shares of the fund
2. Sells and redeems its own shares. Redemption price equals the net asset value per share, assuming no redemption fee.	2. Shares traded on exchanges or traded over the counter after an initial public offering.
3. Price determined by NAVPS and can never be sold at less than NAVPS.	3. Price determined by forces of supply and demand. Could trade at more or less than NAVPS. Investors pay the purchase price in the marketplace plus commission.
4. Sales charge must be stated in the prospectus.	4. Normal brokerage fees apply.
	5. Shares are not redeemable by the issuer.
	6. Shares do not have a redemption fee.

The major difference between closed-end and open-end funds is in their capitalization. Because closed-end funds have a price determined by supply and demand, their price may be more or less than the net value per share. Therefore, if a fund's shares are selling for less than the NAVPS, or if the NAVPS increases but the price declines, the fund must be closed-end. If the purchase price of a closed-end fund is less than its NAVPS, it is said to be trading at a discount. If the purchase price in the marketplace for a closed-end fund is more than the NAVPS, the fund is selling at a premium.

MUTUAL FUND ACCOUNTS

Fund shares can be purchased in one lump sum or through a continuous investment program. The three main types of accounts a mutual fund shareholder can open are

1. Open account
2. Voluntary accumulation plan
3. Contractual plan

Open Account

Regular account holders are investors who have not indicated any intention or desire to make additional periodic investments. They have an **open account** and may make additional purchases on a purely voluntary basis. Normally, under the open account, there is a required minimum amount initially and for subsequent purchase of fund shares. (The minimum may be either in dollar amounts of a specific number of shares.)

The investor must decide how the distributions (dividends and capital gains) are to be treated—whether to take them in cash or in additional shares of the fund. If he does not reinvest the capital gains distributions, the principal may be depleted. The reason is that capital gains distributions are derived from realized gains in the fund's portfolio. Such gains have increased the NAVPS and taking the distribution in cash will reduce the total value of his investment. The investment will not again increase until the assets of the fund appreciate, for which there is no guarantee.

Many mutual funds offer reinvestment plans that permit the shareholder to reinvest capital gains and dividend income distributions in additional shares. These are often automatic and the investor, in lieu of receiving cash, is simply notified of the amount of the distribution and the shares or fractions thereof purchased. Some funds limit the availability of such plans, but such limitation must be so stated in the fund's prospectus.

Funds normally permit shareholders to reinvest dividend and capital gains distributions at NAVPS (no sales charges are levied). The most common limitation imposed by some funds is to require a minimum amount in the shareholder's account before the dividend distributions may be reinvested at the net asset value.

Voluntary Accumulation Plan

As the name implies, the voluntary accumulation plan allows the investor discretion as to subsequent purchase payments into the fund. The investor need not indicate the time or amount of additional payments or the total amount he will eventually invest.

On each payment made into such a plan, a **level** sales charge is made. The investor may obtain the advantage of a reduced sales charge (breakpoints), if rights of accumulation are offered by the fund.

Some funds establish minimum initial payments, minimum dollar amounts for subsequent payments, or a minimum number of periodic investments that must be made.

Under voluntary accumulation programs, the investor may also be permitted to take advantage of a preauthorized check payment plan. The investor preauthorizes his bank to draw checks on his account to make the monthly or periodic payments for open-end investment company shares. A similar arrangement is known as the single-check payment plan wherein the purchaser elects the mode of payment (monthly, quarterly, semiannually, or annually) and one check is drawn to cover both the purchase of the fund shares and life insurance premiums under a program of plan completion.

Contractual Plan

Contractual plans are also known as periodic payment plans. **Front-end load plans** are contractual plans. The characteristics of contractual plans are a fixed total investment (e.g., $48,000), a fixed time period (e.g., twenty years), and fixed payments at regular intervals (e.g., $200 per month). This plan also has a fixed sales charge and fixed custodial fees. Dividends and capital gains distributions are automatically reinvested in fund shares under the contractual plan.

The term **contractual** may be somewhat misleading since the investor cannot be legally required to continue payments and may sell his fund shares at any time. Such plan holders may liquidate up to 90% of their shares at current market value and repurchase them at a later date without a sales charge. This feature is called the **reinstatement privilege**. Moreover, the investor could make a lump-sum purchase under a contractual plan to take advantage of the breakpoints.

Contractual plan prospectuses must fully describe the details of the plan and the underlying mutual fund. It should be noted that a contractual plan is in reality a unit investment trust. The sponsor is called the plan company and is registered under the Investment Company Act as a unit investment trust. The plan company issues redeemable securities, each of which represents an undivided interest in the underlying mutual fund. The plan company actually sells the fund shares to the investor. The company takes the payments, deducts sales charges, and remits the net payments to acquire the fund shares from the underwriter at net asset value. Thus, the underlying asset in the plan company is the mutual fund itself.

Contractual plan custodian. The functions of a custodian were discussed earlier. In contractual plans, the custodian holds the money and securities for the investors. They receive **plan certificates** as evidence of their participation, but the custodian actually holds the fund shares. The custodian is usually appointed to administer the plan and, using the investor's deposit, actually purchases the fund shares. For these services, the custodian deducts a standard processing fee of $0.50 or $1 per deposit.

The custodian, normally a commercial bank, usually acts as the registrar and transfer agent. If the contractual plan investor wishes to assign or transfer the ownership of shares, he so directs the custodian bank. If the contractual plan is trusteed, the custodian bank must have the declaration of trust that legally establishes the trust. Furthermore, the custodian must be directed as to the designated beneficiary in order to properly dispose of the investor's interest at his death.

Plan completion insurance. As the name implies, the insurance provides for a completion of the investor's program even if he does not live until the end of the investment period. The premiums charged are those for group, decreasing term life insurance (i.e., no cash values). The proceeds are not paid to the investor's beneficiary or estate. They are paid to the mutual fund's custodian, who uses them to complete the investment plan. The policy is nontransferable, and, even though the custodian is the beneficiary, the proceeds are includable in the estate of the deceased plan holder for tax purposes. The face amount of the policy is usually the fixed total investment under the accumulation plan.

Sales charges on contractual plans. A contractual plan is a plan in which an investor purchases shares in a fund by making fixed dollar payments. For example, an investor might invest $100 a month for ten years in ABC Fund. A contractual plan is also referred to as a **periodic payment plan**. The Investment Company Act of 1940 limited the maximum sales charge that can be levied on any single-payment voluntary accumulation or completed contractual plan transaction to 9% of the amount invested. The same Act permitted up to 50% of the first twelve payments to be deducted as a sales charge. If this is done, the remainder of the sales charge is deducted over the remaining life of the plan. If an investor decided to terminate the plan and redeem his shares during the first few years, a sizeable loss would be incurred. The **front-end load** penalizes such investors.

The Investment Company Amendments Act of 1970 established two methods of levying sales charges for contractual or periodic payment plans. The prospectus must clearly state which method is to be used. In both, the custodian bank must send the investor a statement of total charges within sixty days after issuance of the plan certificate and inform him that he has the right to withdraw from the plan within forty-five days after the custodian bank mails the notice of that right, and obtain the current value of the fund shares in the investor's account plus a full refund of all sales charges, custodian fees, and insurance premiums. The two methods of levying sales charges for contractual plans are

1. A deduction of up to 50% of the first twelve monthly payments in equal amounts and the deduction of the remainder of the total sales charge over the life of the plan. If this method is used, the investor must be given written notice by the investment company, underwriter, or custodian, if the investor has missed

   a. Three or more payments within fifteen months after issuance of the plan certificate, or
   b. One or more payments between the fifteenth and eighteenth month after issuance of the certificate.

   This notice will inform him of his right to surrender the certificate before the end of the eighteenth month and receive

   a. The current value of the fund shares in his account, plus
   b. A refund of all sales charges the investor has paid in excess of 15% of his total deposits thus far.

2. A deduction of up to 20% as a sales charge from annual payments, but no more than a total of 64% over the first four years (the spread load method). This 64% may be apportioned over the first four years permitting an average of 16% from each payment.

The fund's sponsor must retain reserves of the amount paid in as a sales charge sufficient to make the necessary refund of sales charges, if requested. Under both methods, the investor may get back the current value of his account plus all sales charges within forty-five days after the custodian bank mails the notice of the right. Under the first method, he may get the current value of his account plus a partial refund of his sales charges until the end of the eighteenth month. The Investment Company Act of 1940 establishes specific requirements that must be maintained to provide funds in case an investor does request such a refund. In all cases, the investor, besides a refund of sales charges, is entitled to the current value of the fund shares in the account.

Under the 20% plan, when the customer liquidates the plan after the forty-five-day period expires, he will receive only the current value of his account and will not receive a refund of the sales charge. The reason that the customer is not entitled to any refund after the forty-five-day period is that the investment company has chosen to use the spread load method. The investment company is taking out a smaller percentage of the first year's payments as commission and, therefore, is not required to give refunds on the load other than in the forty-five-day period that applies to both 50% and 20% plans.

Examples

1. Assume Mr. Adams invests $500 monthly in a contractual plan for twelve months. The fund uses a 50% load. He terminates the plan at the end of the twelfth month. The value of the shares acquired is $3,500. The proceeds of the liquidation would be

$$\$3,500 + \$2,100 = \$5,600$$

   $3,000 had been deducted as a sales charge (50% of $500 per month = $250 per month x 12 months).
   The fund must return all sales charges deducted exceeding 15% of the amount invested. Since $6,000 was invested ($500 x 12 months), the return would be the difference between the $3,000 deducted and $900 (15% of $6,000).

2. Assume that Mr. Jones had decided to terminate the plan after the first monthly investment of $500. The value of the fund shares acquired is, at the time of liquidation, $300. The proceeds of the liquidation would be $550 ($300 current value plus all the sales charges deducted—$250).

3. Assume Customer Adams had continued to invest $500 per month in the plan for 15 months. The sales charge of 50% was reduced to 6% at the end of the first year. The shares in his account, at liquidation, had a value of $3,800.

- The total amount deducted as sales charges was $3,090 ($3,000 during the first 12 months and $90 during the last 3 months).
- Mr. Adams would be entitled to a refund of $1,965 (15% of the total $7,500 investment is $1,125. $3,090 – $1,125 = $1,965).
- The proceeds of the liquidation would be $5,765 ($3,800 current value of the account plus the $1,965 refund of the sales charge).

4. Assume Ms. Barnes invests $500 a month in a contractual plan for 12 months. The fund uses a 20% load. At liquidation, the value of the shares acquired is $3,500. Since the fund conformed to the requirements of the spread load method, by deducting no more than 20% sales charge, Ms. Barnes is not entitled to any refund of the sales charge.
5. Assume that, in the preceding example, Ms. Barnes decided to liquidate after the first monthly investment of $500 when the value of the fund shares acquired was $475. The proceeds of the liquidation would be $575. This is the current value of the shares ($475) plus all charges deducted (20% of $500 = $100).

Sales charges. Contractual plans are limited as to the sales charges that can be levied. According to the NASD Rules of Fair Practice

- Mutual fund sales charges may not be "excessive," taking into account all relevant circumstances.
- The maximum sales charge may not exceed 8.5% of the offering price. In order to charge the maximum of 8.5%, the fund must offer all three of the following benefits to customers:

  - Rights of accumulation
  - Quantity discounts on single purchases
  - Dividend reinvestment at net asset value

Members offering both voluntary and contractual plans must file details of any proposed increases in sales charges with the investment companies department of the NASD before implementation. The filings must be clearly identified as an amendment to investment company sales charges.

WITHDRAWAL PLANS

Many mutual funds provide their shareholders with a systematic withdrawal plan. The plan provides for periodic payments from the fund. Most investment companies require the shareholder to have a minimum initial investment in his account (e.g., $10,000). It should be noted that if withdrawals are larger than the investment's appreciation, fund shares will have to be redeemed and there is the danger that the principal can be exhausted. Furthermore, as the total amount invested is reduced, the principal may decrease at an increasing rate. (Shareholders must give the custodian written authorization to redeem shares if necessary to meet the payment requirements under the withdrawal plan. The investor directs the custodian either to redeem shares as a supplement to dividend distributions or to redeem shares and have the dividends reinvested in additional fund shares.)

A withdrawal plan can also be established through a lump-sum investment wherein the investor could take advantage of the breakpoints. Some funds levy a sales charge on dividend reinvestments under a withdrawal plan, but there is no sales charge if the customer uses existing shares he has purchased.

A shareholder of a mutual fund has a choice of four payout options.

1. *Fixed dollar.* The shareholder wants to receive a specific amount from his fund normally on a monthly basis.
2. *Fixed percentage.* For example, 8% per year.
3. *Fixed shares.* For example, 10 shares per month.
4. *Liquidation over a fixed time.* All shares shall be liquidated during a ten-year period at the rate of 1/10 of the account value per year.

Normally, there is no difficulty in liquidating fund shares to provide payments under a withdrawal plan. As discussed earlier, however, the Investment Company Act of 1940 does give fund directors the right to postpone payment of the redemption price.

CONCURRENT PLANS

It is conceivable that an investor could be investing in a contractual or voluntary plan while receiving funds at the same time from a withdrawal plan. Investments are made at the offering price, but redemptions (if any) are at NAVPS. The investor must thus consider the advantages and disadvantages of such concurrent plans and should also consider the possibility of making additional lump-sum investments (which could qualify for reduced sales charges) to provide the invested capital for a withdrawal plan.

As would be imagined, sales literature describing a withdrawal plan must alert the investor to the possible disadvantages.

- Exhausting of invested capital.
- Regular payments received may be more or less than the actual investment return of the fund shares.

INVESTMENT COMPANY ACT OF 1940

The federal act that specifically affects investment companies is the Investment Company Act of 1940. The objective of this Act is to ensure that those investing in investment companies are fully informed and fairly treated. Some of its principal provisions are

- It defines an investment company as a corporation or trust through which investors pool their funds to obtain diversification and supervision of their investments.
- It classifies investment companies in the following categories:

  - Face-amount certificate company
  - Unit investment trust
  - Management company

  Face amount certificate companies issue face-amount certificates of an installment type. The certificate holder pays the issuer periodic payments, and the issuer promises to pay the purchaser the face value at maturity or a surrender value if the certificate is presented prior to maturity. **Unit investment trusts** issue redeemable securities, each of which represents an undivided interest in a unit of a specified security. Most contractual plans are unit investment trusts. Investment companies with no management fee and a low percentage sales charge that invest in a fixed portfolio of municipal or corporate bonds are unit investment trusts. **Management companies** manages a diversified portfolio of various types of securities according to specified investment objectives. This is the most common class of investment company. A diversified management company must have at least 75% of the value of its total assets in cash and securities. No more than 5% of its total assets may be invested in the securities of a single issuer. It may not own more than 10% of the voting stock of any one corporation.
- Investment companies using a vehicle of interstate commerce (not intrastate) must register with the SEC under the Investment Company Act of 1940. (It must be noted that registration does not in any way imply any supervision of management, practices, or policies by the government.)
- Important investment practices and policies and specific investment objectives must be detailed in the registration statement. These cannot be changed without the approval of the majority of the fund's outstanding shares. Shareholders must receive financial reports on a semiannual basis.
- The capitalization of investment companies is restricted in the following ways:

  - An investment company must have a minimum capital of $100,000 before its securities may be offered to the public.
  - Open-end companies may issue only common stock.
  - Bonds may not be issued by a closed-end company unless it has an asset coverage of 300%.
  - Preferred stock may not be issued by a closed-end company unless it has an asset coverage of 200%.
  - Closed-end companies may issue only one class of bonds or preferred stock.
  - Face-amount certificate companies must have a minimum capital of $250,000.
  - Face-amount certificate companies may not issue preferred stocks.

- Membership on the board of directors of an investment company is restricted in the following ways:

  - No more than 60% of the board may be officers or employees of the company or investment advisors to the company.
  - A majority of the board must be independent of any connection with the fund underwriter.
  - A majority of the board may not be persons who are officers or directors of one bank.
  - Directors must be elected by the holders of the outstanding fund shares.
  - Two-thirds of the directors must be chosen at the annual meeting.

- Trading with affiliated persons or underwriters is restricted.

- A fund cannot buy securities of a corporation if a fund officer, director, or investment advisor owns more than 0.5% of the securities of that company.
- The fund cannot buy securities of a corporation if the fund officers, directors, and investment advisors together own more than 5% of the securities of that company.

- The investment company's prospectus must

  - State its important investment practices and policies and specific investment objectives.
  - List all securities owned by the fund.
  - State the management fee to be charged.
  - State that the SEC has not approved or disapproved of the fund's securities nor passed on the accuracy or adequacy of the prospectus.
  - Make it clear that there is no assurance that the fund will be able to attain its investment objectives.
  - Describe the method of computing the NAVPS, offering price, and redemption price.
  - Include a statement of assets and liabilities, a statement of income and expenses, and a statement of changes in net assets.
  - Include a statement warning that the amount the investor receives on liquidation of his shares may be more or less than the original cost.

- The current public offering price must be maintained in principal transactions between dealers and customers in shares of open-end investment company shares.
- Borrowing by an open-end investment company is limited to 33% of its net assets.
- An investment company is required to make payment for shares tendered to it or its agent within seven calendar days.
- Sales charges are limited to certain maximums.

  - A sales charge cannot exceed 9% of the total amount invested on a single payment or completed contractual plan.
  - A sales charge cannot exceed 50% of the first year's payments under a contractual plan.

- All assets of an investment company are required to be deposited with a custodian, usually a national bank or trust company.
- For a person to serve as an investment advisor to a registered investment company, there must be a written contract approved by a majority vote of the holders of outstanding securities.
- The principal underwriter may offer for sale securities issued by an open-end company subject only to a written contract.

MUTUAL FUND SALES LITERATURE

Sales literature concerning mutual funds is broadly defined as any communication used to induce the purchase of investment company shares. Such statements may be oral or written. The important considerations are whether or not these statements are passed on to prospective purchasers or are designed for use in the sale of shares. A piece of sales literature shall be deemed materially misleading by reason of an implication, if such sales literature (1) includes an untrue statement of a material fact, or (2) omits to state a material fact necessary in order to make a statement made, in the light of the circumstances of its use, not misleading.

This broad definition of sales literature is quite inclusive. It includes not only advertising material that would usually be considered to be sales literature, but also the company's annual and quarterly reports. It also includes so-called tombstone advertisements. These are limited to simple statements of fact such as the name of the issuer of the security and its price, as well as where to obtain a copy of the prospectus.

Sales literature will be considered to be materially misleading if it

- Represents or implies that

  - There is any assurance that an investor will receive a stable, continuous, dependable, liberal, or specified rate of return.
  - There is any assurance that the capital invested will increase, be preserved, or be protected against any loss in value.

- Discusses appreciation possibilities, accumulation of an estate, or protection against loss in purchasing power, without including an explanation of the market risks inherently involved in the investment.

- Refers to registration or regulation of any investment company under federal or state laws without explaining that this does not involve any supervision of management or investment practices or policies.
- Implies that custodians provide protection against the depreciation of assets or maintain any supervisory function over management in managing the portfolio or paying dividends or that they provide any trusteeship protection.
- Compares an investment company security with any other investment, index, or average without pointing out the information specified in the regulations.
- Includes a chart or table that is inaccurate in factual detail or tends to create a false or misleading impression of past performance, or of an assumed investment, or appears to represent that the past performance of the investment company will be repeated in the future. Such charts and tables must give effect to the maximum sales commission currently charged.
- Makes extravagant claims concerning the ability or competency of the management.
- Discusses any continuous investment plan without making it clear that such a plan does not assure a profit nor does it protect against depreciation in declining markets.
- Fails to include a clear reference to the prospectus for information concerning the sales commission and, if in other information in sales literature, it fails to state the amount or rate of the sales commission.
- Encourages investors to switch from an investment in shares, or class of shares, of one investment company, to an investment in shares of another company, or class, without a statement that such a switch involves a sales charge on each transaction and that a prospective purchaser should weigh the costs involved against the claimed advantage of the switch.

Sales literature relating to the securities of a particular investment company must be accompanied or preceded by a prospectus. Mutual funds are sold to investors by a prospectus and cannot be sold using only a magazine article or research report.

IMPORTANT POINTS

To summarize important points relating to investment companies

- When a customer purchases an open-end investment company, he pays the ask price or public offering price next computed after receipt of the order by the dealer. If it is a load fund, the sales charge is added to the bid price to obtain the public offering price. In a no-load fund, the bid and ask price are the same.
- The term *mutual fund* refers only to open-end investment companies, not closed-end investment companies.
- If an open-end investment company has increased in value, this is referred to as appreciation; if it has decreased it is called depreciation.
- Unit investment trusts are not managed funds. They do not have a board of directors. They are issued at par and not at a discount. A board of trustees sets overall policies. Unit investment trusts have a fixed portfolio, normally corporate or municipal bonds.
- Most mutual funds offer quantity discounts. The breakpoint is defined as the point where the percentage sales charge is reduced.
- Investment companies must send out financial statements to shareholders at least semiannually. The income statement must itemize each category of income or expense if it is more than 5% of total income or total expenses. Mutual fund expenses include management fees, legal fees, accounting fees, and advertising costs. A money market fund's largest operating expense is normally the management and advisory fee.
- Quantity discounts on the purchase of investment company shares are not available to investment clubs.
- If an investor liquidates an open-end investment company (mutual fund), the redemption value is based on the next computed bid price on the day the order is received. The redemption price for an open-end investment company is equal to the net asset value minus any redemption fee.
- The payment of a cash dividend decreases a mutual fund's net asset value.

NASD RULES CONCERNING INVESTMENT COMPANIES

A number of NASD rules apply specifically to mutual funds, including

- The lowest price at which an NASD underwriter may sell shares of an open-end investment company to another NASD member is the net asset value per share.

- Open-end company shares may be purchased by the dealer from the underwriter, for the sole purpose of covering customers' orders or for his personal investment. A dealer is not allowed to make a market in open-end investment company shares by trading them with other dealers.
- Selling dividends is prohibited under NASD rules. This expression is used to describe the salesman's procedure to influence an investor to buy mutual funds just before a dividend is payable on the incorrect assumption that he will profit. Net assets decline after the dividend is paid, and, therefore, the investor does not benefit. The dividend was already considered in the price.
- The rules concerning the public offering price of an investment company are as follows:

  - No member may purchase an open-end investment company security from an underwriter at a discount from the public offering price unless the underwriter is also a member. No member underwriter can sell such securities at a price other than the public offering price unless

    - The buying broker or dealer is also a member.
    - A sales agreement is in effect between the parties at the time of the sale.
    - The required contents of the sales agreement are specified in the remaining portions of this rule.

  - No underwriter member shall participate in the offering or sale of any such security if the public offering price includes a gross selling commission or load that is unfair if all relevant circumstances are considered.
  - The net asset value on which the public offering price is based is the minimum price at which a member may purchase any such security from the issuer. (The rule then specifies the time of calculation of the net asset value to be used as the basis of the public offering price.)

    - No member shall withhold placing customers orders for any such security so as to profit himself as a result of such withholding.
    - A member may purchase securities of an open-end investment company only to cover purchase orders already received or for investment.

  - No member who is an underwriter shall accept a conditional order for the securities of an open-end investment company on any basis other than at a specified definite price.

- NASD rules cover special deals relating to the sale of investment company shares. These rules hold that giving or accepting anything of material value in addition to the discounts or concessions set forth in the prospectus is conduct inconsistent with just and equitable principles of trade. This applies to a principal underwriter or persons associated with or affiliated with him, members, registered representatives, or associated persons. Examples of items which constitute *anything of material value* are

  - Gifts of more than $100 per person per year. Therefore, gifts of $100 or less per person per year are not considered of material value and may be given.
  - Gifts of management company stock or other security or making such security available on a preferential basis.
  - Loans to a noncontrolled dealer or his associate.
  - Discounts from the offering price more than those set forth in the prospectus and regular selling group arrangement.
  - Wholesale overrides granted to a dealer on its own retail sales unless they are described in the prospectus.
  - Gifts or payments of any kind by a wholesale representative to a dealer firm employee except for

    - Occasional dinner or tickets.
    - Reception or cocktail party given for a group with a bona fide business meeting.
    - Gift or reminder advertising amounting to no more than $100 per person per year.

- Compensation for sales of investment company shares must be reasonably related to the dealer's discount described in the latest prospectus and/or the agreement of the selling group. An RR may receive continuing commissions at retirement provided a bona fide contract exists between him and his employer.
- Members must forward promptly to the underwriter (or custodian) any funds received from customers in payment of shares. Payment must be made within five business days after the date of the transaction;

otherwise, the underwriter must notify the dealer and the NASD office in the district covering the dealer's office. Such transactions are subject to Federal Reserve Board Regulation T.

- In order to avoid the increasing abuse of the withdrawal plan, the NASD prohibits members from suggesting or encouraging the use of the partial withdrawal and reinstatement privilege. This privilege is usually included in single-payment and periodic unit investment trusts. It permits withdrawals of up to 90% of the current value of the planholder's account in cash and return of the money later without a sales charge. Its purpose is to provide emergency funds for the planholder, but it was found that certain planholders were making withdrawals for short-term trades in speculative securities, hence the rule.

- No member is permitted to favor or disfavor the distribution of investment company shares on the basis of brokerage commissions received or expected by the member from any source, including such investment company. However, the **reciprocal brokerage rule** permits members who sell investment company shares to execute portfolio transactions for that investment company as long as such orders are not obtained on the basis of their sales of the investment company shares.

- On open-end investment company shares, the ex-dividend date is the date designated by the issuer or principal underwriter and is not automatically four business days before the record date as it is with corporate shares.

- Assume a mutual fund is quoted $11 bid $11.96 offering price. An NASD member must sell the funds to a public customer or a non-NASD member at $11.96, which is the public offering price or ask price. An NASD member can sell the fund to another NASD member at $11, the bid price.

- The sale of investment company shares in dollar amounts just below the point at which the sales charge is reduced on quantity transactions so as to obtain the higher sales charges applicable on sales below the breakpoint is contrary to just and equitable principles of trade. Furthermore, breakpoints should be fully explained to customers contemplating large purchases of the fund.

- An RR working for a firm that does not distribute a specific fund may, on the customer's instructions, sell the fund shares for the customer to the fund or underwriter at the net asset value and charge the customer a commission.

- Advertisements and sales literature concerning registered investment companies (including mutual funds, variable contracts, and unit investment trusts) must be filed with the NASD's advertising department within ten days of first use or publication, by any member who has prepared or distributed such material in connection with the offer or sale of securities issued by companies for which such member is a principal underwriter. Filing in advance of use is optional.

17 INDIVIDUAL RETIREMENT PLANS

INTRODUCTION

In this chapter we will discuss variable annuity contracts, variable life contracts, and other types of retirement plans. The two main types of annuities are fixed annuities and variable annuities.

FIXED ANNUITIES

In a **fixed-annuity contract**, the insurance company guarantees to pay the annuitant a fixed sum of money for the life of the annuitant. For example, a fixed annuity may pay an annuitant $500 a month for the life of the annuitant. The term *annuity* refers to a stream of payments. For a fixed annuity, the payment is guaranteed by the insurance company. Therefore, a fixed annuity is an insurance product and not a security. With a fixed annuity, the income remains level and the annuitant is exposed to the purchasing power risk. The purchasing power risk is the risk that the purchasing power of the dollar will decrease in the future. Premiums by annuitants into a fixed annuity are invested in the general account after expenses are deducted.

In a fixed annuity, the investment risk is assumed by the insurance company, which provides a guaranteed rate of return, income, interest, and payments to a named beneficiary, if the annuitant dies before annuity payments begin.

To summarize the main points concerning a fixed-annuity contract

- During the distribution period, an annuitant receives a fixed amount monthly for life.
- The insurance company guarantees the rate of return, income, interest, and payments to a named beneficiary, if the annuitant dies before the distribution period begins.
- A fixed annuity is not a security, since the contract is guaranteed by an insurance company. A fixed annuity is an annuity in which the payments are fixed.
- The annuitant takes the purchasing power risk (inflation risk).

VARIABLE ANNUITIES

Variable annuities are securities that attract investors seeking retirement income with inflation protection. However, the investment risk in a variable annuity belongs to the annuitant. Assume Mr. Jones, a single person, is forty-five years old and wants to provide for his retirement needs. He invests in a non-tax-qualified variable annuity. The term *non-tax-qualified* means that Mr. Jones will be investing after-tax dollars. There is no restriction on the amount Mr. Jones can invest in the variable annuity.

Assume Mr. Jones invests $100 a month in the variable annuity for twenty years. The twenty years he invests in the variable annuity is the **accumulation period**. The money purchases accumulation units in the variable annuity. The annuitant owns accumulation units in the separate account of securities. The earnings (interest, dividends, and capital gains) accrue on a tax-deferred basis in the separate account. No taxes are paid during the accumulation period. Over twenty years Mr. Jones will have invested $24,000 in the variable annuity. At the end of the accumulation period, Mr. Jones can take a lump-sum distribution or annuitize the principal. If Mr. Jones surrenders the variable annuity for a lump sum, he will realize ordinary income in excess of his basis (cost). Assume the value of the variable annuity has grown to $80,000. Mr. Jones will realize ordinary income of $56,000.

$$\begin{array}{ll} \$80,000 & \text{Surrender value (sales proceeds)} \\ -\underline{24,000} & \text{Amount invested (cost)} \\ \$56,000 & \text{Ordinary income} \end{array}$$

Assume Mr. Jones takes a life annuity instead of surrendering the annuity for a lump sum. Mr. Jones gives up the rights to the principal of $80,000 and agrees to receive a monthly payment, which will vary according to the performance of the separate account. The payments Mr. Jones receives monthly will be partly taxable and partly a return of capital. The portion that is taxable represents the earnings. The portion of the monthly payment representing a return of capital is not taxable. Variable annuities invest in common stocks and equity mutual funds and are not susceptible to the purchasing power risk that affects fixed annuities. For a person who wants to receive income for life at retirement with inflation protection, a variable annuity is an excellent choice.

A particular variable annuity may have surrender charges for the first five years on a declining scale. Withdrawals prior to age 59½ may result in a 10% tax penalty to the annuitant. The penalty is assessed only on the earnings portion and not on the annuitant's return of capital. Assume Mr. Jones invested $12,000 in his variable annuity, which was cashed in for $40,000 after ten years, when Mr. Jones is fifty-five years old. He is in the 28% tax bracket. His total tax is $10,640.

$$
\begin{array}{lll}
\$28,000 \times 28\% \ = & \$\ 7,840 & \text{Regular tax} \\
\$28,000 \times 10\% \ = & \$\ \underline{2,800} & \text{Penalty tax} \\
& \$10,640 & \text{Total tax}
\end{array}
$$

If Mr. Jones decided to take a lifetime income from the variable annuity, no penalty tax would be assessed even though he is fifty-five years old. He would be able to choose from certain annuity payment options, such as

- *Life annuity.* All payments would cease on the death of Mr. Jones. This payment option would give Mr. Jones the highest cash flow.
- *Joint and last survivor.* If Mr. Jones were married, he might choose this payment option. On the death of Mr. Jones, payments would continue for the life of his spouse.
- *Life annuity—period certain.* Assume Mr. Jones chooses a life annuity—twenty-year period certain. If Mr. Jones dies after eight years, his beneficiary will receive payments for the remaining twelve years or may elect a single payment.

When an annuitant decides to annuitize a variable annuity, accumulation units are converted into a fixed number of annuity units. The annuitant receives a monthly payment, which is the number of annuity units multiplied by the value of each annuity unit. The number of annuity units remains fixed during the annuity or distribution period. However, the value of the annuity unit varies with the investment performance of the separate account. Some insurance companies offer a combination fixed and variable annuity.

A variable annuity is considered to be a security under federal securities laws. The National Association of Securities Dealers (NASD) requires that all persons selling variable annuities have a securities license. A variable annuity must be registered under the Securities Act of 1933 and the Investment Company Act of 1940, since it is both a security and an investment company.

Variable annuitants have the right to vote on any proposed change in investment policy and for the election of the portfolio managers. They must be sent proxies allowing them to vote without attending the annual meeting.

Owners of variable annuity contracts normally have

- The right to vote on proposed changes in investment policy
- The right to vote on the choice of the portfolio manager
- Reduced sales charges on large purchases (sales charge breakpoints)

Investment return in the separate account of a variable annuity consists of dividend and interest income, realized capital gains and losses, and unrealized appreciation or depreciation. The earnings accrue on a tax-deferred basis during the accumulation period.

Since variable annuities are subject to the Securities Act of 1933, their sale must be preceded or accompanied by a copy of the variable annuity's current prospectus. The prospectus contains the investment objectives and investment policies of the separate account and other information of interest to the ordinary investor.

Different methods of purchase apply to variable annuities. There are generally three methods from which to choose, depending on when the annuity payments to the annuitant are to begin. Variable annuities can be purchased by a lump-sum payment or by periodic payments. For example, a person could invest a lump sum now and receive payments at a later date. Or he could invest a lump sum now and receive payments immediately. Another choice would be to invest periodically and receive payments at a later date. If payments are to be received at a later date, it is a **deferred annuity**. If the annuitant receives payments immediately after investing a lump sum, it is an **immediate annuity**.

Charges for services such as premium billing and collecting, recordkeeping, and communications are administrative fees for a variable annuity and are described in the prospectus. For example, a variable annuity would normally have a charge for investment management expenses. Variable-annuity contracts levy administrative fees, which are charges for premium billing and collecting, recordkeeping, and communications.

As with the purchasers of mutual funds, variable-annuity contract holders may get reduced sales charges if their investments exceed the specified breakpoints. The amount of money invested in the variable annuity may permit the investor to obtain a reduced sales charge. Many variable annuities also offer purchasers rights of accumulation.

Mutual funds are valued on a per-share basis; variable annuities have unit values. During the accumulation period, the value of a variable annuity is expressed as an accumulation unit, while valuation during the payout period is expressed as an annuity unit. The value of the units is determined by the value of the investment portfolio in the separate account, calculated once a day at the close of business of the securities markets.

The **accumulation unit** is an accounting measure that determines the contract owner's interest in the separate account. As stated in the prospectus, the units are revalued periodically to reflect changes in the market value of the portfolio's common stock and other investments. The value will change according to changes in market values, realized capital gains and losses, and investment income. Accumulation units are also adjusted daily for the charges and fees, such as mortality and expense. The net value divided by the number of units outstanding yields the value of one accumulation unit. The value of the contract holder's account is determined by multiplying the value of one unit by the number of units the contract holder owns.

The **annuity unit** is an accounting measure that determines the amount of each payment to the annuitant during the payout or annuity period. It is essential to realize that the number of units credited to the annuitant remains fixed. It is the changing value of each unit that results in a variable payout during the annuity period.

If an annuitant chooses to annuitize the contract, immediately before the payout period begins the accumulation units are "converted" into annuity units. This period is known as the **annuity commencement date**.

The number of annuity units the annuitant will receive depends on the

- Value of the accumulation units
- Age and sex of the annuitant
- Type of settlement option selected

If the actual earnings exceed the assumed interest rate (AIR), the value of the annuity unit will increase. The amount of the annuity payment received by the annuitant is found by multiplying the number of annuity units by the value of each unit for that valuation period. For example, if an annuitant had 150 units and each was valued at $8, he would receive a payment of $1,200 for that period. The more risk the annuitant assumes, the higher the payout received for a given sum of money. For example, a **life annuity** will pay an annuitant a larger amount each month than a **joint and last survivor annuity**.

- *Life annuity*. All payments cease at the death of the annuitant. Normally, this option will generate the highest payout because the insurance company has the least amount of risk and the annuitant assumes the greatest risk.
- *Joint and last survivor life annuity*. Payments are made to two annuitants (e.g., husband and wife) as long as either lives. If the husband dies, payments will continue for the life of the wife.
- *Life annuity—period certain*. The annuitant will receive a periodic income for as long as he lives, but if he dies before a specified period (usually ten, fifteen, or twenty years) payment continues to a named beneficiary for the balance of that specified period. The beneficiary also has the right to elect a single payment.
- *Unit refund life annuity*. The annuitant will receive an income for life, but if he dies before receiving the benefits based on the number of annuity units, a named beneficiary receives the value of the remaining units either in a lump sum or in installments.

ADDITIONAL CONCEPTS–VARIABLE ANNUITIES

- During the accumulation period of a variable annuity, the separate account earns interest and dividends and realizes capital gains. However, no taxes are due from the annuitant during the accumulation period. Taxes are paid by the annuitant during the annuity or distribution period.
- The separate account of a variable annuity contains investments that must be consistent with the variable annuity's investment policy described in the prospectus. Variable annuities normally have objectives of growth or growth and income (total return).
- A variable annuity invests mainly in equities and neither the principal nor the payout is guaranteed. Therefore, a variable annuity is an annuity in which the payments vary.

- The surrender value of a deferred variable-annuity contract is equal to the number of accumulation units multiplied by the value of an accumulation unit next computed after receipt of the request for surrender by the issuer.
- Variable annuities offer benefits such as deferral of taxes during the accumulation period, reinstatement provisions, and various settlement options.
- When the value of an accumulation unit in a variable-annuity contract is calculated, components of the separate account include realized and unrealized capital gains and losses and investment income.
- Securities industry regulations require that an advertisement containing variable-annuity total return performance show the disclosure of sales charges, an offer to provide a prospectus, and year-end average annual return.
- Assume a variable-annuity contract holder begins receiving funds during the payout period. The initial payout was $300 based on a 4% net investment rate. In the second month, the contract holder received $325 based on a net investment rate of 10% earned by the separate account. Assume the separate account realizes a net investment rate of 7% during the third month. In this example, the contract holder will receive a payout of less than $325 but greater than $300.
- Some insurance companies offer combination fixed and variable annuities which offer a guaranteed fixed payment with a variable payment from a variable annuity.
- Variable annuities levy charges for premium billing and collecting, recordkeeping, and communications with annuitants. These charges are classified as administrative fees or expenses.

VARIABLE LIFE INSURANCE

Variable life insurance is an innovation in life insurance and allows policyholders an opportunity to earn capital gains on their insurance investment and still maintain death benefit coverage. Therefore, variable life insurance can be defined as a form of life insurance in which the amount of the death benefit and the cash surrender value (benefit) can vary. The variations will occur as a result of the investment performance of the assets in the separate account. The assets in the separate account in a variable life insurance contract are primarily invested in common stock or equity mutual funds. However, a variable life insurance contract guarantees a minimum death benefit regardless of the investment experience of the separate account.

Individuals may consider variable life insurance contracts attractive because the minimum death benefit is guaranteed and the policy offers the opportunity for an increase in the actual amount of the death benefit payable. The increase in the death benefit will depend on the results obtained by the separate account. The opportunity for an increase in the death benefit above its guaranteed amount is a potential hedge against inflation for the purchaser of a variable life insurance contract.

However, the cash surrender value of a variable life insurance contract is not guaranteed. There is no minimum cash surrender value. The cash surrender value will fluctuate according to the investment performance of the separate account. Most other standard policy provisions that apply to whole life insurance also apply to variable life insurance, including reinstatement provisions and changes in ownership and beneficiaries.

Variable life insurance contracts are considered securities and are subject to federal and state regulations. Variable life insurance contracts must be sold by use of a prospectus as required by the Securities Act of 1933. They are also considered investment companies and are subject to the Investment Company Act of 1940. These contracts are also subject to antifraud provisions of the Securities Exchange Act of 1934.

To summarize the main points relating to variable life insurance

- The cash value of a variable life contract will be affected by fluctuating market values of the separate account and any loans taken by policyholders.
- Variable life insurance policies are referred to as *variable* because the death benefit and surrender value will vary based on the investment experience of the separate account. The variable life insurance policyholder bears the investment risk related to the contract. Prospective purchasers of variable life insurance contracts must be provided with a prospectus. However, the cash value of a variable life insurance policy is *not* guaranteed.
- Variable life insurance contracts allow policyholders to select different investment options. They provide a death benefit and cash value, which can fluctuate based on investment performance. Variable life insurance contracts have expense charges for administrative expenses, sales expenses, and expenses charged for mortality premium taxes.

- The two main types of variable contracts issued by insurance companies are variable annuities and variable life insurance. The primary reason a person would invest in a variable annuity is to provide for retirement. The primary reason a person would purchase a variable life insurance contract is for life insurance protection with investment choices.

EMPLOYEE RETIREMENT INCOME SECURITY ACT OF 1974

The Employee Retirement Income Security Act of 1974 (ERISA) is a major piece of legislation that governs the operation of private pension plans. ERISA eased pension eligibility rules for many participants. It also set up the **Pension Benefit Guaranty Corporation** and established rules and regulations relating to the management of private pension funds. Government pension plans are exempt from ERISA provisions.

ERISA was intended to protect employees whose pensions are covered under the Act from imprudent investment decisions of their employers or trustees of the plan. ERISA requires fiduciaries (managers of the plan) to act with prudence when managing pension plan assets. The fiduciary must act in the best interests of the participants of the plan and not in their own best interests.

Fiduciaries who engage in prohibited transactions are subject to penalty excise taxes. The Act specifically defines prohibited transactions. The purpose of prohibiting certain transactions is to prevent a fiduciary from gaining personal benefits at the expense of the plan participants. Non-tax-qualified deferred compensation plans do not have to comply with ERISA provisions. These plans can be discriminatory, and Internal Revenue Service (IRS) approval is not required. Participants in nonqualified deferred compensation plans are generally creditors of the employer.

KEOGH PLANS

Keogh plans allow self-employed individuals to establish a retirement plan on a tax-deductible basis. Keogh plans are also referred to as "HR 10" plans. Keogh plans allow tax-deductible contributions, which grow on a tax-deferred basis.

In addition to tax-deductible Keogh contributions, the Act also permits voluntary contributions (not tax-deductible) by an owner-employee of up to 10% of earned income. Voluntary contributions are available to owner-employees only if they are also available to their employees. Such contributions are non-tax-deductible. However, the earnings on the contributions will accumulate on a tax-deferred basis.

INDIVIDUAL RETIREMENT ACCOUNTS

Beginning January 1, 1998, taxpayers were able to have a traditional or regular individual retirement account (IRA) or a Roth IRA. In a regular IRA, taxpayers who have earned income can deposit money into an IRA. A nonworking spouse can also deposit money into an IRA. Whether the contributions are tax-deductible depends on whether the person is a participant in an employer-sponsored retirement plan and his or her adjusted gross income. The dividends, interest, and capital gains in a regular IRA are tax-deferred until the money is withdrawn. If the money is withdrawn prior to age 59½, the amount withdrawn is subject to a 10% penalty tax and the entire amount withdrawn is taxed as ordinary income. The penalty tax does not apply in certain instances, such as permanent disability, distributions over your life expectancy, distributions used to purchase a first home, or for college expenses.

Distributions from a regular IRA must begin by April 1 following the year in which the person turned 70½. The distributions must be taken according to the person's life expectancy. Insufficient distributions are subject to a 50% penalty tax.

Taxpayers with earned income can open a **Roth IRA,** provided their income is below certain amounts. Contributions to a Roth IRA are not tax-deductible for any taxpayers. If a person maintains a Roth IRA for at least five years and has reached age 59½, withdrawals from a Roth IRA are not taxed. Withdrawals are also tax-free if the distribution is used for a first-time home purchase. Therefore, the earnings on a Roth IRA will not be taxed to the taxpayer if the account has been opened five years and the taxpayer has reached age 59½, or the money is used for a first-time home purchase.

Certain taxpayers can transfer funds from a traditional IRA into a Roth IRA. However, a person must pay taxes on the before-tax contributions in the traditional IRA when transferred to a Roth IRA.

To summarize the main points concerning a traditional IRA and a Roth IRA

- In a traditional IRA, earnings and capital gains grow on a tax-deferred basis. However, taxes are paid at ordinary income tax rates on the earnings in a traditional IRA. In a Roth IRA, there are no taxes on earnings if the account has been open five years and the person has reached age 59½ or the distribution is used to purchase a first home.

- Contributions to a traditional IRA may be tax deductible if the person is not in an employer-sponsored retirement plan or has income below a certain level. Contributions to a Roth IRA are not tax-deductible.
- Withdrawals prior to age 59½ are subject to a 10% penalty tax in a traditional IRA, unless an exemption applies, such as permanent disability, annuity distribution, first home purchase, or college expenses. No penalties apply to a distribution from a Roth IRA, if the account has been open five years and the taxpayer is at least 59½ or the withdrawal is used to purchase a first home.
- Distributions from a traditional IRA must begin by April 1 following the year the person reaches age 70½. With a Roth IRA, there is no requirement to begin distributions by age 70½.
- Funds can be transferred from a traditional IRA to a **Roth IRA**, but taxes will apply to before-tax contributions and earnings.
- If a taxpayer does not qualify to deduct his IRA contribution because of his participation in a retirement plan and his income level, he can still deposit money into an IRA on an after-tax deferred basis. Taxes are paid on the earnings when they are withdrawn from the IRA.
- IRA funds can be invested in gold or silver coins issued by the US government. However, IRA funds cannot be invested in other collectibles, such as diamonds, stamps, paintings, or rugs. Any amount invested in these collectibles will be treated as a distribution from the plan for tax purposes.
- Contributions to an IRA are entirely vested immediately and must be in cash.
- Contributions to an IRA may be made up to the due date of the taxpayer's federal tax return, which is normally April 15.
- The contribution to an IRA can exceed stated limits in the case of a rollover. A rollover occurs when money is transferred from a qualified plan (Keogh, pension, or profit-sharing) into an IRA. A rollover is tax-free if it is placed into an IRA rollover account within sixty days of the distribution. A partial rollover is permitted. The amount not rolled over is taxed as ordinary income.
- The law also allows a person to transfer from one kind of IRA investment to another, tax-free, once a year. If an individual wanted to transfer from an annuity to a savings account, he could do so without tax penalties. If a transfer is made more than once a year, however, the individual will be subject to income taxes on the amount withdrawn, and possibly a 10% penalty tax.

SIMPLIFIED EMPLOYEE PENSION PLAN

The Simplified Employment Pension Plan (SEP) allows employers to annually contribute certain amounts of an employee's income to the employee's IRA. The employer's contribution is deductible under federal tax law. Thus, an employer benefits from an SEP in much the same manner as a Keogh; however, there is usually less work involved in establishing and administering the plan. The employee must include the employer's contribution in his or her gross income. However, the employee can take a deduction for the amount of the employer contribution.

To enjoy the tax-favored status of the SEP, all eligible employees must participate. The plan, as well as the funds in it, belongs to the employee and is vested immediately. Other rules and regulations are similar to those of the IRA.

PENSION AND PROFIT-SHARING PLANS

The two main types of retirement plans offered by employers are defined contribution plans and defined benefit plans. In a **defined contribution plan**, each participant has an individual account, and benefits are paid to that participant based solely on the amount contributed to his or her individual account. Defined contribution plans include

- Profit sharing
- Money purchase pension
- Target benefit
- Stock bonus

A **defined benefit plan** is a pension plan that provides for benefits that are definite and predeterminable. The employer calculates the benefit to be received by the employee and then determines the contributions necessary to provide that benefit level. Defined benefit plans favor high-salaried employees who are near retirement age. Benefits received from pension plans are taxable to the employee to the extent that they are not a return of capital.

Contributions by an employer are tax-deductible to a pension plan. Assets in the plan accumulate on a tax-free basis. Benefits are taxable when received by the employee or beneficiary. Benefits are normally payable to the employee when he retires, dies, or becomes disabled. In certain cases, benefits may be paid to a person when he terminates employment.

A pension plan requires regular contributions by a company regardless of profits. Pension plans must meet IRS regulations concerning benefits, eligibility, and reporting. Pension plans are costly to administer and should be considered only if a company has a stable earnings record. All tax-qualified retirement plans have provisions detailing which employees may participate in the plan, called **eligibility requirement provisions**.

A profit-sharing plan is a qualified retirement plan that offers the employer greater flexibility. A company makes contributions out of corporate profits and allocates the funds to employees participating in the plan according to a formula. The employee, at retirement, receives the balance in his account. A profit-sharing plan is a type of defined contribution plan. If a company loses money in a particular year, it may contribute nothing to the profit-sharing plan for that year.

401(k) PLANS

A **401(k) plan** is a voluntary retirement program sponsored by an employer. It is often referred to as a capital accumulation plan. One reason for their popularity is that the employer does not have the usual pension plan obligation of guaranteeing benefits. They are also popular because they permit considerable growth of assets and allow employees to make tax-deferred contributions into their own retirement programs.

The employee's contribution is made by deferring part of his salary into the plan. The employer may also make contributions. Under a 401(k) plan, employees actually reduce their own salaries. This is why the plan is sometimes referred to as a salary reduction plan.

The basics of a 401(k) plan are as follows:

- A certain amount of pretax money may be deferred to the plan by an employee.
- An additional sum may be contributed by the employer for the employee without the employee's being taxed on the contribution.
- Until distributed, contributions are placed in a trust account for the employee and grow on a tax-deferred basis.

403(b) PLANS

The Internal Revenue Code allows employees of certain nonprofit organizations (hospitals, charities, state and local systems, religious organizations) to invest in tax-sheltered annuities. Therefore, 403(b) plans are retirement plans for employees of nonprofit organizations.

The following employees are eligible to participate in a tax-sheltered annuity under Section 403(b) of the Internal Revenue Code:

- Employees of local school systems, such as a teacher, librarian, or custodian
- Employees of state colleges or universities, such as a professor
- Employees of nonprofit hospitals or charities

However, full-time students who attend state colleges or universities are not eligible to participate in a 403(b) plan, since they are not employees.

Trustees who manage 403(b) plans can invest funds received from participants in mutual funds or fixed or variable annuities. However, limited partnerships are not an eligible investment for a 403(b) tax-deferred annuity.

The maximum contributions that can be deposited into tax-favored accounts are as follows:

	2002 Maximum contribution		2006 Maximum contribution	
Type of account	*Under 50*	*Over 50*	*Under 50*	*Over 50*
Keogh plan	$40,000	$40,000	$40,000	$40,000
Traditional IRA	$3,000	$3,500	$4,000	$5,000
Spousal IRA	$3,000	$3,500	$4,000	$5,000
Roth IRA	$3,000	$3,500	$4,000	$5,000
Education IRA	$2,000 per child	$2,000 per child	$2,000 per child	$2,000 per child
401(k) or 403(b)	$11,000	$12,000	$15,000	$20,000

18 FEDERAL AND STATE REGULATIONS

The public outcry arising from the great decline in stock prices between 1929 and 1933 motivated the passage of the major federal laws regulating the securities industry. During the late 1920s, many investors were speculating in the stock market. About 55% of all personal savings were used to purchase securities, and the public was severely affected when the Dow Jones Industrial Average (DJIA) fell 89% between 1929 and 1933.

During this period, security price manipulation was common, and adequate information concerning securities usually was not available. Regulation was badly needed in the industry. The basic federal acts were passed between 1933 and 1940. However, long before the enactment of legislation by the federal government, individual states had laws on their books concerning the sale of securities. In 1911, the State of Kansas was the first state to pass securities legislation. Today, almost all states have securities divisions regulating the sale of securities within their borders. This chapter will discuss the following securities industry acts and rules:

- Securities Act of 1933
- Securities Exchange Act of 1934
- Securities and Exchange Commission (SEC) rules concerning market manipulation and financial responsibility
- Securities Investor Protection Act of 1970
- Trust Indenture Act of 1939
- Securities Act Amendments of 1975
- State securities laws

SECURITIES ACT OF 1933

The Securities Act of 1933 is sometimes referred to as the **Truth in Securities Act**. Its basic purpose is to make certain that new securities offered to the public are fully and clearly described in the registration statement and the prospectus. Under this law, the SEC attempts to make certain that there is a full disclosure of all significant material facts concerning a security to be offered to the public on an interstate basis. (See Exhibit 18.1.)

Exhibit 18.1: Securities Act of 1933

Does

1. Cover new issues
2. Call for full and fair disclosure
3. Require in a prospectus
   a. The date of the prospectus
   b. A statement concerning any possible stabilizing transactions
   c. A statement that the SEC neither approves nor disapproves of the issue

Does not

1. Regulate trading on national securities exchanges
2. Require copies of underwriting contracts and opinions of counsel to be included in a prospectus
3. Authorize the SEC to determine which securities may be offered to the public
4. Permit telling prospective buyers that SEC approves or endorses the issue or guarantee the prospectus is accurate

Purposes

1. To require registration of securities with the SEC before distribution
2. To require disclosure in a prospectus of information that is important to a prospective investor's assessment of the security offered
3. To prohibit fraud in the sale of securities by any means of communication in interstate commerce

It should be noted that the SEC does not approve securities registered with it, does not pass on the investment merit of any security, and never guarantees the accuracy of statements in the registration statement and prospectus. The SEC merely attempts to make certain that all pertinent information is fully disclosed in the registration statement and prospectus by requiring that

- The issuer file a registration statement with the SEC before securities may be offered or sold in interstate commerce
- A prospectus that meets the requirements of the Act be provided to prospective buyers
- Penalties (civil, criminal, or administrative) be imposed for violations of this Act

REGISTRATION OF SECURITIES

A security may be registered with the SEC by filing a registration statement in triplicate. The registration statement must be signed by the principal executive officer, the principal financial officer, and a majority of the board of directors.

All of the signers are subject to criminal and civil penalties for willful omissions and misstatements of material facts. The information required in a registration statement may be summarized as follows:

- Purpose of issue
- Public offering price
- Disclosure of any option agreement
- Underwriter's commissions or discounts
- Promotion expenses
- Net proceeds of the issuer to the company
- Balance sheet
- Earnings statements for the last three years
- Names and addresses of officers, directors, underwriters, and stockholders owning more than 10% of the outstanding stock
- Copy of underwriting agreement
- Legal opinions on the issue
- Copies of articles of incorporation

PROSPECTUS

A registration statement is normally a very long and complex document for an investor to read. The Act requires the preparation of a shorter document called the **prospectus**. The prospectus summarizes the information contained in the registration statement. It must contain all the material facts in the registration statement, but in shorter form. The prospectus must be given to every person solicited and to every person who purchases or indicates an interest in purchasing securities. The purpose of a prospectus is to provide the investor with adequate information to analyze the investment merits of the security. Even if an investor does not intend to read a prospectus, it still must be given to him. It is unlawful for a company to sell securities prior to the effective date of the registration statement.

RED HERRING PROSPECTUS

A **red-herring prospectus** is a preliminary prospectus. It is given to prospective purchasers during the twenty-day waiting period between the filing date of the registration statement and the effective date.

A red herring is used to acquaint investors with essential facts concerning the new issue. It is also used to solicit indications of buyer interest. However, it *cannot* be used:

- As a confirmation of sale
- In place of a registration statement
- To declare the final public offering price

The red-herring prospectus does not contain information such as the final public offering price, the underwriter's spread, or the date of the due diligence meeting. The term *red herring* was given to the prospectus because the front page contains a statement printed in red ink, which states:

A Registration Statement relating to these securities has been filed with the Securities and Exchange Commission but has not yet become effective. Information contained herein is subject to completion or amendment. These securities may not be sold nor may offers to buy be accepted prior to the time the Registration Statement becomes effective. The Prospectus shall not constitute an offer to sell or the solicitation of an offer to buy nor shall there be any sale of these securities in any State in which such offer, solicitation or sale would be unlawful prior to registration or qualification under the securities laws of any such State.

A registered representative (RR) is not allowed to mark on a preliminary prospectus under any circumstances. He cannot write short summaries or reviews on the preliminary prospectus. The preliminary prospectus must be given to customers without any alterations to allow prospective customers the opportunity to make an informed investment decision on their own.

Unless an exemption applies, it is unlawful for any person to use the mails or any other instrument of interstate commerce to offer a security for sale unless a registration statement has been filed with the SEC. It is unlawful under the Act to sell a security unless the registration becomes effective. Therefore, a security can be offered for sale only after a registration statement has been filed and a security can be sold only after a registration statement is effective.

A security can be offered for sale during the period between the filing and effective date, but a written offer is forbidden unless it meets the requirements of a statutory prospectus as defined under Section 10 of the Act. A preliminary or red-herring prospectus may be used to offer the security because a preliminary prospectus contains all of the material facts in a registration statement and, therefore, meets the requirement of Section 10 of the Act. If the firm uses written offers, such as advertisements in newspapers, this would be considered an illegal offer to sell. The written offers would not meet the requirements of a statutory prospectus and, therefore, would not be permitted under this Act.

However, the Act does permit the use of tombstone advertising between the filing and effective date. The written material that may be used during this period to offer a security for sale is limited to a preliminary prospectus and a tombstone ad. Such a preliminary prospectus or tombstone ad cannot be accompanied by the firm's research report. A firm's research report would not meet the requirements of Section 10 of the Act.

Therefore, to summarize, during the period between the filing date and the effective date of the registration statement

- No sales of the security may take place.
- Offers of the security may take place, but a written offer may be made only through a preliminary or red herring prospectus (tombstone advertising is permitted during this period).
- Brokers may answer unsolicited requests for information by sending out a preliminary prospectus.
- Brokers cannot send out the company's research report or any report projecting the company's future sales and earnings.
- Subscription payments may not be accepted even if the money is held in escrow until the registration statement is effective.

EFFECTIVE DATE OF REGISTRATION STATEMENT

On the date a registration statement becomes effective, securities may be sold to the public by the investment bankers. The effective date of a registration statement is the twentieth day after filing the registration statement with the SEC, provided the registration statement is in proper form. The twenty-day waiting period before the registration becomes effective is called the **cooling-off period**. The purpose of the cooling-off period is to allow the public sufficient time to study the information in the registration statement and prospectus. The SEC may accelerate the effective date of a registration statement if it finds that adequate information with respect to the issuer is available and it is in the public interest do to so.

A copy of the final prospectus must be delivered to each purchaser with a confirmation or with the delivery of the security, whichever occurs first. Additional sales literature may be used by the firm as long as the sales literature is preceded or accompanied by a prospectus. Funds may be accepted by the broker/dealer from customers at this time.

A dealer or underwriter acting as a principal must deliver a prospectus to a purchaser during the forty-day period after the effective date of the registration statement or the beginning of the public offering of the securities, whichever is the later date. If the issuer is distributing securities for the first time, a prospectus must be delivered by the dealer or underwriter when acting as a principal during the ninety-day period following the offering date.

STOP ORDERS

The SEC will issue a stop order when they feel that a registration statement is not complete or is inadequate in a material way. The stop order may be issued prior to the effective date, requiring an amendment to the registration statement. When the amendment has been properly filed, the SEC will state this to the issuer. The registration statement will be effective on the effective registration date or the date the amendment has been properly filed, whichever date is later.

The SEC may issue a stop order to suspend the effectiveness of the registration even after the effective registration date. The SEC would take this action if is feels the registration statement includes any untrue statement of a material fact. The SEC may subpoena the issuing corporation's records to determine whether a stop order is necessary.

SECURITIES EXCHANGE ACT OF 1934

The Securities Act of 1933 was passed to make the sale of new issues to the public in interstate commerce subject to federal regulation. The Securities Exchange Act of 1934 extended this federal regulation to all phases of trading in existing securities. Its objective is to prevent unfair and inequitable practices and to bring trading on securities exchanges and in the over-the-counter (OTC) market under federal control. (See Exhibit 18.2.)

Exhibit 18.2: Securities Exchange Act of 1934

Does

1. Require all securities listed on a national exchange to be registered with the SEC
2. Prohibit manipulative practices, such as wash sales, matching orders, misleading statements
3. Require disclosure of information about a listed security
4. Provide for

   a. Establishment of the Securities Exchange Commission
   b. Registration of stock exchanges
   c. Credit regulation for securities transactions

5. Require publicly owned corporations to provide annual reports to their shareholders

Does not

1. Prevent fraud in the sale of new issues
2. Provide for the registration of new securities

This Act established the SEC, which consists of five persons appointed by the president and administers all federal laws regulating the securities industry, except those regulating the extension of credit, which is handled by the Federal Reserve.

The Securities Exchange Act of 1934 requires many different groups and organizations to register with the SEC. Those required to be registered include

- Corporations having listed securities
- Brokers and dealers operating in interstate commerce (includes those operating on exchanges and in OTC markets)
- Securities exchanges
- National securities associations

MARKET MANIPULATION

The Securities Exchange Act of 1934 outlaws the use of any manipulative, deceptive, or other fraudulent devices. The intent is to prevent any manipulation of securities markets. Specific devices prohibited are listed below.

- **Churning** can be described as a broker/dealer effecting transactions in a discretionary account that are excessive in size or frequency in view of the financial resources and character of the account. This is sometimes referred to as **overtrading** and is prohibited.
- **Wash sales** are prohibited. A wash sale occurs when a customer enters a purchase order and a sale order at the same time through the same broker/dealer. This would, normally, be done to create an appearance of activity in a security. A wash sale for tax purposes is not related to this in any way. A wash sale for tax purposes occurs when a customer sells a security at a loss and repurchases it within thirty days after the sale.
- **Matched orders** are illegal under the Act. Matched orders occur when a customer enters a purchase order and a sale order at the same time, at the same price. In the case of matched orders, the customer places the orders through different broker/dealers. As is the case with wash sales, no change in ownership takes place as a result of the transaction.

- **Pegging, fixing,** and **stabilizing** are prohibited, except when specifically permitted by SEC rules. Such operations attempt to create a price level different from that which would result from the forces of demand and supply.

FINANCIAL RESPONSIBILITY RULES

The SEC has adopted SEC Rule 15c3-1 (uniform net capital rule), which establishes minimum net capital requirements for broker/dealers. The term **net capital** refers to net liquid assets of a firm. In other words, a broker/dealer must, at all times, maintain a minimum amount of net capital for the protection of its customers. If a firm does not have the required net capital under the rule, the SEC will not allow it to operate. Therefore, the purpose of the net capital rule is to protect the customers of the firm by imposing minimum net capital requirements.

The SEC also adopted SEC Rule 15c3-3 (customer protection rule), which requires physical segregation of customer fully paid and excess margin securities, as well as the maintenance of cash reserves. This rule also requires a broker/dealer to buy in a customer if the customer does not deliver a security which was the subject of a long sale within ten business days after settlement date. The purpose of SEC Rule 15c3-3 is the adequate protection of customer assets under the control of the firm.

SECURITIES INVESTOR PROTECTION ACT OF 1970

In the period 1968–1970, the brokerage community was faced with a paperwork crunch as a result of unexpectedly high trading volume. A severe decline in stock prices also hit the industry at this time. Many brokerage firms were forced into mergers or went out of business. Many public customers lost money because the brokerage firms could not meet their obligations. Investor confidence in the securities markets was badly shaken.

In order to restore confidence in the securities markets, Congress created the Securities Investor Protection Corporation (SIPC). The SIPC is a nonprofit membership corporation. The members of the SIPC are, with some exceptions, all persons registered as brokers or dealers under the Securities Exchange Act of 1934, and all persons who are members of a national securities exchange.

The SIPC provides protection for customers of an SIPC member firm in liquidation up to $500,000 per separate customer, except that claims for cash are limited to $100,000 per separate account.

The self-regulatory organizations (exchanges or The National Association of Securities Dealers [NASD]) periodically send reports to the SIPC concerning broker/dealers who are in or approaching financial difficulty. If the SIPC determines that customers of an SIPC member need the protection of the Act, then an application is made to the federal district court having jurisdiction for the appointment of a trustee to carry out the liquidation of the firm. The responsibility of an SIPC-appointed trustee is to

- Liquidate the failed broker/dealer in an orderly fashion.
- Distribute customers' fully paid and excess margin securities.
- Notify customers that the firm is in SIPC liquidation.

The Trustee or the SIPC may arrange to have some or all customer accounts of a failed firm transferred to another SIPC firm. Customers whose accounts are transferred will be notified immediately and will be permitted to deal with the new firm or to transfer their accounts to firms of their own choosing. This procedure is intended to minimize disruptions in customers' trading activities. In many cases (e.g., where there are questions as to the accuracy of the failed firm's records), the transfer of accounts will not be feasible.

Where a transfer of account is not feasible, protection will be afforded the account in the following manner:

- Customers of a failed firm will receive securities that are registered in their names. There is no limit on the value of such property, which will be returned.
- The customers will receive, on a pro rata basis, all remaining cash and securities of customers held by the firm. There is no limit on the value of such customer property, which will be returned.
- The SIPC's funds will be available to satisfy the remaining claims of each customer up to a maximum of $500,000 in cash and securities, but no more than $100,000 for cash claims.
- Any remaining assets after payment of liquidation expenses are available to satisfy any remaining portion of customer's claims on a pro rata basis.

The definition of a **separate customer** for the purposes of protection under the Act requires further explanation. The SIPC provides protection up to limits prescribed in the Act per separate customer, not per separate account. A customer having several different accounts must be acting in a bona fide separate capacity with respect to each account in order to obtain protection for each account.

Consider the following accounts on the books of a broker/dealer:

- Mr. John Jones
- John and Mary Jones
- John Jones, Custodian for Jimmy Jones under the Uniform Gifts to Minors/Uniform Transfer to Minors Act of Massachusetts

Each of these accounts represents a separate customer under the Act, and each is entitled to SIPC protection up to the maximum limits. However, assume John and Mary Jones opened three accounts with the same broker/dealer. Common stocks were purchased in one account. The second account was used to purchase preferred stocks. In the third account, corporate bonds were purchased. In this case, if the broker/dealer goes into an SIPC liquidation, the total of cash and securities in the three accounts would be added together. John and Mary Jones are one separate customer. They are acting in the same capacity in each account and, therefore, are not entitled to separate protection.

The following examples apply to claims remaining *after* the return to customers of securities registered in their names and after the pro rata distribution of customer property held by the firm:

- A remaining claim is for $350,000 in securities. The claim would be satisfied in full.
- A customer has a claim for $350,000 in securities in an individual account and for $400,000 in securities in a joint account with her spouse, as to which each has full authority. The spouse also has an individual account in which there is a claim for $300,000 in securities. All three claims would be fully covered.
- A customer has a claim for $600,000 in securities in a margin account, but he owes the broker $100,000 on those securities. The customer's **net equity** is $500,000 and is fully covered. With the approval of the trustee, the customer may pay the $100,000 and receive the $600,000 in securities.
- A remaining claim is for $280,000 in securities and $120,000 in cash. All but $20,000 would be covered.
- A remaining claim is for $100,000 in securities and $150,000 in cash. The claim would be covered to the amount of $200,000.
- A customer has a claim for $520,000 in securities and $160,000 in cash. The claim would be covered to the amount of $500,000 (the maximum).

In the last three examples, it should be noted that any portion of the claim remaining after (1) the distribution of securities registered in customer name, (2) the distribution of customer property, and (3) the advance of SIPC monies may be satisfied in part from assets of the failed firm, if there are any available for distribution to creditors.

Customers' claims for securities are valued as of a date prescribed by law, in general, at the time of the commencement of procedures to protect customers (valuation date).

To the greatest extent possible, claims for securities will be satisfied by delivery of securities to customers. As a result of the ups and downs of securities markets, when customers receive their securities, they may have a market value higher or lower than their value on valuation date. Similarly, the amount of cash paid in lieu of securities reflects the value on the valuation date and may differ from the value of the securities on the payment date.

Also, the SIPC's funds may not be used to pay claims of any customer who is also: (1) a general partner, officer, or director of the firm; (2) the beneficial owner of 5% or more of any class of equity security of the firm (other than certain nonconvertible preferred stocks); (3) a limited partner with a participation of 5% or more in the net assets or net profits of the firm; (4) someone with the power to exercise a controlling influence over the management or policies of the firm; or (5) a broker or dealer or bank acting for itself rather than for its customer or customers.

The SIPC's funds are available to offer protection to customers of other firms that have had transactions with the firm being liquidated. If a firm being liquidated in a judicial proceeding under the Act has certain open securities transactions with other firms, the SIPC's funds are available to pay the losses of the other firms in closing out these transactions after the proceeding is commenced. The purpose is to minimize the disruption caused by the failure of a broker/dealer by precluding the possible **domino effect** of such a failure on other securities firms.

To summarize important points to remember concerning the Securities Investor Protection Act of 1970 and the SIPC

- The SIPC is a nonprofit corporation.

- Membership in the SIPC consists of registered broker/dealers.
- The SIPC is not an agency of the US government.
- The SIPC does not cover commodity accounts.
- If a customer's claim exceeds the maximum ($500,000 for cash and securities, but no more than $100,000 in cash per separate customer), the customer becomes a general creditor of the firm.
- If customers of an SIPC member need the protection afforded by the Act, a trustee is appointed by the SIPC (with the approval of a federal district court) to liquidate the broker/dealer in an orderly manner.
- A customer must file a claim with the SIPC trustee in order to receive any money for securities or cash under the Act.
- A person is not regarded as a customer under the Act and, therefore, not entitled to any protection if he has a claim for property that, by contract, agreement, or understanding, or by operation of law, is part of the capital of the firm or is subordinated to the claims of creditors of the firm. The SIPC may not advance funds to the trustee to pay any claims of a customer who is

  - A general partner, officer or director of the firm
  - The beneficial owner of 5% or more of any class of equity security of the firm
  - A limited partner with a participation of 5% or more in the net assets or net profits of the firm

- The SIPC maintains a fund that it uses to advance money to the SIPC trustee for payment of customer claims.
- SIPC members are assessed a nominal amount per year or a percentage of their gross revenues from the securities business, and this represents the principal source of revenues for the SIPC fund.
- The SIPC may borrow up to $1 billion from the US Treasury through the SEC, if the SEC feels the loan is necessary to maintain confidence in the US securities markets.

TRUST INDENTURE ACT OF 1939

In order to provide additional protection to investors who purchase debt issues, the Trust Indenture Act of 1939 was passed. This is a separate amendment to the Securities Act of 1933. The Trust Indenture Act of 1939 sets requirements that indentures or deeds of trust must meet. The standards apply to debt issues in excess of $1 million, which must be registered under the Act of 1933. All bonds required to be registered under the Act of 1933 must have an indenture that meets the requirements of the Trust Indenture Act of 1939. Therefore, if a security is exempt from the requirements of the Securities Act of 1933, it is also exempt from the requirements of the Trust Indenture Act of 1939.

If a security is not exempt from the registration requirements of the Securities Act of 1933, the issuer must file an application for qualification of the trust indenture under which the security is to be issued with the SEC. This indenture qualification statement filed with the SEC will become effective on the twentieth calendar day after it is received by the SEC.

The indenture is a contract between the corporation and the trustee who represents the interest of the bondholders. The indenture describes the obligations of the corporation to pay interest on the bonds. It also requires the trustee to take any action (including legal action) necessary to protect the interests of the bondholders.

The other important provisions of the Trust Indenture Act of 1939 can be summarized as follows:

- The trustee representing the bondholders must be independent from the corporation.
- The trustee must be a bank or trust company with a minimum capital of $150,000.
- The trustee must keep the bondholders advised of any important developments concerning the debt issue, such as default.
- The SEC is responsible for the administration of the Act.

SECURITIES ACT AMENDMENTS OF 1975

The Securities Act Amendments of 1975 was signed into law by President Ford on June 4, 1975. The Act amended certain parts of the Securities Exchange Act of 1934 and the Securities Act of 1933. This Act represents the most important changes in the regulation of securities markets since the Securities Exchange Act was passed by Congress in 1934.

The main purpose of this Act is to remove any barriers to competition in the securities industry. The SEC was given much greater power to regulate the securities industry. To summarize the main provisions of the Securities Act Amendments of 1975

- Fixed commission rates were abolished in favor of negotiated commissions on public orders.
- Fixed commission rates were abolished in favor of negotiated commissions on transactions between members.
- The Act directs the SEC to develop a National Market System.
- The SEC is given the power to approve any proposed rule changes by the exchanges or the NASD and refuse to approve any that are a burden on competition.
- The Act requires registration of specialists, floor brokers, floor traders, and municipal securities dealers with the SEC. Previously, these classes of broker/dealers were exempt from registration with the SEC.
- The SEC was given the power to regulate the activities of clearing corporations, securities depositories, and transfer agents.

STATE SECURITIES LAWS

State securities laws are called **blue-sky laws**. Blue-sky laws attempt to protect the public from the fraudulent sale of securities within a particular state. The Securities Act of 1933 does not prohibit any state from enacting laws governing the sale of securities within its borders. Therefore, an issuer that intends to offer securities for sale in several states must comply with the provisions of the Securities Act of 1933 and all securities laws of the appropriate states.

Most states require that, before any securities may be sold within the state, registration of the securities be accomplished by

- Notification
- Qualification
- Coordination

Registration by **notification** is available to issuers of securities that meet certain standards concerning net income, assets, and the number of years the issuer has been in the business.

Registration by **qualification** must be obtained for all securities issues that are not exempted and do not meet the standards to be registered by notification. The issuer must supply the state securities division with financial statements and other information. If the documents filed are acceptable to the state, a permit to sell will be given to the issuer and the securities may be sold to the public.

Registration by **coordination** is accomplished by sending the state securities division copies of documents that are filed with the SEC. The registration becomes effective at the same time it becomes effective with the SEC.

Most states require the registration or licensing of both resident and nonresident broker/dealers and their agents operating within the state. Certain states require broker/dealers to maintain a minimum amount of net capital in order to operate in the state. Some states also require broker/dealers to post bonds in order to do business in the state. A state securities division has the power to revoke the license of a broker/dealer or the license of any salesman for violations of its laws.

To summarize the main points to remember concerning state securities laws (blue-sky laws)

- The securities division of a state has the power to revoke a broker/dealer's and/or salesman's license if state laws are violated.
- An issuer who intends to offer securities for sale in various states must comply with the provisions of the Securities Act of 1933 as well as the securities laws within each appropriate state.
- State securities laws attempt to protect the public against the fraudulent sale of securities within a state.
- The Securities Act of 1933 does not establish standard provisions that must appear in every blue sky law. The individual states set their own requirements that issuers, broker/dealers and salesmen must meet in order to transact business within the particular state.

LAW OF AGENCY

Agency is a relationship by consent or agreement between two parties whereby one party (agent) agrees to act on behalf of the other party (principal). The relationship of a registered representative and a customer, in many transactions, is that of agent and principal.

An agent is always subject to control by the principal. An agent is a fiduciary and, therefore, must always act in the best interests of the principal. The agent generally is given authority by the principal to perform certain legal acts for the principal, and bind the principal contractually with third parties.

An agent normally has certain rights and obligations with regard to the principal, including

- Following the instructions given by the principal
- Acting in a prudent manner
- Properly accounting to the principal for all assets entrusted to him/her
- Keeping the principal advised of important information concerning the transaction

The agent cannot

- Compete with the principal or act on behalf of a third party whose interests are contrary to those of the principal.
- Act beyond the scope of his authority.
- Delegate duties to third parties unless authorized or unless it is necessary or customary to do so, or
- Reveal any confidential information about the principal.

The principal has certain rights and obligations with regard to the agent

- The principal must compensate the agent according to their agreement.
- The principal must pay reasonable expenses of the agent and indemnify the agent against liability or loss for the services performed at the principal's request.
- The principal should not interfere with or discredit the work of his agent.
- The principal should inform the agent of any risks associated with the performance of his duties.

19 DIRECT PARTICIPATION PROGRAMS

OVERVIEW

In recent years, certain types of investments known as **tax shelters** have become very popular with investors wishing to reduce their taxable income. A tax shelter is defined as an investment that provides an investor tax-free or partially tax-free returns, with additional deductions to possibly reduce his taxable income. Tax shelters are attractive investments to persons in high tax bracket rates.

Tax shelters are structured to use available funds to maximize the tax benefits that will flow through to the individual investors, and also meet the financial demands of the business venture. This can be accomplished by using **leverage**. Leverage is using borrowed funds at a fixed rate in order to increase the rate of return earned on total capital invested. In a tax shelter, leverage or borrowed money is used to pay for the deductible expenses of the venture. If the deductible expenses exceed the income, a tax loss will be generated for the investors. A tax shelter investment is referred to as a **direct participation program** because investors directly participate in the gains and losses from the business venture. However, in certain instances, losses from tax shelter investments cannot be deducted against other income of the taxpayer.

TAX REFORM ACT OF 1986

The rules relating to tax shelters in general, and real estate in particular, have been tightened as a result of the Tax Reform Act of 1986. Individuals will no longer be allowed to deduct losses on passive activities (limited partnership interests) from other income. A passive activity, as defined in the Tax Reform Act, is the conduct of a trade or business in which the taxpayer does not materially participate. Any rental activity or an interest in a limited partnership is considered a passive activity regardless of whether the taxpayer materially participates.

Losses from passive activities may be deducted against income from passive activities. However, if the losses from passive activities exceed the income from passive activities, the excess loss may not be deducted from a taxpayer's other income. This is a major change in the federal tax code. Prior to 1987, losses from limited partnership investments were fully deductible.

The excess passive-activity loss of a taxpayer is suspended and carried forward to reduce passive-activity income of the taxpayer in future years. Any unused suspended deductions may be deducted in full when the taxpayer sells his entire interest in the passive activity in a taxable transaction.

Congress provided an exception to the rule that passive-activity losses cannot be deducted against other income of the taxpayer. The tax code allows up to $25,000 of passive losses for rental real estate activities, which can be deducted each year against nonpassive income.

In order for a taxpayer to qualify for this special treatment (ability to deduct up to $25,000 of rental real estate losses), the taxpayer must be an individual and must actively participate in the rental real estate activity.

The $25,000 of deductible losses is allowed after first netting income and losses from all of the taxpayer's rental real estate activities in which he actively participates. Assume a taxpayer has a $25,000 loss from a rental real estate activity in which he actively participates. He also has a $25,000 gain from another rental real estate activity in which he participates. In this case, the taxpayer has no net loss from rental real estate activities in which he actively participates, and no amount is allowed for a deduction under the $25,000 loss rule. This is true even if the taxpayer had net losses from other passive activities for the year.

A taxpayer is considered to be actively participating in a rental real estate activity if he participates in the making of management decisions or arranges for others to provide repairs. Examples of such active participation for a taxpayer include

- Approving new tenants
- Deciding on rental terms
- Approving capital or repair expenditures

Services performed by an agent are not attributed to the principal for determining active participation. The taxpayer must be exercising independent discretion and judgment with regard to the real estate rental activity in order to be considered as actively participating. However, services performed by a taxpayer's spouse are attributed to the taxpayer in determining he is an active participant.

The $25,000 deductible amount is reduced, but not below zero, by 50% of the amount by which the taxpayer's adjusted gross income for the year exceeds $100,000. The deduction for losses on rental real estate activities is completely phased out in a year if a taxpayer's adjusted gross income is $150,000 or greater. The taxpayer's adjusted gross income, for purposes of determining the phase-out, is determined without regard to individual retirement account (IRA) contribution deductions, taxable Social Security benefits, and any passive-activity loss.

A direct participation program may provide flow-through tax consequences, in certain instances, to investors and is normally structured as a limited partnership. Investors purchase certain direct participation programs to obtain possible tax benefits and for profit.

Direct participation programs could include any of the following:

- Real estate syndications
- Oil and gas programs
- Equipment leasing
- Agricultural programs
- Cable TV
- Cattle programs (cattle feeding and cattle breeding)
- Research and development
- Movies
- Subchapter S corporations

An investor, before placing money in a direct participation program, should consider

- The general partner's management ability
- The fact that limited partnerships are nonliquid
- The possible loss of principal
- Possible changes in tax laws

All business enterprises must have a structure in order to conduct their affairs. Capital must be obtained and skillfully managed in order to provide an acceptable return to its owners. The main types of business enterprises are

- Sole proprietorship
- General partnership
- Limited partnership
- Corporation
- Trust

Individuals starting a business will decide on the business structure depending on the type of enterprise, capital available, and the economic risks. However, a tax shelter investment must have a vehicle able to possibly pass through tax benefits to investors. A sole proprietorship or general partnership may be able to provide tax benefits if the taxpayer materially participates in the business. The major disadvantage of a sole proprietorship or general partnership is that investors (owners) are exposed to unlimited liabilities relating to the enterprise. A sole proprietorship or general partner's personal assets are subject to the claims of creditors if the business assets are not sufficient to pay its liabilities.

A partnership is defined as an unincorporated association of two or more individuals who conduct a business for profit. The partnership vehicle allows tax benefits, in certain instances, to flow through to the individual partners. A partnership is not viewed as a separate entity under the Internal Revenue Code. Each partner receives his share of the gain or deducts his share of the partnership loss on his personal tax return.

The flow-through of income and expense tax benefits do not apply to a corporation. A corporation is responsible for federal income taxes on its net income. If the corporation pays a dividend to shareholders, the dividend is taxable to the individual shareholders. Corporations are subject to double taxation of corporate profits. The corporation itself pays a tax on its net income, and the individual shareholders pay a tax on dividends received. Therefore, the corporate vehicle is not normally used for tax-sheltered investments. However, stockholders in a corporation do have limited liability. They can lose only the amount of their investment in the corporation, and their personal assets are not at risk.

There is one type of business structure that combines the flow-through of income and expenses of a partnership with the limited liability of a corporation. This vehicle is a limited partnership. A limited partnership is a partnership made up of one or more general partners and one or more limited partners. Limited partnerships can normally engage in any type of business venture and they are very popular because investors obtain leveraged losses and have no personal liability beyond their capital investment. However, these losses may or may not be deductible against nonpassive income of the taxpayer.

Other advantages of limited partnerships include

- No double taxation of profits as with a corporation
- Deferral of income to lower tax bracket years

Most states have laws concerning the formation of limited partnerships. The laws of most states conform with some variation to the Uniform Limited Partnership Act (ULPA) adopted by the Commission on Uniform State Laws in 1916. State laws regulate the rights and obligations of the partners to each other and to creditors. However, federal law and the Internal Revenue Service (IRS) regulate the limited partnership and the individual partners concerning federal income taxes.

The general partner in a limited partnership has the exclusive right to manage the business of the partnership. S/he is bound by the terms contained in the certificate of limited partnership. The general partner is personally liable for the debts of the limited partnership, except for nonrecourse loans.

Limited partners do not have the right to manage the affairs of the limited partnership. If a limited partner engages in the management of the business, s/he will lose his limited liability and become liable as a general partner. A limited partner can inspect the books and records of the limited partnership and is entitled to receive full and complete information regarding its affairs and finances. A limited partner is entitled to receive his share of the profits, if any, and other distributions described in the certificate of limited partnership.

A limited partnership must be formed pursuant to state law. All states have laws that describe the formation and operation of a limited partnership. If a limited partnership is improperly structured, it may be reclassified as a general partnership by the state and the limited partners would lose their limited liability status.

In order for an entity to obtain the advantages of a limited partnership it must be classified as such for tax purposes. The Internal Revenue Code describes a partnership as a business entity that is not, among other things, a corporation. A corporation, for tax purposes, could include certain unincorporated associations. If a partnership was improperly formed and reclassified as a corporation by the IRS, its tax status would change. The flow-through tax benefit of a partnership would no longer be available, and the entity itself would be responsible to pay taxes on its net income.

There are four major characteristics that are used to distinguish a corporation from other business entities. These factors are

1. Continuity of life
2. Centralization of management
3. Limited liability
4. Free transferability of beneficial interest

If a business organization contains three of these four factors, it will be classified as a corporation for federal income tax purposes. A limited partnership must not possess at least two of these factors to be taxed as a partnership. The corporate characteristic most difficult for a limited partnership to avoid is centralization of management.

A limited partnership does not necessarily possess continuity of life. A limited partnership, under the laws of most states, may be dissolved upon the death, insanity, resignation, or bankruptcy of a general partner. The remaining general partners could continue to operate the business with the consent of other partners. However, the possibility that the limited partnership may have to be dissolved indicates that it does not possess continuity of life. A corporation possesses continuity of life. It has a life separate from its stockholders. If stockholders die or go bankrupt, the corporation is not affected.

A limited partnership is not normally considered to possess centralization of management because a general partner can bind the limited partnership by his action only. Centralization of management does exist in a corporate enterprise because the elected officers and directors act as representatives of the stockholders.

A limited partnership possesses limited liability, but only for its limited partners. A general partner in a limited partnership has unlimited liability for the debts of the limited partnership. A corporation offers limited liability for all of its stockholders. Internal Revenue Code regulations state that an entity will not possess the quality of limited liability if at least one of its owners is personally responsible for the debts of the enterprise.

In a limited partnership it is quite common for restrictions to be placed on the transfer of a person's interest in the limited partnership. A corporation normally possesses free transferability of ownership interests by an investor. If a stockholder wants to liquidate his investment, he sells his shares to another person.

It is a relatively simple matter to set up a limited partnership that does not possess the four main characteristics of a corporation. This is essential to ensure that a limited partnership will be taxed as such by the IRS. Limited partnerships are required by state law to file a certificate of limited partnership, usually with the secretary of state. If the certificate is not filed, a limited partnership will not exist and the investors will not have limited liability. The entity will probably be considered a general partnership.

The reason states require a certificate to be filed is to inform anyone dealing with the entity that certain partners have limited liability and others unlimited liability. The certificate of limited partnership must be signed and attested to by all the partners. The certificate of limited partnership normally contains the following information:

- The name of the partnership. Some states require limited partnerships to use the abbreviation LP.
- The type of business the limited partnership will engage in.
- The location of the limited partnership, which is normally the business address of the general partner.
- The life of the limited partnership must be stated. Limited partnerships do not have a perpetual existence like a corporation. A limited partnership will be dissolved upon the death, insanity, bankruptcy, or retirement of a general partner. The limited partnership may terminate on a date specified in the certificate of limited partnership.
- The name of each partner and his or her home address must be stated.
- The amount of money invested by the limited partners. Limited partners may contribute cash or other property but cannot contribute services. It is not necessary for a general partner to contribute cash or property in return for his partnership interest. The general partners will normally receive his interest in the limited partnership in return for his services.
- The right, if it exists, for substituting limited partners. The Uniform Limited Partnership Act states that a limited partner's interest is assignable only if that right is stated in the certificate of limited partnership. If an interest is assigned by a limited partner to a substitute limited partner, this normally relates only to sharing in the profits or distributions of the original limited partner. The other rights of the limited partner, such as voting rights, are generally not assignable. Many limited partnerships place restrictions on substituting limited partners. Also, the certificate of limited partnership will state whether partners can admit additional limited partners.
- Whether additional contributions of limited partners are required. Some limited partnerships require that limited partners make capital contributions over a number of years. Sometimes, a letter of credit is required from limited partners.
- The time when the contribution of a limited partner will be returned. If no specific date is set for the return of capital, then capital contributions will be returned upon dissolution of the partnership.
- The share of the profits each limited partner is entitled to as a result of his investment.
- Whether any limited partners have a priority over other limited partners relating to contributions or sharing in the profits.
- Whether limited partners can demand property instead of cash in return for their contributed capital.
- Whether remaining general partners can continue to operate the business upon the retirement, death, insanity, or bankruptcy of a general partner. In most cases, this right is granted to remaining general partners. If this right is not granted, the limited partnership would automatically end upon the occurrence of an above-mentioned event.

LIABILITIES OF LIMITED PARTNERS

Limited partners are not personally liable for the debts of the limited partnership. They can lose only the amount of their investment. However, this is not true if a limited partner takes part in the management of the business. In this case, the limited partner would become liable as a general partner. A limited partnership must not allow a distribution if the funds are needed to pay claims of creditors. If funds are distributed to limited partners that are needed to keep the business solvent, these funds must be returned by the limited partners to the business. Upon dissolution of a limited partnership, the assets would be distributed in the following sequence:

- Secured creditors
- General creditors

- Limited partners (first for profits and second for capital claims)
- General partners (first for claims other than profits, second for profits, and third for capital claims)

The priorities for claims of limited and general partners could be changed by agreement. The certificate of limited partnership describes the priority of claims upon dissolution.

To summarize the main points to remember concerning a limited partnership

- A limited partnership must be established pursuant to state law, and a certificate of limited partnership must be filed with the secretary of state.
- A limited partnership must conform to federal law in order to be taxed by the Internal Revenue Service as a limited partnership. Normally, legal opinions are obtained from an attorney concerning the classification of the business organization.
- A limited partnership is defined under the ULPA as a partnership formed by two or more persons consisting of one or more general partners and one or more limited partners.
- Limited partnerships can normally engage in any type of business.
- The management of the limited partnership is exclusively in the hands of the general partner(s). The general partner(s) cannot violate any provision of the certificate of limited partnership or engage in any action that would make it impossible to carry on the business of the limited partnership.
- The general partner is personally responsible for all debts of the limited partnership. The general partner's personal assets could be attached by creditors of the limited partnership, if necessary, to satisfy obligations.
- Limited partners normally have the following rights:

  - To inspect the books and records of the limited partnership.
  - To receive complete information and a complete accounting of the affairs of the limited partnership.
  - To share in the profits and other distributions as stated in the certificate of limited partnership provided the sharing leaves sufficient assets to cover the limited partnership's liabilities.
  - To demand dissolution by court decree.
  - To sue general partners for damages.
  - To remove general partners for good cause.
  - Return of their capital contributions.
  - To receive an agreed-upon disposition of proceeds on the death of a limited partner if stated in the partnership agreement. If this is not stated, the partner's estate will acquire his interest.

- A limited partner does not have the right to take part in the management of the limited partnership. If a limited partner engages in management, he will become liable to creditors as a general partner.
- Upon the dissolution of the limited partnership, claims of creditors are paid first. Secured creditors, if any, would be paid prior to general creditors. Claims of limited partners are normally paid prior to claims of general partners.
- For federal income tax purposes, a limited partnership and a general partnership are taxed in the same manner. All partnerships flow through their gains and losses to the individual partners. The federal government decides how a business organization is to be taxed. It is possible that a limited or general partnership could be classified as such under state law and not taxed as a partnership under federal law. This should not happen because it is relatively easy to qualify as a partnership under federal tax law by following the guidelines set forth in the tax code.
- Some limited partnerships require their investors to sign a written partnership agreement. The agreement must conform to state law and not be in conflict with the certificate of limited partnership.
- Limited partnerships have certain advantages, including

  - Single tax status
  - Professional management
  - Income and expense flows through to the partners
  - Diversification of investment
  - Limited liability for the limited partners, since the capital risk is limited to the investor's initial investment
  - An investor has flexibility concerning the types of investment available
  - Possible tax write-offs against income

- The disadvantages of a limited partnership include

  - Limited partnerships are usually nonliquid investments.
  - An investor could lose principal; the financial risk is normally high.
  - Possible changes in tax laws affecting the limited partnership.
  - Limited partners cannot control the actions of the general partners.

- A limited partnership may be dissolved by

  - The loss of a general partner
  - Actions of limited partners such as a class action suit for damages
  - Winding up of partnership business on agreement of the partners
  - Bankruptcy of a partner, or any event that makes it unlawful to continue the limited partnership
  - Canceling the certificate of limited partnership

- Normally in a limited partnership, general partners cannot, without the approval of the limited partners

  - Admit a general partner.
  - Confess a judgment against the partnership.
  - Contravene the partnership agreement (certificate of limited partnership).
  - Prevent the ordinary business of the partnership.
  - Assign or possess partnership property for other than partnership purposes.
  - Admit a limited partner.
  - Continue the business of the limited partnership on the death, retirement, bankruptcy, or insanity of a general partner.
  - Compete with the limited partnership.

EVALUATING A LIMITED PARTNERSHIP

Many investors, anxious to reap the possible tax savings of a shelter, neglect to carefully evaluate the business objectives and economic viability of the partnership. Such attitudes obviously overlook the fact that the possible tax benefits of a direct participation program are contingent upon the continuing existence of the limited partnership. Therefore, an investor should consider a limited partnership first as an investment and then as a possible vehicle for reducing or deferring taxable income. This is even more important since the passage of the Tax Reform Act of 1986, which restricts the deduction of losses from passive activities, as mentioned previously.

The first factor to be considered in evaluating a shelter should be the basic economics of the industry of which the limited partnership will be a part. For example, an investor in a cattle shelter would want to know the latest trend of beef prices and future prospects of consumer demand.

Of course, an essential element of any evaluation of a limited partnership is an assessment of management. Management should have wide experience in the industry in order that it may control the many risk factors involved in the venture. The manager of a cattle-feeding shelter, for example, must have sufficient knowledge of livestock so he may quickly and effectively deal with any disease that may affect the cattle.

Financial stability of management and the proposed use of partnership proceeds during the operation of the limited partnership should also be carefully examined by prospective participants prior to investment. The front-end load, including organization and selling expenses, asset acquisition, prepaid management, and advance royalty fees, should be computed together with all other initial expenses that do not contribute directly to the value of the partnership.

An investor should take particular note of all sources of compensation to the general partner and sponsor or their affiliates. Management fees are paid on many different bases, often depending on the types of program. For example, partnerships involved in real estate often pay management on a basis of a percentage of gross rental, while those dealing with oil often pay their managers on a per-well basis. In any event, management fees should be carefully analyzed in order to ensure that they are comparable with those in the industry and similar shelters. An excessive management fee often will provide a valuable clue to an unsound program.

The financial stability of the direct participation program may be dependent on the future funding available to the partnership. It is, therefore, necessary to determine who is providing financing to the partnership and to determine the interest rate and the degree of leverage being sought.

A careful review of all financial statements, prospectuses, or offering memoranda provided should be undertaken before a contribution to the partnership is made. Specifically, projected management fees and other expenses must be examined to determine whether or not they are consistent with the information presented in the offering document. The shelter's projected taxable income, internal rate of return, and cash flow should be computed along with discounted cash value and internal rates of projections. The historical figures should be compared with projected values, if both are available, and the rate of return on invested funds should be computed. Prior syndications of the developer should also be reviewed if at all possible. The anticipated length of the investment program must also be determined.

When considering an investment in a direct participation program, the investor must consider a variety of risks. They include such risks as

- The general partner's management ability
- The fact that limited partnerships are nonliquid
- Possible loss of principal
- Unpredictability of income
- Whether the investor will be able to pay future assessments if any occur
- The effect of rising operating costs
- Changes in tax laws

A proper evaluation of a limited partnership investment is not complete without a careful analysis of the investor's tax situation and financial needs. A direct participation program investor must have a substantial net worth and income since an investment in such a partnership is subject to great risk and imposes strict limitations on any transferability of one's interest. Certain states may also restrict entry into a direct participation program by imposing minimum net worth requirements with regard to investor participation in such entities. The investor's sophistication and temperament are also key considerations. An investment program that is confusing and worrisome to an investor is clearly not acceptable in view of the risks and long-term commitment of funds usually required by direct participation programs.

REAL ESTATE

One of the most popular forms of tax shelter investment is real estate. Real estate provides housing for people to live and work in and is important to all of our lives. It has proven to be an excellent hedge against inflation. Real estate also has a limited supply and is expensive to replace.

The main benefits of investing in real estate as a tax-sheltered investment are

- Real estate can produce a tax loss that the investor can use to offset other passive income.
- The investment, while it produces tax loss, can also provide a positive cash flow. This positive cash flow may be tax-free for several years.

Leverage is very important to a successful real estate investment. Leverage is the use of borrowed money to purchase the property. The interest on the mortgage is tax-deductible as an expense in operating the property. However, the principal portion of the mortgage payment is not tax-deductible. Also, income producing real estate can be depreciated using the accelerated cost recovery system (ACRS). The best way to illustrate a real estate investment is by using an example.

Assume two investors form a partnership and purchase an apartment building. The cost of the apartment building is $4 million. Each investor puts up $200,000 and actively participates in the management of the building. Therefore, the total down payment is $400,000 and a mortgage of $3.6 million is obtained for 30 years on the property with an interest rate of 10%. The rental income from the property is $400,000.

The two investors in this apartment building will benefit from increasing equity resulting from amortization of the mortgage. The investors will be reducing the mortgage with rental income from the property. Also, if it is a sound real estate investment, the property will appreciate in value.

Let us assume the results of the first year of operation for the apartment building as follows:

Rental income	$400,000
Interest on mortgage	225,000
Depreciation	185,000
Operating expenses	40,000
Loss	$ 50,000

The taxable loss is divided equally between the two investors. Since a partnership is not a taxable entity, the losses are followed through to the individual investors' personal tax returns. A partnership, under federal tax law, must file Form 1065, which informs the IRS of the partnership profit or loss and each partner's share of the profit or loss.

The partnership does not pay any tax on partnership income, and each partner must report his share of the partnership net profit or loss on his or her individual tax return. Even though a partnership is not a taxpaying entity, it must file Form 1065, which is an informational return. This informational return summarizes the financial transactions of the partnership for the year. Attached to the informational return is Schedule K-1 for each partner, and copies are provided to each partner. Schedule K-1 reports to each partner his share of the partnership gains or losses. Therefore, both the IRS and the individual partners receive a Schedule K-1 from the partnership.

In our example, the loss in the first year of operation is $50,000. This loss is divided equally by the two investors. Each investor's share of the loss is $25,000.

Assume each investor had adjusted gross income of less than $100,000. In this case, each investor could deduct the $25,000 loss against other income on his or her tax return. Each individual is allowed the $25,000 deduction against other income tax because this is an exception provided for in the federal tax code. Up to $25,000 of passive losses from rental real estate activities can be deducted each year against nonpassive income. In our example, each taxpayer had adjusted gross income of less than $100,000. Therefore, the entire $25,000 deduction is allowed against nonpassive income. If the taxpayer's adjusted gross income is in excess of $100,000, the $25,000 deduction is phased out. The deduction is completely eliminated if the taxpayer's adjusted gross income exceeds $150,000.

In our example, for simplicity purposes, we did not allocate a portion of the purchase price of the property for land. Land cannot be depreciated under federal tax law. Therefore, an investor would not purchase raw land for a tax-sheltered investment. Normally, unimproved land is purchased for appreciation purposes or capital gains.

Assume an individual in the 28% tax bracket invested $200,000 in an equipment-leasing limited partnership in 1987. This individual's share of income and expenses are as follows:

$600,000	Revenues
$400,000	Operating expenses
$190,000	Bank interest charges
$110,000	Depreciation

What is the customer's loss?

$600,000	Revenues
– 400 000	Operating expenses
$200,000	Operating income before interest and depreciation
190,000	Bank interest charges
$ 10,000	Net income before depreciation
110,000	Depreciation
$100,000	Loss

The $100,000 loss for the individual is a passive-activity loss and cannot be deducted against nonpassive income. It can be deducted only against other passive income the taxpayer may have.

The cash flow to the investor can be computed as follows:

$(100,000)	Loss for tax purposes
110,000	Depreciation
$ 10,000	Positive or profitable cash flow

The main types of real estate investments include

- Conventional residential real estate
- Commercial real estate
- Government-subsidized housing
- Recreational properties
- Raw land
- Condominium securities

Conventional residential real estate normally involves the purchase or construction of apartment complexes. There are no government subsidies involved in the project. Apartment complexes normally are more risky than commercial properties since residential leases are generally short term. Turnover of tenants can be a problem. Commercial real estate includes office buildings, shopping centers, warehouses, factories, hotels, and motels. Leases in commercial real estate tend to be for longer periods, usually three to five years.

Many commercial leases contain escalator clauses that protect the landlord from increasing costs. Commercial property may be rented on a triple net lease basis. In a triple net lease, the tenant pays all expenses associated with the leased property, except for mortgage payments. Therefore, in a triple net lease the tenant pays taxes, insurance, and maintenance expenses. A triple net lease is many times referred to simply as a net lease.

Government-subsidized housing programs could involve the purchase of existing units or new construction. Low-income housing is eligible for generous depreciation deductions. The government normally provides permanent financing for low-income housing by guaranteeing repayment, and also provides rent subsidies paid to landlords on behalf of low-income families. An investor should be concerned with the location and sound construction of the facility.

Recreational properties normally include vacation homes and condominiums. Under IRS rules, in order for a vacation home or condominium to be considered an investment for tax purposes, it must not be considered a residence. It is considered a residence if it is used by the owner for more than fourteen days or 10% of the number of days for which it is rented at fair market value.

An investment in raw land is generally made by an investor for appreciation purposes. The investor should be concerned with carrying costs (interest, taxes, debt service) and how long the property must be held in order to obtain a reasonable return. Unimproved land cannot be depreciated for tax purposes.

Condominium units, in some cases, are sold to investors by a real estate developer for the purpose of renting them to generate income. The Securities and Exchange Commission (SEC) has declared that the sale of condominiums in this manner is a sale of a security as defined in the Securities Act of 1933. The federal courts have agreed with the SEC.

In a typical condominium arrangement, a developer builds a multifamily dwelling. The developer records a master deed, which gives him the right to create a condominium association. Individual titles are given for each unit in the multifamily structure.

Regulations and bylaws are drawn up, under which each owner shares in expenses and responsibilities relating to the property. The expenses are normally allocated according to each unit's square footage in relation to the total square footage of the entire property.

A master deed is drawn up, which forms the condominium association. It describes the common areas such as hallways or basements. The master deed normally allows for the creation of an owner's association, describes the cost-sharing arrangement, and covers project management. A purchaser of a condominium receives a unit deed that describes the area of which the unit owner has exclusive use. It also describes the common areas that can be used by all of the unit tenants.

If the condominium is used for more than fourteen days or 10% of the rental period, the investor will be subject to the **hobby loss rule**. Under the hobby loss rule, the investor would be able to deduct expenses only to the extent of rental income generated from the property. However, property taxes, interest expense, and any casualty loss is not subject to the limitations imposed under the hobby loss rules.

Many investors choose to invest in a real estate syndication, which is normally formed as a limited partnership. The investors are passive limited partners who are not involved in the management of the properties. The syndicator or sponsor is normally the general partner who manages the property. The sponsor of the program may use securities firms to help him or her obtain money from investors.

The investor in a real estate limited partnership has certain advantages over an investor who directly invests in real estate. These advantages include

- Smaller capital commitment
- Professional management
- Limited liability
- Diversification

The cost of syndicating a limited partnership to investors is not a deductible expense. Syndication costs are those expenses incurred in selling limited partnership interests to investors, including

- Brokerage fees
- Accounting fees
- Registration fees
- Printing fees
- Legal fees

Syndication costs are not deductible for tax purposes. Therefore, the costs associated with issuing and marketing limited partnership interests are not deductible expenses to the limited partnership or to any of the partners. Organization costs incurred in starting up the venture, such as legal, accounting, and filing fees, are deductible over at least a sixty-month (five-year) period.

DEPRECIATION

Real estate tax shelters allow investors to leverage small amounts of invested capital into relatively large depreciation deductions. The useful life of an asset does not have to be estimated to compute the annual depreciation allowance. In real estate, cost recovery items include a building and its components such as heating, plumbing, and wiring. Also, personal property that is used in connection with the business venture (furniture, fixtures, and business machines) are considered cost recovery items. The cost of land cannot be recovered under ACRS.

The depreciable basis of a real estate purchase includes any assumed mortgages and acquisition expenses relating to the property. However, it does not include the cost of the land. The ACRS allows residential real estate to be written off over 27½ years using the straight-line method. Nonresidential real estate can be written off on a straight-line basis over 31½ years. Personal assets not used for business purposes cannot be written off.

The Economic Recovery Act of 1981 substantially changed the rules for computing depreciation on business assets. The net method (ACRS) reduced the time required to write off the cost of business assets. This was an attempt to encourage investment in certain areas of the economy.

The tax benefits of depreciation in general are

- Deferral of tax liabilities on income
- Conversion of ordinary income to capital gains
- Deductions possibly in excess of income

Some of the main points relating to ACRS deductions include

- Business assets that may be depreciated are assigned useful lives by the tax code. However, component depreciation under ACRS is not allowed. In other words, structural components of a building must be depreciated in the same manner as the building itself.
- The basis for depreciation is the cost of the property, and the concept of salvage value has been eliminated.
- ACRS deductions are allowed whether the property is new or used.

It is important to remember that a sale or foreclosure of real estate property could result in a taxable gain to the owners. The gain would be the difference between the amount received by the owner and his adjusted basis on the property. The adjusted basis is the original cost of the property minus all depreciation or ACRS deductions. Normally, this gain will be taxed at capital gains rates. A portion of the gain may be taxed at ordinary income tax rates and is referred to as **recapture**. The IRS is recapturing some of the tax benefits allowed as a result of depreciation or ACRS deductions. Recapture is disadvantageous to an investor in a direct participation program.

AT-RISK RULES

The at-risk rules contained in the federal tax code allow an investor to deduct a loss for tax purposes only to the extent he is at risk at the end of the tax year with respect to that activity. The amount an investor is at risk in a tax shelter is

- The amount of his original investment
- The adjusted basis of any property contributed
- Any borrowed amount for which the investor is personally liable for repayment
- Any property pledged other than tax shelter property to secure payment

Under federal tax law, the concept of adjusted basis is important when a cash distribution is made from the limited partnership. The portion of a cash distribution paid to a partner that exceeds the partner's adjusted basis is subject to tax. Distributions that are equal to or less than a partner's adjusted basis are nontaxable. Those distributions are treated as a nontaxable return of capital.

A partner's adjusted basis in a tax shelter investment is increased by

- The original cash or property invested
- Debt for which the partner is personally liable (recourse debt)
- Additional cash or property invested
- Profits generated by the limited partnership

A partner's adjusted basis in a tax shelter investment is decreased by

- Losses generated by the limited partnership
- Cash distributions to partners

Assume a limited partner invests in an oil and gas limited partnership and his initial basis is $5,000. In the first year the partnership generates for the limited partner $3,000 of taxable income. The limited partner's adjusted basis at the end of the first year is $8,000. In the second year, the limited partner receives a cash distribution of $9,000. Since the distribution is greater than the limited partner's adjusted basis, the excess distribution is taxable to the limited partner.

$9,000   Cash distribution
$\underline{-\,8,000}$ Adjusted basis
$1,000   Amount of distribution subject to tax

The limited partner's adjusted basis is reduced to zero as a result of the cash distribution. A limited partner's adjusted basis is never reduced to an amount less than zero.

Also, when the limited partnership reduces a liability, each limited partner is considered to have received a cash distribution equal to his share of the liability reduced. This can create phantom income for the limited partner. The limited partner is then taxed on income he does not receive.

Assume a limited partner has an adjusted basis in a limited partnership of $8,000. The limited partnership pays off a $100,000 nonrecourse loan of which the limited partner's share is $10,000. The transaction generates a $2,000 taxable gain to the limited partner, even though no cash was received.

$10,000   Limited partner's share of loan reduction
$\underline{-\,8,000}$ Adjusted basis
$ 2,000   Taxable gain

OIL AND GAS PROGRAMS

Oil and gas programs have been a popular tax shelter investment. An investor in an oil and gas program generally bears more risk than an investor in a real estate program. However, an investor normally can write off a large portion of his investment in the early years.

To understand how an oil and gas program is created, we will trace a typical example. Assume Mr. Jones owns a large piece of land in Texas. Along comes Mr. Barnes, a leasehound, who puts together leases for drilling companies and limited partnerships. Mr. Barnes offers Mr. Jones cash plus a royalty interest in return for a working interest on the land. The royalty interest provides income to Mr. Jones, the landowner, based on a percentage of oil and gas production, but it does not share in the costs of the operation or management. Mr. Barnes, the leasehound, has obtained a working interest in the property. The working interest, also called an operating interest, bears the costs of operating or management of the mineral property.

Mr. Barnes sells his working interest in Mr. Jones's property to a limited partnership. Mr. Barnes receives cash plus an overriding royalty interest. An overriding royalty interest represents a percentage of the production that is created out of a working interest.

The limited partnership that owns the lease on the property can now begin drilling. A drilling contractor is hired by the limited partnership. The operator of the limited partnership is the person who supervises the drilling and is normally the general partner. Remember, a limited partnership must have at least one general partner.

The drilling contractor supplies the labor, tools, drilling rig, and machinery necessary for the drilling operation. The drilling contractor could be paid on a per diem basis, or for a fixed price, which is referred to as a **turnkey** contract or arrangement.

The main advantages to investors of oil and gas programs as a tax shelter investment are

- Intangible drilling costs
- Depletion allowances
- The possibility of capital gain

Intangible drilling costs are deductible expenses for labor, supplies, fuel, repairs, and other items with no salvage value. Equipment costs such as machinery, tools, pipe, and casing are capital expenditures, and the costs must be recovered through ACRS deductions. Intangible drilling costs incurred on a well that does not produce oil are referred to as *dry hole costs*. These costs are deductible as they are incurred and paid.

When oil and gas production begins, depletion deductions are allowed that generally produce tax-free income. Under federal tax law, two methods of depletion are allowed.

1. Cost depletion
2. Percentage depletion

Cost depletion is similar in nature to straight-line depreciation. It is computed by dividing the total value of reserves into the value of oil and gas that is produced during the year. Assume 10% of the total partnership reserves are extracted in a particular year. The investor's depletable basis is $10,000. An investor's depletable basis is his original investment minus any previous depletion and losses claimed. The investor's cost depletion is $1,000 ($10,000 x 10%). Under cost depletion, an investor cannot deduct more than the amount he is at risk in the venture.

Under the percentage depletion method, an investor can claim a flat percentage of the depletable basis during each year of production. Percentage depletion almost always provides larger deductions than cost depletion. Percentage depletion on oil and gas wells cannot be greater than 50% of the taxable income generated on the oil and gas property or 65% of the total taxable income of the taxpayer.

The main types of oil and gas limited partnership programs available to investors are

- Exploratory drilling
- Developmental drilling
- Balance drilling
- Oil and gas income

An exploratory drilling program is an oil and gas program that drills for oil and gas in an area without proven reserves. This practice is referred to as *wildcatting*. Therefore, a wildcat program is an oil and gas program that drills in a completely unproven area. Some exploratory programs drill extension or step-out wells. These are wells drilled in unproven areas adjacent to a producing field. This is done to the limits of the oil and gas field that is already producing. In some exploratory programs, deeper test wells are drilled. These are wells drilled in a proven field but to deeper unproven zones. If oil is discovered, but the well produces only ten barrels or less per day, it is referred to as a *stripper well.*

Exploratory programs offer an investor the greatest risk, but the potential for the greatest returns. Investors in exploratory programs experience more dry holes. Even in a successful exploratory program, cash flow to investors may be several years away. This is because money generated from early development may be needed to finance development of the well. This type of program is suited only for investors who can bear the risks associated with it.

A developmental drilling program drills new wells in an area of proven reserves. The probability of finding oil or gas is much higher than for an exploratory program. However, the cost of acquiring leases in areas of proven reserves is higher than the cost of acquiring leases in unproven areas. Therefore, returns to investors are less under a successful developmental program than a successful exploratory program.

A balanced drilling program drills both exploratory and developmental wells. In other words, a balanced drilling program is mixing high-risk exploratory drilling with lower-risk developmental drilling.

An oil and gas income program buys already-producing properties with proven oil and gas reserves. An oil and gas income program does not drill for oil and gas. An income program does not generally produce any intangible drilling costs or depletion deductions for investors and is technically not a tax shelter investment. An oil and gas income program possesses the least risk to an investor.

Some oil and gas limited partnerships provide for assessment of the limited partners for additional capital contributions. The assessment is a demand to limited partners for additional cash contributions if needed by the program for additional drilling or completion costs. If the investor does not meet the assessment by depositing the additional cash, his share of the revenues will be automatically reduced.

Sharing arrangements between general and limited partners vary depending on the particular oil and gas program. The term **sharing arrangement** refers to the agreement between the general and limited partners that will determine the manner in which revenues and costs will be shared by the partners. A sharing arrangement may allocate capital costs to the general partners and tax-deductible costs to the limited partners. The IRS requires that a sharing arrangement have a substantial economic effect if it is to be allowed for tax purposes.

The main types of sharing arrangements in oil and gas programs include

- Overriding royalty interest (carried interest)
- Disproportionate working interest (promoted interest)
- Subordinated working interest (reversionary interest)
- Functional allocation

In an overriding royalty-sharing arrangement, the sponsor or general partner does not pay any costs related to drilling the wells, but shares in revenues as soon as the first oil and gas is removed from the well. An overriding royalty interest is also referred to as a **carried interest** since the general partner's costs are carried by the limited partners.

In a disproportionate sharing arrangement, the general partner receives a share of the revenue that is greater than his participation in costs. A general partner might pay 10% of the costs and share in 25% of the revenues.

In a subordinated working interest, the general partner or sponsor does not bear any costs relating to drilling the wells. However, he does not share in revenues until the investors or limited partners recover the cost of their investment. A subordinated working interest is also referred to as a **reversionary interest**.

In a functional allocation-sharing arrangement, the general partner bears all of the capital or tangible costs of drilling the wells. These are costs that must be capitalized for tax purposes. The limited partners or investors bear the intangible costs, which are deductible as they are incurred. Therefore, in a functional allocation sharing arrangement, nondeductible costs are allocated to the general partner and deductible costs are allocated to the limited partners. Most public offerings use functional allocations to make the program attractive to investors. However, since a functional allocation-sharing arrangement is a **special allocation** according to the IRS, it must have a substantial economic effect separate from the tax consequences of the allocation. Otherwise, the IRS may choose to disallow the functional allocation-sharing arrangement.

EQUIPMENT LEASING

Equipment leasing as a tax shelter is similar in certain ways to a real estate program. Both equipment leasing and real estate involve renting property and rely on ACRS deductions, interest deductions, and leverage. Losses are generally spread over a number of years. However, in most cases, losses generated in an equipment-leasing deal are for a much shorter period than for a real estate deal. Usually, a few years after investing in an equipment-leasing program, ACRS deductions decline or disappear and the taxpayer receives phantom income that must be reported for tax purposes. But the taxpayer receives no cash to make the tax payment. Phantom income is a product of a leveraged tax shelter investment and normally occurs after a program reaches the crossover point. The crossover point refers to the point at which a tax shelter investment that had been generating losses begins to generate taxable income without cash flow to pay the tax liability. The crossover point is also referred to as the **burnout** or turnaround.

An equipment-leasing program allows a business to obtain the use of an asset such as an airplane or computer equipment without incurring the risk of ownership of the asset. In a blind pool arrangement, investors do not know the identity of the assets until after the partnership is formed. An equipment-leasing tax shelter program is attractive to investors because it can generate substantial ACRS or depreciation deductions over a relatively short period of time.

An equipment-leasing tax shelter could invest in any of the following types of assets:

- Aircraft
- Computer equipment
- Railroad cars
- Drilling rigs
- Barges
- Oil tankers
- Medical equipment
- Farm machinery

Equipment-leasing programs contain risks an investor should consider. The credit standing of the company that is renting the equipment is very important. Will the company or lessee be financially able to meet the lease payments? Equipment leasing is subject to the at-risk rules. Therefore, for an investor to claim a loss in excess of his cash contribution in the program, he must be personally liable for the repayment of the borrowed funds used in the purchase of the equipment. The at-risk limitation on deducting losses applies to equipment-leasing and oil and gas programs.

There are normally two types of leases used in an equipment-leasing program.

1. Finance lease
2. Operating lease

In a finance lease, the limited partnership (lessor) anticipates receiving the entire cost of the equipment (including financing costs) and to earn a reasonable profit from the rentals charged. A finance lease could be leveraged or nonleveraged. If it is leveraged, up to 80% of the equipment's cost is financed with a nonrecourse debt. A nonleveraged finance lease uses equipment that is purchased for cash or for cash plus recourse debt.

A finance lease is normally structured as a net lease. This means the lessee (company) pays maintenance, property taxes, and insurance in addition to the rent. The limited partners, in a finance lease, receive tax benefits and any residual value that the equipment might have at the end of the term of the lease. The limited partners bear the risk of the company's not meeting the lease payments or that the equipment might be destroyed or without residual value at the end of the lease term.

With an operating lease, the limited partnership does not receive a full return of the equipment cost over the initial lease term. In order to earn a profit, the limited partnership (lessor) must profitably re-lease or sell the equipment at the end of the initial lease term. An operating lease may or may not be structured as a net lease. An operating lease is riskier for the limited partnership than a finance lease. The lessor runs a risk from obsolescence of the equipment or the inability to re-lease the equipment on favorable terms.

Equipment-leasing deals are generally not suitable for an investor seeking long-term tax deferral. The shorter the cost recovery period, the faster the crossover point is reached. Equipment leasing generally provides possible tax deferral in the early years. However, once the crossover point is reached, the investment generates taxable income instead of a tax loss. Also, an investor may have a problem with recapture since the gain on the sale of the equipment is ordinary income to the extent of previous cost recovery deductions taken. Equipment-leasing deals are normally suitable for investors in a high tax bracket.

RETURN ON INVESTMENT ANALYSIS

A person investing in a tax shelter can analyze his or her return on investment under several methods. The most common methods used to compute return on investment in a tax-sheltered investment are

- Payback method
- Present value method
- Internal rate of return
- Cash-on-cash method

Under the **payback method**, an investor measures the time required for the after-tax income generated from the investment to equal the after-tax cash expenditure for the investment. The **present value method** attempts to measure future returns in relation to today's value. The present value method is concerned with the time value of money. A dollar received today is worth more than a dollar that will be received sometime in the future. The **internal rate of return** on an investment is the rate that discounts future cash flows from an investment to an amount that equals the amount invested. The internal rate of return analysis results in a net present value of zero. The internal rate of return analysis measures only the amount that remains invested. The true return on an investment will differ from the internal rate of return unless cash distributions can be reinvested at a rate that equals the internal rate of return. Both internal rate of return and present value analysis take into consideration the time value of money.

The **cash-on-cash method** is the easiest of the four methods used to analyze returns on tax shelters. The annual return on the investment is divided by the amount of cash invested in the shelter. The effect of taxes is disregarded in this analysis. Certain investors use this analysis because of its simplicity.

TAX SHELTER OFFERINGS

The tax aspects relating to a tax shelter are regulated by the IRS. However, tax shelter offerings are also subject to federal and state securities laws. The federal securities laws applicable to tax shelters are enforced by the SEC and the National Association of Securities Dealers (NASD). State securities laws are enforced by individual state securities regulators.

Offerings of direct participation programs are either managed offerings or nonmanaged offerings. A managed offering is sold through one soliciting broker/dealer or wholesaler. In a nonmanaged offering, the sponsor of the program hires individuals or broker/dealers who assemble dealers and educate them about the benefits of the program. If a sponsor or manager hires wholesalers, under NASD rules, the wholesaler must be registered.

A public tax shelter offering must be registered with the SEC. A registration statement is filed with the SEC, and a prospectus is sent to customers. The purpose of the prospectus is to provide full disclosure to potential purchasers.

Federal securities laws exempt the following two types of tax shelters from the registration requirements of the Securities Act of 1933:

- Intrastate offering
- Private placement

An **intrastate offering** is made by a limited partnership organized in one state and offered only to residents of the same state. A private placement is made under Regulation D, and investors must meet certain suitability standards. In a private offering, an offering memorandum is sent to investors instead of a prospectus.

A sale of a limited partnership interest is not normally final until the general partner accepts the subscriber as a limited partner by signing the subscription agreement. This agreement contains representations relating to the following:

- That the subscribing limited partner has read the prospectus and understands the risks involved in the agreement
- That the subscriber has sufficient net worth and income to invest in a direct participation program
- That the investment is suitable for the person
- That the investor's taxpayer identification number or Social Security number has been obtained
- That the subscriber's state of residency is correct
- That the investor, by signing the subscription agreement, grants the general partner a power of attorney to conduct partnership affairs
- That the subscriber understands how the general partner may be indemnified against liabilities or penalties
- The amount of the limited partner's initial contribution
- That the limited partner, by signing the subscription agreement, agrees to the terms and representations contained therein

Public tax shelter offerings are normally available to investors in minimum amounts of $5,000. Private limited partnership offerings normally require a minimum amount of $20,000, sometimes payable in a series of annual installments. Therefore, private offerings are normally available only to investors of substantial means while public offerings are available to investors of moderate means. Public offerings normally diversify in a pool of properties offering moderate returns and seeking capital gains on the disposition of the property. A private tax shelter normally invests in a single piece of property with the major objective being the realization of tax benefits.

ALTERNATIVE MINIMUM TAX

Certain taxpayers obtain tax advantages that reduce or eliminate their tax liability. The alternative minimum tax is designed to recoup some of these tax advantages by imposing a minimum tax on certain tax preference items. Individual taxpayers are required to pay an alternative minimum tax if it exceeds the regular income tax.

TAX SHELTER REGISTRATION

As a result of the Tax Reform Act of 1984, certain tax shelter investments must now be registered with the IRS. In general, a tax shelter must be registered if it offers a greater than two-for-one tax deduction or it has five or more investors and a total offering of more that $250,000.

The tax shelter organizer is the person principally responsible for registering the tax shelter. If the tax shelter organizer fails to register the shelter, then any person who participates in the organization of the tax shelter is required to register it. Penalties will be imposed on organizers who fail to timely register a tax shelter.

Once the shelter is registered, the organizers must maintain a list identifying all investors. This list must be maintained for seven years and available for inspection by the IRS. Investors must include the tax shelter identification number on their tax returns when claiming the tax benefit.

ABUSIVE TAX SHELTERS

An abusive tax shelter is one that lacks economic reality and viability. Without the promised tax benefits, the investment considered by itself would be worthless. The most important characteristic an investor should be concerned with in any tax shelter investment is the economic soundness of the program. If the IRS determines that a particular tax shelter investment is abusive, then

- The tax deductions will be disallowed.
- Additional tax will be owed by investors.
- Interest will be charged on underpaid taxes.
- Investors may be subject to fraud or negligent penalties.

SUBCHAPTER S CORPORATION

Normally a corporation is not a suitable business enterprise for a tax shelter investment. A corporation is normally a separate taxpaying entity. However, the subchapter S corporation is an exception since it functions very much like a partnership for tax purposes.

A subchapter S corporation is not subject to a corporate income tax. The stockholders of a subchapter S corporation report their share of the corporation's net income or loss. Therefore, a subchapter S corporation can flow through tax benefits to its shareholders similar to a limited partnership. However, a subchapter S corporation cannot have more than thirty-five shareholders or stockholders. The stockholders in a subchapter S corporation can be individuals, estates, or certain trusts. A corporation cannot invest in subchapter S corporations. A corporation is allowed to invest in a limited partnership.

A subchapter S corporation can issue only one class of stock. The subchapter S corporation must be a domestic corporation and its shareholders U.S. citizens or residents. Shareholders cannot be nonresident aliens.

Subchapter S corporation shareholders can deduct losses only to the extent of their adjusted basis in the stock. A shareholder's adjusted basis is reduced by losses in previous years.

SOLE PROPRIETORSHIP

A sole proprietor is an individual who owns a business directly without any other owners. The sole proprietor is his own boss and makes his own decisions. S/he has unlimited liability for the debts of the sole proprietorship if the debts are not satisfied by business assets. The sole proprietor can draw money out of the business at any time provided creditor claims can be satisfied.

GENERAL PARTNERSHIP

A general partnership is established by agreement of two or more persons to operate a business enterprise for profit as co-owners. A written partnership agreement is drawn up and signed by all partners. The partnership agreement governs the activities of the individual partners throughout their partnership relationship. Partners may invest money in the partnership, or their investment may consist of services in lieu of money. It is not mandatory that a written partnership be drawn. However, it would be extremely unwise to conduct partnership business without a written agreement. The partnership agreement must contain the essential elements of a contract to be enforceable under state law.

A partnership enters into contracts in its own name. Each partner owns an undivided proportionate share of partnership property unless there is an agreement to the contrary. Normally, all partners obtain an equal share and equal rights in the management of the business. Partners share proportionately in the profits and losses of the business. Each partner is entitled to complete information relating to partnership business. The books and records relating to the partnership should be kept at the partnership's place of business.

Partnership differences are settled by a majority vote of the partners unless otherwise agreed. Each partner acts as an agent of the partnership in all business transactions. In other words, any partner can bind the partnership by his acts within the scope of the business. All of the partner's personal assets are subject to claims of partnership creditors. However, a partner's personal creditor can only attach the individual partner's interest in the partnership.

A partnership is dissolved when a partner dies or withdraws from the partnership. A partnership could terminate at the end of a specific period. If no particular period is specified in the partnership agreement, then the partnership continues at the will of each of the partners.

CORPORATION

A corporation is a business organization created under the laws of a particular state. Ownership in a corporation is divided into shares of stock. The stockholders elect the board of directors, which appoints the officers to manage the corporation. Direct participation programs are not normally set up as corporations because income and expense cannot be flowed through to individual stockholders. A corporation is a very popular form of business organization since its stockholders have limited liability. They are not responsible for the debts of the corporation.

The rights and obligations of stockholders of a corporation were presented earlier in the text and need not be reviewed here. It is sufficient to state that corporations are not effective tax shelter vehicles.

TRUSTS

A trust may be set up to carry on a business or to own property or for any lawful purpose. A trust is set up pursuant to a trust agreement. The trust assets are managed by a trustee. Ownership in the trust may be evidenced by shares called **certificates of beneficial interest**.

The trustee and beneficiaries of the trust are not responsible for debts incurred by the trust. A creditor must look to the trust assets for settling claims against the trust. However, a trustee could be liable for debts incurred in violation of the provisions of the trust agreement. A trustee is a fiduciary and must act in the best interest of the beneficiaries of the trust.

The trust agreement or deed of trust normally covers the following relating to a trust's activities:

- Name of the trust and trustees
- Duration of the trust
- Purpose of the trust (such as dealing in real estate)
- Directions concerning the management of trust property
- Provisions relating to the sale of trust property
- Any limitations placed on the trustee
- The compensation of the trustee
- Distributions from the trust to beneficiaries

SUMMARY—TAX REFORM ACT OF 1986

The following are the main provisions of the Tax Reform Act of 1986 relating to direct participation programs:

- Losses from tax shelter investments such as limited partnerships are generally deductible only against other passive income. Losses from passive activities, with an exception for rental real estate activities up to a certain amount, cannot be deducted against other income of the taxpayer.
- Deductible losses from rental real estate activities are limited to $25,000 provided the taxpayer actively participates in the management. The $25,000 deductible limit is phased out if the taxpayer's adjusted gross income exceeds $100,000. It is eliminated when his adjusted gross income exceeds $150,000.
- Residential rental property must be depreciated over 27½ years and commercial real estate over 31½ years. Both must be depreciated using the straight-line method.
- Real estate investments are not subject to the at-risk rules. This means that a taxpayer cannot deduct losses in excess of the amount he has invested or his adjusted basis in the real estate investment.
- Taxpayers may be subject to an alternative minimum tax.

SERIES 63 STUDY GUIDE

20 UNIFORM SECURITIES AGENT STATE LAW EXAMINATION STUDY GUIDE

INTRODUCTION

Most states have enacted some form of legislation designed to protect investors by preventing the sale of fraudulent securities. Such legislation intends to exercise control over those selling securities and over the securities themselves. The term **blue sky laws** is often used when referring to such state laws. The term itself originated in a Kansas law of 1911 where it was apparent that farmers had been exploited by promoters who sold the farmers securities of companies having as assets only the "blue sky."

The Uniform Securities Act, also referred to as the **Uniform Practice Code** or the Act, has been adopted in most states. Prior to its adoption in the late 1950s there were 47 individual state laws—each different. These presented a horrendous problem to those persons or companies wishing to sell, issue, or underwrite securities nationally.

The Uniform Securities Agent State Law Examination is prepared by the North American Securities Administrators Association (NASAA) in cooperation with securities industry representatives. The examination consists of 50 multiple-choice questions. The passing score is 70% (35 correct answers). One hour is allotted for the examination. The relative importance given in the examination to particular sections of the Uniform Securities Act is as follows:

20%	Definitions of Terms
15%	Licensing or Registration Requirements for Broker/Dealers, Agents, and Investment Advisors
10%	Registration of Securities; Exempt Securities and Exempt Transactions
45%	Fraudulent and Other Prohibited Practices
10%	Regulatory Oversight, Criminal Penalties, Civil Liabilities, Scope of the Act and General Provisions

The purpose of the Uniform Securities Act is to protect the public against fraudulent transactions within a state. In order for an agent to solicit business within a state, both the agent and the broker/dealer must be registered in that state or exempt from registration.

An **issuer** who sells securities to the public must make certain disclosures in the form of registration. The **purchaser** of a security can read the available information on the issue, such as a registration statement and prospectus, and decide whether to purchase the security.

The purpose of the Uniform Securities Act is to regulate securities transactions within a particular state. The individual states regulate the sales of securities within the state. They also regulate the activities of broker/dealers and their agents and investment advisors and investment advisor representatives. The purpose of the Uniform Securities Act and state regulation is to prevent fraudulent or unethical business activities within the state. For an issuer to sell securities to the public, the issuer's securities must either be registered in the state or qualify for an exemption from registration (exempt security). An issuer of securities is the corporation selling the securities such as Coca-Cola, Johnson & Johnson, or XYZ Manufacturing Company. If the securities must be registered in the state, certain information must be filed with the administrator, the state official who enforces the provisions of the Uniform Securities Act on behalf of the state. It is a violation of the Uniform Securities Act to "offer to sell" or "sell" unregistered nonexempt securities in a particular state.

The same rules apply to broker/dealers and their agents. The broker/dealer is the business entity such as Merrill Lynch or Paine Webber. The broker/dealer employs agents who are also referred to as registered representatives (RRs) or brokers. The broker/dealer is an entity and the agents are individuals. Both the broker/dealer and the agents must be registered to solicit business within a state, unless they qualify for an exemption from registration. The burden of proving any exemption is on the issuer, broker/dealer, agent, or any other person claiming an exemption under the Act.

Investment advisors and investment advisor representatives must be registered to do business within the state, unless they qualify for an exemption from registration. The investment advisor is a business entity and an investment advisor representative is an individual. The broker/dealers and investment advisors are responsible for the activities of their agents and investment advisor representatives. The term *person* under the Uniform Securities Act refers to a "legal person" as well as a natural or human person. Therefore, under the Uniform Securities Act, the term *person* includes a corporation, partnership, sole proprietorship, business trust, government, political subdivision of a government such as a city or town, joint-stock company, an unincorporated association, a trust in which the beneficial interests are evidenced by a security, and a natural person.

When a broker/dealer, investment advisor, agent, or investment advisor representative is initially registered in a state, two forms must be completed. One form is a registration application, and the second form is a **consent to service of process,** which allows the administrator to receive service of process (notice of a lawsuit or legal proceeding) on behalf of the entity or person being sued in a noncriminal suit. The administrator will notify the entity or individual of the legal proceeding. The consent to service of process allows a public customer to deliver notice of a lawsuit to the administrator against an out-of-state broker/dealer or investment advisor. The out-of-state broker/dealer or investment advisor must defend the lawsuit within the public customer's state. Therefore, assume a public customer in Vermont filed a lawsuit against a Montana broker/dealer doing business in Vermont. The public customer delivers the legal documents to the administrator in Vermont. The Vermont administrator notifies the Montana broker/dealer of the lawsuit. The Montana broker/dealer must defend the lawsuit in Vermont.

The US Congress in 1996 passed a federal law entitled **The National Securities Markets Improvement Act of 1996.** The purpose of the Improvement Act of 1996 was to allocate regulatory responsibility between the Securities and Exchange Commission (SEC) and the state securities administrators.

A security defined as a **federal covered security** (covered security) is exempt from state regulation and will be regulated by the SEC. A federal covered security is defined as

- Securities listed on the New York Stock Exchange (NYSE), American Stock Exchange, or National Association of Securities Dealers Automated Quotation (NASDAQ) National Market Securities
- Securities issued by investment companies registered under the Investment Company Act of 1940
- Sales to qualified purchasers, which are individuals or businesses with assets at certain levels
- Certain offerings and transactions exempt from the Securities Act of 1933

However, the individual states will be able to collect fees and require notice filings. The individual states will still be able to enforce antifraud provisions of the Uniform Securities Act against entities or individuals, even if they are exempt from state regulation.

Investment advisors managing $25 million or more in client assets or who advise a mutual fund must be registered with the SEC. Investment advisors managing less than $25 million in client assets will register only with the state in which the advisor maintains its principal place of business.

The SEC regulates all investment advisors not registered in any state, such as a large foreign investment advisor doing business in the United States. Therefore, investment advisors with assets of $25 million or more will be registered only with the SEC. Investment advisors with assets of less than $25 million register only with the state. The Improvement Act also created a national standard for investment advisor registration outside of his or her home state. An investment advisor would not have to register in a particular state if he or she has no place of business in the particular state, and during the preceding twelve-month period has had fewer than six clients who are residents of the particular state.

The SEC can deny registration to an investment advisor or investment advisor representative or other person who has been convicted of a felony within the previous ten years. The SEC denies registrations to persons who have served jail sentences of one year or more.

Investment companies as a result of the Improvement Act are subject to SEC regulation only and will not be subject to state regulation. Broker/dealers will be exempt from state registration and regulation if the client has less than thirty days' temporary residency in a state.

IMPORTANT TERMS

The Uniform Securities Act defines the following terms as they relate to the purchase or sale of securities within a state

- Administrator
- Agent
- Broker/dealer
- Guaranteed

- Investment advisor
- Issuer
- Person
- Sell or offer to sell
- Security

The administrator is the top state official who is given the power to enforce the provisions of the Uniform Securities Act for the protection of the public. The administrator and his officers and employees may make public or private investigations within his own state or even outside of his own state. For example, the administrator in the state of Idaho could conduct an investigation in Idaho or in another state.

The administrator can require persons to give oral or written statements or affidavits under oath relating to an investigation. The administrator can subpoena books, records, papers, and correspondence relevant to a matter under inquiry. The administrator can subpoena witnesses who live within or outside of the state. The administrator is allowed, under the Uniform Securities Act, to begin an investigation if he feels a violation will occur, even if it has not yet occurred. The administrator may have jurisdiction for a violation of the Uniform Securities Act, provided the transaction occurred in the state, regardless of where the customer or agent resides.

The administrator is given the power to summarily suspend or revoke the registration of an agent, broker/dealer, or investment advisor. However, the person whose registration is suspended or revoked must receive notification of the order and receives the right to a hearing. The administrator may deny or suspend a registration based on factors such as

- The public interest
- Training
- Knowledge of the securities business
- Experience

The administrator is not allowed to deny or suspend a registration *solely* on the basis of lack of experience, provided the applicant or registrant is qualified by training, knowledge of the securities business, or both. An applicant or registrant is never allowed to state that a security registered with the SEC or a state securities administrator has been approved by virtue of such registration. This type of statement is misleading and prohibited under the Uniform Securities Act (Uniform Securities Code).

The administrator registers a security, but never passes upon the accuracy or adequacy of the prospectus, never approves the security, and never states that the registration statement or prospectus is true and complete.

If a person feels that a state securities administrator has ruled incorrectly concerning a matter, the administrator's order may be appealed. The person may file for review of the order with the appropriate court within sixty days after the entry of the order.

The term **agent** under the Act means any individual, other than a broker/dealer, who represents a broker/dealer or issuer in effecting or attempting to effect purchases or sales of securities. This includes an individual, such as the secretary of a salesman, who is authorized to accept orders. The secretary must be registered as an agent under the Act to accept orders and transact business with customers.

The term *agent* does not include an individual who represents an issuer in effecting transactions in a security that is classified as exempt by the Act or in effecting transactions which are themselves considered by the Act to be exempt transactions. A person is also not considered to be an agent if he effects transactions with employees, partners, or directors of the issuer, if no commission or remuneration is given for soliciting any person in the state. If an individual is not considered to be an agent under the Act, registration as an agent is not necessary.

The term *agent* under the Uniform Securities Act would normally include

- A person who sells registered securities to the general public
- A secretary of a salesman who is authorized to accept orders
- A person who sells securities such as common stock in a Canadian mining company or one-year commercial paper
- A person who engages in any transaction for the benefit of the issuer of the securities

The term *agent* under the Uniform Securities Act would *not* include

- A person who represents an issuer in an exempt transaction
- A bank, savings institution, or trust company

- An officer of a broker/dealer who does not effect or attempt to effect purchases or sales of securities
- A clerical person with no authority to accept orders
- A secretary to an officer of a broker/dealer
- A person who represents an issuer in effecting transactions in which no commissions are paid
- An officer selling his own company's stock to his employees and no commission is paid to the officer for soliciting purchasers
- A person who represents an issuer in transactions with an underwriter

If an agent violates the Uniform Securities Act, the agent could be subject to

- A criminal penalty
- A civil penalty
- Suspension or revocation of his license
- Disgorgement of commissions or profits

The term *agent* under the Uniform Securities Act is synonymous with broker or salesman. When a person is acting as an agent, he is purchasing securities for the account of a customer and earning a commission on the transaction.

The term **broker/dealer** means any person engaged in the business of effecting transactions in securities for the account of others or for his or her own account. The term does not include an agent, issuer, bank, savings institution, or trust company. The term also does not include a person who has no place of business in a particular state if

- He effects transactions in the state exclusively with or through

  - The issuers of the securities involved in the transactions
  - Other broker/dealers
  - Banks, savings institutions, trust companies, insurance companies, investment companies, pension or profit-sharing trusts, or other financial institutions or institutional buyers, or

- During any twelve-month period he does not direct more than fifteen offers to sell or buy into this state to persons other than issuers, broker/dealers, or institutional buyers.

Assume Montvale Securities Corporation is a broker/dealer registered in Arkansas with its only office in Little Rock. Montvale Securities has three bank customers in Texas and during a twelve-month period, directs four offers to sell to individuals living in Texas. For purposes of the Uniform Securities Act, Montvale Securities is not required to be registered in the state of Texas.

Therefore, under the Uniform Securities Act, the following are considered to be broker/dealers:

- Any person engaged in the business of executing or effecting transactions for the account of others or for his or her own account.
- A broker/dealer who has a place of business in a particular state even if his or her only clients are financial institutions.

However, under the Uniform Securities Act, the following are not considered broker/dealers

- An agent
- An issuer
- A commercial bank
- A savings bank
- A person with no place of business in the state who does not direct more than fifteen offers to sell or buy into this state in any twelve-consecutive-month period.

The word **guaranteed** under the Act means guaranteed as to the payment of principal, interest, or dividends. For example, a parent corporation could guarantee the payment of principal and interest on bonds issued by a subsidiary corporation. This action by the parent corporation would make the bonds more marketable and give the purchaser a higher-quality security.

The term **investment advisor,** under the Uniform Securities Act, includes any person who, for compensation

- Engages in the business of advising others, either directly or through publications or writings, as to the value of securities or as to the advisability of investing in, purchasing, or selling securities, or

- As part of a regular business, issues analyses or reports concerning securities.

Therefore, an investment advisor *advises others on securities for compensation.* The investment advisor must advise others either orally or in writing. The advice must be on securities. Securities are not insurance contracts, residential real estate, collectibles, or commodity futures contracts. The advice must be for compensation, either direct compensation or indirect compensation.

The term *investment advisor* does not include the following:

- Bank, savings institution, or trust company
- Lawyer, accountant, engineer, or teacher whose performance of these services is solely incidental to the practice of his profession and who receives no special compensation for the advice
- Broker/dealer whose performance of these services is solely incidental to the conduct of his business, if he receives no special compensation for them
- Publisher of any bona fide newspaper, newsmagazine, or business or financial publication of general, regular, and paid circulation
- Any person whose advice, analyses, or reports relate only to securities exempted by the Act
- Any person who has no place of business in this state if

  - His only clients in the state are other investment advisors, broker/dealers, banks, savings institutions, trust companies, insurance companies, investment companies, or other financial institutions or institutional buyers, or
  - During any twelve-month period he solicits fewer than six clients.

- Any person whom the administrator designates as not within the definition of an investment advisor

This definition of investment advisor is modeled after that used in the Investment Advisors Act of 1940. It recognizes the fact that broker/dealers commonly give a certain amount of advice to their customers as part of their regular business and that this should not bring them under the Investment Advisors Act. However, if the broker/dealer is specially compensated for such advice, he would be subject to the Act. The important distinction concerns why the compensation was paid. Was the compensation paid for the advice itself or for other services to which the advice is merely incidental?

In the description of **publisher,** it should be noted that "paid" circulation is an integral part of the definition. A person who distributes a "hot-tip" sheet to attract clients would not, for example, be considered a publisher. The publishers of *U.S. News & World Report* would not be considered to be investment advisors, but anyone selling subscriptions to a market letter providing investment advice would be considered an investment advisor under the Uniform Securities Act.

Investment advisors under the Act cannot take or have custody of any securities or funds of any client if

- The administrator, by rule, prohibits the investment advisor from taking custody, or
- The investment advisor fails to notify the administrator that he has custody of the securities or funds.

An investment advisor's compensation under the Act may be based on the average value of funds managed over a period of time. The investment advisor's compensation cannot be based on a percentage of the capital gains or losses generated in a client's account except for private investment companies.

The term **issuer** under the Act means any person who issues or proposes to issue any security. The term **nonissuer transaction** refers to a transaction not directly or indirectly for the benefit of the issuer. For example, an isolated nonissuer transaction is exempt from the registration requirements of the Uniform Securities Act. Assume John Jones sells 100 shares of XYZ to his brother. This is an isolated nonissuer transaction and not subject to the registration requirements of the Act since it is an exempt transaction.

The term **person** under the Uniform Securities Act refers to an individual, a corporation, a partnership, an association, a joint-stock company, or a trust wherein the interests of the beneficiaries are evidenced by a security, an unincorporated organization, a government, or a political subdivision of a government. The term **person** refers to both a natural person and a legal person (business entity).

The terms **sale** and **sell** include every contract of sale of, contract to sell, or disposition of, a security or interest in a security for value. In other words, the definition includes any disposition of a security for consideration.

The terms **offer** and **offer to sell** include every attempt or offer to dispose of, or solicitation of an offer to buy, a security or interest in a security for value.

The terms *sale, sell, offer,* and *offer to sell* include the following:

- A security given or delivered with, or as a bonus on account of, any purchase of securities. Such securities are considered to constitute part of the subject of the purchase and to have been offered and sold for value.
- A purported gift of assessable stock is considered to involve an offer and sale under the Act. A gift of nonassessable stock is not considered a sale under the Act.
- The sale or offer of a warrant or right to purchase or subscribe to another security or a security convertible into another security is considered to include an offer of the other security.

The terms *sale, sell,* and *offer to sell* do not include

- A bona fide pledge or loan
- A stock dividend, if nothing of value is given by stockholders for the dividend
- Mergers, consolidations, reclassification of securities, or sale of corporate assets in consideration of the issuance of securities of another corporation

The term **security** under the Uniform Securities Act means, but is not limited to, any

- Note, stock, treasury stock, bond, debenture, or evidence of indebtedness
- Certificate of interest or participation in any profit-sharing agreement
- Collateral trust agreement, certificate of deposit for a security, or transferable share
- Preorganization certificate or subscription
- Investment contract, voting trust certificate, or interest in farmlands or animals
- Certificate of interest or participation in an oil, gas, or mining lease
- Oil and gas drilling programs, real estate condominiums, and cooperatives
- Commodity option contracts or whiskey warehouse receipts
- Multilevel distributorship arrangements or merchandise marketing schemes
- Listed stock options
- Interest in a real estate investment trust
- Limited partnership interests
- Interest in a unit investment trust

In general, the term **security** applies to any interest or instrument commonly known as a security, or any certificate of interest or participation in, temporary or interim certificate for, receipt for, guarantee of, or warrant or right to subscribe to or purchase, any of the foregoing.

Investment contracts may be considered securities under certain circumstances. The federal courts have determined that the basic test to be used to determine whether an investment is a security concerns the following two questions:

1. Is the investment in a common enterprise?
2. Is the investor led to expect profits because of the managerial efforts of a third party, such as a promoter?

Investments that are considered securities, since they affirmatively answer these two questions, include commodity option contracts, whiskey warehouse receipts, oil and gas drilling programs, real estate condominiums, cattle programs, equipment-leasing programs, multilevel distributorship arrangements, and merchandising marketing schemes.

The term *security* does not include any insurance or endowment policy or annuity contract under which an insurance company promises to pay a fixed sum of money, either in a lump sum or periodically for life, or some other specified period. Therefore, a fixed annuity is not considered a security under the Act, but a variable annuity is a security. The term *security* includes items previously mentioned such as listed stock options, limited partnership interests, an interest in a real estate investment trust, a certificate of interest in an oil well lease, an investment contract, and an interest in a unit investment trust. It would not, however, include Keogh plans, individual retirement accounts, or fixed-annuity contracts. The term *security* under the Act does not include collectibles, such as paintings, rugs, antiques, or precious stones, and does not include real estate bought for residential use.

A **private placement** under the Uniform Securities Act is defined as any transaction pursuant to an offer directed to not more than ten persons in the state during any period of twelve consecutive months. The private placement exemption under the Uniform Securities Act is narrower in scope than the federal securities exemption. A private placement is an exempt transaction provided the provisions of the Act are complied with.

LICENSING/REGISTRATION REQUIREMENTS

It is unlawful for any person, broker/dealer, or issuer under the Uniform Securities Act to

- Transact business in a state as an agent unless that person is registered as an agent under the Act or exempt from registration. An agent cannot sell securities based on a pending application in a state. The application must be approved before the agent can transact any business in the state. This is true even if the agent has passed the Series 63 examination. No business can be conducted until the application is effective.
- Transact business in a state as a broker/dealer unless he or she is registered as a broker/dealer under the Act or exempt from registration.
- Employ an agent unless the agent is registered or exempt from registration

  - An agent's registration is not effective during any period when he is not associated with a registered broker/dealer or an issuer. If a broker/dealer's license is suspended the licenses of all of the agents are not effective. The agents would have to transfer to a properly registered broker/dealer in order to effect transactions.
  - When an agent begins or terminates a connection with a broker/dealer or issuer, or begins or terminates those activities which make him an agent, the agent and the broker/dealer or issuer must promptly notify the administrator. The requirement to notify the administrator is placed on both the broker/dealer and agent concerning a change in registration.

- Transact business in a state as an investment advisor unless

  - He is registered as an investment advisor or exempt from registration.
  - He is registered as a broker/dealer.
  - He has client assets of $25 million or more (federal registered only).

The Uniform Securities Act permits the same person to exercise both broker/dealer and investment advisory functions without dual registration. It authorizes the administrator to condition a particular applicant's registration as a broker/dealer upon his not acting as an investment advisor, if the administrator finds he is not qualified to act as an investment advisor.

Every registration of a broker/dealer, agent, or investment advisor expires on December 31 unless renewed. An initial or renewal registration may be obtained by filing an application with the administrator together with a consent to service of process for an initial registration.

In some states, applicants for initial registration are required to publish an announcement of their application in specified newspapers. If there is no denial order or pertinent pending proceeding, a registration of a broker/dealer, agent, or investment advisor becomes effective on the thirtieth day after the application is filed. Of course, the Administrator may specify an earlier effective date. He may also defer the effective date until the thirtieth day after the filing of any amendment.

Registration of a broker/dealer or investment advisor automatically constitutes registration of any agent who is a partner, officer, or other person of similar status or similar functions. Every applicant must pay a filing fee specifically established for that applicant's category (broker/dealer, agent, or investment advisor). If the application is denied or withdrawn, the administrator retains the fee.

CAPITAL REQUIREMENTS

The administrator may require a minimum capital for registered broker/dealers and investment advisors. The administrator may also require registered broker/dealers, agents, and investment advisors to post surety bonds and may determine their conditions.

A **surety bond** is a contract issued by an insurance company whereby the insurance company agrees to make good the default or the debt of the insured party. For example, if money is stolen from a broker/dealer by an employee, a surety bond will normally cover the loss up to certain limits.

Surety bonds must provide for suit thereon by any person having a cause for action arising under the civil liabilities sections of the Act and, if the administrator requires, by any person who has a cause of action not arising under the Act. The surety bond shall also provide that no suit may be maintained to enforce any liability on the bond unless the suit is brought within two years after the sale or other act on which the suit is based.

RECORDKEEPING

Registered broker/dealers and investment advisors are required to make and keep such accounts, correspondence, memoranda, papers, books, and other records as the administrator prescribes. Such records must be preserved for three years unless the administrator prescribes otherwise. They must also file any financial reports required under the Act.

If information in any document filed becomes inaccurate or incomplete in any material respect, the registrant must promptly file a correcting amendment unless notification of the correction has been properly made under the rules. All required records are subject at any time to such reasonable periodic, special, or other examinations by representatives of the administrator as the administrator deems necessary or appropriate in the public interest, or for the protection of investors. To avoid unnecessary duplication of examinations, the administrator may cooperate with the securities administrators of other states, the SEC, and any national securities exchange or national securities association registered under the Securities Exchange Act of 1934. The SEC and state administrators can engage in joint examinations, joint rulemaking, joint investigations, hearings, or proceedings and can share personnel and have a central records depository.

ADMINISTRATIVE SANCTIONS

The administrator has the authority to deny, suspend, or revoke any registration of a broker/dealer, agent, or investment advisor, if he finds that the order is in the public interest and that the applicant or registrant

- Has filed an application for registration that contains an untrue statement of a material fact.
- Has willfully violated or failed to comply with any provision of the Uniform Securities Act.
- Has been convicted, within the past ten years, of any misdemeanor involving a security, or any aspect of the securities business, or any felony. A person would not be denied a registration if he or she had been *charged* with a felony but not convicted of the felony.
- Is permanently or temporarily enjoined by a court of competent jurisdiction from engaging in the securities business.
- Is the subject of an order of the administrator denying, suspending, or revoking his registration.
- Is the subject of an order entered within the past five years by the securities administrator of another state or the SEC denying or revoking registration or is the subject of an order of the SEC or national securities association registered under the Securities Exchange Act of 1934, or is the subject of a US Post Office fraud order.
- Has engaged in dishonest or unethical practices in the securities business.
- Is insolvent, either in that his liabilities exceed his assets or in that he cannot meet his obligations as they mature. Such an order entered against a broker/dealer, or investment advisor would require a finding of insolvency.
- Is not qualified on the basis of factors such as training, experience, and knowledge of the securities business.
- Has failed to reasonably supervise agents if he is a broker/dealer, or employees if he is an investment advisor.
- Has failed to pay the proper filing fee. The registration will be denied until the fee is paid.

The administrator may not institute a suspension or revocation proceeding on the basis of a fact or transaction of which he is aware when registration becomes effective, unless the proceeding is instituted within the next thirty days.

In applying the rules concerning denial or revocation, other pertinent provisions include

- The administrator may not enter an order
  - Against a broker/dealer on the basis of the lack of qualification of anyone other than the broker/dealer (if he is an individual) or an agent of the broker/dealer.
  - Against an investment advisor on the basis of the lack of qualification of any person other than the investment advisor himself (if he is an individual) or any person representing the investment advisor in actions making him an investment advisor.
  - Solely on the basis of lack of experience if the applicant or registrant is qualified by training, knowledge, or both.

- The administrator shall consider that

- An agent who will work under the supervision of a registered broker/dealer does not need to have the same qualifications as the broker/dealer.
- An investment advisor is not necessarily qualified solely on the basis of experience as a broker/dealer or agent. If he finds that an applicant for registration as a broker/dealer is not qualified as an investment advisor, he may condition the registration as a broker/dealer on his not doing business in the state as an investment advisor.

- The administrator may provide for an examination, written, oral, or both, to be taken by persons representing an investment advisor.

The administrator may summarily postpone or suspend registration pending the final determination of any proceedings. In this case, the administrator shall promptly notify the applicant or registrant as well as the employer or prospective employer that such order has been entered, the reasons for the order, and that within fifteen days after the receipt of a written request the matter will be set down for a hearing. If a hearing is not requested or ordered, the order remains in effect until modified or vacated by the administrator. The administrator may cancel the registration or application if he finds that a registrant or applicant is no longer in existence; has ceased to do business; is subject to an adjudication of mental incompetence or control of a committee, conservator, or guardian; or cannot be located after a reasonable search.

Withdrawal of a registration becomes effective thirty days after receipt of an application (or shorter period as determined by the administrator) unless a revocation or suspension proceeding is pending or a proceeding to revoke or suspend or to impose conditions on the withdrawal is instituted within thirty days after the application is filed. The administrator may institute a revocation or suspension proceeding within one year after the withdrawal became effective and enter a revocation or suspension order as of the last date on which the registration was effective.

For the administrator to enter an order related to denial or revocation of an application, there must be

- Appropriate prior notice to the registrant or applicant
- Opportunity for a hearing
- Written findings of fact and conclusions of law

The administrator is given broad powers to enforce the Uniform Securities Act. To summarize, the administrator, under the Act, may do the following:

- Subpoena witnesses, books, records, papers, and correspondence relating to a securities investigation.
- Require affidavits to be filed by persons relating to a particular investigation.
- Cancel a registration if a registrant or applicant is no longer in existence or has ceased doing business as a broker/dealer or agent.
- Deny, suspend, or revoke a registration if he finds that an applicant or registrant has violated any provisions of the Act, engaged in dishonest practices, or has been convicted within the past ten years of a felony or misdemeanor relating to securities.
- Subpoena witnesses whether they live within or outside the state.
- Begin an investigation if he feels a violation will occur even if it has not yet occurred.
- Summarily suspend the registration of an agent, broker/dealer, or investment advisor. However, the person suspended will receive notification of the order and must be given the opportunity to have a hearing on the matter. Hearings are public unless both parties request that it be private. The administrator can grant the request that the hearing be private.

REGISTRATION OF SECURITIES

It is unlawful for a person to offer or sell a security in any state unless it is either registered or exempt from registration. There are different methods of registering a security—by notification, coordination, or qualification.

Notification (Filing)

Registration by notification is also called **registration by filing**. To qualify for registration by notification or filing, the issuer must meet certain tests concerning earnings and must not have had a default in the payment of principal, interest or dividends in the past three years. Generally, high-quality securities registering in one state would be registered by notification or filing.

If there is no stop order in effect and no proceeding pending under the Act, a registration by notification, becomes effective at 3:00 P.M. Eastern time on the second full business day after filing, or at an earlier time if the administrator so determines.

Coordination

If a registration statement has been filed under the Securities Act of 1933 concerning an offering, a security may be registered by coordination. If the security is to be registered by coordination, copies of the registration statement and prospectus are filed with the administrator.

The registration statement must provide any information specified in the Act including a consent to service of process. The registration statement automatically becomes effective when the federal registration statement becomes effective, if no stop order is in effect or no proceeding is pending.

Qualification

Any security may be registered by qualification. In this case, the registration statement must contain certain information concerning officers, directors, and the capital structure of the issuer.

If a security is registered by qualification, the registration statement becomes effective when the administrator so orders. The administrator may require that a prospectus be sent to specified persons participating in the distribution. A newly formed company registering securities for the first time in a state would have to register its securities by qualification.

Registration Provisions

A registration statement may be filed under the Uniform Securities Act by any of the following:

- The issuer
- Any other person on whose behalf the offering is to be made
- A registered broker/dealer

The person filing must pay a filing fee. If the registration statement is withdrawn before the effective date or a preeffective stop order is entered, the administrator shall retain part or all of the fee.

So long as the registration statement is effective, the administrator may require the person filing to file reports, not more than quarterly, to keep the information in the statement reasonably current, and to disclose the progress of the offering.

Denial of Registration

The administrator may issue a stop order denying effectiveness to, or suspending or revoking the effectiveness of, any registration statement if it is found that the order is in the public interest, that material facts are misleading, or that provisions of the Uniform Securities Act have been violated.

The administrator may not institute a stop order proceeding against an effective registration statement on the basis of a fact or transaction known to him when the statement became effective, unless the proceeding is instituted within the next thirty days.

The administrator may postpone or suspend the effectiveness of the registration statement pending final determination of any proceeding. In such case, the appropriate persons must be notified that the order has been entered and the reasons for entering the order, and that within fifteen days after receipt of a written request, there will be a hearing. If no hearing is requested or ordered, the administrator, after notice of and opportunity for hearing to each person, may modify, vacate, or extend the order until final determination.

Except in the preceding case related to the final determination of a proceeding, no stop order may be entered by the administrator without

- Appropriate prior notice to the applicant or registrant, the issuer, and the person on whose behalf the securities are to be or have been offered
- An opportunity for a hearing
- Written findings of fact and conclusions of law

The administrator may vacate or modify a stop order if he finds that the conditions prompting its entry have changed or that it is otherwise in the public interest to do so.

EXEMPT SECURITIES

Securities exempt from registration and advertising filing requirements of the Uniform Securities Act, but not its antifraud provisions, include

- Securities issued by the US government, federal agencies, and any state or political subdivision of a state
- Securities issued by the government of Canada or any other foreign government with which the United States currently maintains diplomatic relations
- Securities issued by banks, savings institutions, and credit unions organized in the United States
- Securities issued by insurance companies, not including variable annuities, organized in the United States
- Securities issued or guaranteed by any common carrier, public utility, or holding company that is subject to jurisdiction of the Interstate Commerce Commission
- Securities listed on national securities exchanges such as the NYSE, American Stock Exchange, and regional stock exchanges.
- Securities issued by nonprofit organizations. The administrator under the Act has the power to revoke this particular exemption if he feels it is in the public interest to do so.
- Commercial paper maturing within nine months of the date of issuance
- Any investment contract issued in connection with an employee's stock purchase, savings, pension, profit-sharing, or similar benefit plan so long as required notice is given to the administrator
- Federal covered securities (covered securities)

A **federal covered security** is exempt from state regulation as a result of the National Securities Markets Improvement Act of 1996. Federal covered securities are defined as

- Securities listed on the NYSE or American Stock Exchange
- NASDAQ National Market Securities
- Securities issued by an investment company registered under the Investment Company Act of 1940
- Securities sold to qualified purchasers. Qualified purchasers are individuals, married couples, or family-owned businesses that have at least $5 million in investments as well as a business or trust with $25 million in investments.
- Certain securities exempt under the Securities Act of 1933 including securities issued by the US government; federal or state banks; savings and loans and cooperatives; common carriers; employee pension, profit-sharing, and stock purchase plans; municipal securities outside of the home state of the issuer; private placements; secondary market transactions; fixed-annuity contracts and other insurance contracts; and commercial paper with a maturity of nine months or less. However, the following securities are *not* defined as federal covered securities:

  - Securities issued by nonprofit organizations
  - Intrastate offerings (offerings sold exclusively in one state)
  - Municipal securities offered within the issuer's home state

An **exempt security** is exempt from the registration requirements and the advertising requirements of the Uniform Securities Act. However, no security is exempt from the antifraud provisions of the Uniform Securities Act. Therefore, if a person commits fraud with a US government security, common stock, municipal bond, oil and gas drilling partnership, corporate bond, or any other security, he is subject to criminal, civil, or administrative penalties.

EXEMPT TRANSACTIONS

Transactions exempt from registration and advertising filing requirements of the Uniform Securities Act, but not its antifraud provisions, include

- Any isolated nonissuer transaction, such as one individual selling stock to another individual. For example, John Jones sells 100 shares of stock to his sister. This is an isolated nonissuer transaction.
- Any nonissuer distribution of an outstanding security if

  - A recognized securities manual contains specified information.
  - The security has a fixed maturity or a fixed interest or dividend provision and there has been no default during the current or preceding three fiscal years in the payment of principal, interest, or dividends.

- Any nonissuer transaction by or through a registered broker/dealer pursuant to an unsolicited order or offer to buy (the administrator may require that the customer acknowledge in a specified manner that the sale was unsolicited).
- Any transaction between the issuer and an underwriter or among underwriters. For example, XYZ Corporation sells stock to ABC Broker/Dealer relating to an underwriting. This is an exempt transaction.
- Any transaction secured by a real or chattel mortgage or deed of trust.
- Any transaction by a court-supervised person such as an executor, administrator, sheriff, marshal, receiver in bankruptcy, guardian or conservator.
- Any transaction executed by a bona fide pledge without any purpose of evading the Uniform Securities Act.
- Any offer or sale to a bank, savings institution, trust company, insurance company, investment company, pension or profit-sharing trust, or other financial institution or institutional buyer or to a broker/dealer. To be considered an institutional buyer, no specific level of assets is necessary for the bank, insurance company, or other institutional buyer.
- Any transaction pursuant to an offer directed to not more than ten persons (other than institutional buyers) in the state during any twelve consecutive months if

  - The seller reasonably believes that all the buyers in the state are purchasing for investment other than institutional buyers.
  - No commission or other remuneration is paid or given for soliciting any buyer. This is the definition of the private placement exemption under the Uniform Securities Act.

- Any offer or sale of a preorganization certificate or subscription if

  - No commission or other remuneration is given for soliciting any prospective subscriber.
  - The number of subscribers is ten or less.
  - No payment is made by the subscriber.

- Any transaction pursuant to an offer to existing security holders of the issuer if no commission is paid for soliciting any stockholders in that state and the administrator does not disallow the exemption.
- Any offer (but not sale) of a security for which registration statements have been filed under the Act and the Securities Act of 1933, if no stop order or refusal order is in effect and no public proceeding looking toward such an order is pending.
- Any transaction exempted by the National Securities Markets Improvement Act of 1996.

Upon specified conditions, an administrator may deny or revoke certain exemptions. The burden of proving an exemption or exception from any definition is on the person claiming it. As previously mentioned, no security is exempt from antifraud provisions of the Act.

FRAUDULENT AND OTHER PROHIBITED PRACTICES

It is unlawful under the Uniform Securities Act for any person, in connection with a securities transaction, to

- Employ any device or scheme to defraud any person
- Make any untrue statement of a material fact or omit stating a material fact necessary to make statements made not misleading
- Engage in any act, practice, or course of business that operates or would operate as a fraud or deceit on any person

It is unlawful for an investment advisor to enter into or to be a party to an investment advisory contract unless it provides in writing that

- The investment advisor shall not be compensated on the basis of a share of the capital gains or capital appreciation on the client's funds with an exception for private investment companies.
- No assignment of the contract may be made without the consent of the other party to the contract.
- The investment advisor, if a partnership, shall notify the other party to the contract of a majority change in the membership of the partnership.

An investment advisory contract may provide for compensation based on a percentage of the average total value of the funds managed over a definite period of time. If an investment advisor is a partnership, no assignment is considered to be made if a death or withdrawal represents only a minority interest of the partnership, or the admission of new members to the partnership is only a minority interest.

An investment advisor is prohibited from having custody of securities or funds of a client if the administrator prohibits custody or the investment advisor fails to notify the administrator of the custody.

Agents are prohibited from engaging in dishonest or unethical business practices. These prohibitions apply to both purchases and sales and may or may not be specifically described in a state's securities law. Some practices are easy to identify while others are not. Some of the actions that have been held to be fraudulent, dishonest, or unethical are

- Failing to state important facts of making inaccurate statements concerning commissions, markups, or markdowns.
- Telling a customer that if a security is registered with the SEC or state securities administrator, it means that it has been approved by the regulator.
- Making recommendations on the basis of material inside information about the issuer not available to the public.
- Rendering incorrect market quotations to clients or engaging in false trades or market manipulation.
- Sharing in the profits or losses in a customer's account

  - Without the written consent of the customer
  - Without the written consent of the agent's employing broker/dealer
  - In an amount not related to the agent's personal investment in the account

- Exercising discretion without first obtaining prior written permission from the customer.
- Telling a customer that a security will be listed on an exchange without any knowledge that such listing is to occur.
- Selling securities prior to the effective date of a new securities issue.
- Guaranteeing a profit in a customer's account or guaranteeing that the customer will not lose money on a transaction.
- Promising to perform services for a customer without being qualified or without really intending to perform such services.
- Borrowing money or securities from a customer even with his or her permission.
- Not telling a customer that commissions and taxes on a transaction may be larger than usual.
- Making transactions not recorded on the employer's records without disclosing such actions to the employer and receiving written permission.
- Not making the employer aware of a customer's written complaint.
- Soliciting orders for securities that are unregistered and nonexempt.
- Participating in market manipulative transactions such as "wash sales," which create a misleading appearance of active trading in a security.
- Misrepresenting the status of a customer's account to the customer.
- Telling a customer that dividends from a mutual fund will always exceed interest earned on a savings account.
- Accepting orders for a customer from a third party without first obtaining written authorization.
- Commingling the agent's funds with customer funds. The term **commingling** refers to a situation in which an agent deposits customer money into his own personal checking account.
- Making unsuitable recommendations or transactions such as

  - Churning customer accounts, recommending "excessive" transactions
  - Not making reasonable inquiry of customers as to their financial situation, needs, and objectives
  - Not explaining important facts and risks to customers
  - Recommending transactions without reasonable grounds

Under the Uniform State Securities Act, an agent is prohibited from engaging in the following activities because they are fraudulent, dishonest, or unethical business practices

- Guaranteeing a customer against loss, misrepresenting a return on a security, employing any device to defraud, or performing any act that would operate as a fraud on any person.
- Paying commissions to an investment advisor without disclosing this to the customer. Any potential conflict of interest must be disclosed to the client.

- Backdating records such as confirmations or order tickets, making untrue statements of a material fact or failing to state a material fact. Records cannot be backdated even one day.
- Recommending tax shelters to persons in low tax bracket rates.
- Engaging in securities transactions based on inside information or material nonpublic information. It is a violation under the Uniform Securities Act to trade any security based on inside information, including US government securities, municipal bonds, limited partnerships, and common stock.
- To state that the administrator has approved an offering, found a registration to be true and complete, or passed upon the accuracy or adequacy of a prospectus.
- Attempting to obtain a written agreement from a customer that he will not sue the agent or broker/dealer even though the sale of securities is in violation of state law. Any agreement of this type is null and void under the Act.
- Deliberately failing to follow a customer's instructions.
- Selling speculative common stock to clients with income objectives.
- Backdating confirmations even if they are backdated only one day.

SUITABILITY

For an investment to be suitable for a customer, the investment must meet the customer's investment objectives, financial situation, and needs. For an older person seeking current income with safety of principal, an agent might recommend US government securities or high-quality municipal bonds. The agent should *not* recommend to the older person investments such as speculative growth stocks, tax shelter investments, precious metals, or options.

Assume an agent recommends that a customer purchase $12,000 worth of a mutual fund. The recommendation exceeds the customer's available cash position. The customer is forced to sell the security prior to settlement date since he does not have the available funds to pay for the purchase. In this example, the agent has made an unsuitable recommendation. Assume an agent has discretionary authority over a customer's account. The customer's investment objective is current income only. The agent invests $14,000 in a speculative security that pays no interest. The agent has engaged in an unsuitable transaction.

An agent, when recommending a securities transaction, must inquire as to whether the customer can pay for the purchase by settlement date. To recommend purchases beyond a customer's ability to pay for them is a clear violation of the Uniform Securities Act.

In certain instances, an agent may make a suitable recommendation to a customer. However, the customer requests that an order for another security be executed. The agent feels that the security the customer wants to purchase is not suitable. The agent, in this case, can execute the order, but it would be wise to obtain a written statement from the customer. The written statement should make clear that the transaction was unsolicited and not recommended by the agent.

Assume an agent recommends a suitable investment to a customer and the customer decides to purchase the security. Three days after the purchase, his spouse calls and wants to cancel the trade. She states that her husband has lost his job and cannot pay for the trade. Since it is an individual account, the agent cannot sell the security without instructions from the husband. The agent is not allowed to give the husband a personal check to pay for the purchase. Also, the agent cannot arrange a loan for the husband to pay for the trade.

Assume an agent calls a customer and offers the customer a security for the customer's portfolio. The customer offers resistance to the purchase of the security. The agent cannot, in order to convince the customer to purchase the security

- Guarantee the customer against loss in the transaction.
- Offer to repurchase the security at a fixed price in the future.
- Offer to repay the amount of the commission to the customer if the transaction is not profitable.

All of those actions would be clear violations of the Uniform Securities Act. The agent could explain the features of the security in an attempt to demonstrate suitability to the customer. However, the final decision on whether to purchase the security belongs to the customer.

REGULATORY OVERSIGHT

The Uniform Securities Act is administered by a specified administrative agency. The administrator and his officers and employees are prohibited from using for their own benefit any information that has not been made public.

The administrator may make public or private investigations within or outside the state if he believes it necessary to determine whether the Act has been violated or to aid in enforcing the Act. If he so desires, he may require a person to file a statement in writing, under oath, as to the facts and circumstances concerning a matter under investigation and may publish information concerning any violation of the Act or rules or orders under the Act.

If a person refuses to obey a subpoena, the appropriate court, on application of the administrator, may order the person to appear before the administrator and produce requested evidence or else be held in contempt of court. If an individual has claimed his privilege against self-incrimination, he may not be prosecuted or subject to any penalty or forfeiture. He, of course, is not exempt from prosecution and punishment for perjury or contempt committed in testifying.

If it appears that a person has engaged or is about to engage in an act or practice that violates the Act or any rule or order under the Act, the administrator may bring action in the appropriate court to enjoin the act or practice and enforce compliance with the Act. A permanent or temporary injunction, restraining order, or writ of mandamus may be granted and a receiver or conservator appointed for the defendant or the defendant's assets. The administrator may not be required by the court to post a surety bond.

CRIMINAL PENALTIES

A person who willfully violates the Uniform Securities Act on conviction may be fined not more than $5,000, or imprisoned not more than three years, or both. No person may be imprisoned for a violation if he proves he had no knowledge of the rule or order. No indictment may be returned under this Act more than five years after the alleged violation. The administrator may refer evidence concerning willful violation to the attorney general or proper district attorney, who may institute appropriate criminal proceedings.

CIVIL LIABILITIES

Any person is subject to civil liabilities if he or she offers or sells a security

- In violation of specified sections of the Act or rule or order under specified sections
- By means of any untrue statement of a material fact or omission to state such a fact necessary to make statements made not misleading

A person subject to civil liabilities is liable to the person buying the security from him. The buyer may sue either at law or in equity to recover the amount paid, together with interest at 6% per year, costs, and reasonable attorney's fees, less the amount of any income received on the security. If he no longer owns the security, he may sue for damages. Damages are the amount that would be recoverable on a sale less the value of the security when the buyer disposed of it, and interest at 6% per year (rescission of the contract).

Those persons subject to civil liabilities include not only the individual selling the security, but also

- Every person who directly or indirectly controls a seller who is liable
- Every partner, officer, or director of such seller or person performing similar functions
- Every employee of such seller who materially aids in the sale
- Every broker/dealer or agent who materially aids in the sale

These individuals are liable jointly and severally unless they can prove that they did not know, and by exercising reasonable care could not have known, of the existence of the facts on which the liability is alleged to exist.

A person may not sue under the civil liability section of the Uniform Securities Act more than two years after the contract of sale, and a person may not sue

- If the buyer received a written offer, before the suit when he owned the security, to refund the consideration plus interest at 6% less any income received on the security, and he did not accept the offer within thirty days of its receipt
- If the buyer received such an offer when he did not own the security unless he rejected the offer in writing within thirty days of its receipt

Therefore, if an entity or individual violates the Uniform Securities Act, the entity or individual could be subject to

- Criminal penalties
- Civil penalties
- Administrative penalties

Criminal penalties could result in imprisonment or fines. Civil penalties could result in fines or injunctions. Administrative penalties could be censure, fines, suspension of licenses, or a bar from the securities industry.

JUDICIAL REVIEW OF ADMINISTRATIVE ORDERS

Any person aggrieved by a final order of the administrator may obtain a review of the order in the appropriate court by filing in court, within sixty days after the entry of the order, a written petition requesting that the order be modified or set aside. A copy of this petition is served on the administrator, who then certifies and files in court a copy of the filing and evidence on which the order was entered. After this, the court has exclusive jurisdiction to affirm, modify, enforce, or set aside the order. The court may order additional evidence to be taken and the administrator may modify his findings and order on the basis of such additional evidence. Unless the court so orders, the commencement of proceedings does not operate as a stay of the administrator's order.

Assume the administrator suspends an agent in Pennsylvania for thirty days for violations of the Uniform Securities Act. The agent immediately appeals the order to the appropriate court (Pennsylvania Court of Appeals). The Pennsylvania Court of Appeals would have jurisdiction to affirm, modify, enforce, or set aside the order. The fact that the agent has filed an appeal does not operate as a stay of the administrator's order. This means the penalty of suspension is in effect unless the Pennsylvania Court of Appeals orders a stay of the administrator's order. In other words, the court could order that no penalty go into effect until they had an opportunity to review the matter. Assume the Pennsylvania Court of Appeals reviews the matter and modifies it by requiring only a ten-day suspension. The agent would only have to serve a ten-day suspension instead of a thirty-day suspension.

SCOPE OF THE ACT

The Scope of the Act section of the Uniform State Securities Code defines what "in this state" means concerning offers and acceptances of offers to buy or sell securities. The Act applies to an offer to buy or sell and acceptances of offers to buy or sell provided

- They originate from a state.
- They are directed to anyone in the state.
- They are accepted in a state.

The entire transaction will be subject to the Act if any part of an offer is considered "in this state." Assume a customer who lives in Massachusetts receives a soliciting telephone call from an agent in Vermont. The statutes of Massachusetts would apply because the solicitation was received in Massachusetts. However, if the agent in Vermont were operating fraudulently, the state of Vermont could institute action against him on the theory that a state should not be used as a base of operations for defrauding persons in other states. An administrator can investigate the activities of a broker/dealer or investment advisor within or outside of his or her state. The administrator does not need the permission of another state's administrator to conduct an investigation.

Under the Uniform Securities Act, an advertisement in a regular newspaper or periodical is not an offer in any state other than the state of publication. A person could place an advertisement in the *New York Times* and have it freely circulated in other states without being considered offers in other states. Radio and television programs are considered to be offers only in the state from which they originate. In other words, they are treated in the same manner as a newspaper or periodical.

Under the Uniform Securities Act, an offer to buy or sell is not made in a state when

- The publisher circulates any bona fide newspaper or other publication of general, regular, and paid circulation, either not published in the state or having more than $2/3$ of its circulation outside the state.
- The offer is broadcast on a radio or television program originating outside the state but received in the state.

CONSENT TO SERVICE OF PROCESS

Every applicant for registration and every issuer proposing to issue a security in that state must file with the administrator in prescribed form, an irrevocable consent appointing the administrator to be his attorney and to receive service of any lawful process in any noncriminal suit, action, or proceeding that arises under the Act after the consent has been filed. Service may be made by leaving a copy of the process in the office of the administrator. For such service to be effective, the plaintiff must send notice of the service and a copy of the process by registered mail to the defendant.

If a person (including a nonresident) engages in conduct prohibited or made actionable by the Act and has not filed a consent to service of process, and personal jurisdiction over him cannot be otherwise obtained in the state, the conduct is considered equivalent to his appointing the administrator to be his attorney to receive service in any noncriminal suit.

ADDITIONAL CONCEPTS—UNIFORM SECURITIES ACT

The following points are presented to increase a person's understanding of the provisions of the Uniform Securities Act. They are purposely not in any particular order.

- Under no circumstances can a prospective customer be told that dividends from a particular stock or mutual fund will always be greater than interest earned on a savings account. The customer cannot be told this even if past history supports such a claim. Remember, past performance in the securities industry is never an indication of future performance. A prospective customer cannot be assured by an agent relating to a particular rate of return on a security investment. Common stocks and mutual funds can decrease in value and an investor can lose principal. An investor cannot lose principal on a savings account.
- A broker/dealer, agent, investment advisor, or investment advisor representative who violates the Uniform Securities Act may be subject to

  - Criminal penalties
  - Civil liabilities
  - Suspension or revocation of their registration
  - Disgorgement of commissions

- The Uniform Securities Act states that an agent may share in the profits and losses in a customer's account provided

  - Such sharing is approved by the customer.
  - Such sharing is approved by the agent's employing broker/dealer.
  - The extent of the sharing is limited to the agent's proportional contribution to the account. In other words, if an agent contributes 50% of the funds to the account, he can share in 50% of the profits and losses in the account. The agent and the customer cannot mutually agree on a different profit-and-loss sharing percentage.

- Assume an agent makes an intentional omission of a fact relating to the sale of a security. Under the Uniform Securities Act, the intentional omission would constitute **fraud** if a reasonable person would attach decision-making importance to the information that was omitted.
- Under the Uniform Securities Act, the administrator can require a qualification examination for a person, which can be written, oral, or both.
- An agent can state that the administrator has registered the security. The agent can also state that he is a registered agent in the state. However, the agent can never imply or state that the security or the agent has been approved by virtue of the registration.
- Under the Uniform Securities Act, the following are considered to be securities. They are considered securities even if they are exempt securities.

  - US government bonds
  - Shares of stock in closely held companies
  - Limited partnership interests in a new movie entitled *Discussions of the Uniform Securities Act*
  - Certificates of interest in an oil well
  - Certificates of deposit for a security

However, the following are *not* considered to be securities under the Uniform Securities Act:

- Condominium units purchased exclusively for residential purposes
- Collectibles such as diamonds, paintings, rugs, or precious metals

- Under the Uniform Securities Act, assume no denial is in effect and no other securities-related proceedings are pending. In this case, an application filed for registration of a broker/dealer automatically becomes effective thirty days after the application is completed.
- Assume Mr. Kilpatrick has had his agent's registration revoked for violating the Uniform Securities Act. The administrator may deny any future application by Mr. Kilpatrick for registration as

  - An agent
  - A broker/dealer
  - An investment advisor
  - A financial and operations principal
  - An investment advisor representative

- Under the Uniform Securities Act, the term *guaranteed* means guaranteed as to the payment of principal, interest, and dividends.
- An individual or corporation is not considered to be an investment advisor if it gives advice only about annuity contracts. The term *annuity contract* means fixed-annuity contracts that are not securities. Variable annuities are securities.
- Under the Uniform Securities Act, the term *market manipulation* includes making false trades, giving false quotations, and disseminating false information. However, commingling a client's funds with the agent's funds is not market manipulation. Commingling and market manipulation are both prohibited under the Act but are defined differently.
- Under the Uniform Securities Act, a person can sell securities for more than one broker/dealer only if that person becomes registered as an agent of each broker/dealer.
- Under the Uniform Securities Act, a registered agent cannot offer to sell securities in a pending underwriting. The agent cannot sell unregistered, nonexempt securities unless the underwriting has become effective.
- Assume a customer has $1 million of net worth. The customer's investment objective is income only. A registered agent has discretionary trading authority for the account. Discretionary trading authority allows the agent to make purchase and sale decisions for the account. The agent purchases $6,000 of a noninterest-bearing speculative bond issue. Under the Uniform Securities Act the agent has effected an unsuitable securities transaction for the customer. Even though an agent has discretionary authority over a customer's account, the agent still must purchase securities that are suitable for the customer.
- Under the Uniform Securities Act, an investment advisor's compensation may be based on a percentage of the average total value of funds managed over a definite period of time. Investment advisors cannot share in the capital gains generated in a public customer's account. This rule does not apply to an investment advisor managing a private investment company.
- Under the Uniform Securities Act, if a person knowingly makes a misleading filing with the administrator, that person may be fined not more than $5,000 and imprisoned not more than three years, or both.
- An investment advisor is a person who advises others on securities for compensation. The term *investment advisor* under the Act excludes banks. The definition of investment advisor also excludes lawyers, accountants, teachers, or engineers whose performance of advisory services is solely incidental to the practice of their profession. A broker/dealer who gives investment advice is not considered to be an investment advisor under the Act, provided such advice is incidental to the conduct of its business and receives no special compensation for such advice. Also, a publisher of a bona fide newspaper or magazine with a regular and paid circulation is not considered an investment advisor under the Uniform Securities Act.
- Any person who makes an untrue statement of a material fact in connection with the sale of a security has violated the Uniform Securities Act.
- An administrator, under the Uniform Securities Act, may deny or revoke a registration if

  - An agent or investment advisor representative has been convicted within the past ten years of a felony or misdemeanor involving a security or relating to the securities business.
  - An agent or investment advisor representative has wilfully violated provisions of the Uniform Securities Act.
  - An investment advisor or broker/dealer has engaged in unethical or dishonest practices.

ABOUT THE CD-ROM

INTRODUCTION

The CD contains questions and answers to review the material in the book and to prepare for the actual exams. To master the material most efficiently, we suggest you study the chapter review questions for the Series 7 exam prior to reading each chapter and then answer the questions following your reading of the chapter. Make sure that you understand the answers to all the review questions before proceeding to the next chapter.

There are six sets of exams comprised of 50 multiple-choice questions. These exams correspond to the layout of the actual test. After completing the book and chapter review questions, we suggest you take each exam individually. Again, make sure you understand the answers to all the questions before taking the next exam. These series of exams are designed to identify areas of the Series 7 material where you may need more study. Once you have mastered these exams and done additional study, if necessary, you are prepared for the final exam.

The final exam consists of 250 multiple-choice questions. The actual Series 7 exam consists of two segments of 125 questions. A candidate is given three hours for each segment. We suggest you simulate test conditions and give yourself an uninterrupted block of time to take the exam.

To reinforce your understanding, six sets of additional practice questions are provided. Each set has 125 multiple-choice questions with answers and explanations provided.

Once you've mastered the Series 7 material, you are well on your way to mastering the Series 63 material. Comparatively, the Series 63 material comprises a smaller body of knowledge than the Series 7. We have provided three 50-question exams and one 25-question exam.

SYSTEM REQUIREMENTS

- A computer with a processor running at 120 Mhz or faster
- At least 32 MB of total RAM installed on your computer; for best performance, we recommend at least 64 MB
- A CD-ROM drive
- A color monitor with at least 800x600 resolution

NOTE: Many popular word processing programs are capable of reading Microsoft Word files. However, users should be aware that a slight amount of formatting might be lost when using a program other than Microsoft Word.

USING THE CD WITH WINDOWS

To install the items from the CD to your hard drive, follow these steps:

1. Insert the CD into your computer's CD-ROM drive.
2. The CD-ROM interface will appear. The interface provides a simple point-and-click way to explore the contents of the CD.

If the opening screen of the CD-ROM does not appear automatically, follow these steps to access the CD:

1. Click the Start button on the left end of the taskbar and then choose Run from the menu that pops up.
2. In the dialog box that appears, type *d:\setup.exe*. (If your CD-ROM drive is not drive d, fill in the appropriate letter in place of *d*.) This brings up the CD Interface described in the preceding set of steps.

WHAT'S ON THE CD

Chapter Review Questions: There are 683 chapter review questions with answers and explanations for all nineteen chapters. The number of review questions per chapter fluctuates to correspond to the amount of material covered, with some chapters requiring 90+ questions and others needing only 10 questions.

Examinations: There are six sets of examinations comprised of 50 multiple-choice questions with answers and explanation included. The six examinations are ordered with the intention of corresponding to the layout of the actual test.

Final Examination: Upon completion of the six examinations, a final examination of 250 multiple-choice questions is included on the CD. Answers and explanations are provided.

Additional Practice Questions: For added assurance, six sets of additional practice questions are provided. Each set has 125 multiple-choice questions with answers and explanations included.

Series 63 Test Review: Examinations: 1 – 4. Three 50-question multiple-choice exams and one 25-question multiple-choice exam.

CUSTOMER CARE

If you have trouble with the CD-ROM, please call the Wiley Product Technical Support phone number at (800) 762-2974. Outside the United States, call 1(317) 572-3994. You can also contact Wiley Product Technical Support at **http://www.wiley.com/techsupport**. John Wiley & Sons will provide technical support only for installation and other general quality control items. For technical support on the applications themselves, consult the program's vendor or author.

To place additional orders or to request information about other Wiley products, please call (877) 762-2974.

INDEX